Oswald Mathias Ungers

For Lo

OSWALD MATHIAS UNGERS

works and projects 1991 1998

with essays by
francesco dal co
oswald mathias ungers

Electaarchitecture

Editor
Giovanna Crespi

Copy Editor
Gail Swerling

Translations
Melissa Thorson Hause
David Stanton

Distributed by Phaidon Press
ISBN 1-904313-00-0

www.phaidon.com

www.electaweb.it

First published in English 2002

Contents

Per artem et ex voluntate: Through Art, According to Will

Francesco Dal Co

Architecture behaves like nature. Like nature, it has the capacity to transform itself from one form to another. The essence of architecture is discovery rather than invention. If one's processes of reasoning are based on subtraction, one easily comes to the conclusion that architecture is a question of materials and geometry.

With his "Aphorisms on Architecture," some of which are published as an introduction to this book, I could complete my task of presenting the second volume of the complete works of Oswald Mathias Ungers. The first volume, published in 1991, described the buildings and projects of the years 1951–1990 (from the complex on Aachener Strasse in Cologne-Braunsfeld to the remarkable library that Ungers sited in the garden of his house at Cologne-Müngersdorf). This second, which documents the work of the years 1990–1998, also comprises projects that will be completed after the end of the twentieth century. It offers a complete survey of the work of Ungers, an aloof, proud, and uncompromising protagonist of the history of architecture from 1950 on.

If Ungers's work is considered against this background, it will not be difficult for readers to note that he has reacted with steadfast, coherent indifference to the ripples, as fleeting as they are light, that have ruffled the surface of the sea in which modern architecture risks foundering. Few architects have such an individual style as his, which is, however, the result of a professed aversion to the intellectual proclivities and professional laxity that have recently almost nullified the difference between style and fashion. Rigorously modern, Ungers's architecture takes the form of a constant rejection of the allure of up-to-dateness. Its key characteristics are subtraction and geometry; measure and function its antipodes; number and proportion its foundations, as the architects who most influenced Ungers were well aware. On the basis of these premises, he contends, as tradition requires, that the behavior patterns of architecture are similar to those of nature. This assertion has nothing to do with the organicism and naturalism with which a large part of contemporary architecture concerns itself. No ideology resounds through it, but rather the observation that each project is nothing more than the aspiration to imitate hidden geometric measures and comply with the laws governing the unity of the world to which construction attests. This correspondence is the theme of Ungers's research, and explains the process of continuous subtraction of which his architecture is expression and result. By obstinately focusing on the analogy between nature and the project—beginning with recognition of the primacy of the numbers on which each "act of creative delimitation" rests, as is, once again, suggested by tradition—Ungers counters every attempt made by contemporary culture to represent the decadence of architecture as a consequence of the oblivion of its sacred and symbolic values.

Ungers's works are proportioned numerical constructions that, however, shun numerology; they are assemblages of geometry, the aim of which is meaning, and they refuse to be summed up by the recognition of the primacy of objective and function. His architecture possesses artful essence, to which nothing is more extraneous than the aspiration to carry out the task of consoling (or entertaining). It is an expression—not merely metaphorical—of the cohesion of the world, of the continuous procession from the unit to the square, and it does not wish to demonstrate anything but the fact that measuring, ordering, designing, and constructing derive from a single root. Its presence is a manifestation of its existence.

It is no coincidence that, with the passing of the years, a form that is extremely eloquent from this point of view has assumed a central role in Ungers's works. This is the dome, evoked or used explicitly in several variants and in numerous projects. In any analysis of the dome, it is interesting to note that Ungers has placed, in the center of the *Wunderkammer* set up in his house for models of a number of the great monuments of Western architecture, a model of the Pantheon. The model, made by Ungers in recent years, is not the result of a collector's whim. A perfect demonstration of the power of architecture to counter the oblivion that threatens its future, the Pantheon expresses in the highest form the insight that the Indonesian monument Borobudur communicated over fifty years ago to Mus: "The house and the world are two equivalent sums." No construction makes this equivalence more evident than the Pantheon. No form other than the dome, which shows that it is possible to "proceed from the unit to the square by means of a triangle," truly demonstrates the potential of geometry. In the shape of the dome, the knowledge of the surveyor is materialized as the art of combining simple figures that give life to what the Austrian art historian Alois Riegl describes as "the concrete representation of the tangible unity of the form"—the objective of Ungers's work. "More than any other interior in the world," Riegl continues, "that of the Pantheon has conserved the completeness and perfection of antiquity, which has no need for reflection." In the Pantheon there is the proof that "discover" and "build" are consequential synonyms of "contemplate," from which the solution to the problem of interior space is derived in the Roman monument treated "as cubic material, fixed with measurements that are absolutely equal and therefore clear." The obsession with the square, in which Ungers's architecture is steeped, is a consequence of the interminable reverberations of these living memories and a demonstration that the severe rigor of the architect's designs has its roots in acute nostalgia. The research he carried out regarding the shape of the dome—in which the process of transformation "from one form to another" is clearly evident and in which architecture and nature do behave in the same manner—indicates that each of Ungers's projects is nothing more than an opportunity for reasserting the immutability of the grounds on which this original, necessary coincidence rests.

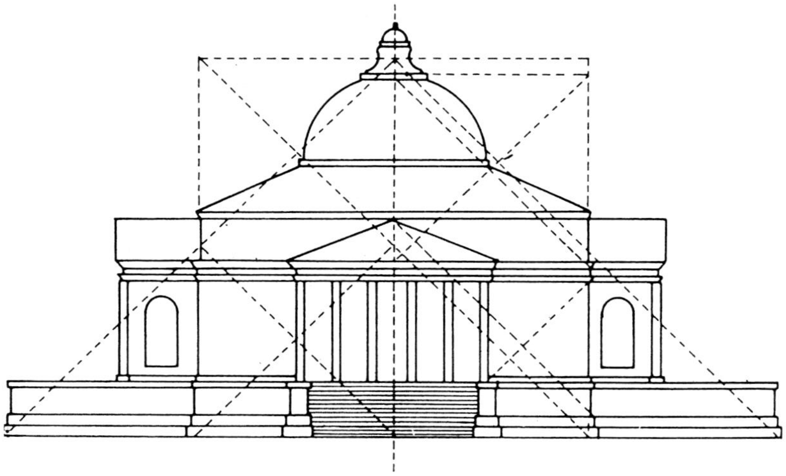

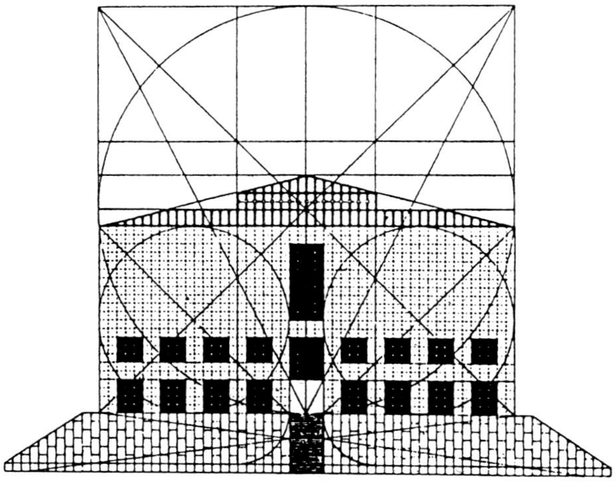

Aphorisms on Architecture

Oswald Mathias Ungers

Architecture is influenced by two essential references: on the one hand, the relation to the place—not only the real, material place but also its spiritual and historical dimension—and on the other, the formal type expressed in the particular building.

Architecture means not only to invent but to discover, to reinterpret familiar concepts over and over again, to see the world with new eyes, to experience it anew, to rediscover and enliven it with fresh content. To create architecture is also to infuse reality with an idea, a new and different view. In this process, typological thinking is both a prerequisite and a method.

Morphological thought and action presuppose two things: first, the recognition and discovery of archetypes, and second, a view of realities in complementary relations.

There are two basic types in architecture: the ark and the box. The first symbolizes the abiding and constant; it is lasting and bound to its place. The other type, the box, is movable and has something temporary and changeable. It can constantly shift location and has no established place. The ark expresses permanence, the box transience.

Humanistic thinking is based not in exclusivity but rather, on account of its historical references, in the diversity of spiritual and artistic contexts. This way of thinking seeks ruptures and discontinuities. Nothing could be further removed from it than to neutralize opposition in the manner of fanatics and systematizers, who seek a common denominator for every value and want to reduce all flowers to a single form and color.

The search for a unified, comprehensive building style, a single method and a single idea, is not only anachronistic but represents a loss of values and a regression to a dogmatic atavism. We must learn to live and deal with contradictory theses. We must know that there is not just one way to build, but many ways that are diametrically opposed and will endure.

Thinking in reduced dimensions, one arrives at the conclusion that architecture is material and geometry. These are the two components that determine the architectural design. The handling and development of material gives the building its concrete form; the geometry—its logic, proportion, and relationships—gives it its inner structure. The geometry defines the arrangement, size, and form of the spaces and solids. It is the grammar, the syntax of the architectural design. The material determines the execution, the reality.

At the beginning of the modern age, Alberti asserted the principle of *varietà nell'unità*, diversity in unity. In the same period, Nicolas of Cusa propagated the convergence of opposites. Both paradigms, Alberti's *varietà nell'unità* and the *coincidentia oppositorum* of Cusa, proceed from the same premise: a basic principle common to everything and its unlimited variation, the essential, unified form and its diverse adaptation to different circumstances. This principle embraces not exclusivity, the exclusion of opposites, but their integration. It requires not only contrary but complementary thinking.

The architect is a craftsman, an archaeologist, an adventurer, a discoverer. One false step, one false decision, and his work is in vain. Every motion requires the highest level of concentration and experience. He is a craftsman in the best sense of the word—an artisan whose handwork mutates into a work of art. He strives for completion, flawlessness, perfection. Even when he fails in the service of perfection, this does not relieve him of his ethical and moral duty to conceive the work as carefully and as enduringly as possible.

Gestalt, or form, stands at the foreground of thought and action. "The problem of form is the problem of art in general," says Hildebrand. The archetypal geometric forms—circle, straight line, sphere, cone, cylinder, cube, and ellipse—provide a framework for the translation of a mental and spiritual conception into a symbol. Already the humanists sought for the ideal shape, the perfect form, in order to represent the idea of creation. The essence of art and architecture is number, measure, and proportion. Sublimity is expressed through them alone.

The formal language of architecture is a rational, intellectual one, a language of reason. Emotions and fantasy are controlled by *ratio*, which in turn stimulates the imagination. The dialectical process between these two polarities—reason and emotion, *ratio* and imagination, idea and reality—is inherent in the creative act and results in the continual development of ideas, concepts, spaces, elements, and forms. It involves the idea of abstraction, the recognition of the object in its elementary form, and appearance in its clearest Gestalt.

The gale of the cybernetic apocalypse has blown off the roofs and pierced the walls, has destroyed the streets and the squares. Public life now takes place before the computer screen, where any reality can be simulated. Virtual worlds, not real places, are represented.

The places that create and bestow identity have disintegrated and dissolved. They have disappeared into a network of information, without orientation or history. Nothing new can arise when there is no longer a stable framework of place or time. Dissolution, chaos, continual change—the immanent process hinders every attempt, every historical reference.

Architecture is not a function of something else. It is no substitute, and can solve neither economic nor social problems. Architecture has its own language. It is autonomous. The spiritual in architecture takes no consideration of practical questions. Otherwise, how could the Parthenon, the Pantheon, the basilica, the cathedral, and many other architectural marvels have been created? What has shaped architecture is not the concern for function, but the "will to art." The idea.

Architecture that merely functions is trivial. What is function, anyway, and why this all-dominating dictatorship of function, when one can just as well perform theater in a factory, live in a church, and govern from a waterworks? The function adapts itself to the space, the form. The space, the Gestalt, have value in themselves. The beauty of the Pantheon endures eternally, independent of its function.

Just as the seed is a part of the life cycle of the plant, so also the block of stone and of glass, the firm and the perforated, the closed and the open, the new and the old, the articulated and the strict, clarity and intricacy, the labyrinthine and the absolute, the natural and the artificial, the empirical and the idealistic, abstraction and empathy are part of one and the same cycle. The architecture of morphological idealism is contradictory in its uniformity. It is not pluralistic and arbitrary but dialectical and complementary.

The idea of a stage set applies to the urbanistic aspect of architecture. Every spatial arrangement of buildings can also be viewed as a stage design. The arrangement of objects in space is simultaneously the creation of a backdrop for human activities, for the actors' roles, for the life that takes place on this stage. Seen in this way, every site, every place becomes an architectural stage for the drama of the individual, in the case of a private stage, or of all, in the case of the public stage, the city.

The new abstraction in architecture uses a rational geometry with clear and regular forms in both plan and elevation. In this context, the plan is the result not of the literal interpretation of functions and constructive conditions but of logical geometric systems. The latter are based on proportional relationships and coherent sequences, as was the case in the "modular system" of medieval architecture, the floor plans of Palladio, and the architectural theory of Durand.

Any building that has as its theme something other than itself is, from a spiritual point of view, trivial. It may fulfill legitimate purposes and needs; it may satisfy justifiable technical demands. But if it does not also fulfill itself as an idea, above and beyond the mere discharge of duty, it remains banal, incapable of satisfying the claim of architecture to be an expression of spiritual universality. In his architecture, Schinkel was concerned not only with the fulfillment of needs, but above all with the universality of ideas.

"Ars sine scientia nihil est." With this proposition, the French architect Jean Mignot made a decisive contribution to the understanding of art in the Renaissance. In antiquity, the mathematical rule and geometrical principle of order were the foundation of architecture. The antique conception of beauty was based not only on appearance but on a system of rules and proportions. "Arte sine scientia esse non posse," says Cicero, and Plato writes: "If one were to separate the doctrine of number, measure, and balance from all the arts, then proverbially everywhere only a miserable remnant would remain."

New development can arise only from a consciousness of history—assuming that history is not perverted into a reservoir of forms and styles. If we want to draw from history, then it can only be by recognizing the metaphysical values and basic principles behind outward appearances. History is not a recipe book but an encyclopedic lexicon of the development of the human spirit. This lexicon contains the vocabulary for the creative response to reality. But it also contains the key to the challenge of the tasks of the present. An architecture that renounces this spiritual foundation cannot itself be the bearer of spiritual values. Every creative architecture is incorporated into a historical *continuum*. The essential insight of humanism lies in the consciousness of this temporal *continuum*.

Unlike the village, the town, or the ideal city, the present-day metropolis no longer has a unified form. It is a heterogeneous aggregation of different elements, systems, and functions. The metropolis consists of fragments. It is a fragmentary, open structure, whose diverse and self-contradictory claims can no longer be apprehended in a coherent system. The present-day city is dialectical; it is thesis and antithesis at the same time. In it become visible not only the contradictions of society but those of technical systems as well. No longer can unified forms be found, non-contradictory solutions consisting of a single system.

My concern is for pure form, for the abstraction, the basic type, the elementary building. No natural materials burdened with associations, no architectural details that tell the history of the window, the entrance, or the building with cornices, copings, and jambs, the differences between base and crown.

My concern is the pure box, the simplest form for the interpretation of a constantly recurring element. Without agitation, without forward or backward leaps, without the usual distinctions. An element as clear and unambiguous, as direct and undisguised as possible.

No overtones, no courtesies; radical and without decorative accessories. The box in its elementary form. Not an expression of something, not a synonym for anything; polished down to the absolute core, as pure and unequivocal as possible.

Nothing metaphysical, no symbol for a condition of whatever sort. Only the direct, unadulterated form. Nothing moves, nothing is obscured, encoded, or concealed. There is no hidden meaning; everything that is meant is visible, unmediated, evident.

There is nothing to decipher or interpret; the things are what they are and are not intended to be anything else. All the spaces are the same, the content is different. The facades are the same. No longer is there a front or a rear side.

The aim is a non-objective architecture: space in itself, a building without qualities, encumbered by nothing, defined only by geometry and proportion, dependent on the rules of number and relation.

It is not mystical and didactic themes, however conceived, that are invoked and exploited, whether signaling freedom, openness, or creativity. Only the order of the numbers is determinative, their relation among themselves, the proportions of length, breadth, and height.

At the end of a long, changeful history, laden with meaning and full of symbols and metaphors, stands the geometrically purified building.

Projects

Berlin Tomorrow— The New Berlin, 1990

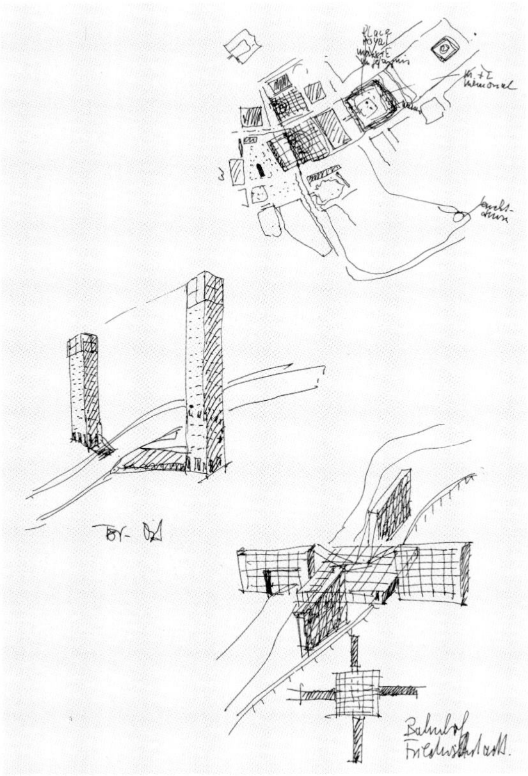

Project team: Volker Busse, Michael Croce, Andreas Geitner, Walter Noebel, Martina Röhr, Karl-Heinz Winkens

Berlin is the typical example of a city shaped by the vicissitudes of fate; the changes it has experienced in its seven-hundred-year history explain its present appearance better than any functional analysis. In the beginning, Berlin consisted of two cities: one for fishers, the other for merchants. Soon it became a market town of free citizens, then an aristocratic residence and the seat of the king, who transformed it into a military stronghold, the capital of his realm, and finally a fortification. It grew into the imperial city of a new empire, and then into the greatest industrial center in Europe. It became a metropolis and the capital of a new, "thousand-year" Reich. Its reduction to a rubble heap—the largest in Europe—at the end of World War II was followed by its division into East and West Berlin. Now, it can once again become a metropolis and, for the third time, a capital—this time of a reunified Germany.

The urban structure of Berlin thus represents the result of ideas, decisions, and historical processes; planned and chance events, constructive and destructive powers have shaped it and produced its wide-ranging diversity. Its plan is like a book of events in which all the significant moments in its history are inscribed; it is more like a gigantic puzzle with countless parts than a logically ordered whole. Each generation has bequeathed a continually evolving accumulation of fragments to the next; none, however, has succeeded in writing a genuine conclusion. The city is and remains—fortunately—a fragmentary, discontinuous, mutable ensemble; therefore it is and remains vital and richly faceted. An element of continuity is found only in the dialectical process, in which thesis is always opposed by antithesis.

Any project for Berlin must therefore come to terms with the problem of its history and develop corresponding strategies for the future. First, however, two illusory notions must be dispelled. The first is the idea that it is possible to reconstruct the city in its historic form, a conception that by no means corresponds to actual demands and expectations. Nor, on the other hand, should random renovation be allowed free rein, giving rise to chaotic, unregulated, and therefore destructive development. A new orientation is unavoidable; this realization is what lies behind every manifestation of a simulated and therefore false vitality. The same realization, however, can also result in something like an experimental project, one that intensifies the experience of the city as an architectural and urban environment in the sense of a composed ensemble. Because of its extreme and idiosyncratic character, Berlin, more than other cities, seems predestined to serve as a laboratory for the exploration of new problems. As so often in its history, Berlin could once again assume the role of a pilot project, demonstrating new and exemplary solutions in the larger European context of the dialectical city.

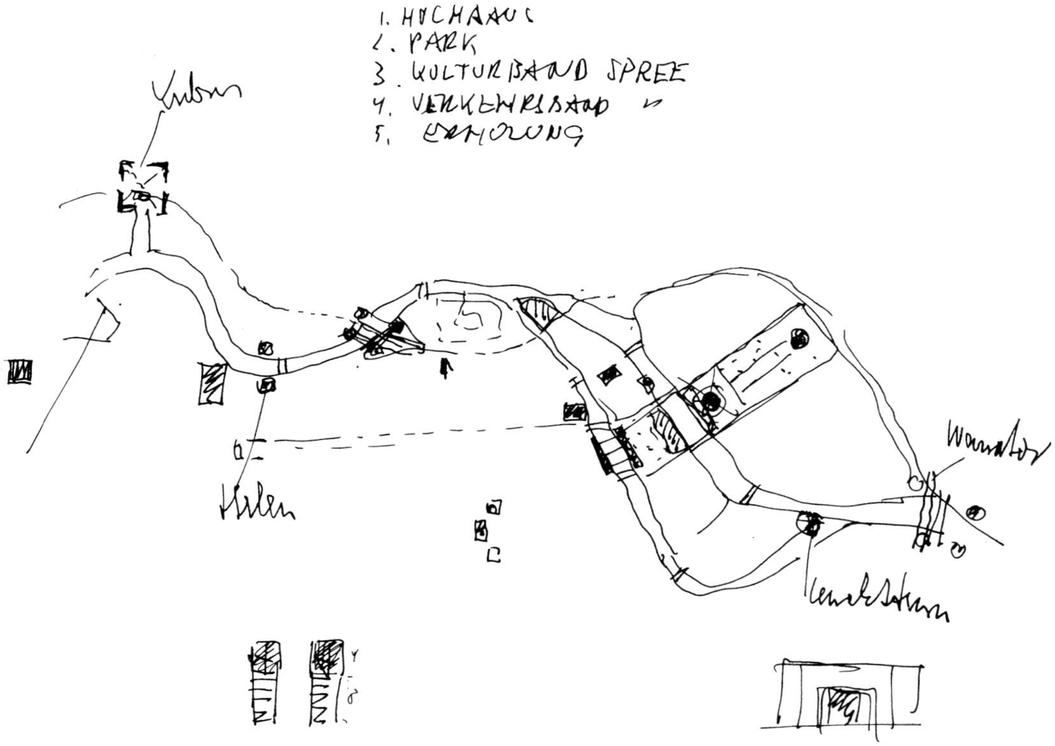

Conceptual development: identification of functions and meanings; completion of fragments; demonstration of typologies through historic examples; development of models.

DAS NEUE BERLIN

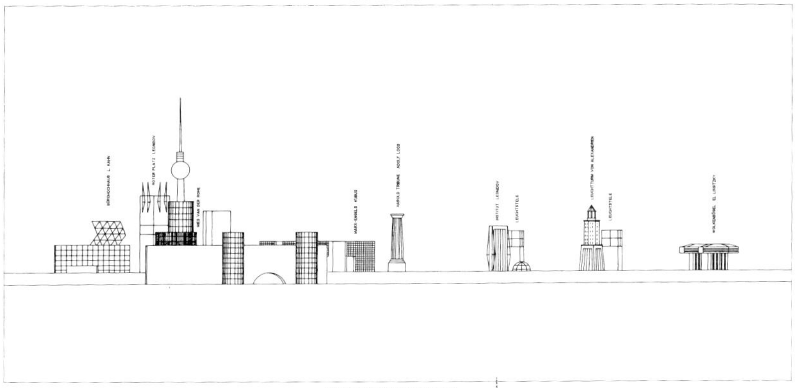

IKONEN DER ARCHITEKTUR

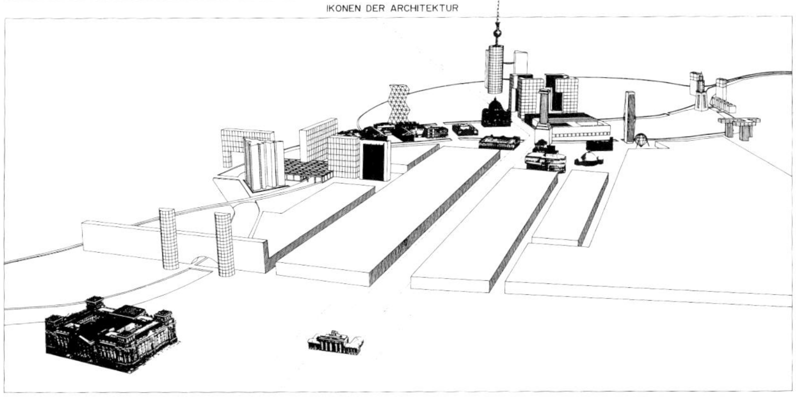

DAS NEUE BERLIN

CHICAGO TRIBUNE A. LOOS

MIES VAN DER ROHE

LEUCHTTURM VON ALEXANDRIA

WOLKENBÜGEL EL LISSITZKY

ROTER PLATZ LEONIDOV

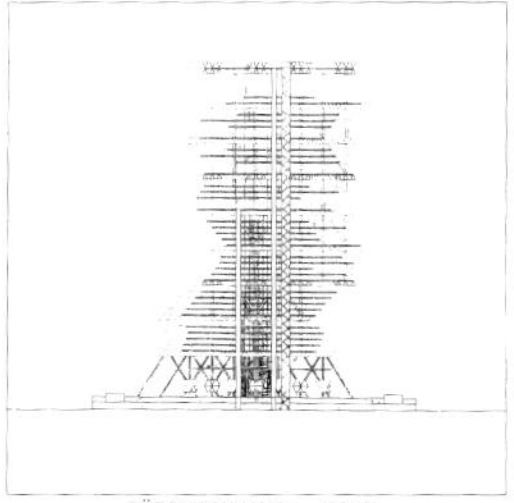

BÜROHOCHHAUS L. KAHN

INSTITUT LEONIDOV

DAS NEUE BERLIN

BAHNHOF FRIEDRICHSTADT — PROF. O.M. UNGERS

DAS NEUE BERLIN

VOLKSHAUS — PROF. O.M. UNGERS

Competition Design for Potsdamer/Leipziger Platz, Berlin, 1991, 1992

With: Stefan Vieths

Project team:
Urban design competition: Volker Busse, Andreas Geitner, Jarno Nillesen, Lukas Baumewerd, Markus Müller, Katja Schulz, Thomas Duda

Daimler-Benz site: Benedikt Baumewerd, Lukas Baumewerd, Albert Brauns, Volker Diekmann, Knud Ehm, Johannes Götz, Kai-Uwe Lompa, Georg Malat, Johannes Martini, Jarno Nillesen, Ingo Schweers, Joachim Sieber, Philippe Vernin, Frank Wieschemann

No other German—or even European—city has seen so many conflicts within such a concentrated area as the city center of Berlin. Before World War II, the area around Potsdamer Platz was densely populated and boasted the busiest square in Europe; from the end of the war until 1989, this same area was reduced to a desolate wasteland, disfigured with rubble. After the fall of the Berlin Wall, it was sold to four major investors. The first competition in 1991 included the entire area, while the second focused on the design of the Daimler-Benz site.

This singular location cannot be understood, analyzed, or reinterpreted without understanding the history of Berlin as a whole, for the urban history of Berlin is the history of a city of many different places. Within the planning area, a variety of urbanistic structures is relevant. The first is the historic block grid of the Friedrichstadt area with its corresponding configuration of buildings as well as the strict geometric dominance of Leipziger Platz. The second is the original parcel structure of the buildings outside Friedrichstadt, a system of coordinates that has maintained its urbanistic influence. A third factor is the streets and traffic routes established between Kemperplatz and Leipziger Platz after the war, effecting a reconfiguration of the property lines.

The new plan takes these historic structures as its point of departure. The superimposition of the block structure Friedrichstrasse, the current network of streets and transit lines, and an additional grid of high-rise buildings based on the coordinates of the historic parcel structure bordering on the Tiergarten result in a dense, complex, and differentiated network with streets and blocks of varying size, form, and significance. The differentiated block and street structure takes account of the existing property lines and various functional requirements, allowing a maximum of flexibility in building and open space. The plan unites every conceivable type of urban open space, ranging from the central park to smaller squares, avenues (the former

Model for urban design competition; use diagrams; perspective views.

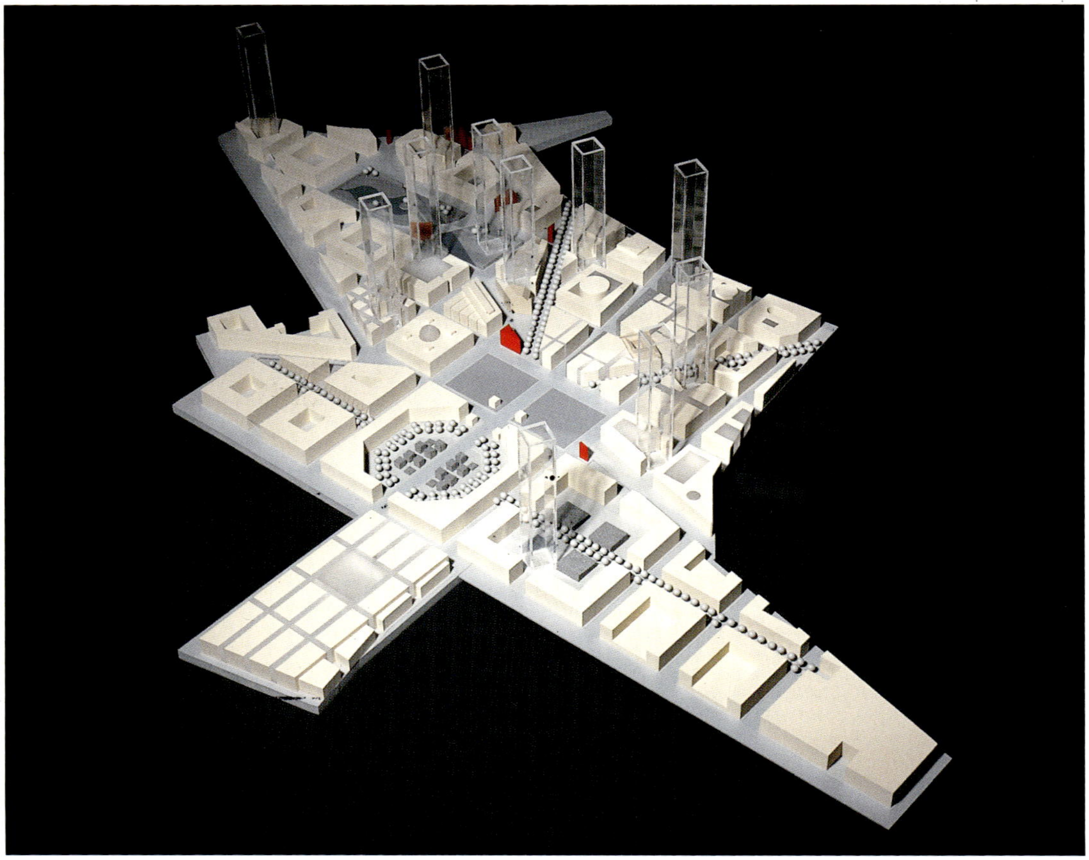

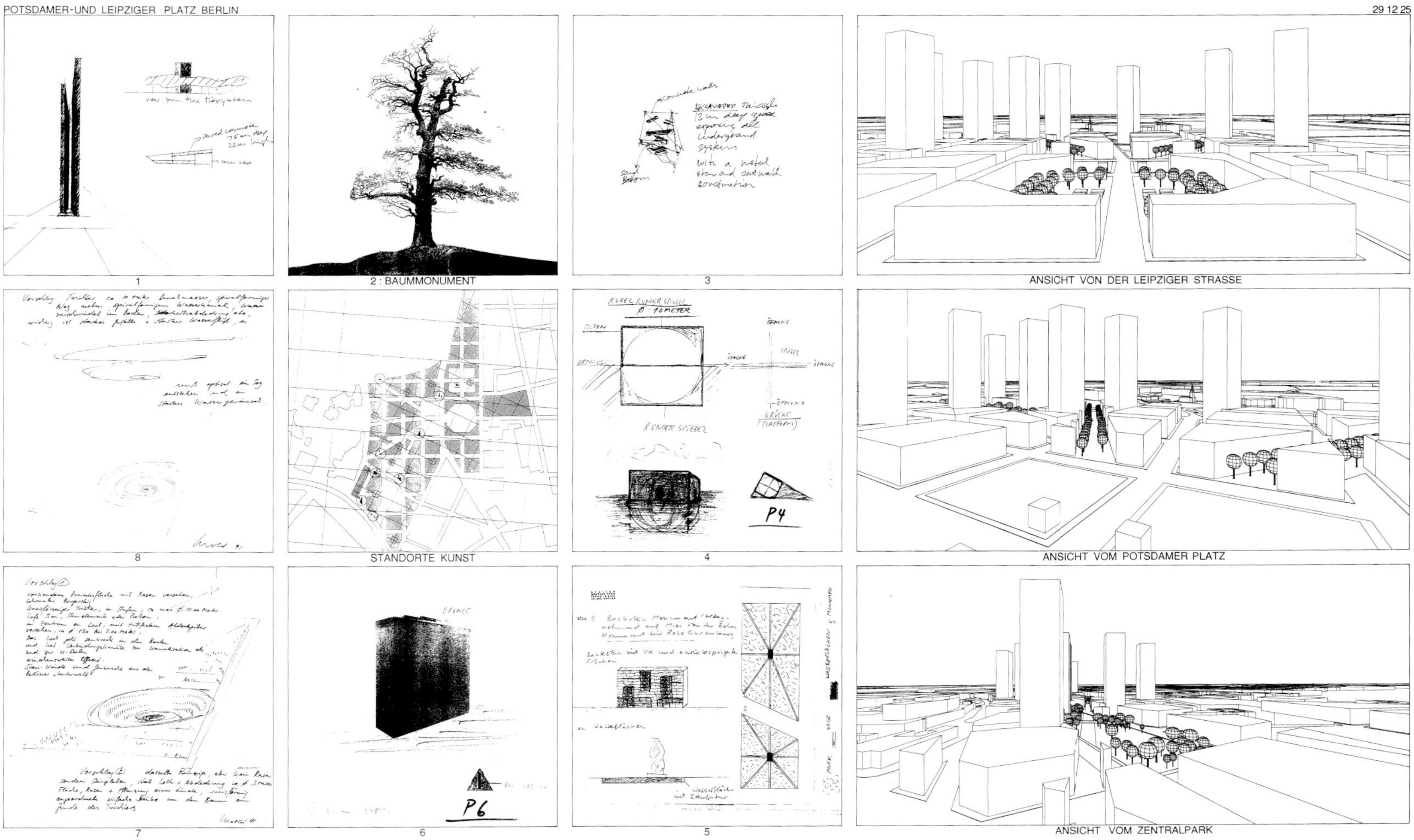

Potsdamer Strasse), boulevards, pedestrian streets, and passages and to traffic axes and monumental plaza complexes (Potsdamer/Leipziger Platz). A wide range of functional demands can be met within a richly variable architectural structure. In this scheme, the individual building (Weinhaus Huth on the former Potsdamer Strasse), the historic legacy (the esplanade), the superblock with maximum office space, and the complex, mixed-use block constitute integral elements of the overall urban structure.

The design makes possible the maximum individuality in the choice of materials and architectural style. The height limit is 22 meters for the block structures and 180 meters for the towers. The towers have identical "footprints" in the dense weave of the block structure. The contrast between tower and block structure is intentional and produces the chance configuration necessary for a complex plan.

In this context, art serves not as mere decoration but as an integral element of the urban concept. The superimposition of structures results in residual areas of varying size; at the boundary between functional and useless space, art steps in and continues the architectural and urbanistic design with its own means, reinterpreting extreme situations with over- and understatements and creating plazas with integrated sculptures, individual objects, edges, and corners. Architecture, urbanism, and function, history and reality are conceived as a complex unity.

The winner of the 1991 urban design competition was the office of Hilmer and Sattler. Their project provided the basis for a second competition focusing on the Daimler-Benz site at Potsdamer Platz, in which Ungers also participated. The competition specified certain formal criteria: preservation of the existing street system; superimposition of a grid of block structures onto the Friedrichstadt area; differentiation of the grid according to size and function of the individual blocks; and accentuation through high-rises at strategically important points.

Thus the project was developed, differentiated in a number of areas, completed, and adapted to the specific demands of the program. The centerpoint of the new plan is Potsdamer Platz. Both it and Leipziger Platz remain well-defined geometric figures, with the historic octagon of Leipziger Platz connected with the new quadrangular form of Potsdamer Platz.

The former is conceived as a green area for pedestrians, business, and leisure; the latter is a communications node with streets radiating in different directions. It is accentuated by a ring of high-rises positioned at the pointed ends of the wedge-shaped blocks encompassing the square. On the one hand, these isolated towers constitute an element of the block system; on the other, they represent autonomous structures, rising above and distinguished from the surrounding buildings by their division into two parts: a socle corresponding to the surrounding architecture, and a superstructure in the form of a climate-controlled, glass-enclosed cube.

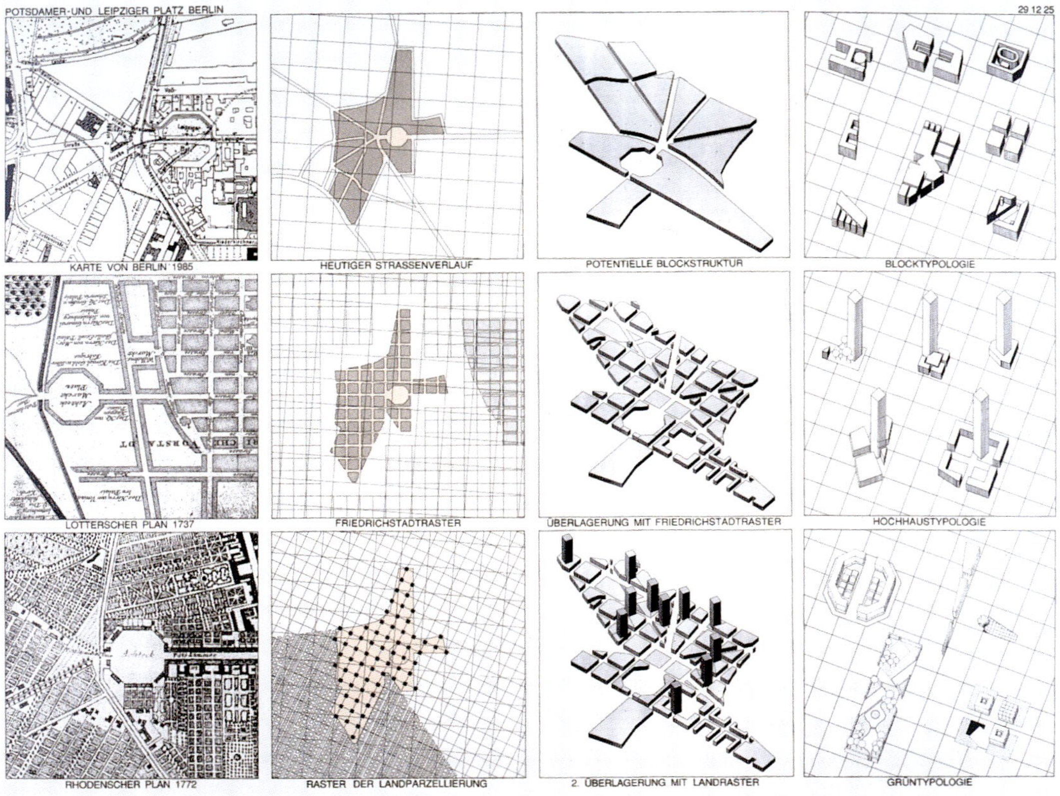

Use diagrams.

Sketch.

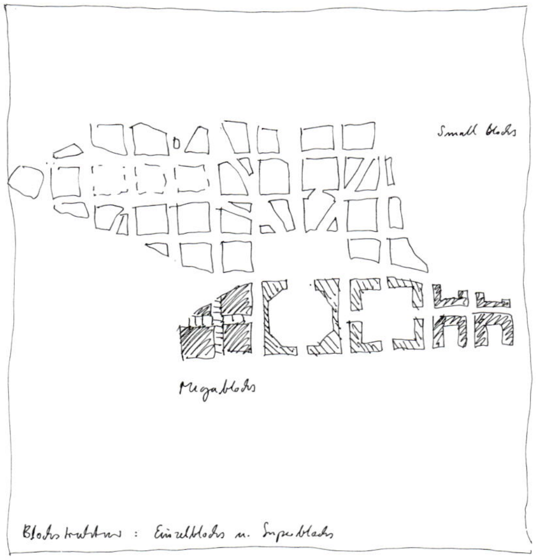

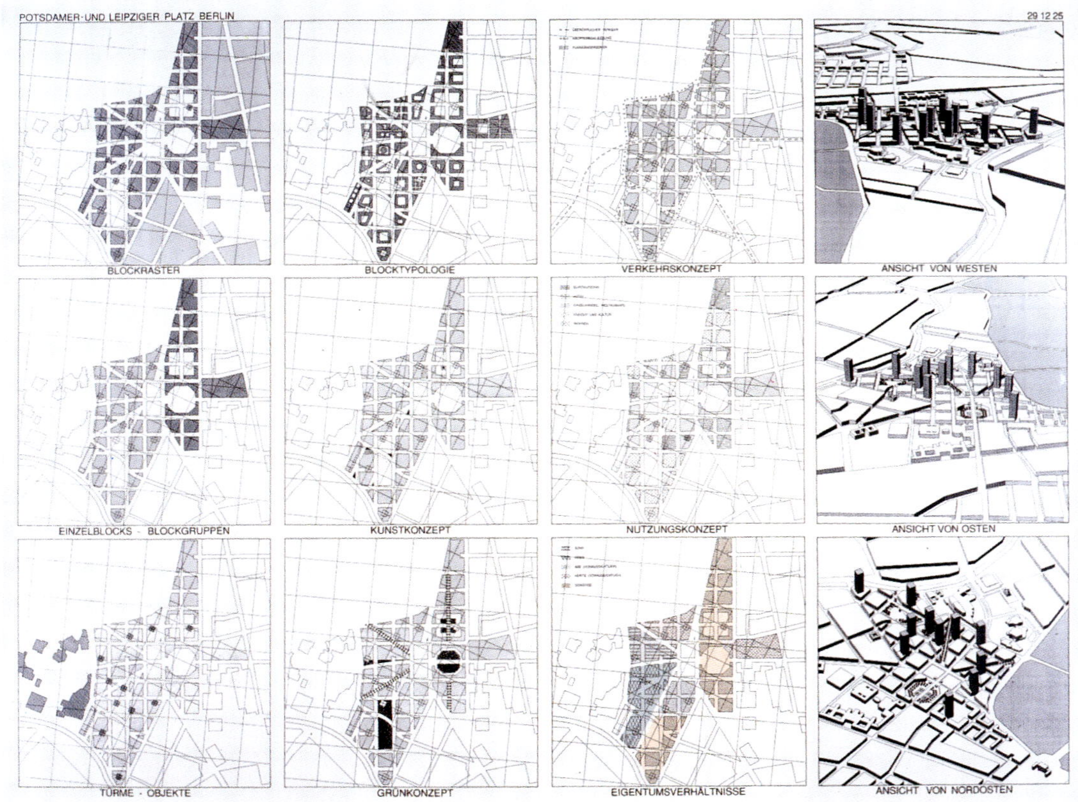

Use diagrams;
perspective views.

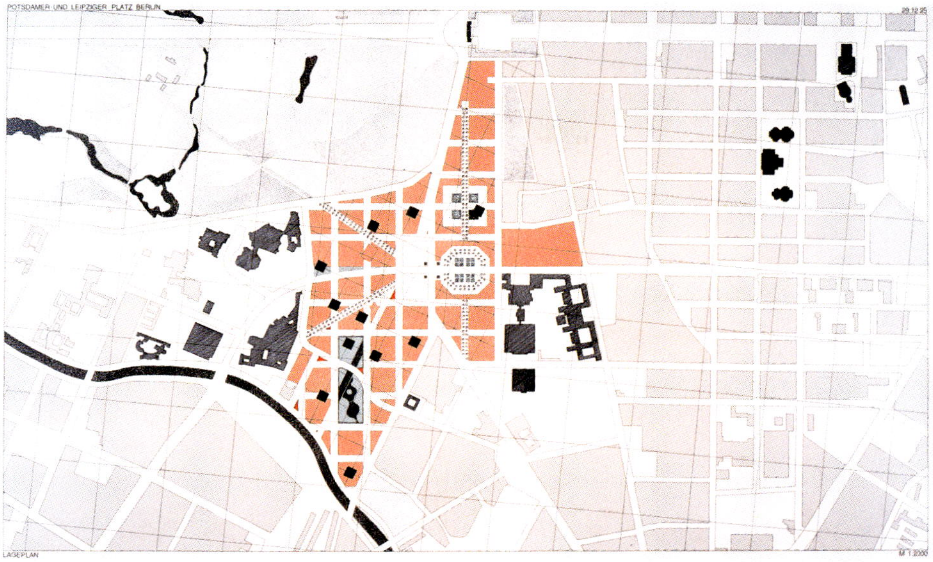

Site plan.

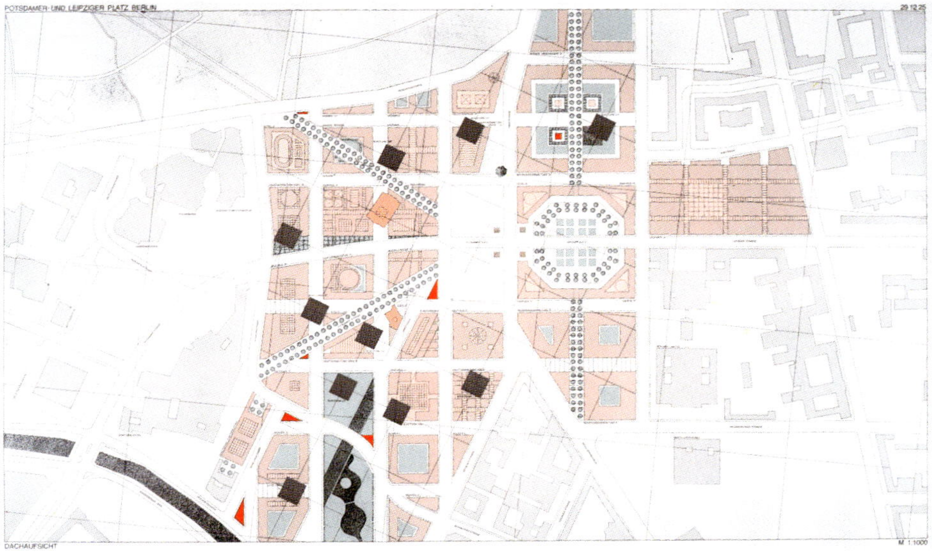

View from above; sketch.

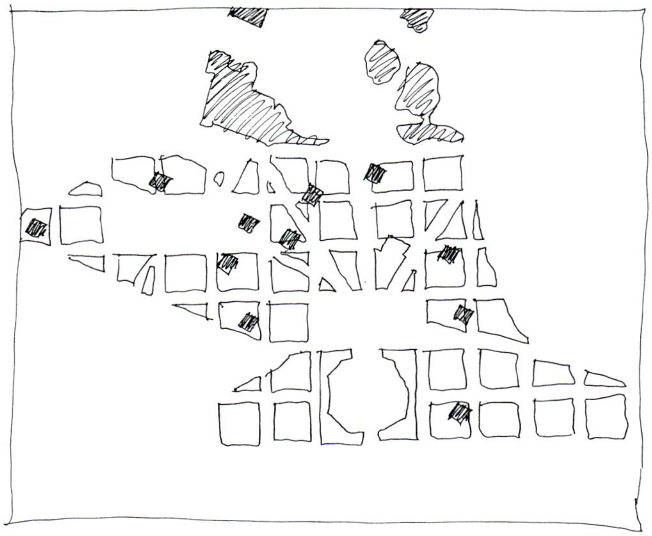

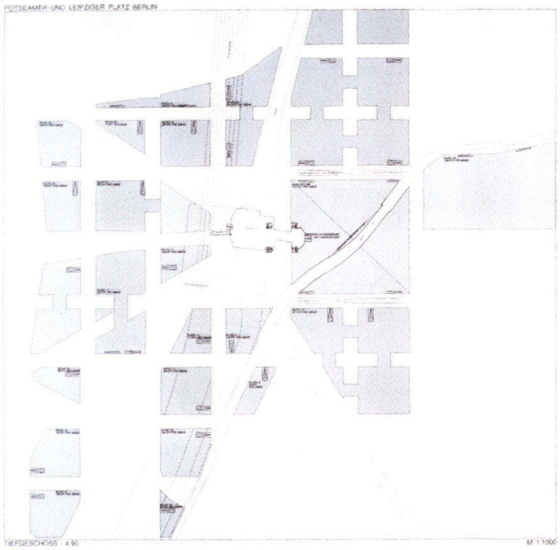

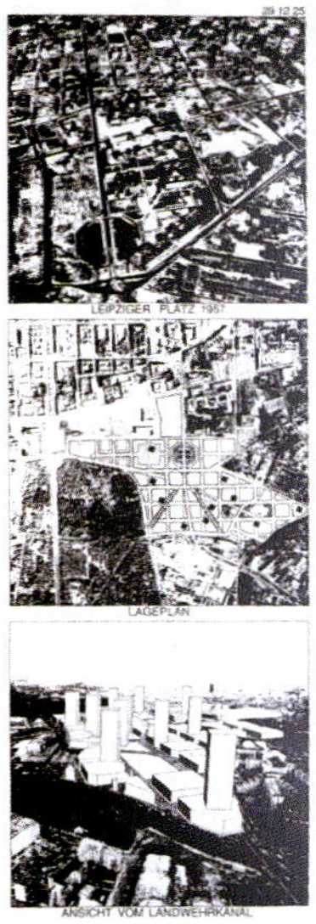

Plan of basement level; view of Leipziger Platz in 1957; site plan, photomontage.

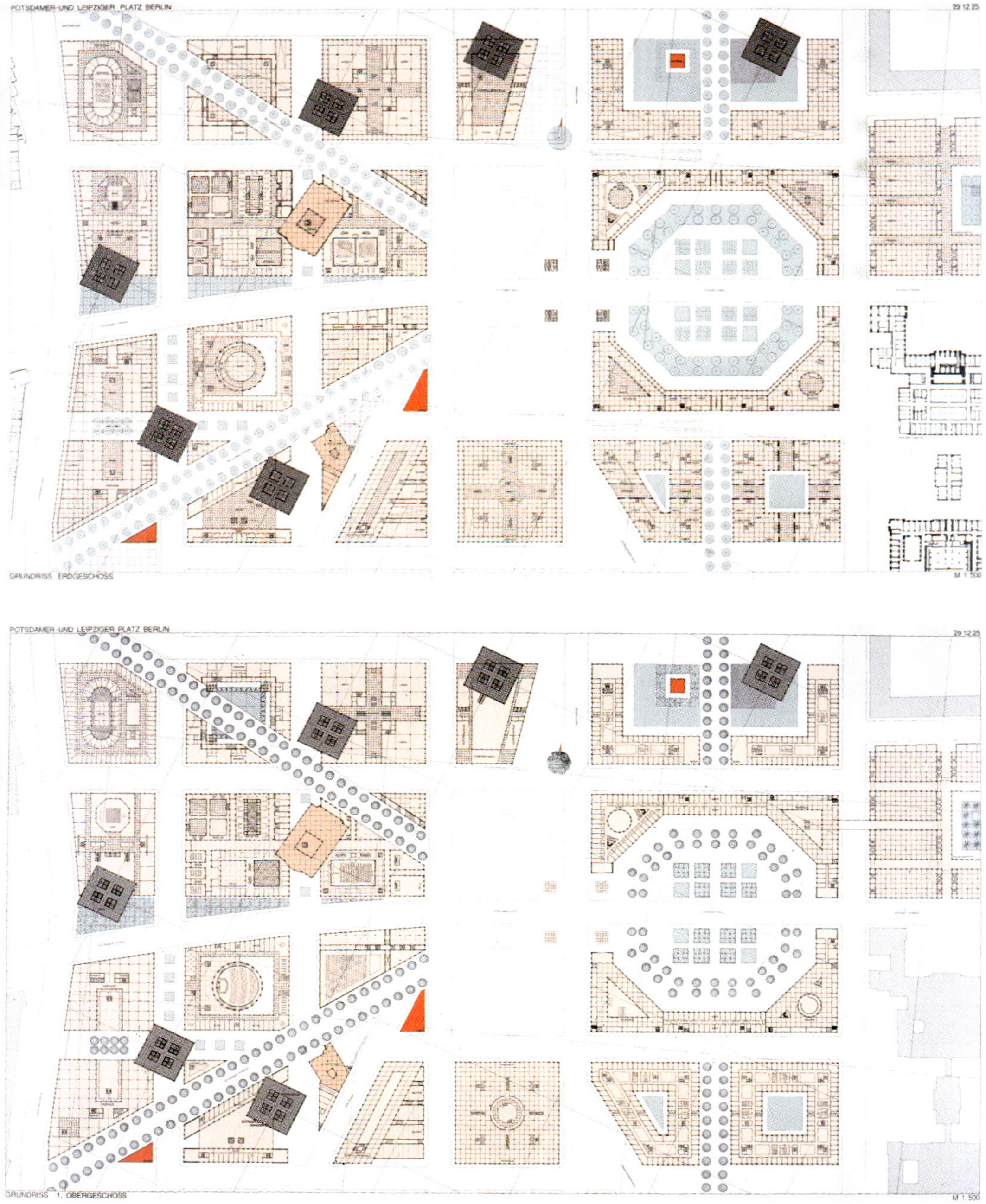

Project for Daimler-Benz site: ground-floor plan; first upper floor plan.

This ring of high-rises on Potsdamer Platz finds its counterpoint in a double tower outside the competition area in the vicinity of the Kulturforum. It marks the entrance to the city center and—in its visible connection with the towers of Potsdamer Platz—the new Potsdamer Strasse as well, an axis that likewise serves as a plaza. The result is a triad of open areas consisting of the octagon of Leipziger Platz, the square of Potsdamer Platz, and the long rectangle of Potsdamer Strasse. At the end of the old Potsdamer Strasse, which preserves its original character as an avenue, is a rectangular park with a semicircular termination, intended to have the character of a city garden and bounded laterally by the rear side of the Staatsbibliothek.

The underlying block grid, based on units of fifty by fifty meters each, provides the module for a radial figure that, proceeding from Potsdamer Platz, creates three spatially similar but functionally different traffic rings. The first, immediately adjacent to the plaza, is a covered gallery; the second is a normal, tree-lined city street that also accommodates incoming traffic; the third is a high-traffic road, establishing a relationship to the main traffic axes of the city. Between the old and the new Potsdamer Strasse, an extensive system of galleries is proposed, comprising three blocks arranged around interior courtyards with shops on the lower floors and offices above.

At the south end of Potsdamer Strasse is a business center with a domed atrium, accentuating the location with respect to both form and content. At the north entrance to the old Potsdamer Strasse is the exhibition building of the Deutsche Bahn; the two lower stories at the tip of the block, oriented toward Potsdamer Platz, accommodate service facilities as well as exhibition spaces.

A conservatory is incorporated into the top story of the Mercedes office tower. The upper stories are naturally ventilated with climate-controlled paneling. The historically significant architecture of the former Weinhaus Huth is reconstructed to accommodate a number of restaurants. Beneath the large gallery ceiling, the roof of the Enothek serves as an open-air bar.

The large open foyer of the musical theater is oriented toward the old Potsdamer Strasse. A lower entrance area with a cloakroom provides access to the building-high foyer, which in turn leads into the audience

Opposite:
Project for Daimler-Benz site: sketch; general plan.

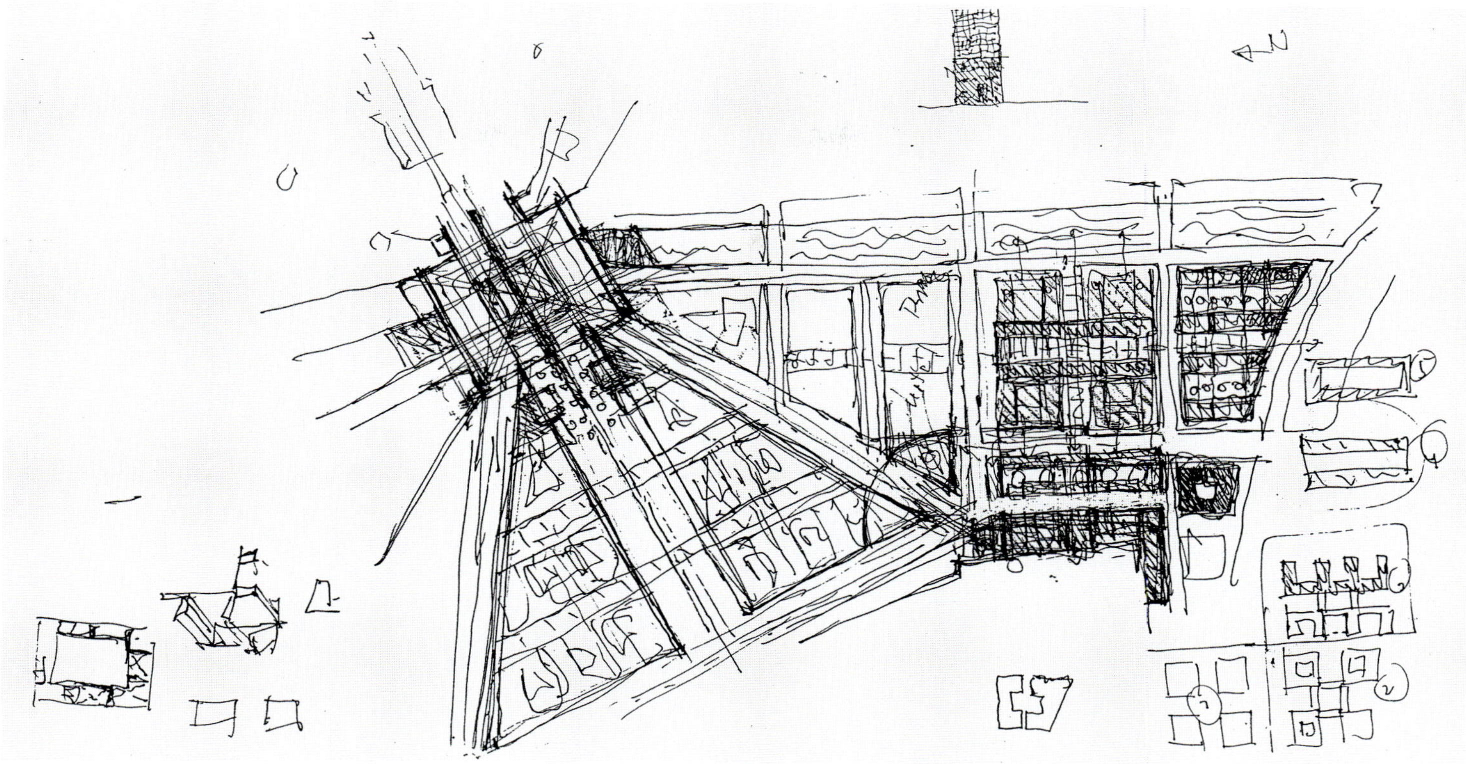

M 1:200
UBERSICHTSPLAN

Project for Daimler-Benz site: view from above; sketch.

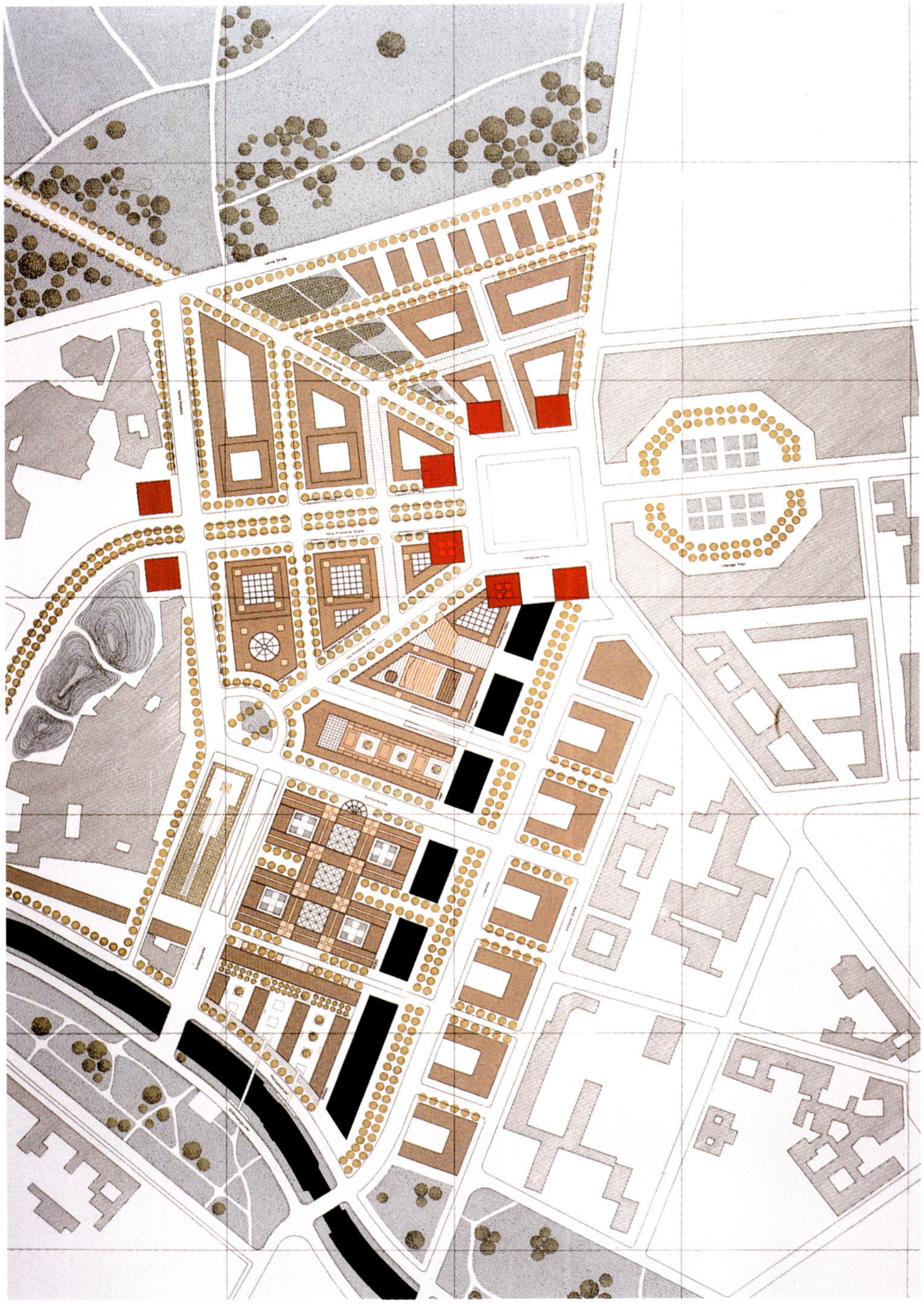

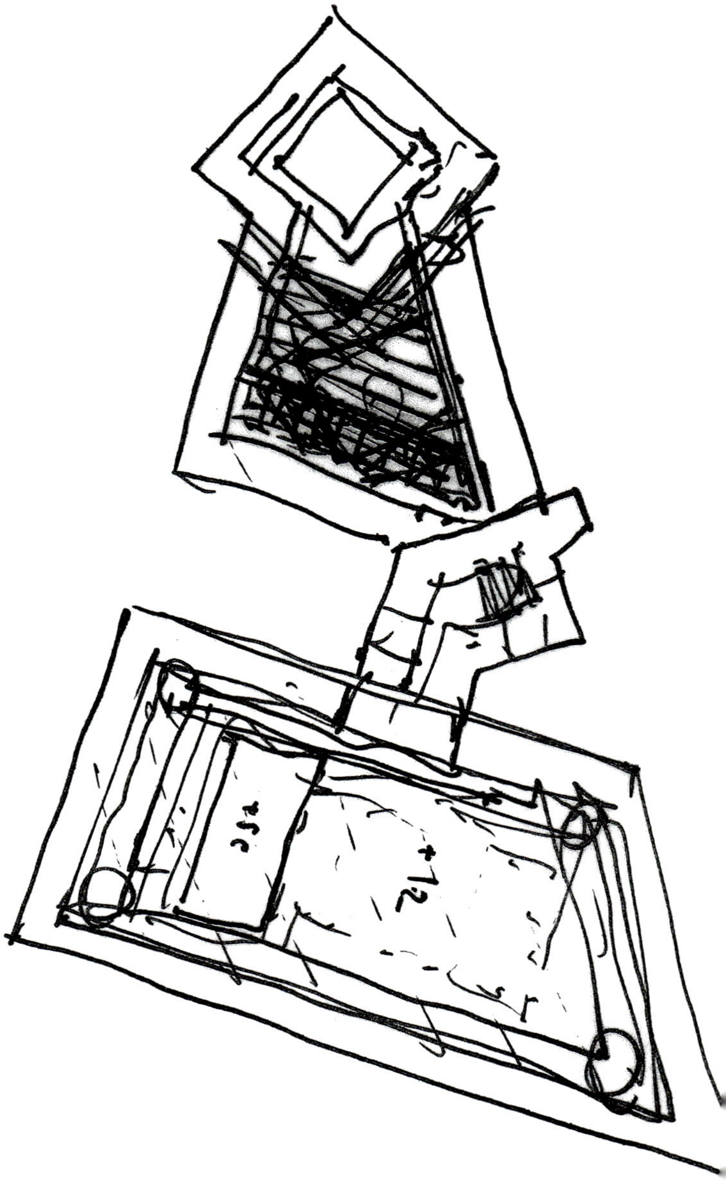

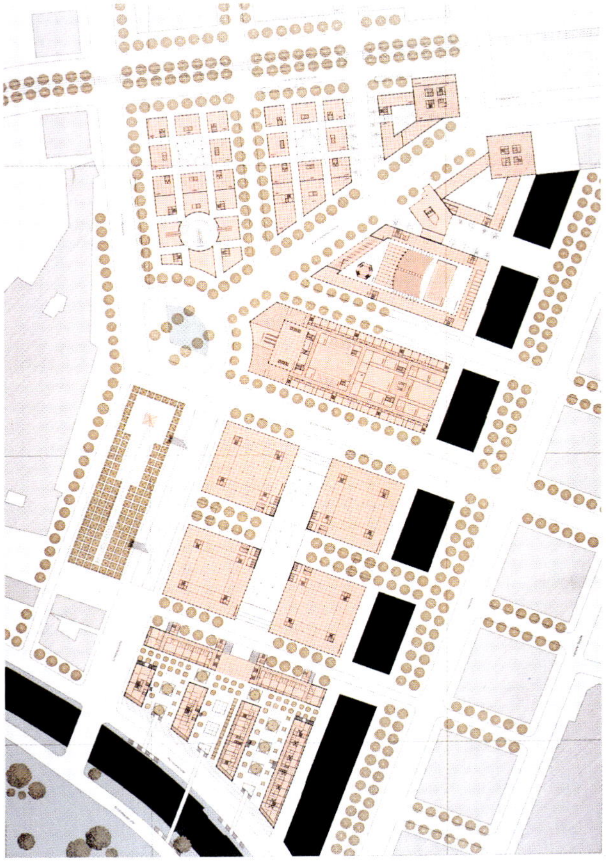

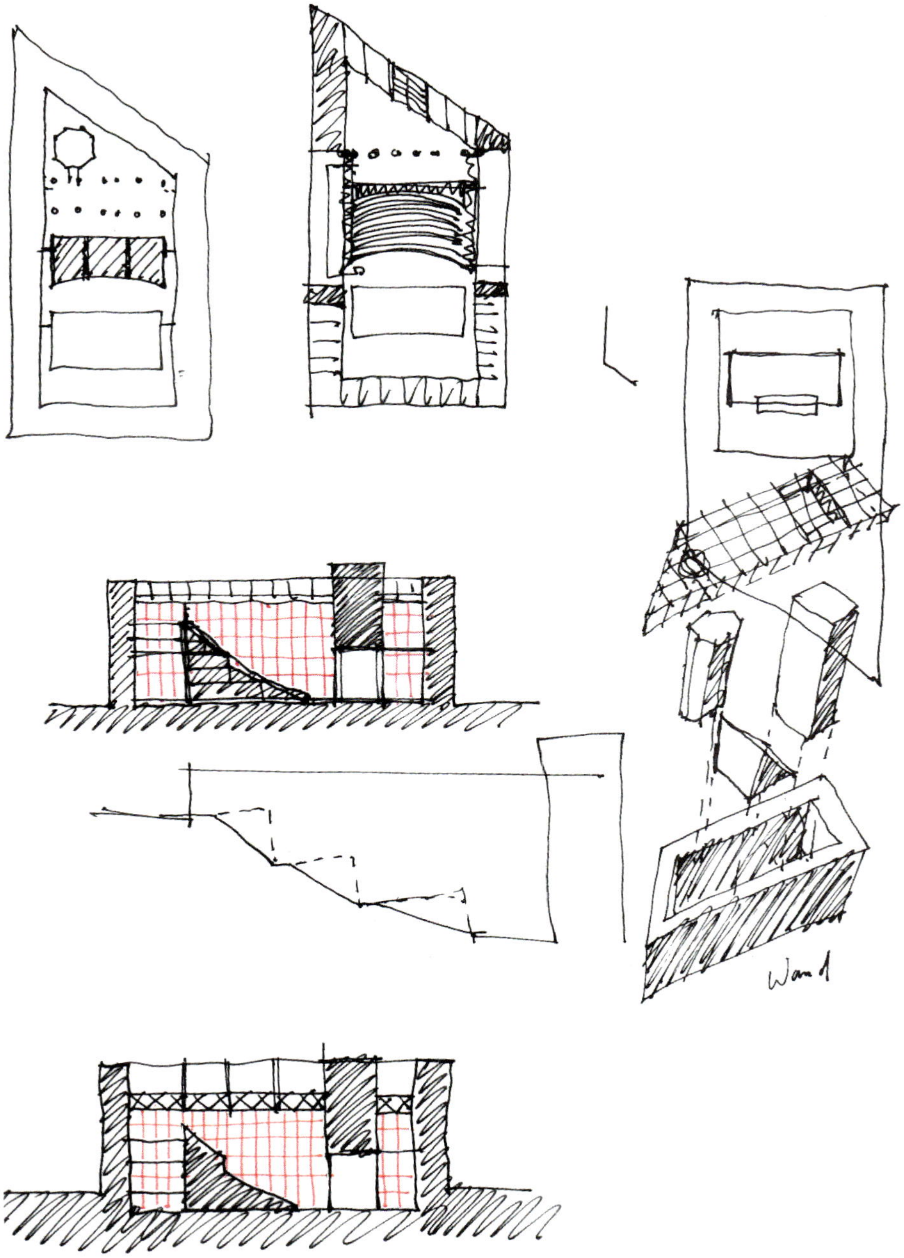

Project for Daimler-Benz site: ground-floor plan; first upper story plan; sketches for musical theater.

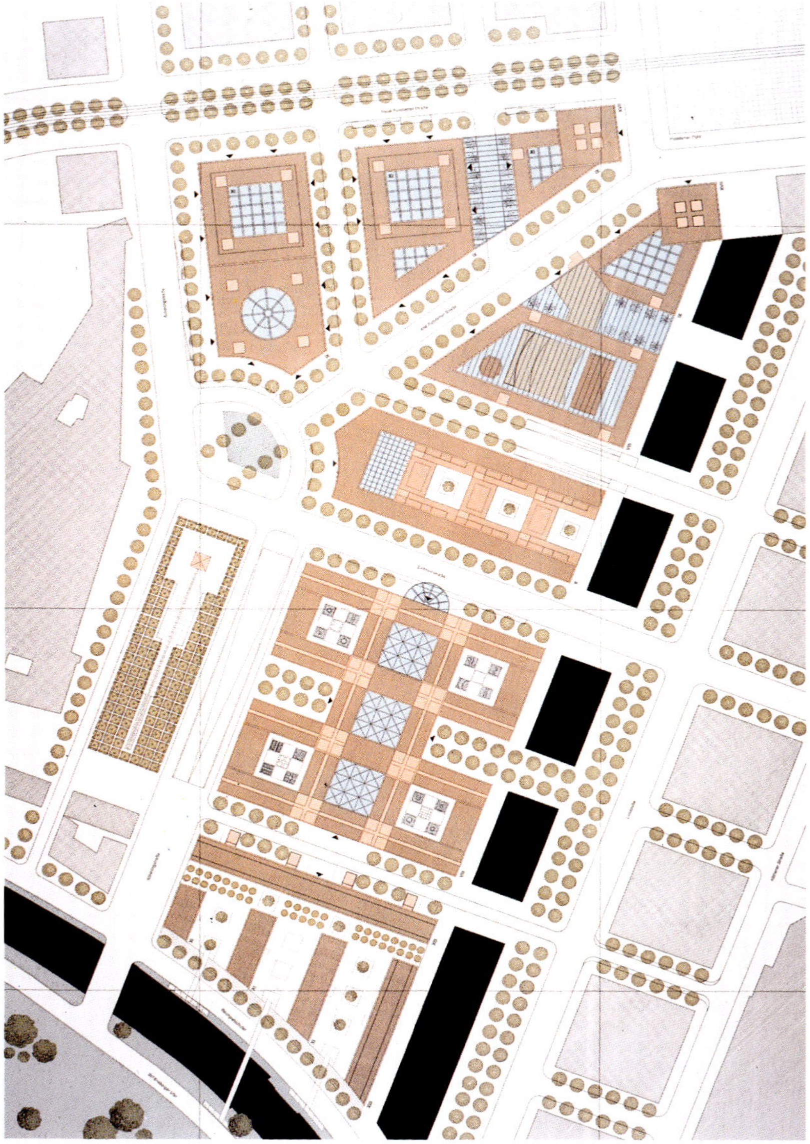

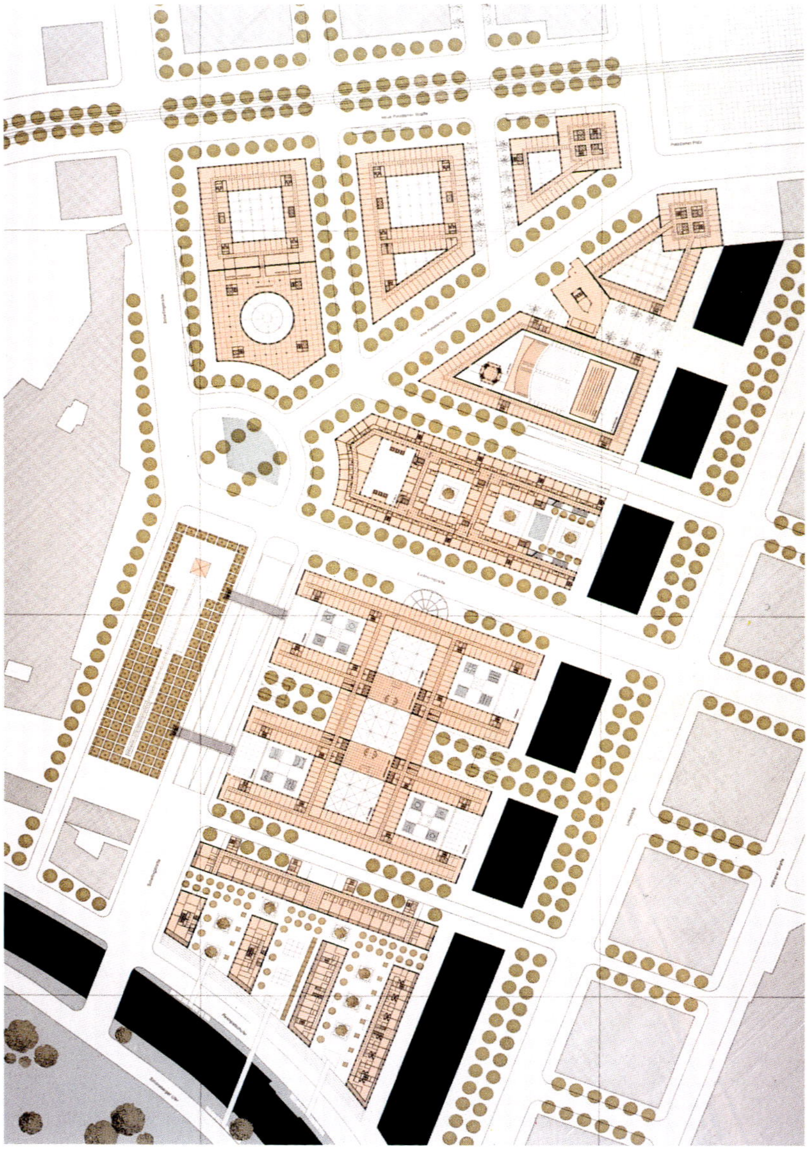

spaces located at the same level.

The hotel is oriented toward the plaza containing Hans Scharoun's Staatsbibliothek. Together with the business center, it defines this new urban space. The hotel itself occupies the upper stories, which are structured by a system of courtyards and a cascade-like arrangement of terraces; the basement level accommodates conference spaces and a fitness center.

The Debis complex is composed of four structures arranged around a shared entrance gallery. The U-shaped buildings with their terraces are oriented on the one hand toward the gallery and on the other toward the park on Schellingstrasse and the green area on Linkstrasse.

The comb-shaped residential complex along the Landwehrkanal accommodates a diverse residential program, including senior citizens' dwellings, maisonettes, and other dwellings of differing size. The buildings stand on a socle that accommodates service facilities and shops as well as a therapy area for the senior citizens. At the same time, it provides a public terrace with a view of the Landwehrkanal.

The proposed reorganization of the built structure is not confined to the zone around Potsdamer Platz; the Kulturforum also is incorporated into the overall project. The reference point and point of departure is Mies van der Rohe's Nationalgalerie. Two measures emphasize the special historic and cultural significance of this building: the extension of the residential buildings to the south to form a spatial boundary along the Landwehrkanal, and the inclusion of a plaza in the area of the Kulturforum, across from the Nationalgalerie. Mies's building thus finds itself at a strategically and geometrically dominant point, while the amorphous, out-of-scale mass of the Staatsbibliothek takes its place in a spatial structure that makes it more urbanistically tolerable, a jagged mountain range, as it were, within a large, urbanistically circumscribed area.

Overleaf:
Project for Daimler-Benz site: two examples of elevation and section along Linkstrasse with residential buildings, Debis complex, hotel, musical theater, and Daimler-Benz building.

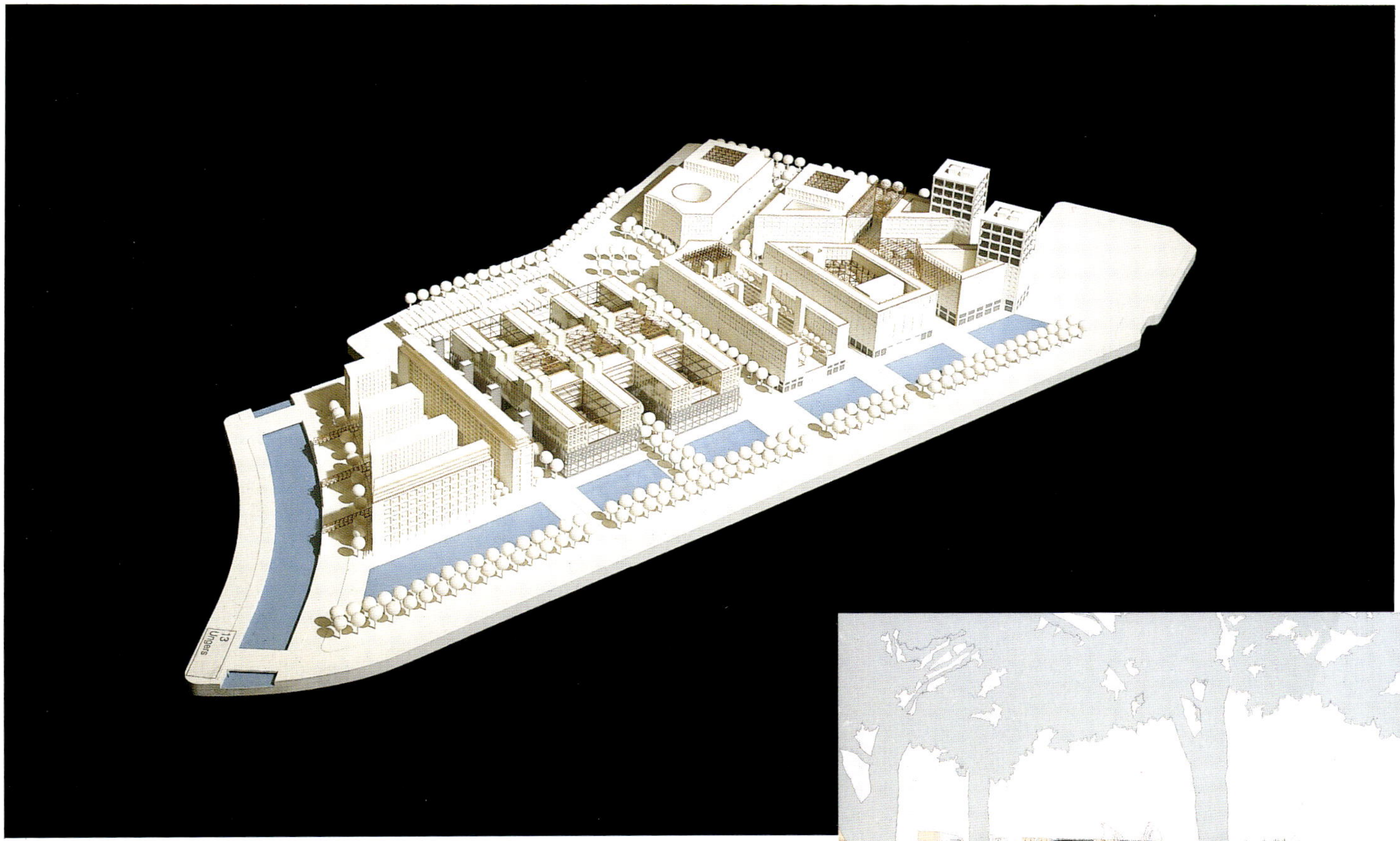

Project for Daimler-Benz site: view from above; ground-level plan; model; perspective views.

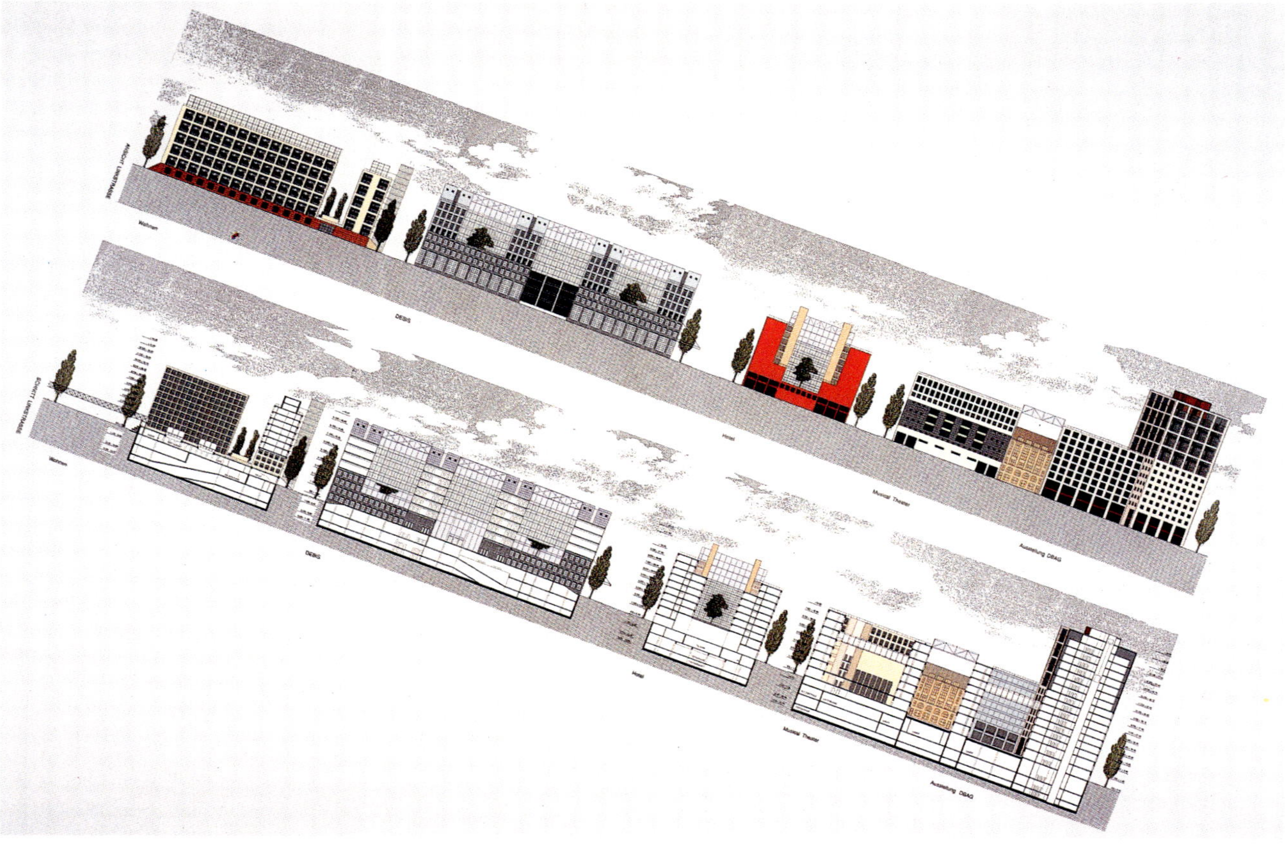

Competition Design for Olympia Arena, Berlin, 1991

Project team: Axel Balzereit, Benedikt Baumewerd, Lukas Baumewerd, Sharon Chung-Klatte, Johannes Götz, Sebastian Klatt, Jörg Lenschow, Ulrich Müller, Joachim Sieber, Dominic Snellgrove, Tanja Treversian

Use diagrams of Olympia area.

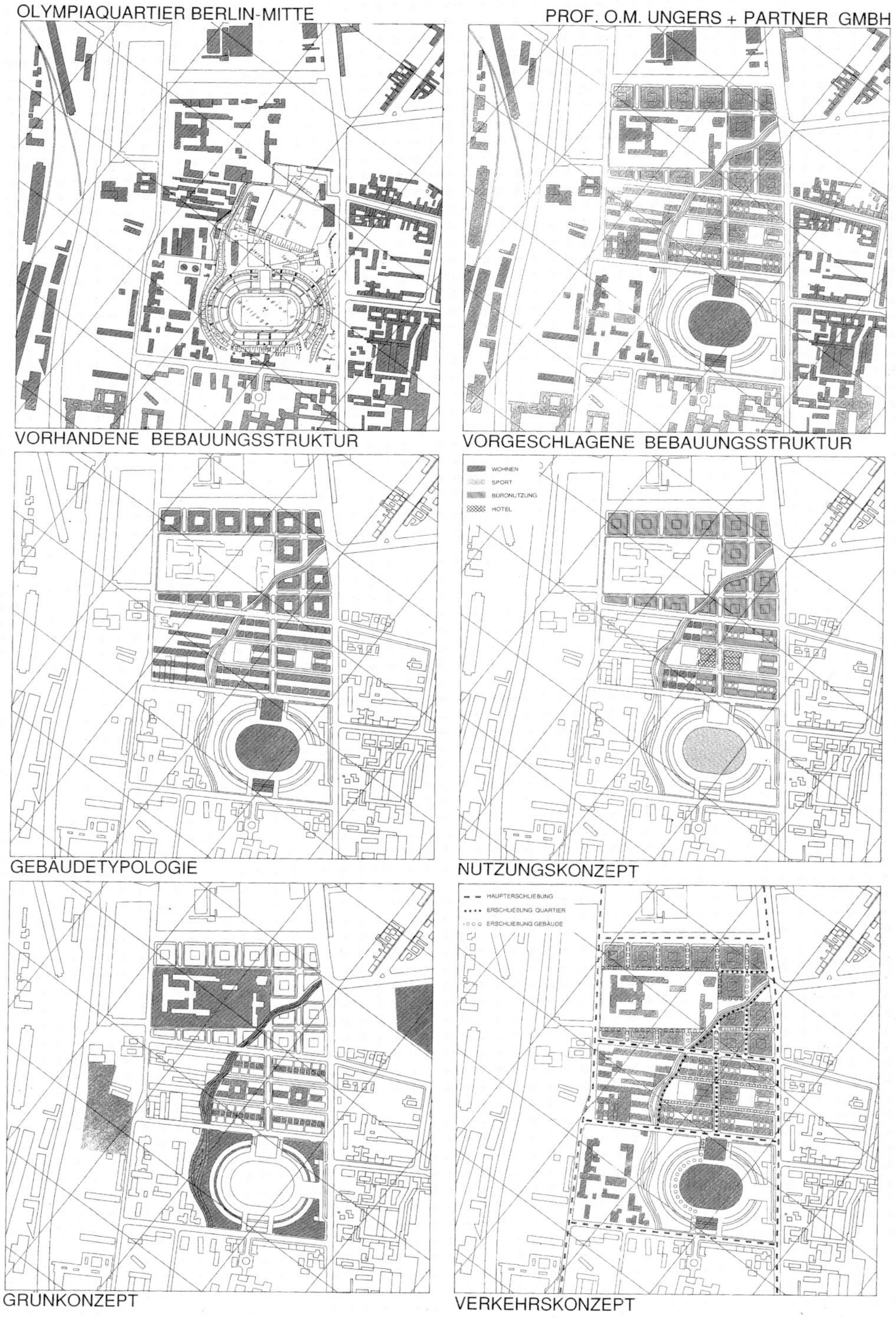

The program called for a multipurpose arena with fifteen thousand seats, adjoining spaces, and additional buildings with approximately eighteen thousand square meters of total floor space, designated for a mixture of commercial and residential uses. The site lies at the edge of the actual urban core (Friedrichstadt, Unter den Linden, Spreebogen, and so forth) and is bounded by Chausseestrasse to the east, Scharnhornstrasse and the Berlin-Spandau shipping canal to the west, Boyenstrasse to the north, and Habersaathstrasse to the south. It evinces the mixture of residential building and large-scale institutions and facilities typical of the Moabit district. The block structure of the historic city, particularly Friedrichstadt, exists here only in a rudimentary form.

The area is dominated by individual buildings such as the Charité, the Hamburger Bahnhof, Eltron, the natural history museum, and the Schering building. The urban image is as unarticulated and heterogeneous as the street plan, which is incomplete, incoherent, and much too coarse-grained for sensible architectural use, a character that has resulted not only from the years of division by the Wall, but also from the insertion of larger built areas into the network of streets. Accordingly, the plan first of all calls for an augmented, reorganized street grid, that provides better articulation for the out-of-scale built areas and also creates a differentiated block structure.

Two new streets are introduced parallel to Habersaathstrasse, linking Chausseestrasse and Scharnhornstrasse. Together with Sellerstrasse and Boyenstrasse, they serve to create five blocks of approximately equal size and differing function, thus reflecting the high level of complexity of the surrounding urban structure. The principle of dialectical urban form defines the proposal, reflecting diversity in unity.

The first block between Invalidenstrasse and Habersaathstrasse comprises mainly dwellings and the natural history museum. The second block is occupied by the new Berlin-Arena, built into the existing embankment of the Stadion der Weltjugend. Its position within the embankment serves not only to visually reconcile the large structure with its residential surroundings but above all to create ecologically advantageous conditions (sound insulation). The third block consists of east-west rows of buildings about thirty meters in height in a mixture of residential and commercial usage. The rows are interrupted by two green plazas opening up toward the reconstructed watercourse of the Panke River, a greened, recreational strip extending throughout the entire area. The fourth block accommodates an extended hospital complex and an additional structure

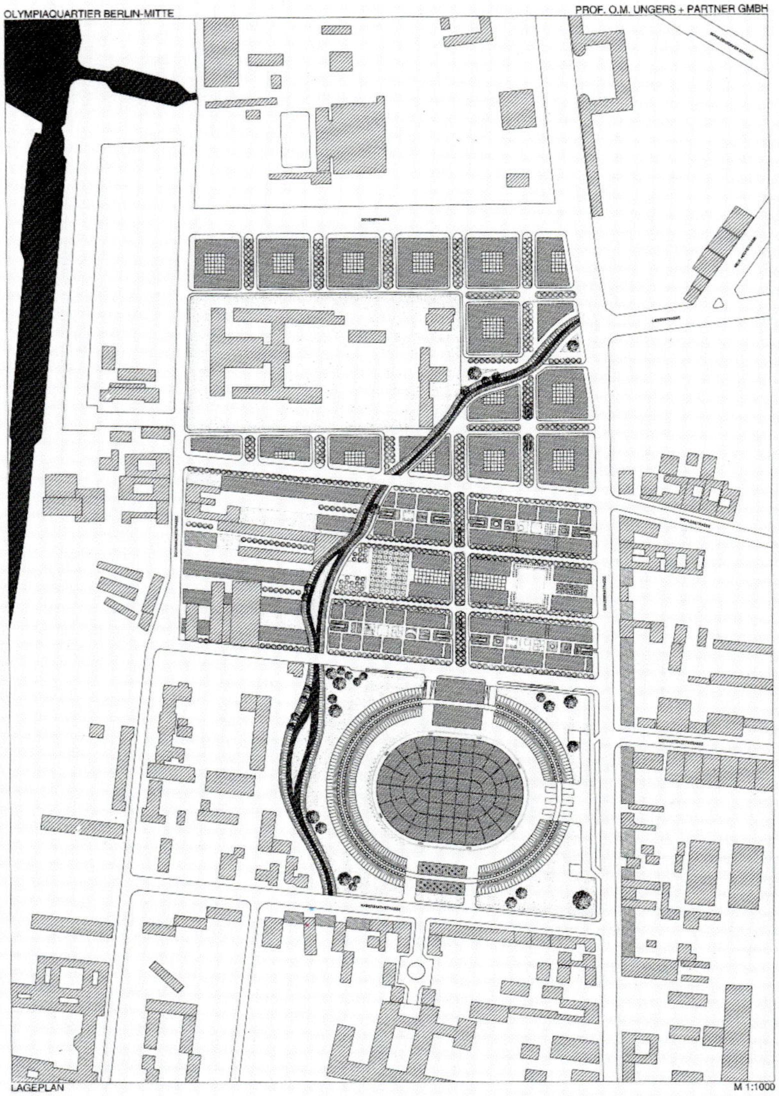

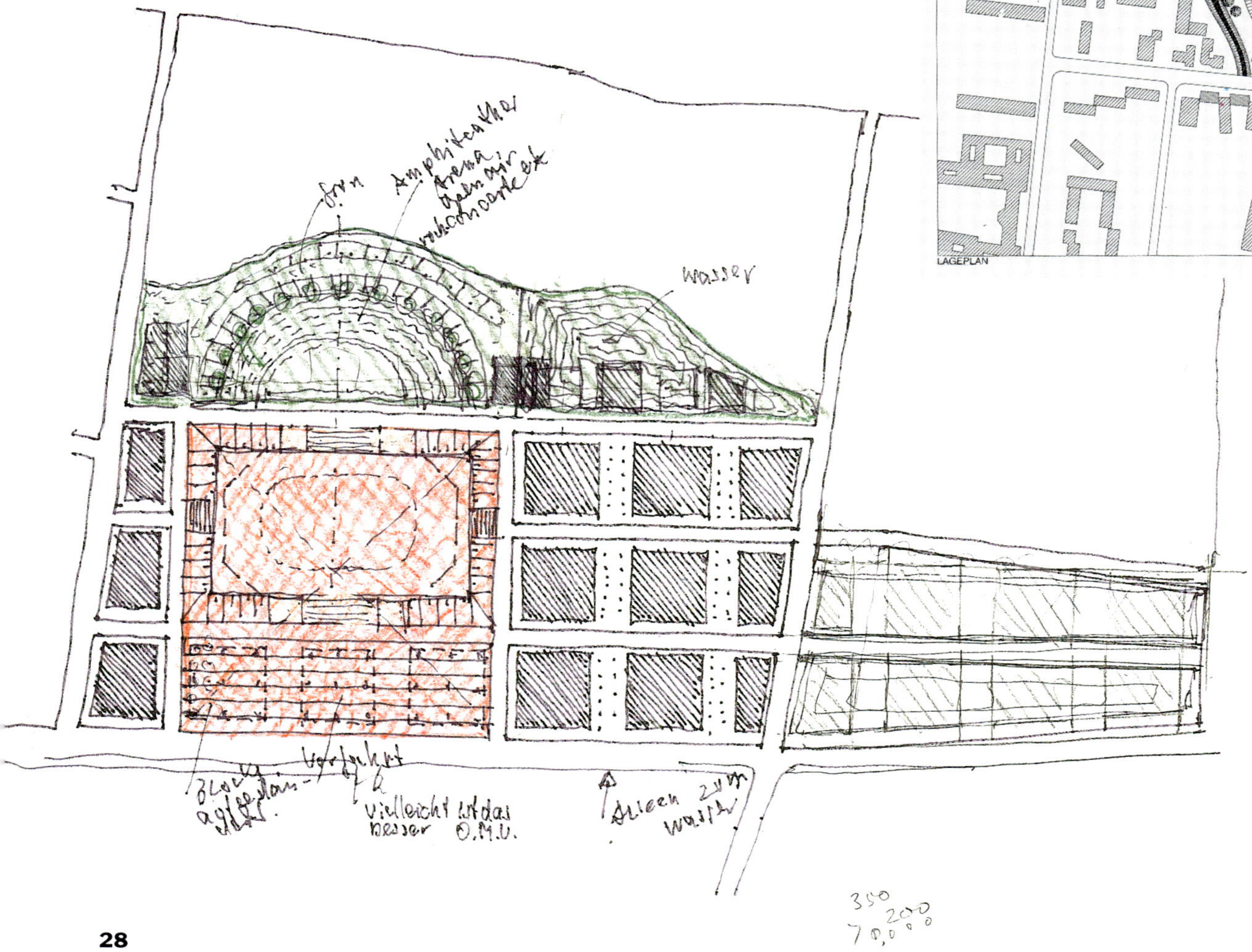

Sketch; site plan.

Perspective views; model views.

OLYMPIAQUARTIER BERLIN-MITTE PROF. O.M. UNGERS + PARTNER GMBH

ANSICHT VON NORDOSTEN

ANSICHT VON SÜDWESTEN

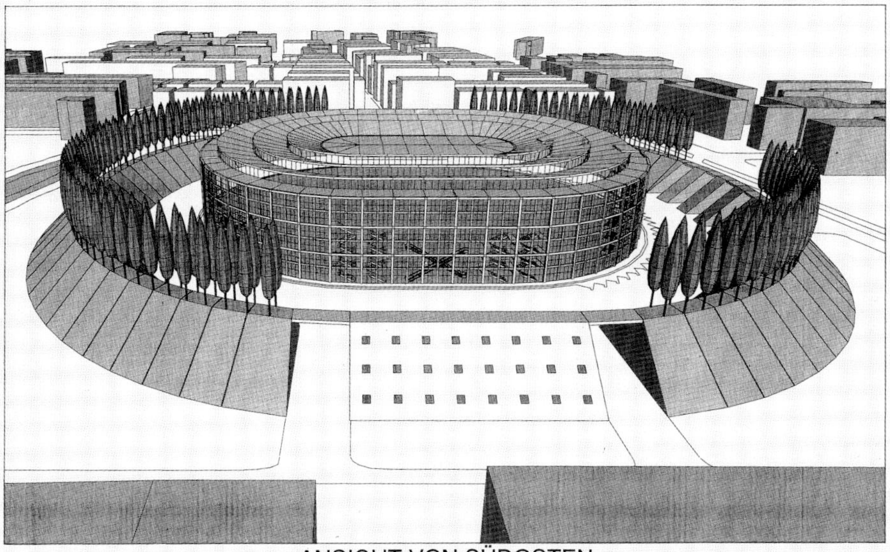

ANSICHT VON SÜDOSTEN

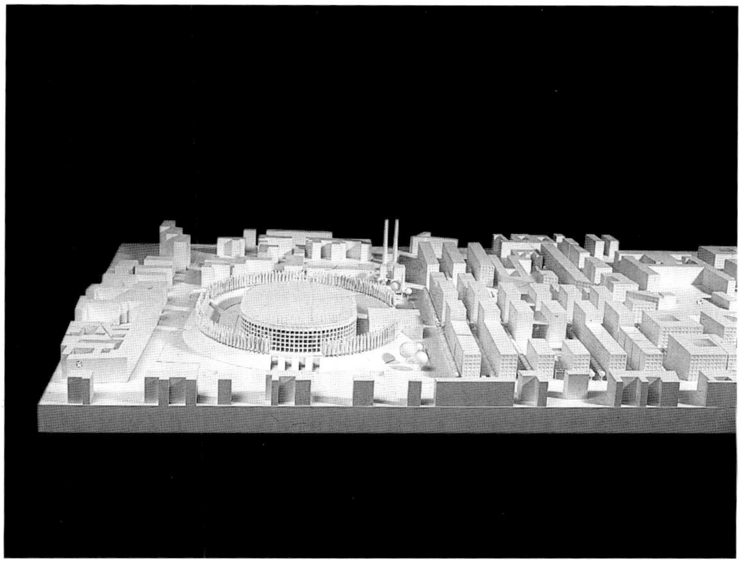

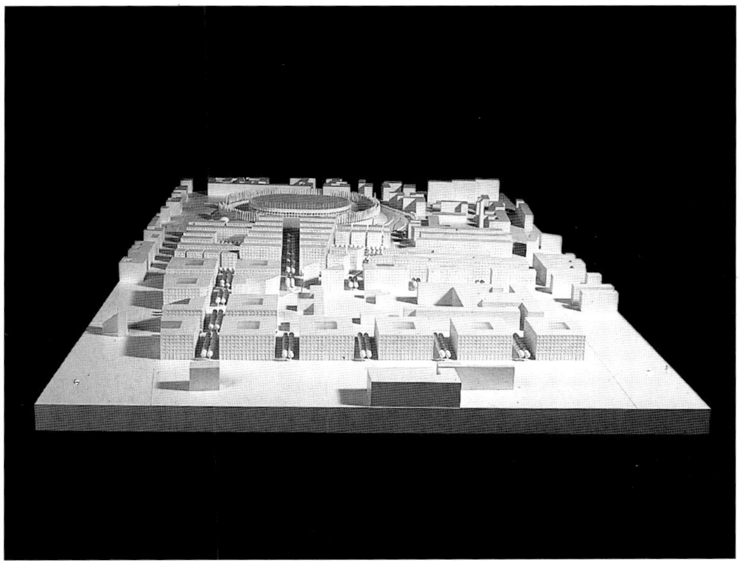

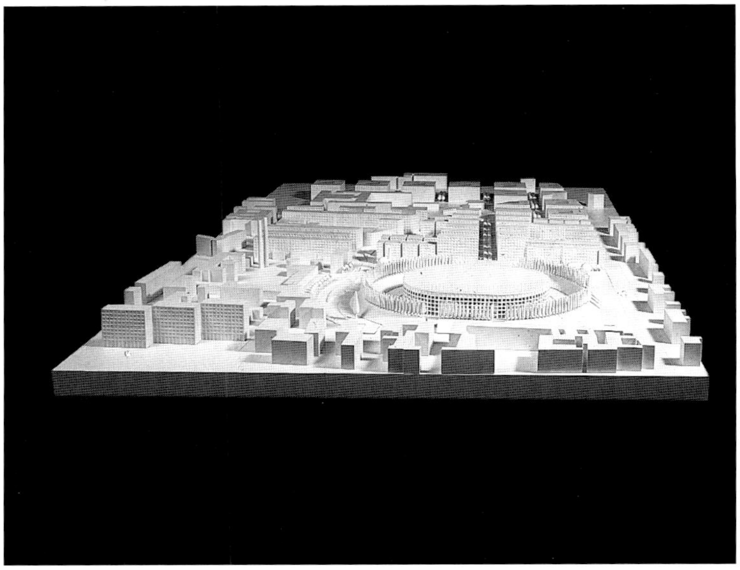

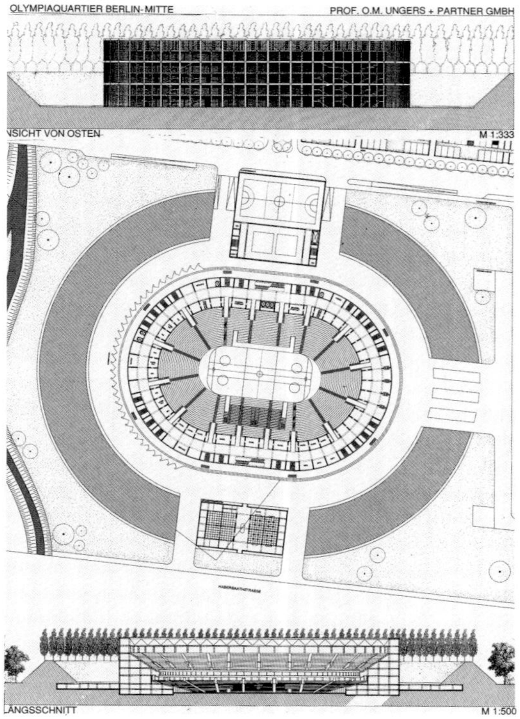

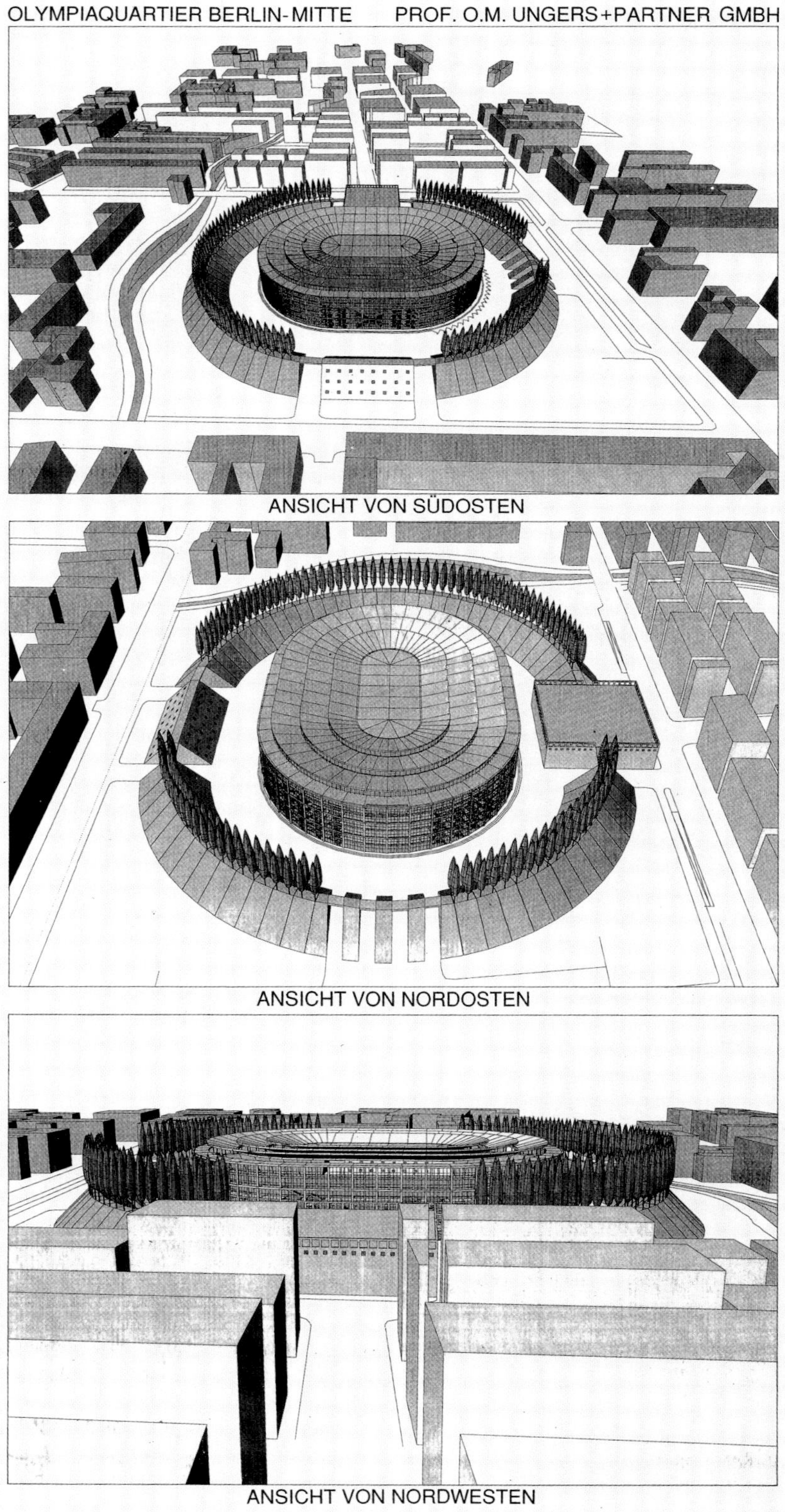

Sketch; elevation, plan, and section; perspective views.

of blocks measuring fifty by fifty meters each, suitable for office, institutional, and residential use. The fifth block contains a variety of different structures, with an existing ice rink, transformer substation, and various components of the Schering corporation. Dwellings could be added as well.

Within the urban ensemble, the grounds of the arena also function as a public park. The arena itself is embedded in a green embankment, the top of which serves as a tree-lined jogging path. In addition, the Panke River is transformed into a strip of green extending throughout the individual blocks in a continuous band. This park area is to be enlivened with flowing water, small islands, and above all small works of architecture (bridges, footpaths, plateaus, terraces, benches, rest areas, pavilions) designed by different artists. The image of the classicist or mannerist garden serves as a model here—a small, artistically embellished piece of nature in the city.

Competition Design for High-Rise at Landtag, Düsseldorf, 1991

With: Volker Busse

Project team: Stefan Vieths, Lukas Baumewerd, Benedikt Baumewerd

The objective was to design a building that will mark the approach to the city center, complete a high-caliber architectural ensemble, point the way to the future, radiate attractiveness and novelty, convey a sense of identity, and simultaneously serve as a symbol and trademark for the city of Düsseldorf. The metaphor is that of a "magic cube"—a floating cubic form, by day a mysterious black box and by night an illuminated glass body above the city, a point of light, a glowing cube; a building with two faces: both light and dark, closed and open, transparent and opaque; a hovering ideal form, detached from the exigencies of the place and therefore of the highest rationality and perfection; a technological "miracle cube," marked by the absolute laws of geometry and purity of proportion, connected to the earth by a scaffolding of slender steel supports and glass shafts, fragile-seeming legs that suggest the instability of the cube.

Below, a massive four- to six-meter-high socle of red granite imitates the irregular form of the street and the site, an intentional opposition to the ideal form of the cube. The entrance, with the reception area, is located in the socle, with escalators leading to the entrance hall at the plateau level. The socle area accommodates technical facilities and thirty-four parking spaces.

Site plan.

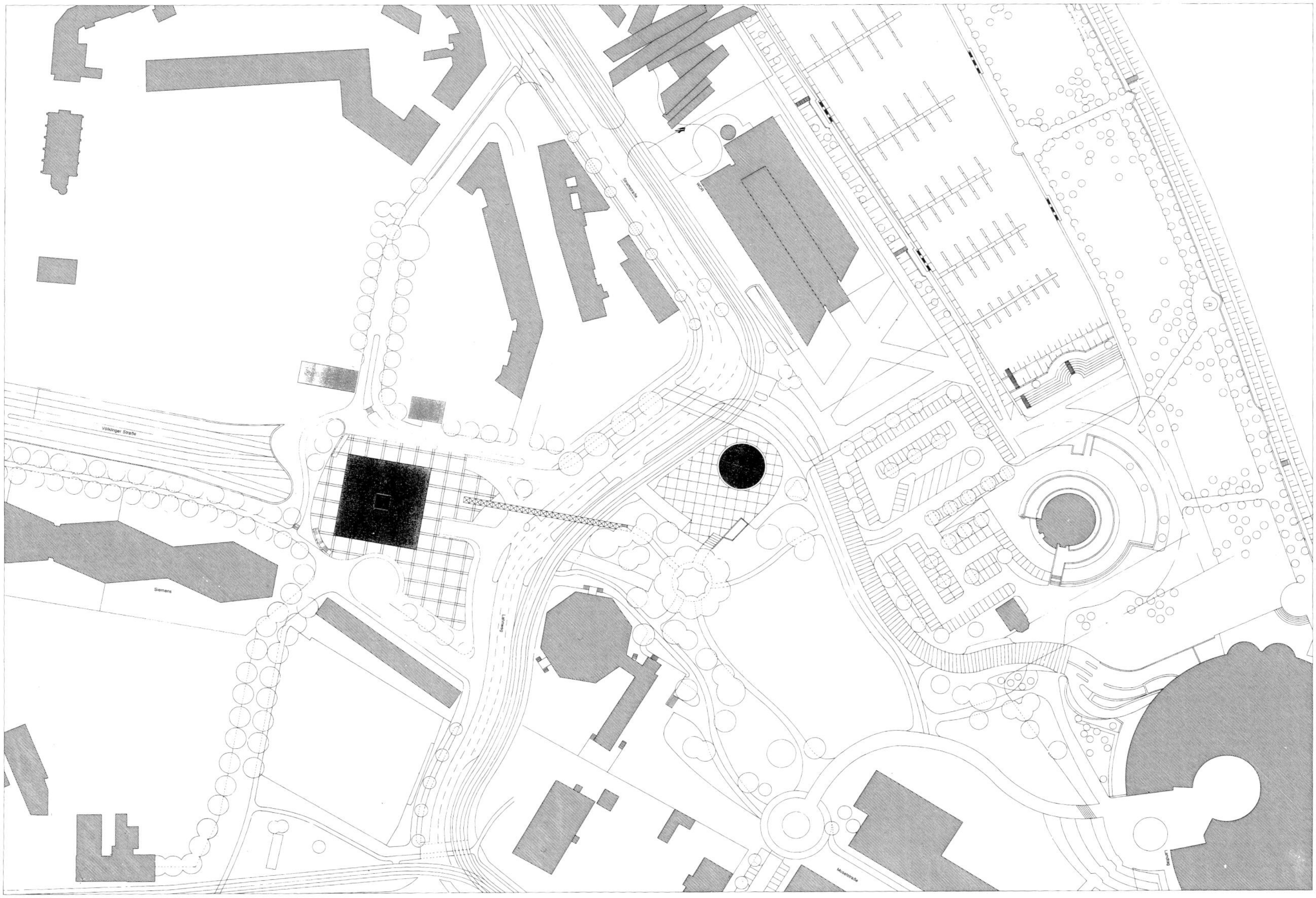

Views by night and by day;
plan at socle level; section.

Model views.

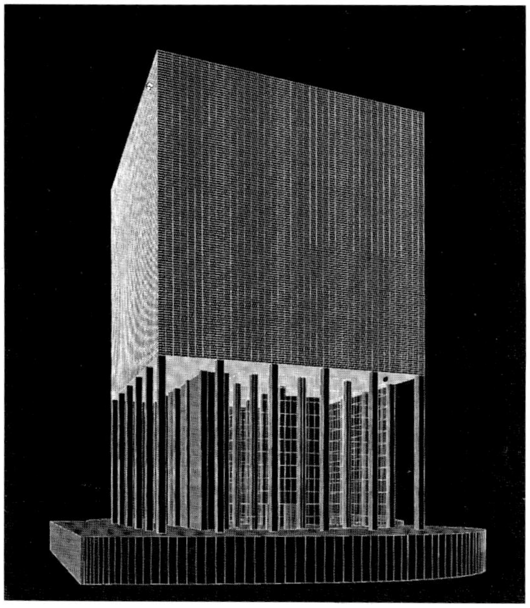

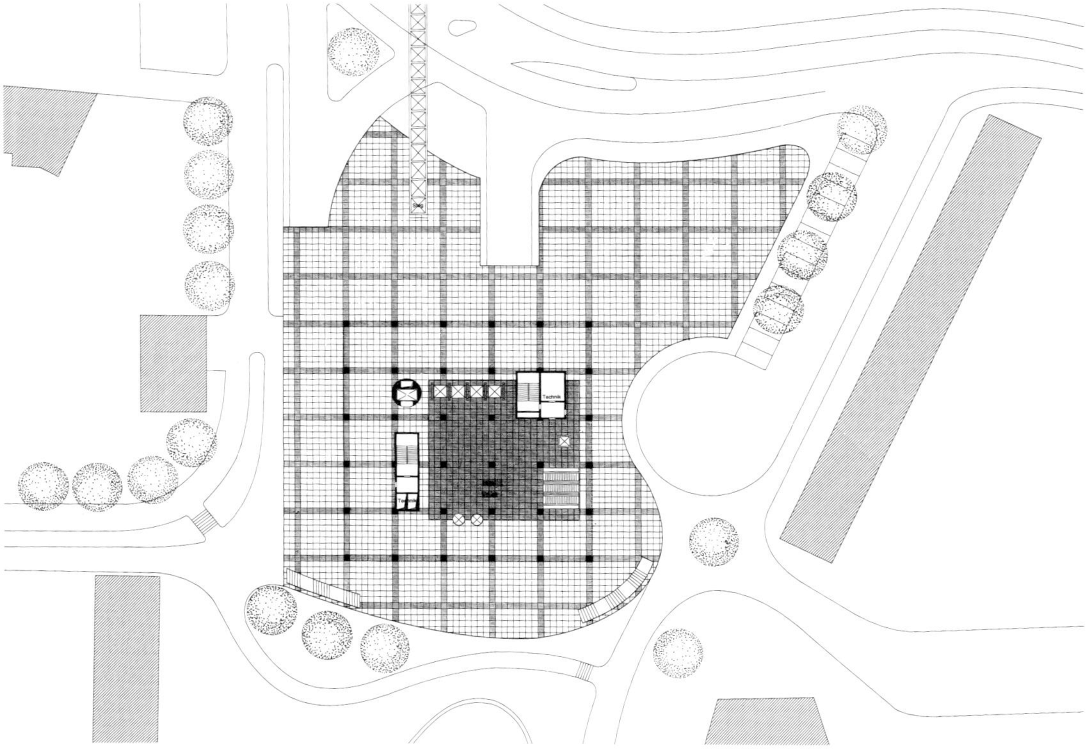

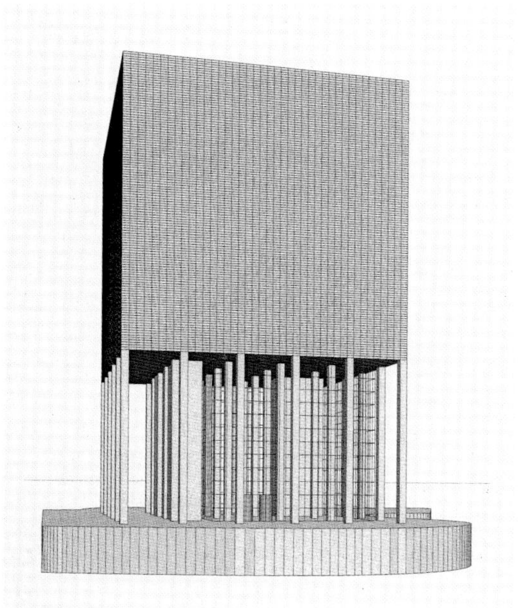

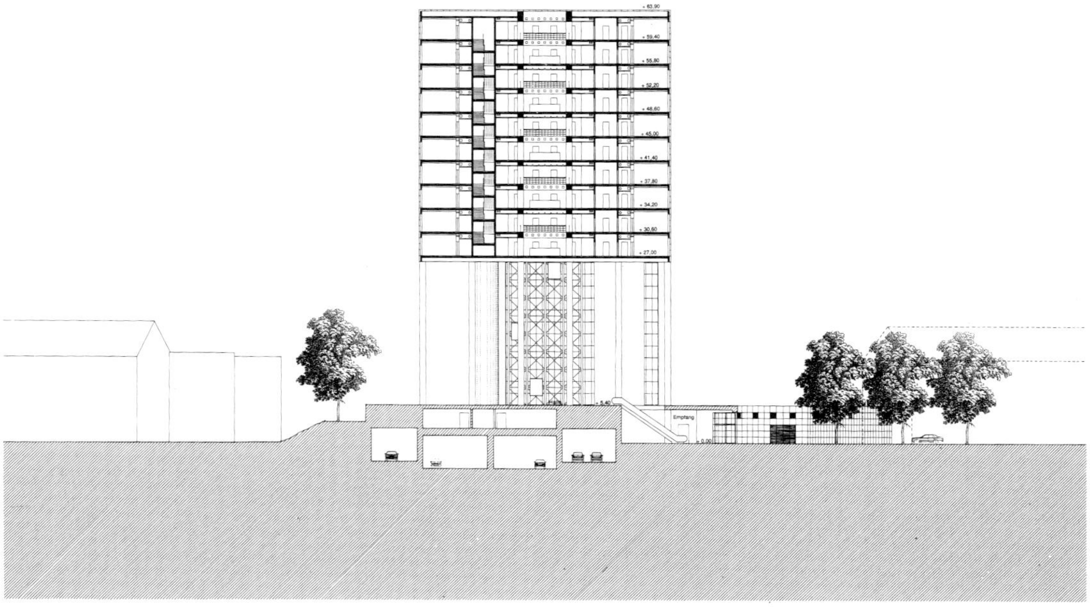

Competition Design for City Portal Buildings, Frankfurt am Main, 1991

With: Stefan Vieths

Project team: Benedikt Baumewerd, Lukas Baumewerd, Kai-Uwe Lompa, Markus Müller, Axel Steudel

The design is the result of various interpretive possibilities based on an analysis of the formation of a gate structure. The two high-rise buildings mark the western entrance to the city on Theodor-Heuss-Allee at the Emserbrücke. While the buildings have the same basic form and height, their differing construction and design are defined by their differing integration into the urban context, functional usage, and technological conditions.

The trade fair tower—an office building—completes the missing corner of Hall 8 of the trade fair grounds and emphasizes its northeast edge. With a solid interior core and an outer shell of light steel construction, the

Model view; plan.

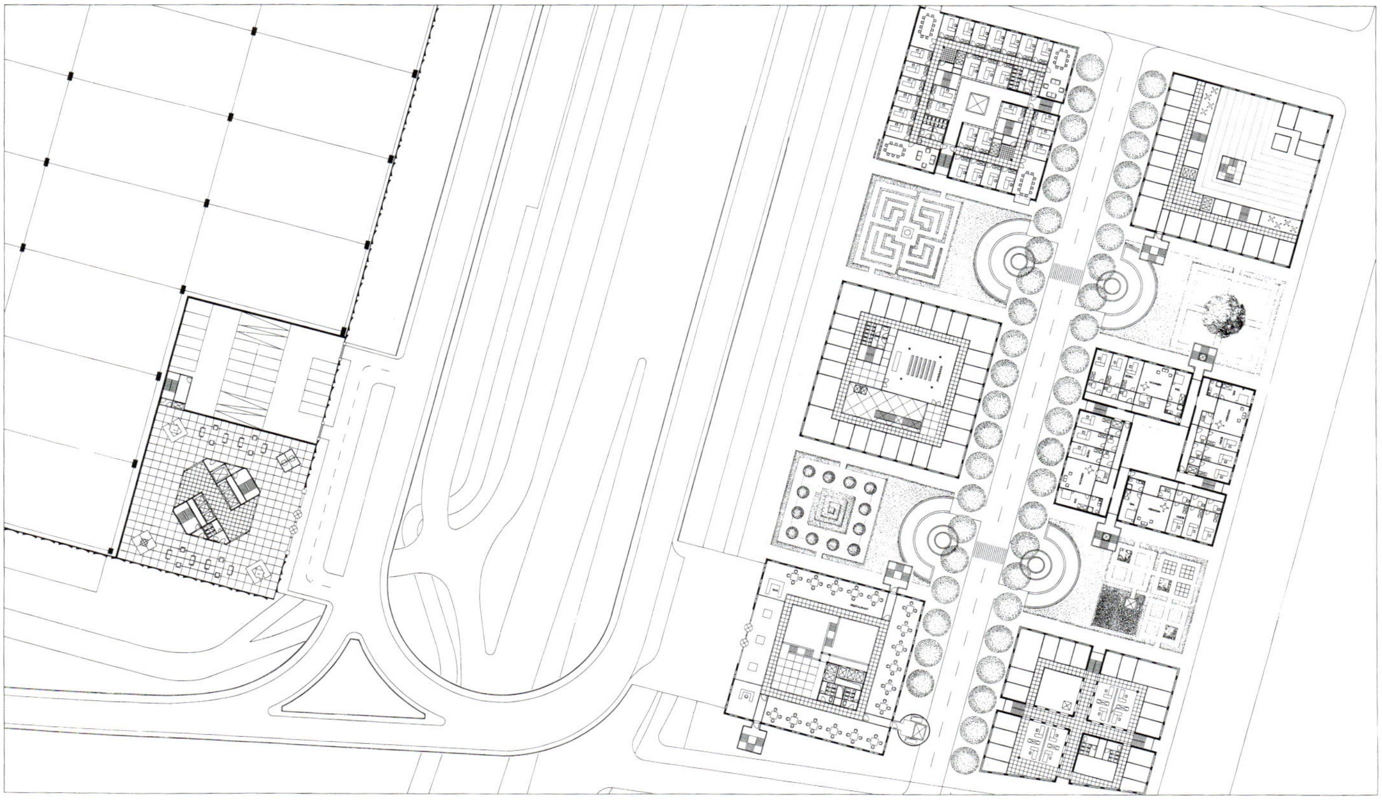

Opposite:
Plans of various levels with trade fair tower on left and Bosch tower on right; facade detail of Bosch tower; sketches.

building has a climate-controlled sheath over its entire height. In the upper ten stories, the basic form changes from a quadratic to a rectangular plan. The continuous climate-controlled sheath around the exterior is in two-story segments and contains green plants. The trade fair tower has an entrance and a driveway at the +6.50 meter level. A separate garage stands next to the high-rise. The ground floor under the tower remains open, accommodating the covered service entrances for Hall 8 of the trade fair.

The Bosch tower marks the southeast edge of a six-building complex on a single block. With a minimized core and exterior disposal towers, it evinces three different technical concepts from bottom to top. The lower area is a solid shell with random openings and natural ventilation. The middle area is supplied with partially natural and partially artificial ventilation, to be used as needed. The upper area consists of a climate-controlled shell, and is mechanically ventilated. The tower has two entrances: one at the ±0.00 meter level facing the interior of the block, and the other at the +6.50 meter level, accessible from the new trade fair bridge. The parking areas for the entire block are consolidated into a linear, two-story underground garage below the internal access road.

The high-rise functions as both a hotel and an office building. The two lobbies for the office and the hotel are connected. The office spaces are flexible, accommodating individual, combination, or open-plan offices, or a mixture of types. Individualized functions over a number of floors can also be accommodated.

The remaining five buildings on the Bosch grounds have a usable area of about ten thousand square meters each. Function and design can be varied, as long as the basic form—a cube measuring thirty-five by thirty-five meters, solid construction—is followed. The building entrances open onto an internal avenue, which unites the complex into an urban ensemble. Between the buildings are architectural gardens composed of hedges and trees.

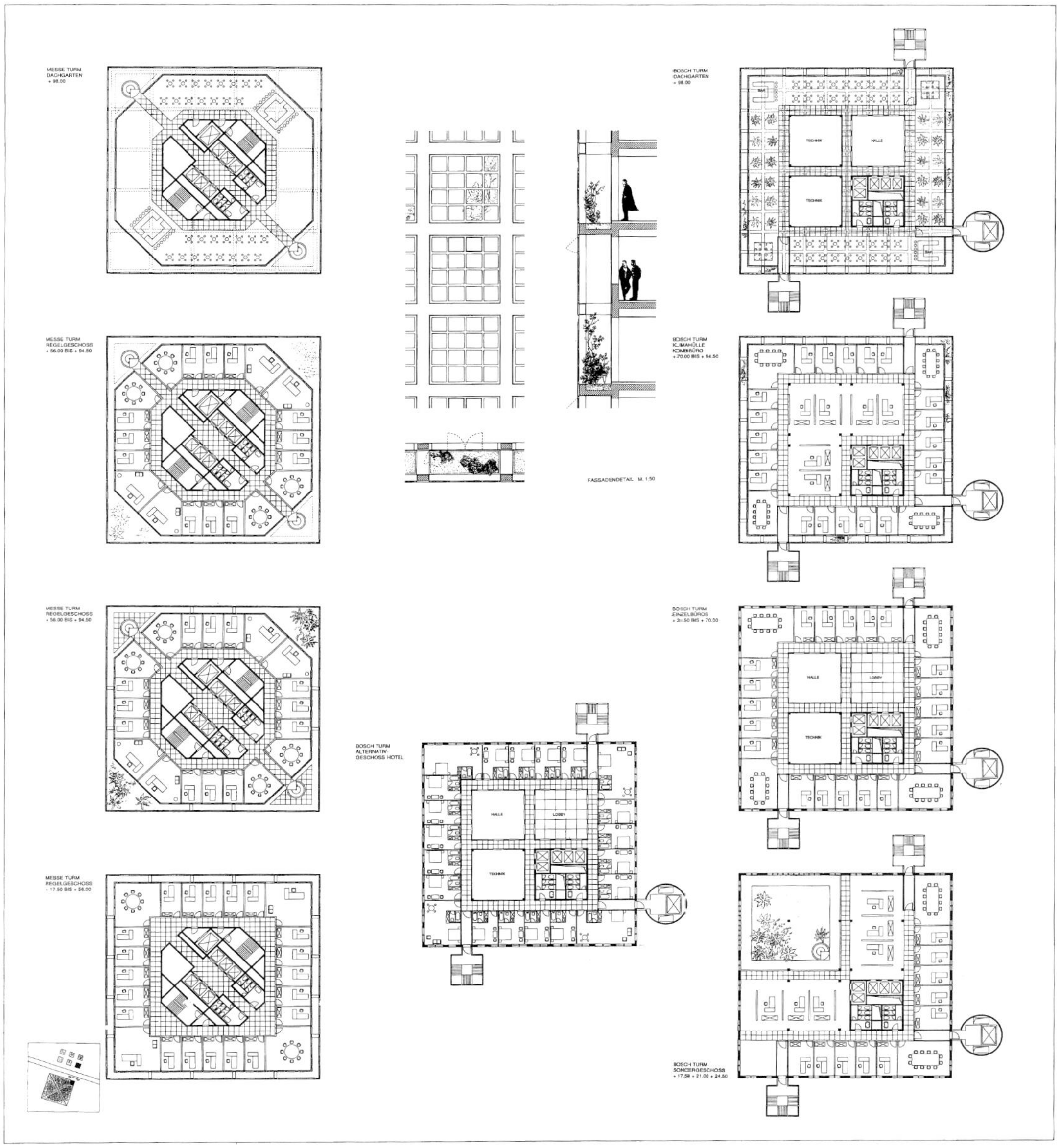

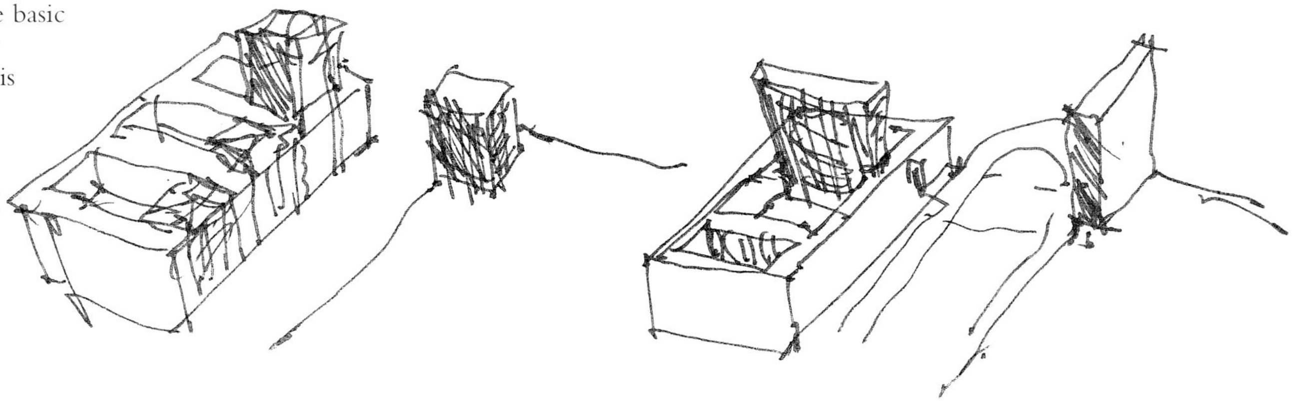

Bosch complex: sketches; elevation.

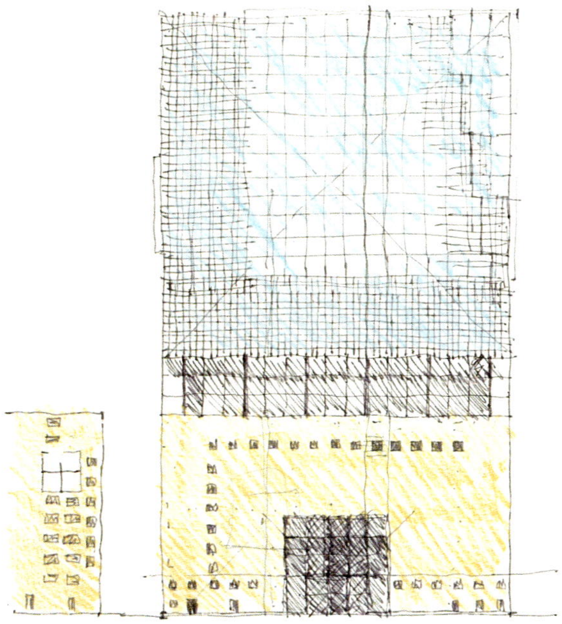

Elevations and sections of Bosch tower (right) and trade fair tower (left).

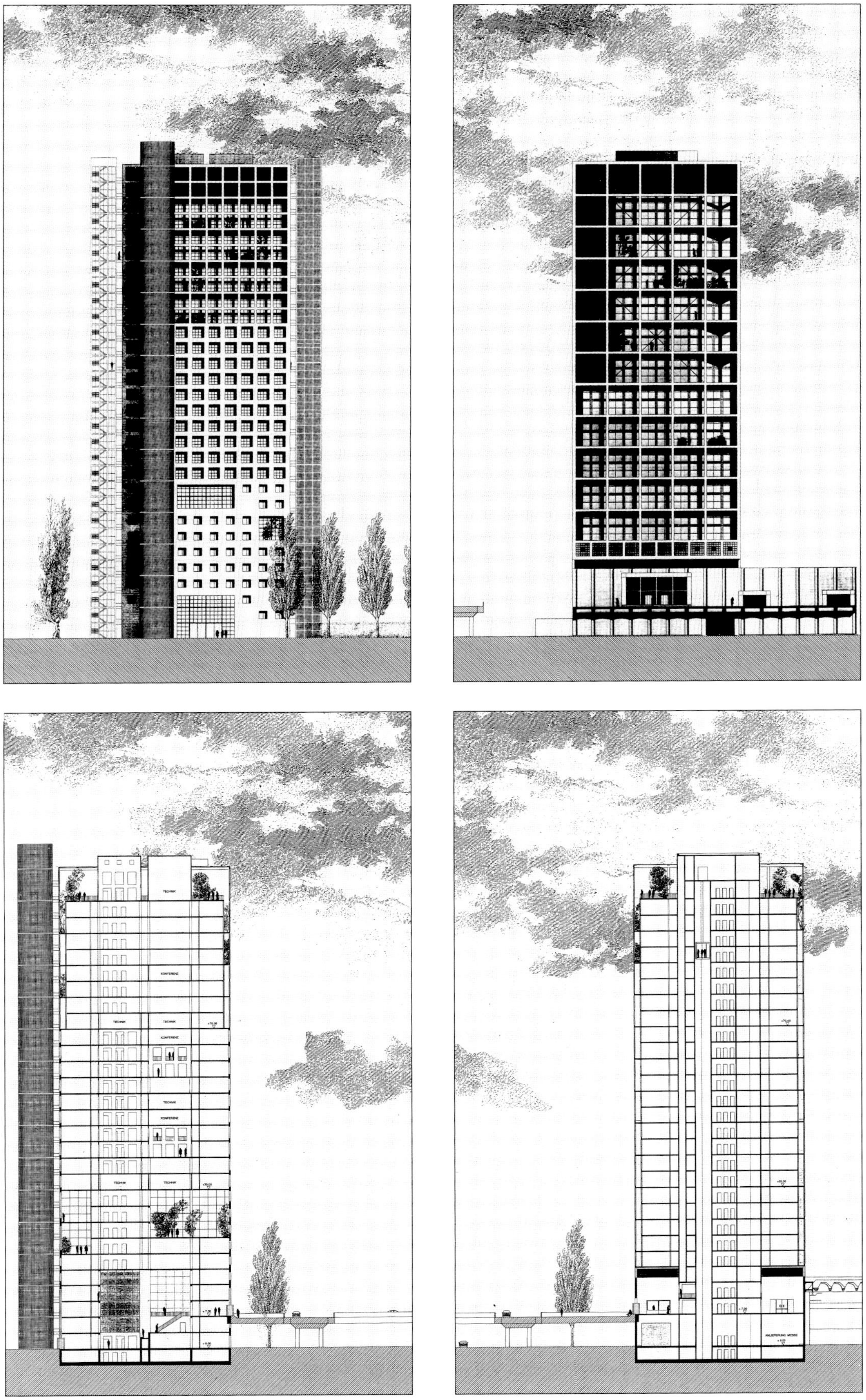

Neuss Projects, Neuss-Hammfeld, 1991, 1994, 1995

Project team:
Urban development master plan:
Lukas Baumewerd, Andreas Geitner, Volker Busse, Eun Young Yi
Neuss-Hammfeld II and III: with Stefan Vieths
Project team: Marvin Keim, Peter Pfertner, David Koralek, Philippe Vernin, Kai-Uwe Lompa, Frank Wieschemann, Michael Laudert
Neuss tower: Lukas Baumewerd, Boris von Glasenapp

In 1991, a design was developed in the context of an urban project for Neuss-Hammfeld, a new area on the urban periphery marked by a heterogeneous building development of office and commercial buildings. Ungers's concern was to design three different building forms that refer to historic building typologies: the castrum, the campanile, and the gate. The project is an attempt to make these building

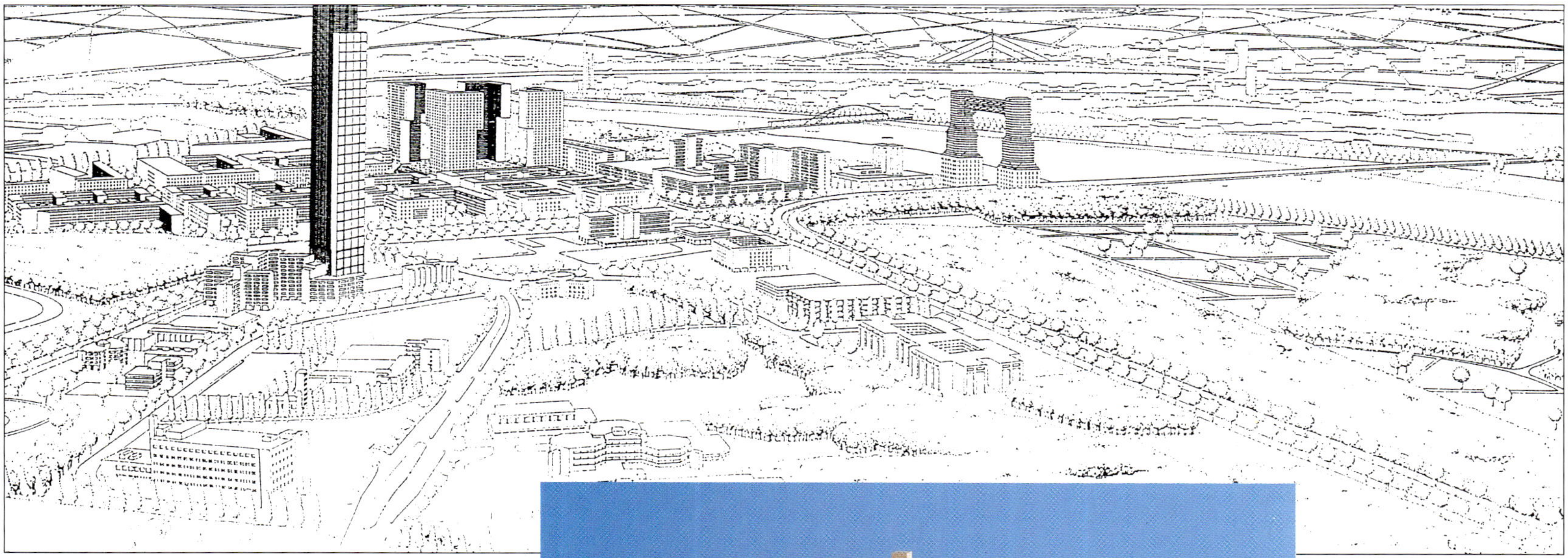

Model views; perspective drawing of urban design project.

Typologies of high-rises for urban design project: castrum, campanile, city gate.

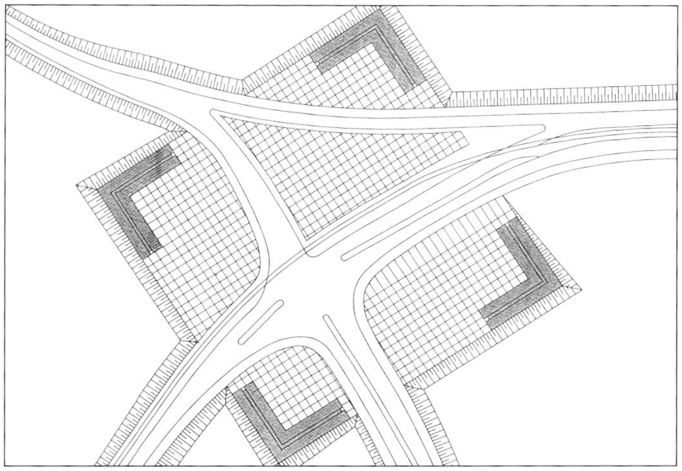

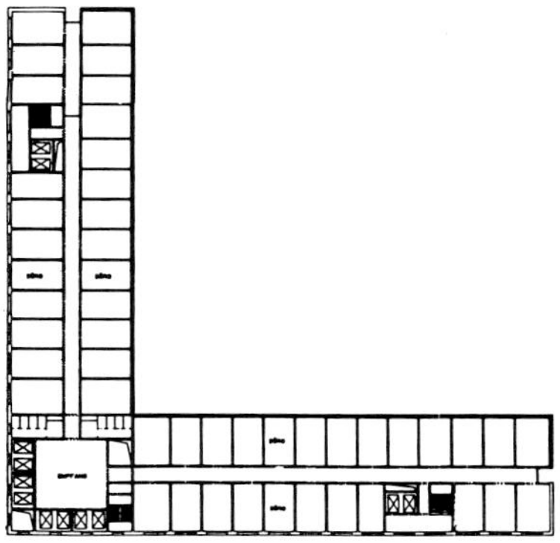

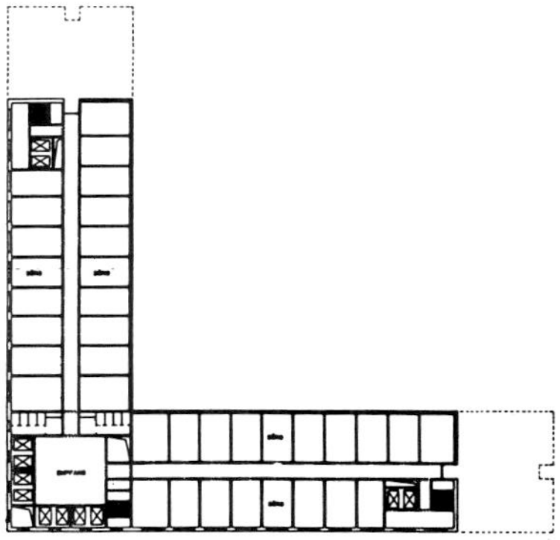

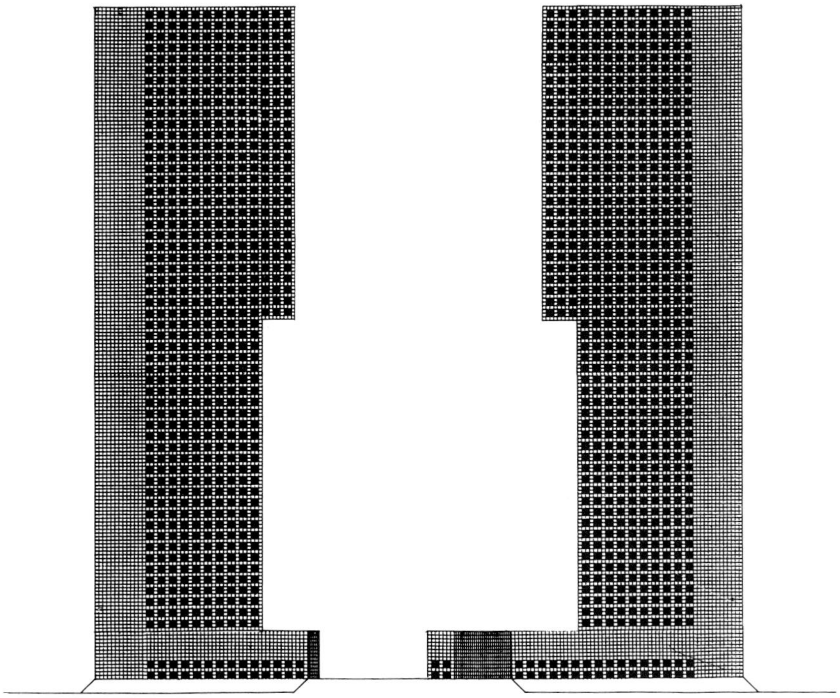

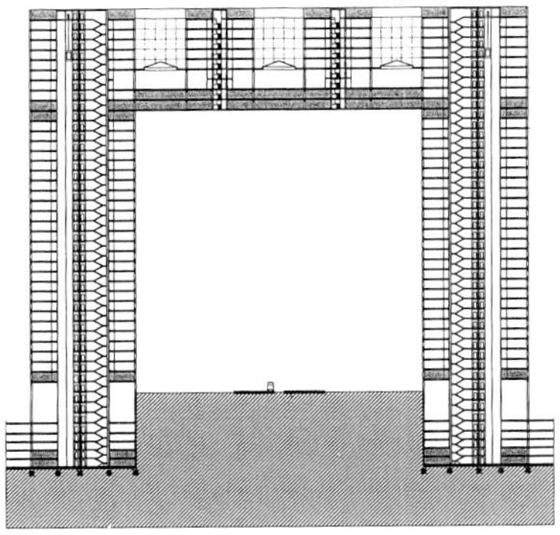

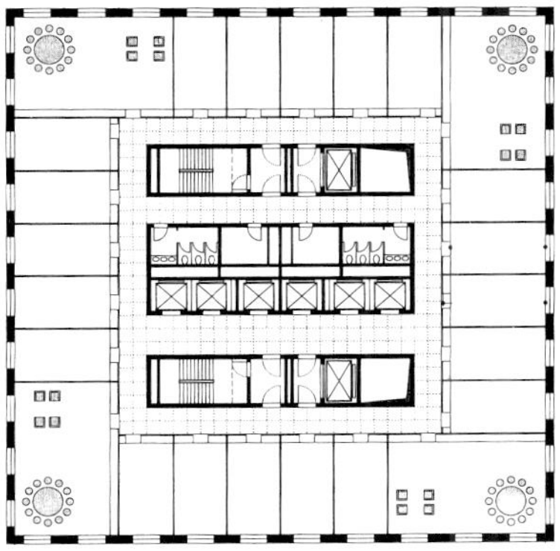

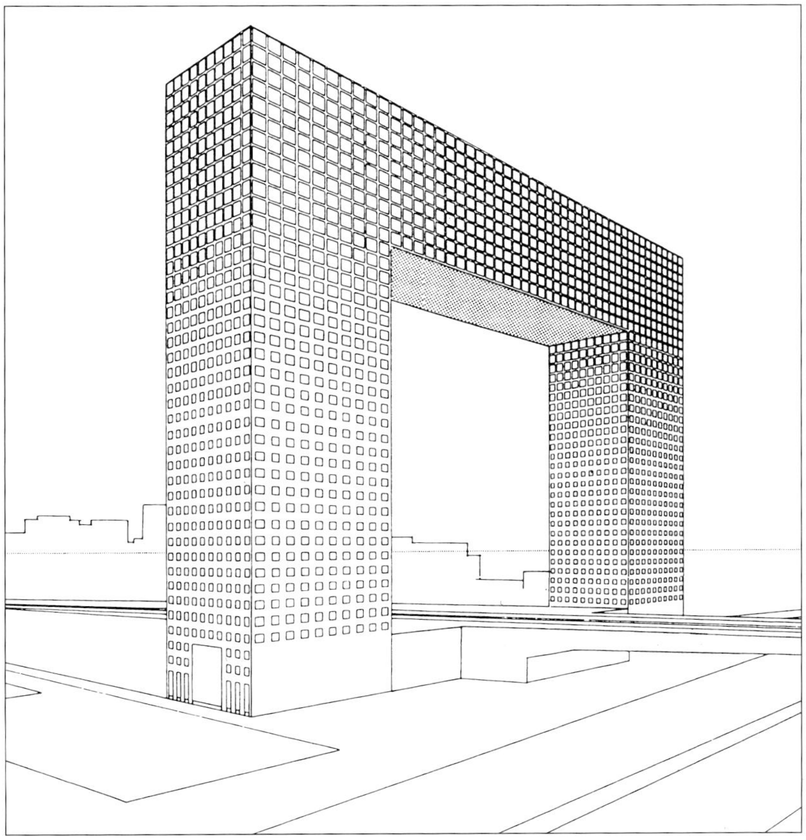

Campanile project: plans, elevation.

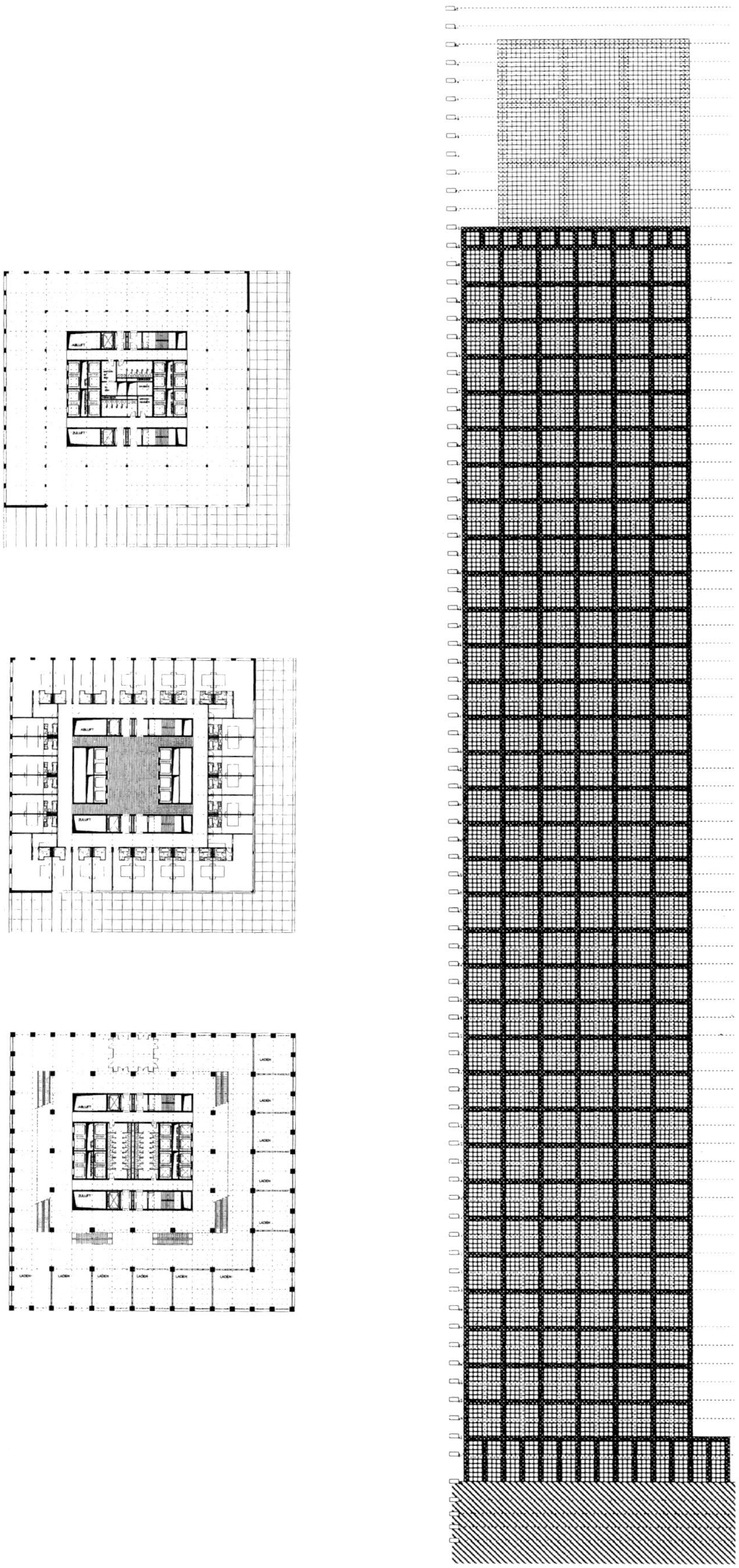

types visible in the urban realm in a transformed and oversized form, to evoke images that associate themselves with the silhouette when viewed from a distance. As with the trade fair tower in Frankfurt, this "enlargement" process is justified by the technical possibilities and can result from the function of a high-rise. The potential high-rise is based on a single theme that is elaborated throughout. Here Ungers takes the idea of the gatehouse to an extreme: the abstraction is readable as the primeval architectural motif of "post and lintel"—"load and support" or "standing and lying." In a further level of abstraction, the dimensions and the resulting gate opening are based on a gigantic square module. A final abstraction is added in the vertical dimension: the bays between the windows, gradually narrowing toward the top, slowly dissolve the heavy wall (as a perforated facade) into a kind of grid. The articulation can be read as the transformation of a grid, formed by the shift from a positive to a negative complementary form.—*Martin Kieren.*

In 1994, Ungers presented a design for the planning area Neuss-Hammfeld II and III, which is divided into four quadrants by the intersection of the streets Am Pfauenhof and Hammer Landstrasse. These quadrants form the basic structure for the proposed urbanistic development. Except in the unbuilt southwestern quadrant (Hammfeld II), the project accepts the existing architecture and completes it to form a coherent urban image. The existing green areas and streets with sidewalks are likewise preserved. Stipulations required that construction follow the outline of the blocks and called for a unified roof height of about twenty-five meters. In accord with further stipulations, primarily office usage is envisioned for Hammfeld II and III, with an additional cinema, hotel, musical theater, and a few dwellings. Building types are derived from these different functions.

Hammer Landstrasse serves as a central axis connecting the new urban district with the old city of Neuss. The proposal calls for the transformation of the street into a generous boulevard leading from the old city to the Rhine and ending in a pedestrian bridge over the river. This main axis is framed by two high-rises, one establishing a gateway to the old city, the other a gateway to the Rhine. An additional high-rise is proposed for

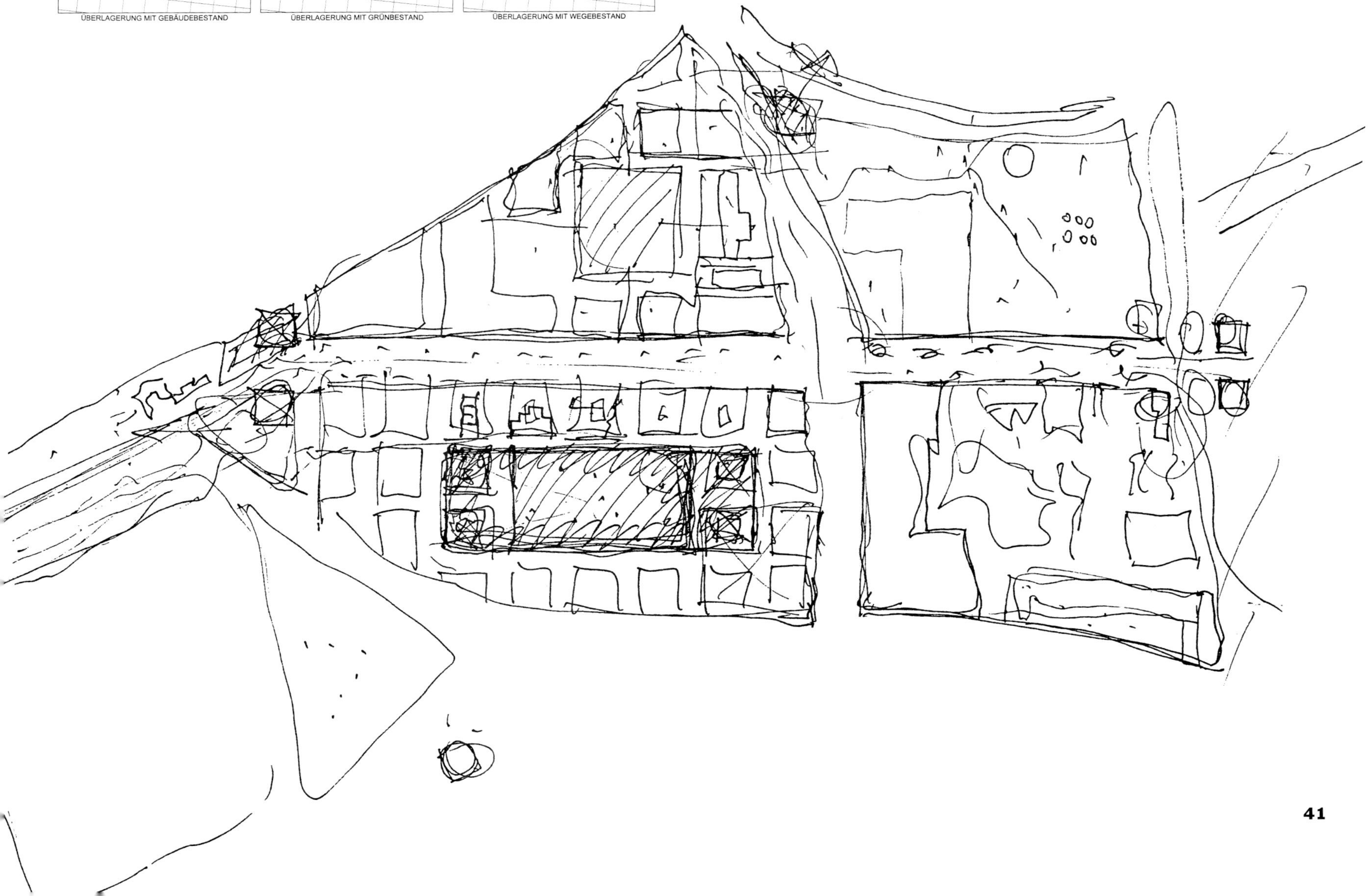

Function plans for Neuss-Hammfeld II and III; sketch.

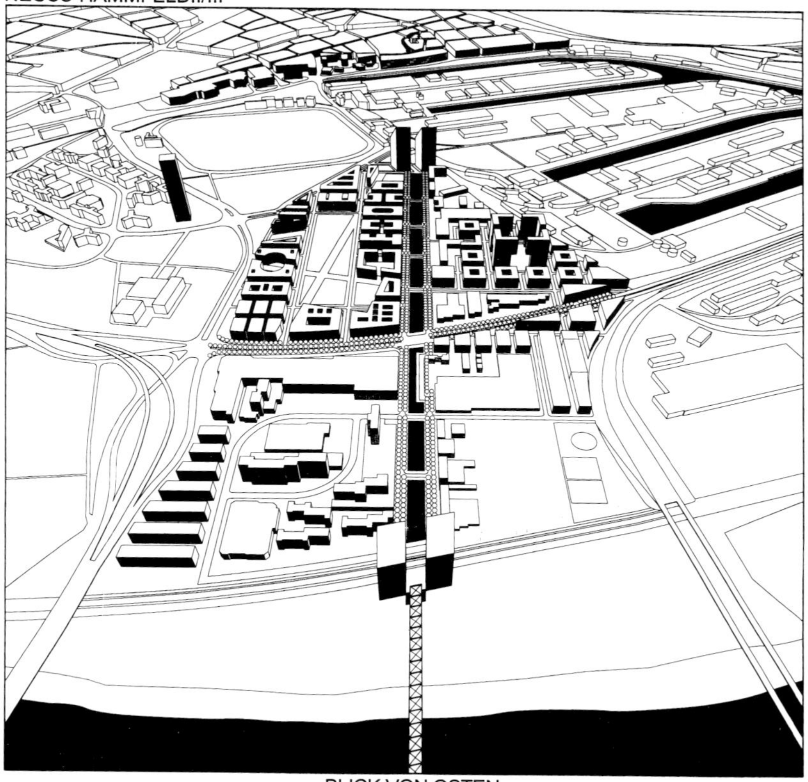

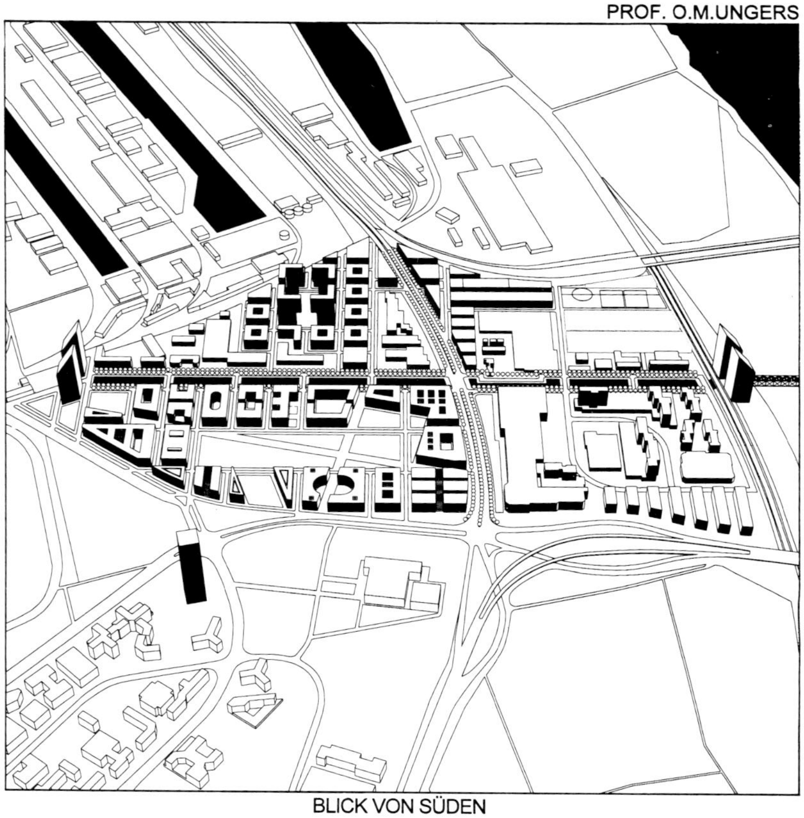

Perspective views;
model views.

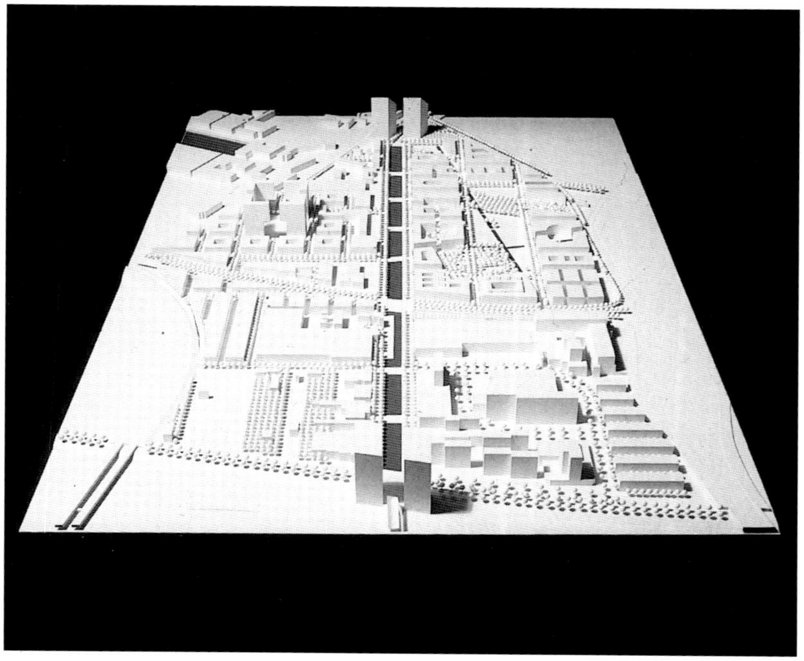

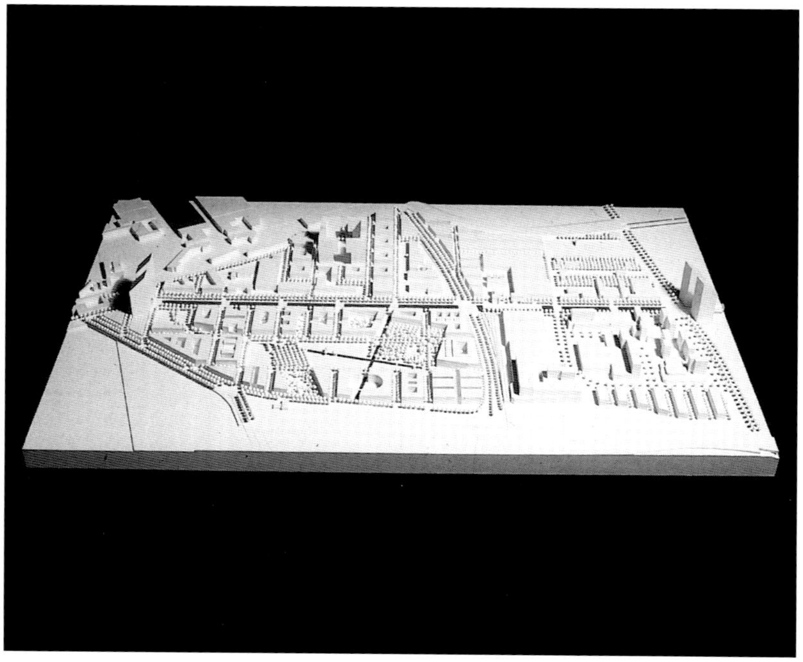

General plan for Neuss-Hammfeld II and III; ground-level plan; plans and typologies of individual blocks.

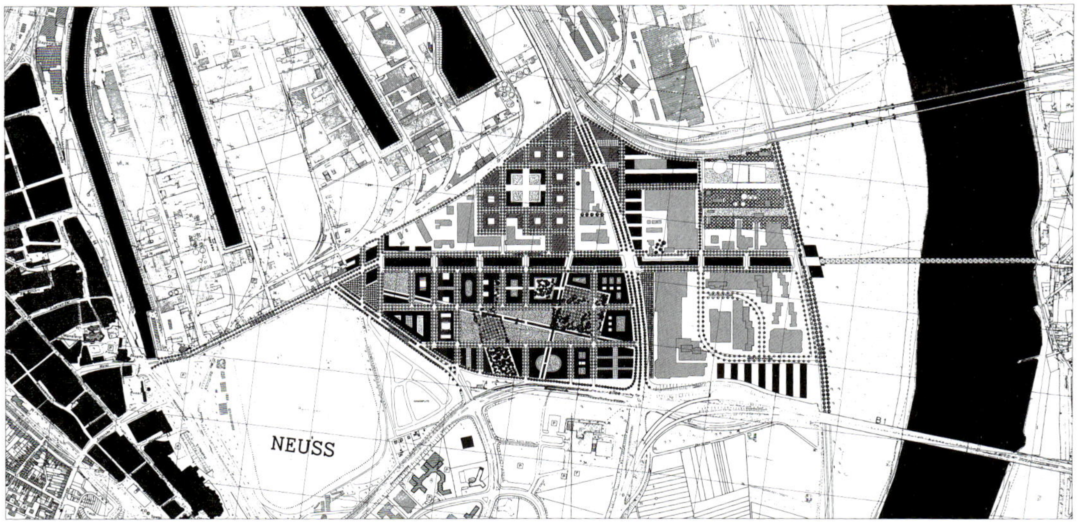

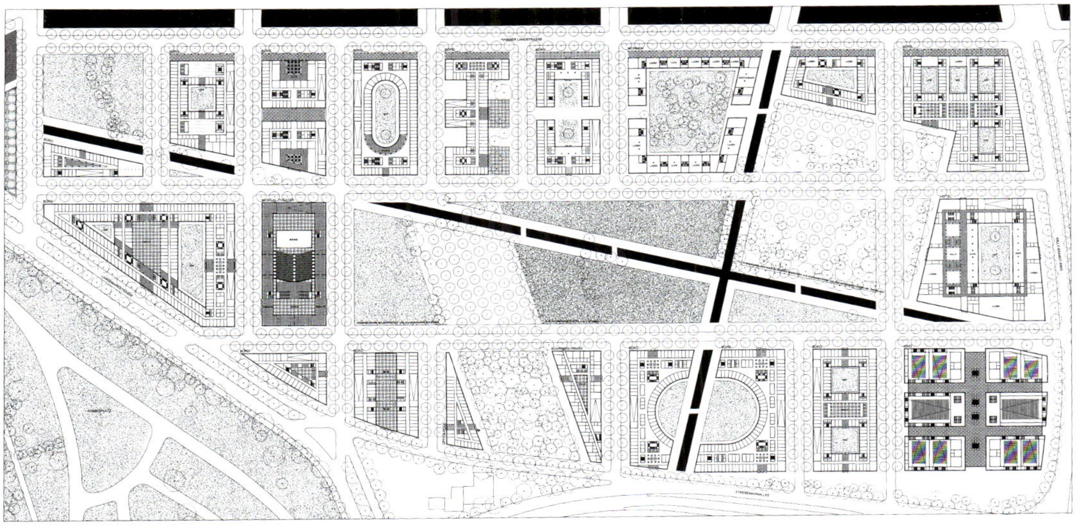

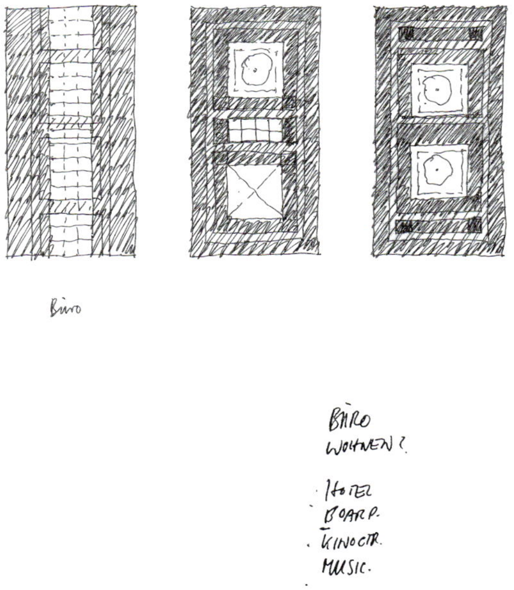

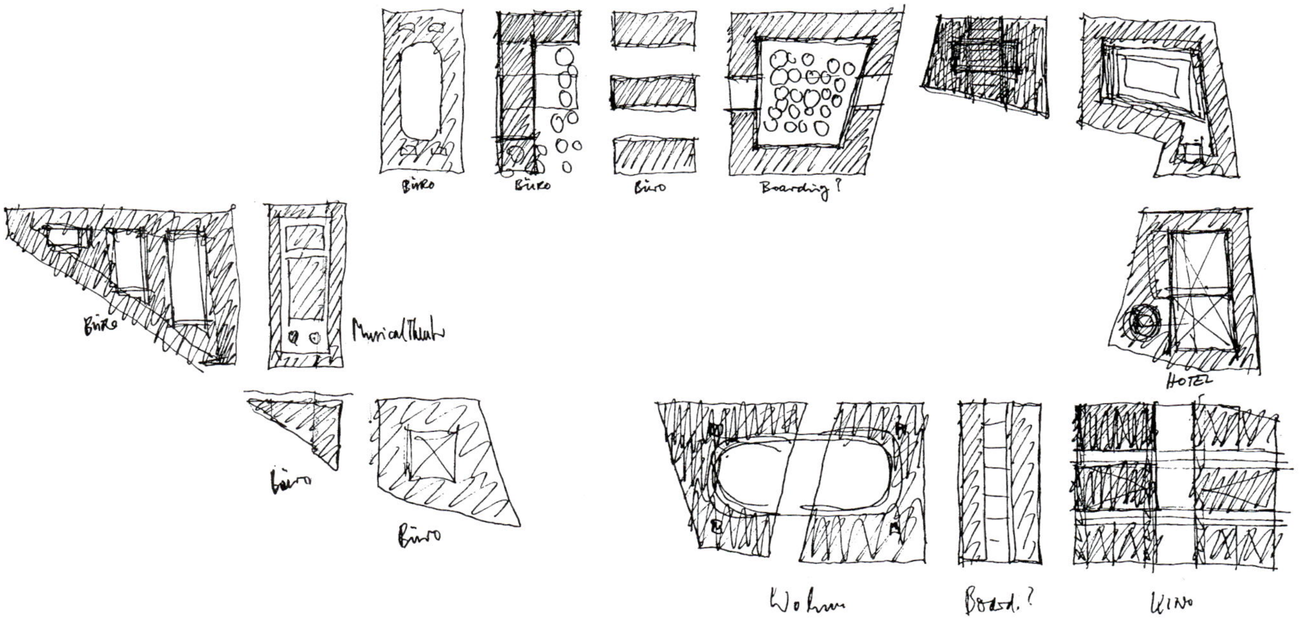

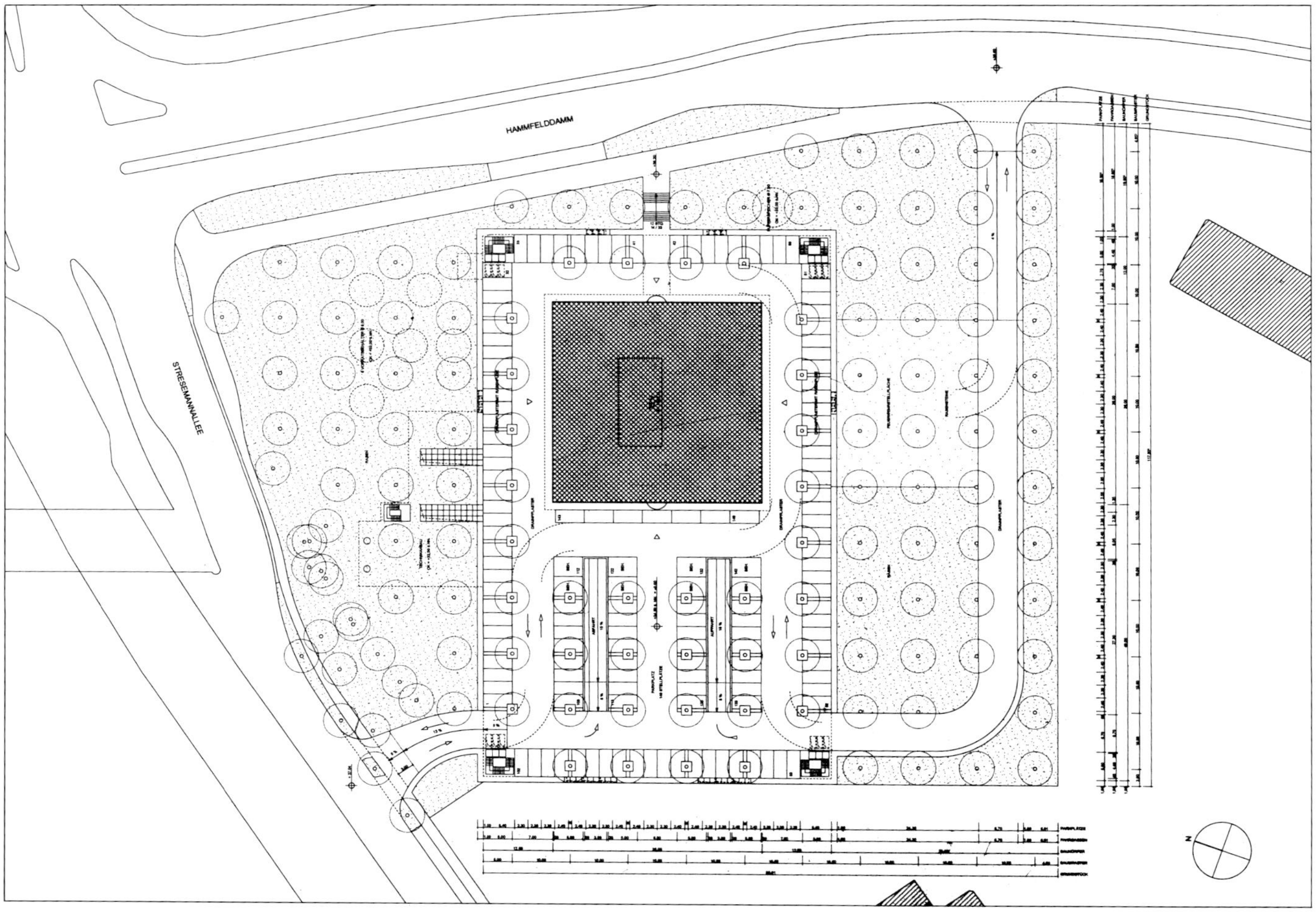
HAMMFELDDAMM
STRESEMANNALLEE

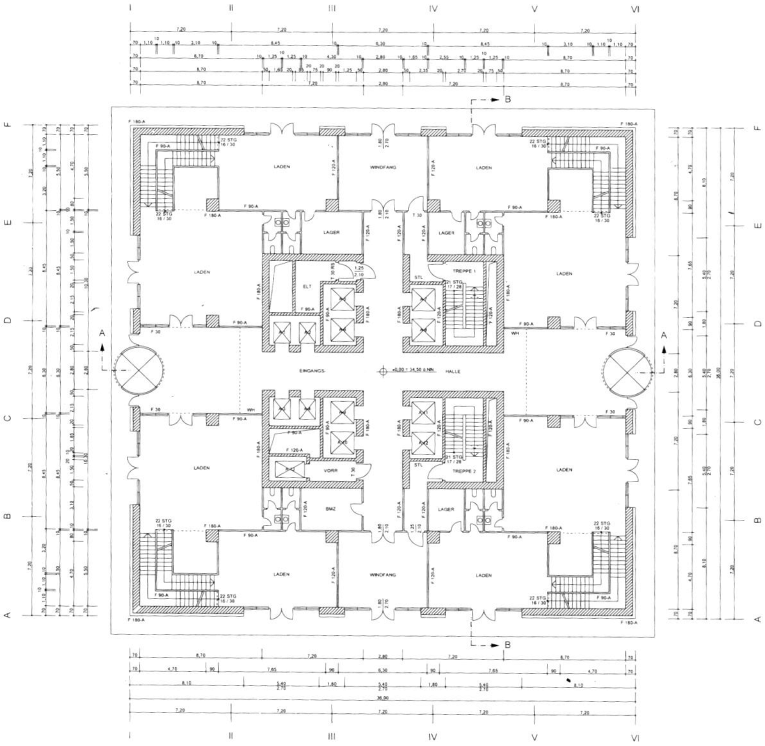
LADEN
WINDFANG
LAGER
TREPPE 1
TREPPE 2
EINGANG
HALLE
ELT
VORR
BMZ

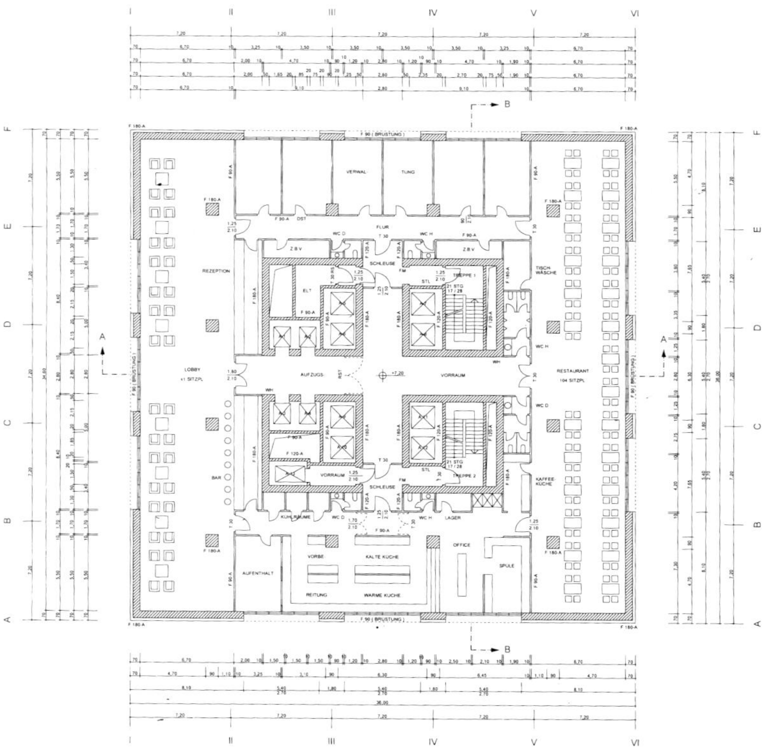
VERWAL
TUNG
REZEPTION
LOBBY
BAR
AUFZUGS
VORRAUM
SCHLEUSE
RESTAURANT
KAFFEE KÜCHE
KALTE KÜCHE
WARME KÜCHE
AUFENTHALT
OFFICE
SPÜLE
LAGER

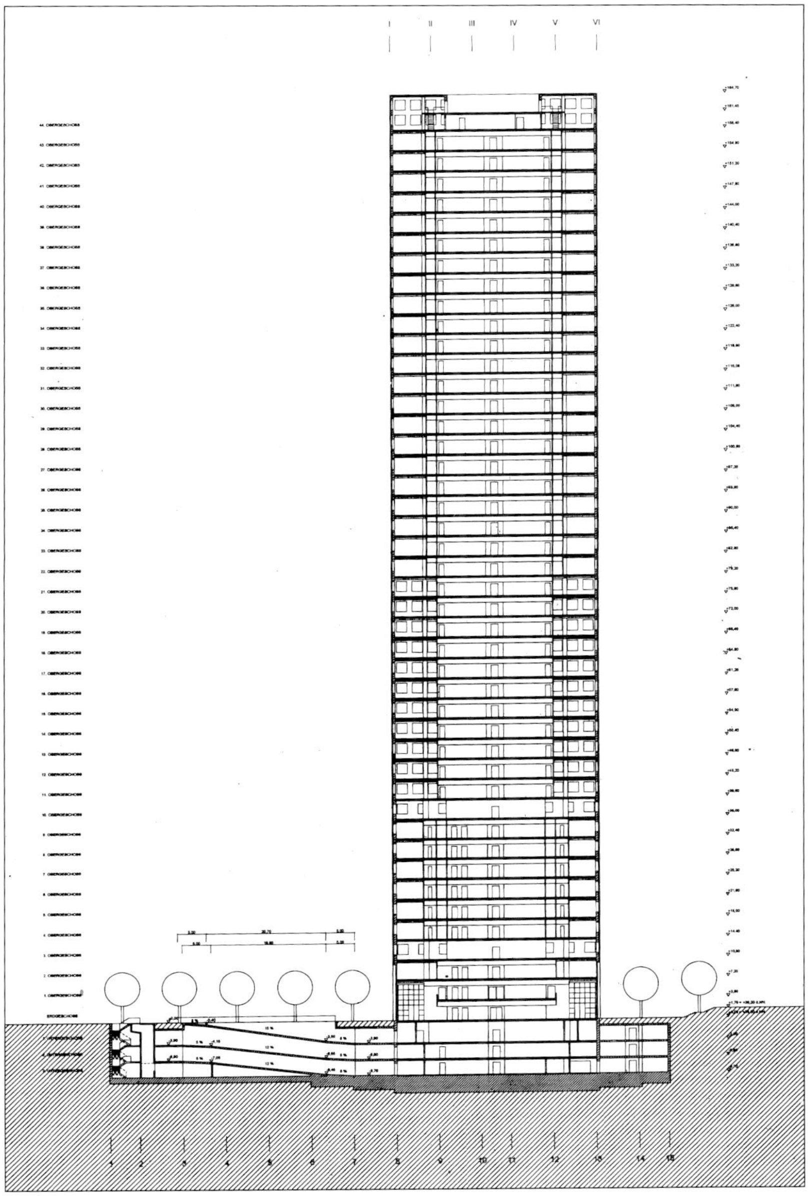

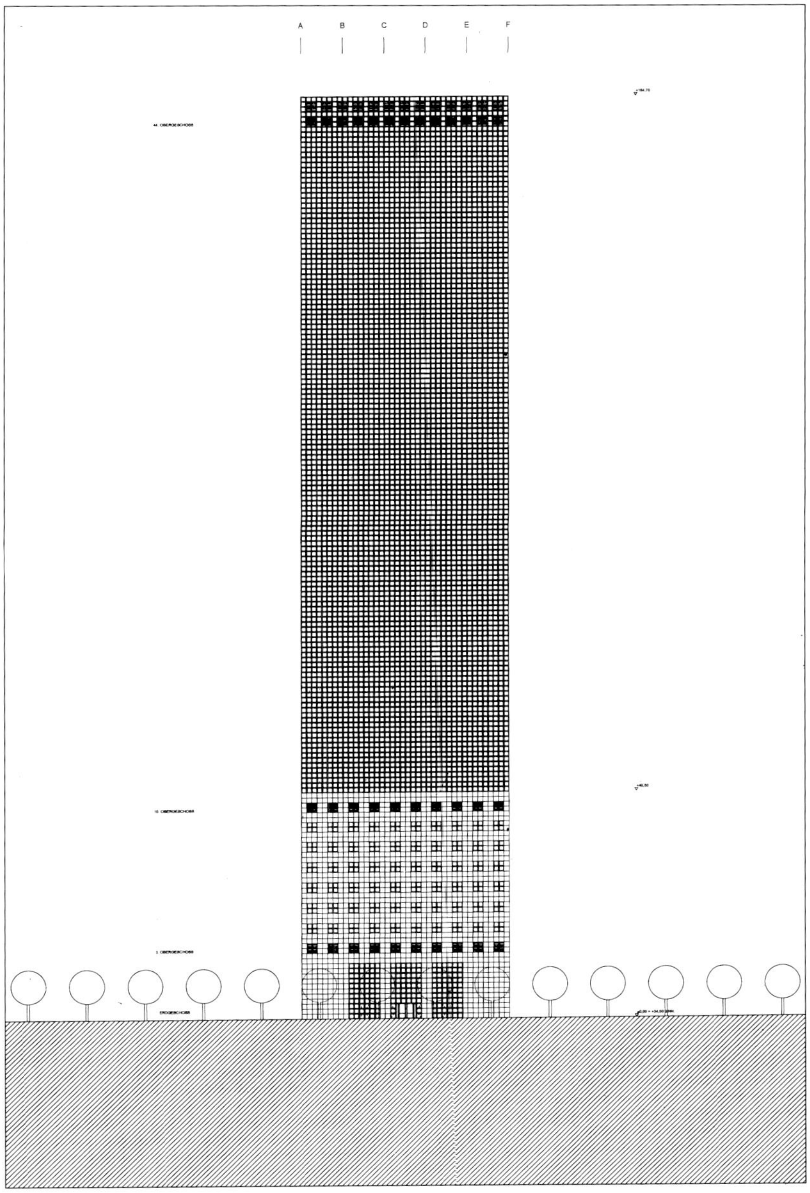

Neuss tower: site plan; plan of ground level and second upper level; section; elevation.

the center of the Hammfeld III and four angles form a castrum, giving this small quarter its own clear identity. Together with the proposed Neuss tower, the gatehouses and the castrum form an ensemble of striking buildings that clearly positions the new urban district within the Rhenish landscape.

In 1995, Ungers took up the project again, this time with reference to the Neuss tower proposed for a corner parcel in the vicinity of the Hammfeld planning area. The tower is intended to lend visible unity to the surrounding buildings and, by emphasizing the otherwise undifferentiated and unarticulated urban profile, provide a point of identification for the entire zone. The building, intended for offices and a hotel, is 165 meters in height and consists of two parts: a solid stone socle in the form of a cube, whose height corresponds to that of the neighboring buildings, and the glazed body of the tower proper. In contrast to the facade of the tower, which is perforated with hotel windows, the entire surface of the socle is closed. On the interior of the socle is a large hall with the hotel reception as well as eight shops in each of the four corners of the building; the floors in the glazed part accommodate offices. The socle is faced with light-colored sandstone, harmonizing with the gray-green glass of the tower. The rest of the parcel is occupied by a parking lot planted with trees, below which additional parking is available in three underground garage levels.

Competition Design for Urban Planning of KHD Euroforum, Musical Theater, Cologne, 1992, 1995

With: Stefan Vieths

Project team:
Competition design: Frank Wieschemann, Don Dimster, Lukas Baumewerd, Johannes Götz, Joachim Sieber, Philippe Vernin, Albert Brauns, Kai-Uwe Lompa
Urban planning: Peter Pfertner
Musical theater: Marvin Keim, Axel Steudel, Kai-Uwe Lompa, David Koralek, Frank Wieschemann

The competition site occupies a prominent place within the urban structure of Cologne. Located directly on the Rhine, it is spanned by the thoroughfare leading to the Zoobrücke and thus represents one of the main entrances to the city center. At the same time, the urban context of the site—marked by large industrial complexes and transportation buildings immediately adjacent to residential areas and trade fair facilities—stands in a relationship of tension and opposition to that of the city center. The design is intended to give the new area its own spatial order and identity, integrating those buildings that are worth preserving. An additional, autonomous architectural element is to be added to the pattern of existing structures.

A large park in front of the KHD building marks the center of the Euroforum. The large gate structure is intended to create a dominant urbanistic feature, establishing a relationship between the Euroforum and other large buildings in the city (cathedral,

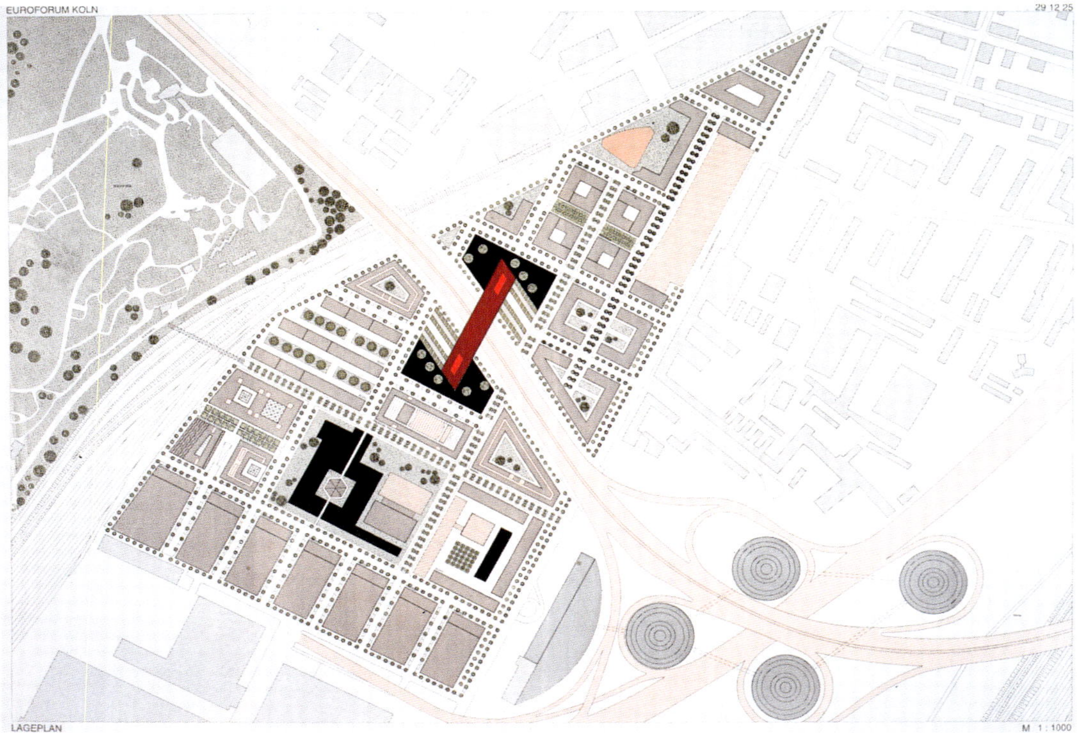

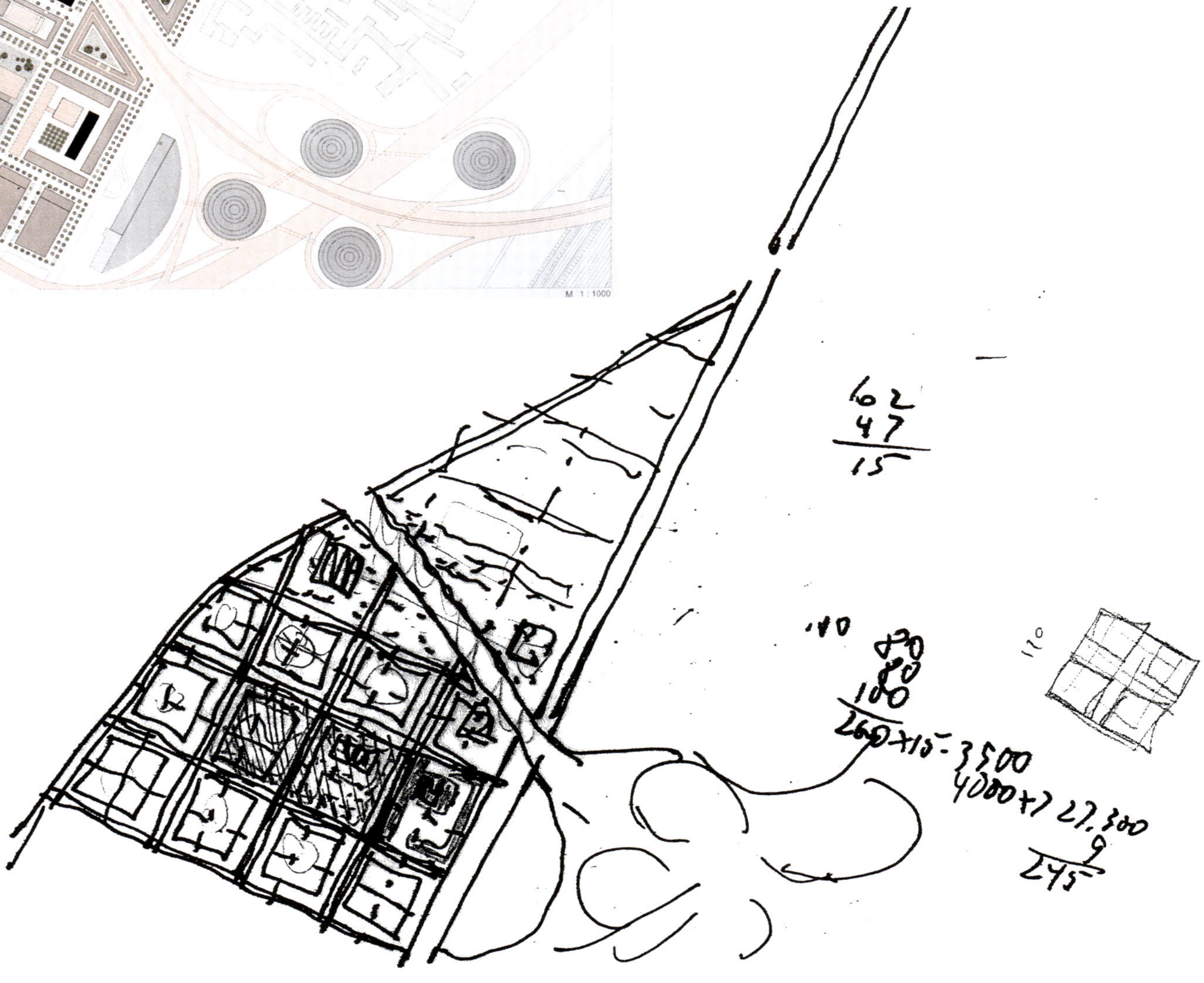

Site plan; sketch.

Opposite:
Perspective view; ground-level plan.

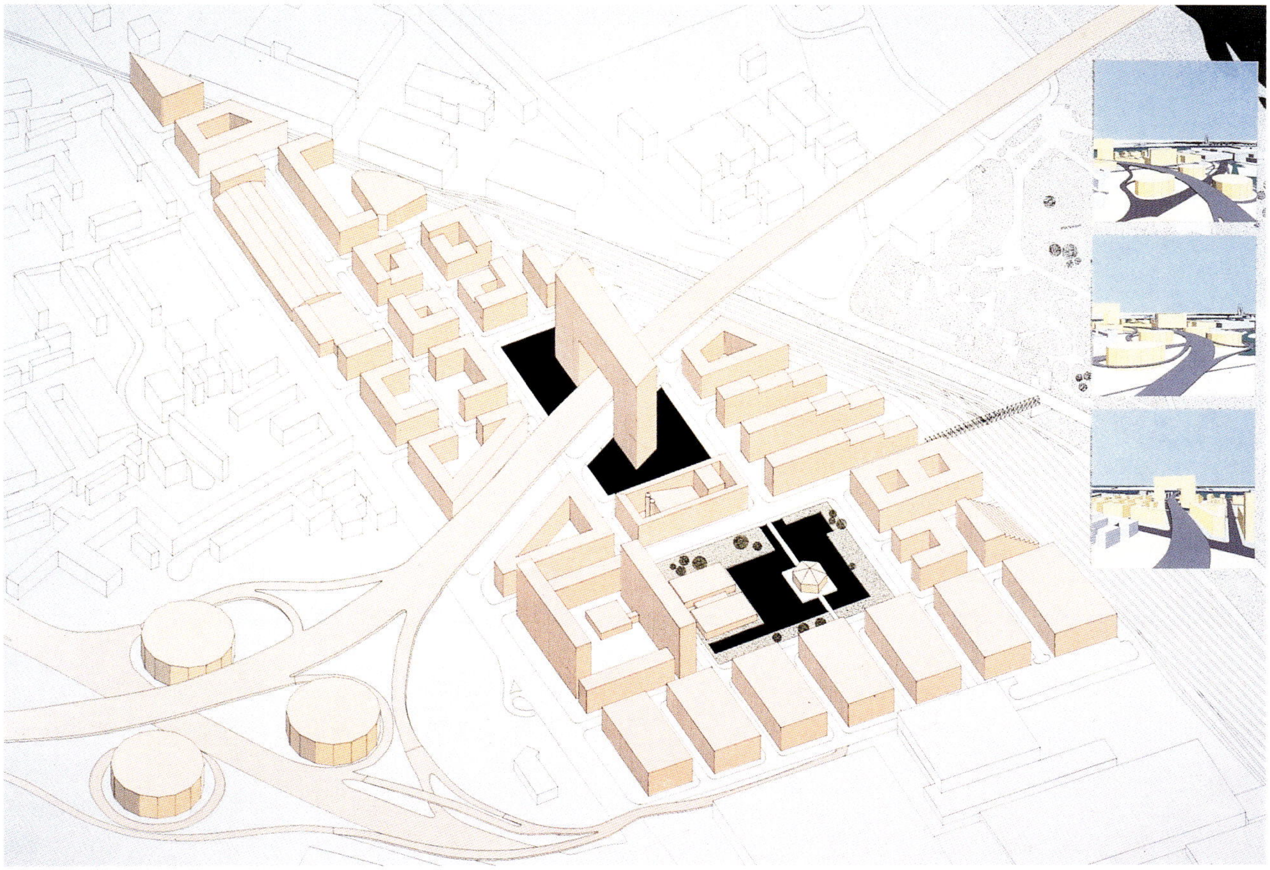

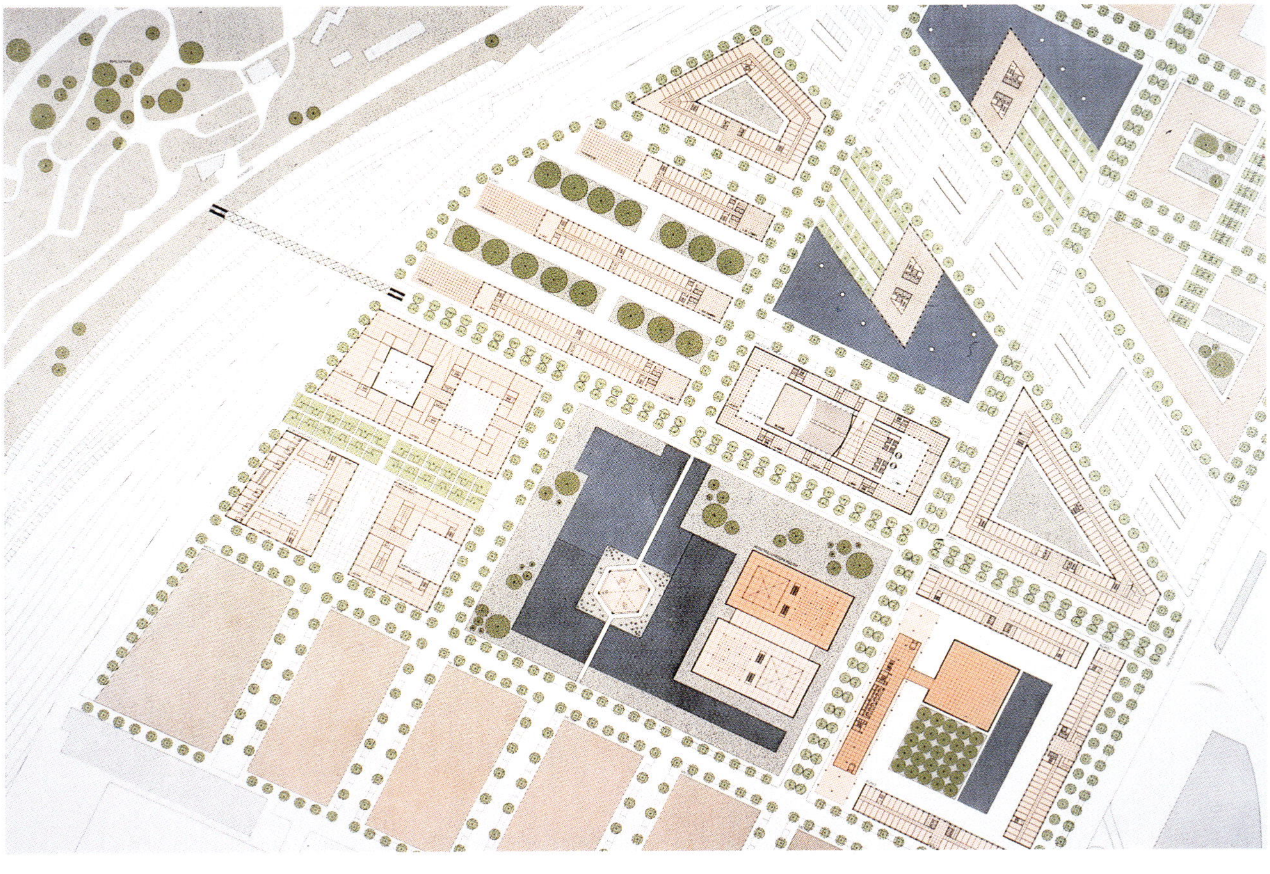

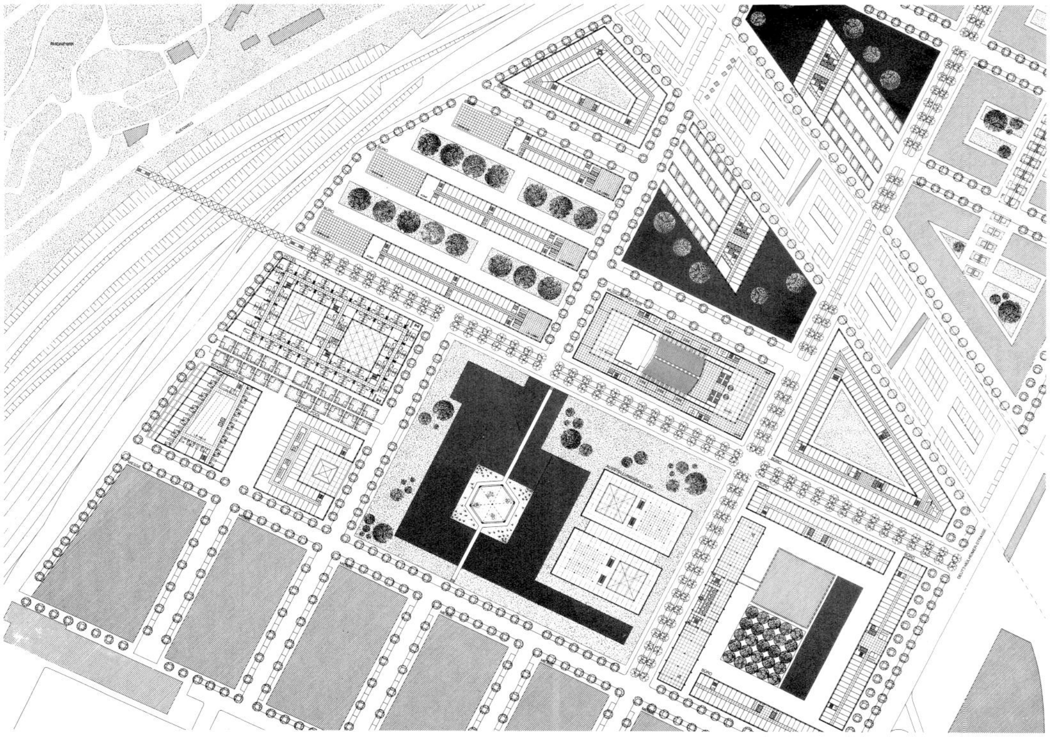

Ground-level plan; sketches for two building typologies.

Elevations; sections; sketches for hotel and musical theater.

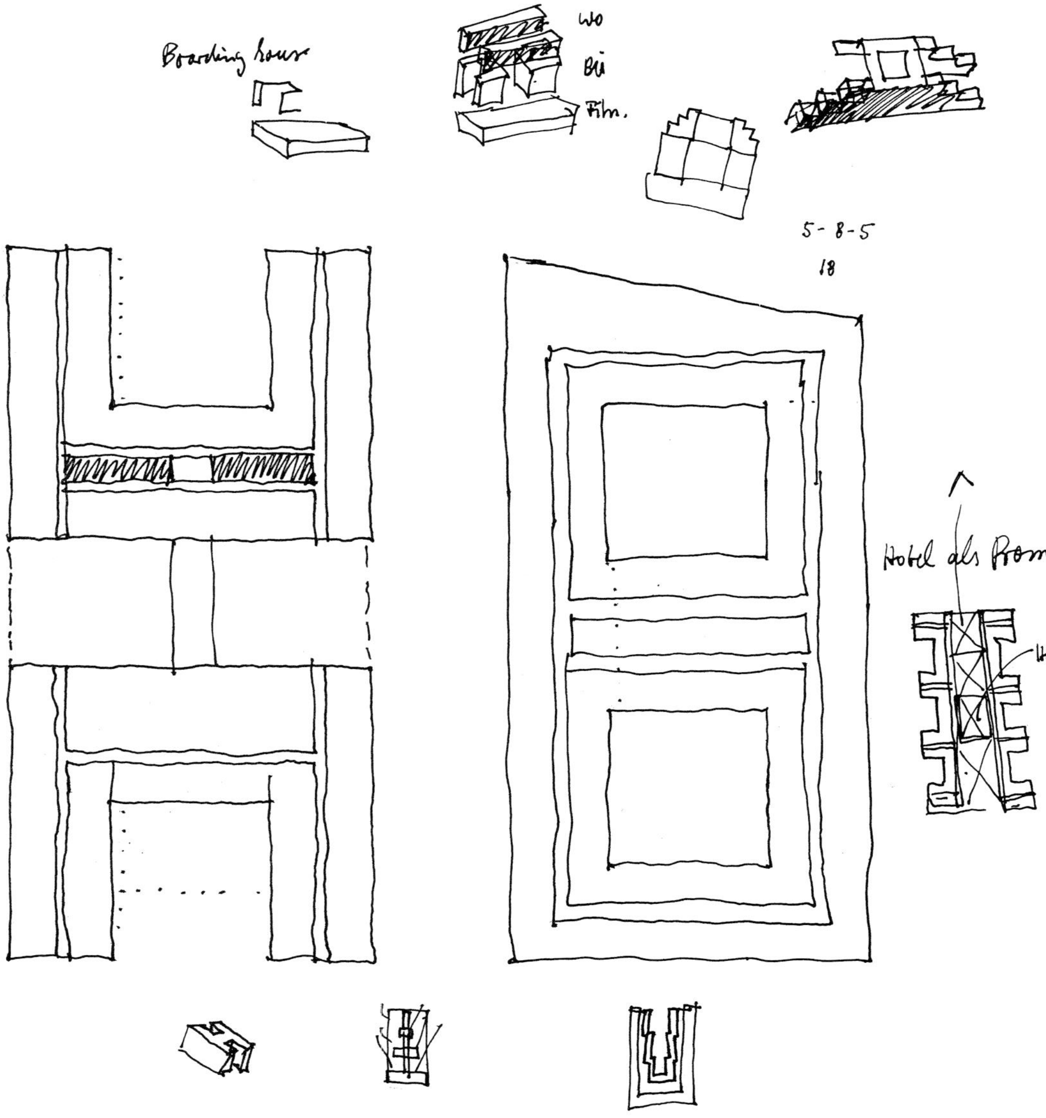

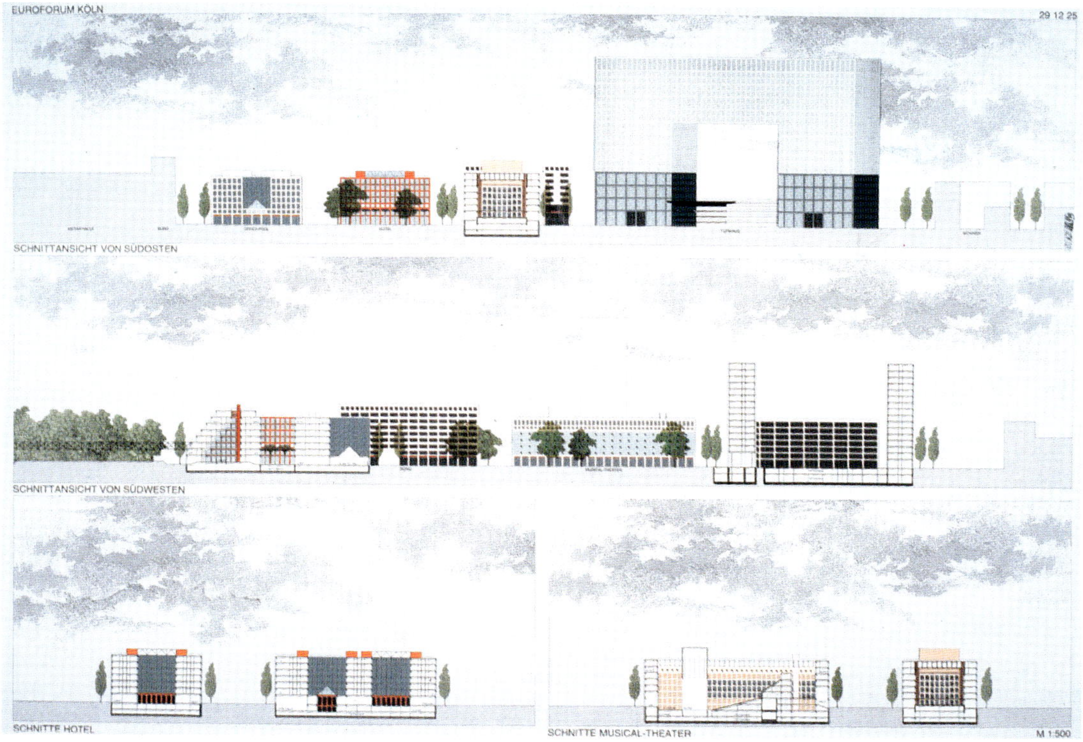
EUROFORUM KÖLN
29 12 25
SCHNITTANSICHT VON SÜDOSTEN
SCHNITTANSICHT VON SÜDWESTEN
SCHNITTE HOTEL
SCHNITTE MUSICAL-THEATER
M 1:500

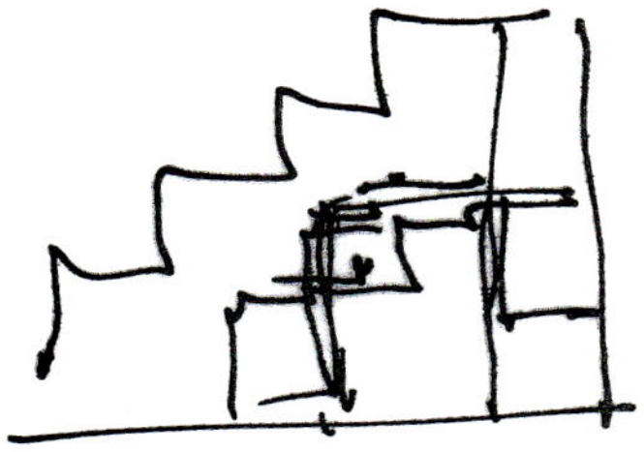

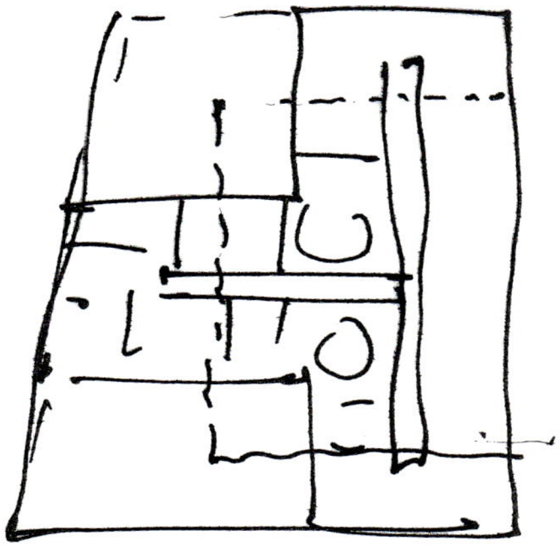

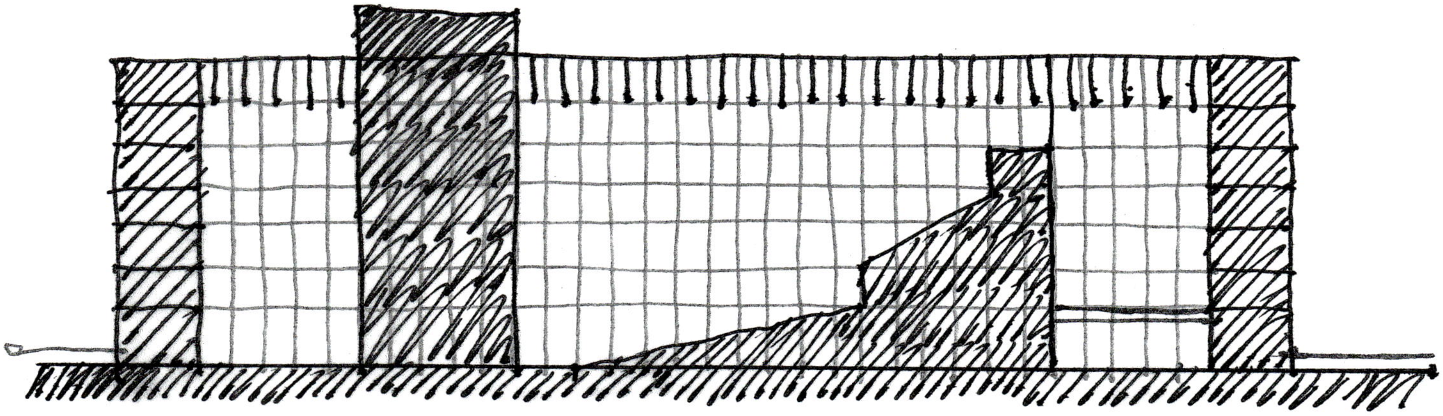

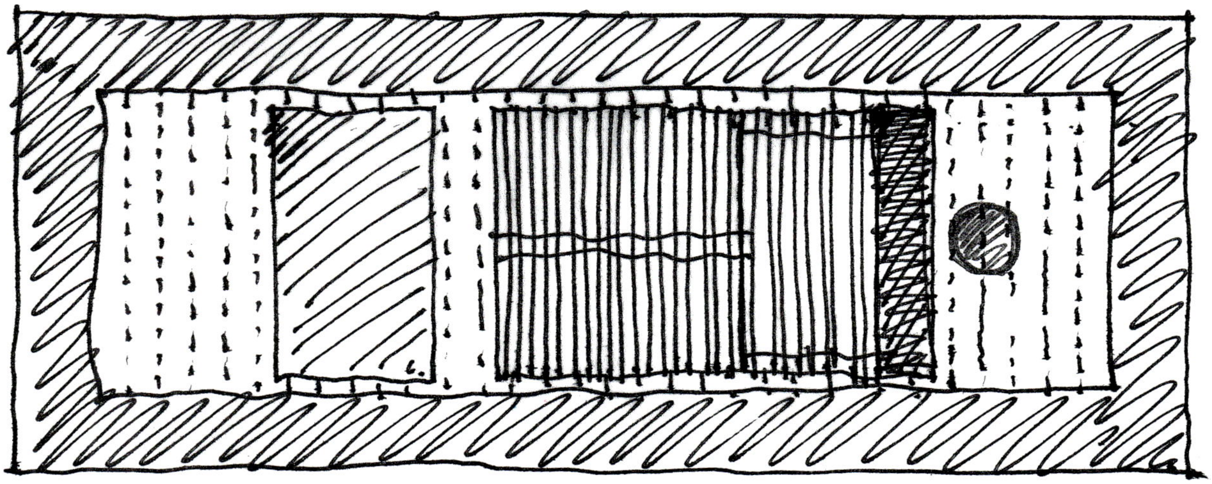

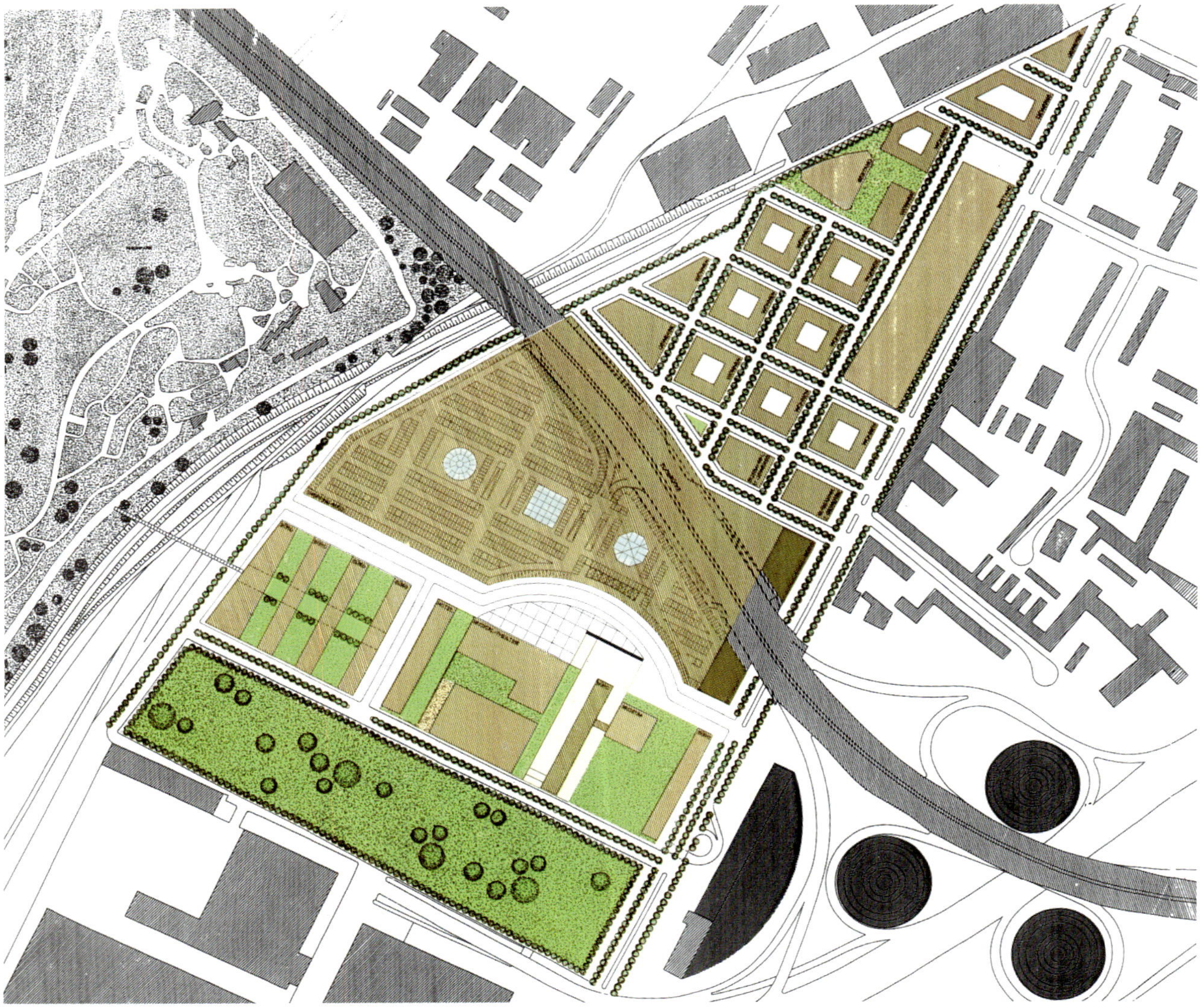

Site plan; ground-level plan; model view.

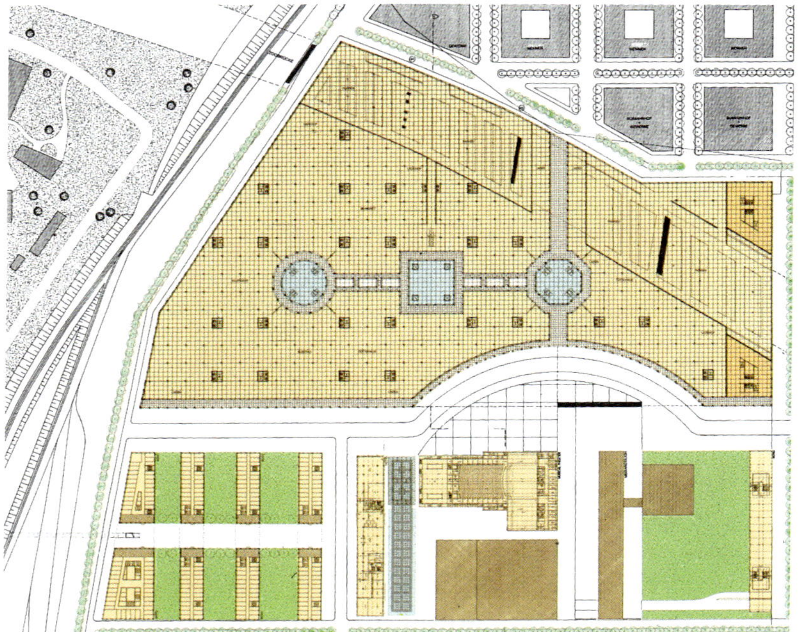

television tower) while at the same time marking the entrance to the city.

A basic module of 2.7 by 2.7 meters provides the foundation for a strict block grid oriented to the existing KHD structure. The standard size of a block is 41 by 41 meters but can be varied according to the specific nature of the plot and the demands of the program. The blocks for office buildings can take a variety of forms. In the four-wing block, three new wings are added to the KHD wing to form an inner courtyard; the U-shaped block opens toward the park, while the perimeter blocks frame the area toward the autobahn and the three-row block affords a view to the Rhine. A hotel forms a double block between the park and the Rhine, while a boarding house with terraces facing the river functions as a separating block. The musical theater is a block with inserted elements. A wall-like perimeter structure defines an inner plaza, in which the stage and tiers of seating are arranged as objects.

The construction in the inner competition area (plot A) continues in plots B and C, with blocks adjacent to the trade fair grounds conceived as additional halls for the expansion of the fair. An office tract is positioned in front of them. Angled blocks on plot C accommodate dwellings that combine with existing buildings to form an ensemble arranged along a quiet residential street.

A street typology corresponds to the typology of blocks. Two boulevards with rows of trees in the center mark the main axes of the area; avenues are of the standard type, while the trees that extend like a roof over the quiet residential streets give these spaces an almost interior quality. The park features a number of water-lily pools as well as an island with a hothouse for lotuses. A continuous system of paths leads past bamboo groves to footbridges.

The design for the musical theater originated in connection with these urbanistic plans. The objective was to design a classical theater building with complete stage facilities and an audience capacity of 1,800. With only two tiers, the audience space is extremely compact, providing good visibility from all seats. The proposed design unifies audience space and foyer into a single spatial continuum. Lateral colonnades effect a flowing transition from the foyer into the audience space. The latter is conceived as a large, urban space, in which interior facades are elaborated. The critical connection to the stage is established through a perspectival staggering of the area in front of the stage. The solid inner core of the theater is enclosed by a glass circulation zone with the main staircase as well as the necessary emergency exits.

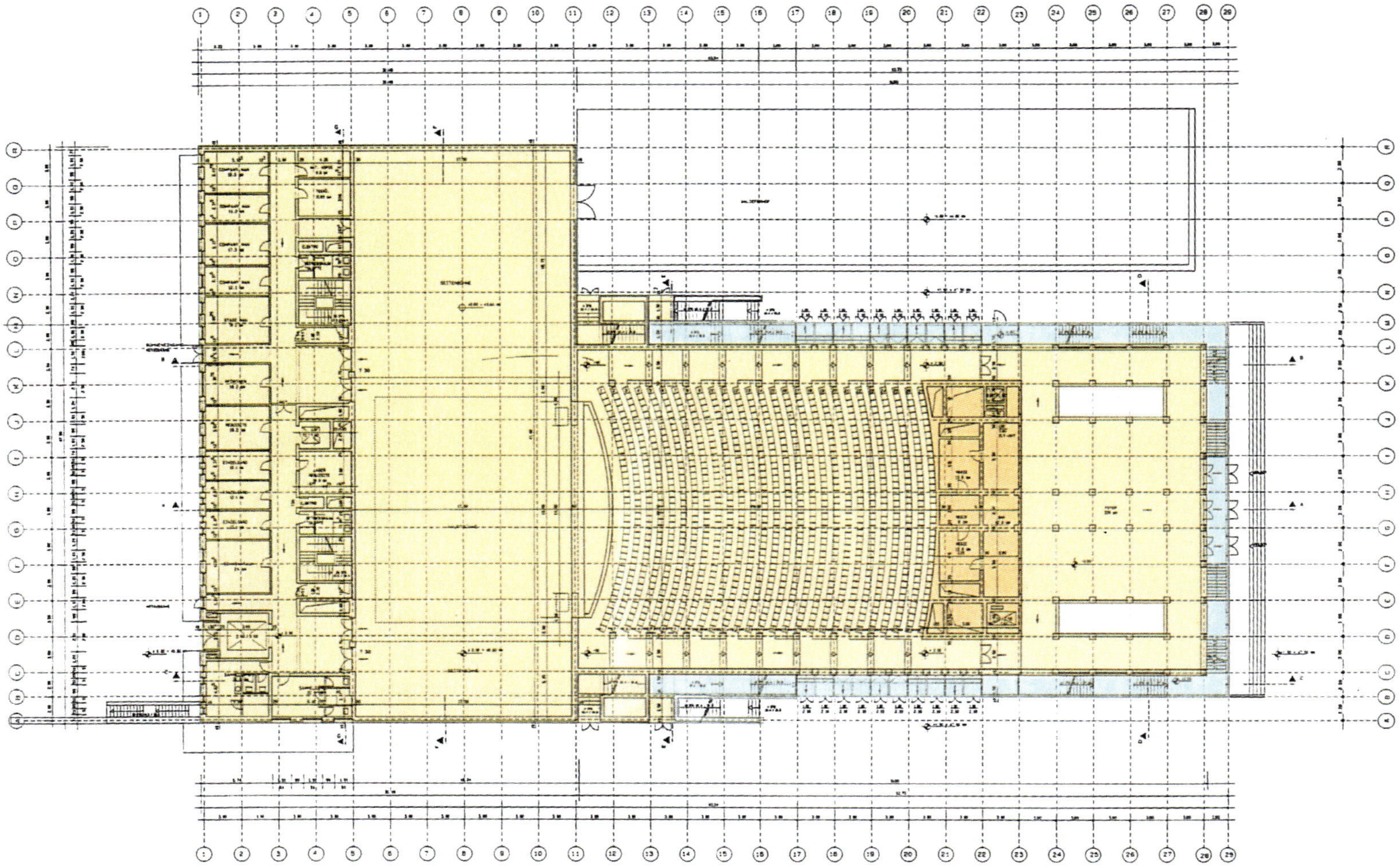

Musical theater: plan; elevations; section through stage area.

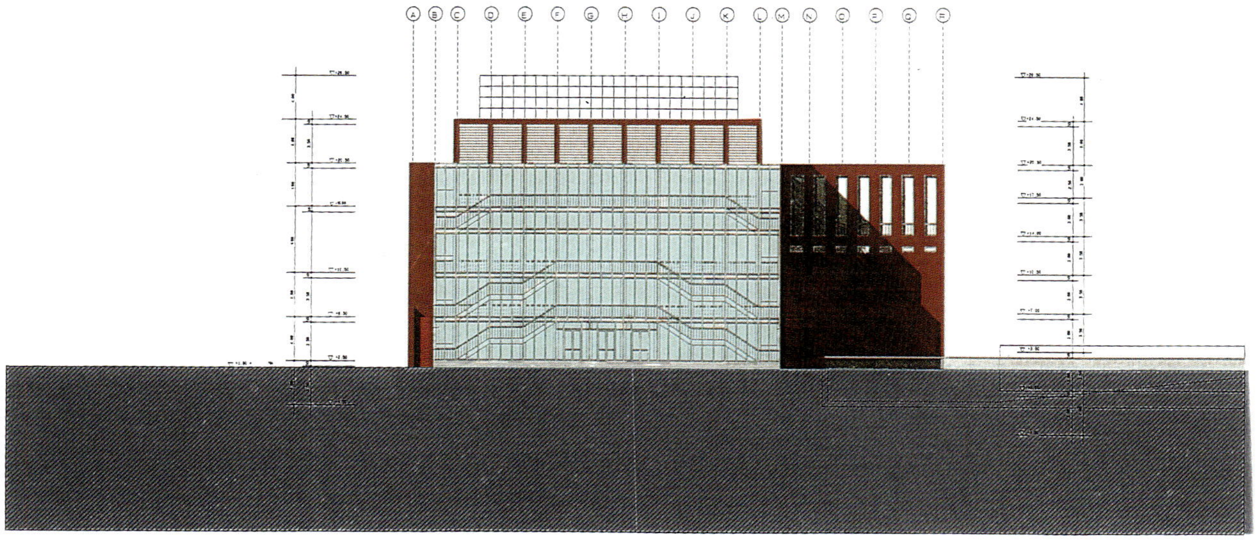

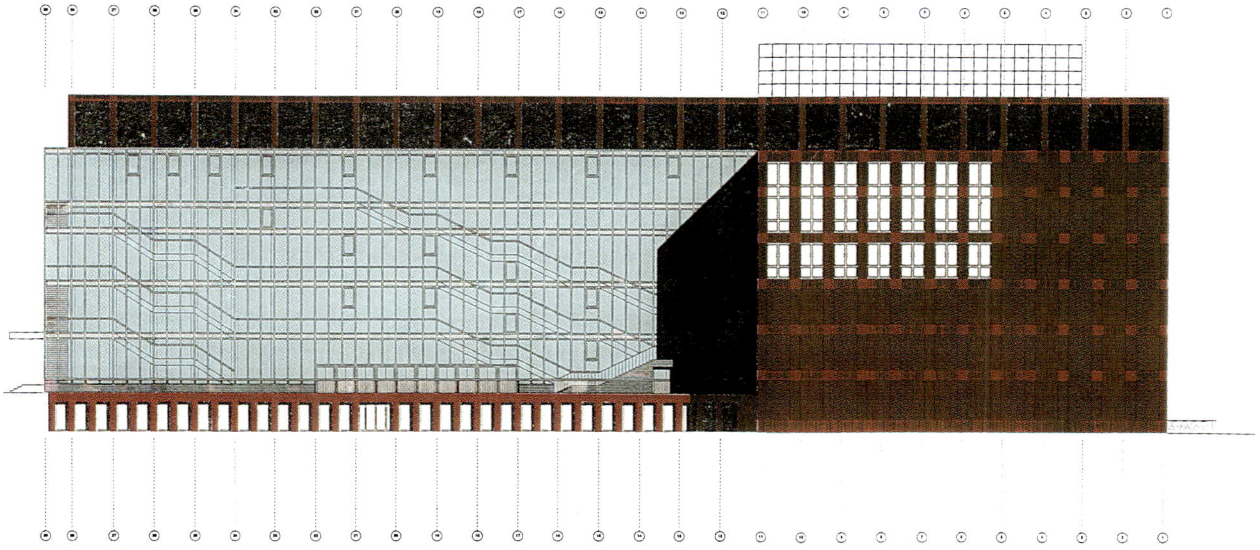

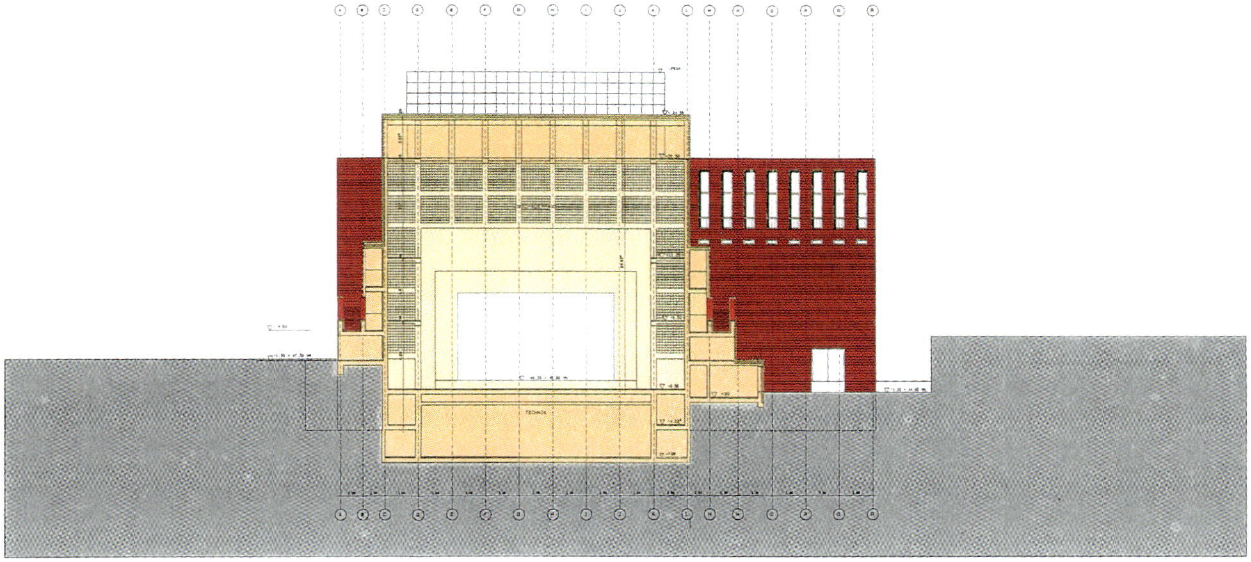

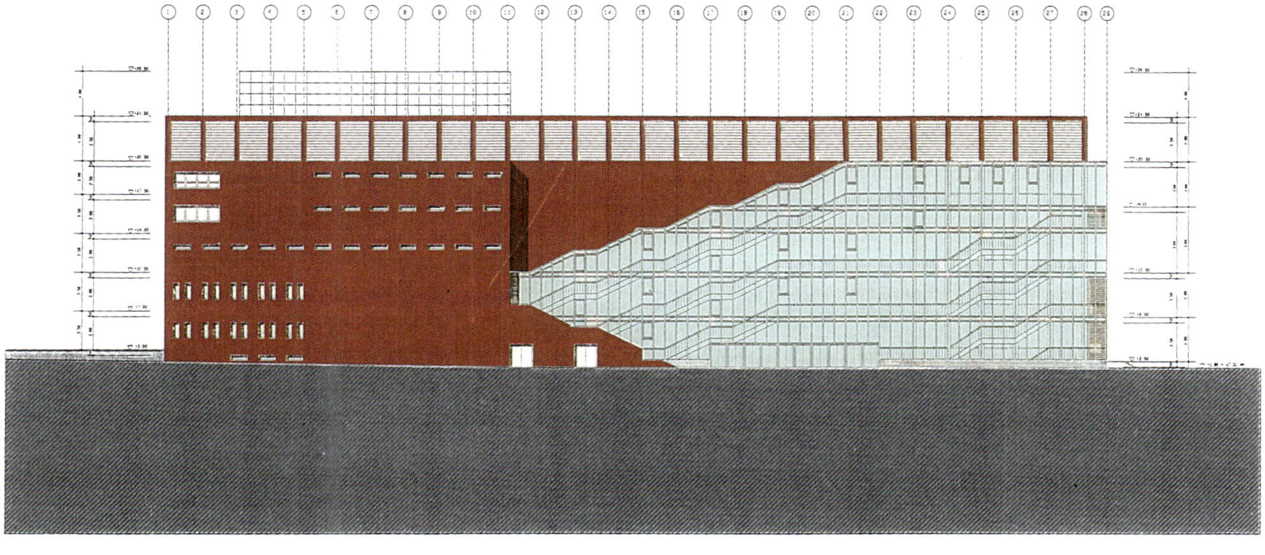

Competition Design for Cathedral Square, Magdeburg, 1993

With: Stefan Vieths

Project team: Don Dimster, Lukas Baumewerd, Johannes Götz, Frank Wieschemann, Raimund Fein, Michael Haase, Volker Diekmann

The urban setting of the cathedral of Magdeburg stands in stark contrast to the cultural and historic significance of the place. The existing structures are often incoherently juxtaposed and evoke little sense of space, causing the urban texture to dissolve into vast, unarticulated areas that almost assume the character of a landscape. The desolate overall situation contrasts with the variety and quality of the existing urban fragments, which include objects of great cultural and historic significance such as the cathedral and the Convent of Our Lady. In addition, however, there are also secular buildings of the most diverse types for residential and commercial use. All represent prototypical elements from the urban schemes of the Middle Ages, the baroque era, the nineteenth century, and the period of postwar reconstruction. The latent potential of the competition area lies in the dense, contrasting juxtaposition of these built urban ideas.

The design concept refers to and completes the existing urban fragments. Three urbanistic areas are identified, each representing a particular city type: the cathedral district, the residential structures around the Convent of

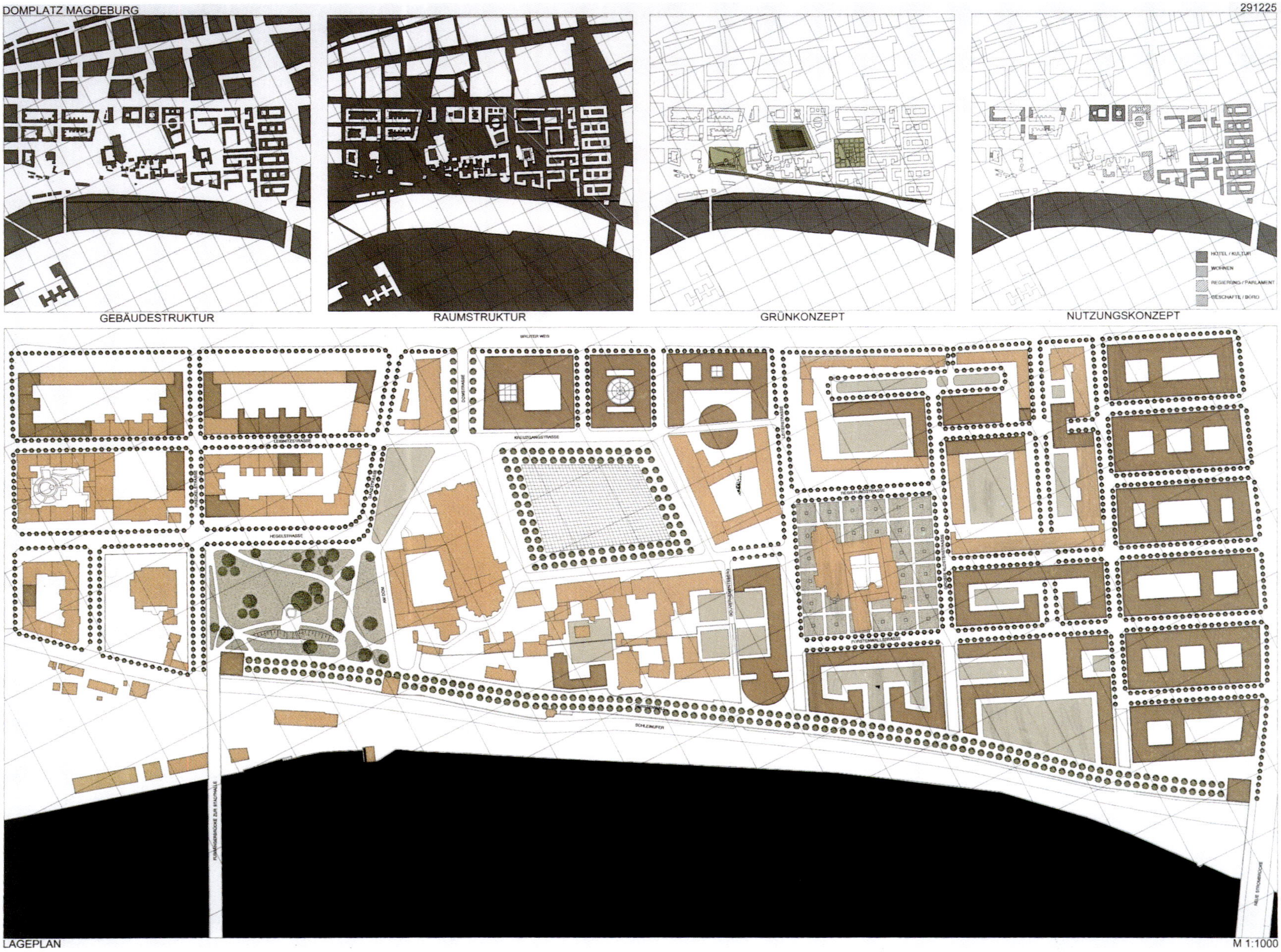

Site plan with use diagrams.

Views; elevation from the Elbe; architectonic typologies.

Our Lady, and the late-nineteenth-century buildings south of the cathedral. Each of these areas is characterized by a specific building type and spatial structure. In a second step, new buildings are incorporated into the syntax of each of the spatial and block typologies. In this way, three sectors of differing identity are created, each of which is organized around its own spatial center.

The cathedral district, as the central sector, is altered so as to provide once again a clear frame for the cathedral square and consolidate the overall architectural form toward the Elbe River. The new buildings adopt the motif of the poché block characteristic of the existing buildings. The new elements consist of four buildings that correspond to the functional demands of the location: the hotel on Domstrasse offers elegant accommodation for visitors to the cathedral square and guests of the state government; a museum documents the history of the cathedral district and its cultural significance; the parliament house on Breiter Weg supplements the existing government building and provides additional space for parliament and government; a newly created courtyard accommodates a library and a café. The building complex on Fürstenwall is completed by the parliament building, its plenary hall oriented toward the river as a half-round volume. Parking garages are located in the socle of the building. Around

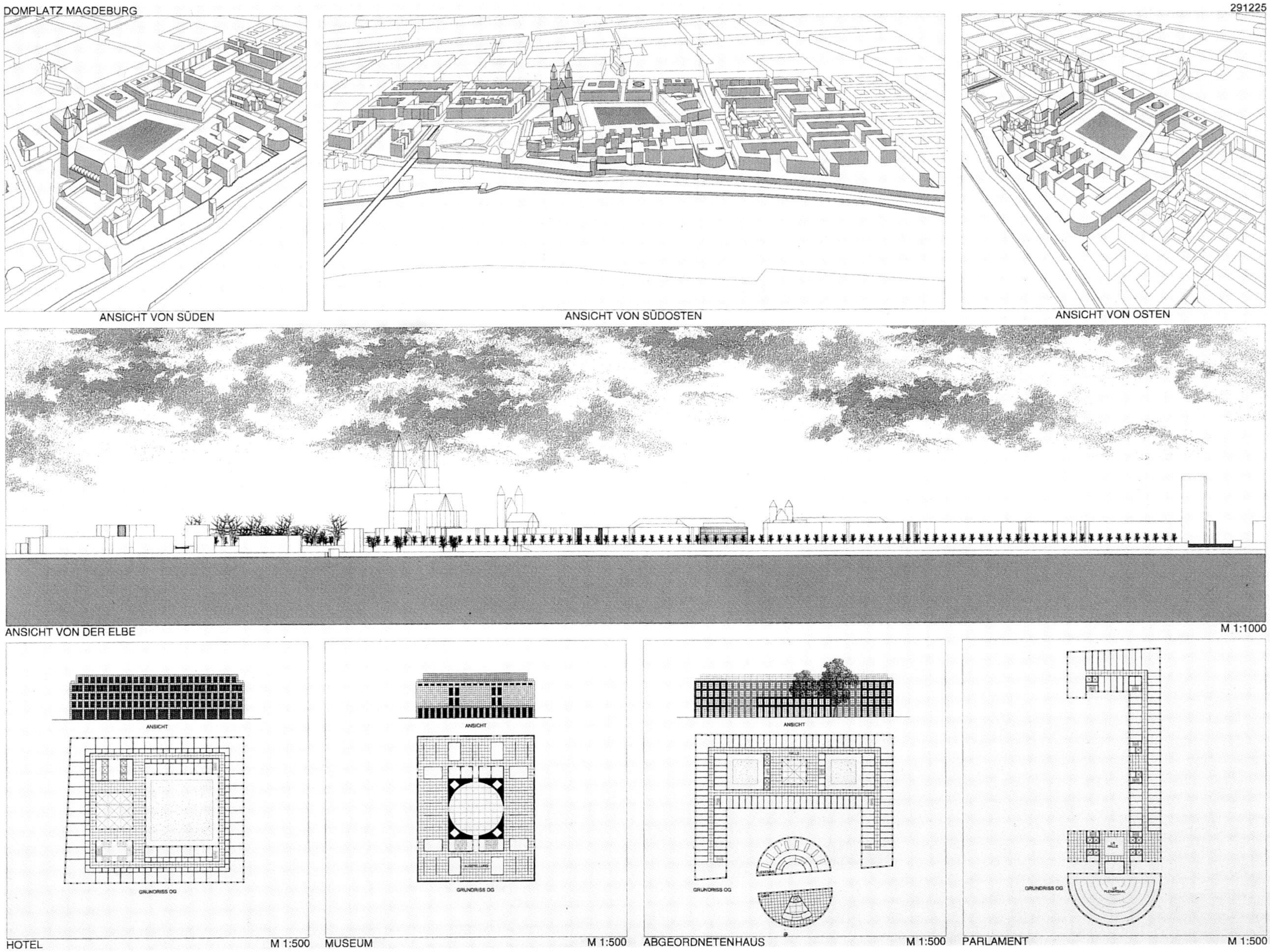

Sketch of site plan
with green areas;
studies for museum.

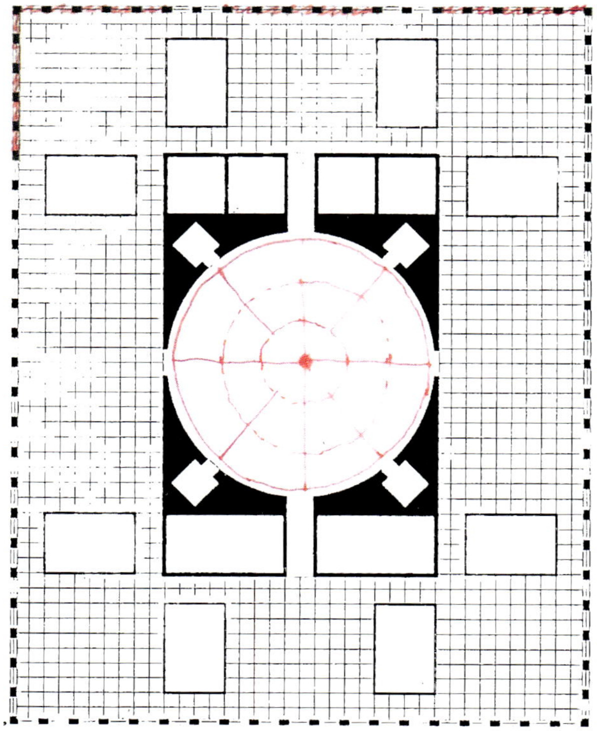

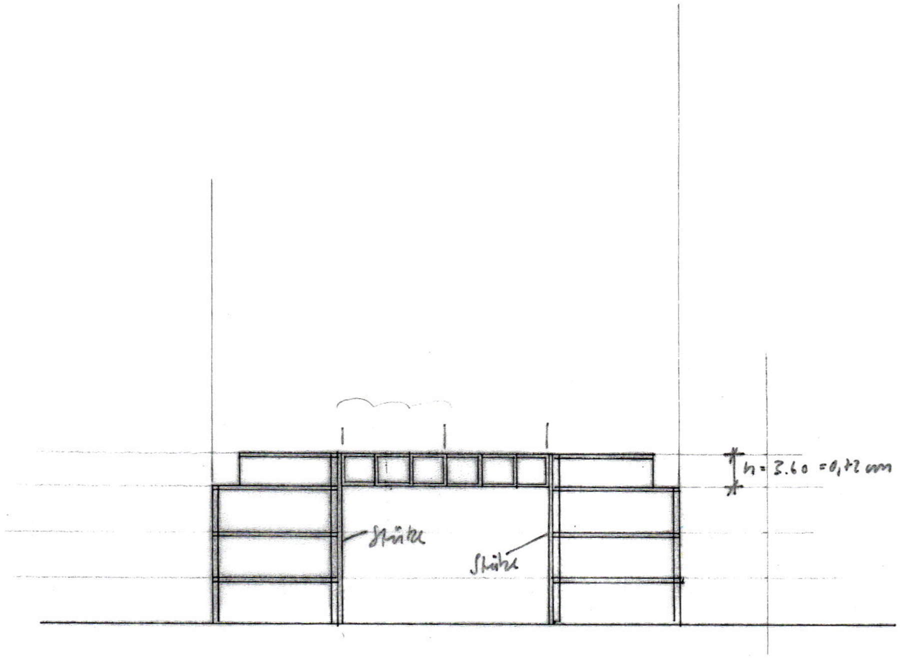

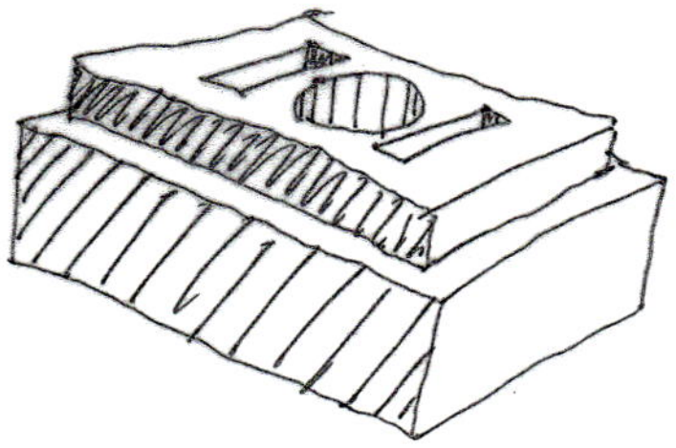

1:500

Opposite:
Plan and sketch for
parliament building; use
diagrams; model view.

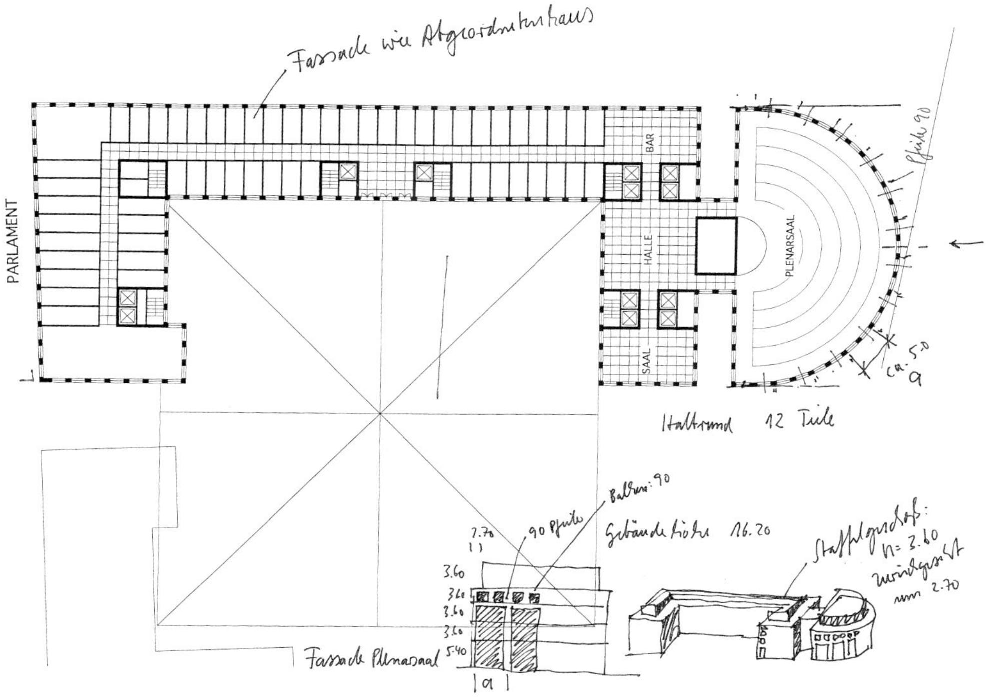

the Convent of Our Lady, the open, rowlike buildings from postwar reconstruction are transformed into meandering blocks extending to Fürstenwall. A sculpture park in the middle presents the monastic complex as an object. The new buildings contain dwellings, shops, and restaurants on the ground floors, with the block at the parliament building accommodating housing for the delegates. South of the cathedral square at the Materlik complexes, the urban expansion of the nineteenth century, with its orthogonal street grid and parceled perimeter blocks, is still clearly discernable. The plan calls for the completion of these blocks and the removal of construction over the street in the area of Leibnizstrasse and Danzstrasse. In analogy to these three areas, an additional block type is proposed for the central urban area along the Ernst-Reuter-Allee, which accommodates a high concentration of office and commercial spaces.

These urbanistic elements are unified by the augmentation of the street network and the establishment of spatial relationships between the three central green areas. They also receive a common basis in the promenade along the river embankment, which extends the existing promenade to the Neue Strombrücke. The necessary elevation of the terrain is achieved by means of a built socle containing parking garages. The south end of the promenade forms a new pedestrian bridge connecting the government district and the municipal hall.

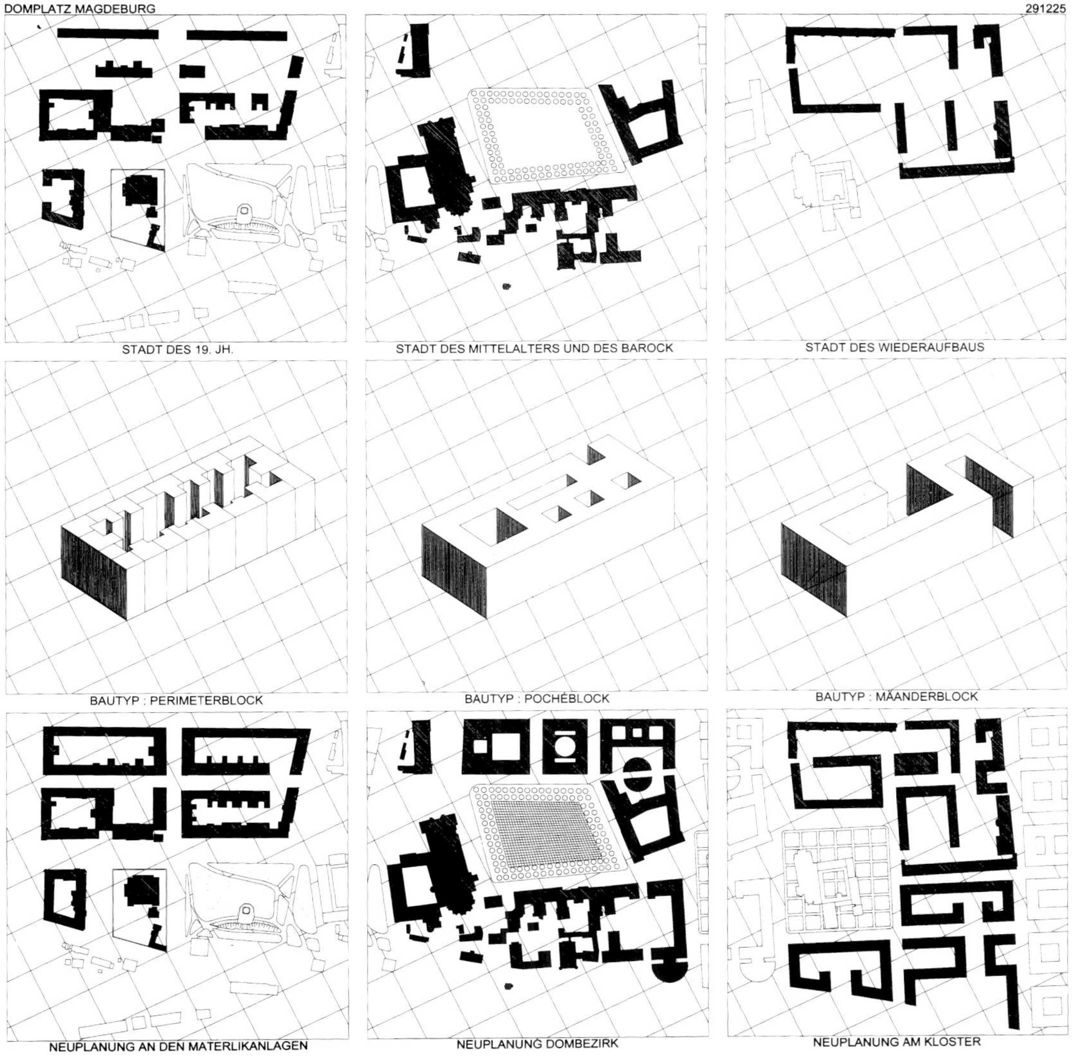

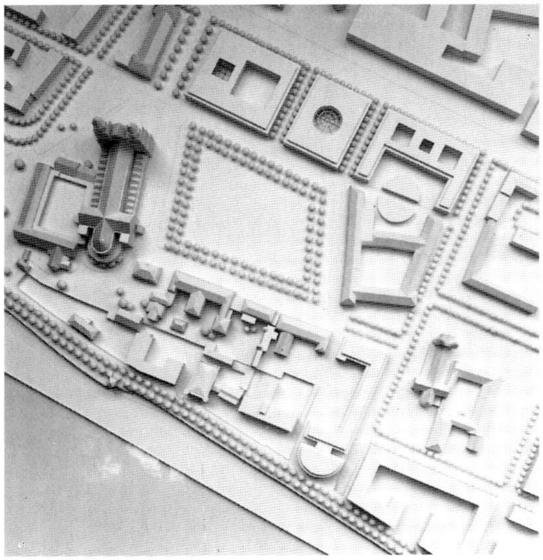

Feasibility Study for Alfred-Wegener-Institut, Potsdam, 1993–1998

Project team: Tobias Scheel, Karl-Heinz Winkens, Birgit Schindler

The Potsdam research station of the Alfred-Wegener-Institut für Polar- und Meeresforschung (AWI) in Bremerhaven was established in 1992 to preserve and develop the scientific potential of Antarctica research in the former East Germany. Its research activities focus primarily on geoscientific studies at the edges of the inland ice areas and in the permafrost regions, as well as the physics and chemistry of the atmosphere over the polar land masses—areas of study that augment the research program of the AWI, which previously focused on oceanography. The East German polar researchers no longer study only the Antarctic, but to an increasing extent the Arctic as well, a region crucial to the understanding of climatic events in Europe.

The new project consists of an extension of the existing building and the construction of warehouse facilities for duty-liable goods, equipment, and chemicals. Both buildings receive above-ground parking lots; a central lounge space is provided as well. The design for the expansion on the Telegraphenberg hill derives its form and location from the functional demands of a laboratory and administration building, but above all from the relation to the existing terrain and its historic scientific research buildings. The new architectural configuration results from a seemingly random yet ordered mixture of freestanding buildings that combine to produce an overall organism. The main urban feature is the arrangement of freestanding structures, which enter into axial relationships with the neighboring buildings to form individual ensembles. The latter, in turn, are integrated into their spatial context through an overarching system of axes, which combine with the topographical position of the buildings to create a unique image. Temporary annex buildings disturb this arrangement perceptibly. The following considerations of historic preservation are taken into account: the new structure should not dominate the hill but should be tailored to the existing buildings in volume and height and should sensibly enhance the existing architectural arrangement at a moderate elevation. Positioned at the edge of the institute grounds, the new building now defines the eastern edge of the Telegraphenberg.

Historic plan ca. 1890; perspective showing new planning; phases of construction.

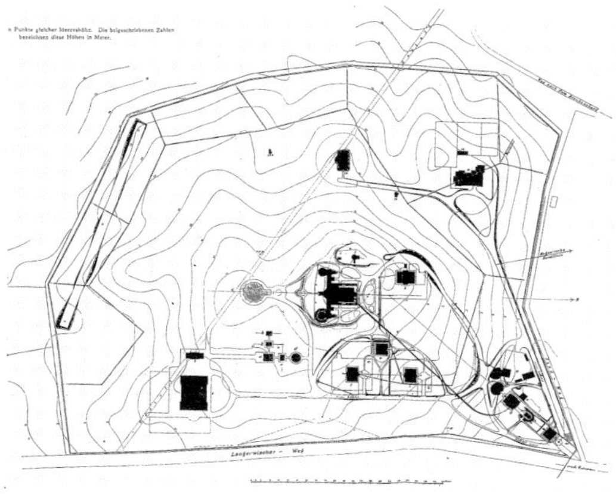

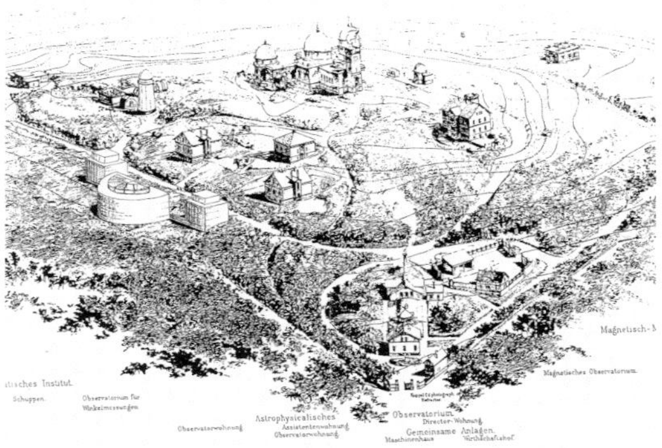

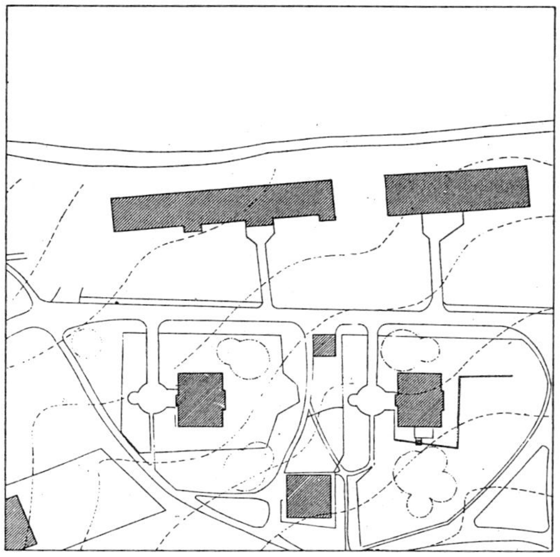

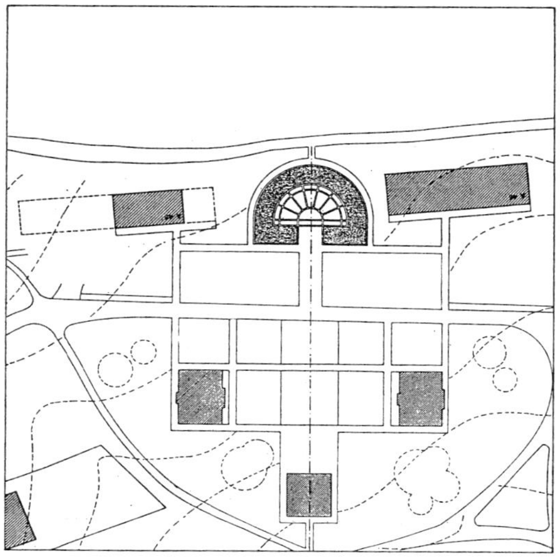

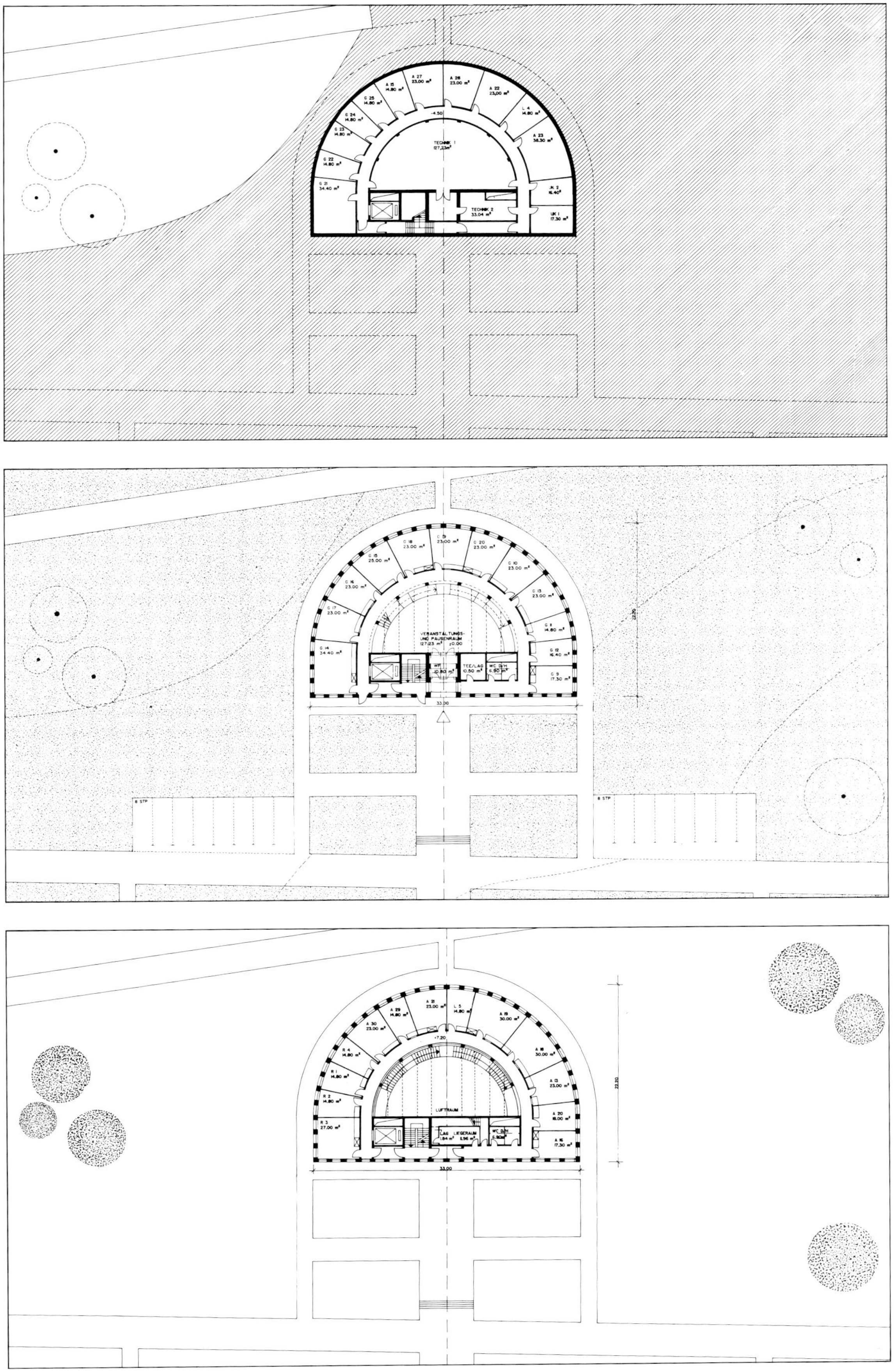

Plans.

Section; elevations.

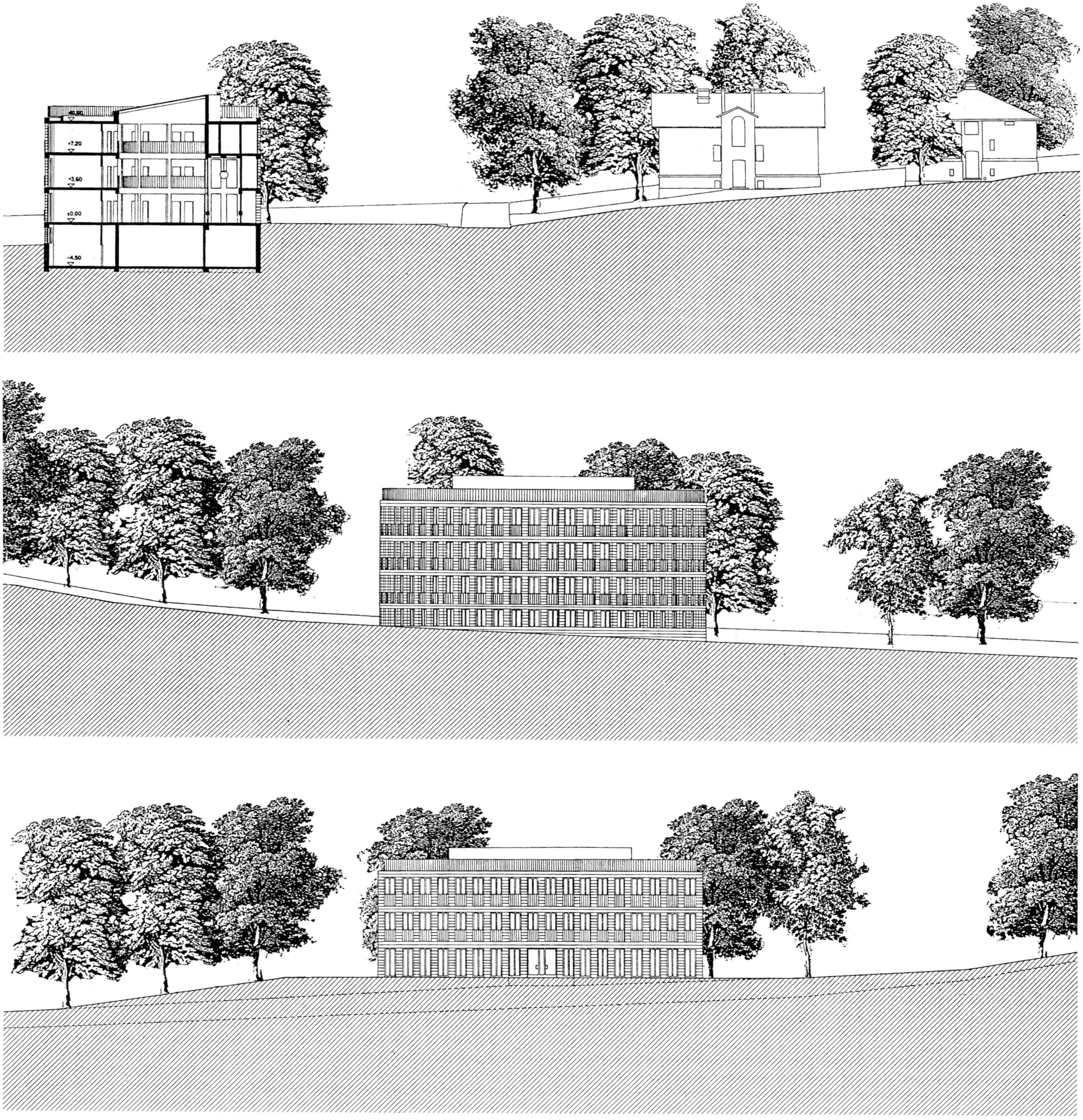

Competition Design for Expansion of Königliche Porzellan-Manufaktur (KPM), Berlin, 1993

With: Stefan Vieths

Project team: Don Dimster, Axel Steudel, Johannes Götz, Frank Wieschemann

The grounds of the Königliche Porzellan-Manufaktur (Royal Porcelain Manufacturers) are located at a central juncture within the urban organization of Berlin. The site on Strasse des 17. Juni—the great urban axis of Berlin, here intersected by the S-Bahn—is distinguished by its position on the boundary between the densely built district of Charlottenburg and the expansive Tiergarten landscape, as well as by its place in the area between the Spree and the Landwehrkanal. This configuration of boundaries and intersections is reflected in the morphology of the existing buildings. Here, structures of the most diverse typology, function, and orientation confront each other directly.

The old KPM complex, from the

General plan; perspective views; use diagrams.

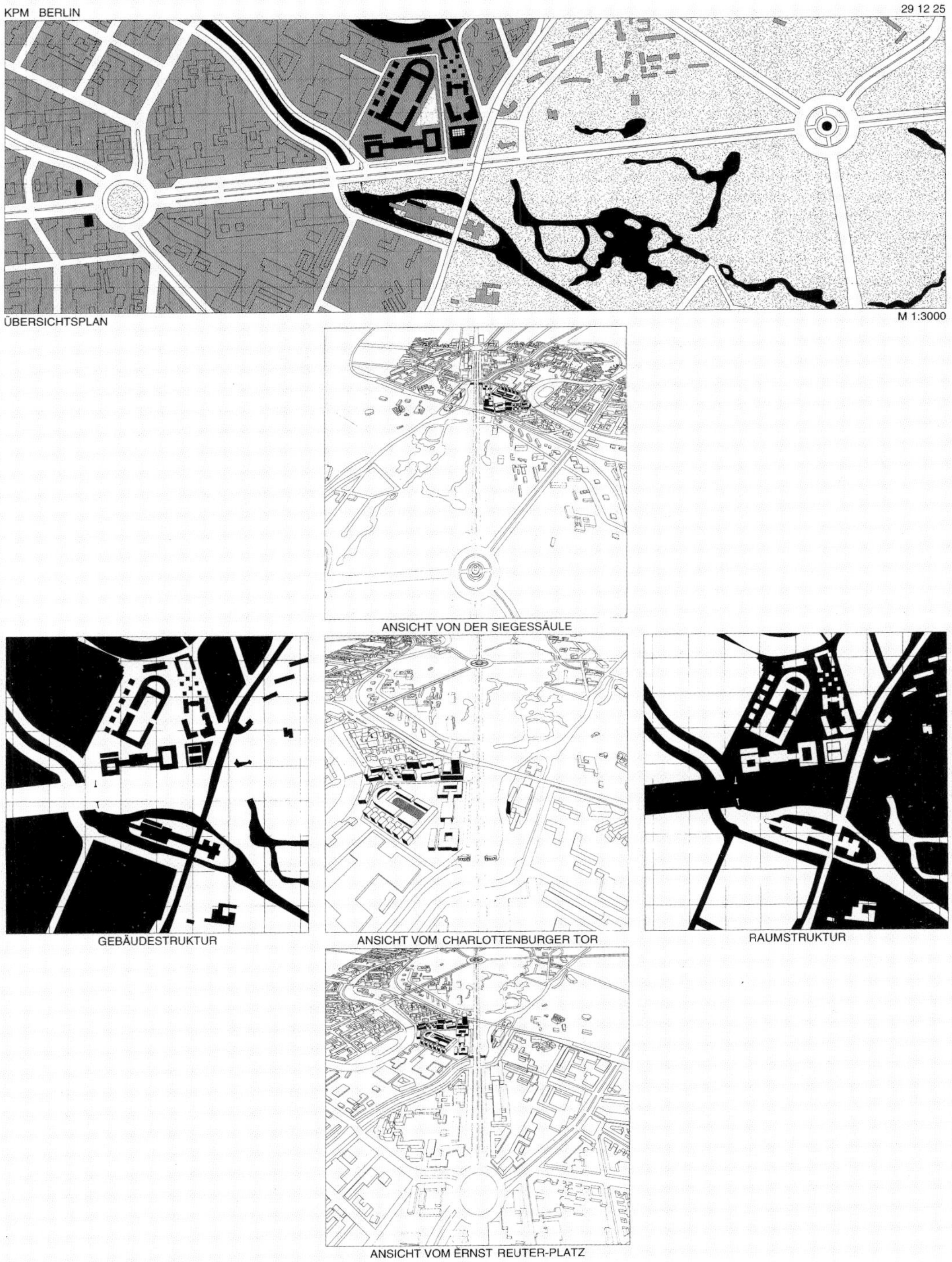

Crossectional study; site plan.

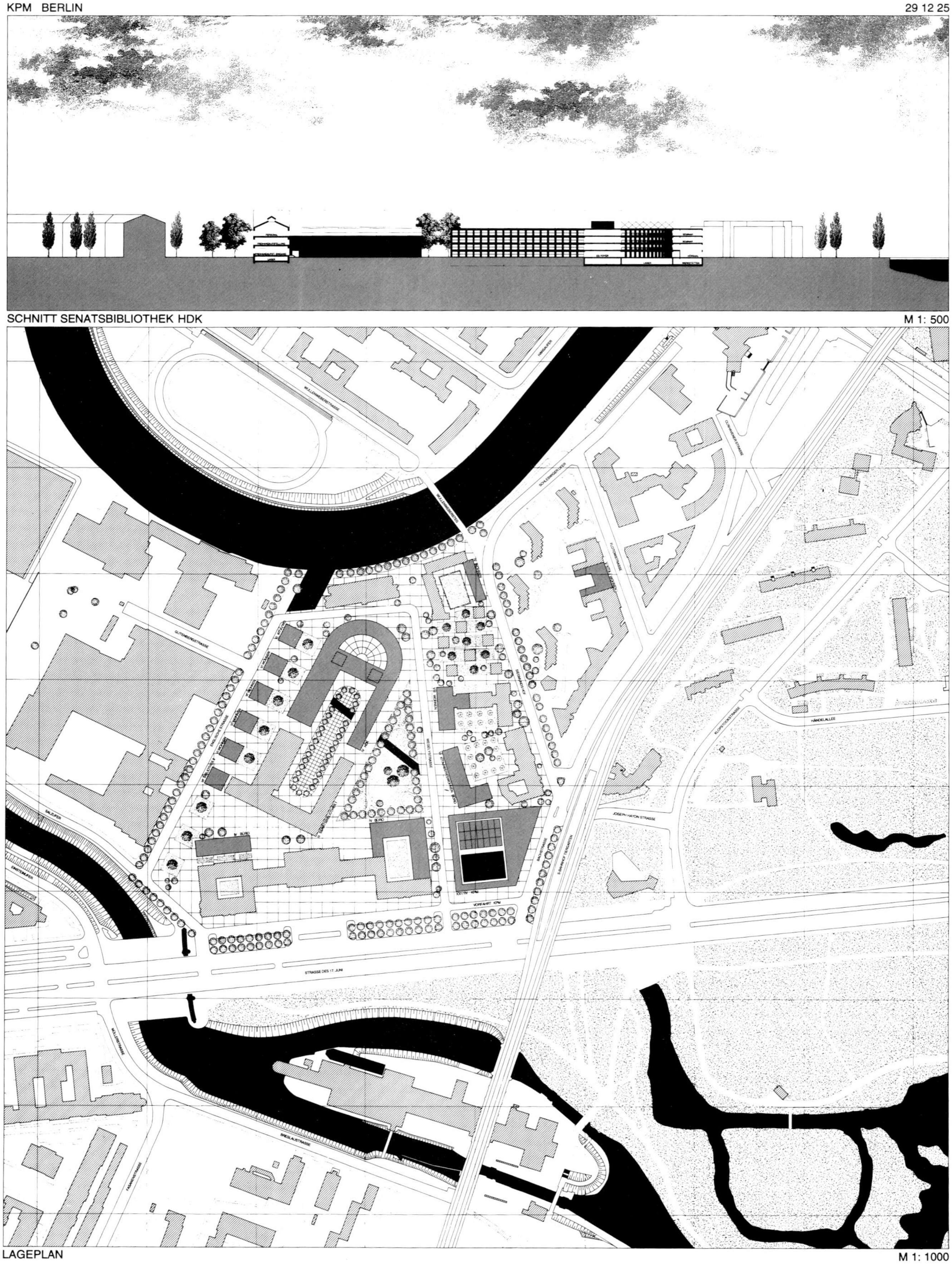

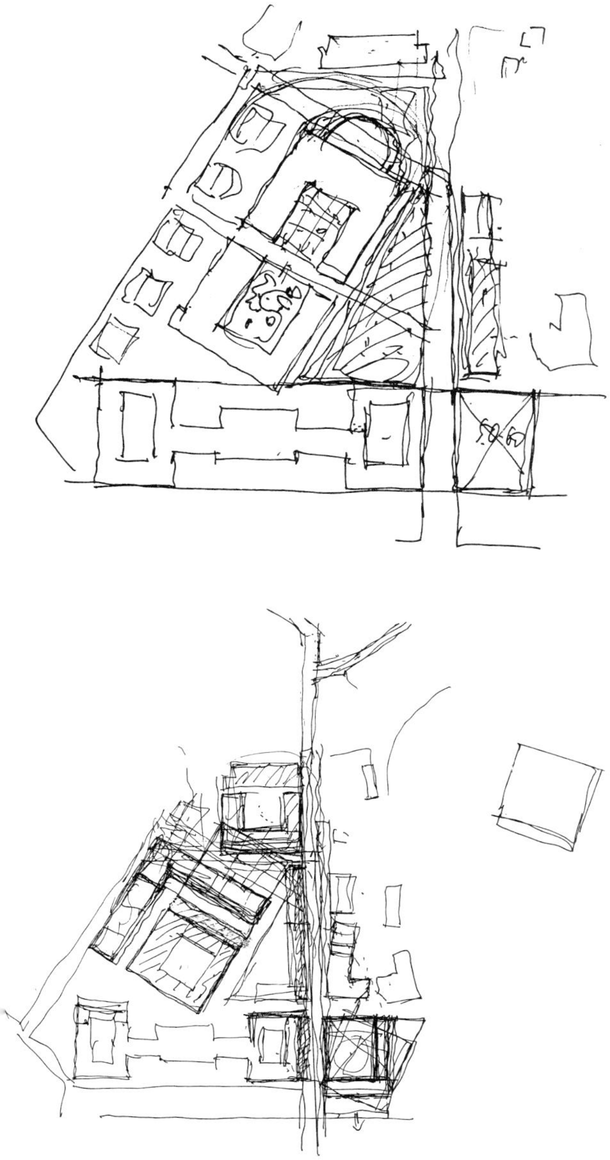

Sketches.

nineteenth century, consists of the commercial buildings west of the site, as well as buildings added in the 1950s.

The residential buildings on Siegmunds Hof present a compendium of residential types from the nineteenth century to the 1950s and generally reflect the lower density of the Hansa area to the east. The freestanding university building on the Spree was erected in the 1970s, while Ernst-Reuter-Haus, clearly oriented to Strasse des 17. Juni, is a prime example of an imposing administrative building from the turn of the century. Portions of these fragments are of high quality and represent—each in its own way—a specific idea of the city and the history of Berlin. The immediate juxtaposition of these contrasting individual objects constitutes the architectural and spatial potential on which the design concept is based.

The proposed design accepts and emphasizes the fragmentary and contradictory structure of the complex as a specific urban quality. Rather than being systematically unified, the chance features of the existing structure are used as opportunities to develop an urbanistic scheme composed of freestanding buildings, inspired by Schinkel's design for the Spreeinsel. In this process, chance elements are integrated into a rational composition, while existing fragments are incorporated into urbanistic units and supplemented with new objects. This concept permits an unbroken continuation of the building tradition by largely preserving the existing structures and incorporating them into a new overall concept. In addition,

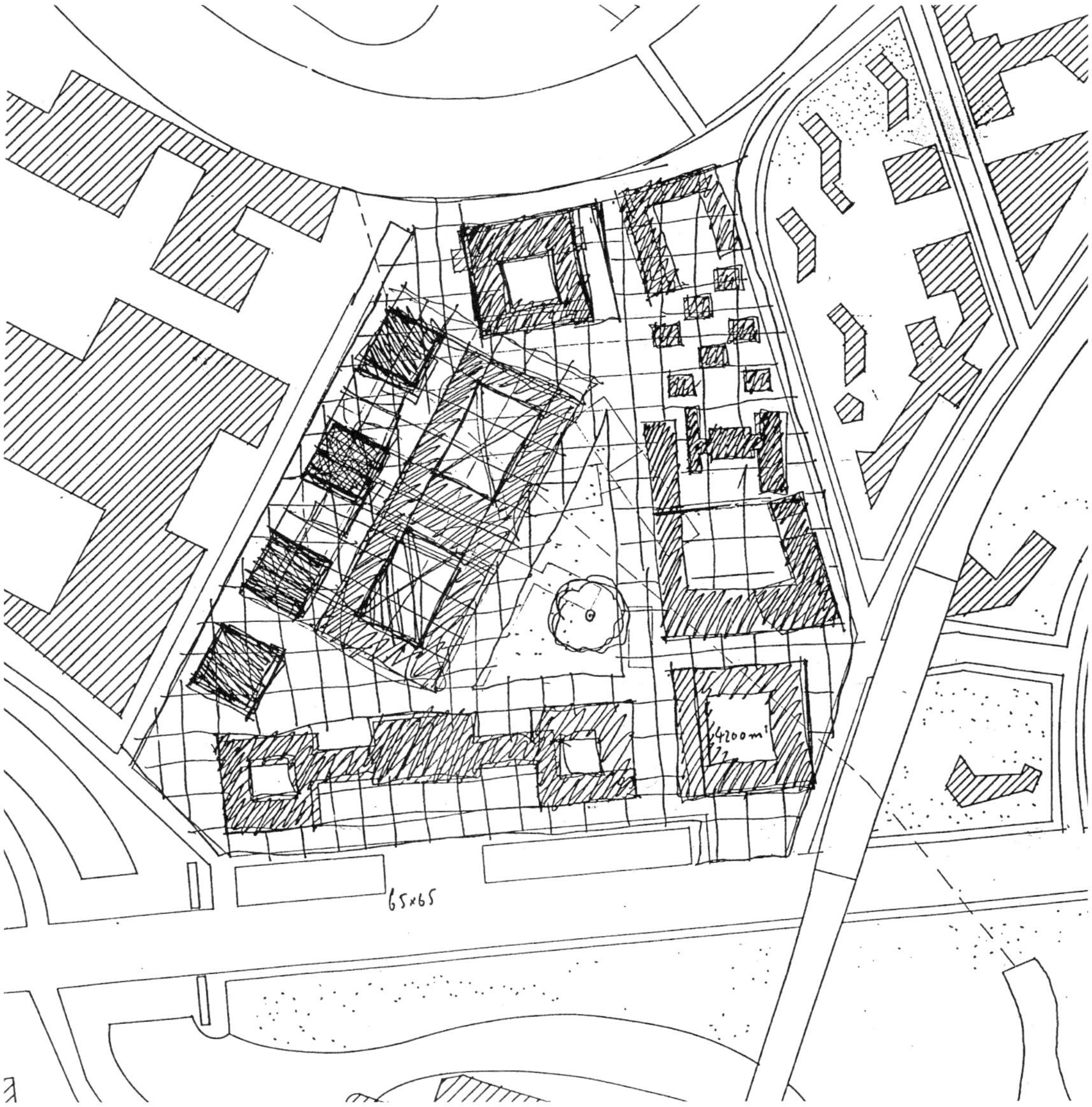

Ground-level plan; sketch.

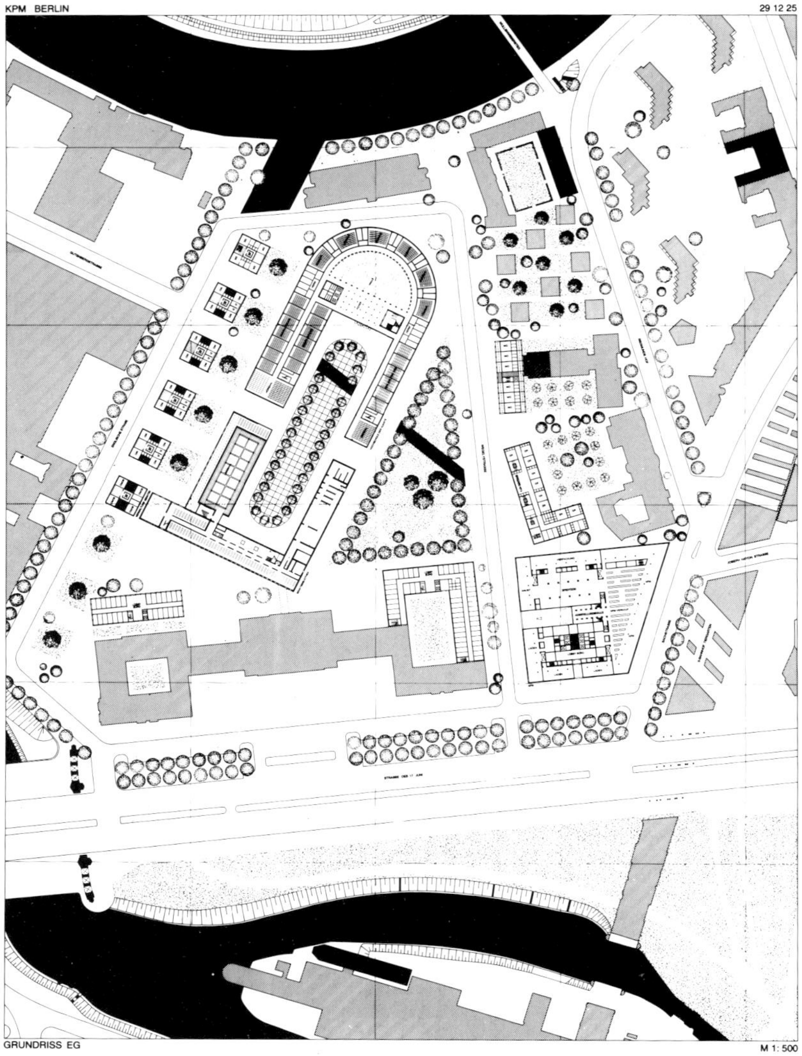

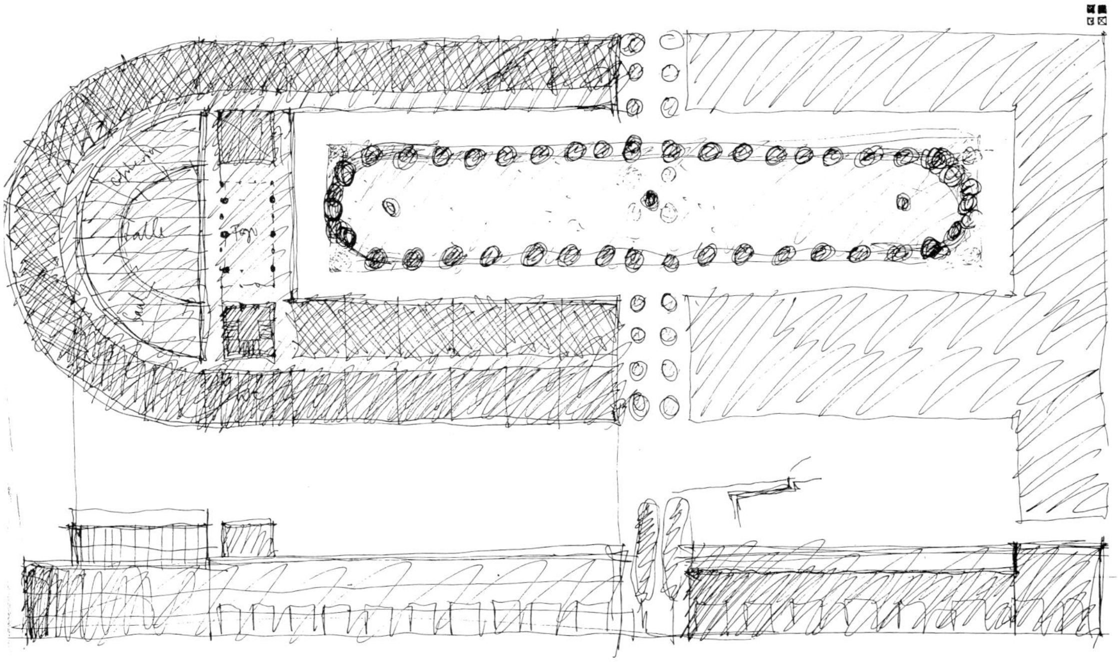

the scheme makes possible a building typology whose variety satisfies the range of planned usages. In analogy to the buildings, a typology of precisely defined exterior spaces is devised as well, ranging from the garden to the interior courtyard to the campus.

The center is marked by a triangular area, a green, open space defined by freestanding buildings. It connects the preexisting student housing with the Hochschule der Künste (HdK) and the Senatsbibliothek into a new, self-contained academic complex, supplementing the other institutions in the immediate vicinity. The urbanistic composition revolves around freestanding structures, each of which represents a specific building type. The plan calls for a high-rise building, the KPM tower, at the urbanistically significant entrance to the Tiergarten. The relation to Ernst-Reuter-Haus is established by the socle, which supports both the slender office tower and the closed cube of the firing hall. The hippodrome is a building ensemble with a long, hippodrome-like interior courtyard, incorporating the U-shaped KPM building as well as the Senatsbibliothek and the HdK. As a monumental double-courtyard complex, Ernst-Reuter-Haus is augmented with extensions that likewise serve for office space. The west wing is intended as a replacement building for the plot reserved for the Deutsche Bahn on Englische Strasse. The addition of a new angled structure to the buildings at the edge of the block on Siegmunds Hof results in a double-angled courtyard complex, while a second wing transforms the neighboring eight-story building into an H-shaped ensemble.

West of the hippodrome, six villas are planned, consisting primarily of housing that will close off the complex toward Englische Strasse. The KPM facilities are concentrated in the tower on Strasse der 17. Juni; together with the tower of the research institute by Ludwig Leo, the building serves to establish a gateway to the Tiergarten. This architectural conception offers a number of advantages: the KPM receives an urbanistically outstanding building appropriate to the firm's historical significance for Berlin while the commercial function makes optimal use of the prominent location on Strasse der 17. Juni at the Tiergarten S-Bahn station. In this way, the residential and institutional buildings at the rear of the site are kept free from disturbances. The functional concentration in a tower structure also leaves space for a generous campus.

Typologically speaking, the KPM tower represents a reinterpretation of the traditional Berlin residential and commercial structure, a hybrid, multifunctional building accommodating a wide range of functions beneath a single roof. The tower itself contains offices and dwellings, while the socle area accommodates production and exhibition spaces interlocked by means of a generous stair complex, so that the KPM production facilities become a part of its self-representation. At the end of the stair is an exhibition area and a restaurant, both of which open out onto a large roof terrace with a view of the Tiergarten.

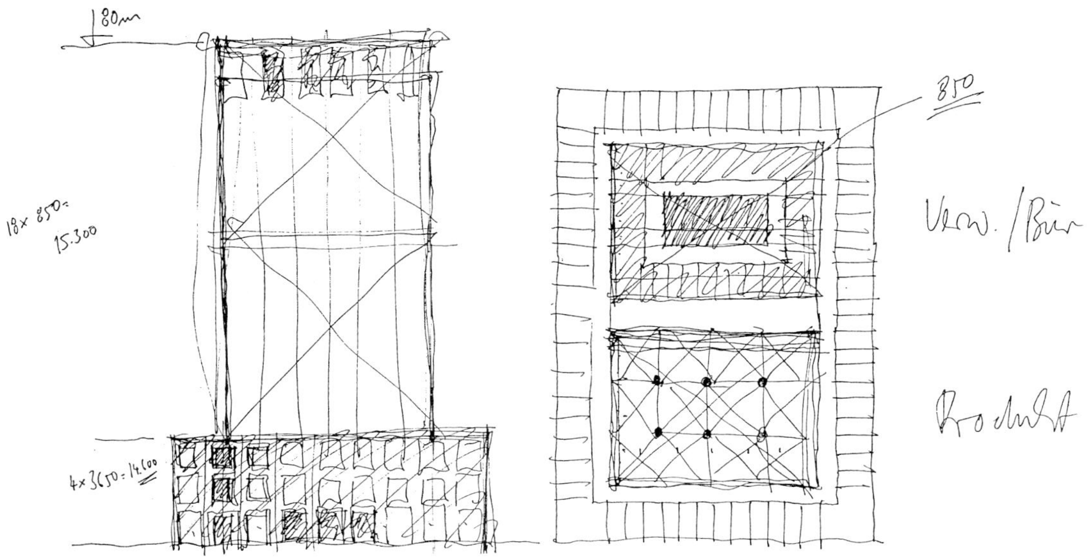

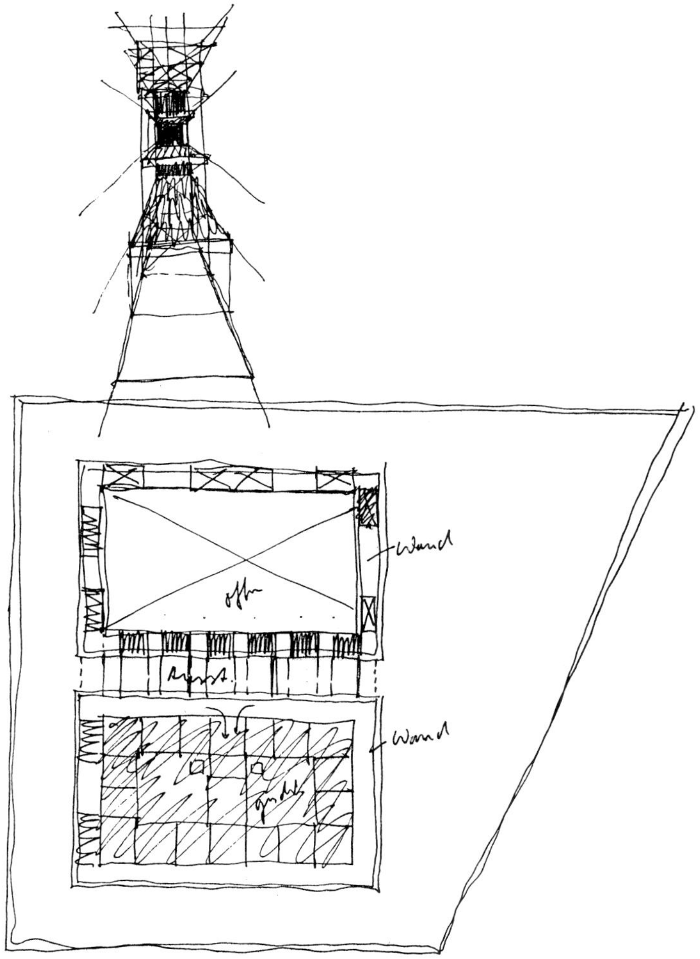

Sketches for KPM tower; plans; elevations; sections.

Competition Design for Spreeinsel, Berlin, 1993, 1994

With: Stefan Vieths

Project team:
First phase: Peter Pfertner, Johannes Götz, Axel Steudel, Frank Wieschemann
Second phase: Peter Pfertner, Marvin Keim, Don Dimster, Kai-Uwe Lompa, Axel Steudel, Elke Stumm, Frank Wieschemann, Johannes Götz, Michael Laudert

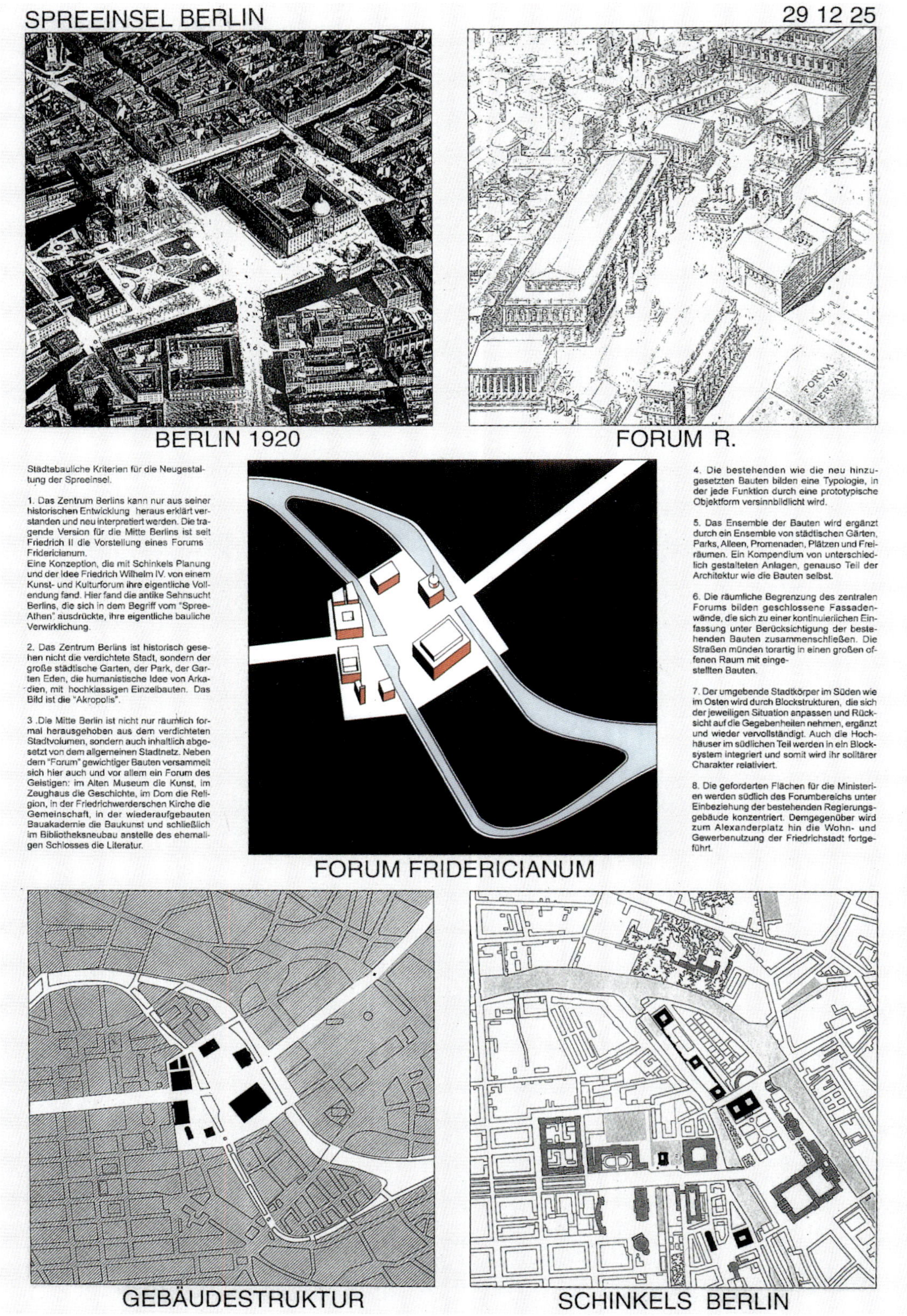

The Spreeinsel is an area of prime significance for the historic center of Berlin. One of the earliest areas of settlement and the location of the palace of the Prussian kings, it is a site that can be reinterpreted only on the basis of its historical development. Since Frederick II, the underlying concept has been that of the Forum Fridericianum, a scheme that found its fulfillment in Schinkel's plan and Frederick William IV's idea of a forum for culture and art. Here, Berlin's longing for an "Athens on the Spree" came to architectural expression as well in a kind of "acropolis." Now, in addition to the forum of politically significant buildings, a spiritual and intellectual forum is to be established here as well, with the Altes Museum, the Zeughaus, the Friedrichwerdersche Kirche, the Bauakademie, and a new library.

The objective of the competition was to find an urban solution for the future Mitte district of Berlin. A central question is whether the Palast der Republik should be demolished or preserved and whether the historic Stadtschloss should be reconstructed or replaced. For many, the Palast der Republik, contaminated with asbestos and already scheduled for demolition, nonetheless represents a significant, if problematic, document of the former East Germany. Its main assembly hall was the site of the historic decision to reunify Germany in 1990; it served as a seat of parliament, congress center, and showpiece all in one—a building for the people constructed with the greatest effort, the visible expression of the achievements of an entire generation disadvantaged by fate.

The value of the Palast der Republik for collective memory is incalculable and should not be minimized. The Schloss, still preserved as a ruin after the war, was forced to yield to a new political consciousness. Its reconstruction is impossible, not only out of respect for history, but also for technical and economic reasons. A fake could not replace the reality, nor could a painful loss be compensated by a bad copy. Such a reconstruction could only take place at the cost of destroying the other historical document.

In view of this difficult situation, the design calls for the Palast der Republik to be placed under historic preservation and maintained in

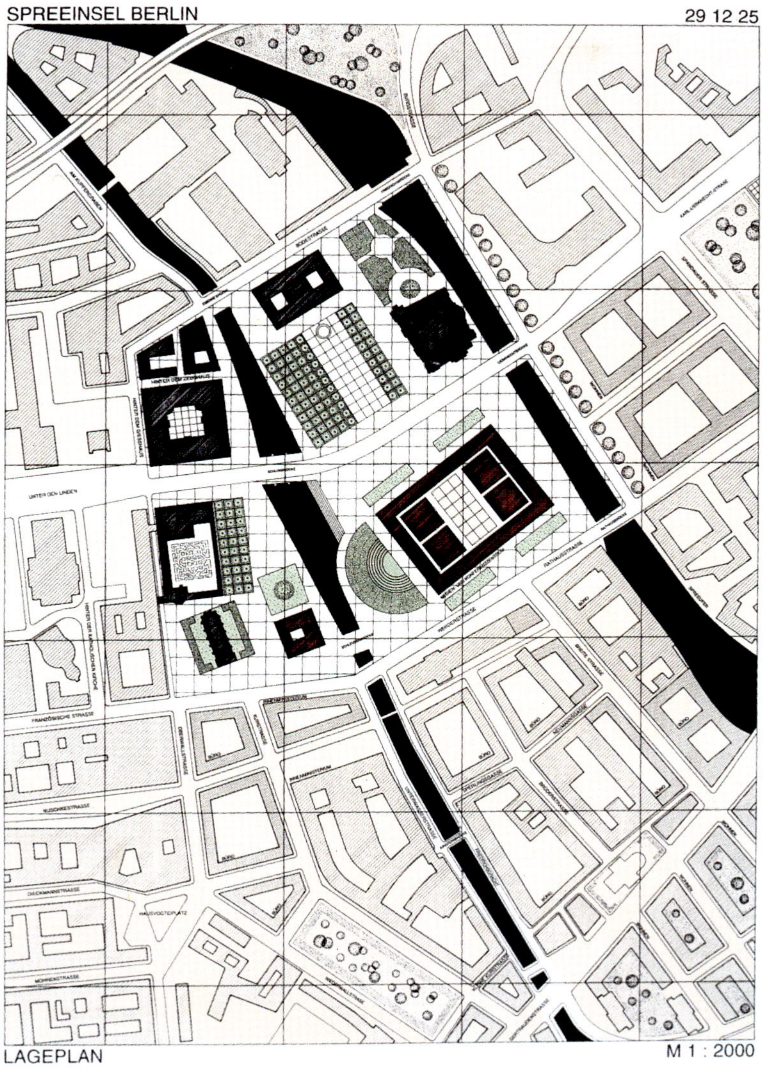

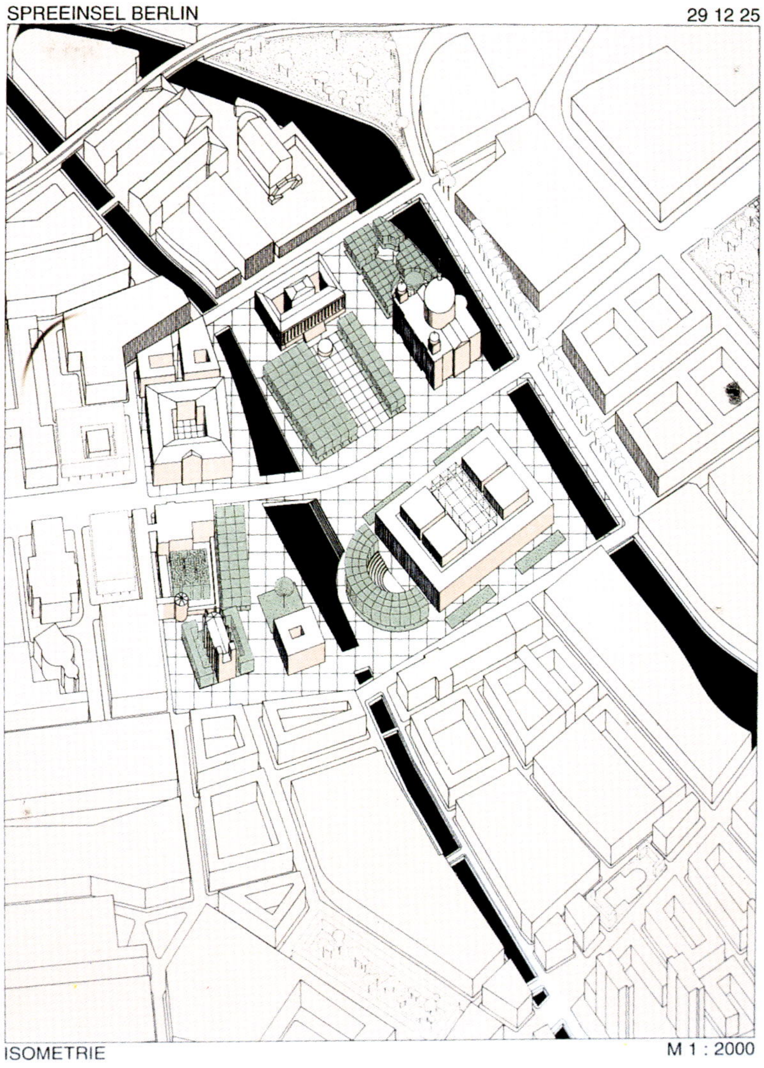

Site plan; isometric.

Opposite:
Use diagrams.

Overleaf:
Site plan with use diagrams; typical floor plan; ground-level plan; elevations, plans, and sections of media center and ministries.

its original form. The aesthetics of both interior and exterior should remain untouched and should be carefully restored in accord with the original design. The building's monumental position, however, should be compromised in order to integrate it into a closed urban volume—not as a freestanding building but as part of a street block. Accordingly, the buildings at the edge of the block are brought forward to the street line of Unter den Linden, forming a closed backdrop for the Lustgarten together with the short side of the Palast. In this way, the dense architectural network of the Spreeinsel is continued up to this edge, and the Lustgarten receives a spatial frame into which the freestanding buildings of the cathedral, the Altes Museum, and the Zeughaus are placed.

Respect for history likewise prohibits construction on the site of the former Schloss, which thus remains empty, constituting a negative space within the block structure. The site of the Schloss appears in the plan as an open space surrounded on all sides by buildings; enlivened with surviving architectural elements (columns, capitals, bases), it can be used as a historic park. The historic underground vault, which served among other things as the state treasury, is to be exposed and made accessible. Above all, however, the surviving Eosander Gate in the form of a triumphal arch is to be erected in its old location again, while the monument of St. George once again occupies its original place in the inner courtyard. In addition to the great architectural relics of the Museumsinsel—the Pergamon altar, the Egyptian temple complexes, the Ishtar Gate—an exhibition area for architectural elements from the Prussian past will be established here as well. The fusing of two mutually destructive historical ideologies into an

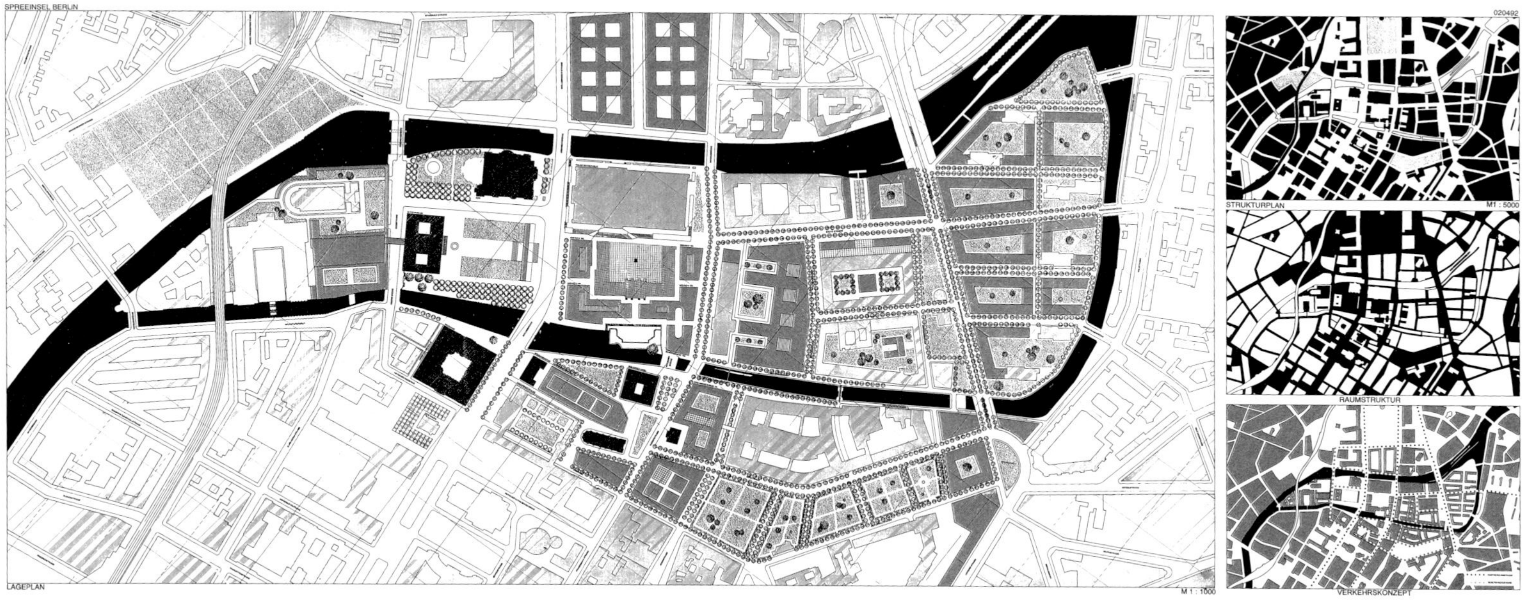
SPREEINSEL BERLIN
020492
LAGEPLAN
M 1 : 1000
STRUKTURPLAN
M1 : 5000
RAUMSTRUKTUR
VERKEHRSKONZEPT

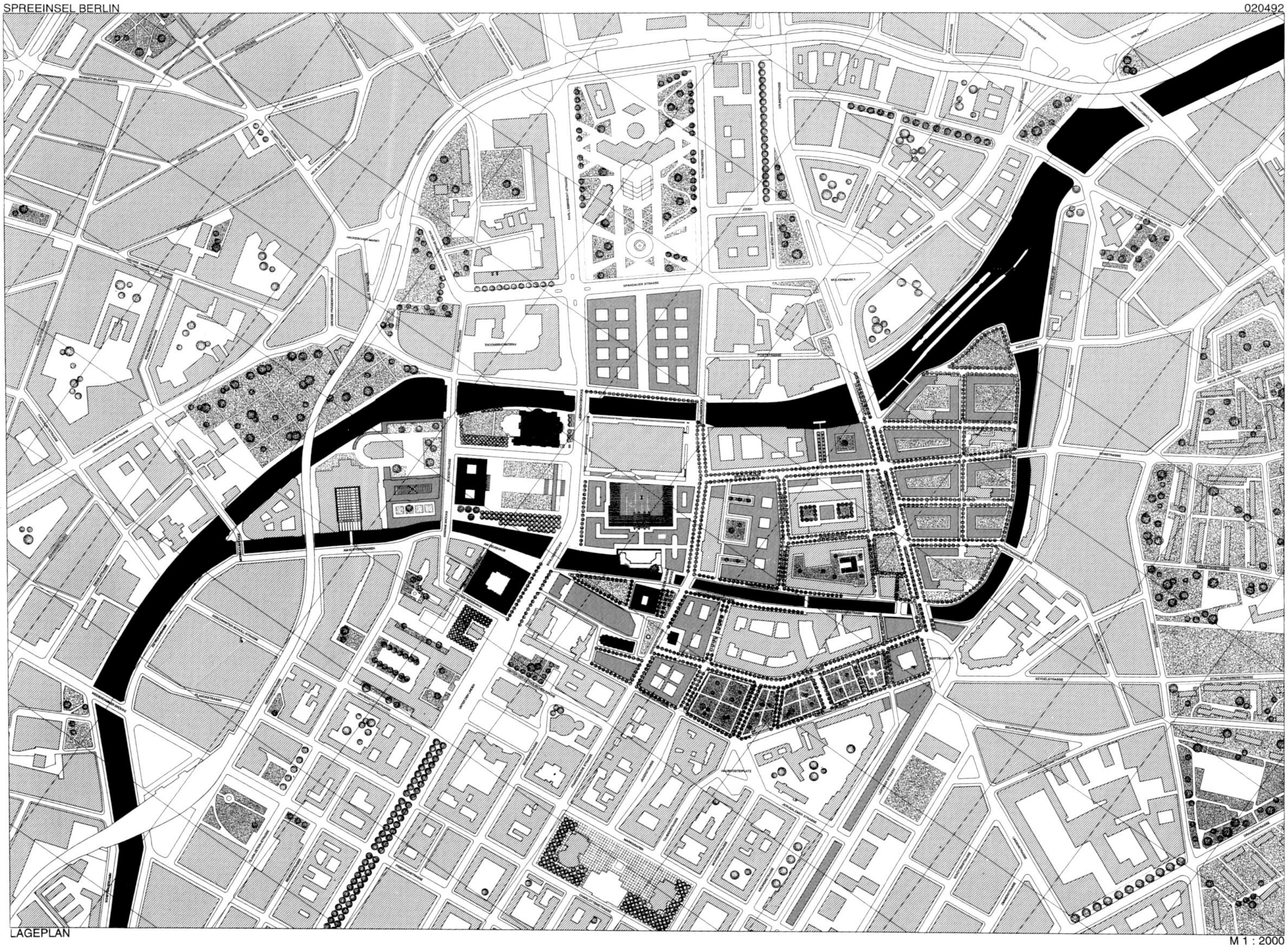
SPREEINSEL BERLIN
020492
LAGEPLAN
M 1 : 2000

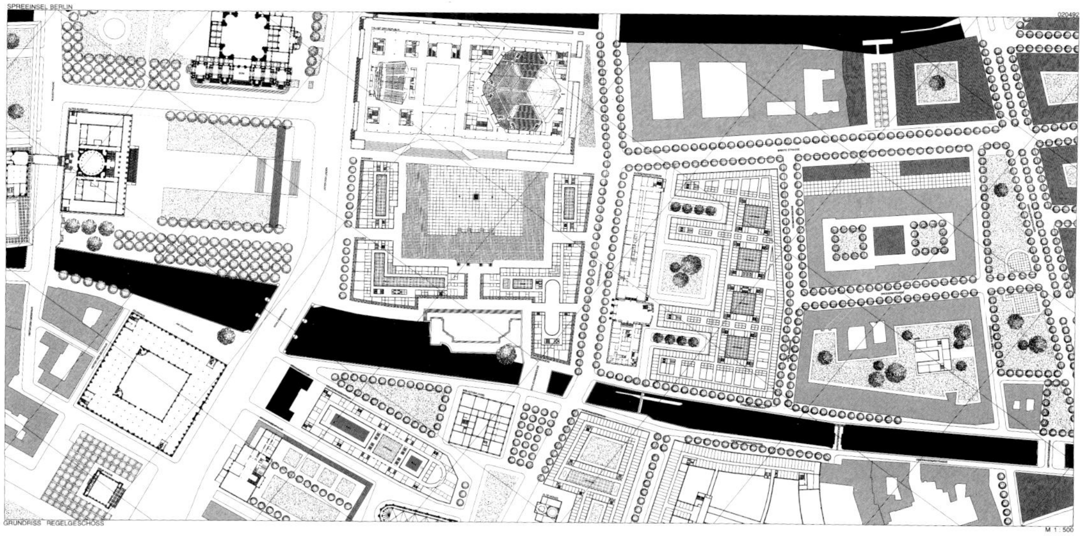

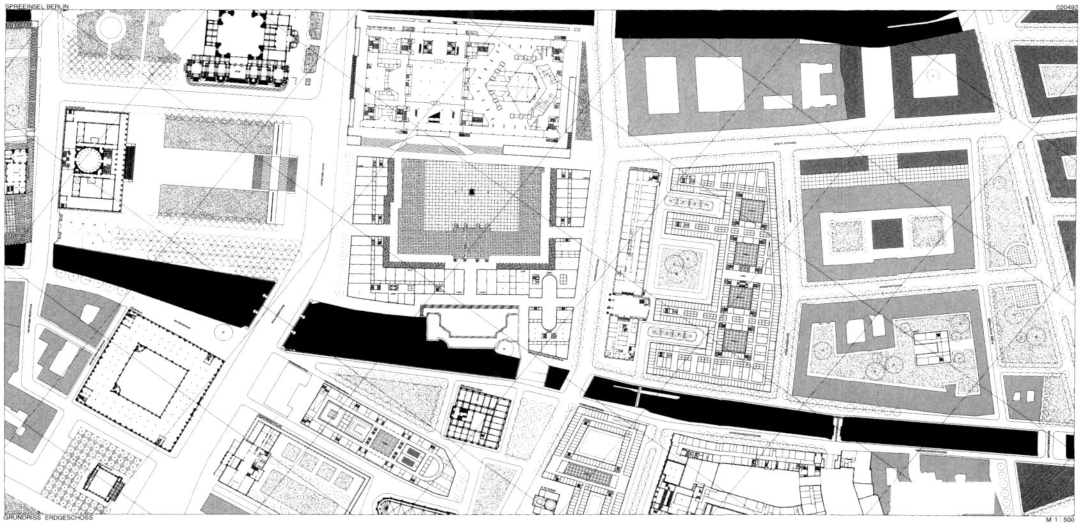

urbanistic unity not only will serve to illustrate the historical process, but can still function even if the advocates of demolition have their way. Assuming that the Palast der Republik, for whatever reason, was demolished, and that ethical or other considerations prohibited the reconstruction of the Schloss, the concept of negative space would still remain viable. The open space in the form of the plan of the Schloss would then function as a historic park in the midst of the dense urban volume.

The urbanistic idea for the reorganization of the Spreeinsel is based on the concept of freestanding buildings inserted into the overall urban structure, an idea anticipated by Schinkel in his 1851 plan for Berlin. Through the careful addition of individual buildings, Schinkel accentuated the overall plan of the city and created a variegated counterpoint of architectural monuments and normal block construction. The present design functions in the same way: freestanding buildings such as the Friedrichswerdersche Kirche and the Staatsratsgebäude together with the proposed reconstruction of the Kommandantur, the Bauakademie, the Alte Münze, the pedestal for the monument of Wilhelm I, and a few architectural gems on the interior of the block represent spatial and architectural high points within the profane urban structure. The reconfiguration into closed blocks establishes a clear system of public street space, block-edge construction, and planted interior courtyards. Together with the

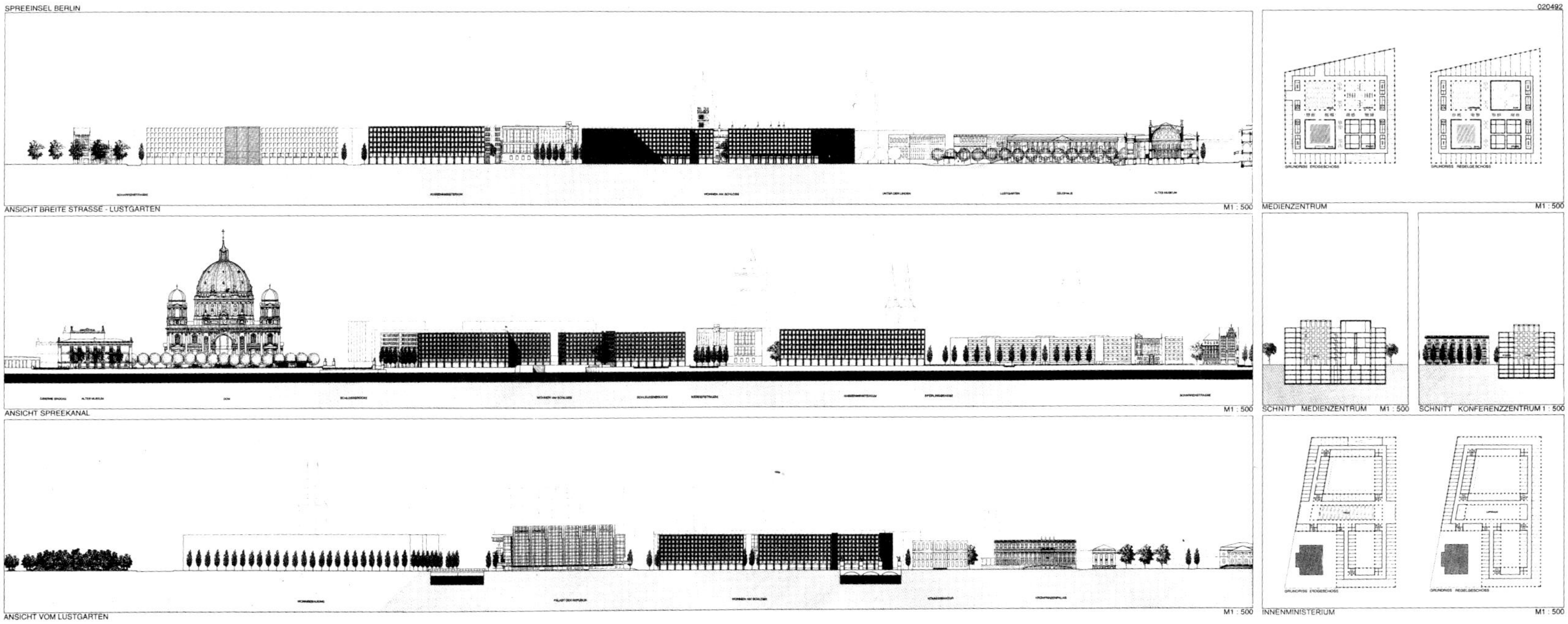

SPREEINSEL BERLIN

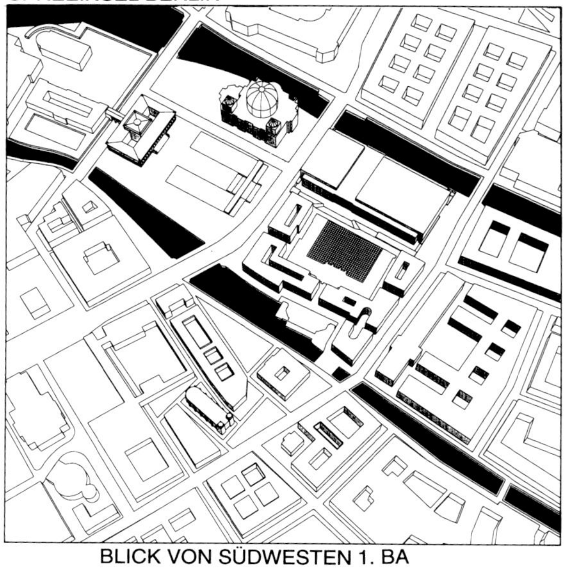

BLICK VON SÜDWESTEN 1. BA

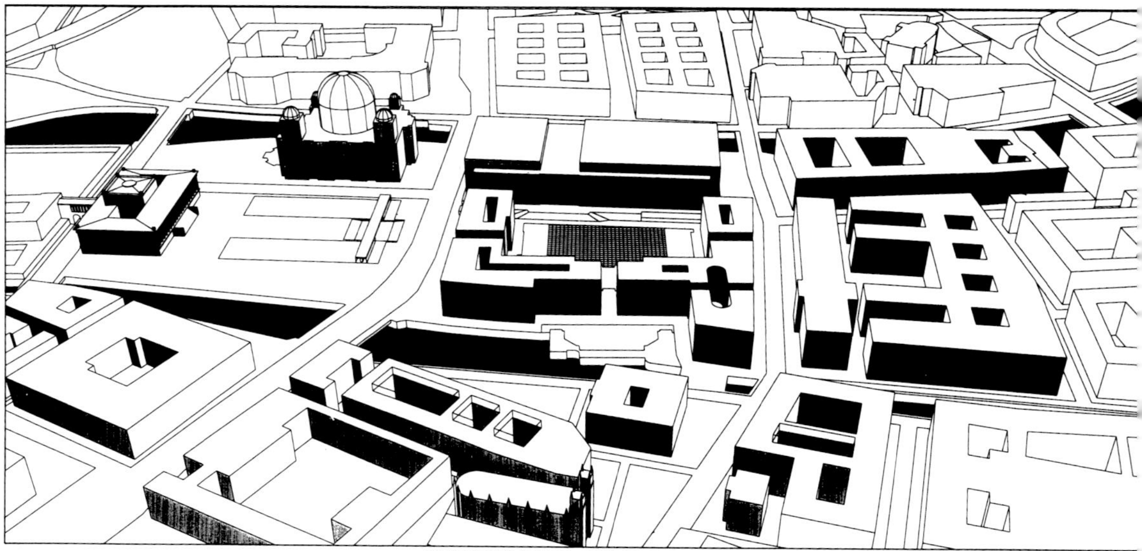

PERSPEKTIVE KUPFERGRABEN

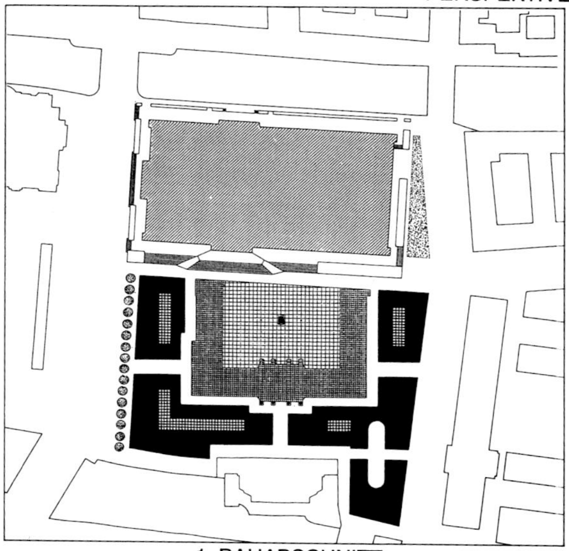

1. BAUABSCHNITT

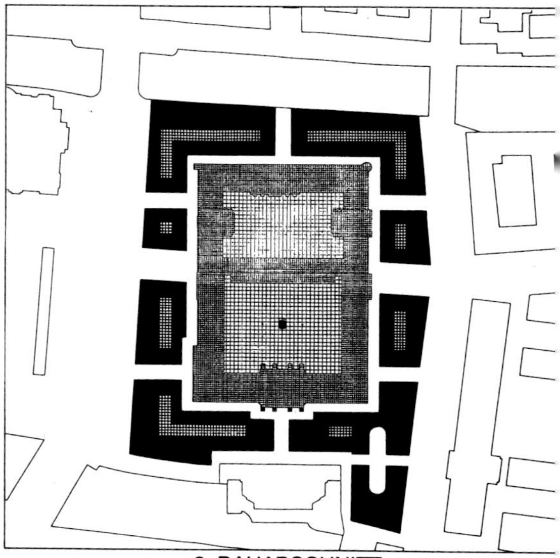

2. BAUABSCHNITT

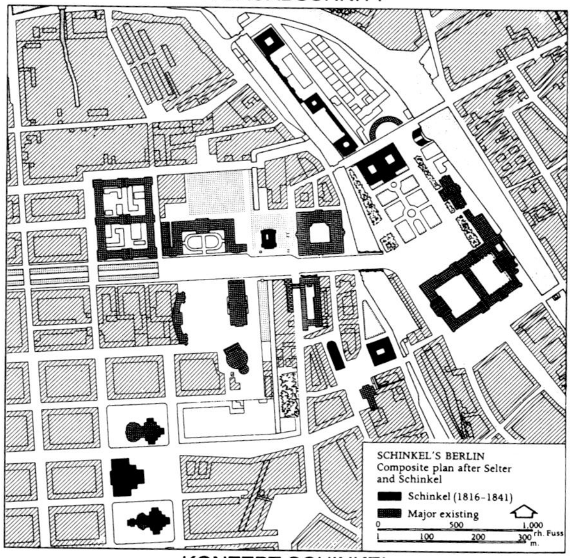

KONZEPT SCHINKEL

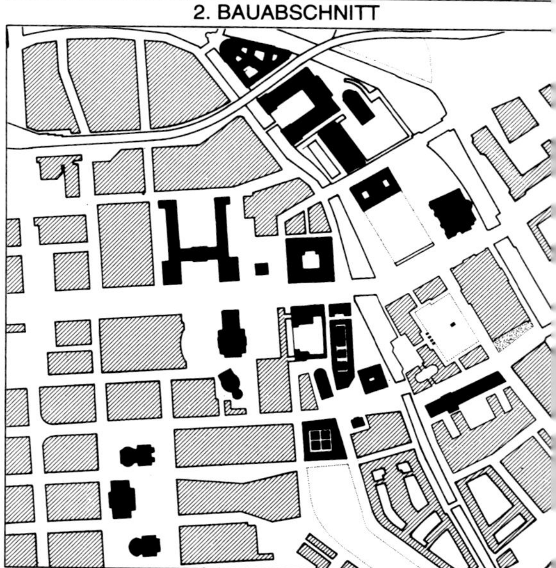

ENTWURFSVORSCHLAG

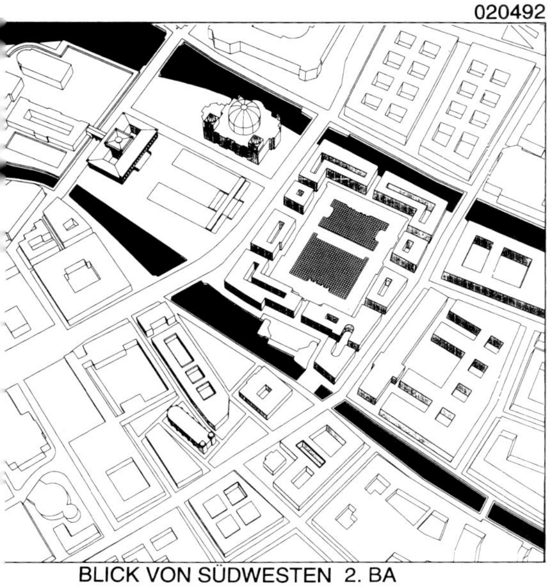

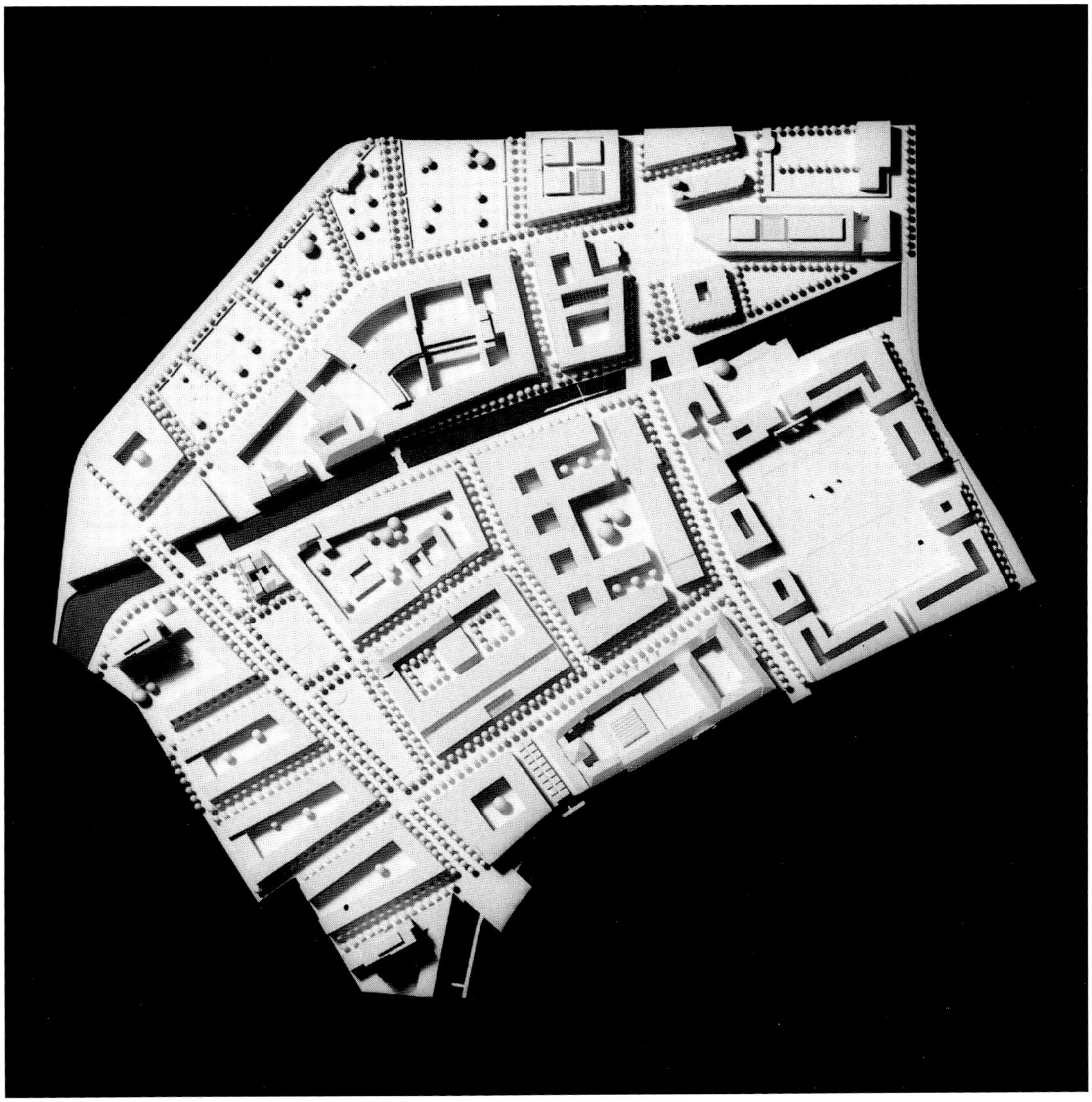

Proposed solutions for the Schloss area; photo of the Stadtschloss in 1916; photo of the Place des Vosges in Paris; model view.

Aussenministerium, the Staatsratsgebäude forms a diverse block with inner courtyards, plazas, and passages. The old Reichsbank building serves as the new Ministry of the Interior, while an entrance block with an interior passage establishes the connection to the Werderscher Markt. Within this ensemble, the Alte Münze, by Gentz, could be reconstructed and used as a reception building.

An effort is made to recapture the character of the old Werderscher Markt. In addition to the church, the reconstruction of the Bauakademie represents an important element, which could be used as an Amerika-Gedenkbibliothek (America Memorial Library). The old structures on the block could be used as a conference center, with the media center as a finishing touch.

The architecture surrounding the future Schlossplatz should accommodate a dense variety of urban functions, with shops and cultural installations on the ground floor with arcades opening onto the "Schlossplatz," and offices, medical practices, and residences above.

The closed block structure of the Spreeinsel is framed to the east by the Spree River and to the south and west by a ring-shaped strip of green following the course of the old fortification wall, into which individual buildings are incorporated. The plan of the Petri-Kirche is traced in the park area, its foundations exposed along with existing remains of the city. The plan is an attempt to complete the Mitte district of Berlin with careful additions in the interest of a multifaceted urban system.

Competition Design for Lehrter Bahnhof District with Humboldt Colonnades and "Kubus," Berlin, 1994, 1995

With: Stefan Vieths

Project team:
First phase: Karl-Heinz Winkens, Marvin Keim, David Koralek, Axel Steudel, Peter Pfertner, Philippe Vernin, Michael Laudert, Frank Wieschemann, Chase McCarthy, Bill Mannarelli, Volker Diekmann, Kai-Uwe Lompa
Second phase: Karl-Heinz Winkens, N. Cadez, Axel Steudel, David Koralek, Marvin Keim, Chase McCarthy, Philippe Catoir, Volker Diekmann, Johannes Götz, Michael Laudert, Kai-Uwe Lompa, Bill Mannarelli, Peter Pfertner, Joachim Sieber, Philippe Vernin, Frank Wieschemann
Kubus: Karl-Heinz Winkens, Hugo Daiber, Tobias Scheel, Robert Beyer

The competition area for the new urban district around the Lehrter Bahnhof railway station lies at the north edge of the Tiergarten in the Spreebogen area, in the immediate vicinity of the Reichstag and the future government precinct of Berlin. At present the site is essentially unbuilt and receives its character from the waterfront areas of the Spree River and Humboldthafen harbor, whose strict geometric design goes back to nineteenth-century plans by Lenné. The new Lehrter Bahnhof is scheduled for construction on the site within the next few years; its central location will make it a key node in the Berlin transit system. The site and built form of the station have already been established; along with its urbanistically dominant system of tracks, the plans for the Lehrter Bahnhof thus constitute a given for the competition design of the surrounding urban district. In essence, the competition has two objectives: to effect the large-scale spatial definition of the Spreebogen and Humboldthafen areas, and to integrate the planned railway station into a new area.

In its basic urbanistic idea, the project continues and reinforces the spatial design of the Spreebogen already devised by Lenné. Existing elements include the semicircular area of the Spreebogen as well as the shipping canal and Humboldthafen axially related to it. An additional element is the linear architectural structure of the government buildings planned by Axel Schultes. Like the nearby Reichstag and Bundesrat buildings, the government complex refers to the north-south axis running through the middle of the Humboldthafen.

As an appropriate boundary to the north, the project calls for a colonnade framing the Humboldthafen, transforming the attractive, but at present hardly perceptible, urbanistic presence of the harbor into an urban space of unique character. A precise architectural edge following the semicircular course of the Spree lends clear spatial definition to the Spreebogen and the Tiergarten in a manner suited to the urban character of this largest Berlin park.

In Ungers's first proposal, the colonnade extended along the entire Spreebogen; in the second, it defines only the plaza in front of the railway station. This plaza, flanked on the east by a park and on the west by an additional plaza, participates in an urban composition that includes two other forms as well: an office tower and a cube, the latter accommodating a hotel. At the west end of the station, the plan calls for a block of office buildings.

The design results in a configuration of three urbanistic "bands" extending from Invalidenstrasse to the Spree. The first is the colonnade, whose architectural form represents a direct response to the existing structure of the place. The second is the composition of the planned railway station (bridge, cube, and water artery). The third consists of the compact structure of the blocks. The diversity of these elements lends the new area a very urban character, full of tension and contrast, typical of the area around a railway station. The redesign of the Humboldthafen creates an urban space whose striking form alludes to the Berlin tradition of large geometric plazas such as Leipziger Platz, Pariser Platz, and Mehringplatz.

The design explores the theme of the colonnade in all its variations: some colonnades are open, while others surround buildings with passages and plazas on the water. A change in grade between outer and inner colonnades makes it possible to walk around the Humboldthafen at the level of the old loading areas. In this way, a diverse spatial structure is created, one that formulates the relationship to the water in a wide variety of ways and accommodates a number of different functions (restaurants, cafés, offices, hotels).

The concept of the railway station plaza as an open space into which architectural objects are inserted creates an optimal spatial connection with Invalidenstrasse, an important through street, as well as with the

HUMBOLDTKOLONNADEN BERLIN 291225

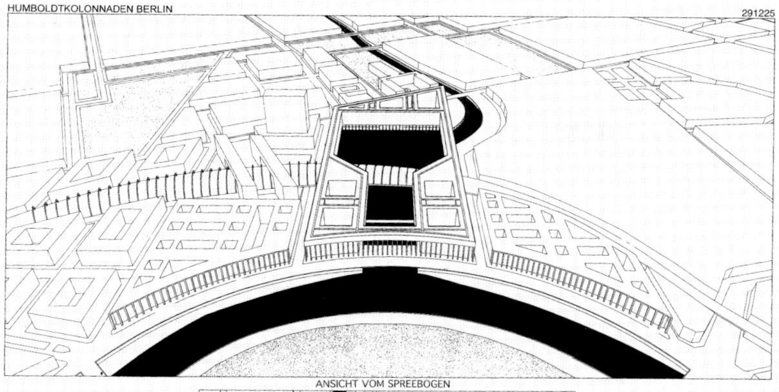

ANSICHT VOM SPREEBOGEN

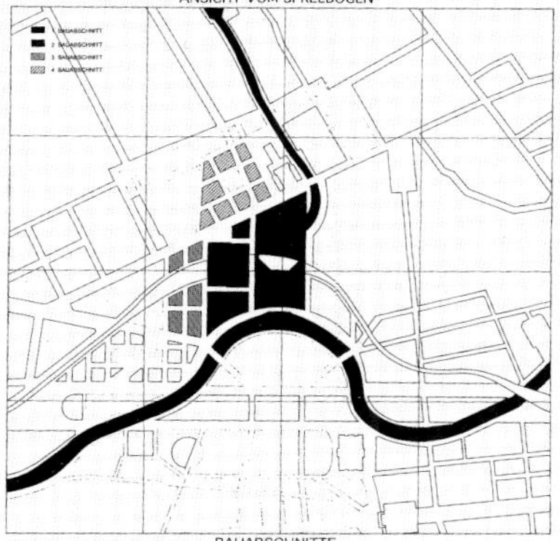

BAUABSCHNITTE

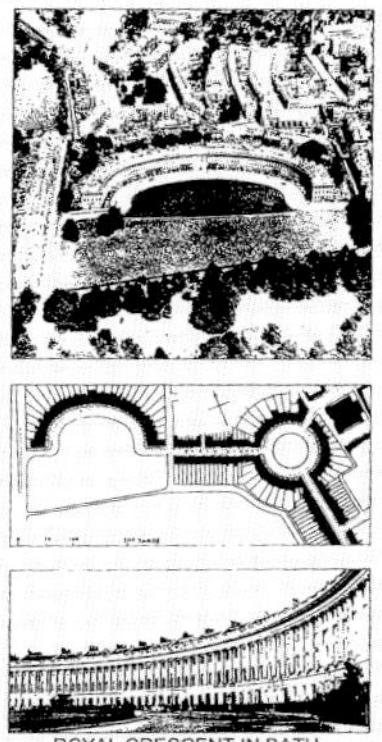

ROYAL CRESCENT IN BATH

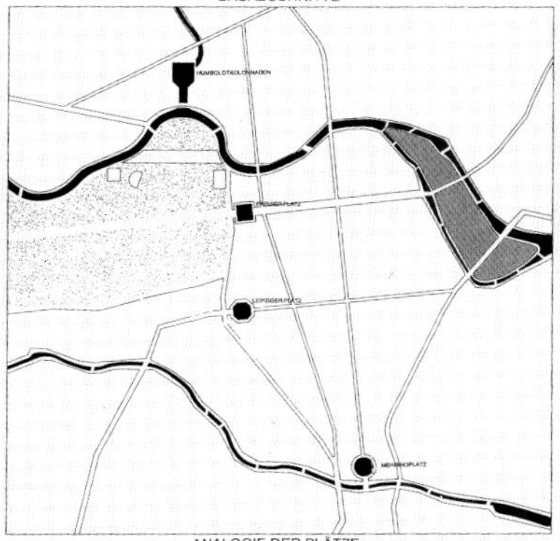

ANALOGIE DER PLÄTZE

ALSTERARKADEN IN HAMBURG

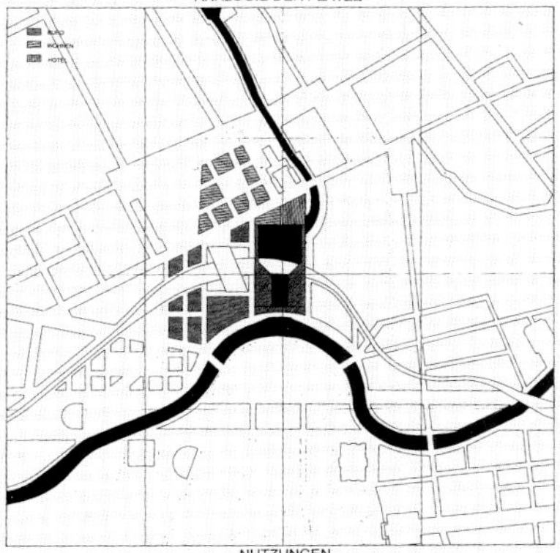

NUTZUNGEN

HUMBOLDTKOLONNADEN BERLIN 291225

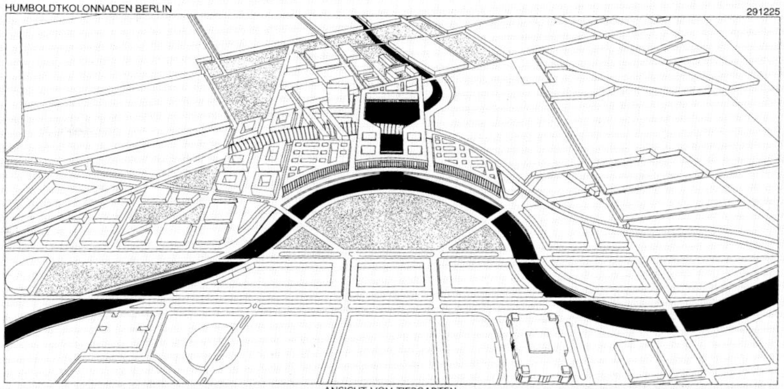

ANSICHT VOM TIERGARTEN

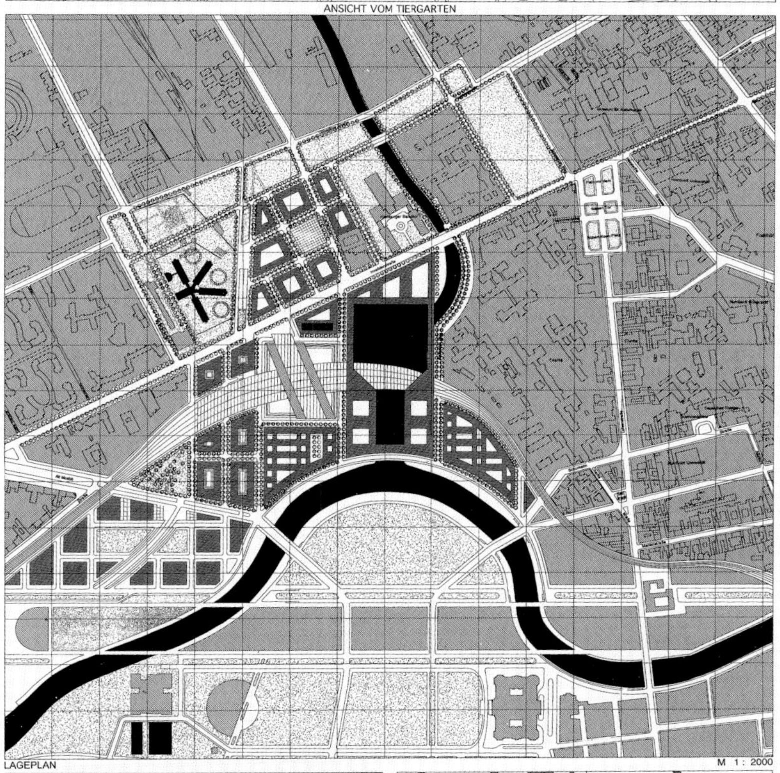

LAGEPLAN M 1 : 2000

GEBÄUDESTRUKTUR

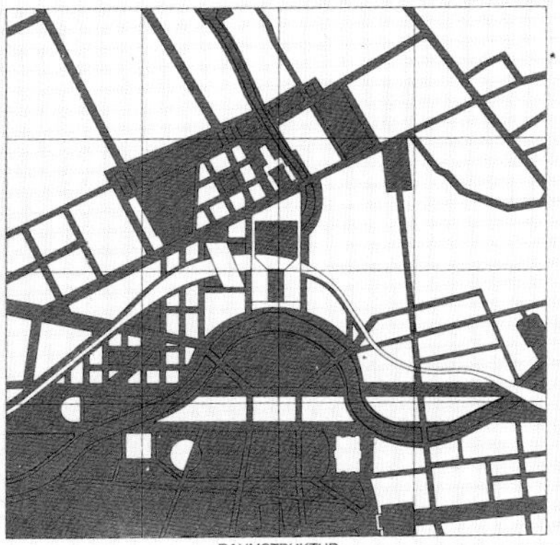

RAUMSTRUKTUR

First proposal:
perspectives;
site plan;
use diagrams.

First proposal: ground-level plan; elevation; section; views.

Second proposal: site plan with perspective views; sketches; model view.

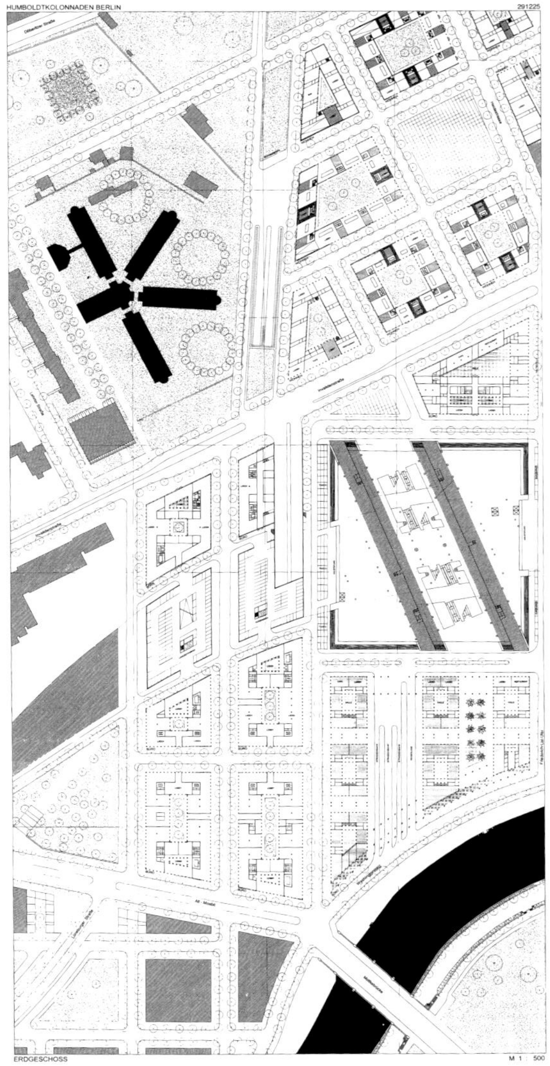

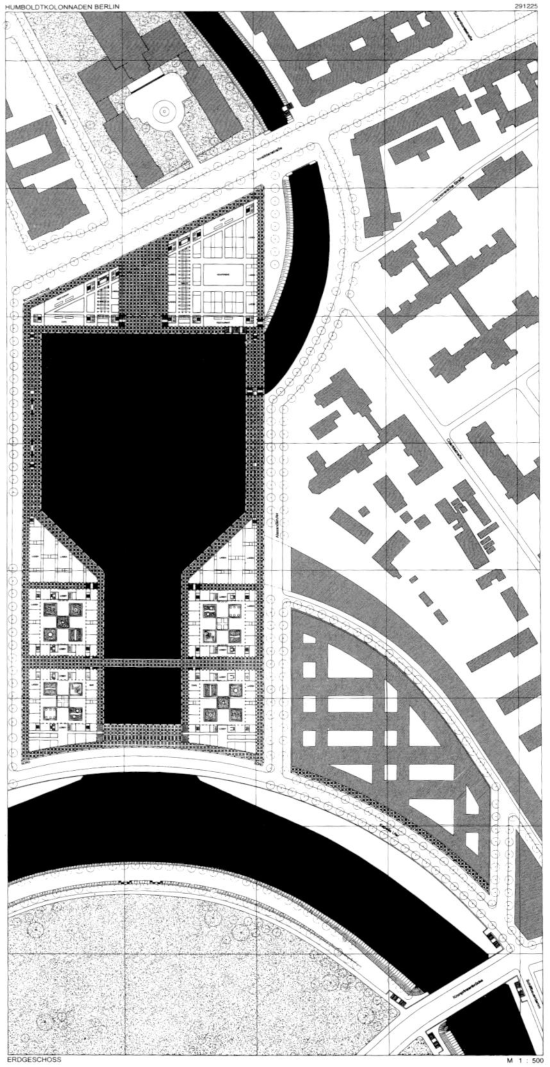

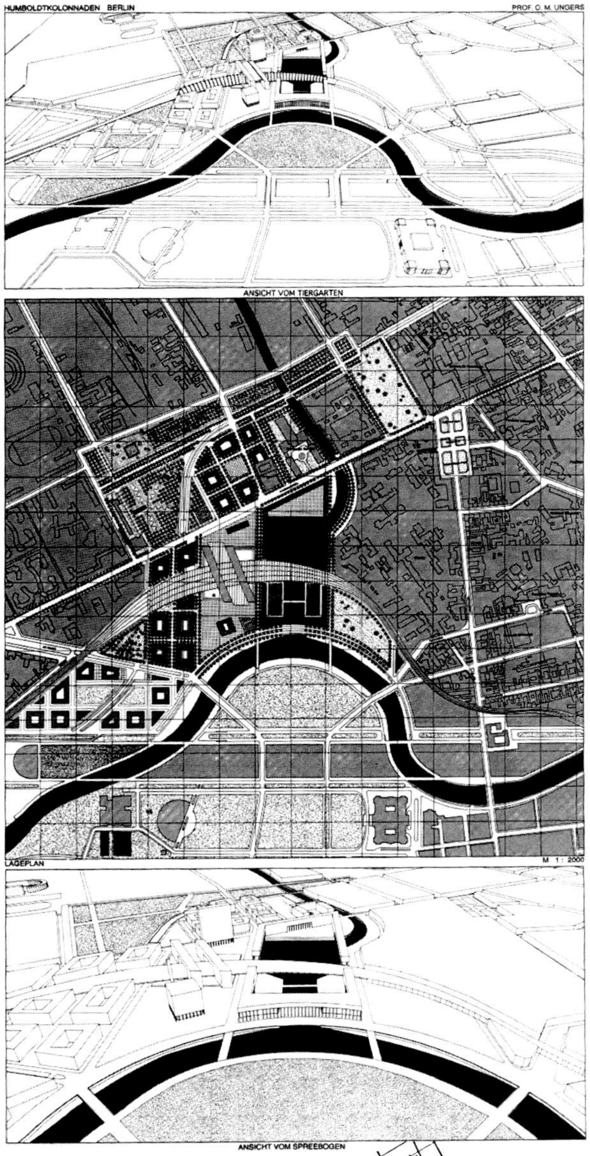
HUMBOLDTKOLONNADEN BERLIN
PROF. O. M. UNGERS
ANSICHT VOM TIERGARTEN
LAGEPLAN
M 1:2000
ANSICHT VOM SPREEBOGEN

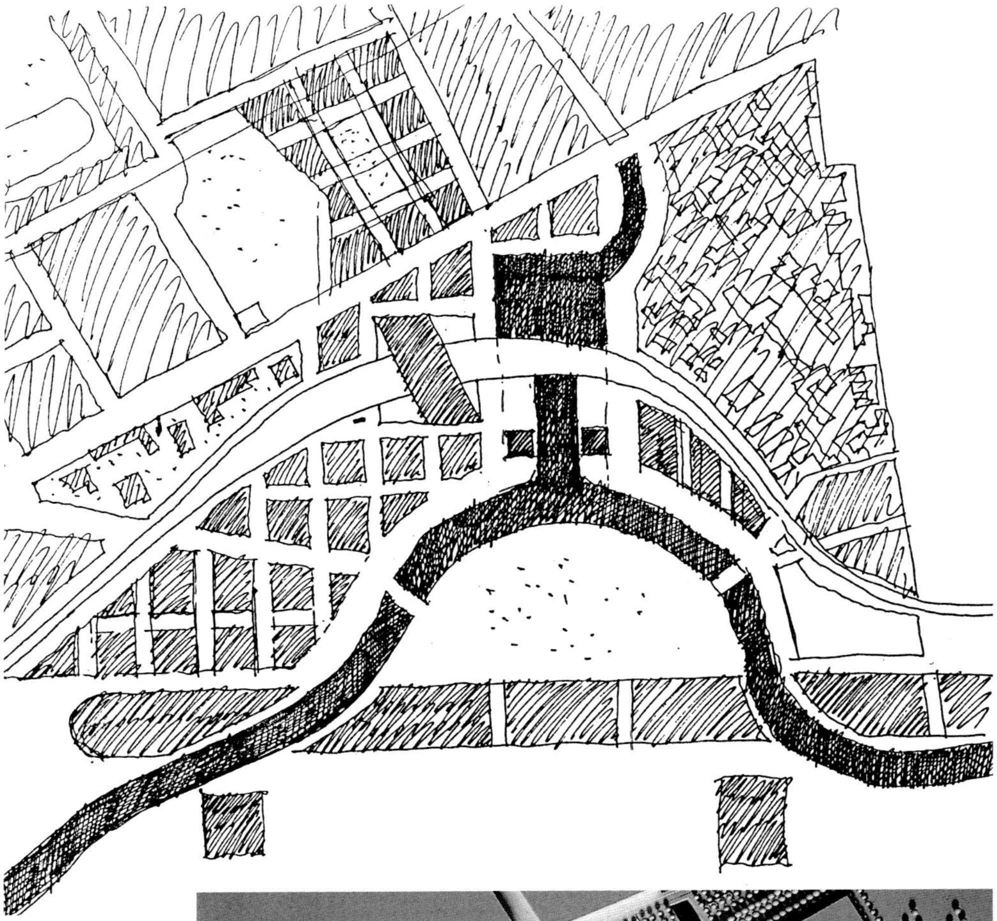

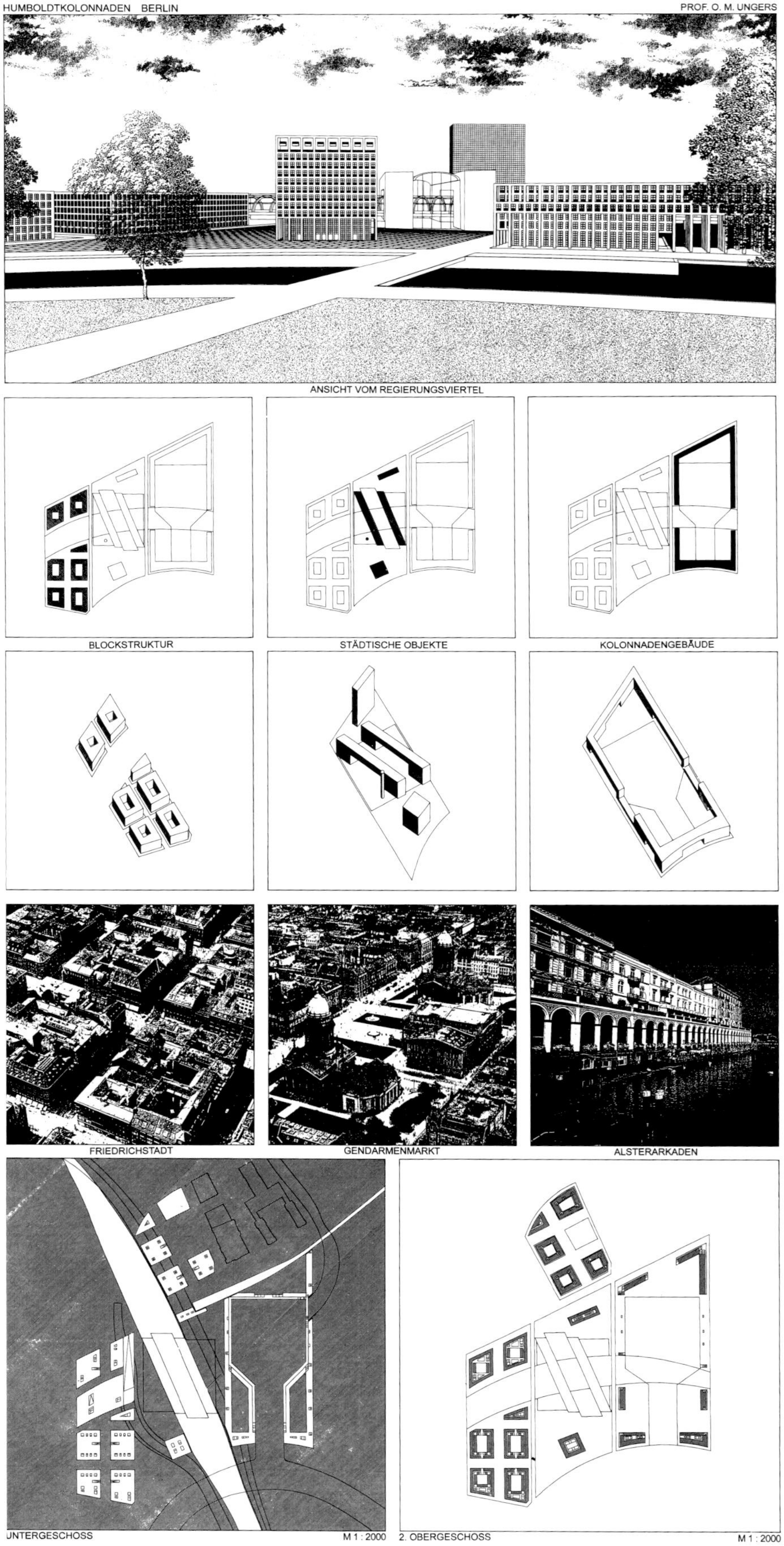

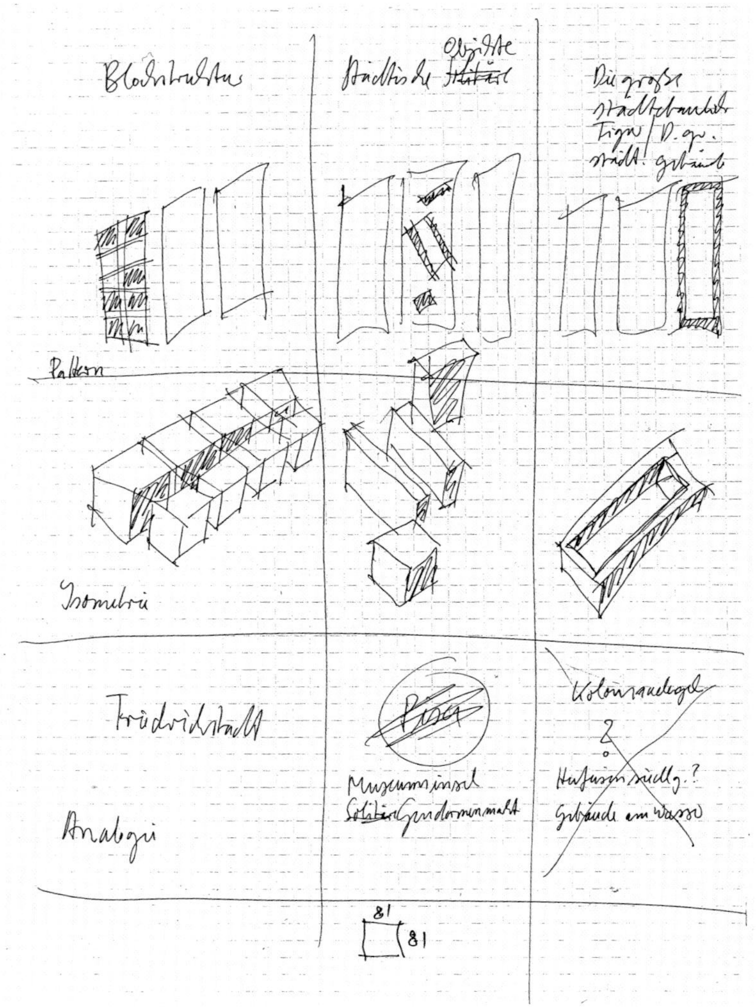

Second proposal: perspective; use diagrams; historic prototypes; plans; sketches.

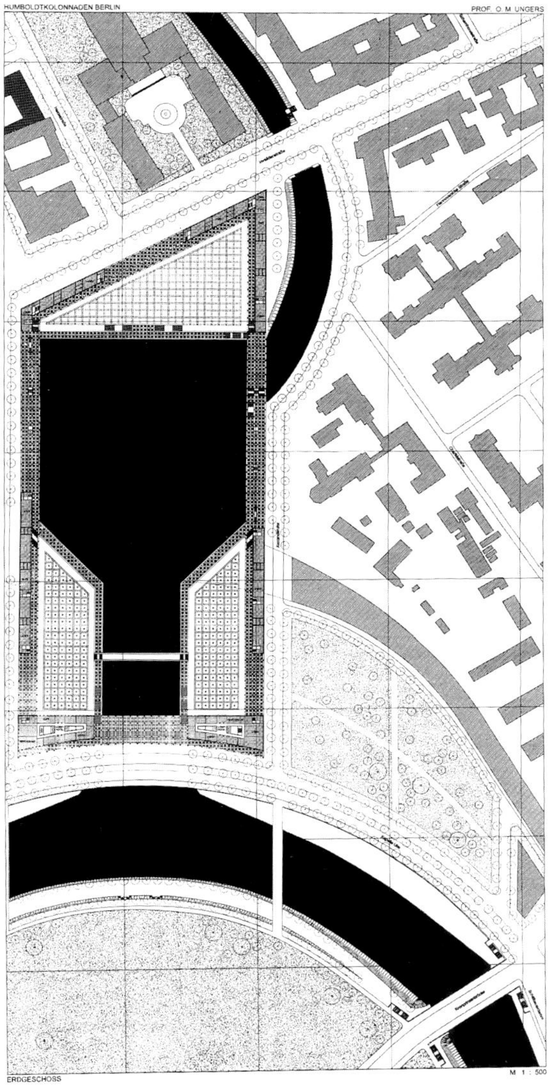

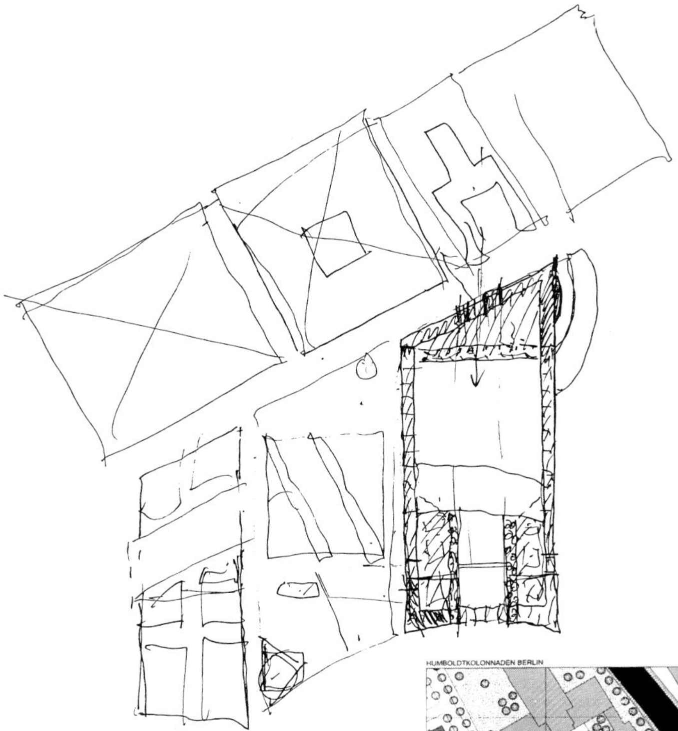

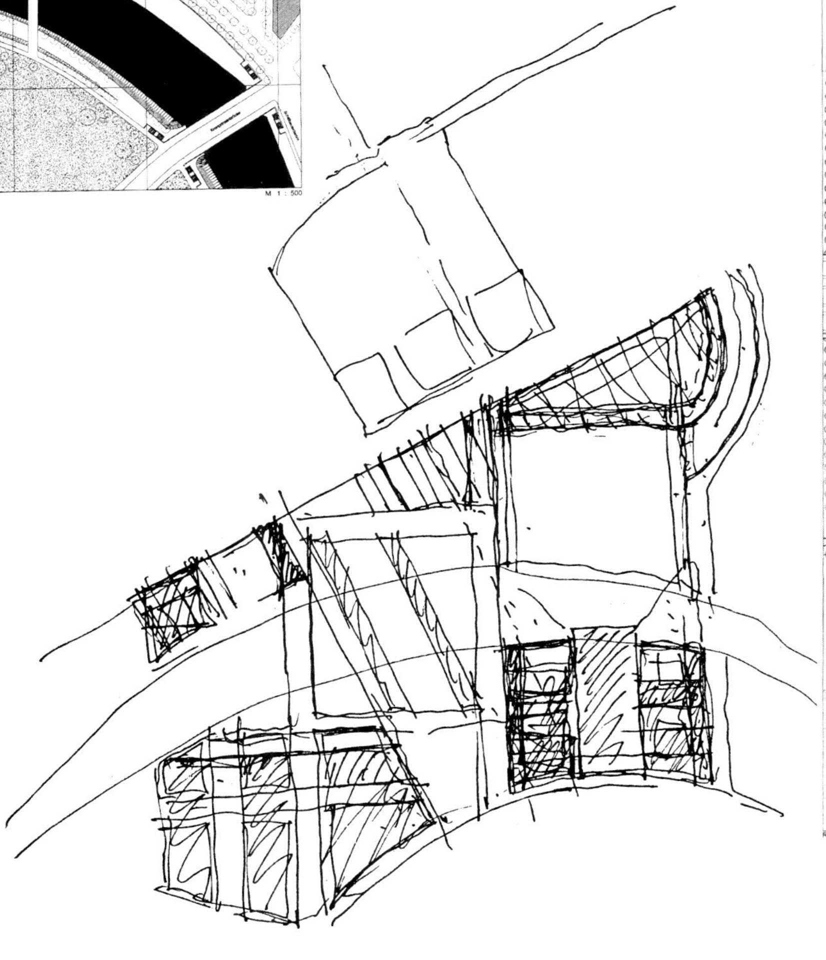

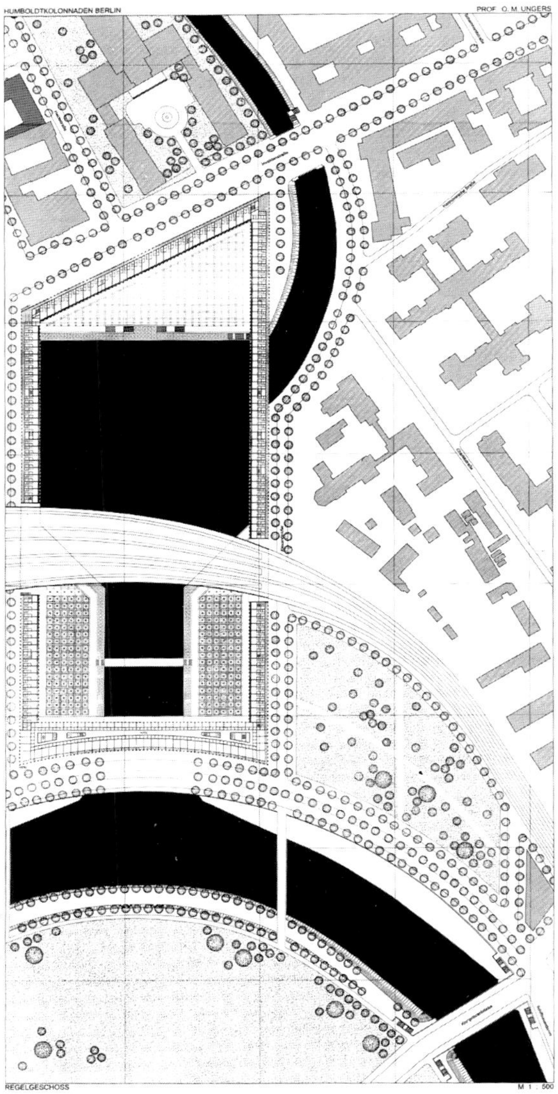

Ground-level plan; sketches; typical floor plan.

Ground-level and typical floor plan; view from the Spree; section; perspective.

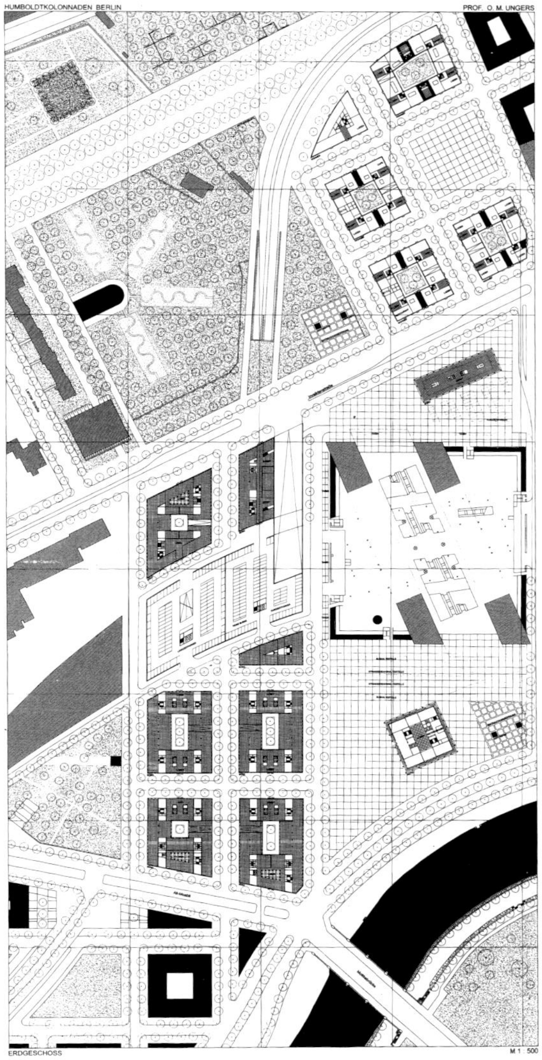

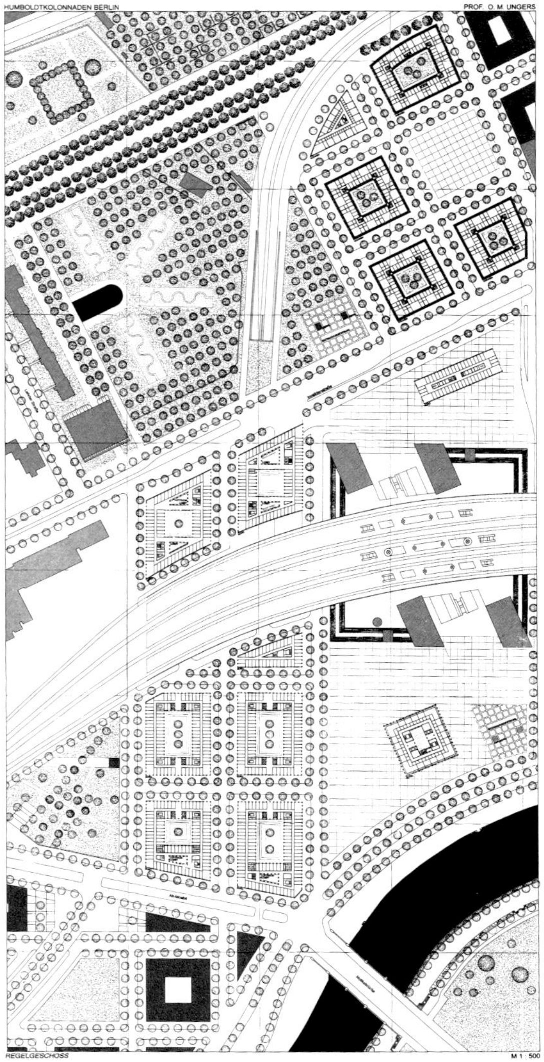

Opposite:
Elevation; section; perspective views; model view.

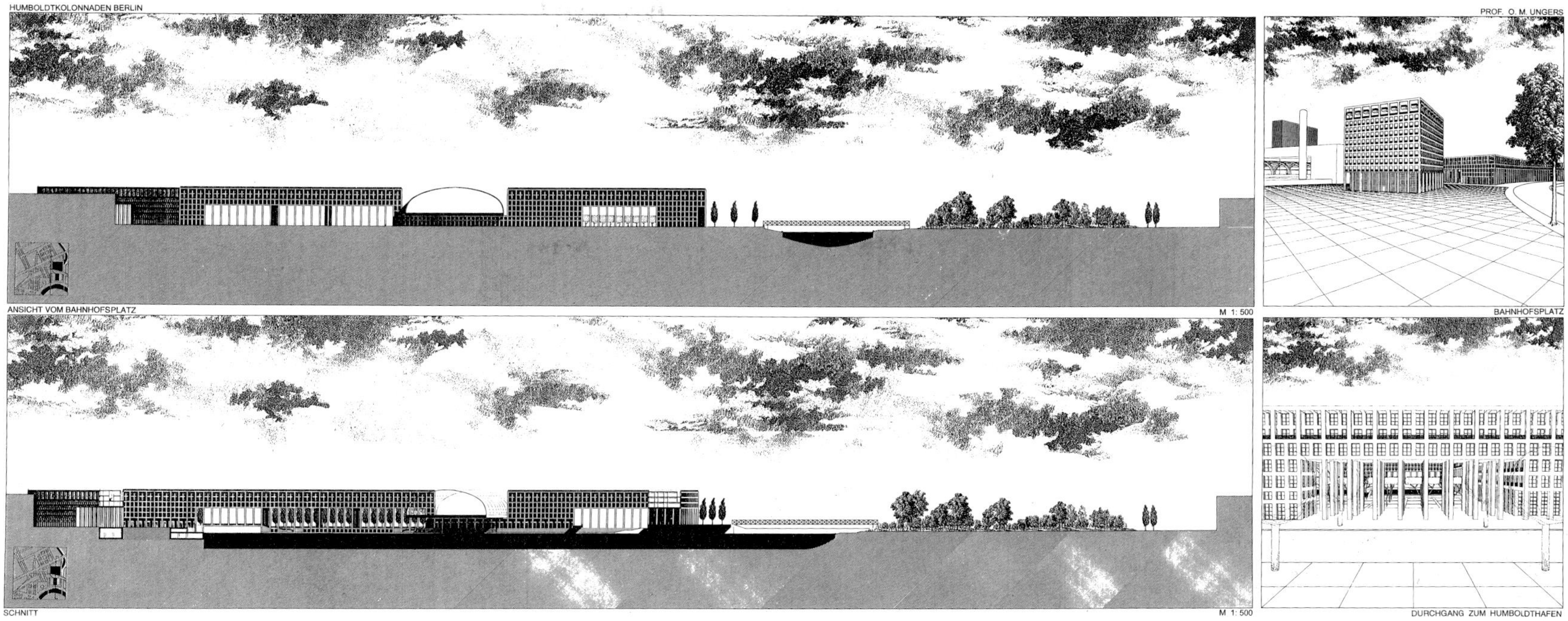
HUMBOLDTKOLONNADEN BERLIN
PROF. O. M. UNGERS
ANSICHT VOM BAHNHOFSPLATZ
M 1: 500
BAHNHOFSPLATZ
SCHNITT
M 1: 500
DURCHGANG ZUM HUMBOLDTHAFEN

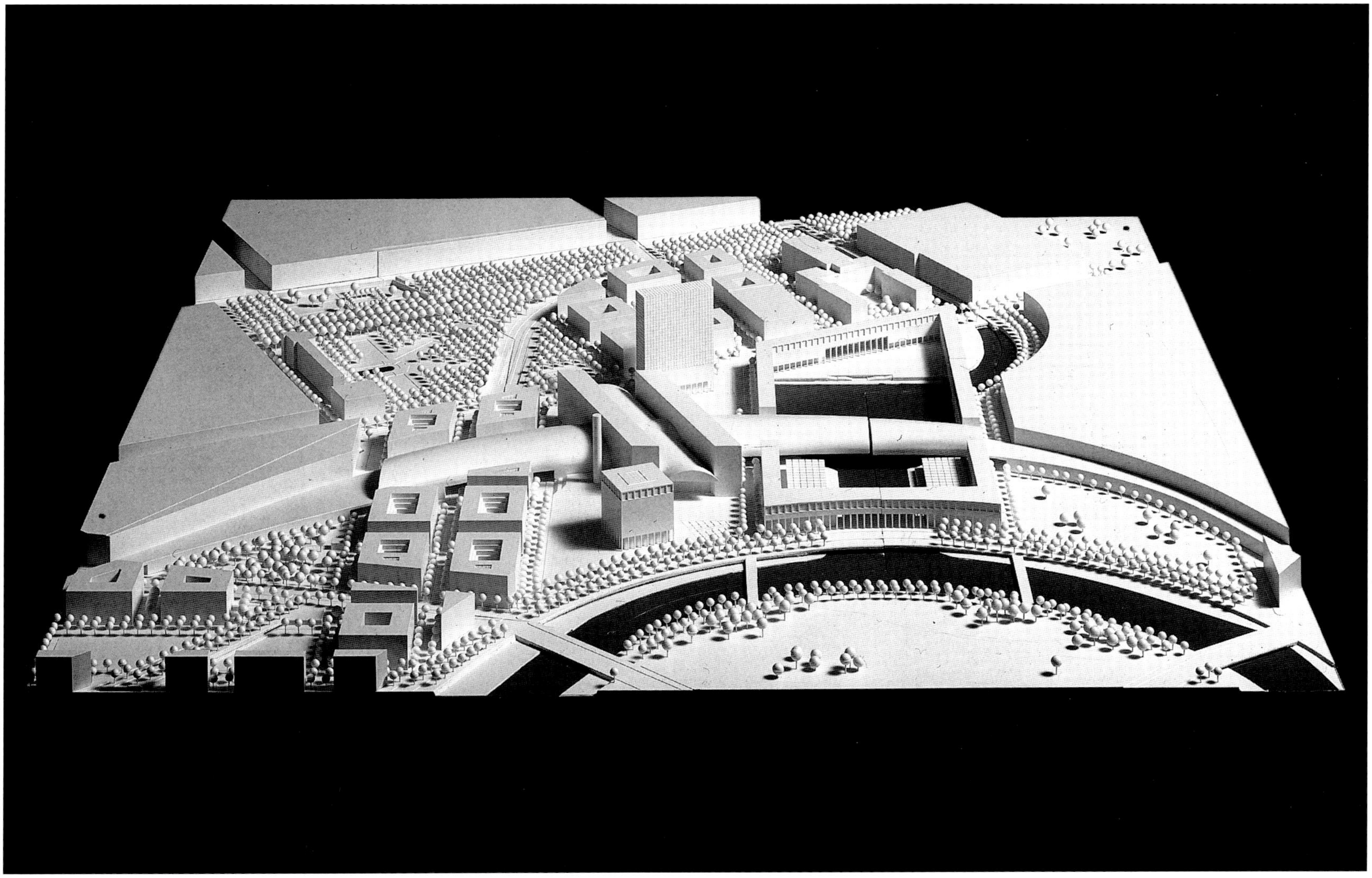

Computer rendering; studies for office building.

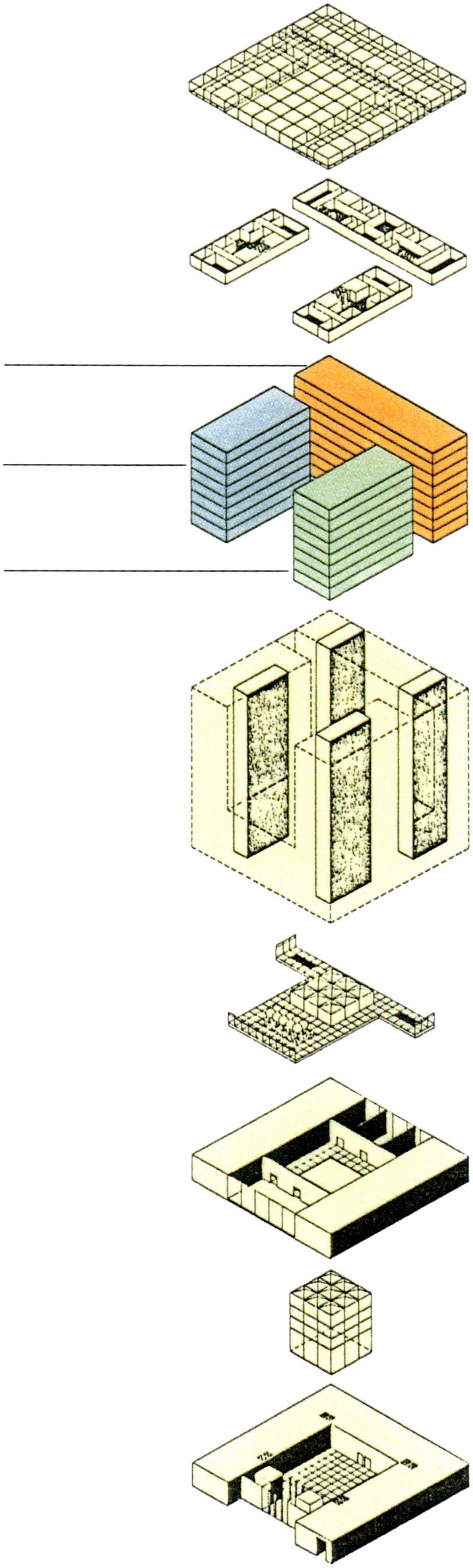

Tiergarten and the government precinct to the south. The high-rise to the north marks the position of the railway station on Invalidenstrasse, while the cube of the hotel marks the transition from the station to the large open space of the Tiergarten. Together, the station plaza and the Humboldt colonnades form a double plaza consisting of two conflicting urban spaces. In analogy to the Leipziger Platz/Potsdamer Platz pair, an engaging spatial composition arises from the contrast between a quiet, enclosed water plaza and a pulsating traffic node.

The new urban area is divided in two by the Invalidenstrasse. Both halves have a closed block structure that reflects the typical Berlin building height of twenty-two meters. In use and orientation, the block structure of the southern section is defined by the design of the railway station and the Humboldt colonnades. At the center is the Lehrter Bahnhof with the Humboldt colonnades adjacent to the east, accommodating offices, a boarding house, a hotel, a restaurant, shops, and cafés, as well as a dock for the tourist boats of the "Weisse Flotte." To the south and north, the area is defined by the three architectural objects of the colonnade, tower, and cube.

In 1995, Ungers was commissioned to design a freestanding building west of the Humboldthafen. The cube-shaped building is clearly articulated into a five-story socle and three tower structures rising above it with nine stories each. The building represents a conscious attempt to establish an urban landmark projecting high above the twenty-two-meter Berlin roofline. In this way, the "Kubus" becomes a freestanding high-rise building that not only relates to its immediate architectural surroundings and the Tiergarten but also establishes a connection to the buildings planned for Potsdamer Platz and Alexanderplatz.

In accord with a historic building type, the three tower structures arranged on a common socle are oriented toward Lenné's urban landscape around the Spree and the park areas

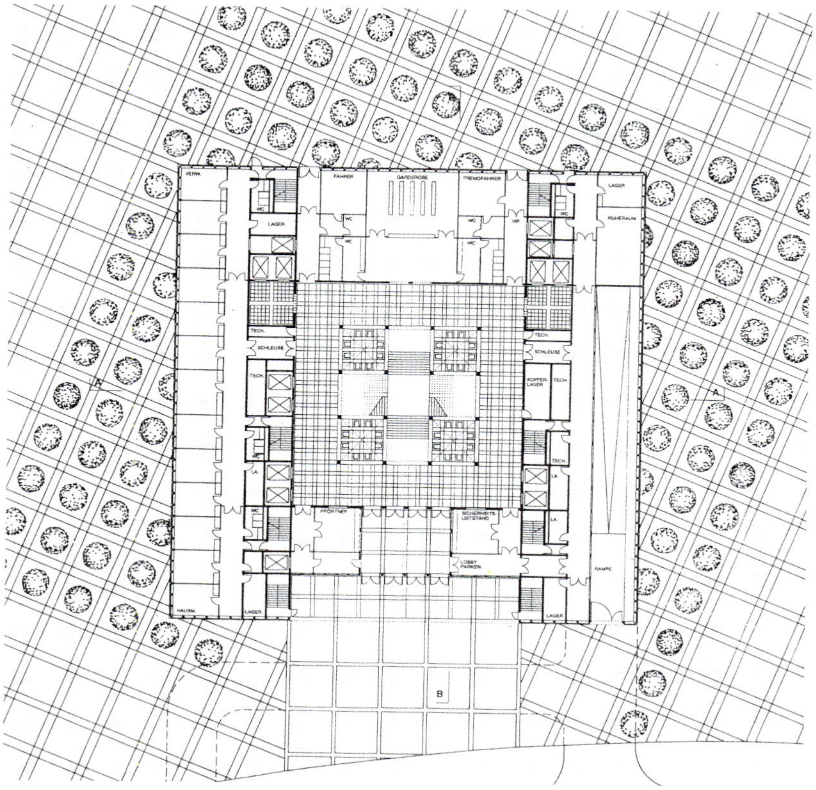

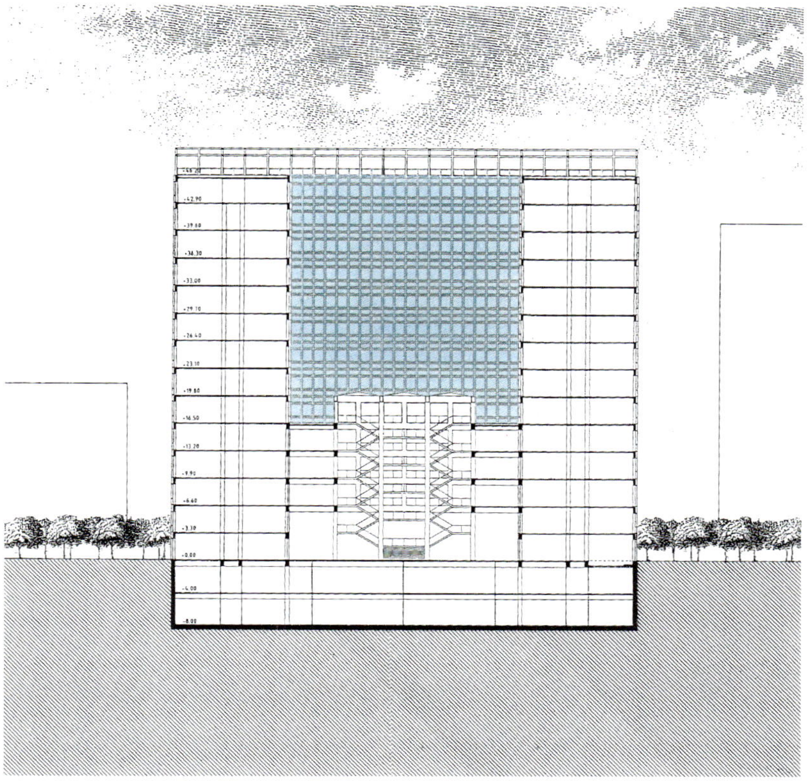

Ground-level plan; section; computer rendering of large central atrium.

to the south. The freestanding building opening up to its environs calls attention to its special location: the surrounding urban scenery becomes an elementary part of the design concept. The motif of the closed socle and the three towers rising up from it represents the desire of different institutions to share a single building while at the same time demonstrating their organizational autonomy.

The main entrance, located in the deeply recessed bay facing the Spree, leads into the large hall. Inside, areas of water and plants define this space as a belvedere with a view of the government buildings. By day, the material—transparent glass—heightens the contrast between the cube and the urban landscape, where stone predominates as the building material; by night, the building appears as a light-filled cube. The transition from light to dark and the contrast between transparency and opacity define the character of this urbanistically important building.

Competition Design for Federal Chancellery, Berlin, 1994

With: Stefan Vieths

Project team: Peter Pfertner, Marvin Keim, Axel Steudel, David Koralek, Kai-Uwe Lompa, Philippe Vernin, Frank Wieschemann, Michael Laudert, Joachim Sieber, Volker Diekmann

The site of the Federal Chancellery marks the western end of the linear government complex planned by Axel Schultes north of the Reichstag. The Spree River divides the site almost in half: the western portion on the Moabiter Werder is the Chancellor's Park, while the chancellery itself occupies the eastern area. Together with the buildings planned for the forum and the Abgeordnetenhaus (Delegates' Offices), the complex creates an urban edge on the Spreebogen, in front of which the freestanding buildings of the Reichstag, Bundesrat, and congress hall are arranged.

The character of the location is thus ambiguous: on the one hand, it constitutes part of an urban pattern; on the other, it is defined by the landscape around the Spree. This ambiguity becomes the theme of the architectural design, which consists of a colonnade and a freestanding structure placed within it. The design thus establishes the urbanistic edges required by the linear scheme of the government buildings while at the same time making use of the prominent location on the Spree. In addition, the striking composition of framing structures and individual architectural objects serves to define the functional disposition of the Federal Chancellery itself, which consists of two buildings: to the west, a freestanding building on the Spree that accommodates directorship functions, and to the east, a building incorporated into the framing structure to serve administrative and subsidiary functions. This two-layered architectural configuration also corresponds to the rigorous security requirements of the Federal Chancellery.

The two buildings flank the official ceremonial plaza, which thus takes on an unequivocally urban character. The framing structure itself is dissolved into rows of

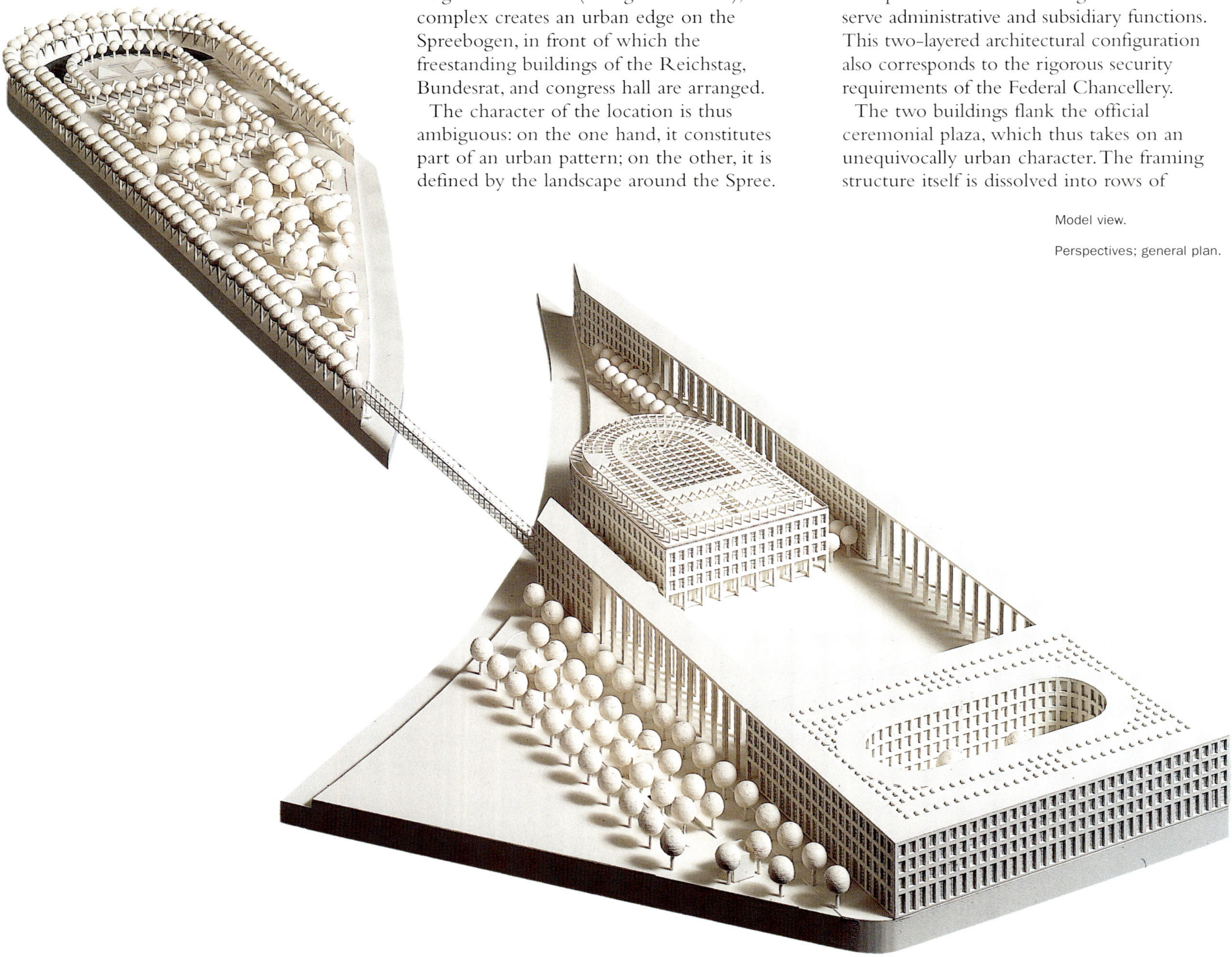

Model view.

Perspectives; general plan.

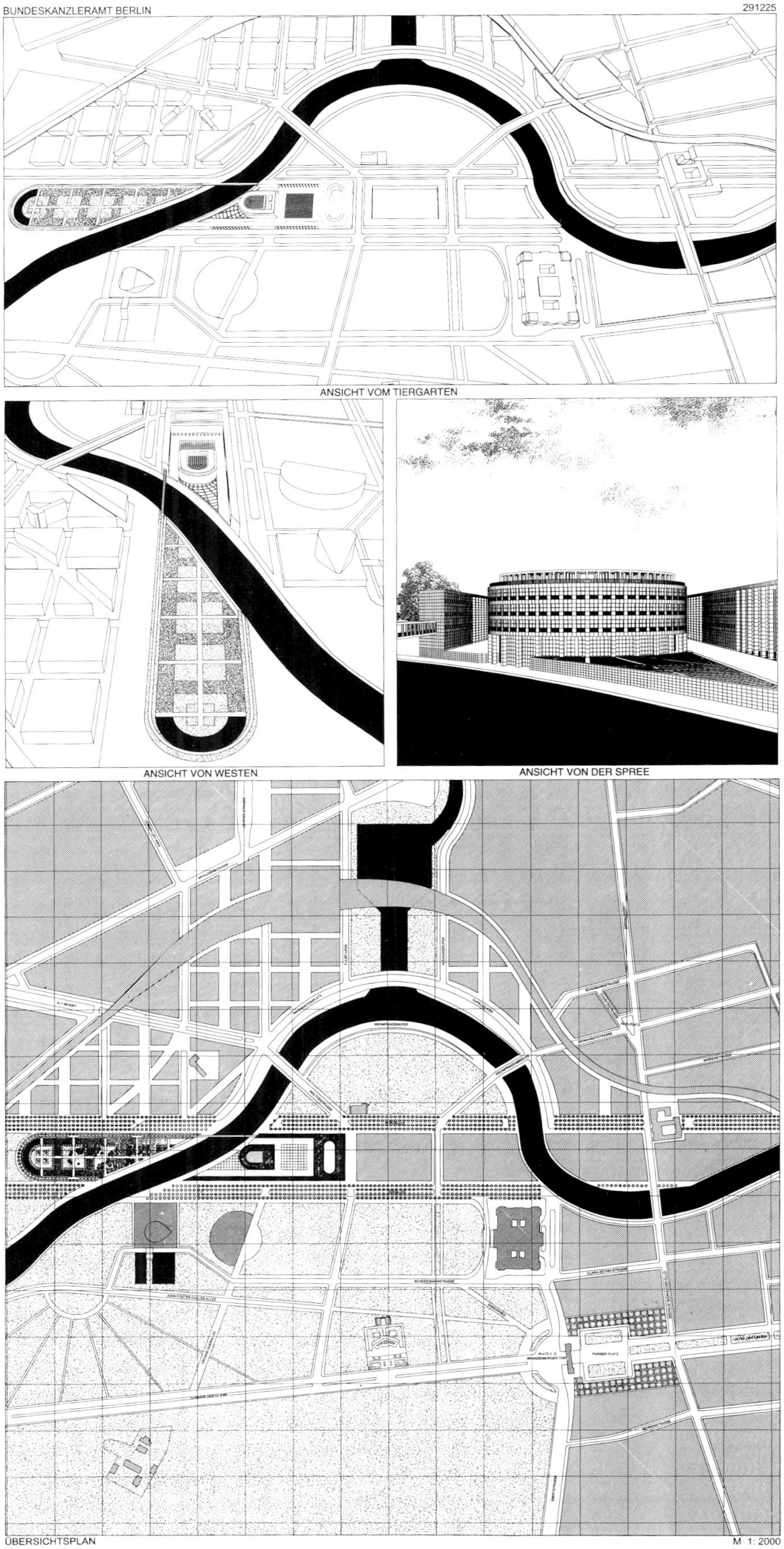

colonnades, helping to maintain the visual connection to the Tiergarten and the Spreebogen park. On the west side of the directorship building, an open terrace on the Spree forms a counterpoint to the strictly composed ceremonial plaza.

West of the Spree, the Federal Chancellery finds its complement in the Chancellor's Park. Here, a tree-lined embankment defines a park space into which green volumes in various geometric shapes are inserted. The design is inspired by the motif of the ministerial gardens traditionally located at the edge of the Tiergarten. The planted areas encompass a grove of locust trees and augment it with compact green spaces, creating a thematic sequence ranging from dense grove to rose garden.

The distribution of functions arises from the conception of two independent structures. The directorship functions are assigned to the freestanding building on the Spree, which is organized around a generous roofed hall. The international conference hall is located on the ground level with direct access to the Spree terrace. The floors above it accommodate, from bottom to top, official meeting rooms, spaces for the Federal Cabinet, and the offices of the Federal Chancellor, spaces that are likewise oriented toward the Spree.

The administrative division occupies the east wing of the colonnade structure in a building with an arena-like courtyard. Most of the central special-purpose areas are on the ground and basement levels, and others occupy the lateral wings: the north wing accommodates the chauffeur service, and the south wing contains the main security office, the federal border police, and rooms for the press. An underground garage adjoins the north side of the complex and lies open under the northern avenue with direct access to the chauffeur service and the central special-purpose areas of the administrative building. The cafeteria occupies the southwestern tip of the colonnade structure, directly on the Spree.

The planned central hall between the office and special-purpose areas serves as a vertical and horizontal circulation space for personnel and visitors and as a waiting and rest area with cafeteria, reception, and exhibition areas. It has a glass roof at about the level of the roof story and adjoins the exterior facade at the central entrance area at the ground and upper levels.

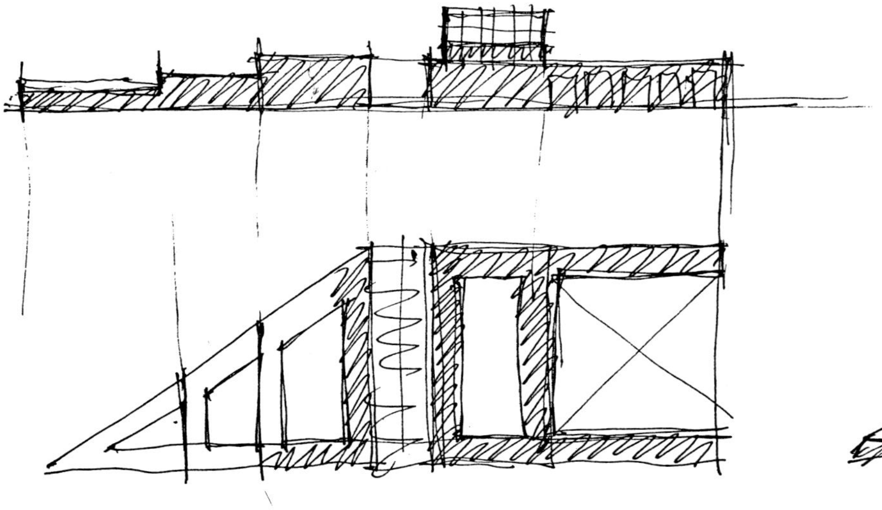

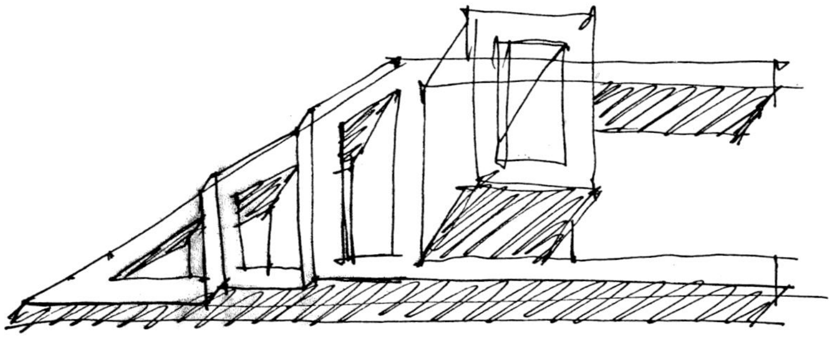

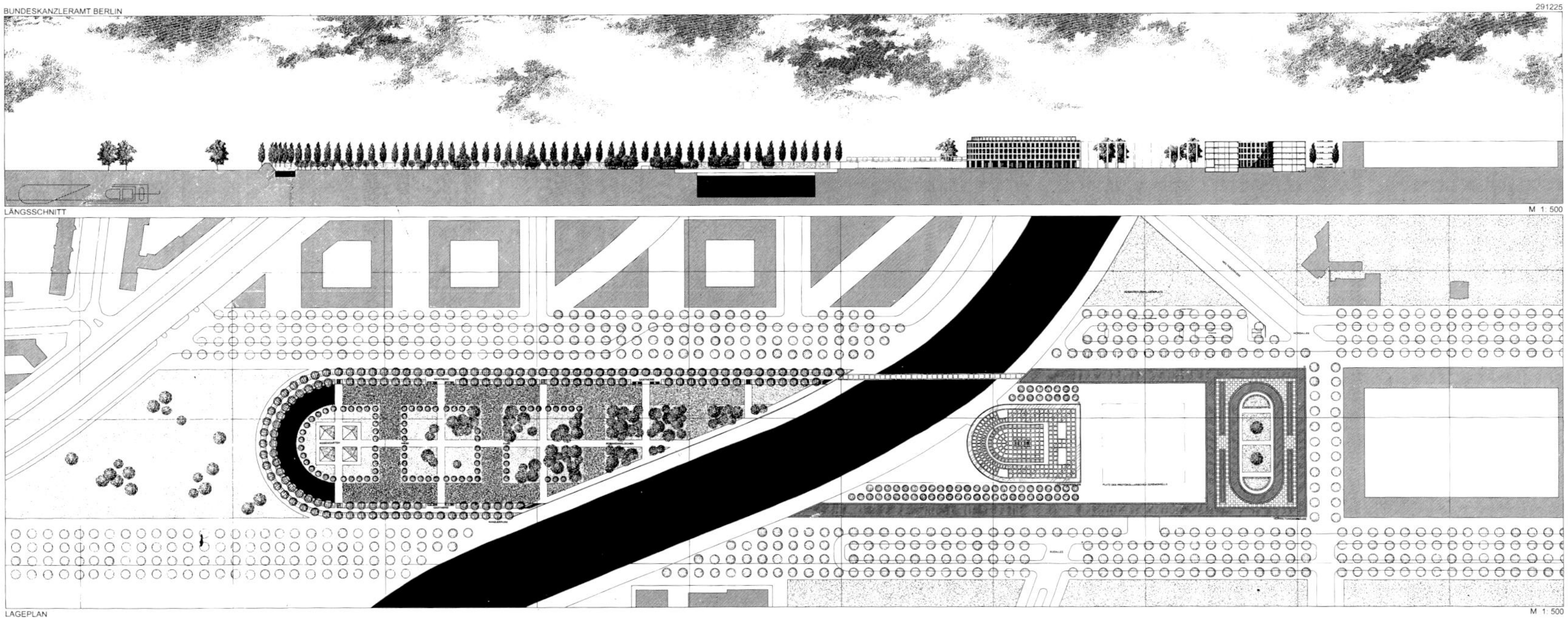

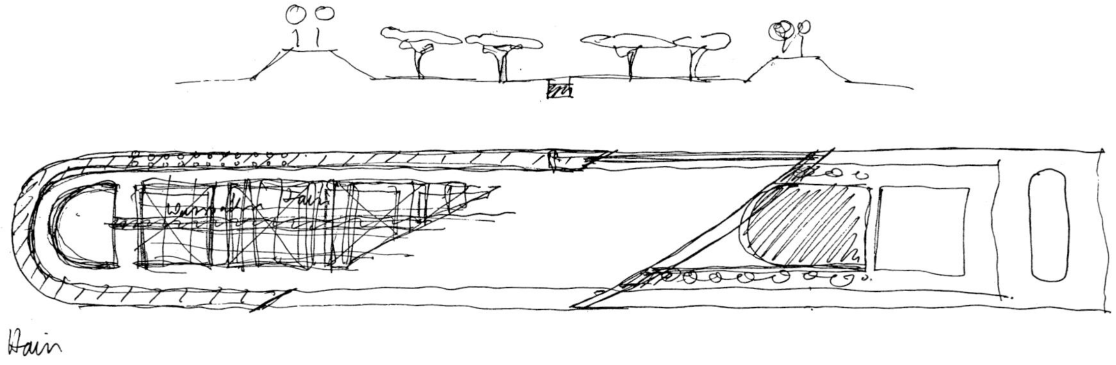

Sketches; section; site plan; ground-level plan.

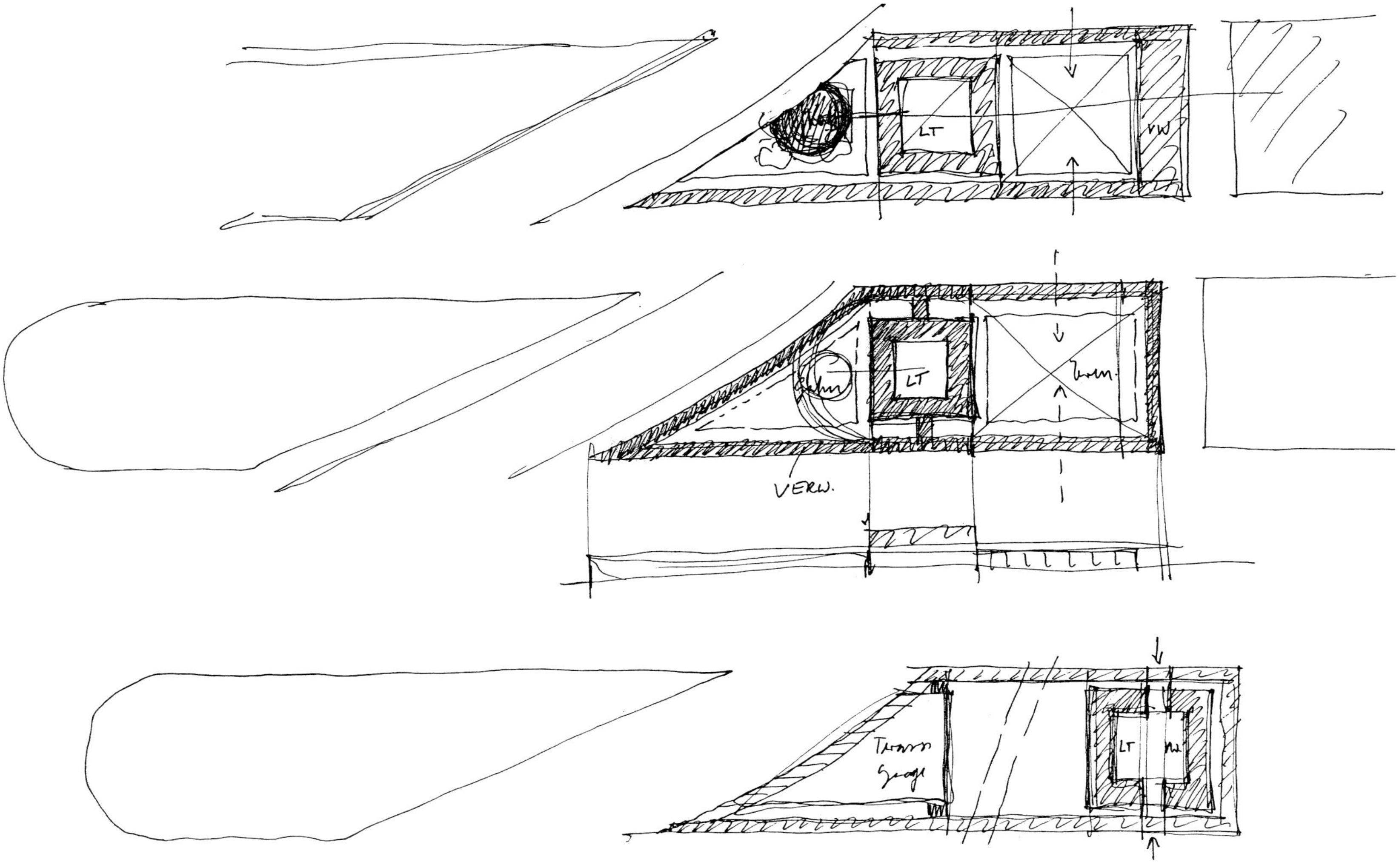
LT
VW
LT
VERW.
LT

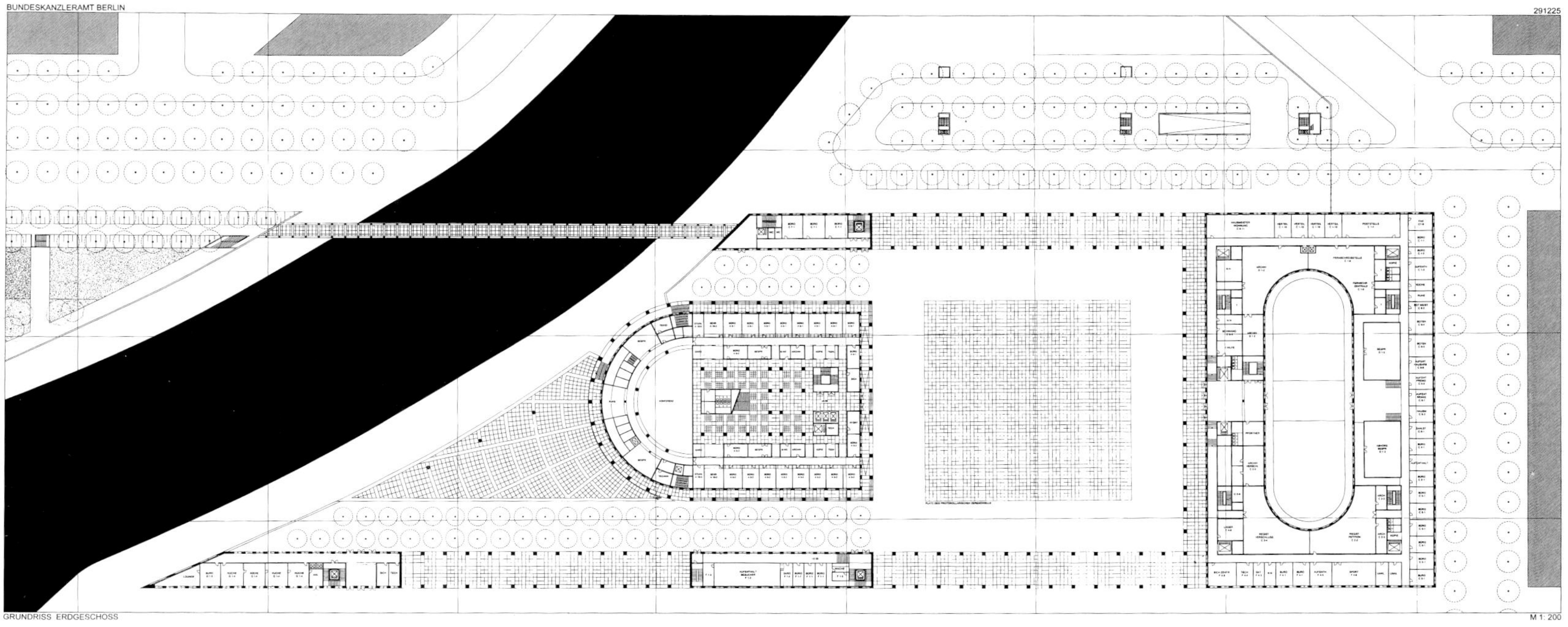
BUNDESKANZLERAMT BERLIN
291225
GRUNDRISS ERDGESCHOSS
M 1: 200

Competition Design for Dresdner Bank, Pariser Platz, Berlin-Mitte, 1994

With: Karl-Heinz Winkens and Tobias Scheel

Model view.

Opposite:
Site plan; use diagrams

Project team: Chase McCarthy, Christoph Sauter

The Pariser Platz was constructed as one of three geometric plazas marking the city gates of Berlin in the course of the great baroque expansion of the city beginning in 1734. With the Brandenburg Gate—completed in 1791 after a design by Langhans—and other, primarily nineteenth-century buildings tailored to the gate structure in scale, proportion, and height, Pariser Platz marked the central, monumental entrance to the historic center of Berlin along the axis Charlottenburger Chaussee/Unter den Linden. In the second half of the nineteenth century, the original residential usage of the palatial buildings along the edges of the blocks gradually yielded to governmental and diplomatic functions. The destruction and alterations of World War II and the postwar period have transformed the plaza into an urban fragment containing the isolated structures of the Brandenburg Gate and the Akademie der Künste.

In the coming years, Pariser Platz is to be reconstructed in accord with its original classicistic form. Detailed design statutes subordinate the architecture of the individual buildings to the design of the urban plaza as a whole. Against this background, the competition posed essentially two tasks: to find a balanced urbanistic solution for the reconstruction of the Pariser Platz, and to lend the Dresdner Bank a monumental appearance on both interior and exterior. In order to arrive at an optimal solution for the narrow plots in question, the design includes the entire block.

The typology of the single courtyard

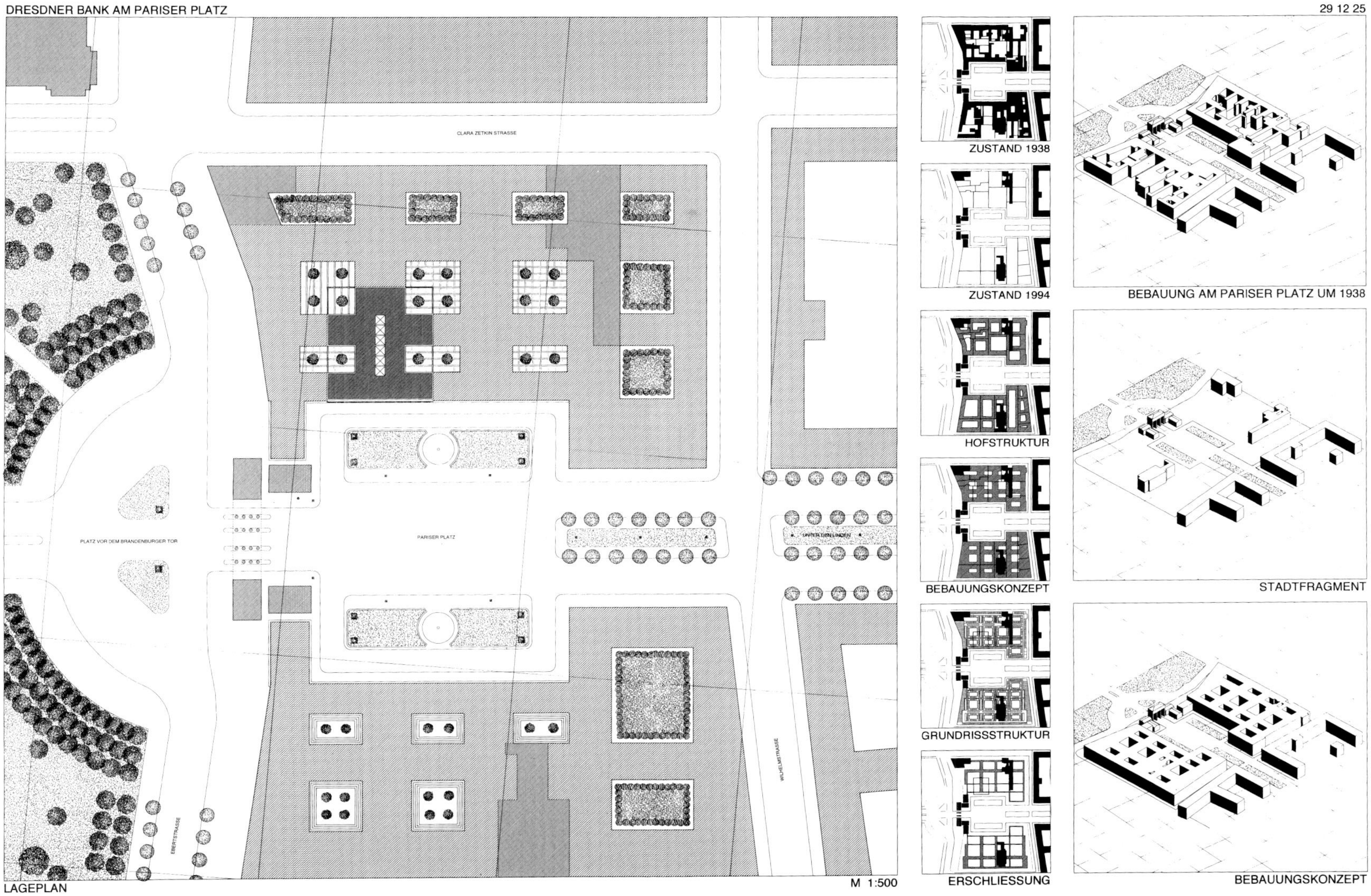

confined to the individual parcel is abandoned in favor of a more spatially expansive courtyard structure, in which various smaller courtyards adjoin one another, providing optimal utilization and illumination for the individual buildings. The design proposal evinces a simple but engaging form. The gap between buildings is closed with a clear structure that adheres to the design statutes and exudes an unpretentious elegance. Thus despite its disciplined integration into the overall urban scheme, the building receives a memorable individual appearance in keeping with its significance.

The proportioning and material of the facade allude to the great Berlin tradition of functional but elegant office buildings. In classical fashion, the facade is divided into three parts. The socle is covered with large slabs of natural stone; the middle part with its french windows is faced with smaller panels of lighter Jurassic limestone; the recessed top story is covered in finely finished plaster.

At the center is a large hall with an inset stairway marking the central axis of the building. This staircase is a monumental exhibition area and at the same time a public space, providing access to zones with double rows of offices grouped around a series of square courtyards. The organization of the building is programmatic: the top story accommodates representative living suites oriented to Pariser Platz, as well as club and conference rooms with corresponding service installations.

The first to third upper stories are occupied by offices. The ground level includes spaces for the Ponto Foundation and the consulate, also oriented to Pariser Platz, as well as two clubrooms and the business office for investment consulting clients. The basement level is spatially connected to the ground floor and receives adequate illumination through the square atriums and ceiling-high glass doors.

Sections; plans; isometrics.

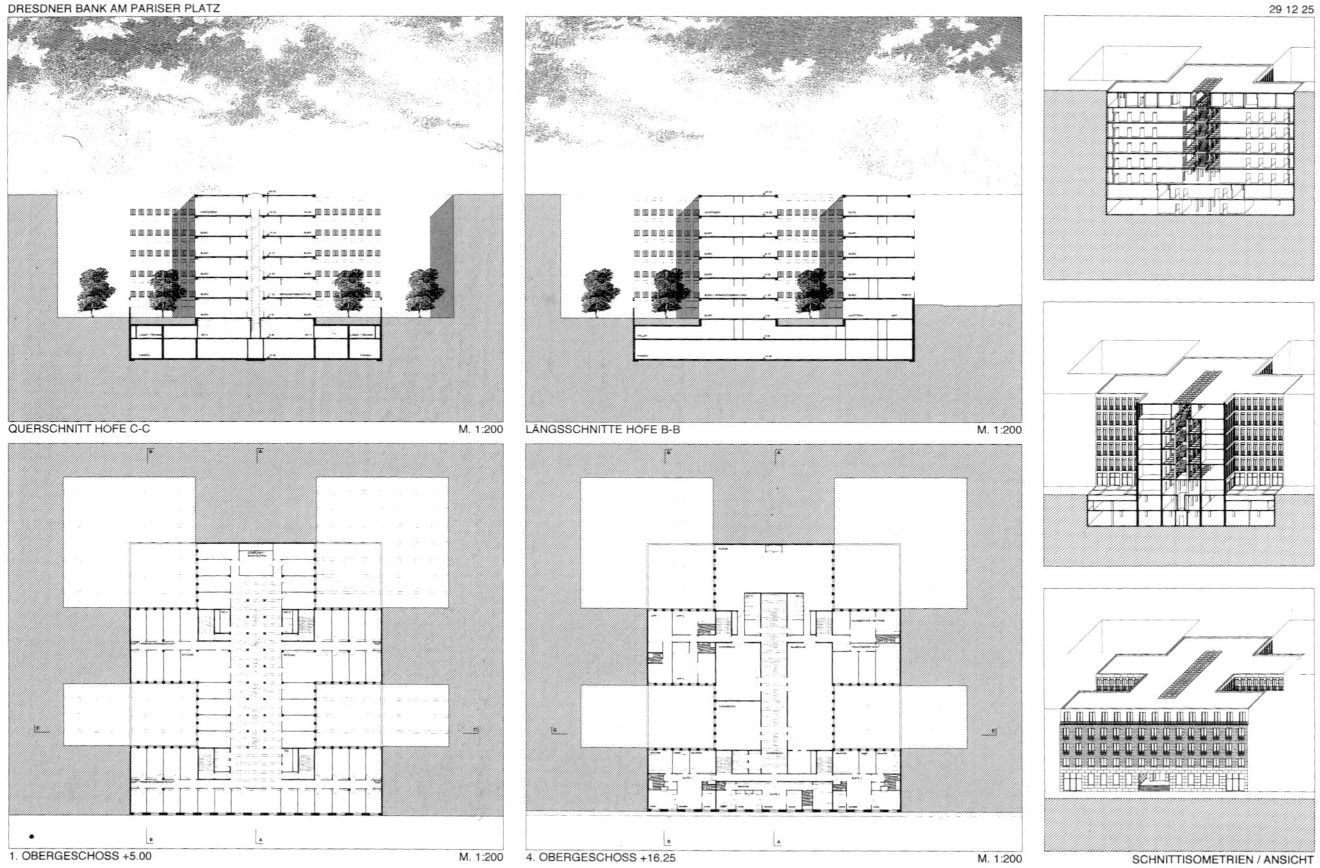

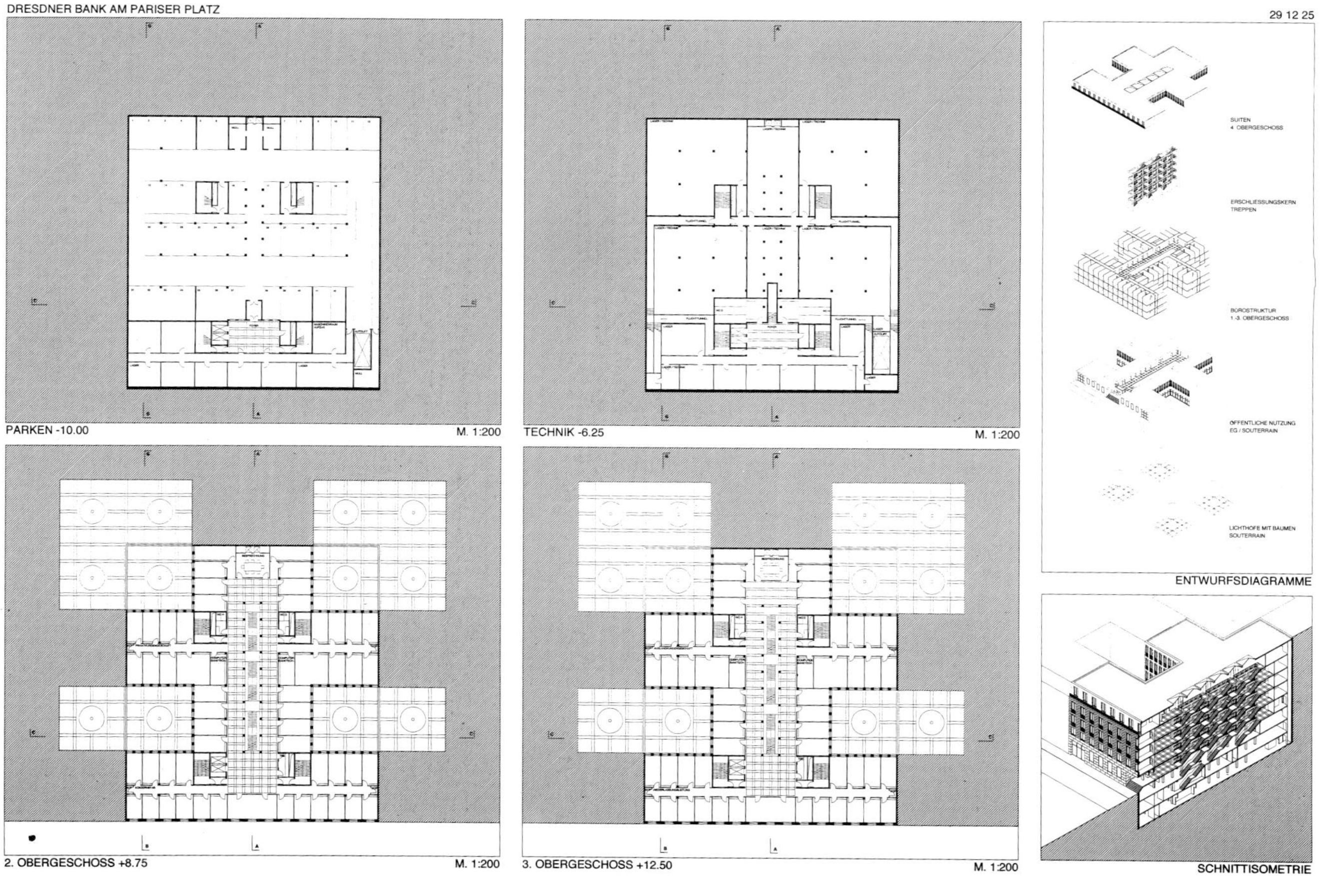

DRESDNER BANK AM PARISER PLATZ

29 12 25

ANSICHT PARISER PLATZ M. 1:200

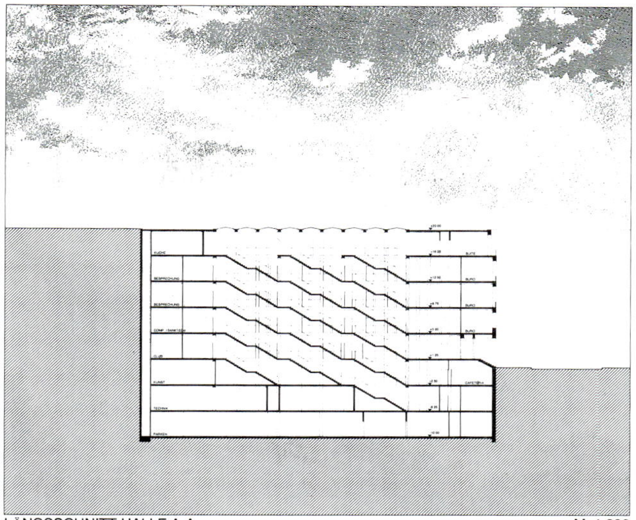

LÄNGSSCHNITT HALLE A-A M. 1:200

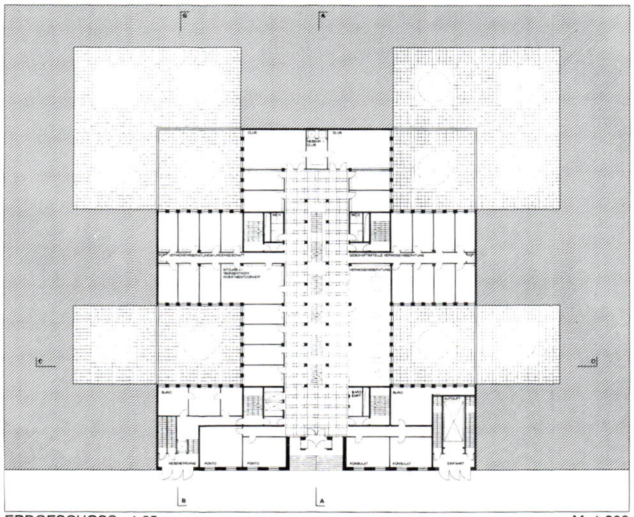

ERDGESCHOSS +1.25 M. 1:200

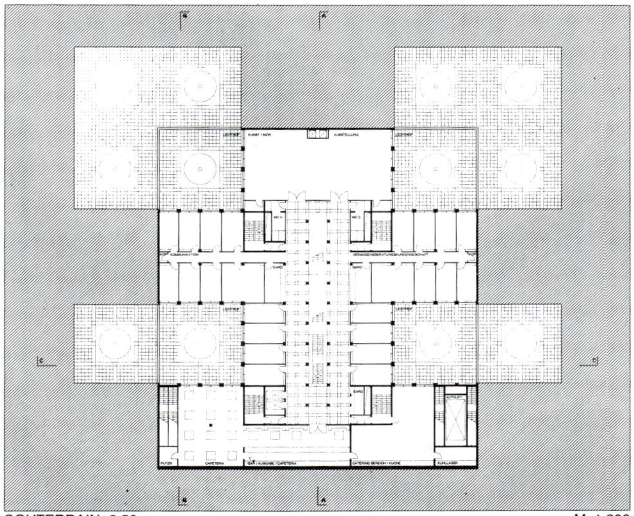

SOUTERRAIN -2.50 M. 1:200

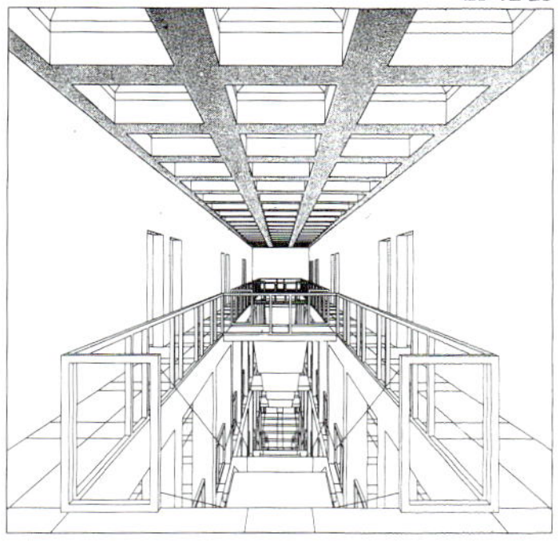

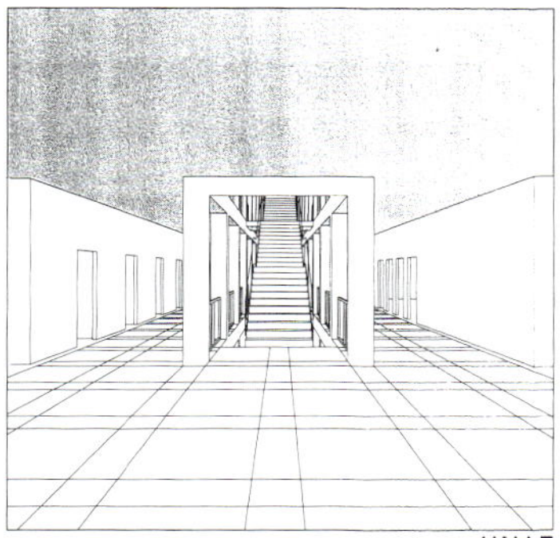

HALLE

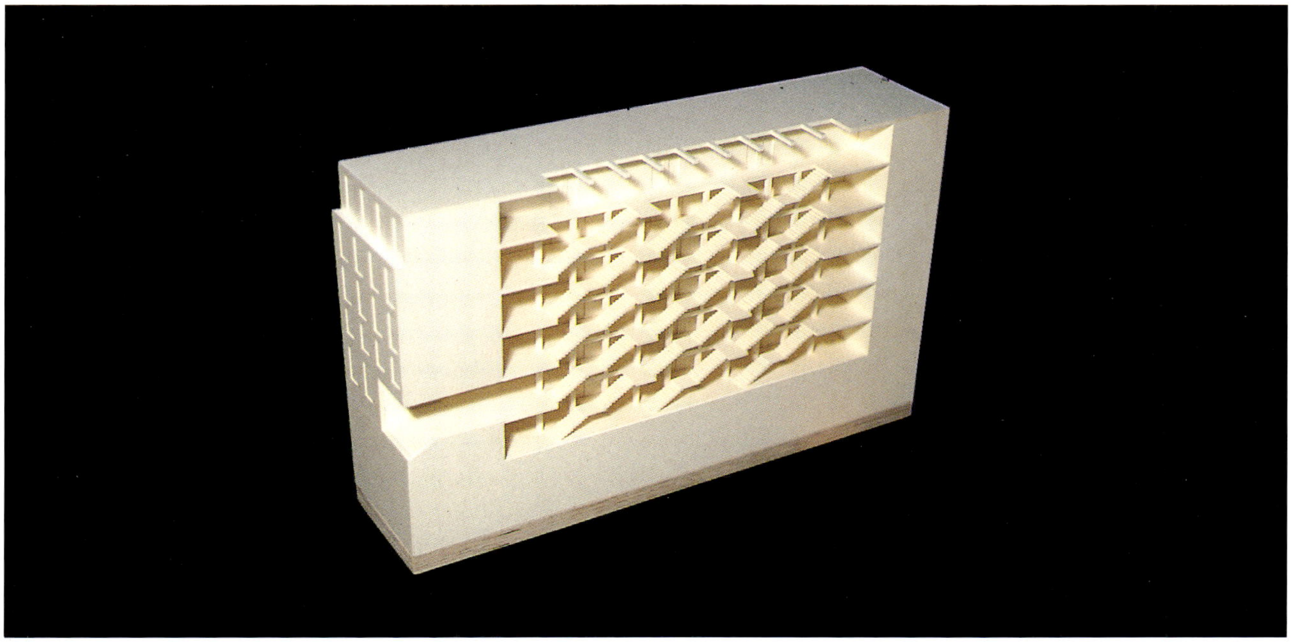

Elevation; section; plans; perspectives; model view.

Design for Residential Tower, Heerlen, Netherlands, 1995

Project team: Boris von Glasenapp

The residential tower in Heerlen is part of a comprehensive design that calls for the reurbanization of the Heerlen city center, a district marked by the planning measures of the 1960s and 1970s. The tower is located at the edge of the Burgemeester von Grunsvenplein plaza. This plaza forms the transition from the historic town, which goes back to Roman times, to the surrounding urban expansions of the twentieth century.

The plaza is bounded by uniform residential construction. To the east lies the old town center with its small-scale, differentiated structures, while across from it the city theater dominates the plaza as a freestanding individual element. On the northern edge, a lack of spatial definition causes the plaza to merge with Geerstraat, a street that leads toward the train station. In this location, the planned residential tower marks the corner of the plaza and, together with the neighboring high-rises on Apollolaan and Het Loon, forms an ensemble of tall buildings at the entrance to the Heerlen city center. The residential tower is the highest building in the city; its lower, broader section corresponds to the height of the surrounding high-rises, while its slimmer upper part towers above them. A two-story arcade forms the socle zone of the building on Burgemeester von Grunsvenplein. On the rear side, toward the heavily trafficked Geerstraat, the stair tower projecting from the facade functions as a landmark visible from afar. Like the rest of the building, it is uniformly faced with clinkers.

In addition to the large three-bedroom apartments in the upper stories, each of the lower fifteen stories accommodates a pair of two-bedroom apartments. A café with an outdoor terrace on the ground level and office spaces in the first upper story take advantage of the attractive location.

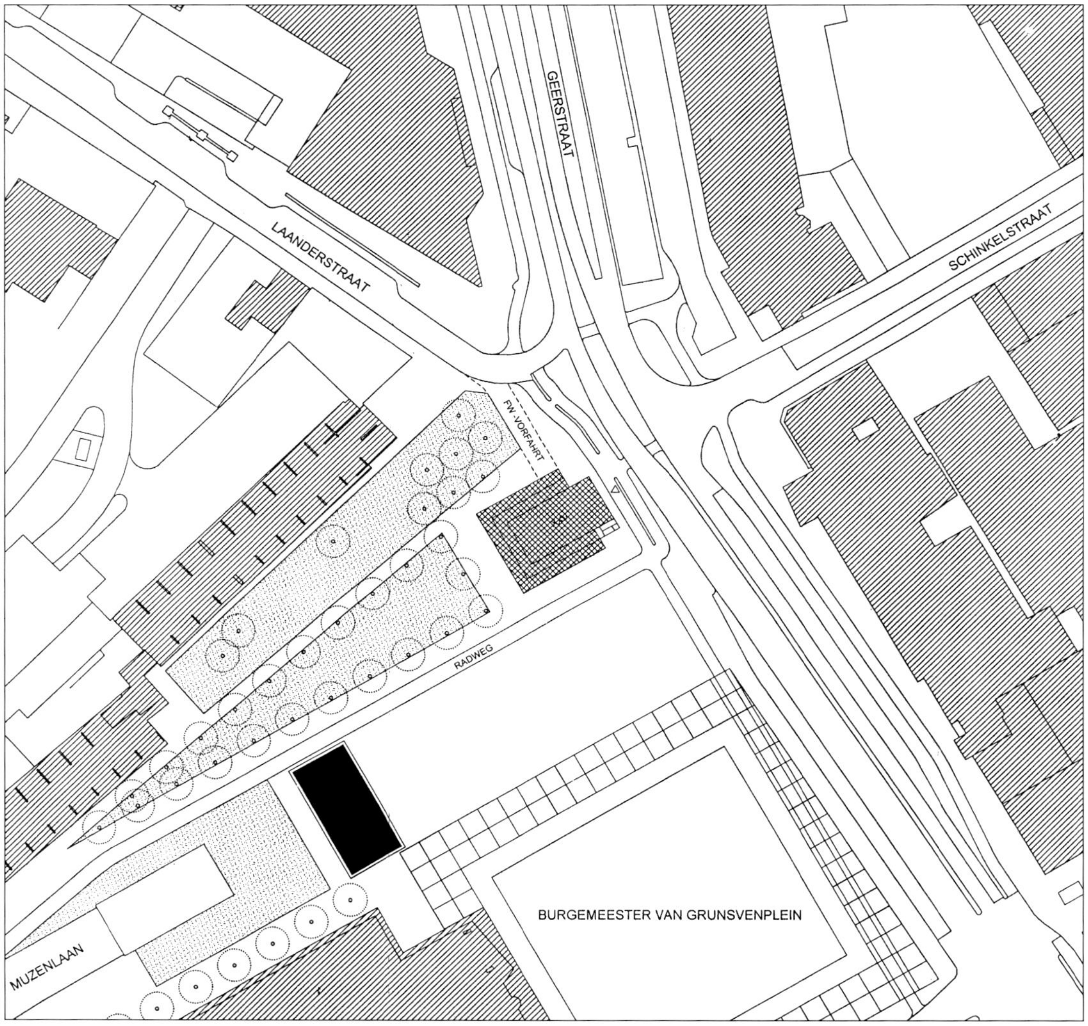

Site plan.

Opposite:
Elevation; perspectives.

Overleaf:
Plans; section.

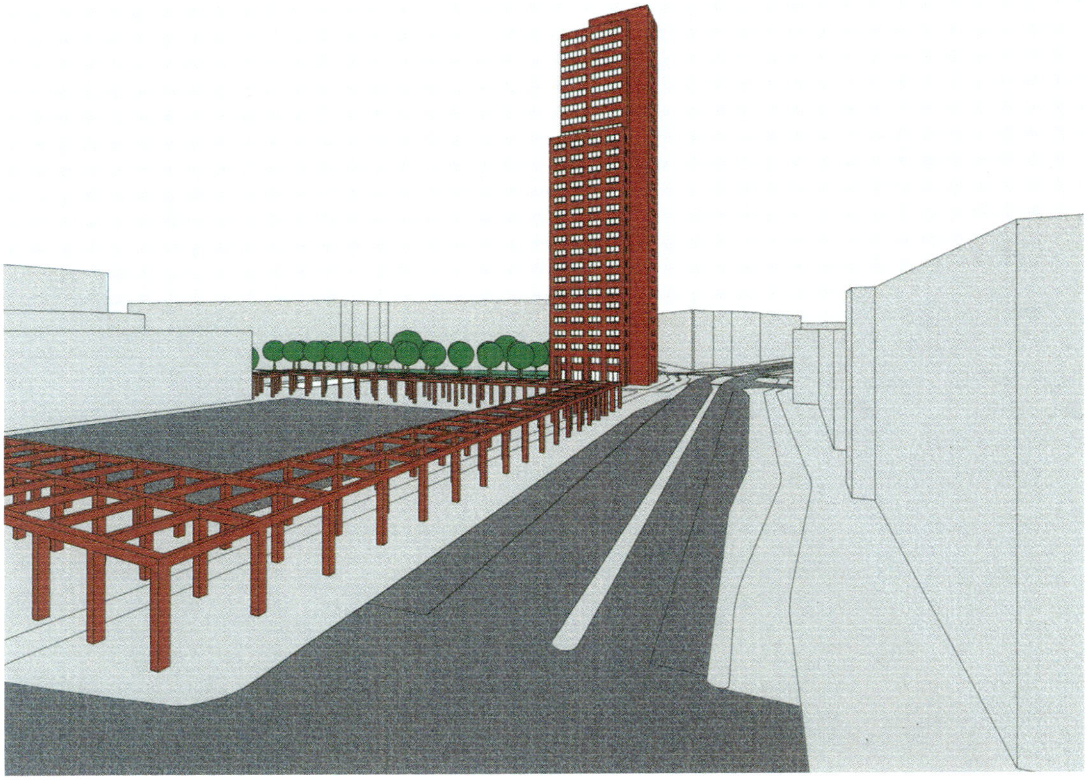

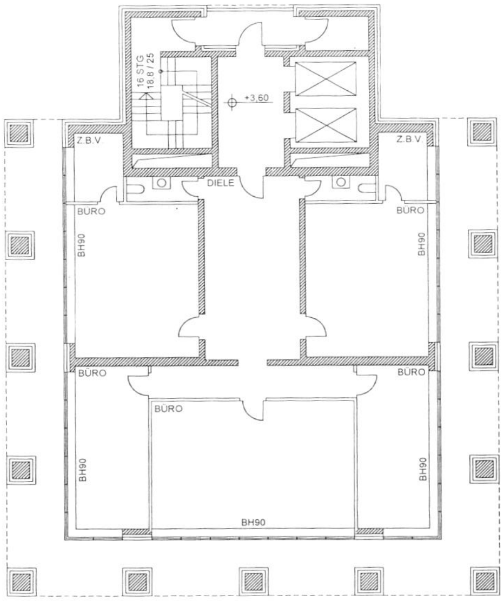
16 STG
18.8 / 25
+3,60
Z.B.V.
Z.B.V.
DIELE
BÜRO
BÜRO
BH90
BH90
BÜRO
BÜRO
BÜRO
BH90
BH90
BH90

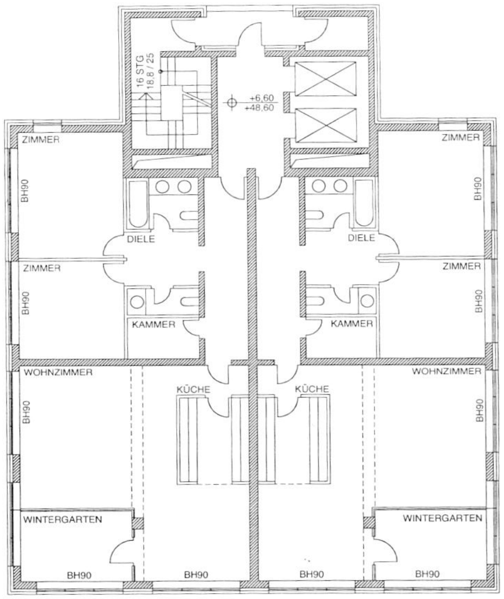
16 STG
18.8 / 25
+6,60
+48,60
ZIMMER
ZIMMER
BH90
BH90
DIELE
DIELE
ZIMMER
ZIMMER
BH90
BH90
KAMMER
KAMMER
WOHNZIMMER
KÜCHE
KÜCHE
WOHNZIMMER
BH90
BH90
WINTERGARTEN
WINTERGARTEN
BH90
BH90
BH90
BH90

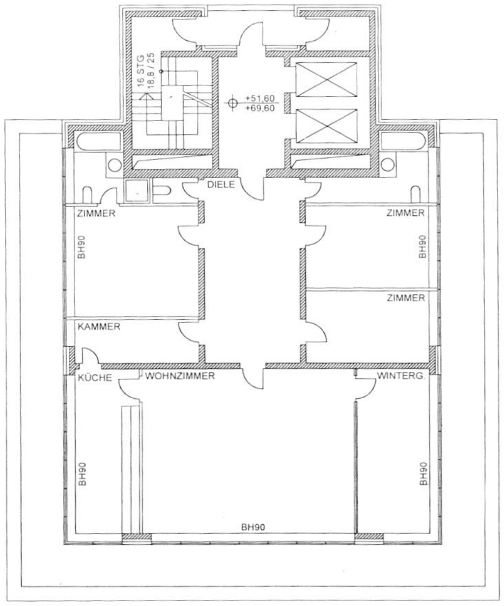
16 STG
18.8 / 25
+51,60
+69,60
DIELE
ZIMMER
ZIMMER
BH90
BH90
ZIMMER
KAMMER
KÜCHE
WOHNZIMMER
WINTERG.
BH90
BH90
BH90

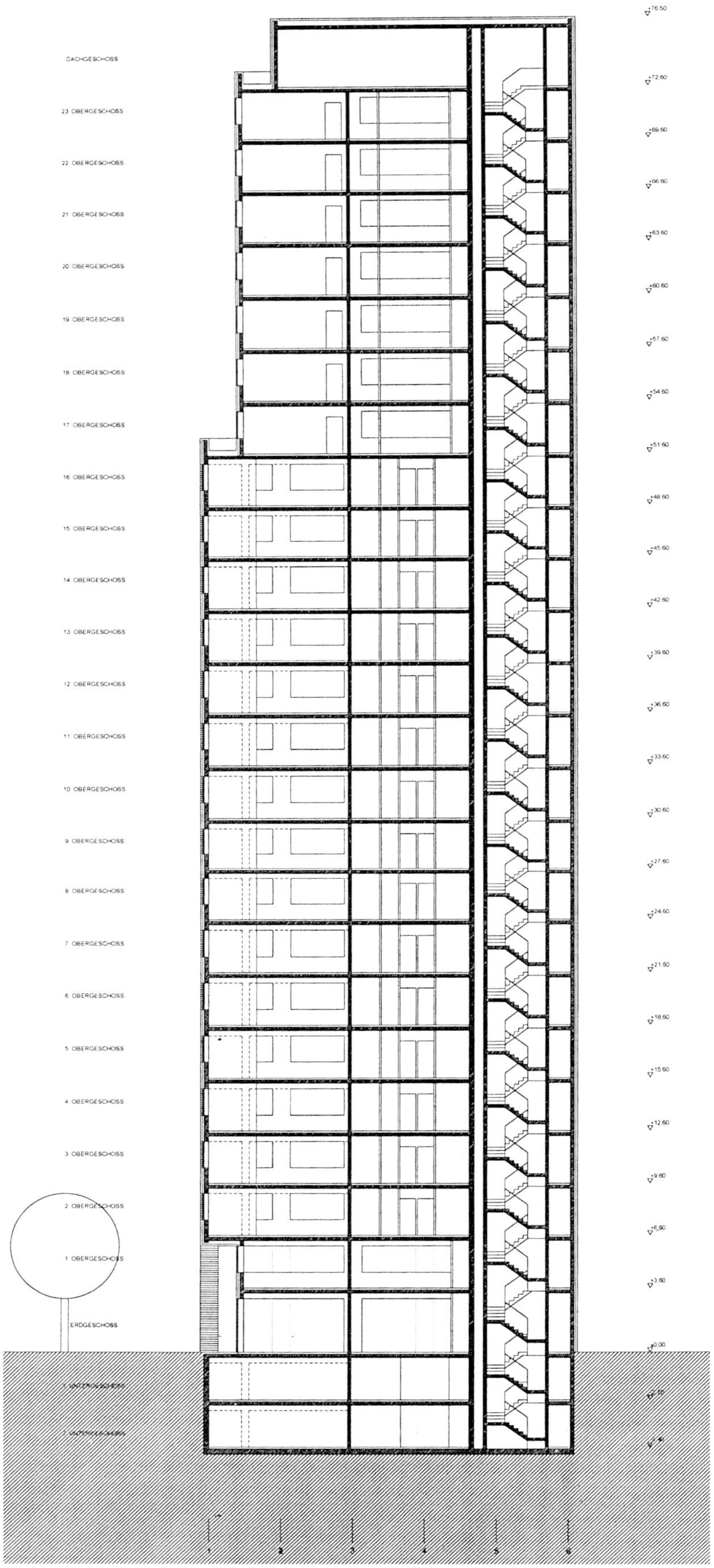
DACHGESCHOSS
23 OBERGESCHOSS
22 OBERGESCHOSS
21 OBERGESCHOSS
20 OBERGESCHOSS
19 OBERGESCHOSS
18 OBERGESCHOSS
17 OBERGESCHOSS
16 OBERGESCHOSS
15 OBERGESCHOSS
14 OBERGESCHOSS
13 OBERGESCHOSS
12 OBERGESCHOSS
11 OBERGESCHOSS
10 OBERGESCHOSS
9 OBERGESCHOSS
8 OBERGESCHOSS
7 OBERGESCHOSS
6 OBERGESCHOSS
5 OBERGESCHOSS
4 OBERGESCHOSS
3 OBERGESCHOSS
2 OBERGESCHOSS
1 OBERGESCHOSS
ERDGESCHOSS
1 UNTERGESCHOSS
1 UNTERGESCHOSS
1
2
3
4
5
6

Feasibility Study for Rostock-Reutershagen, 1995

With: Stefan Vieths

Project team: Axel Steudel, Marvin Keim, Christine Combe, Peter Pfertner, Volker Diekmann, Frank Wieschemann, Anja Albers

The competition area comprises the central area of Reutershagen, a northern district of Rostock built essentially during the postwar era. Its structure reflects the principles of the modernist, open urbanism of the period, with its objectlike buildings and loosely defined urban spaces. This holds true especially for the city center investigated here, which constitutes a fallow area occupied by temporary structures. The design seeks to fill this "empty" center by implanting a new urban core.

Like the historic city center, the new urban core of Reutershagen also represents an independent, clearly legible unit whose autonomous structure receives additional emphasis from the clarity of its basic form. Like the city center, it is marked by compact buildings, here of six stories each, into which precise urban spaces cut, thus contrasting vividly with the open, flowing spaces of the surrounding buildings.

An intersection of existing streets divides the urban core into four blocks, within which two plazas are defined. The first is the Marktplatz, whose function as well as proportions and design characterizes it as the center of public life in Reutershagen. A second plaza on axis with Ulrich-von-Hutten-Strasse marks the entrance to the urban center and is conceived as a decorative and traffic plaza. The design adopts a precise approach to the existing structures, creating an integral connection between existing substance and new planning. Like the former fortified area of the Rostock city center, the urban core is surrounded by a tree-lined ring street, which effects the transition to the existing

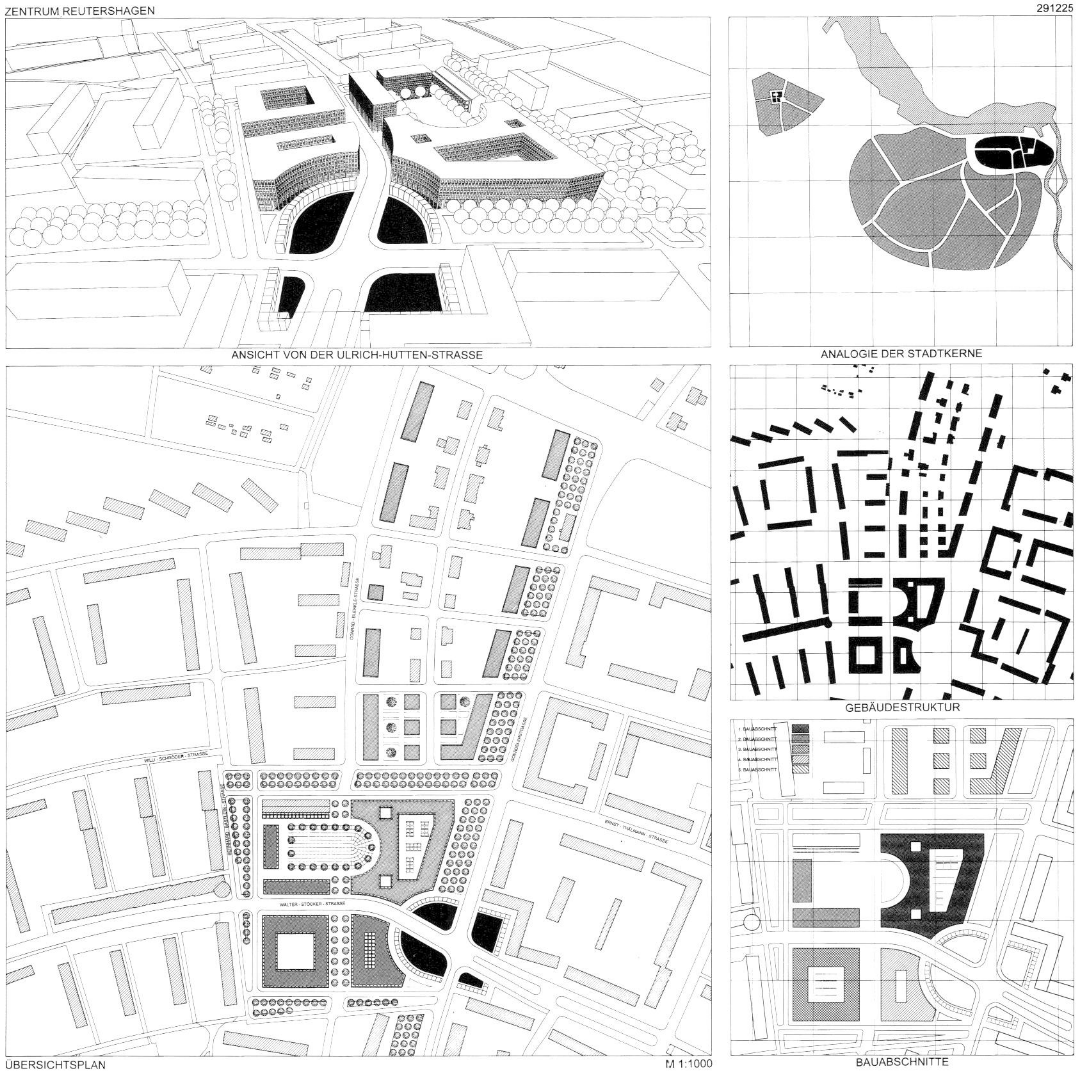

Perspective view; general plan; use diagrams.

Overleaf: Perspective view of Marktplatz; site plan; use diagrams; elevation; ground-level plan; sections.

ZENTRUM REUTERSHAGEN 291225

ANSICHT MARKTPLATZ

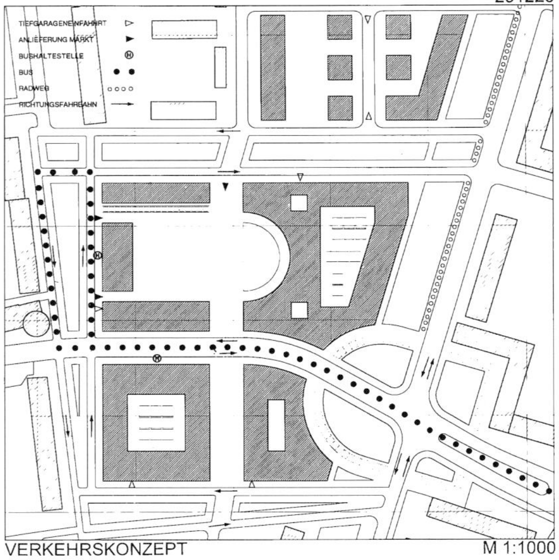

VERKEHRSKONZEPT M 1:1000

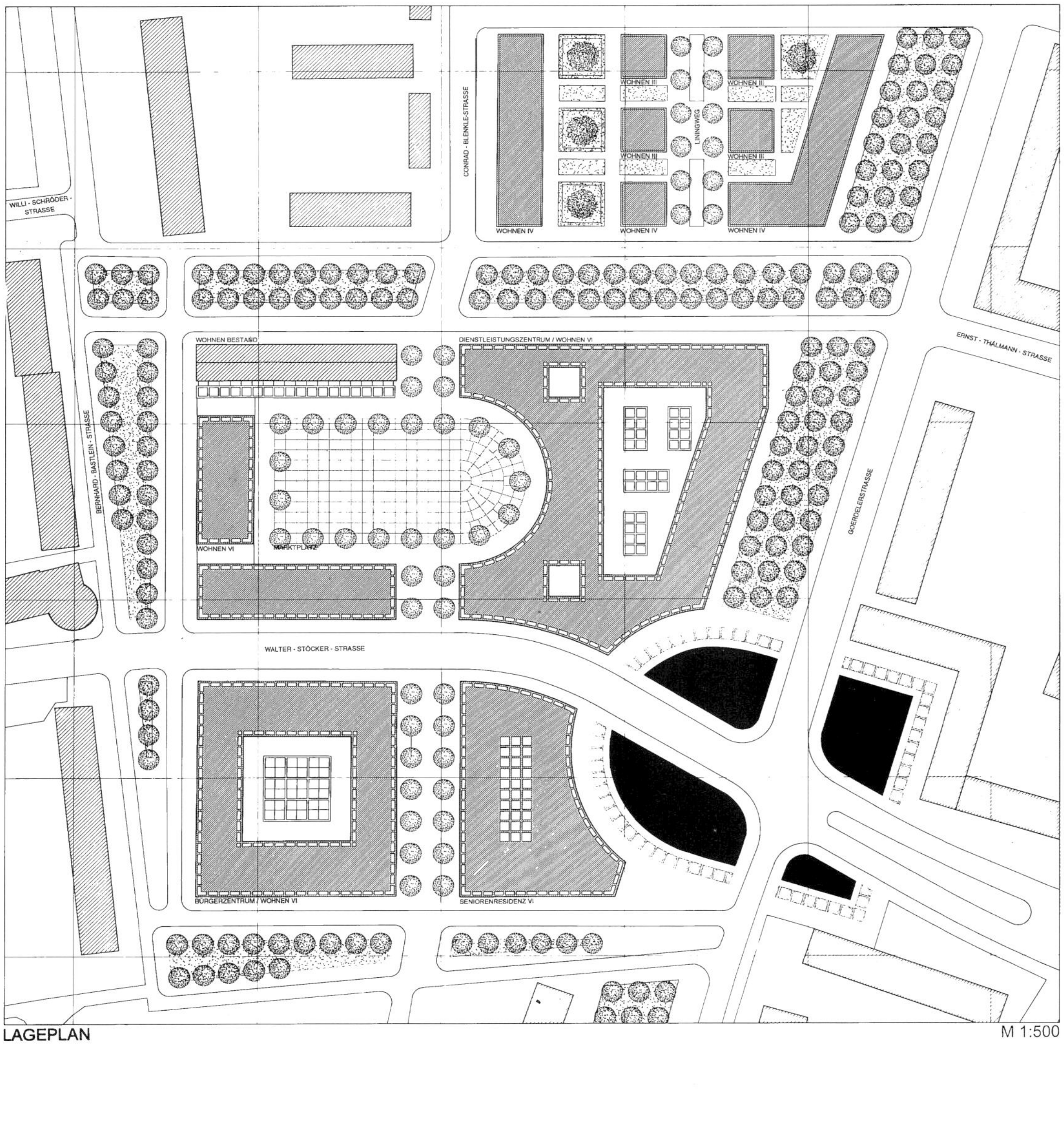

LAGEPLAN M 1:500

GRÜNKONZEPT M 1:1000

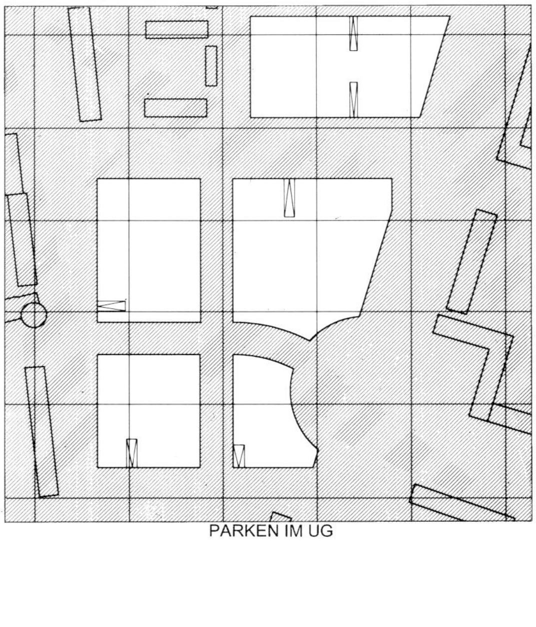

PARKEN IM UG

ZENTRUM REUTERSHAGEN

291225

ANSICHT VOM MARKTPLATZ M 1:200

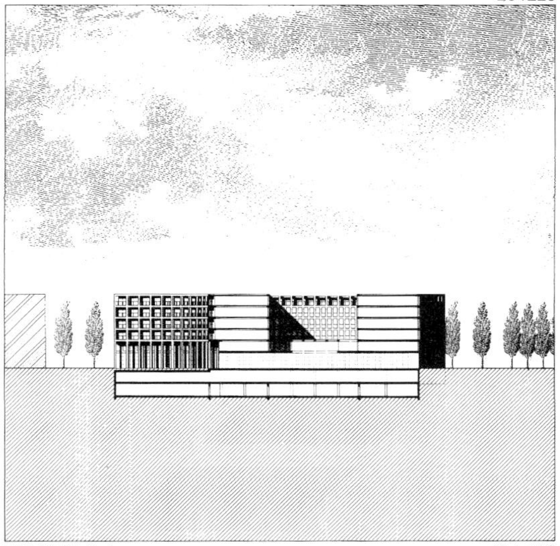

SCHNITT A-A M 1:500

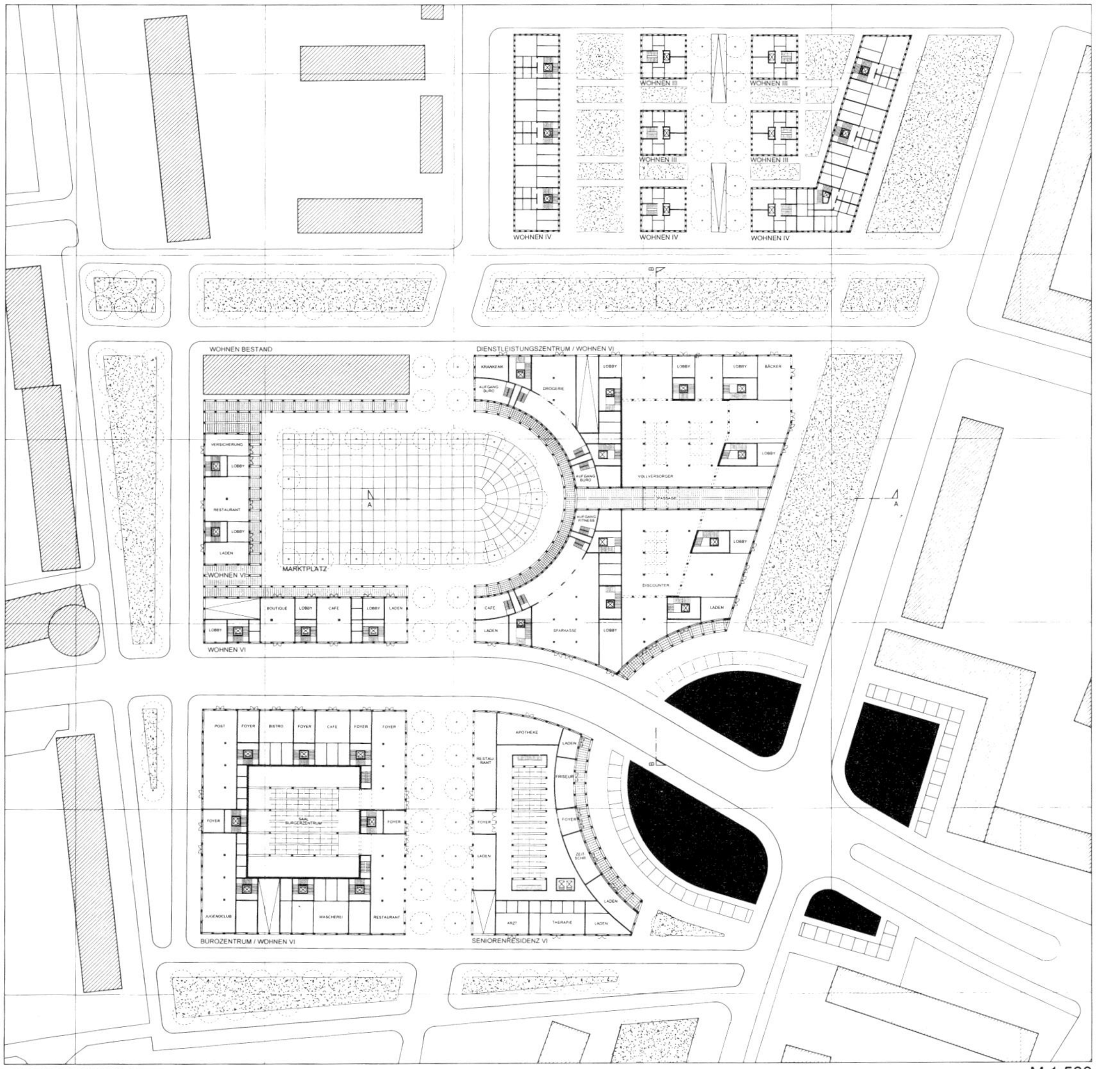

ERDGESCHOSS M 1:500

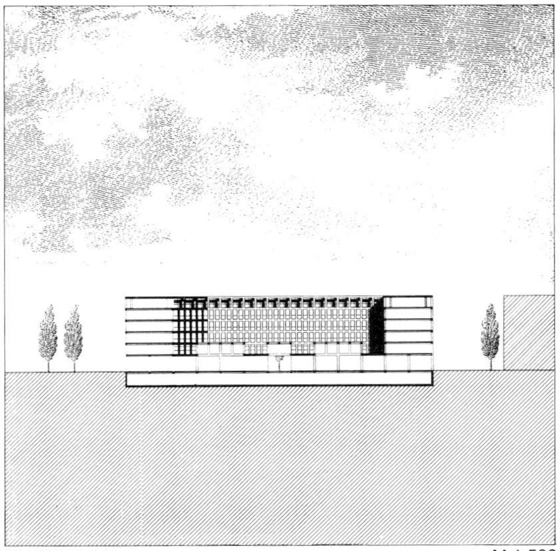

SCHNITT B-B M 1:500

ZENTRUM REUTERSHAGEN 291225

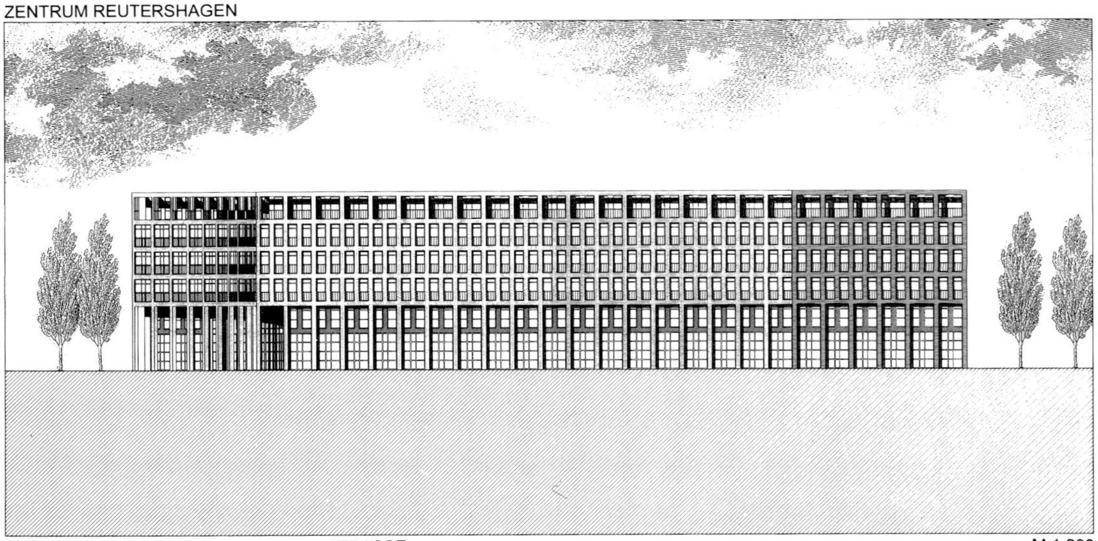

ANSICHT VON DER C.-V.-GOERDELER-STRASSE M 1:200

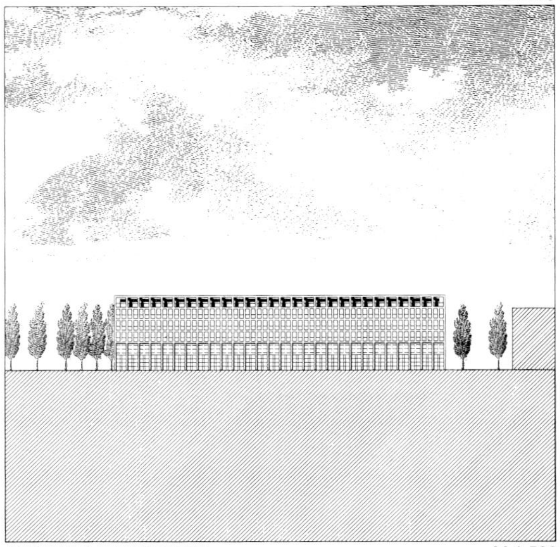

ANSICHT VON NORDEN M 1:500

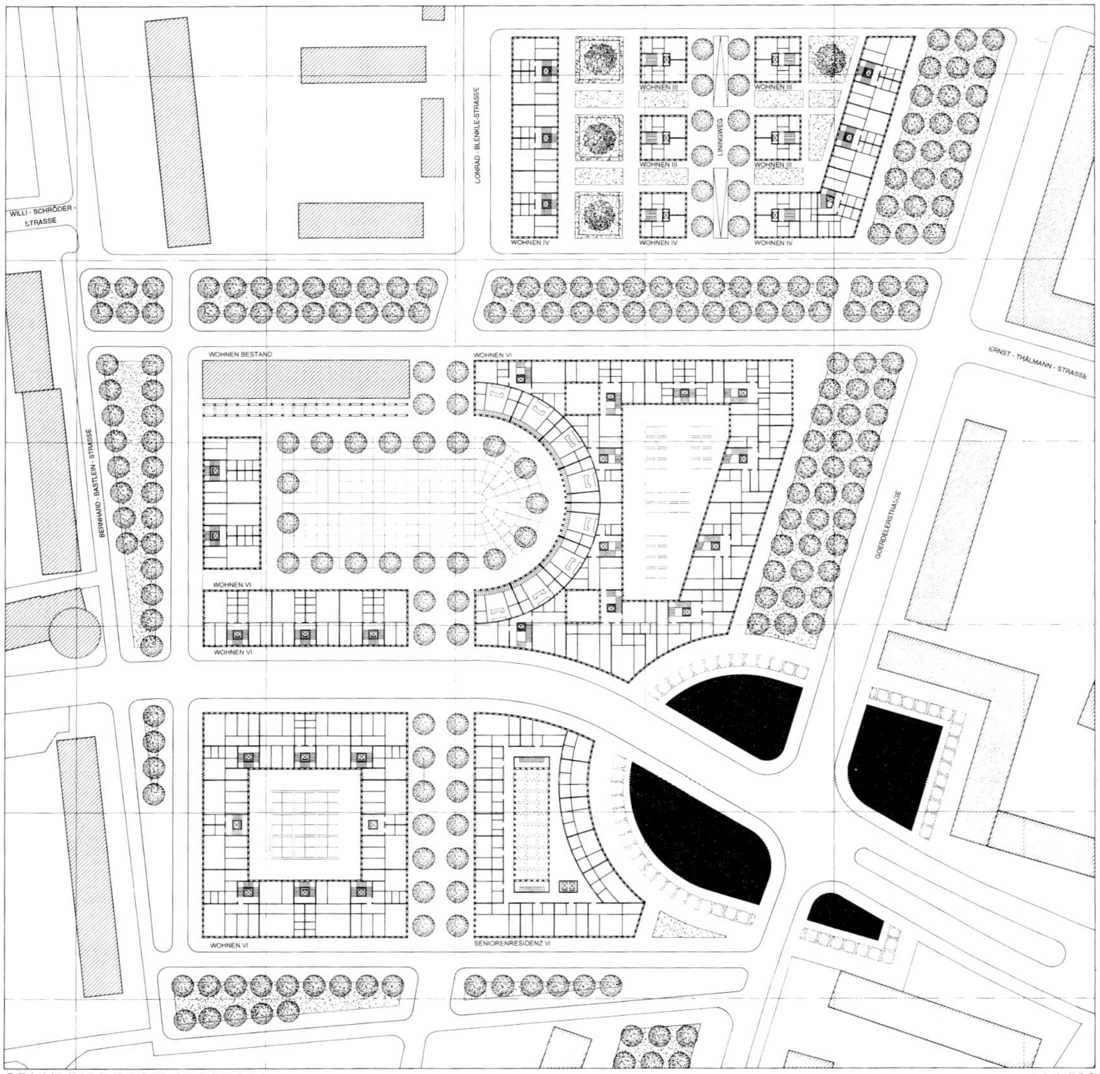

GRUNDRISS REGELGESCHOSS M 1:500

ANSICHT VON SÜDEN M 1:500

buildings and serves to organize traffic in the center.

The functional concept calls for a concentrated urban mixture of different uses. The northeast block at the intersection of Ulrich-von-Hutten-Strasse and Carl-Goerdeler-Strasse accommodates a shopping center with supermarket, discounter, bank, drugstore, café, and various smaller shops and medical practices occupying the ground level and first upper story. The upper stories accommodate residences. The building delimiting the Marktplatz to the west shows a similar, if more finely differentiated, functional structure.

The southern blocks of the urban core augment the commercial spaces around the Marktplatz with senior citizens' housing and a municipal center. North of the urban core, the existing buildings are supplemented with

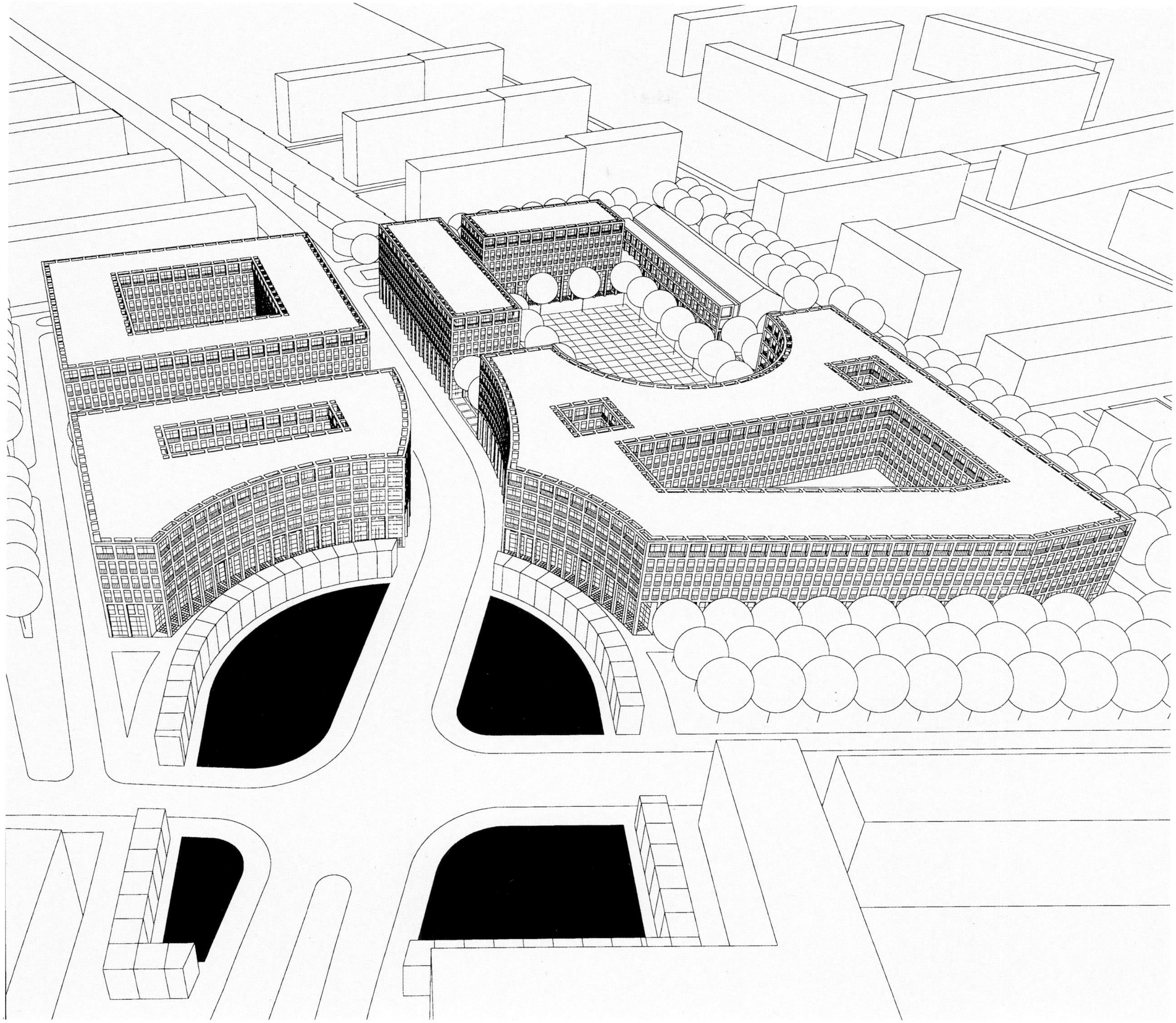

Perspective.

Opposite:
Elevations; typical
floor plan.

a number of residential structures that continue the design of the existing objectlike buildings. On Carl-Goerderler-Strasse, row buildings form a clear spatial edge, providing a frame for this important urban boulevard. On the interior of the block, the finely differentiated residential building is supplemented by urban villas.

The park area along Carl-Goerdeler-Strasse is transformed into a premenade and becomes an urban boulevard connecting the district center with Hamburger Strasse.

Competition Design for Kunstpalast, Düsseldorf, 1995–2000

With: Stefan Vieths

Project team: Kai-Uwe Lompa, Boris von Glasenapp, Frank Wieschemann, Marvin Keim, Johannes Götz, Guido Lohmann, Matthias Weiher, Gloria Amling

The proposed design of the Kunstpalast complex in Düsseldorf involves two main features: the addition of a new wing to the monumental courtyard to accommodate the Kunstpalast itself, and the construction of a freestanding semicircular building in the interior urban space behind the new Kunstpalast. The new wing preserves and continues the historic facade of the existing complex. The spacious urban configuration along the Rhine between the monumental courtyard and the Tonhalle is carefully augmented without disturbing its effect. The frugal articulation of the new Kunstpalast transforms the area behind the new building into a clearly framed courtyard space. Placed within this space is a gallery building whose clear geometry adds an element of order to the random, heterogeneous complex of Victoria-Versicherung building, residential architecture, and Kunstpalast.

The structure of the Kunstpalast is developed from the rhythm of the historic facade of the monumental courtyard, with the alternation of wall and window forming the basic module for the new building.

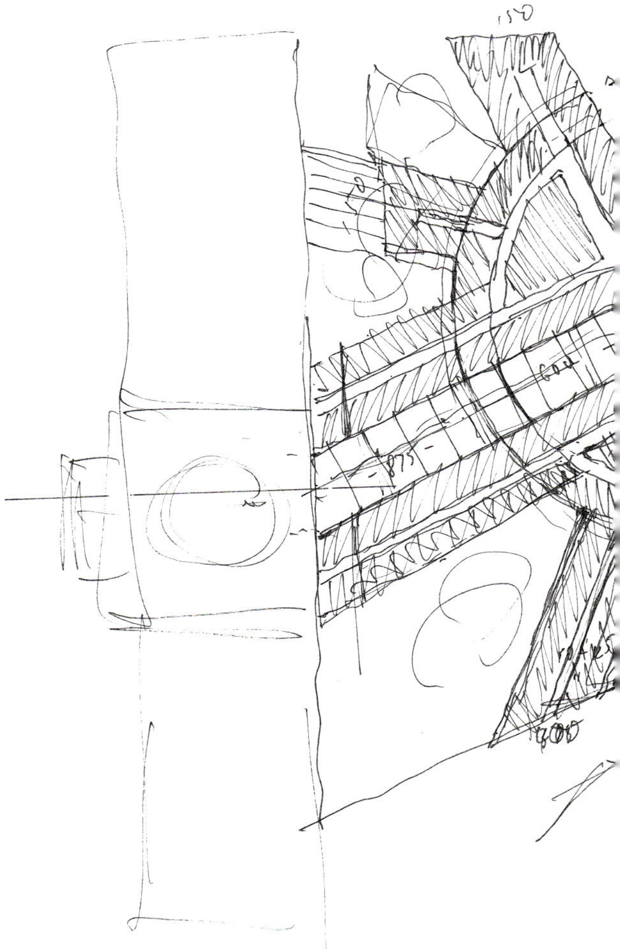

Model view; sketches; perspective; view from above.

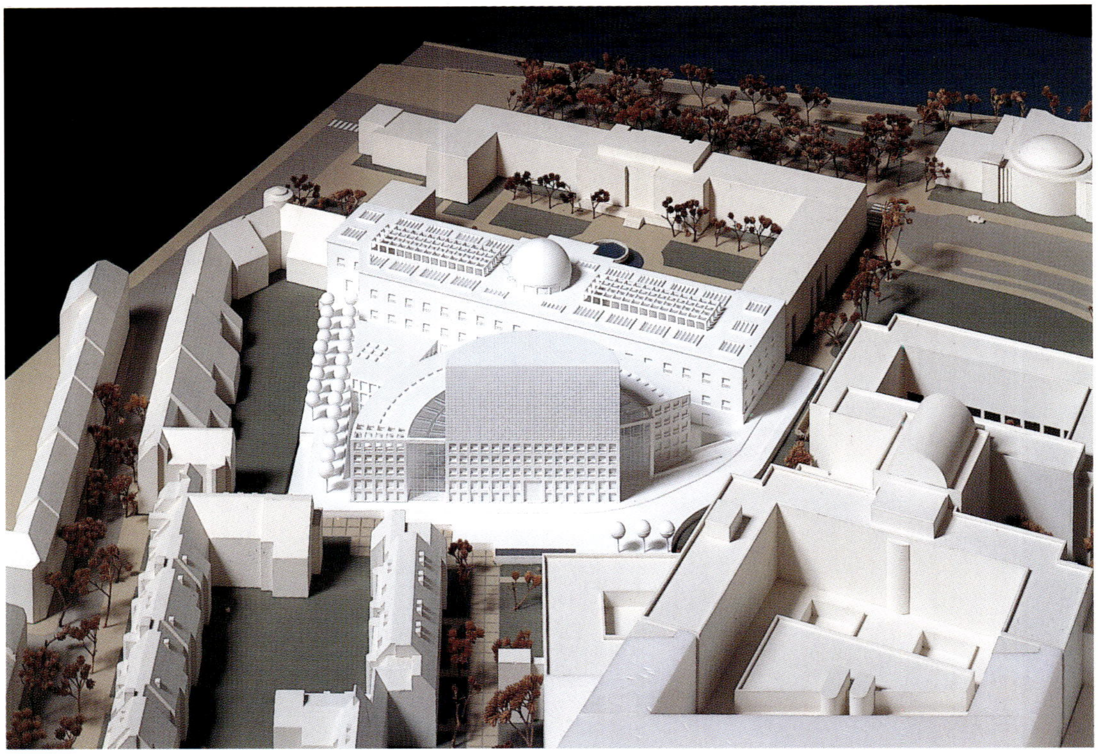

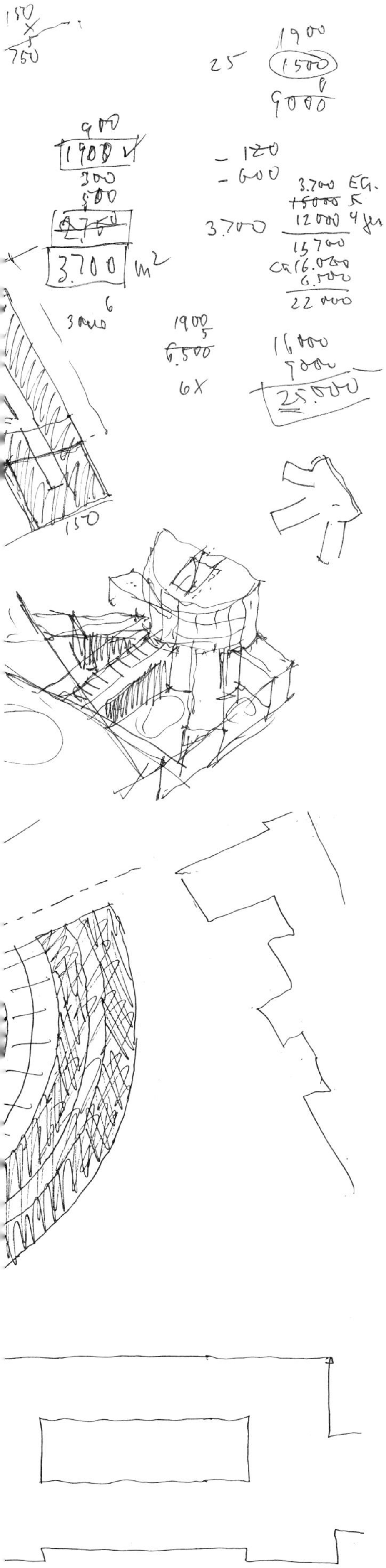

KUNSTPALAST DÜSSELDORF

PROF. O.M. UNGERS

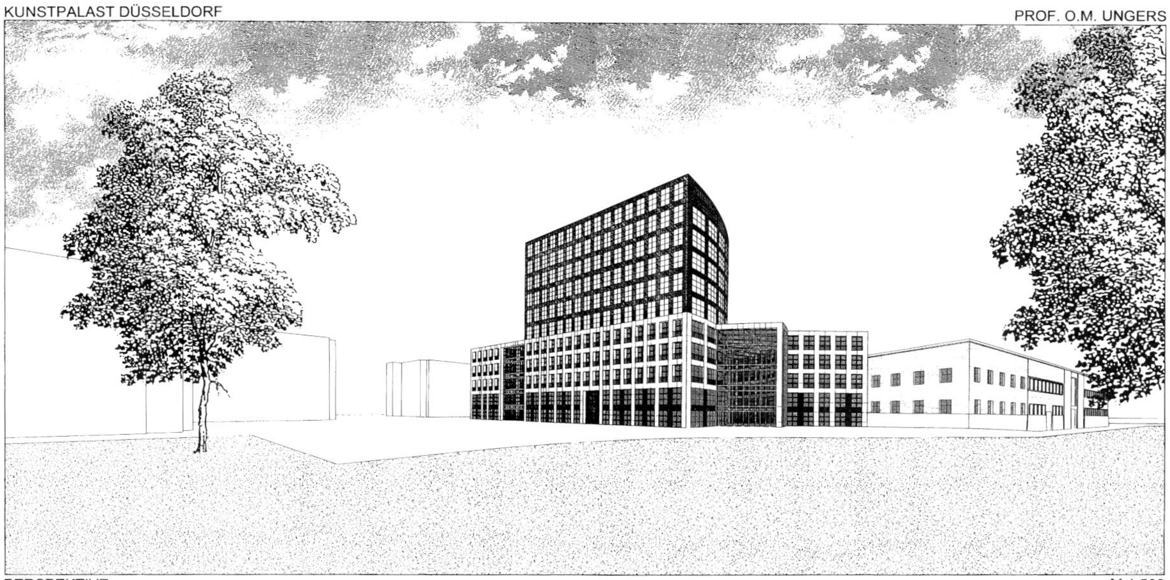

PERSPEKTIVE

M 1:500

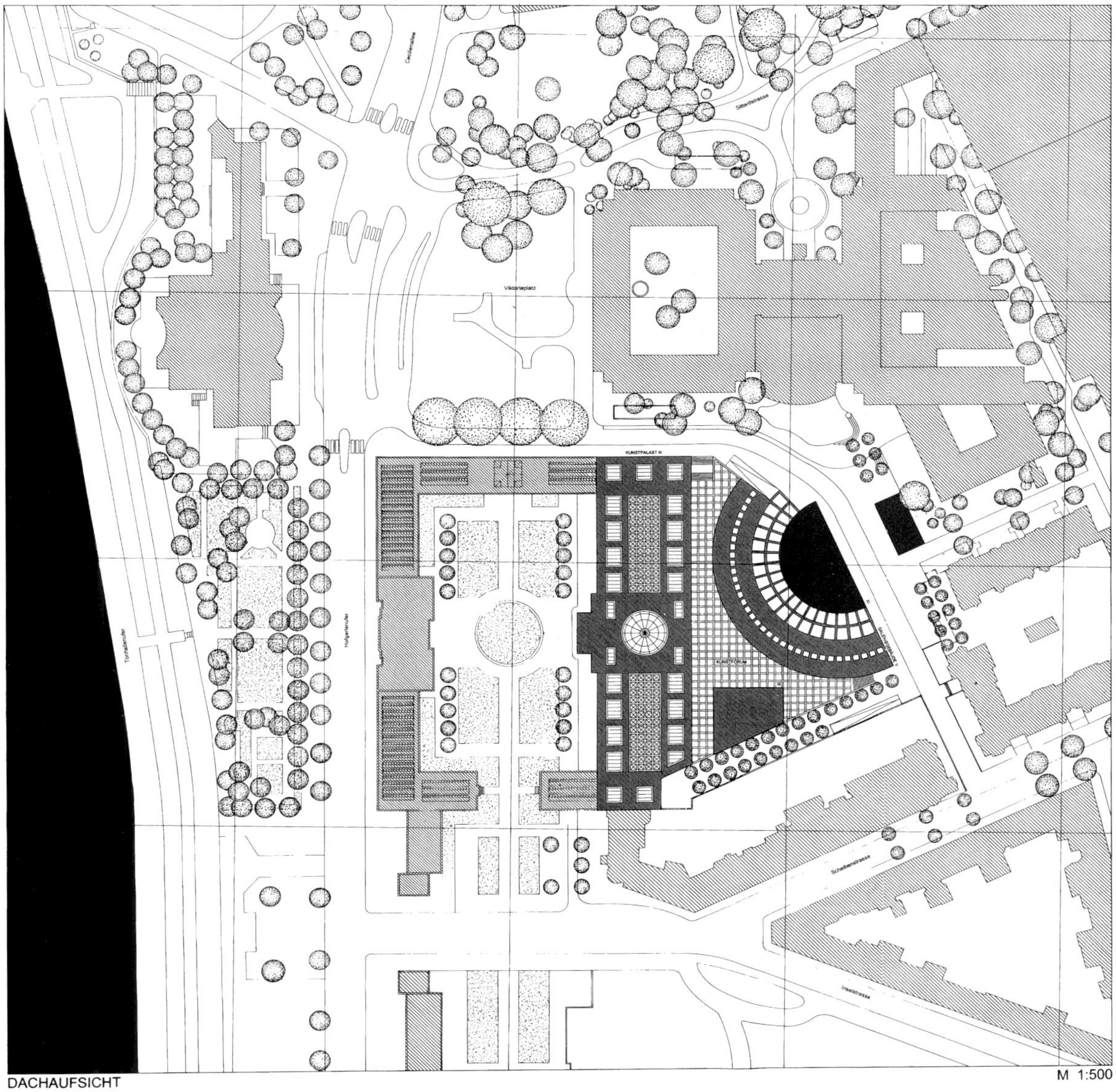

DACHAUFSICHT

M 1:500

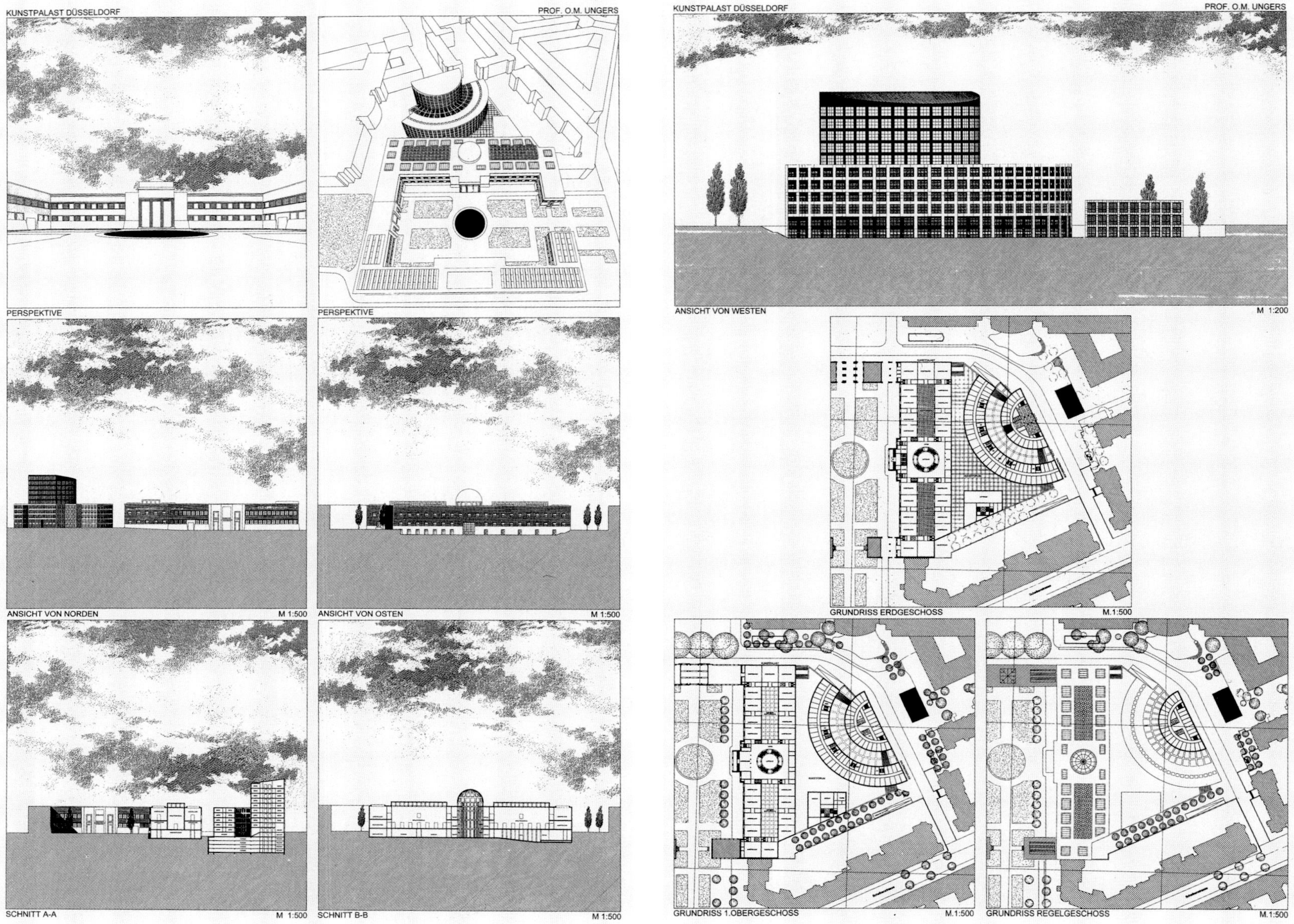

Accordingly, the entrance hall is oriented toward the existing portico. It connects the different floors with one another and is crowned by a dome recalling the historic dome of the Kunstpalast. Sculpture courtyards with glass roofs adjoin the central entrance hall on either side, with the remaining exhibition spaces arranged around these areas in two stories.

Access to the Robert-Schumann-Saal in the basement level is provided by a building-high foyer connected with the entrance level of the Kunstpalast. This foyer area has additional entrance and emergency exits facing the Kunstforum. The service entrance to the Kunstpalast is located on Brüderstrasse in the area of the restoration workshop. The use of clinkers for the facade of the new building corresponds to the facade of the monumental courtyard.

The semicircular gallery building is composed of three parts: a lower wing of the same height as the Kunstpalast, a tower structure whose slanted roof is defined by the lines of sight from the monumental courtyard, and a gallery connecting the tower and the circular wing. The gallery building is conceived as an office structure, with galleries, ateliers, and shops proposed only for the ground and basement levels. The entrance to the building is on Brüderstrasse. The facade of the gallery building is faced in natural stone up to the height of the circular wing, with glass above.

The Kunstforum, a sunken plaza between the Kunstpalast and the gallery building, is intended as a place of exchange for culture and business. It accommodates galleries, the entrances to the Kunstpalast and the Robert-Schumann-Saal and a seminar building, resulting in a functionally dense and complex urban space.

Perspectives; elevations; sections; plans.

Perspective of gallery building; plan of first upper story.

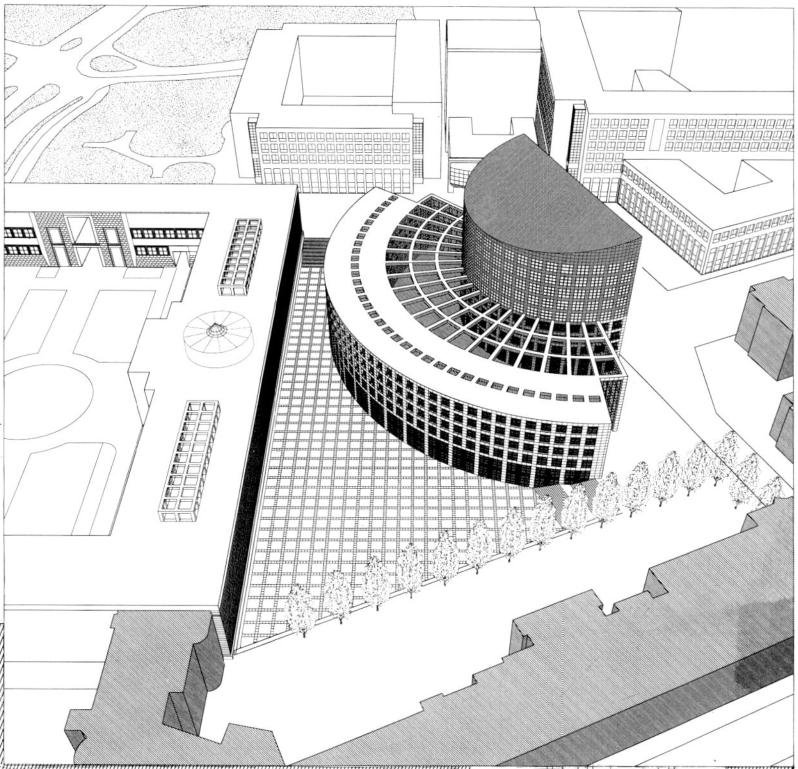

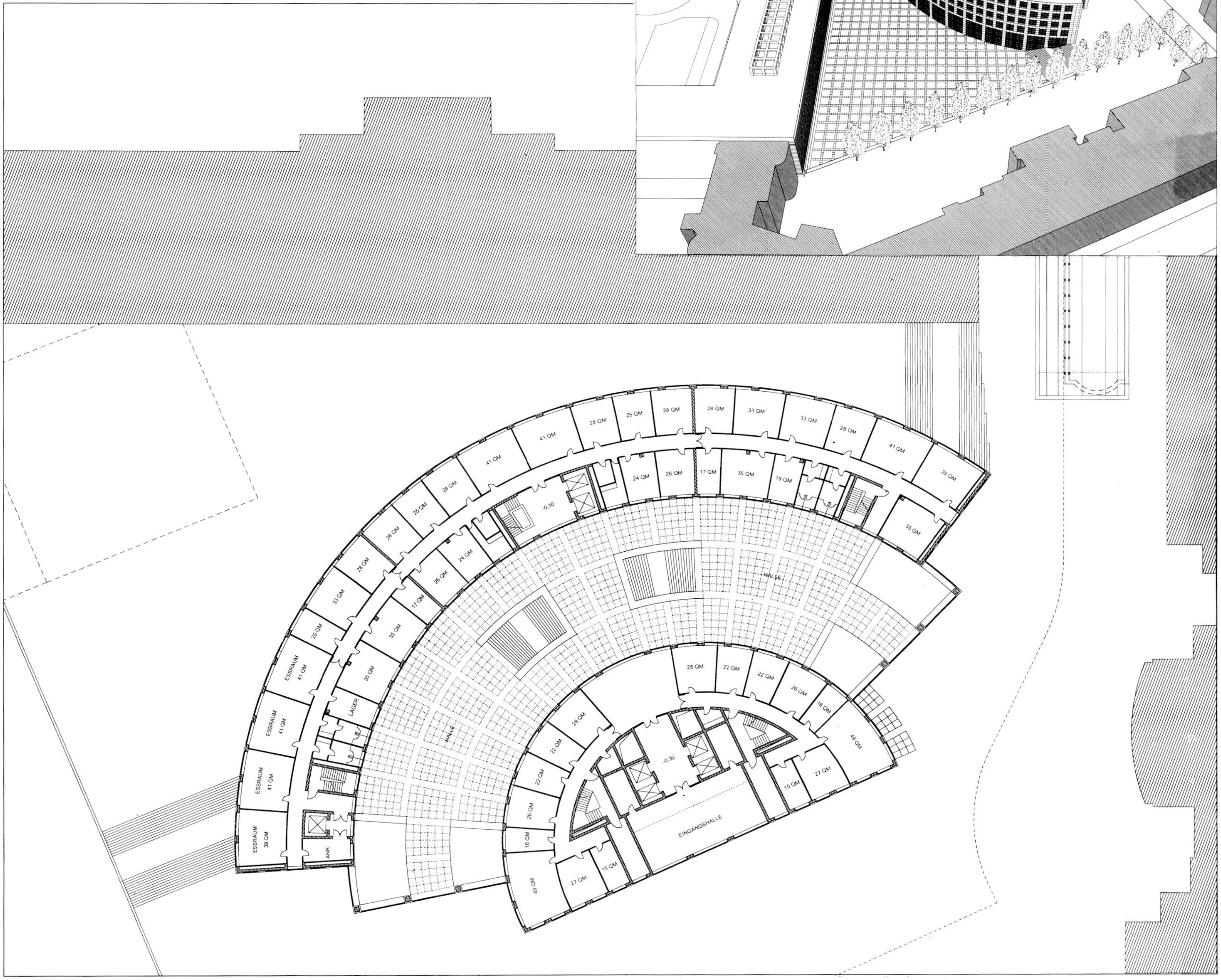

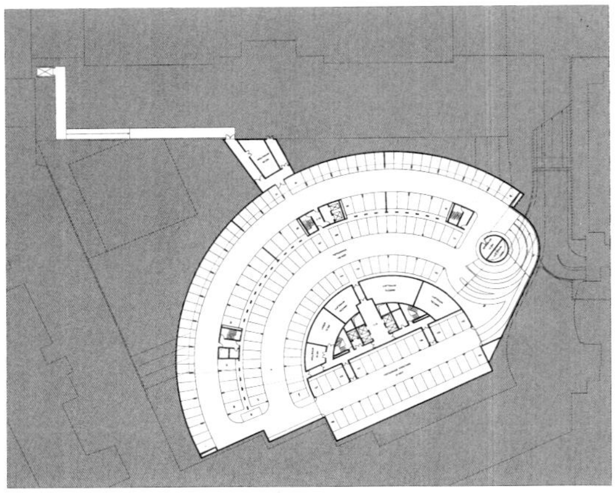

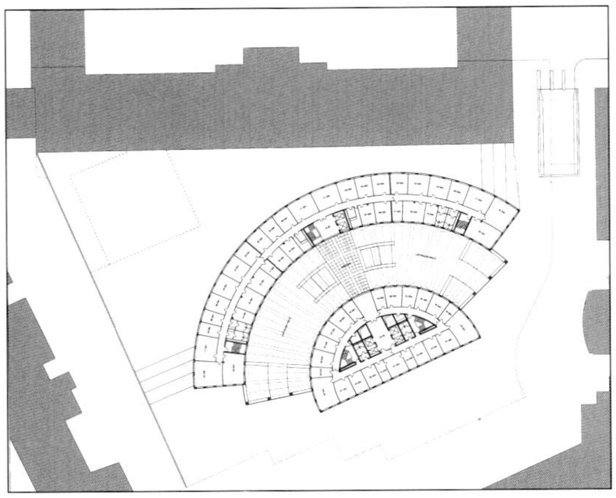

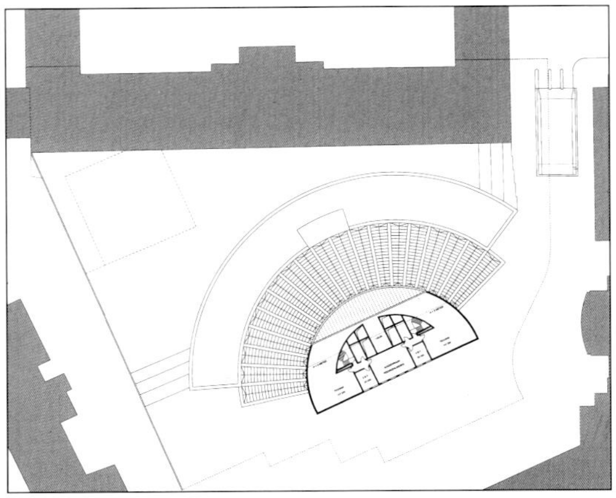

Gallery building: plans; elevations; section.

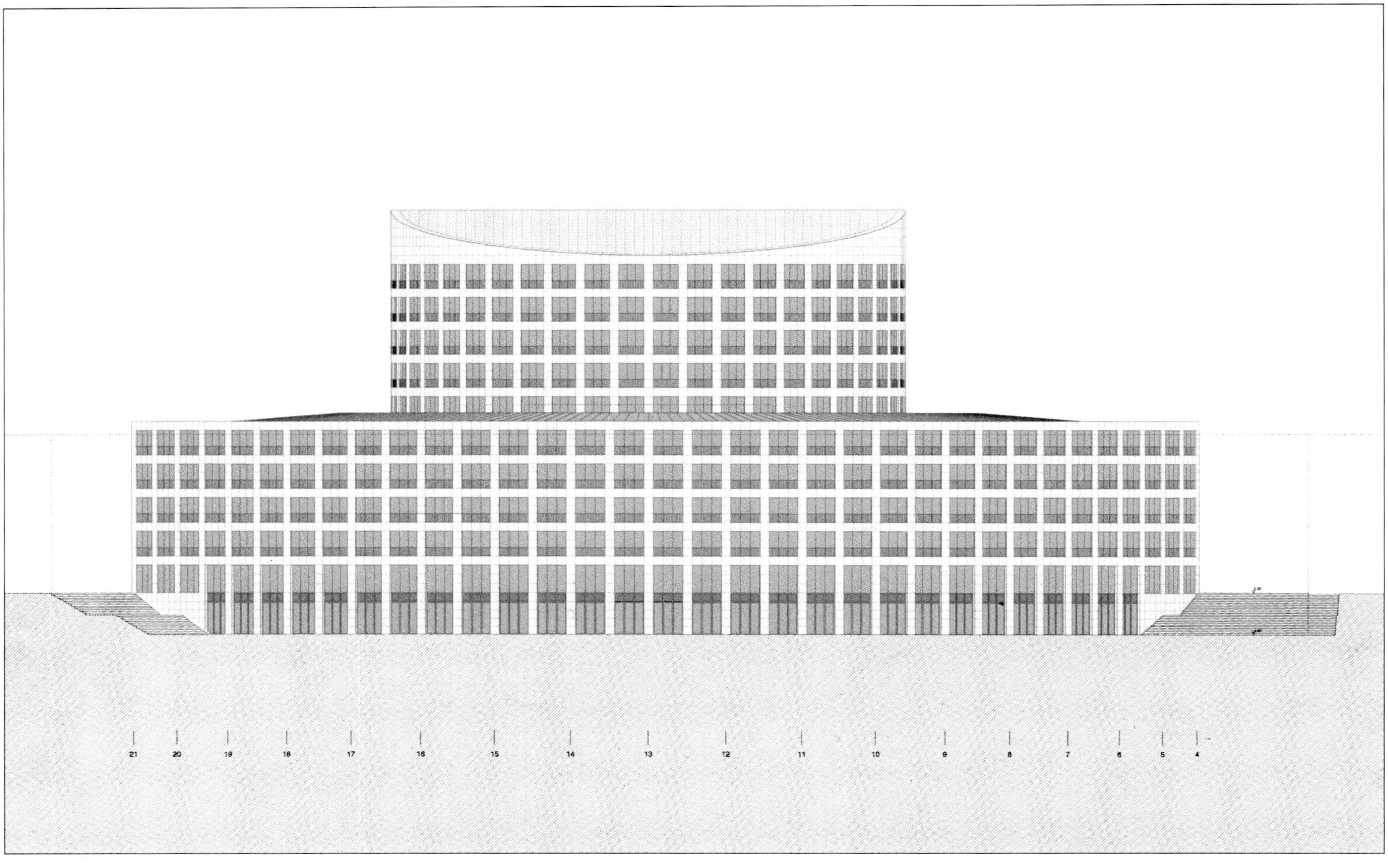

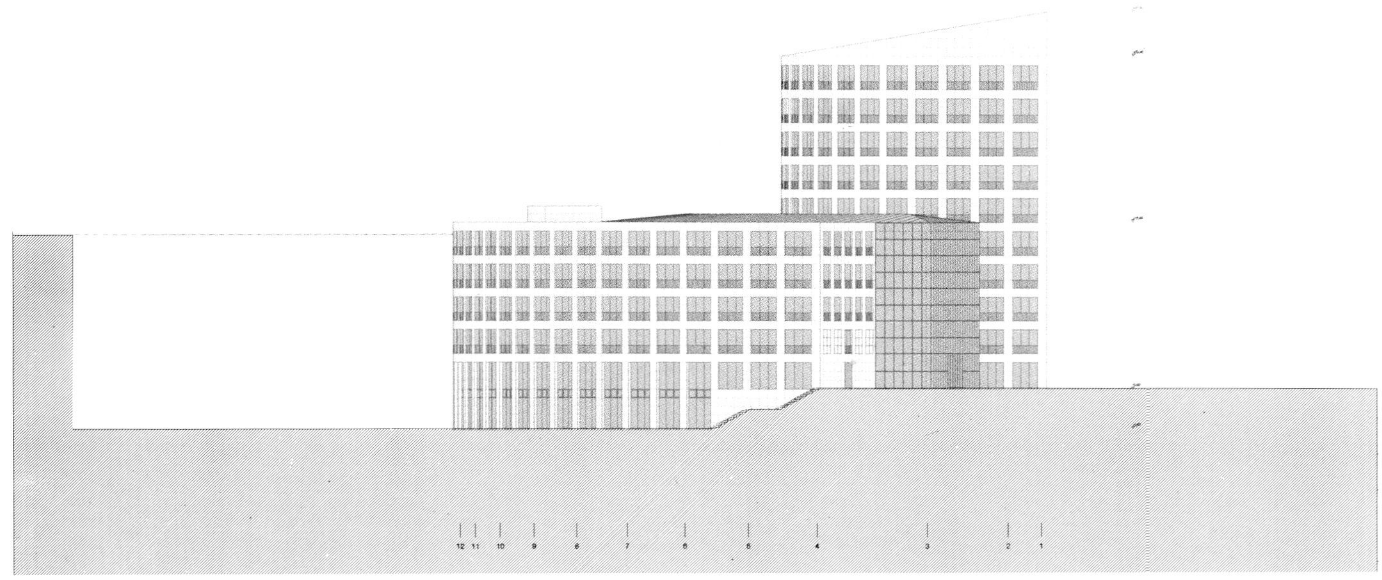
12 11 10 9 8 7 6 5 4 3 2 1

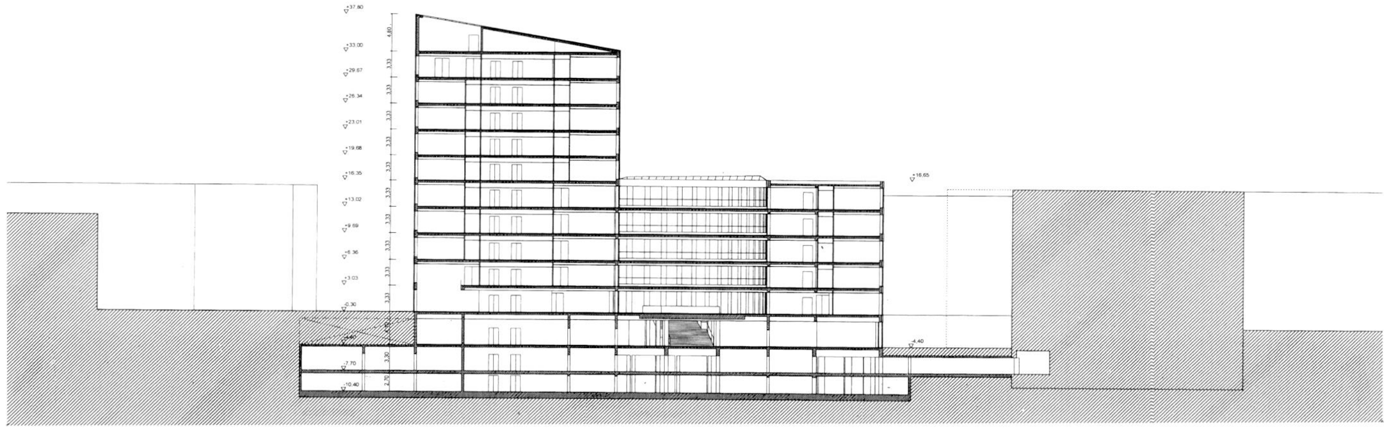

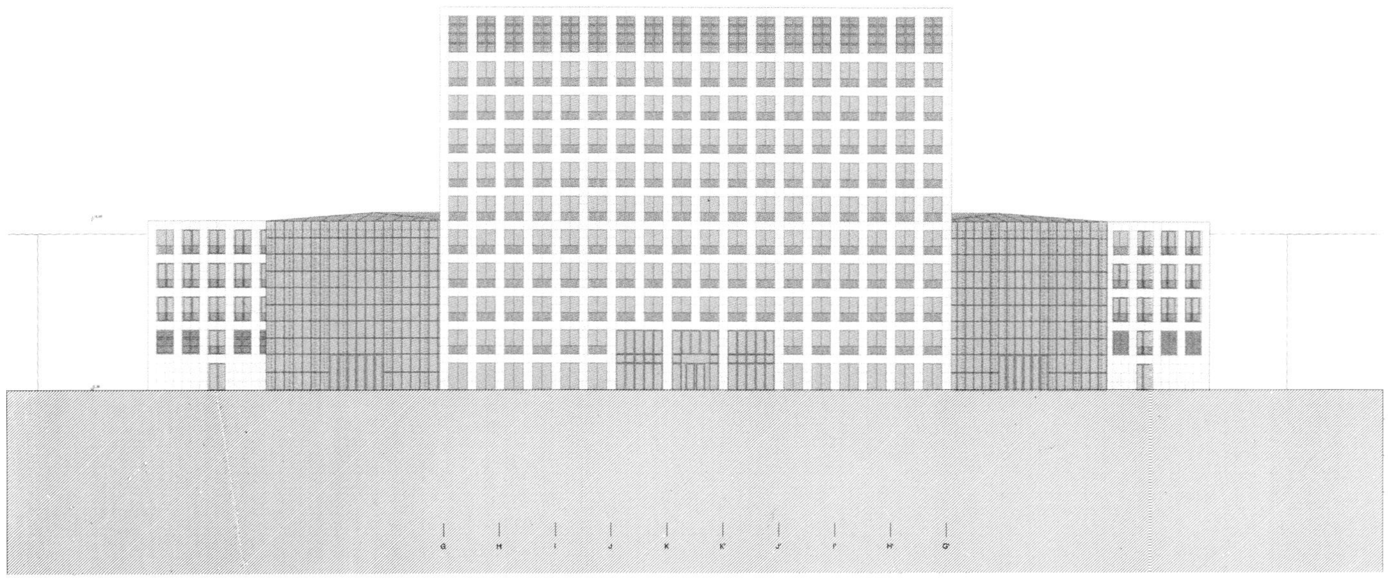

Computer renderings of interior spaces of the gallery building; plans of the Kunstpalast.

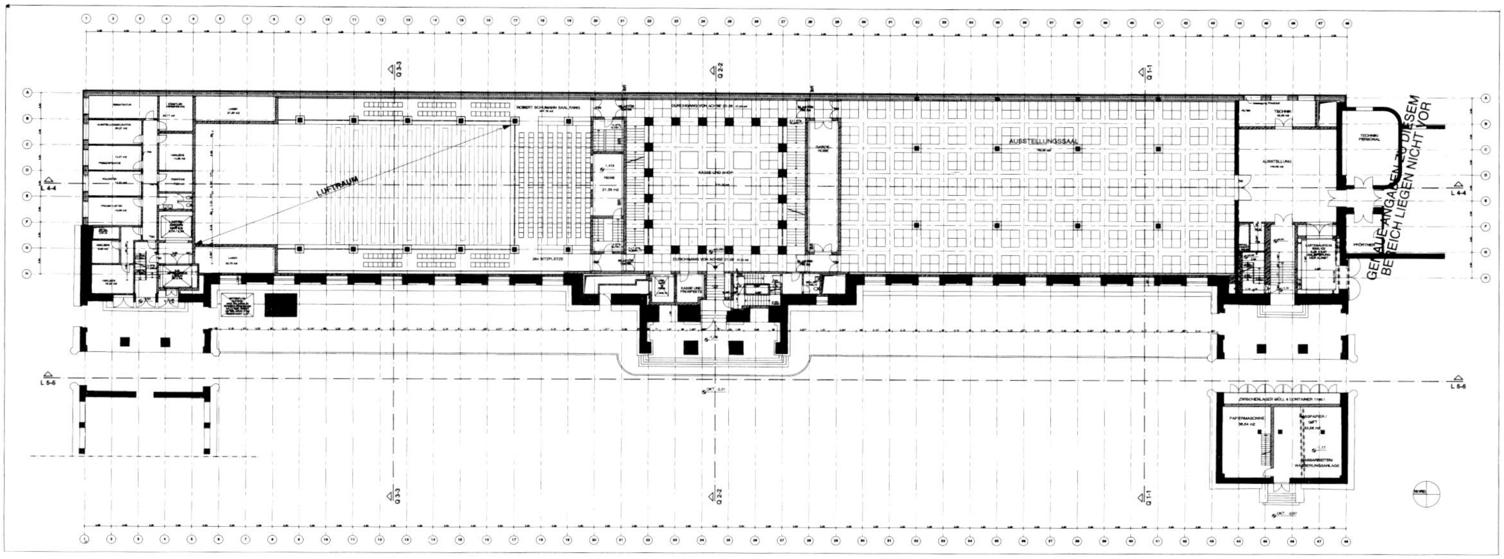
LUFTRAUM
AUSSTELLUNGSSAAL
GENAUE ANGABEN ZU DIESEM
BEREICH LIEGEN NICHT VOR

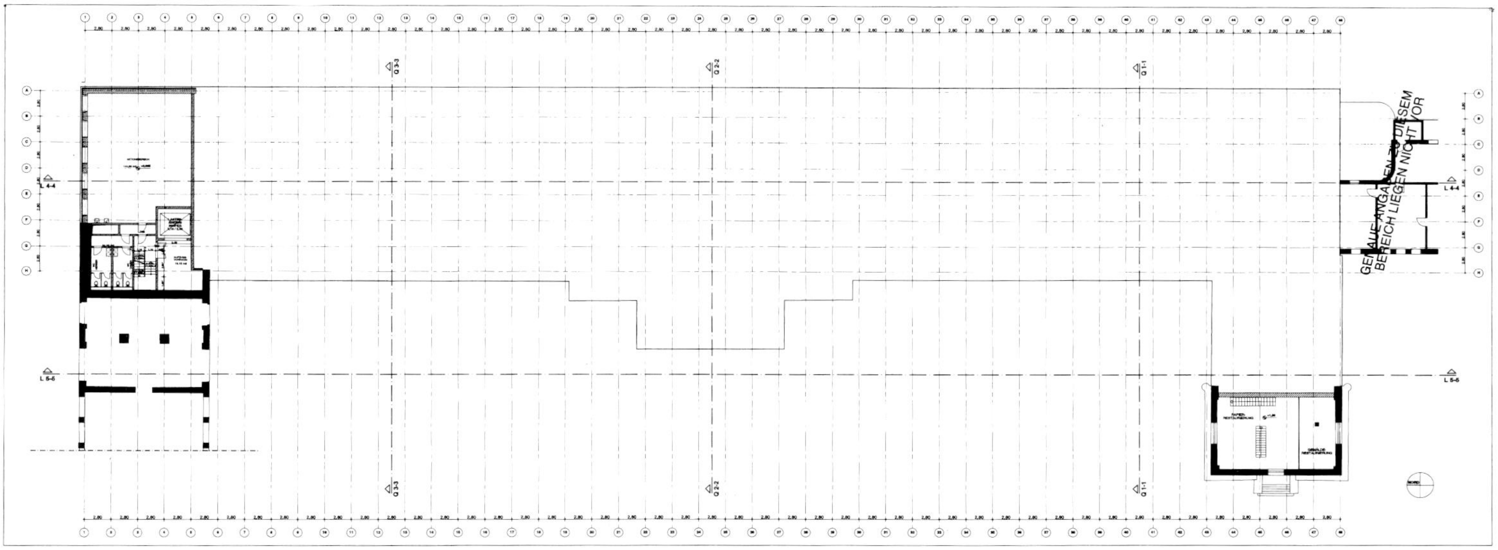
GENAUE ANGABEN ZU DIESEM
BEREICH LIEGEN NICHT VOR

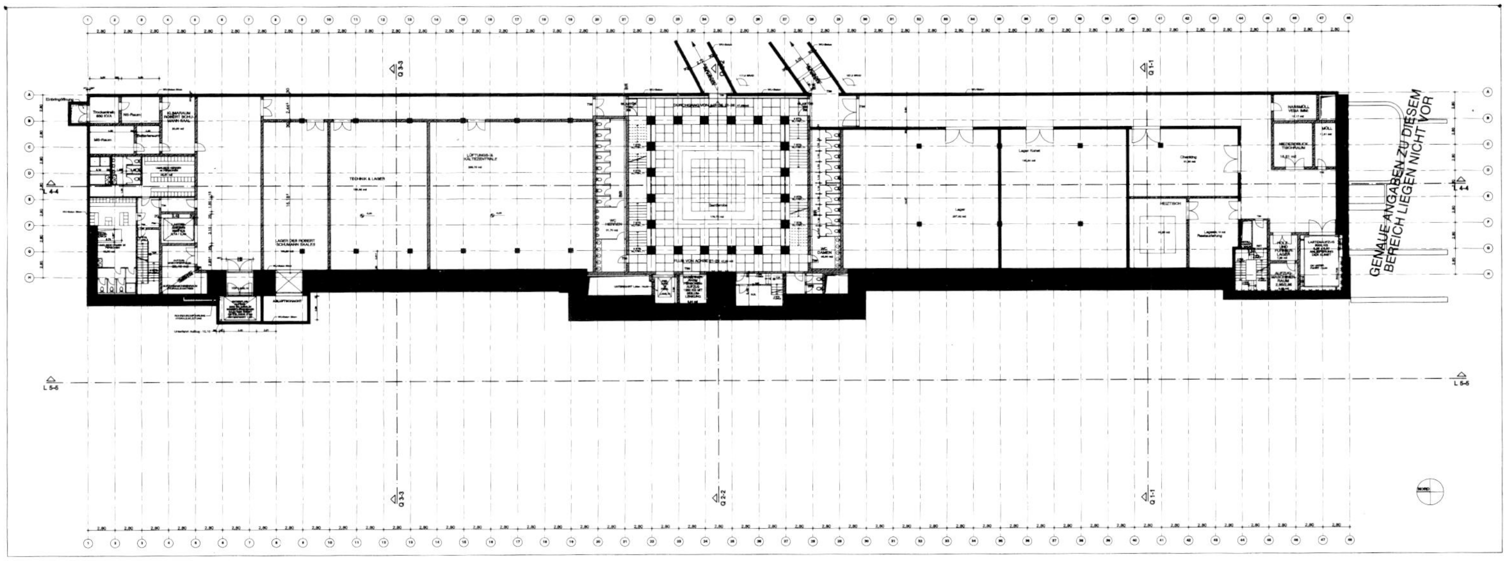
GENAUE ANGABEN ZU DIESEM
BEREICH LIEGEN NICHT VOR

Kunstpalast:
elevations;
sections.

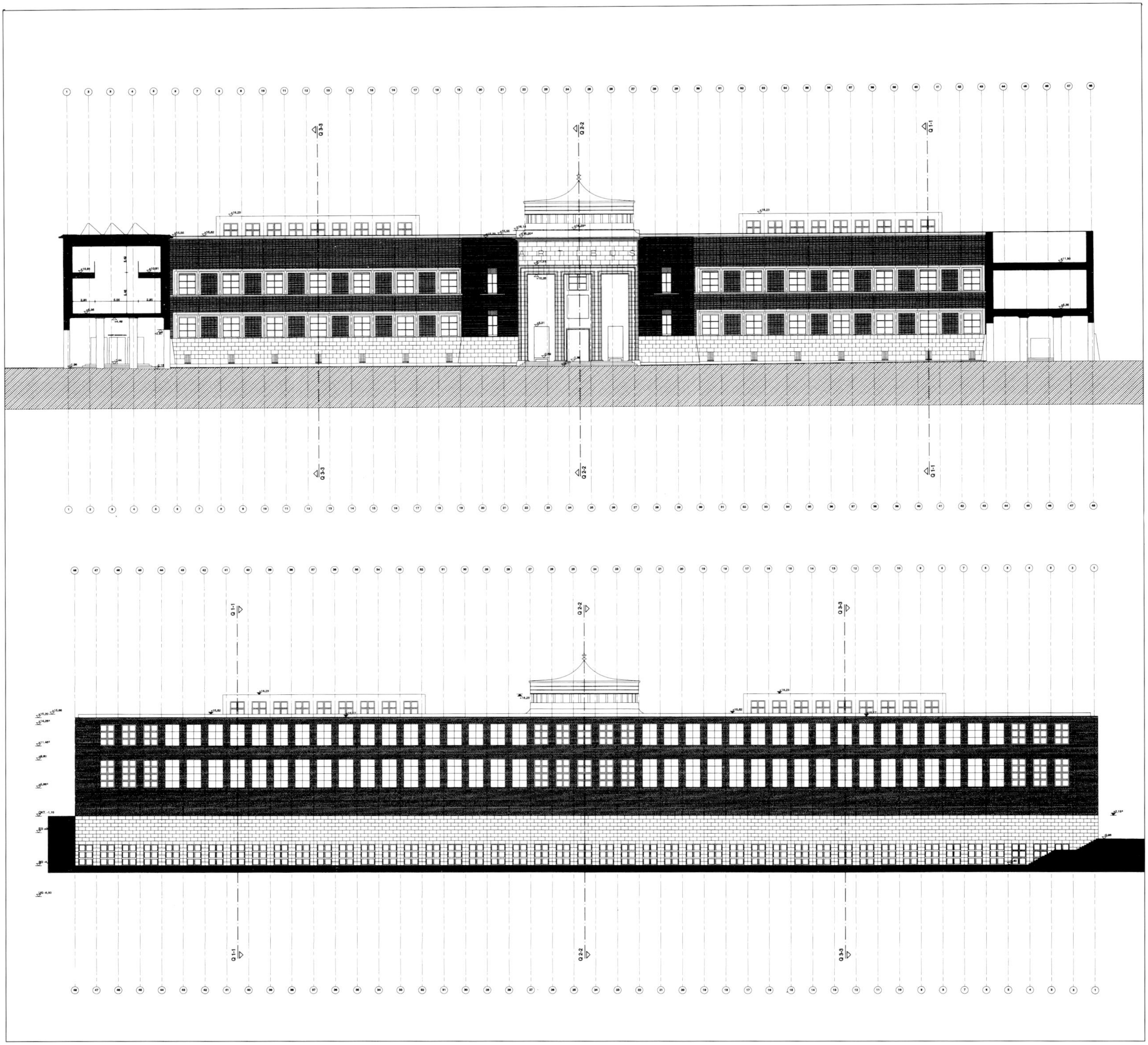

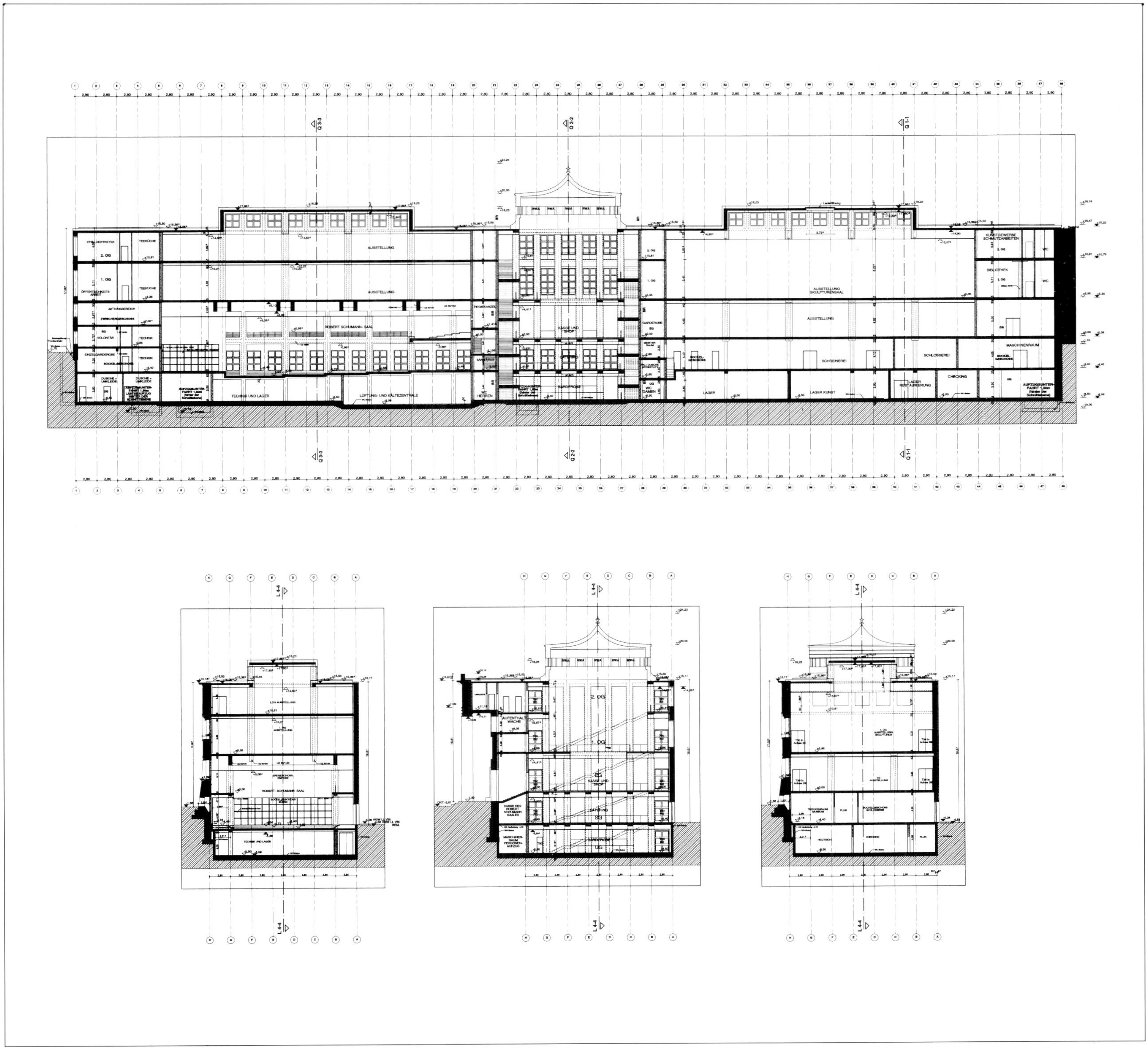

Feasibility Study for Gatehouses at Leipziger Platz (Entrance to Potsdamer Platz U-Bahn Station), Berlin, 1995

With: Stefan Vieths

Project team: Marvin Keim

The design calls for two pavilions reduced to their essential elements: a shaft for the elevator, three supports, and a roof slab. The buildings are homogeneously constructed of smooth, anthracite-gray exposed concrete, with floor slabs of concrete as well. The unpretentious form of the buildings corresponds to functional necessities. The similarity of material and form lends them a sculptural quality, reflecting their urbanistic significance as gatehouses. The proposal calls for fluorescent lights in the area around the openings to the underground passage, thus staging the transition from the subterranean to the above-ground realm. In this way, the buildings become light sculptures by night. The playful transformation of a simple form into an art object is continued in the band of brass letters running around the edge of the roof slab.

Model views.

Opposite:
Perspectives;
ground-level plan.

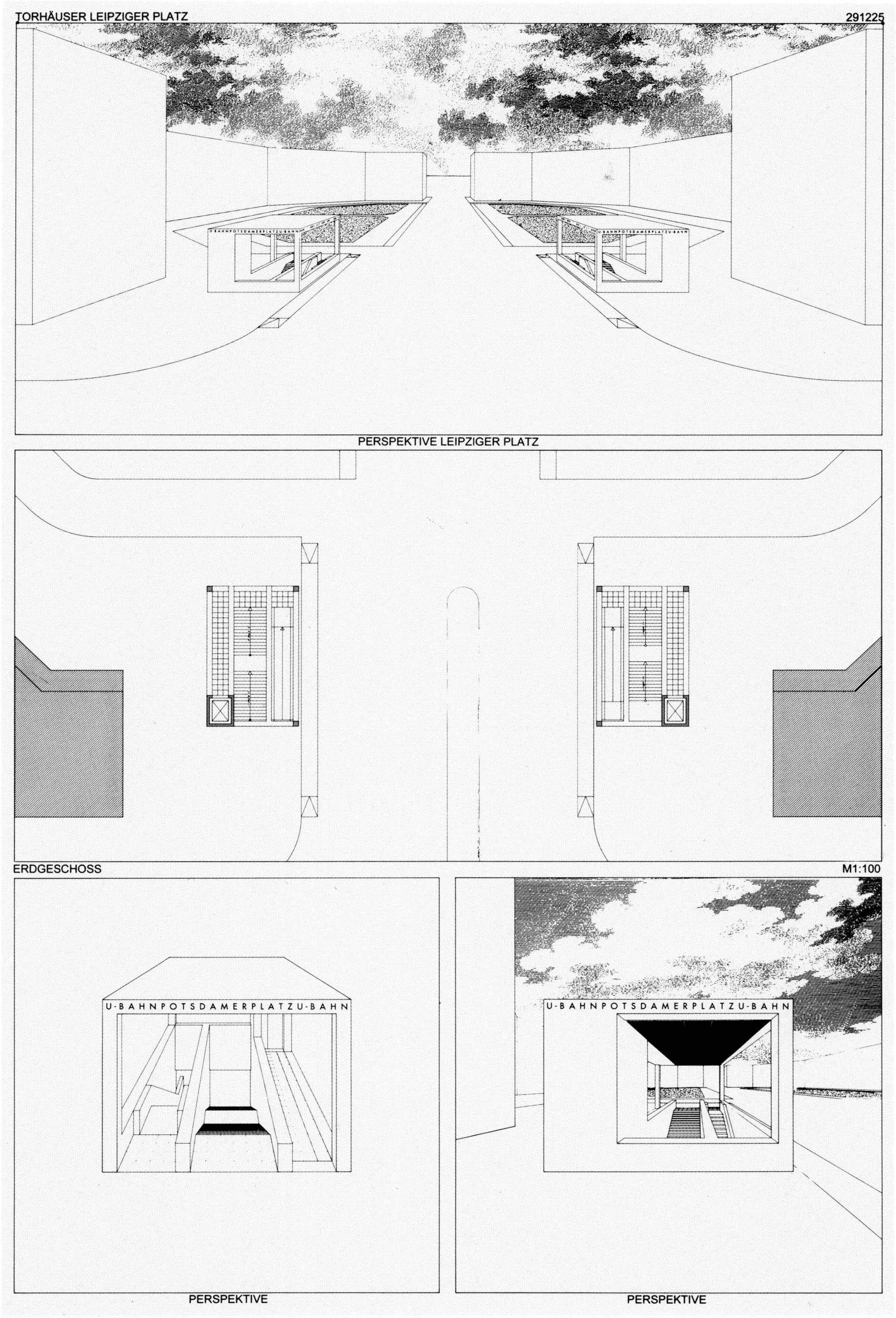
TORHÄUSER LEIPZIGER PLATZ
291225
PERSPEKTIVE LEIPZIGER PLATZ
ERDGESCHOSS
M1:100
U-BAHNPOTSDAMERPLATZU-BAHN
PERSPEKTIVE
U-BAHNPOTSDAMERPLATZU-BAHN
PERSPEKTIVE

Sections; plans.

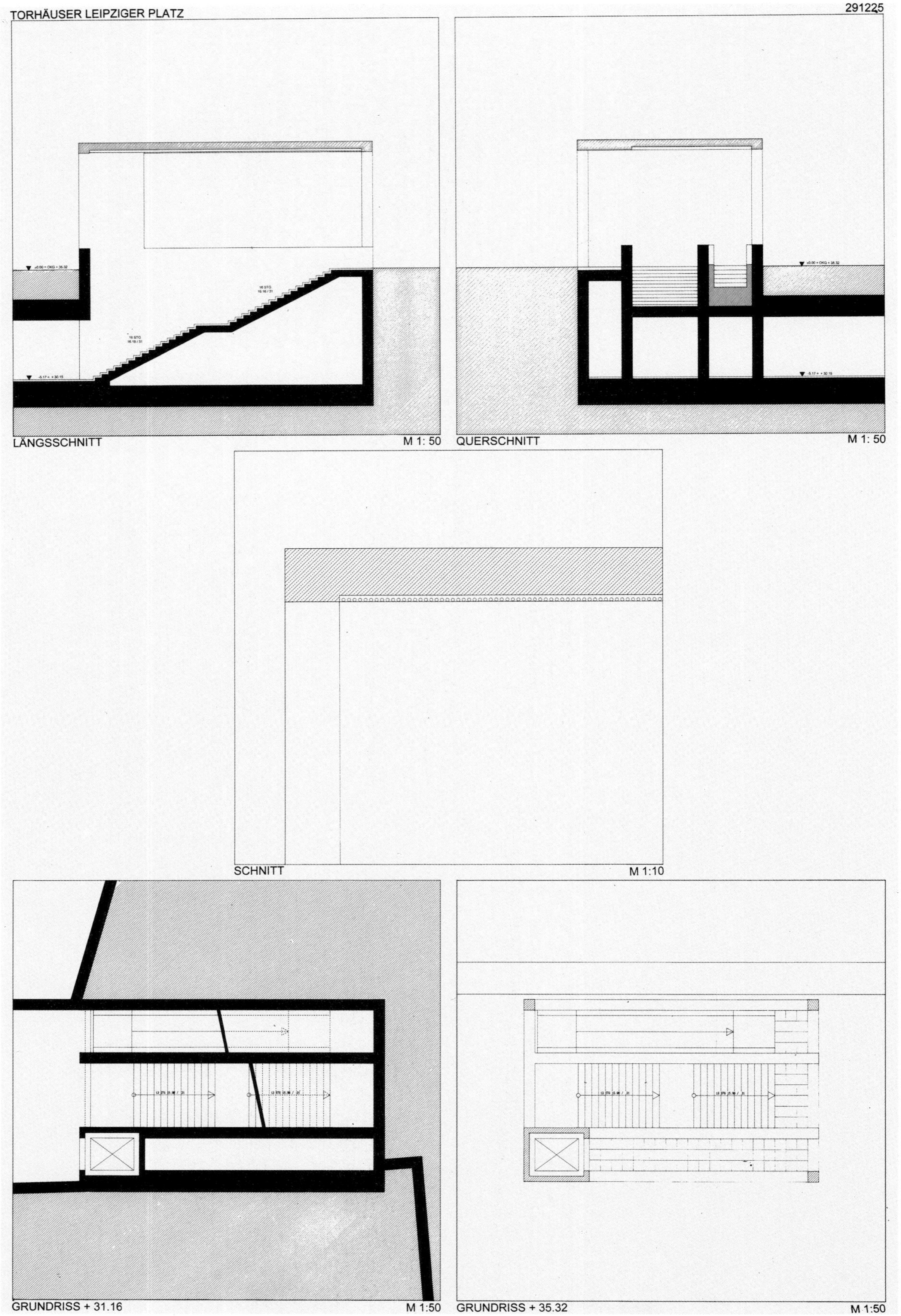

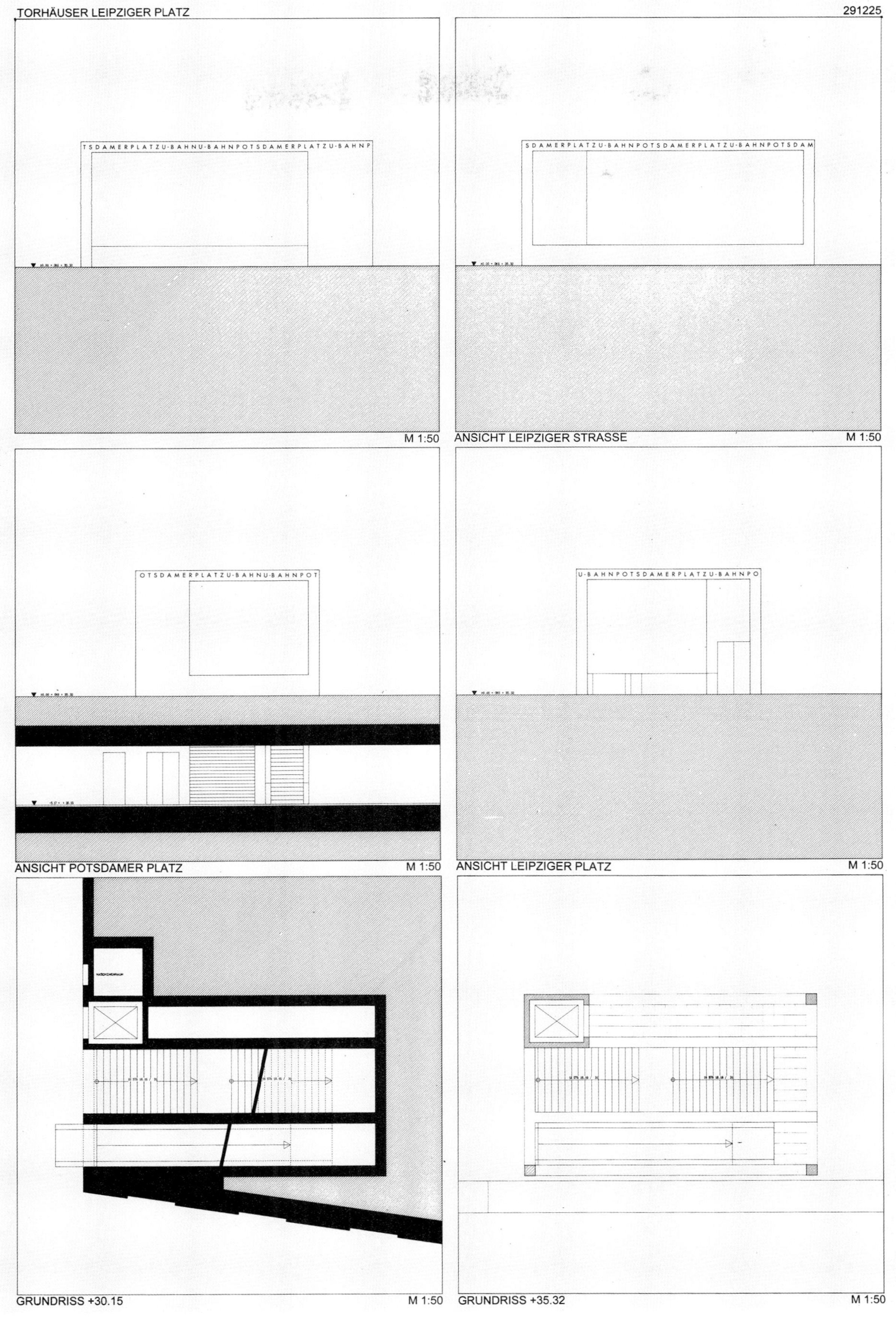

Elevations; plans.

Feasibility Study for Postcenter at Münsterplatz, Bonn, 1995

With: Stefan Vieths

Project team: Marvin Keim, Michael Garçon

The competition area, a largely built-up block in the center of the old city of Bonn, marks the northwest edge of the Münsterplatz. The existing buildings consist of freestanding, typologically diverse structures from different epochs, including the Fürstenbergpalais, which dominates the Münsterplatz side of the block. The objective of the competition was to complete and restructure the block as a whole.

The design concept for the "Fürstenberg passages" is derived from the collagelike structure of the existing buildings, including post office buildings from the nineteenth century, the Münsterschule, corner construction on Vivatgasse, and the Fürstenbergpalais. These existing structures are supplemented by two freestanding buildings—an angle shape and a stepped pyramid—and connected with each other by a system of passages, resulting in a sequence of volumes and spaces that suggest a "city within a city."

The angle-shaped corner structure along the edge of the block, though conceived as a freestanding building, clearly subordinates itself to the Fürstenbergpalais on the facade toward Münsterplatz, forming as it were the

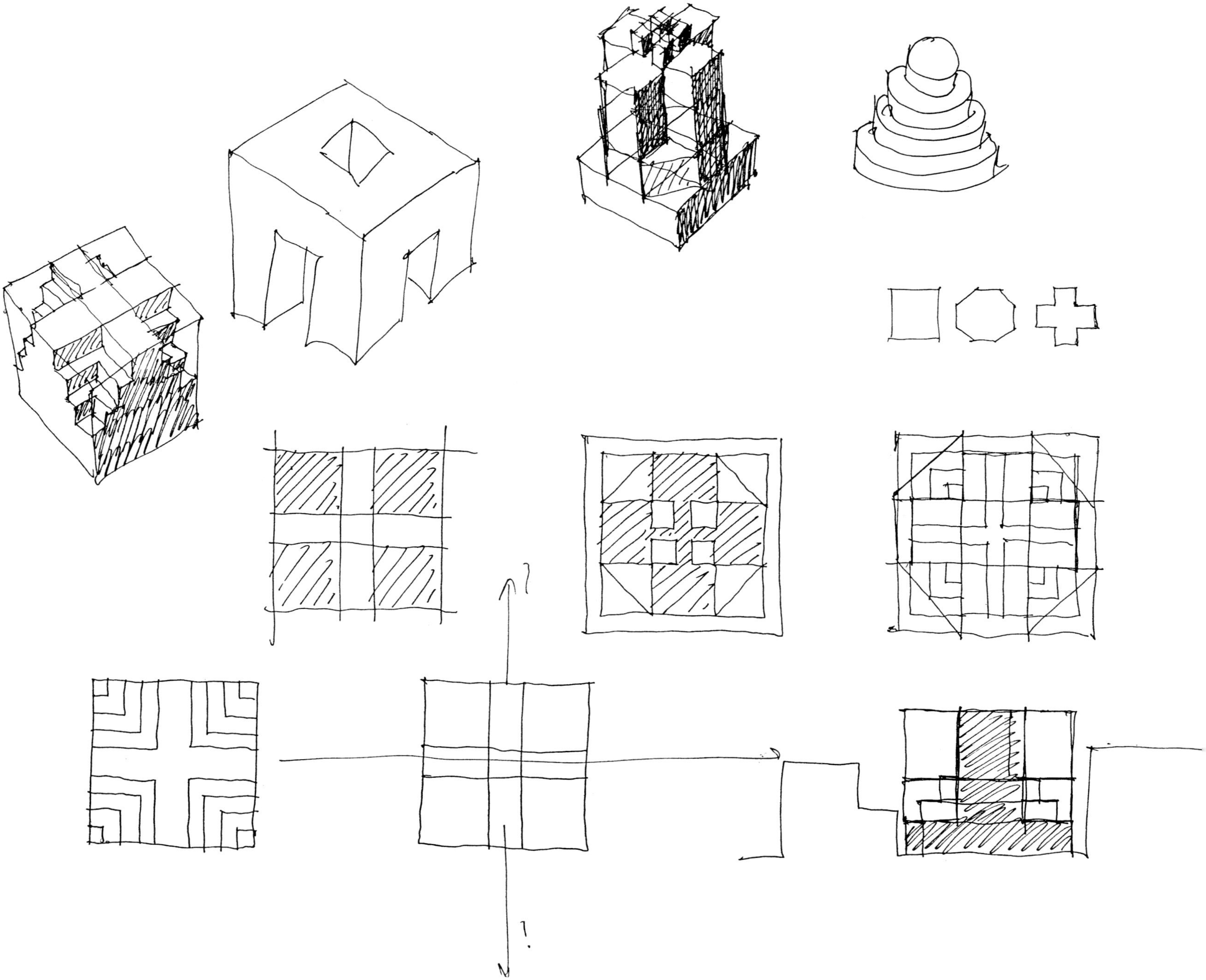

left wing of the Palais. The stepped pyramid inserted into the almost square interior courtyard of the block establishes a center and a clear system of order for the patchworklike structure of the existing buildings; at the same time, however, it leaves the existing historic buildings intact and underlines their significance with a respectfully receding form. The goal of the conception is to conceive old and new as elements of equal importance and in this way to create a new urban unity. The ground level and first upper story accommodate trade and restaurants, while the other floors contain offices.

FÜRSTENBERGPASSAGE BONN

PROF. O. M. UNGERS

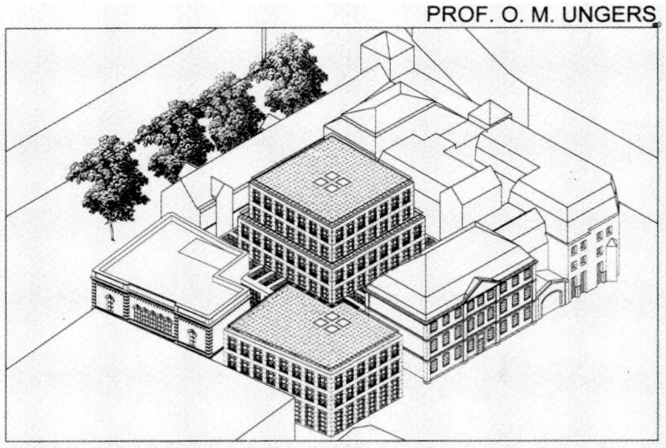

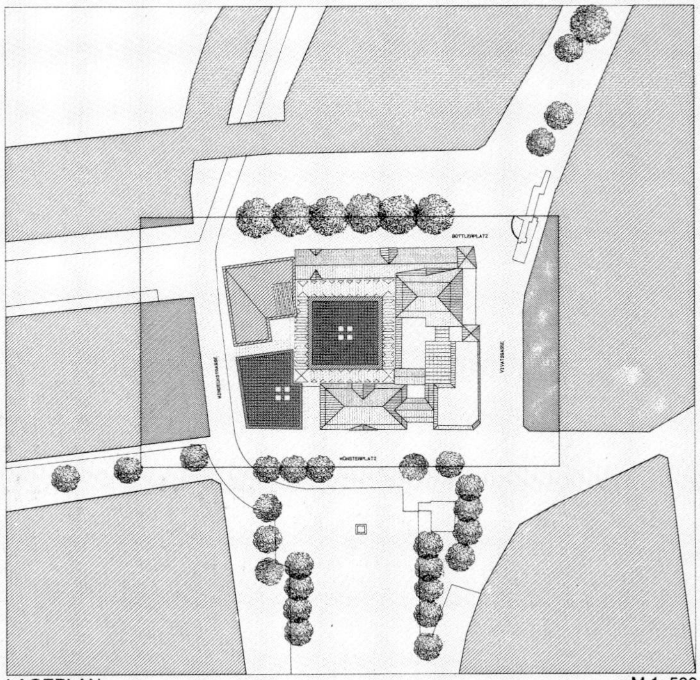

LAGEPLAN

M 1: 500

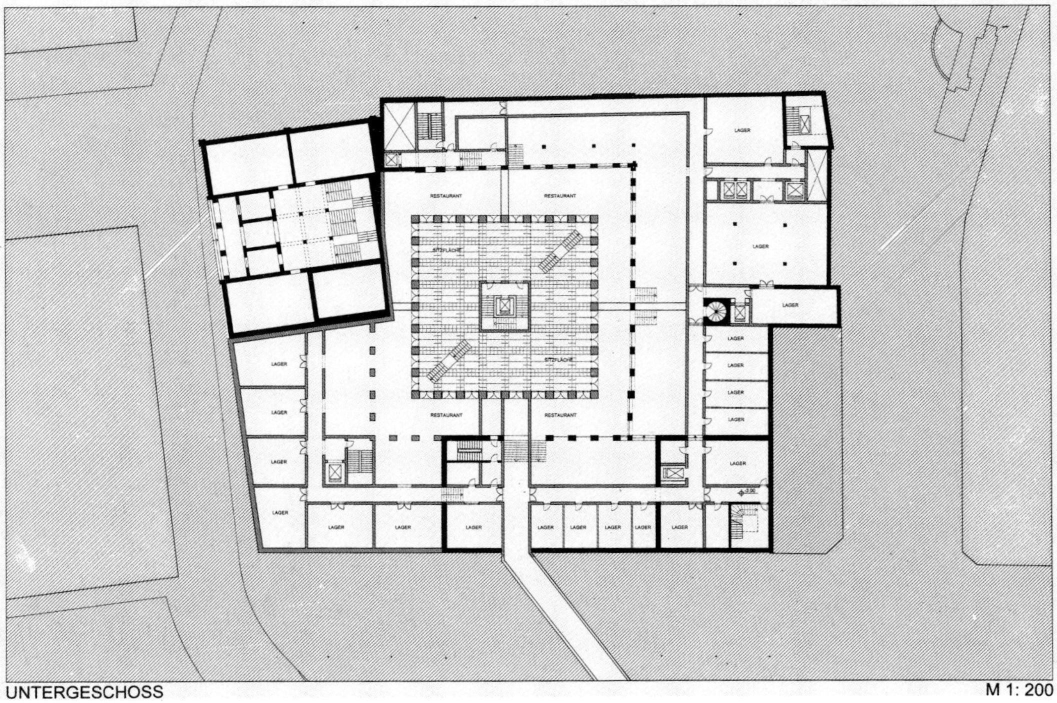

UNTERGESCHOSS

M 1: 200

Sketches; perspective; site plan; basement-level plan.

Plans; sketch; elevation.

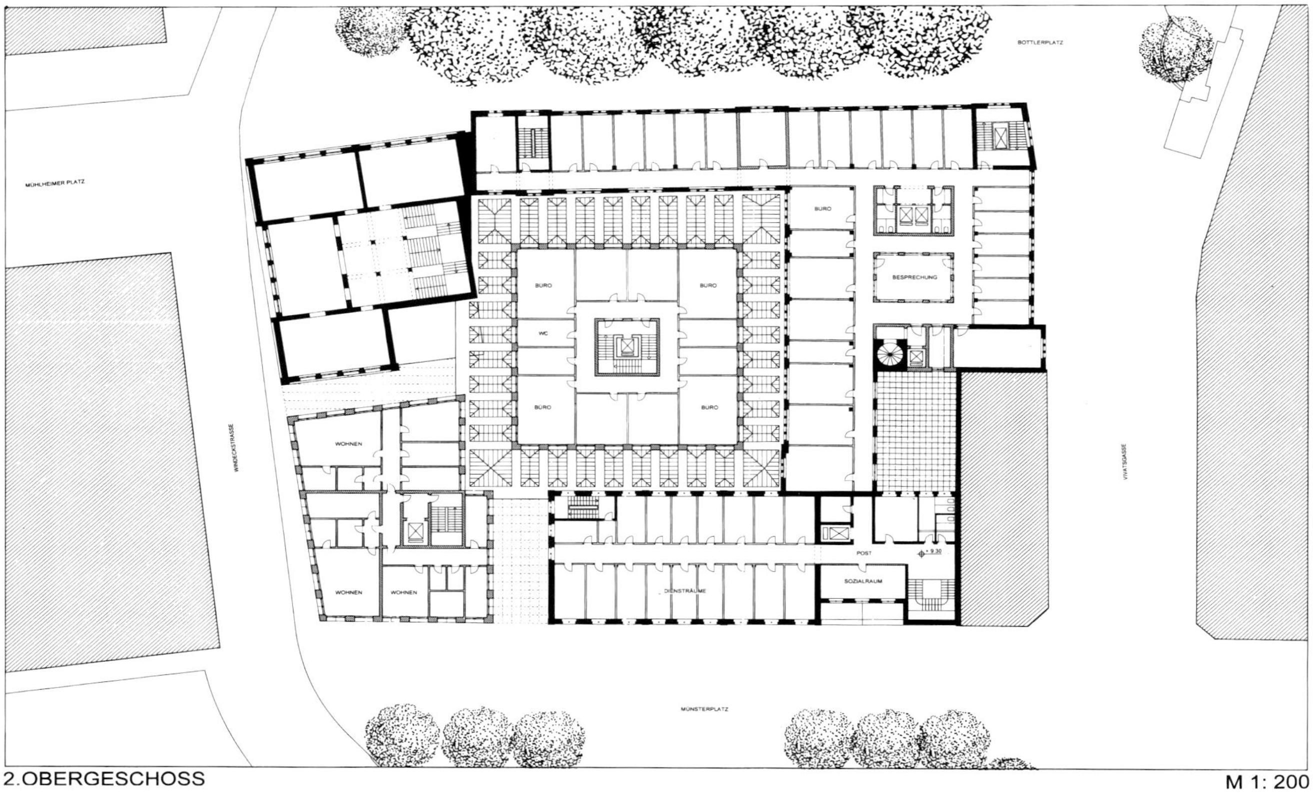

2.OBERGESCHOSS M 1: 200

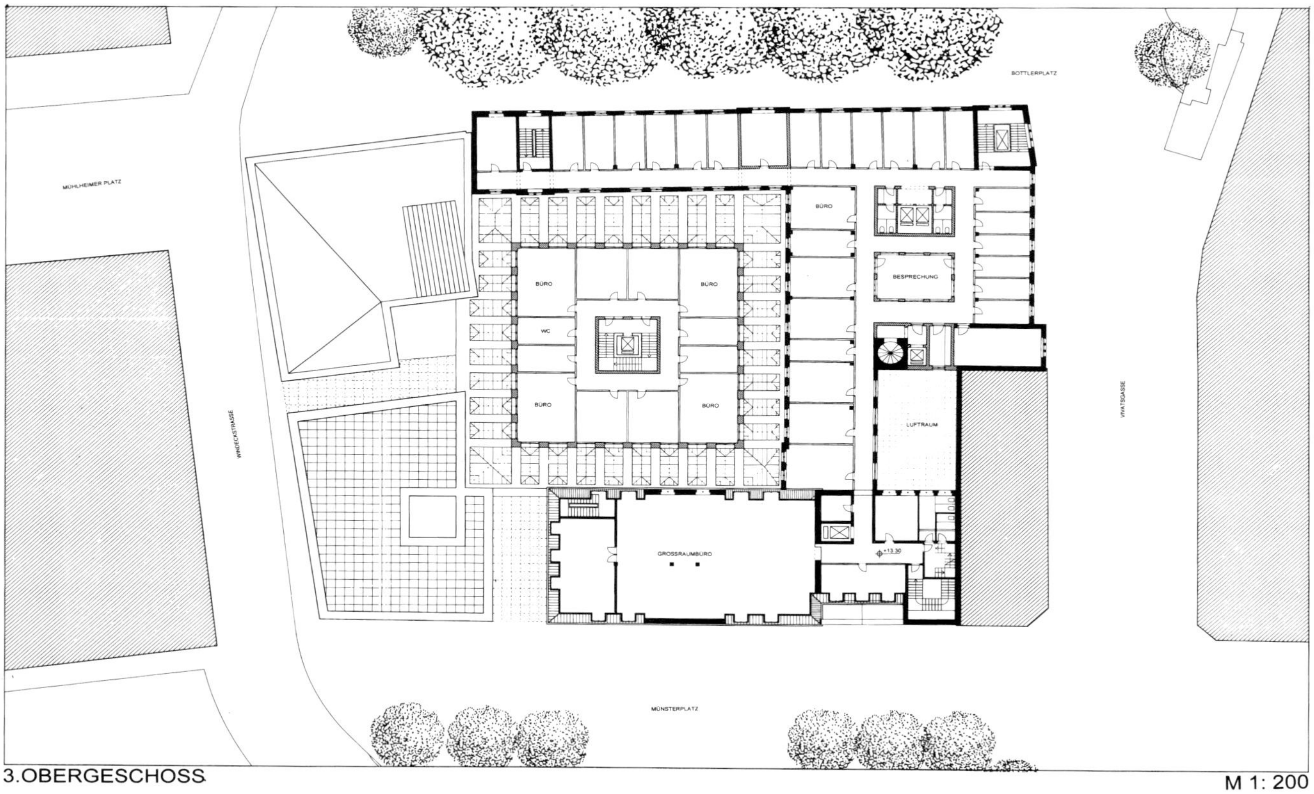

3.OBERGESCHOSS M 1: 200

FÜRSTENBERGPASSAGE BONN PROF. O. M. UNGERS

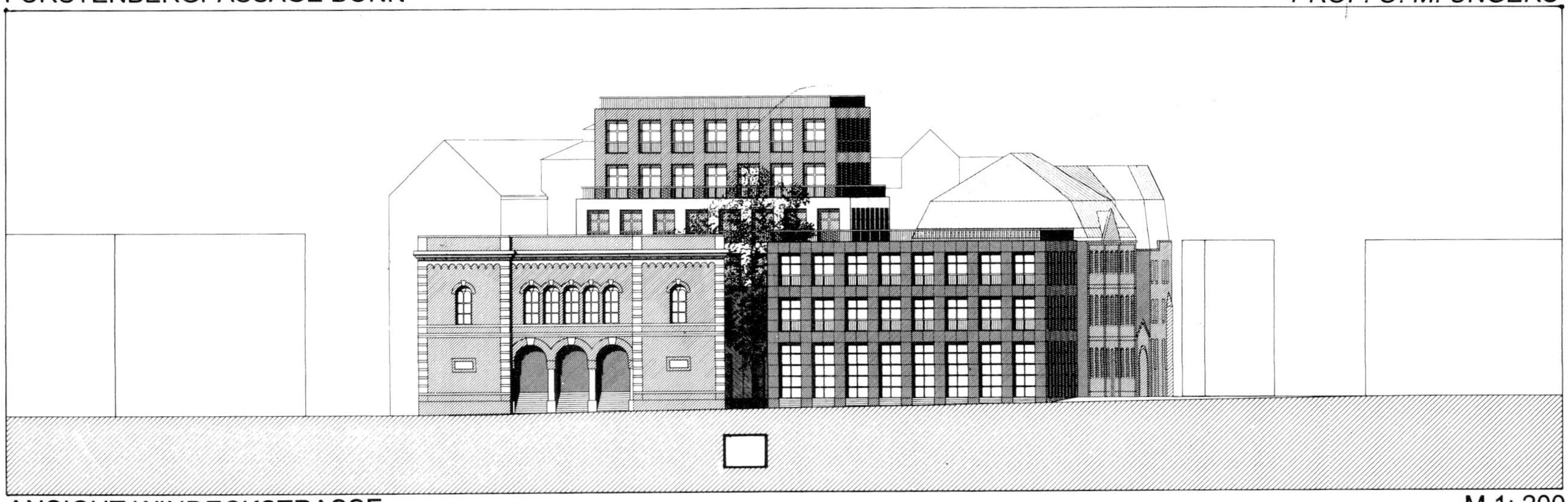

ANSICHT WINDECKSTRASSE M 1: 200

Section; plans.

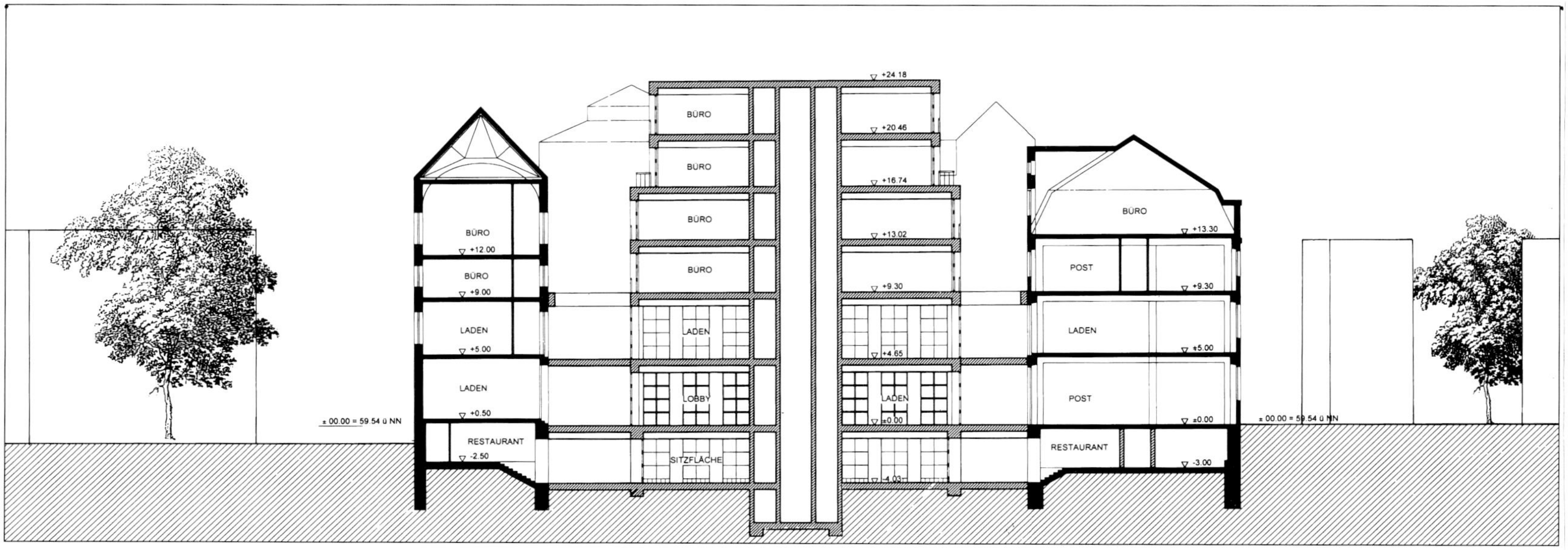

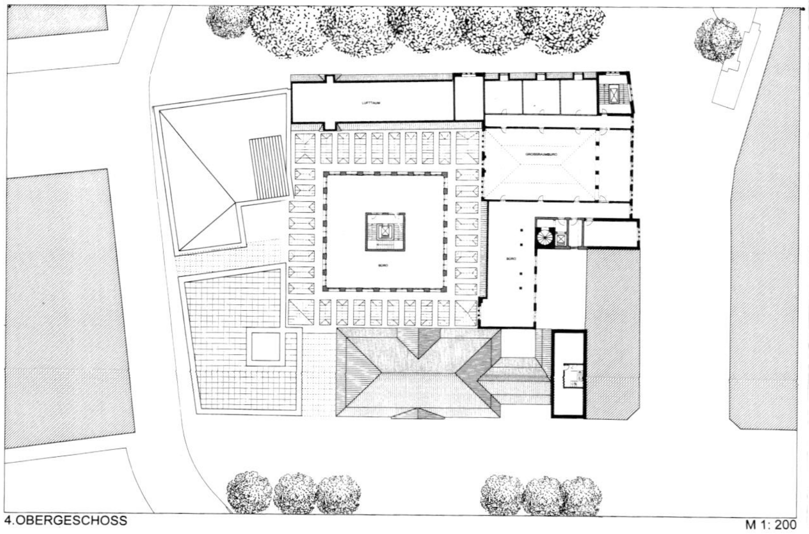

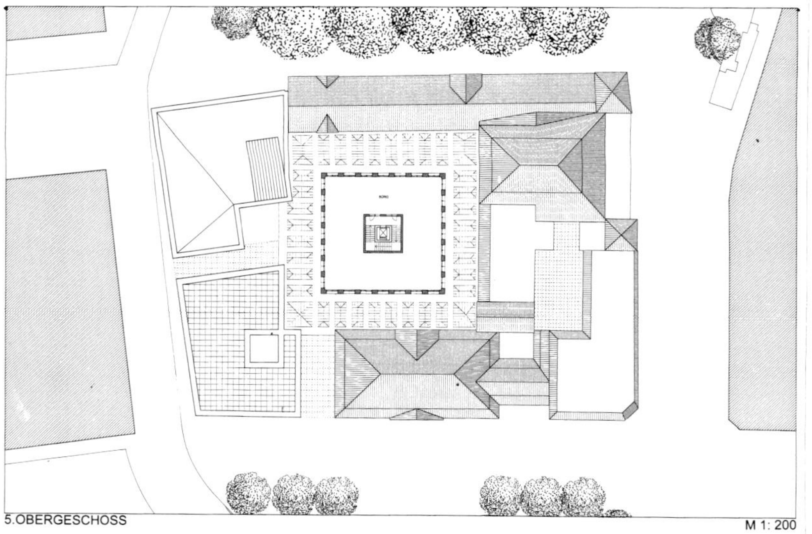

Competition Design for Federal Foreign Office, Berlin, 1996

With: Stefan Vieths

Project team: Marvin Keim

The new Federal Foreign Office occupies a pivotal site in the urban structure of the historic center of Berlin. The competition area is bounded to the west by the park area along Kurstrasse and to the east by the former Schlossplatz, while the north edge of the site adjoins the Werderscher Markt, where the Bauakademie is to be reconstructed. With the Bauakademie and the Friedrichswerdersche Kirche, classical and Gothic revival architecture once defined the urban character of the historic Werderscher Markt. In order to establish clear spatial contours in relation to these significant urban spaces, a closed city block is proposed in accord with current urban planning. The Foreign Office is conceived as an interior courtyard complex opening toward the Werderscher Markt. The Werderscher Markt thus becomes not only the address but also the spatial point of reference for the new Foreign Office. In the tradition of the Forum Fridericianum, the square is transformed into a place where culture (the Bauakademie), religion (the Friedrichswerdersche Kirche), and politics (the new Foreign Office) are concentrated and incorporated into an urban ensemble.

The reference to Enlightenment traditions also raises the central question of the competition, namely the approach to be taken to the monolithic monumentality of the former Reichsbank building, which has now

Sketches.

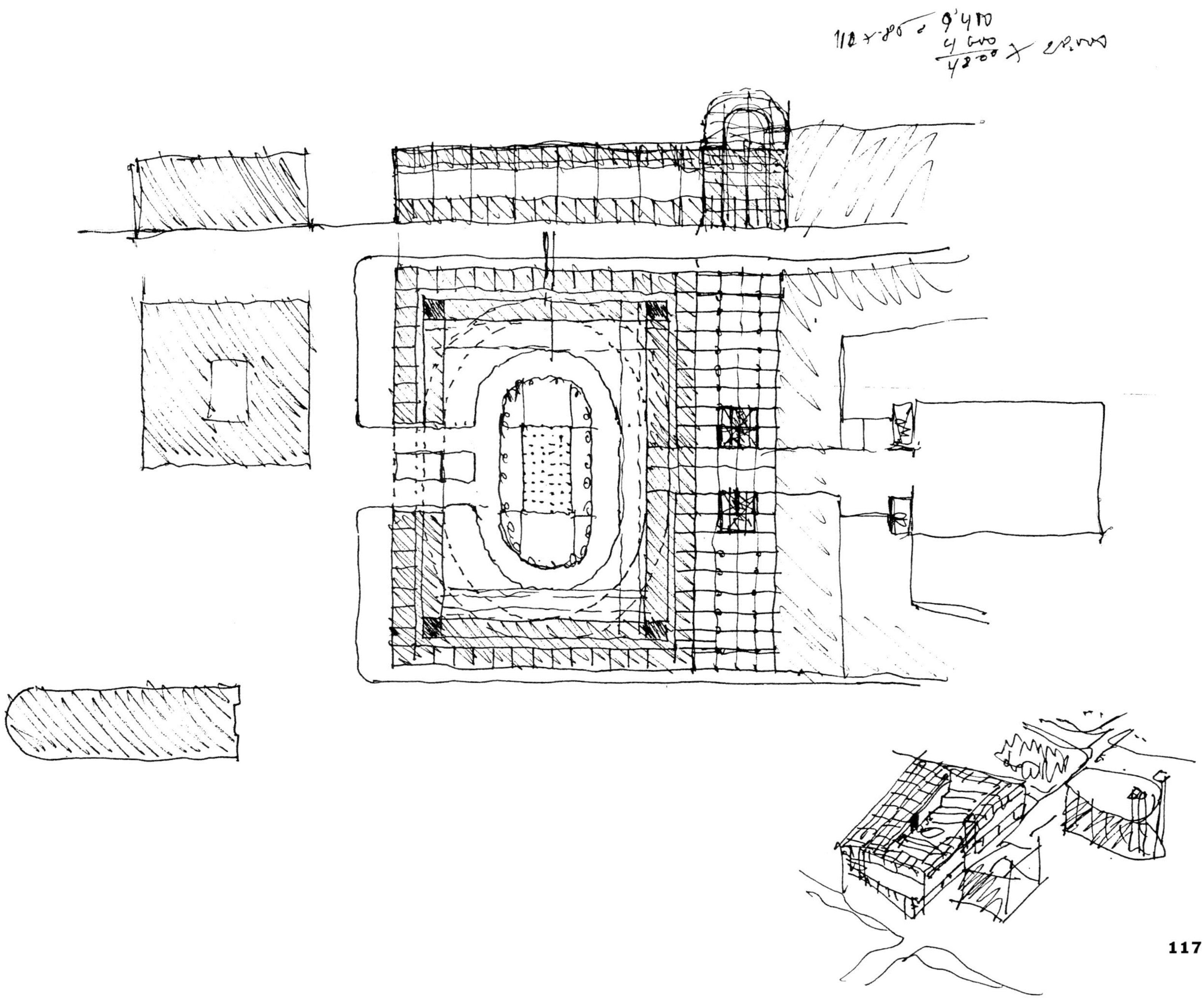

Sketches.

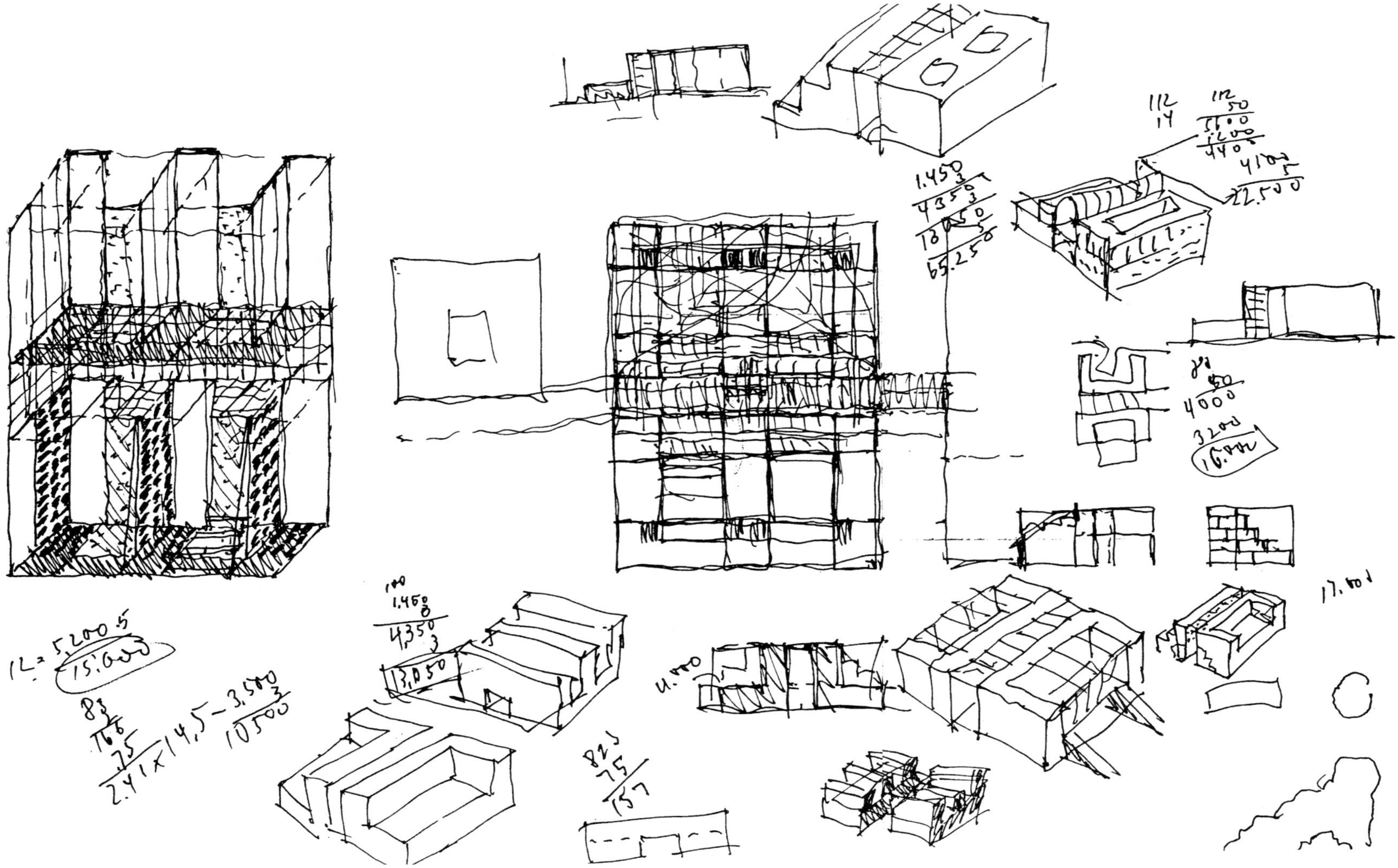

become the main building of the Foreign Office. Put more precisely, it is the question of political self-representation in a reunified Germany. The proposed design answers this question by relativizing the existing building, that is, reducing it to the status of a functional building through the addition of an entrance courtyard. The main facade of the Foreign Office will no longer be the oversized pillared colonnade of the former Reichsbank but the new driveway, whose formal language alludes to the Reichsbank design of Mies van der Rohe and therewith to the other, modern, enlightened tradition of this place. Corresponding materials are part of the design, with the closed surfaces in light travertine and the flush windows in natural anodized aluminum. The old and new buildings are connected by a glass hall that serves as the actual monumental entrance area with the main stairway but that can also accommodate receptions and the like. A large roof terrace offers a panoramic view of the historic center of Berlin.

The building shows a simple configuration of double rows of offices with a center-to-center distance of 1.35 meters. The four above-ground stories accommodate the three divisions of the Foreign Office, which are horizontally organized. The areas open to the public (passport office and information office) are located on the ground level of the wing toward the Werderscher Markt and are entered from the front side. These entrances are thus within viewing range of the central security office, positioned in the driveway of the monumental courtyard as an independent volume. The driveway continues over the courtyard and is thus completely controlled and protected, despite the approach from the Werderscher Markt. The basement level accommodates the library, which is entered from the glass hall. The book stacks and reading area are on a single level; two atriums provide the reading zones with natural illumination. The entrance to the underground parking garage is located on Kurstrasse, with the areas under historic preservation remaining untouched. If necessary, the roof terrace can be remodeled to provide additional office space.

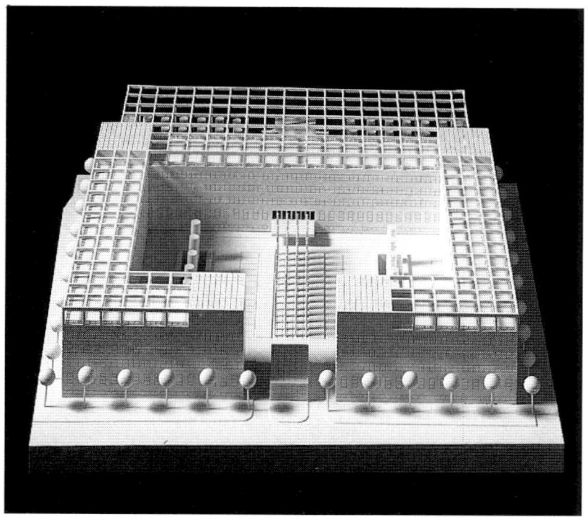

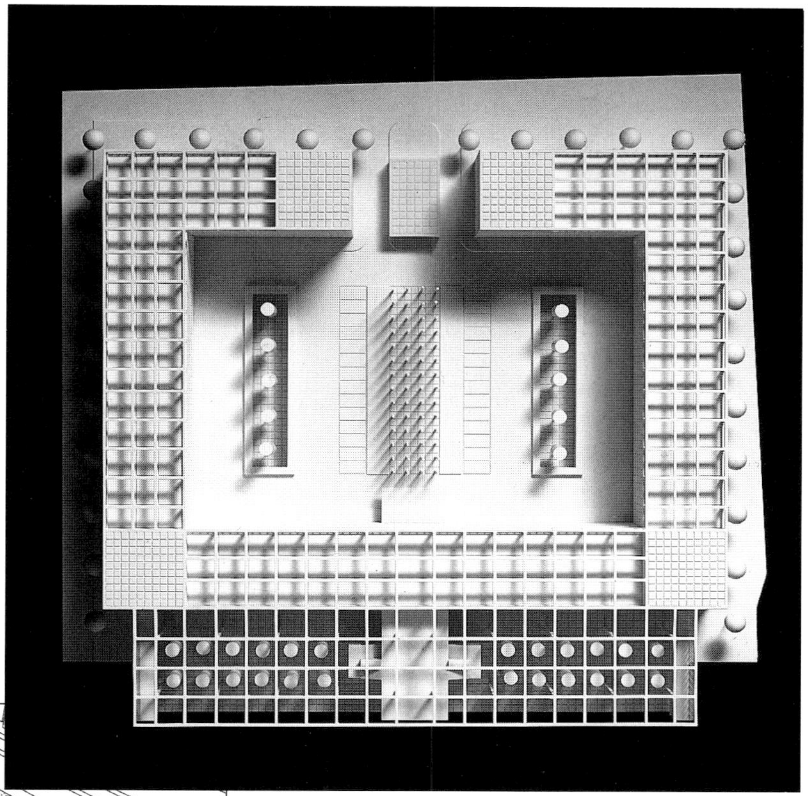

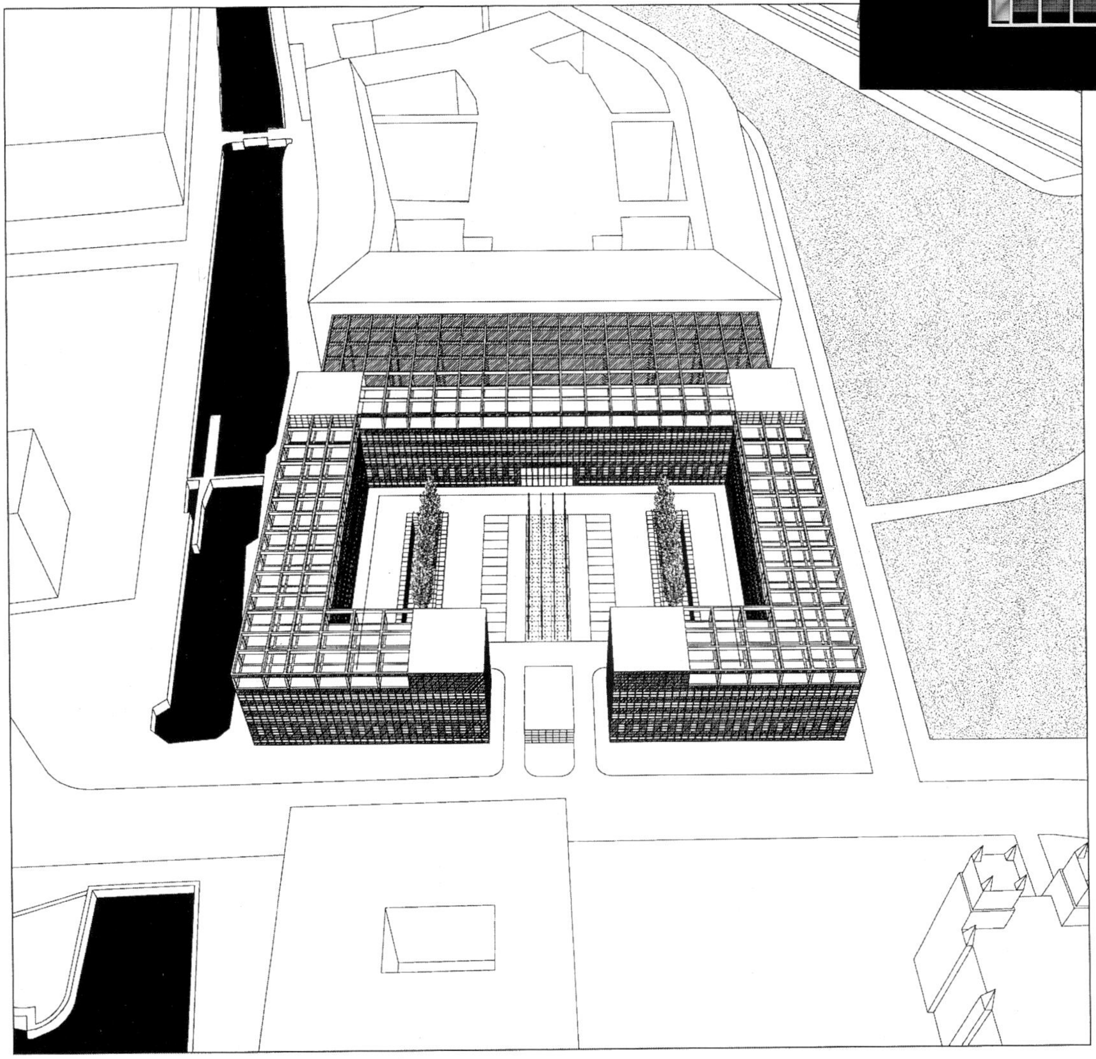

Model views; perspective.

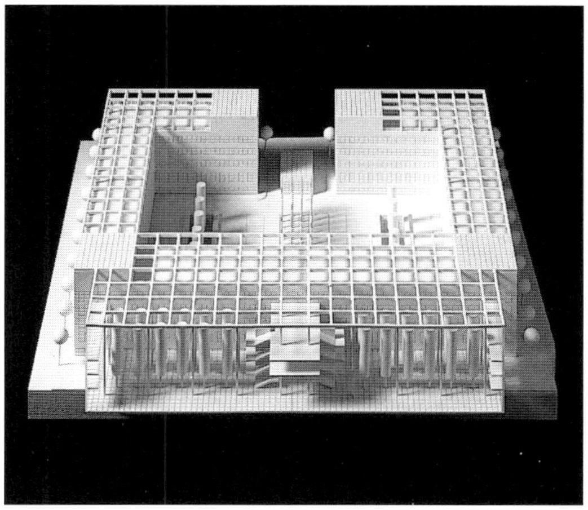

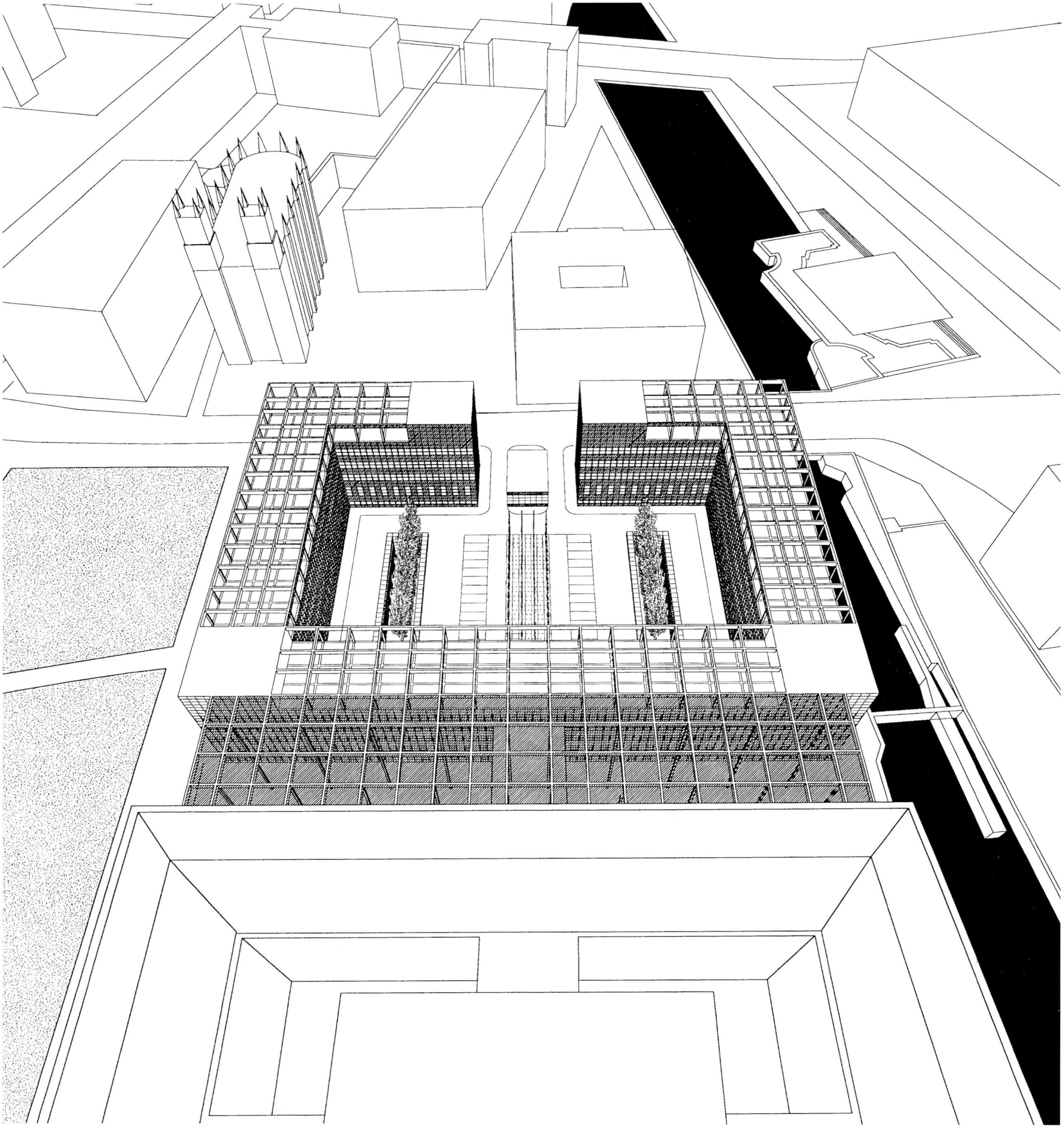

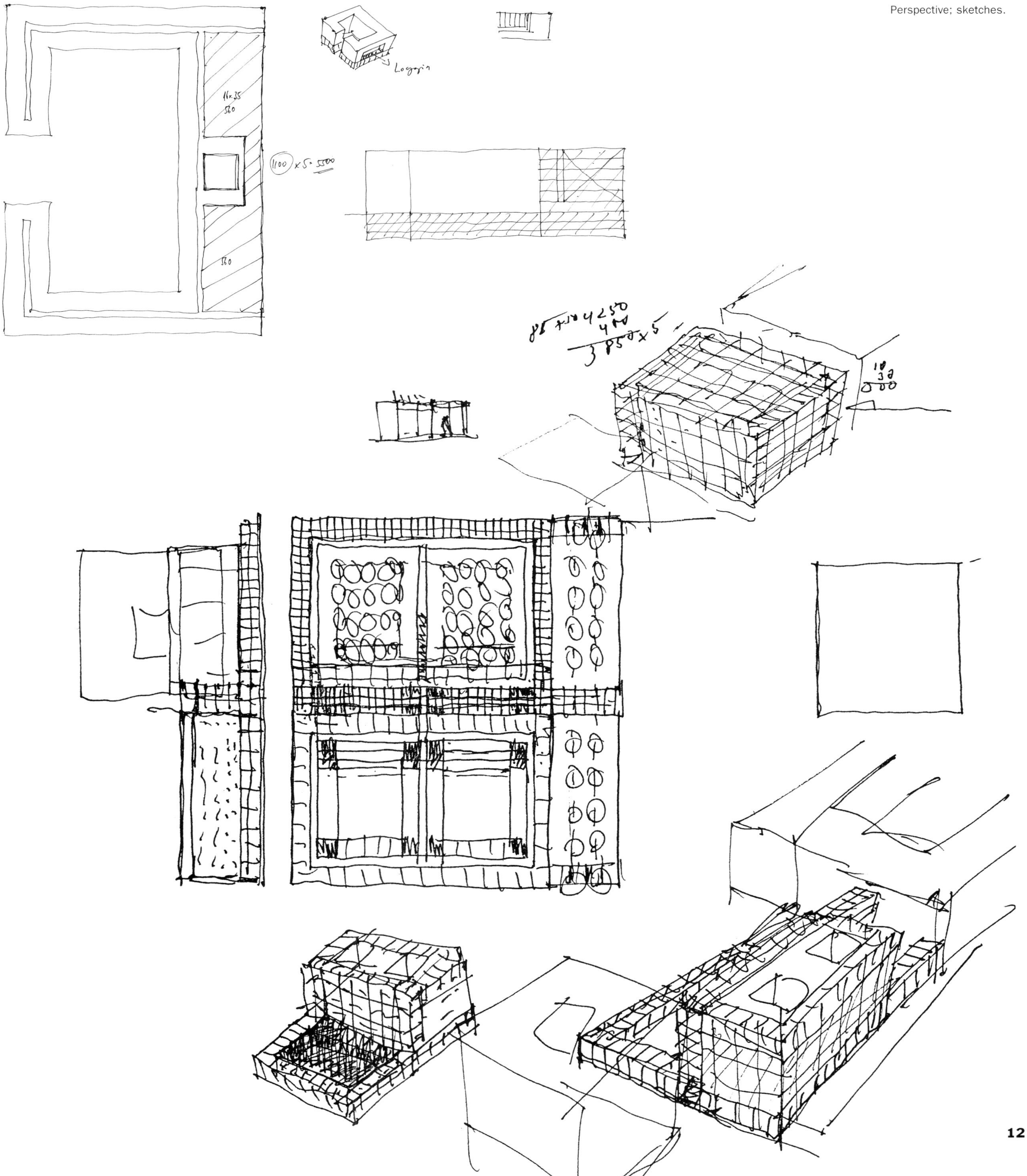

Perspective; sketches.

Sketches; elevations; sections; plans.

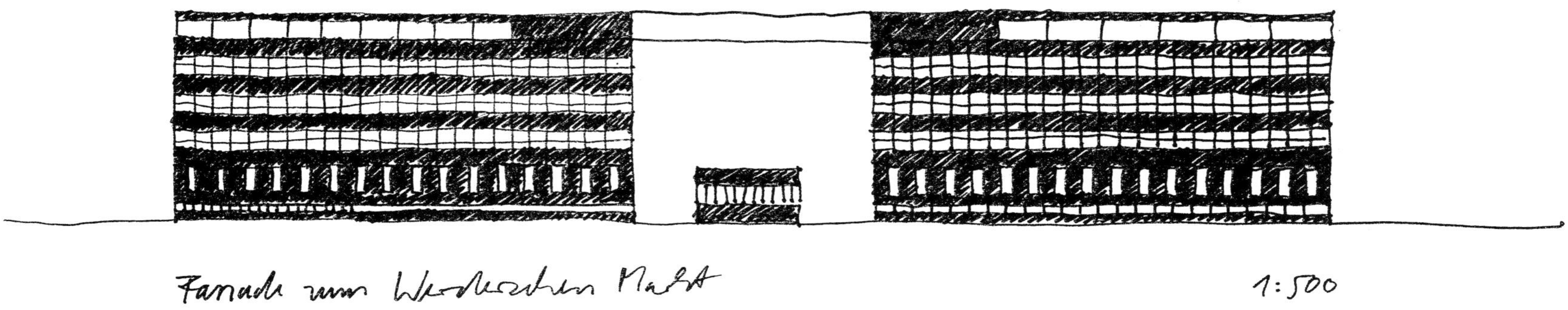

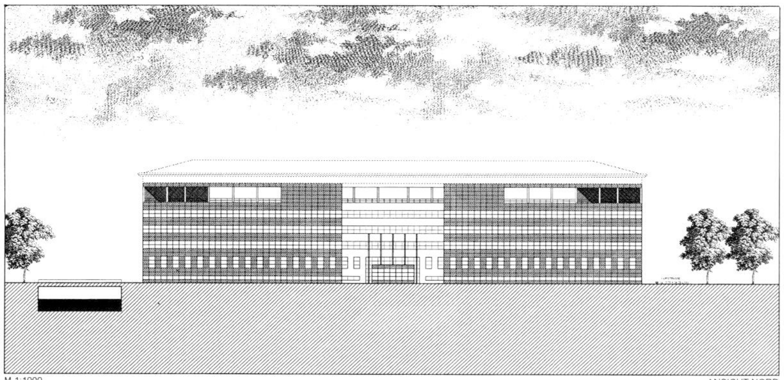

M 1:1000 ANSICHT NORD

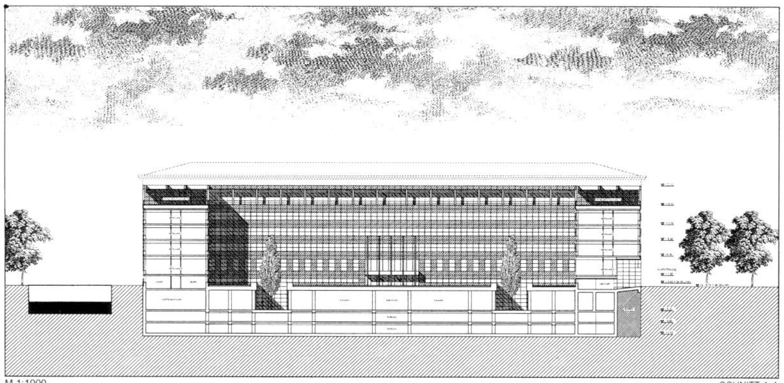

M 1:1000 SCHNITT A-A

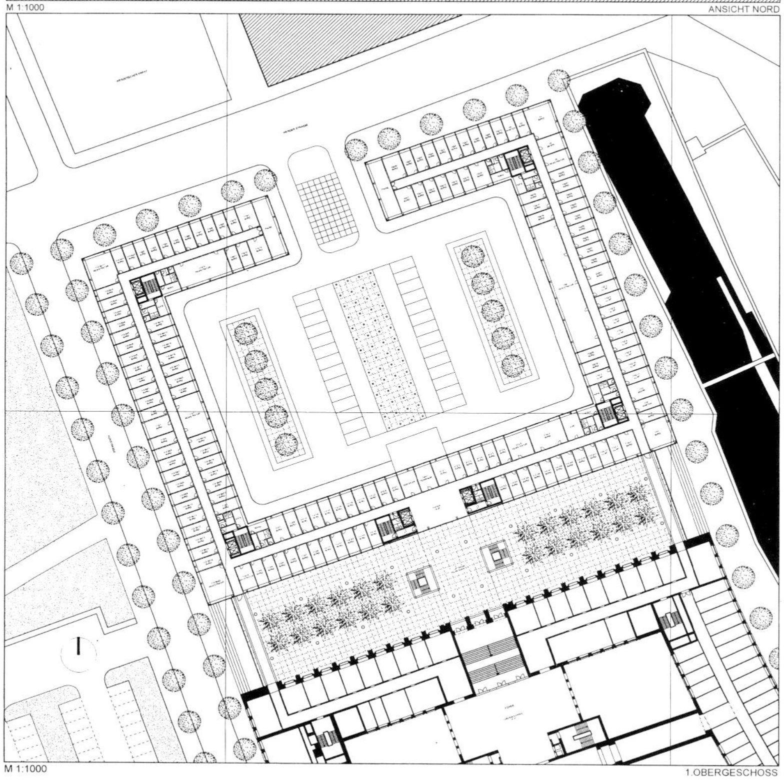

M 1:1000 1.OBERGESCHOSS

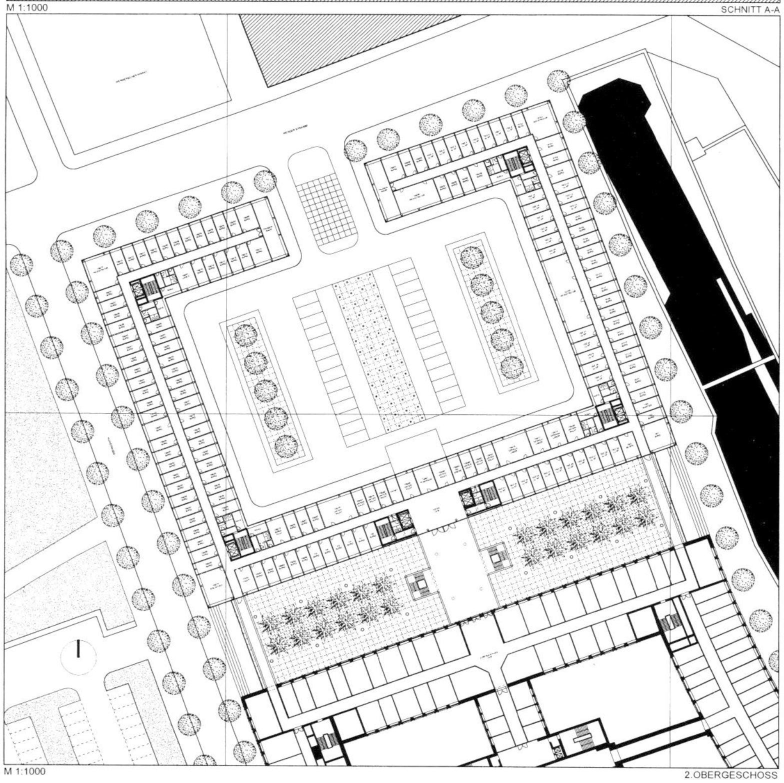

M 1:1000 2.OBERGESCHOSS

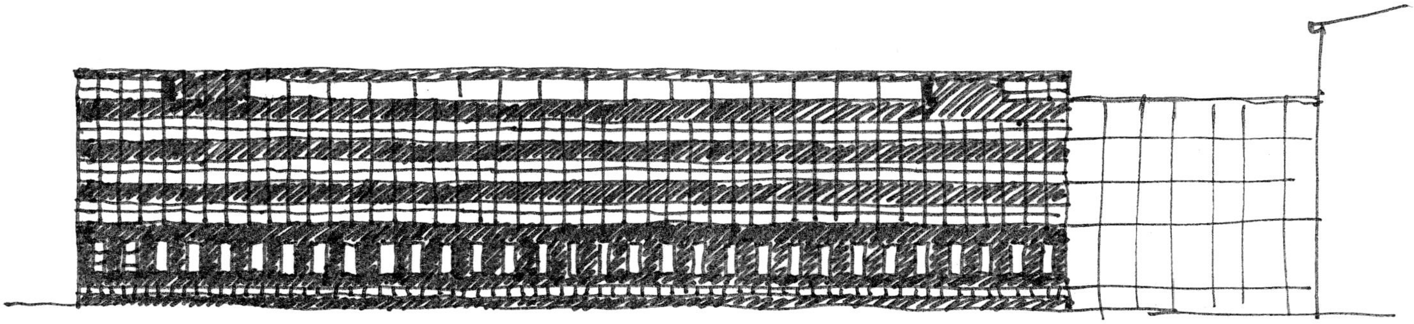

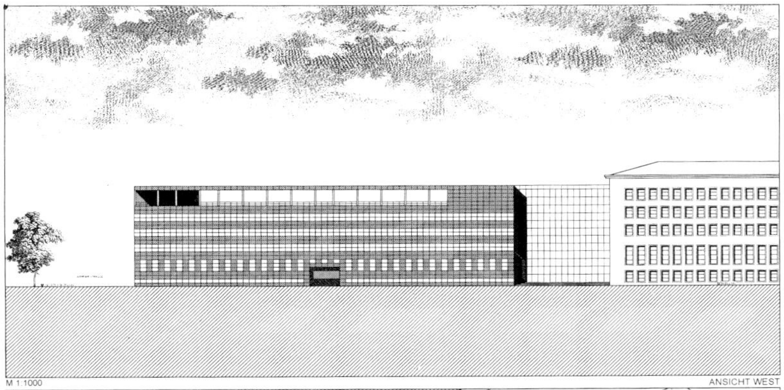

M 1:1000 ANSICHT WEST

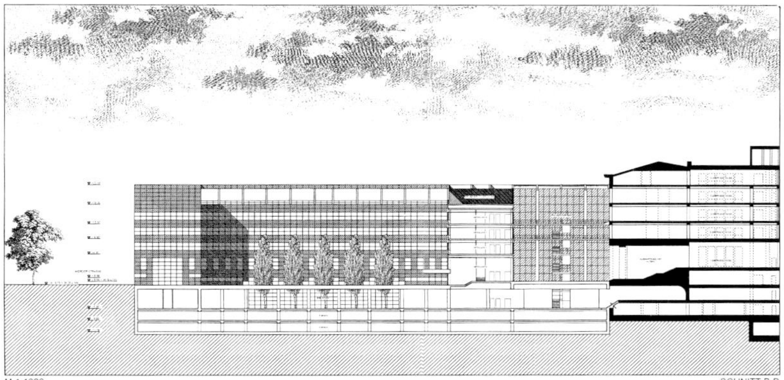

M 1:1000 SCHNITT B-B

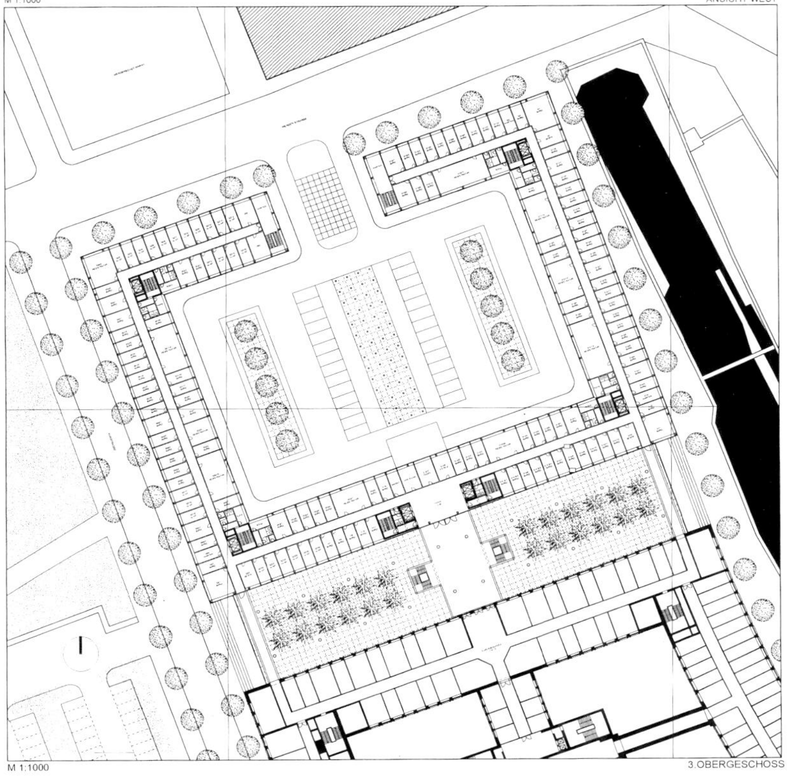

M 1:1000 3.OBERGESCHOSS

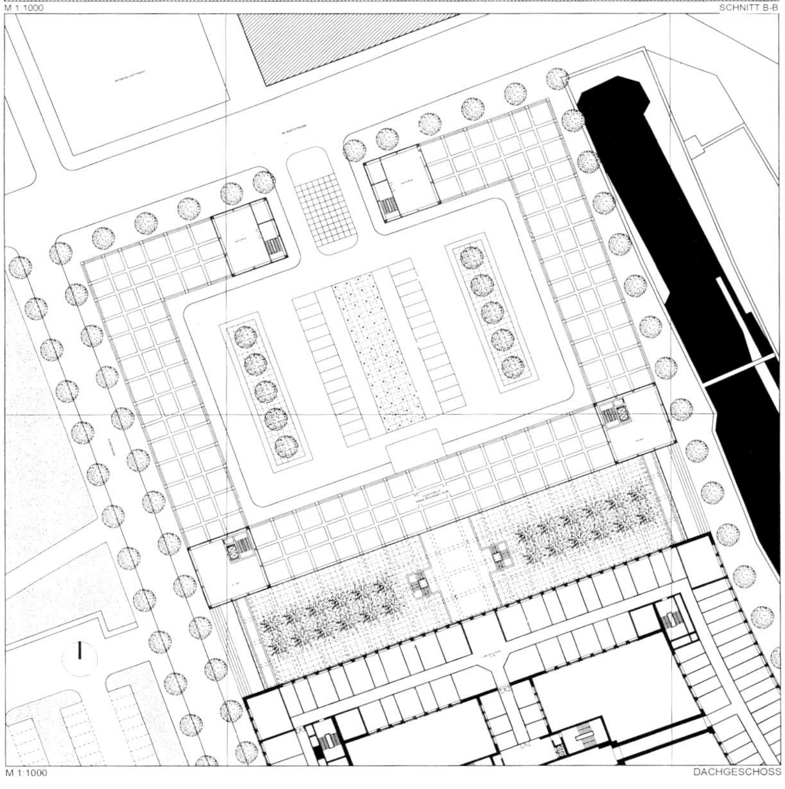

M 1:1000 DACHGESCHOSS

Competition Design for Wallraf-Richartz-Museum, Cologne, 1996–1999

With: Stefan Vieths

Sketches; perspectives; site plan; variable exhibition layouts.

Project team: Michael Garçon, Marvin Keim, David Koralek, Peter Pfertner, Jan Rogler, Axel Steudel, Wilfried van der Bel, Mehmet Yalcin

The site of the new Wallraf-Richartz-Museum forms the boundary of the historic Gürzenich complex toward Rathausplatz. The complex consists of the Gothic hall structure of the Gürzenich with its various postwar additions and the ruined Church of St. Alban. The approach to this heterogeneous architectural structure and the historic surroundings of the Rathausplatz constitute the focus of the competition.

The proposed design calls for dividing the planned building mass into two volumes. One building is inserted into the cleft in the existing buildings and forms a clear boundary toward the north, while the second is freestanding and is positioned in front of the newly created spatial edge. The juncture between the two buildings occupies the site of the historic street "In der Höhle," which is thus revived as a circulation area. In this way, the Gürzenich complex is augmented and completed: the southern edge of the complex with the striking Gürzenich hall finds its complement in the new main building of the Wallraf-Richartz-Museum. Between these two main buildings, the smaller-scale structure subordinates itself to the surrounding spaces of the city as an urban mass and alludes to the facade of old St. Alban in its sculptural articulation. Old St. Alban also defines the structure of the new building, with scale and orientation derived from the crossing square of the ruin. The proposed facade material is the light tufa stone of the great Romanesque churches of Cologne, with natural anodized aluminum for the windows.

The main building on the Rathausplatz accommodates the entire exhibition area; the other building, the subsidiary spaces. A double stair complex at the juncture between the buildings provides circulation. The exhibition building is conceived to allow the greatest

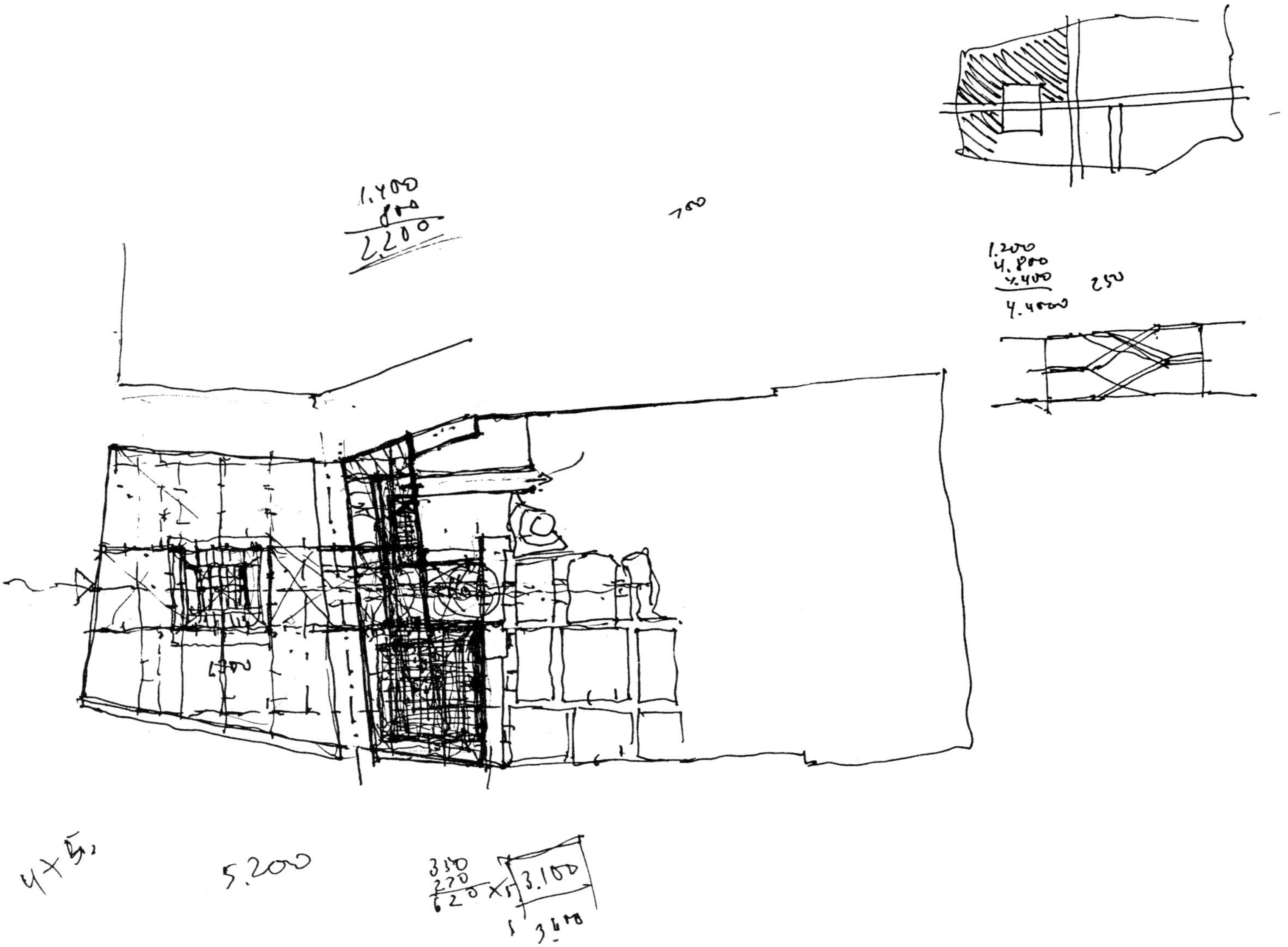

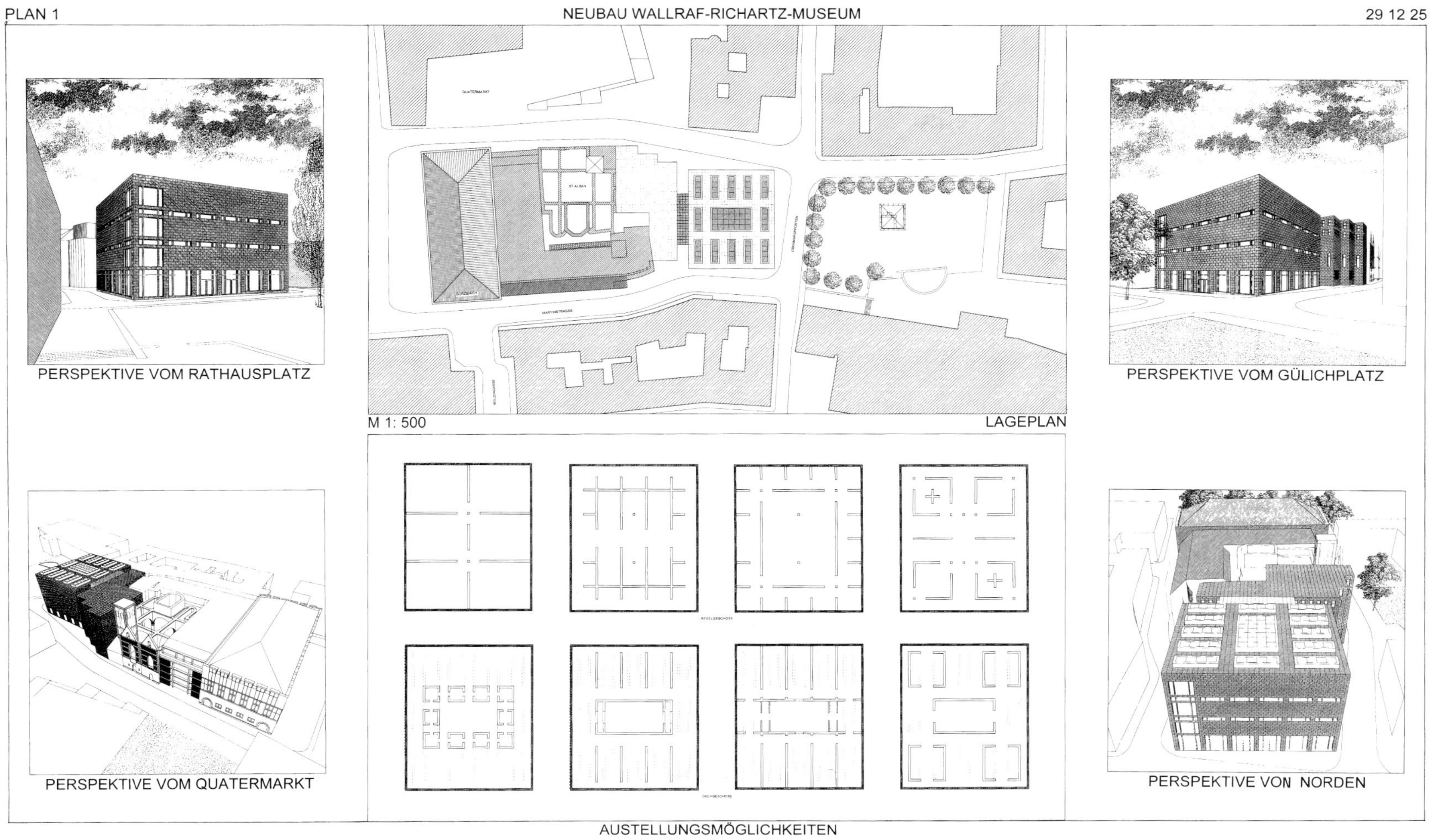
PLAN 1
NEUBAU WALLRAF-RICHARTZ-MUSEUM
29 12 25
PERSPEKTIVE VOM RATHAUSPLATZ
M 1: 500
LAGEPLAN
PERSPEKTIVE VOM GÜLICHPLATZ
PERSPEKTIVE VOM QUATERMARKT
PERSPEKTIVE VON NORDEN
AUSTELLUNGSMÖGLICHKEITEN

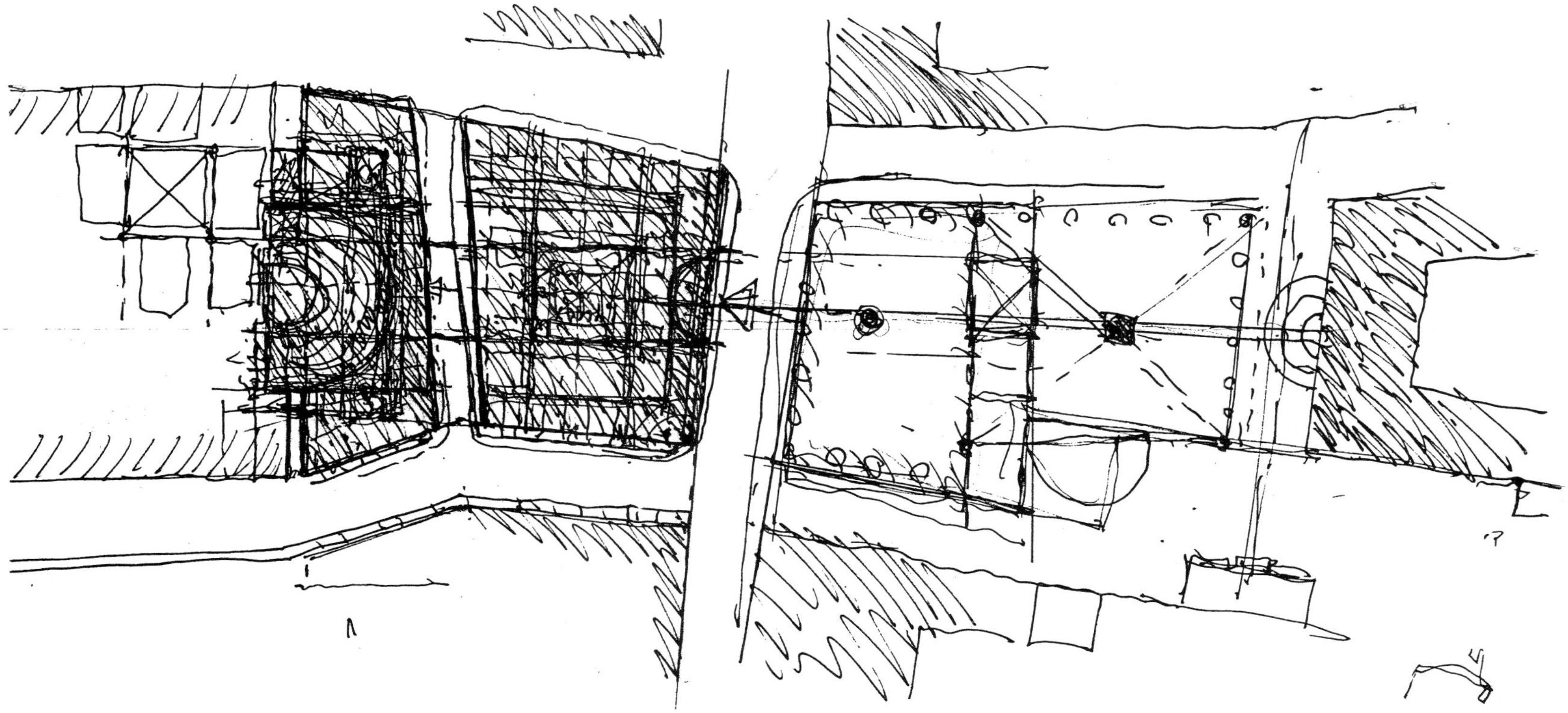

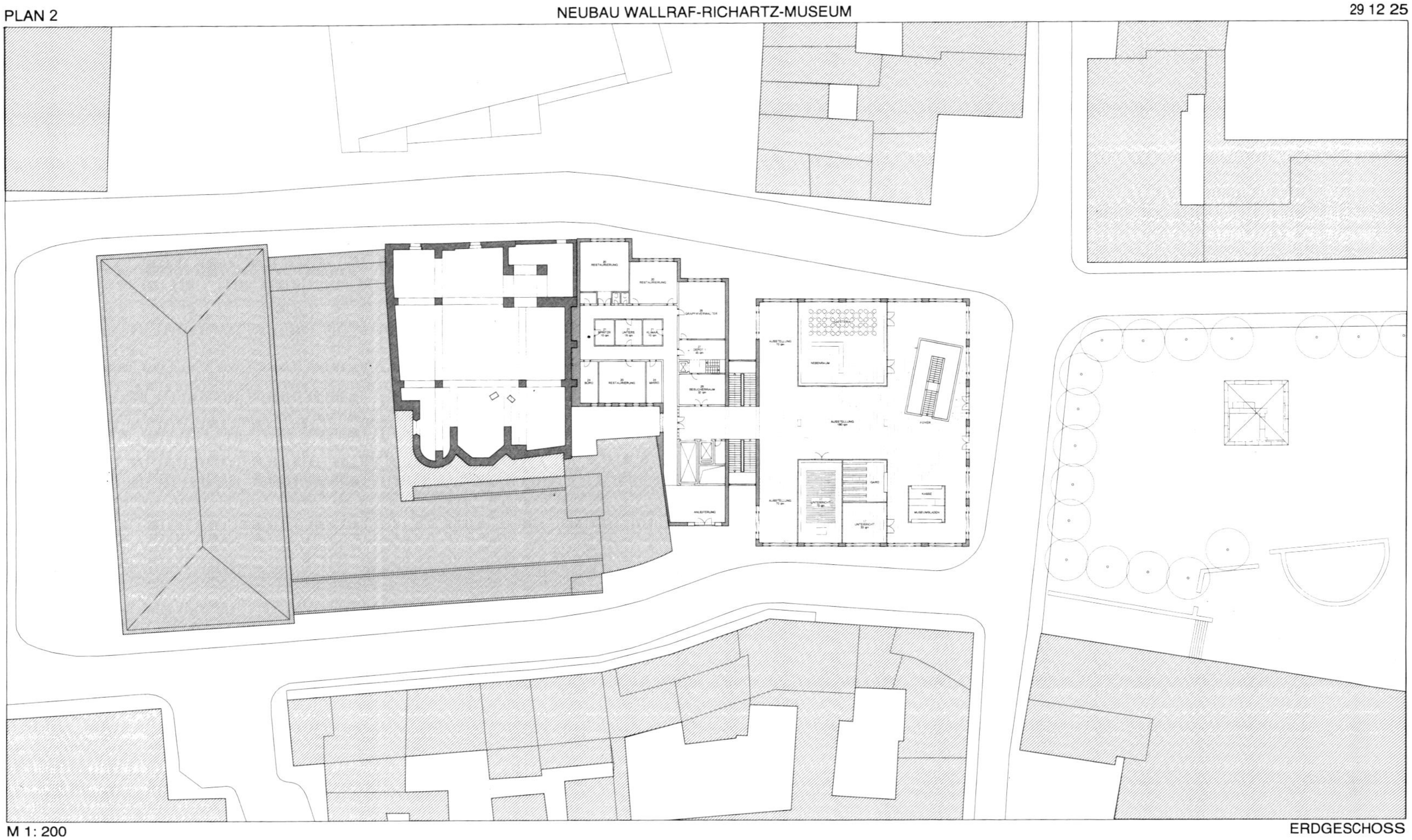

Ground-level plan;
model view.

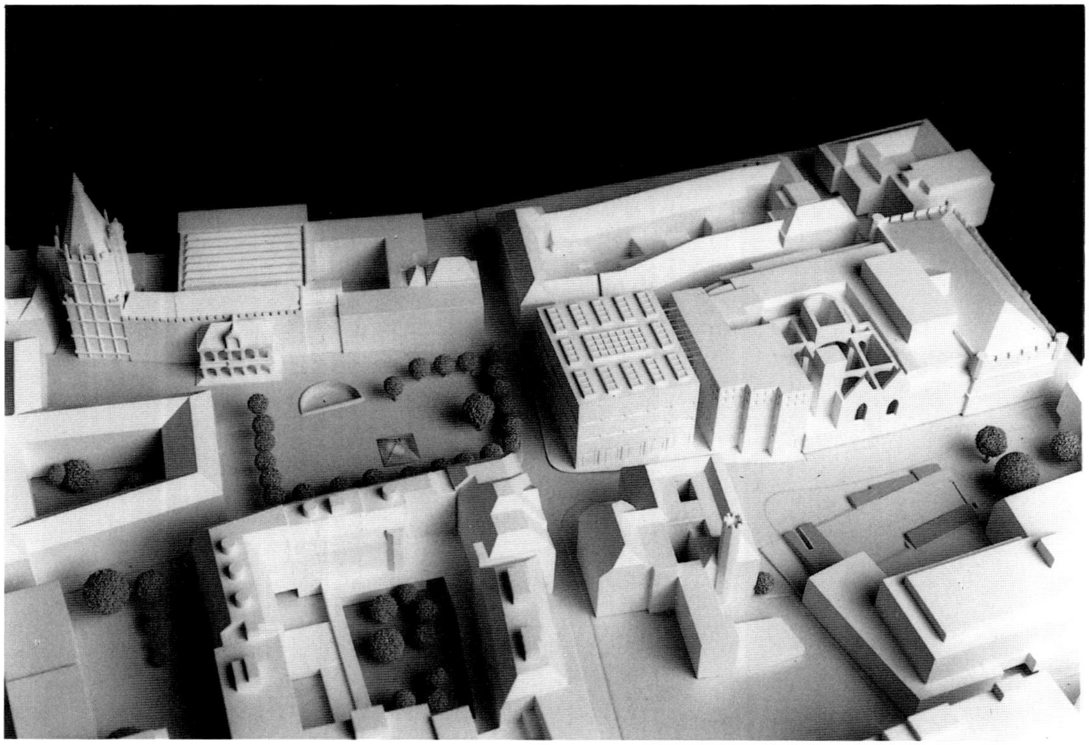

Elevations; sections; plans; sketch.

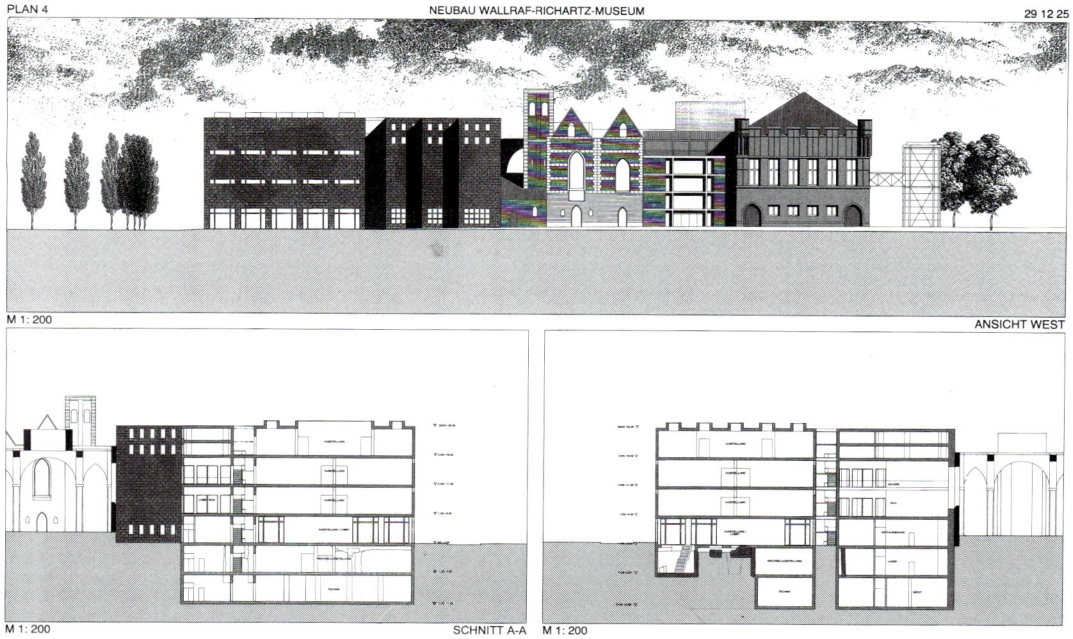

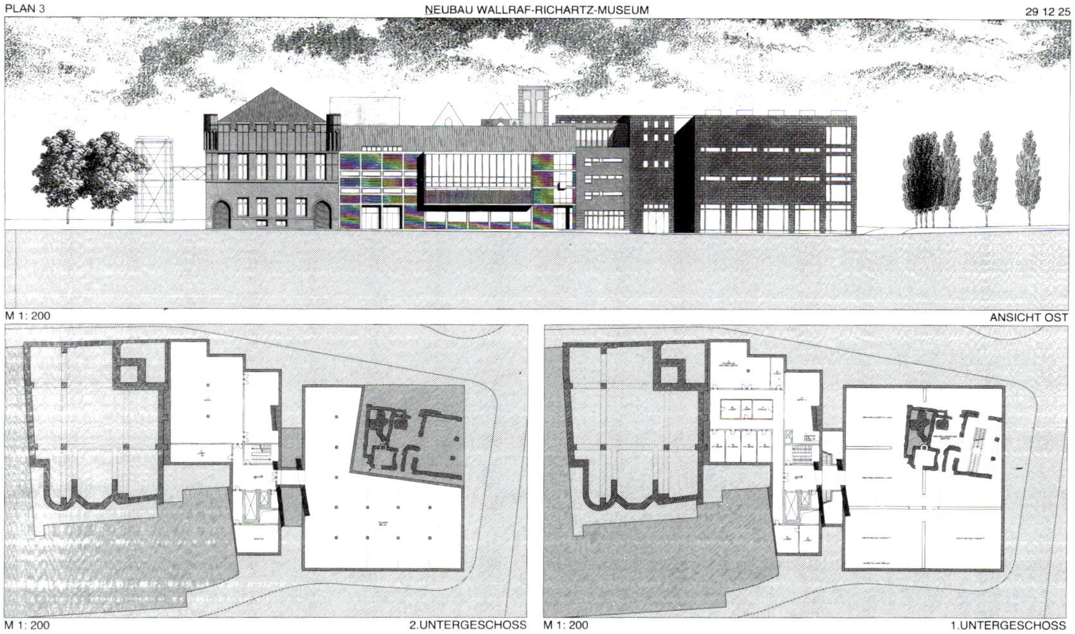

WALLRAF-RICHARTZ-MUSEUM

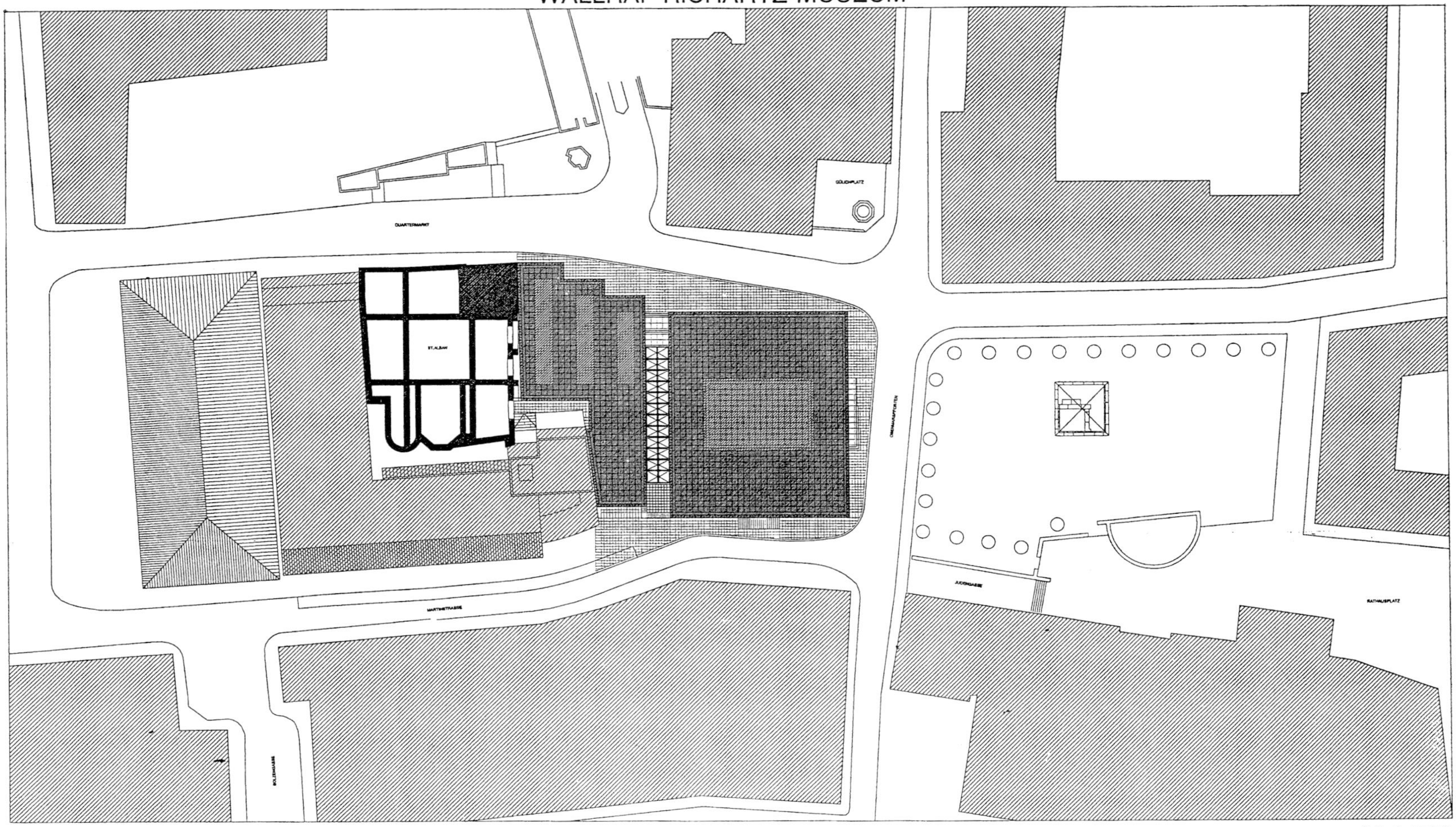

LAGEPLAN M 1:600

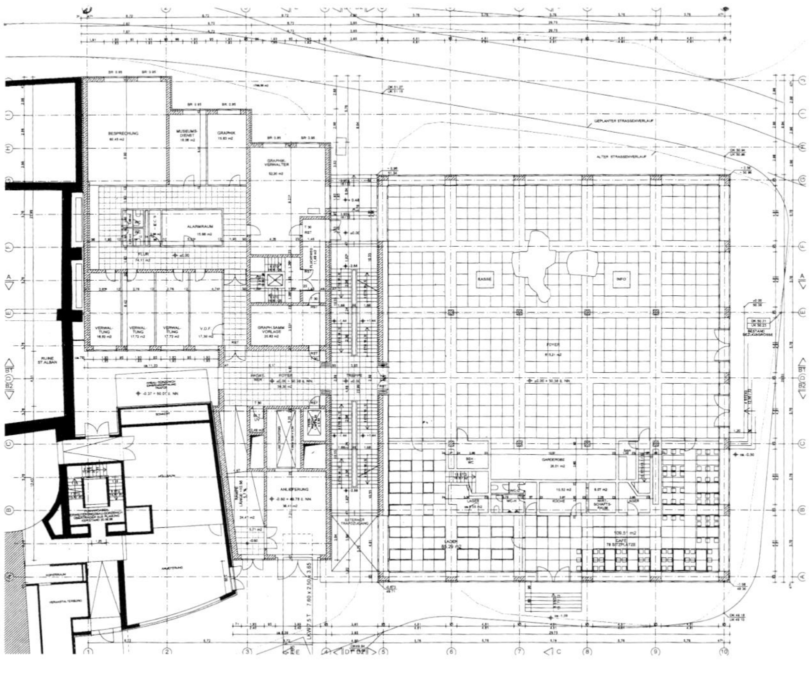

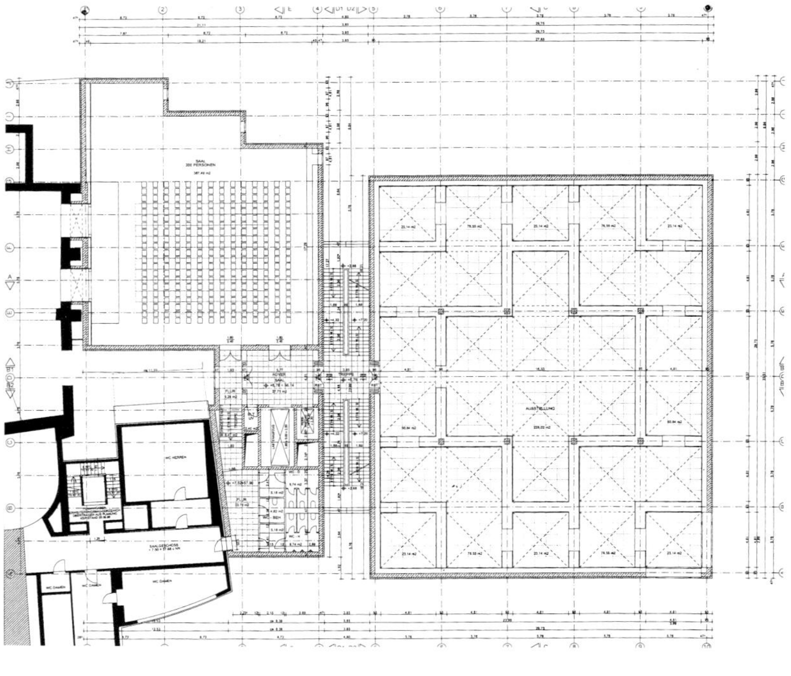

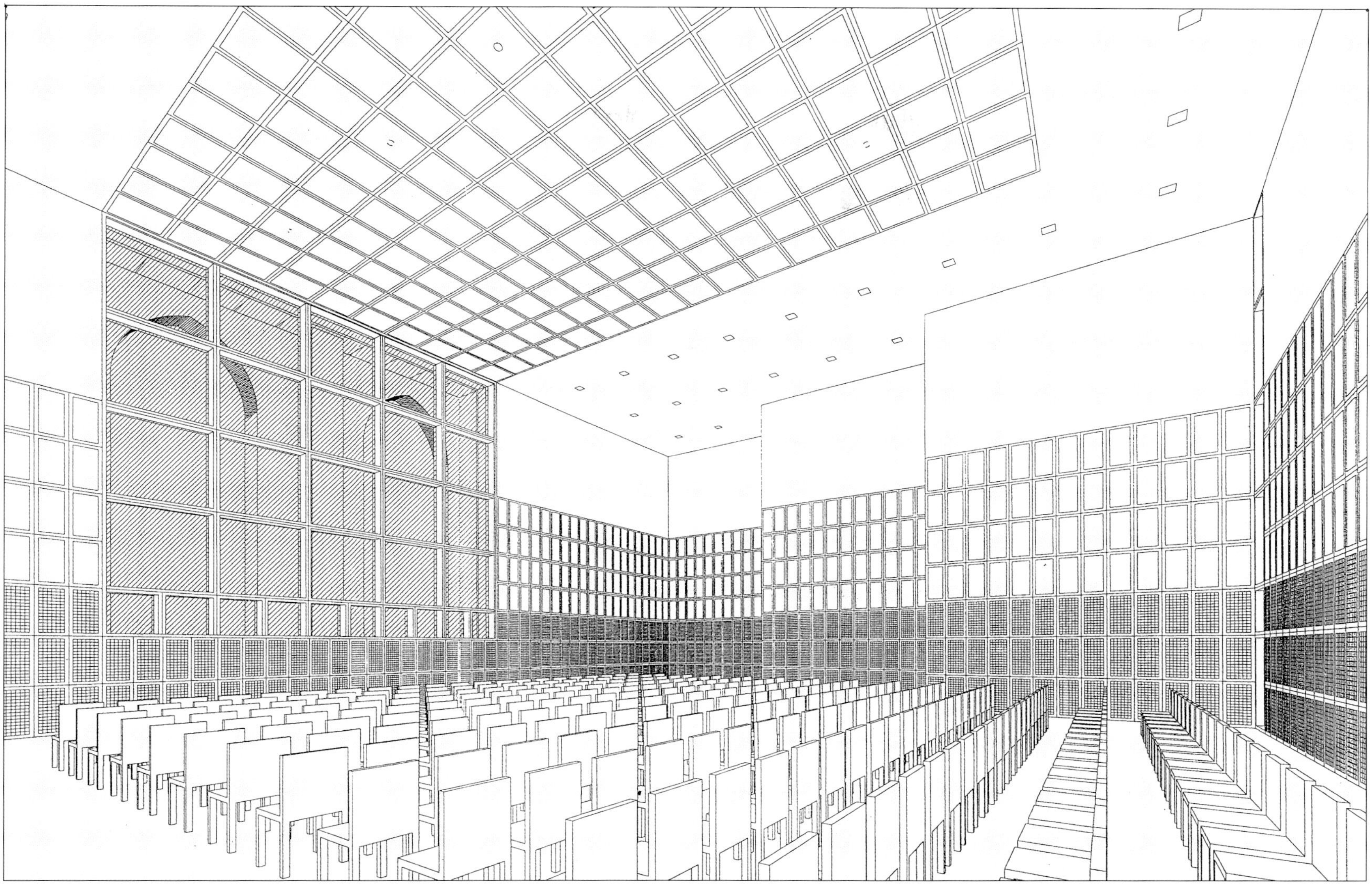

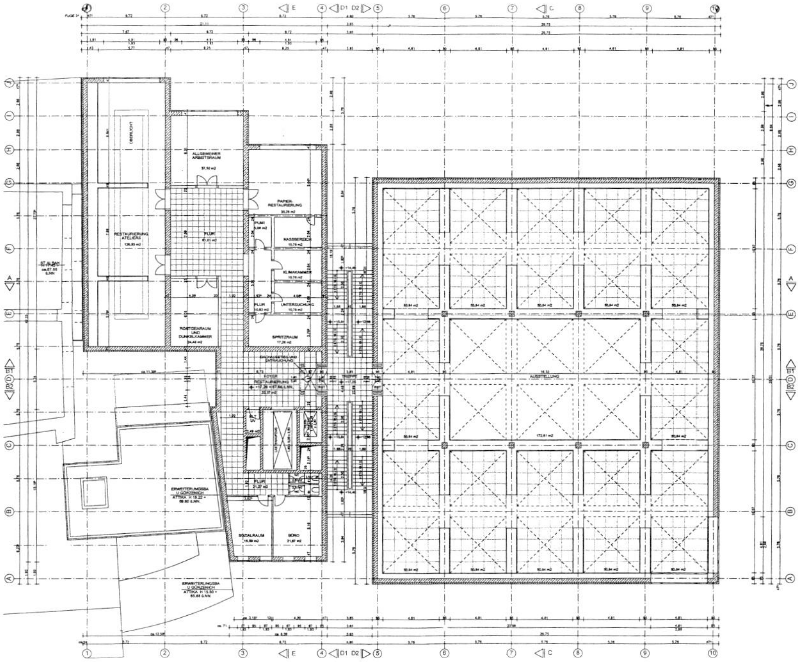

Site plan; ground-level plan; second- and fifth-upper-story plans; perspective of conference hall.

Section through stairwell;
perspective of building;
perspective of stairwell.

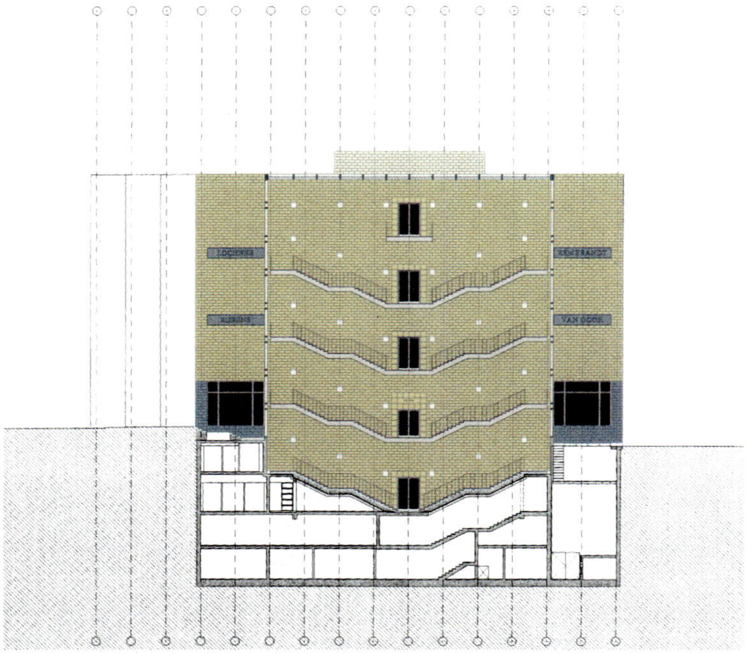

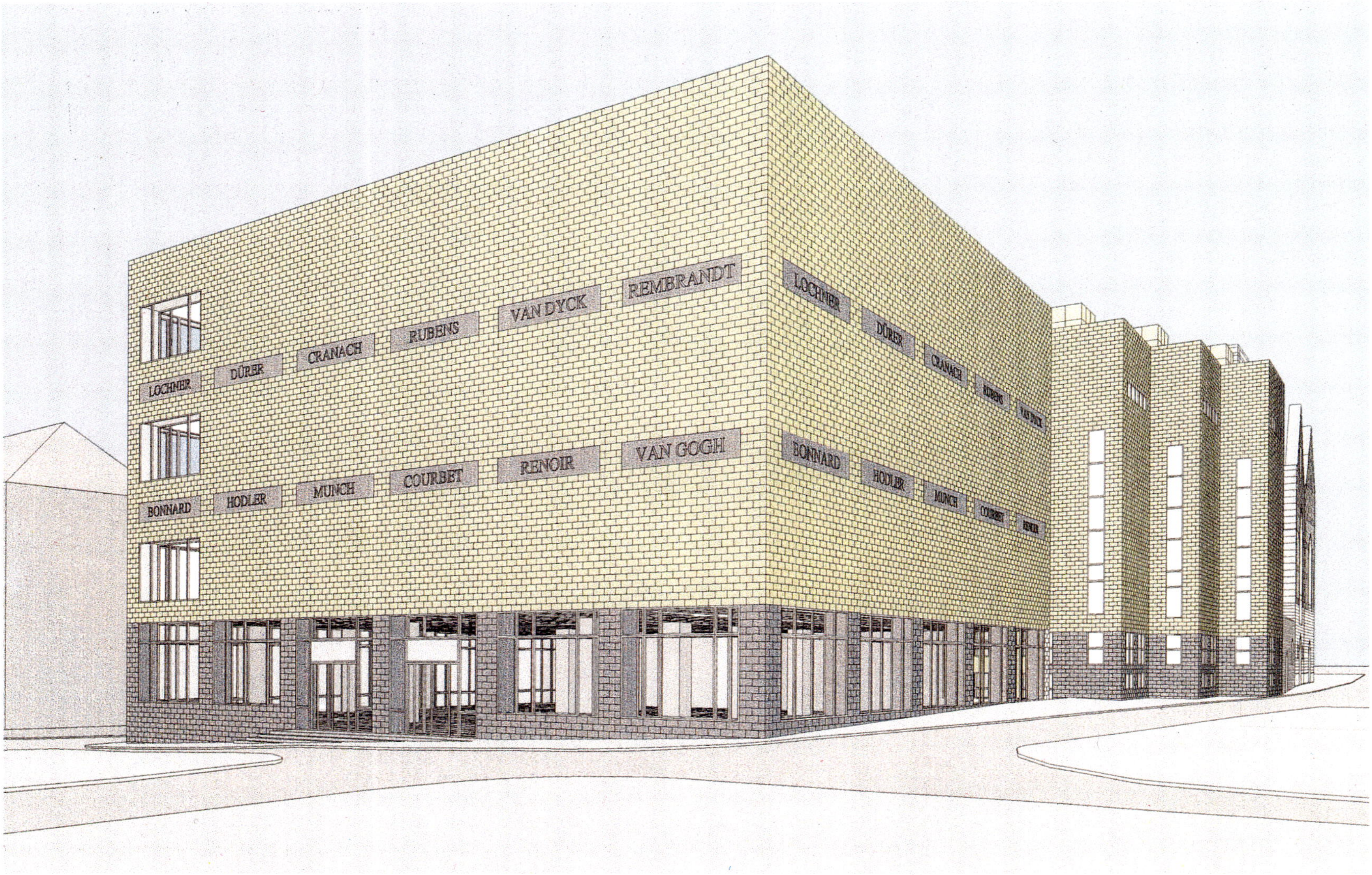

possible degree of flexibility. A high sidelight illuminates the spaces of the permanent collection in the first and second upper stories, while skylights are provided for the third upper story. The spaces for temporary exhibitions are located in the basement level and are accessed separately from the entrance hall. On the northeast corner, panorama windows in the upper stories of the otherwise largely closed facade provide a view of the city, cathedral, and Rhine river, expressly emphasizing the close relationship of the museum's collection to the city and its historic development. A lecture hall occupies the first upper story of the functional building and adjoins the foyer of the Gürzenich. The location and height of the hall are devised in such a way that the church windows of old St. Alban can be incorporated into the new architecture. In analogy to the Gürzenich additions of the 1950s, the historic facade is thus integrated into the architectural structure of the Wallraf-Richartz-Museum. Important archaeological remains are integrated into the temporary exhibition: the cellar of the "Zur roten Tür" house serves as an entry space, while the remains of the large Roman building constitute freestanding objects within the space.

Details of facade design; axonometric of exhibition spaces.

Competition Design for Parish Church of St. Theodor, Cologne-Vingst, 1997

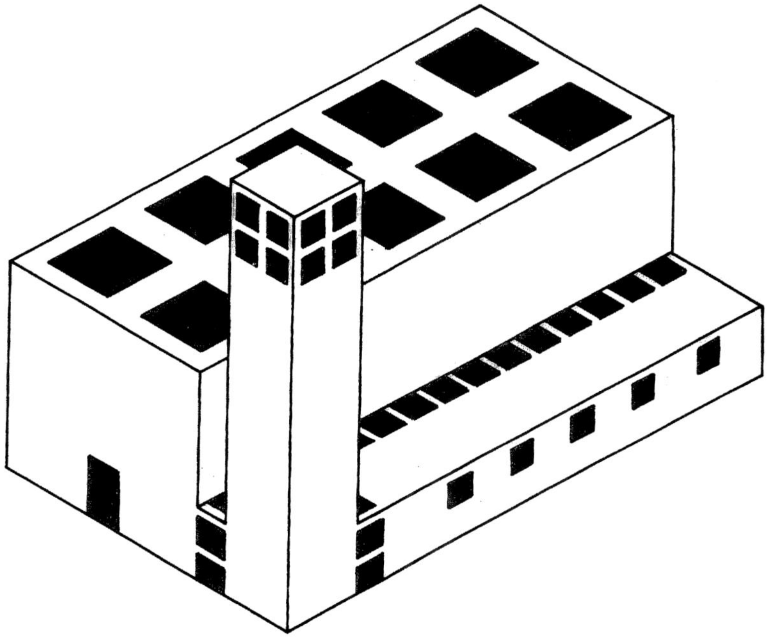

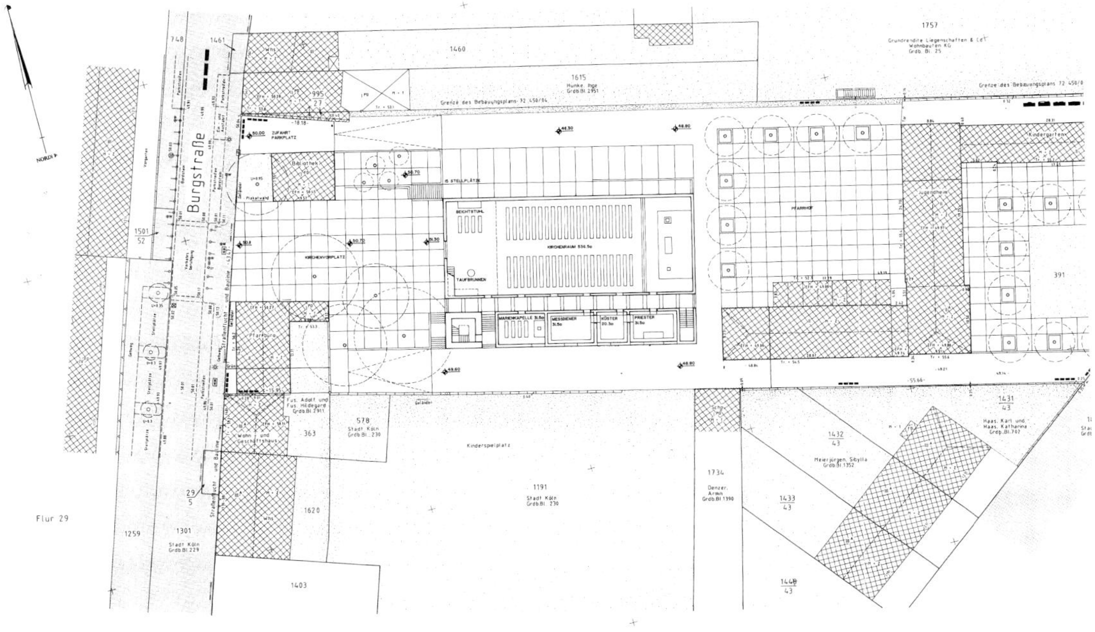

Axonometric; plan.

Project team: Johannes Götz, Volker Dieckmann

The design for the new Catholic parish church in Cologne-Vingst represents a building type different from that envisioned in the Vatican competition for a "church for the year 2000." Both projects called for the design of a parish church for a poor congregation. The Vingst project, however, aims not at impressive effects but rather at a simple, unspectacular, and dignified space whose exterior appearance is free of all sensationalism. Just as the liturgy is a solemn yet momentous act, one that focuses on the essentials, the building in which it is celebrated should be conducive to a spiritual, worshipful state of mind through extreme concentration of form. It should be a serious space, a simple building. Simplicity, dignity, and clarity are the features of this design. It consciously seeks to continue the tradition of great church designs by Rudolf Schwarz and to recall his noble and monumental ecclesiastical architecture.

The spirit of Romano Guardini and Burg Rothenfels informs the design, which is intended to revive that spirit again. The plan explains itself. There are no secret, concealed metaphors, no pagan, symbolic, or hidden spatial tricks. The church space is lucid and comprehensible at a single glance, with the altar area in the east and the organ loft in the west, as has always been the case in almost every village church. One important element, however, is the uniformity of the basic module, derived from the module of the existing tower. This module defines the entire building as well as its individual parts.

The church is entered through a low side aisle and, on feast days, through the main portal. The building consists of four parts. A socle structure of basalt accommodates garages, storerooms, dressing rooms, and a parish workshop. Surmounting the socle is the tower and a flat building containing the sacristy, a small chapel, and side rooms, as well as the actual church space. Next to the vertical form of the tower, the structure with the side rooms lies horizontally like a shadow, its dimensions corresponding to those of the tower. All the above-ground portions of the building are connected by the side aisle. Inspired by the buildings in the surrounding area, the design calls for brick facing. The church is white-plastered on the interior and is illuminated from above through skylights of glass brick. The space is pure and without decorative interruption. The essential furnishings from the previous church—altar, tabernacle, ambo, baptismal font, images of saints, and pews—are reused. Urbanistically speaking, the original situation remains largely unaltered. In effect, the new plan is derived from that of the old building. Only a row of trees is added to enclose the adjacent complex with the parish hall and other facilities.

Elevations; details; plans; sections.

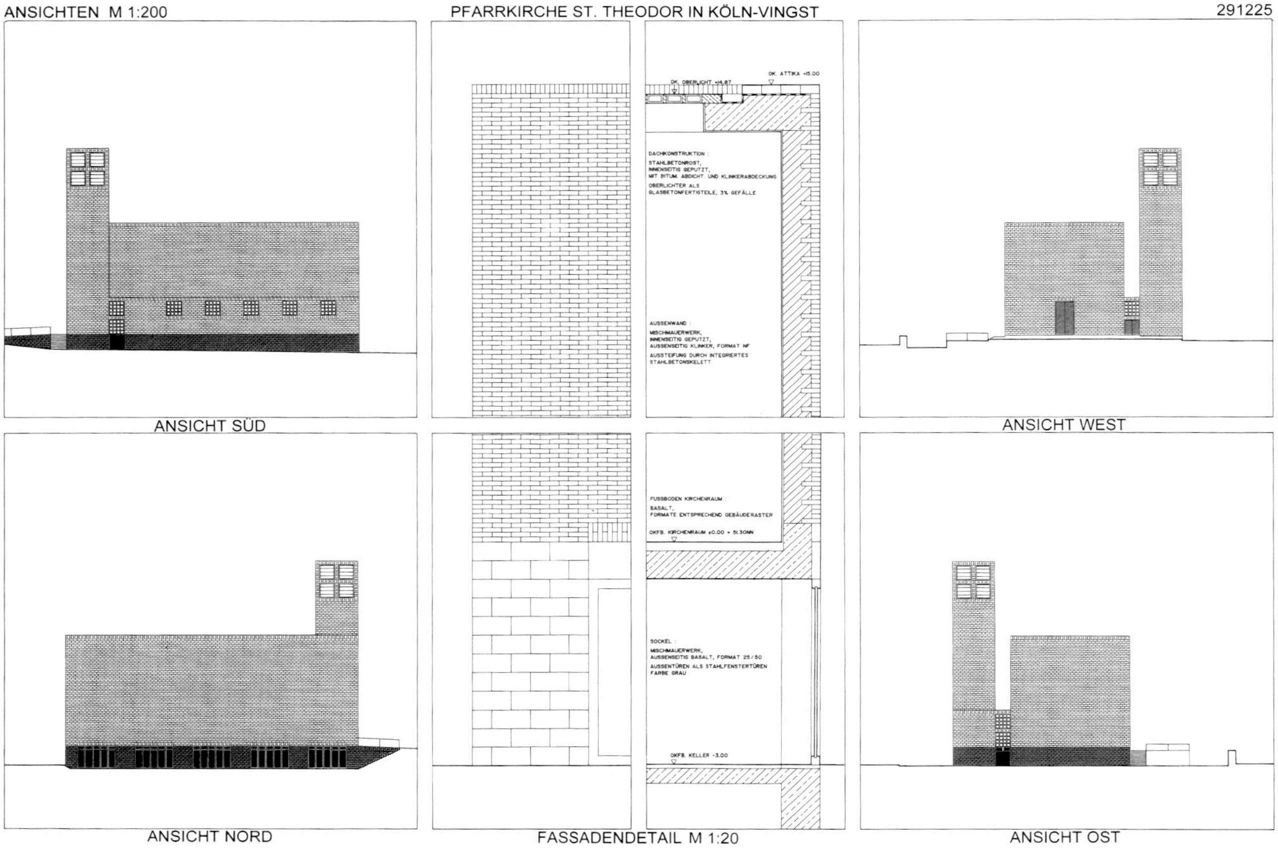

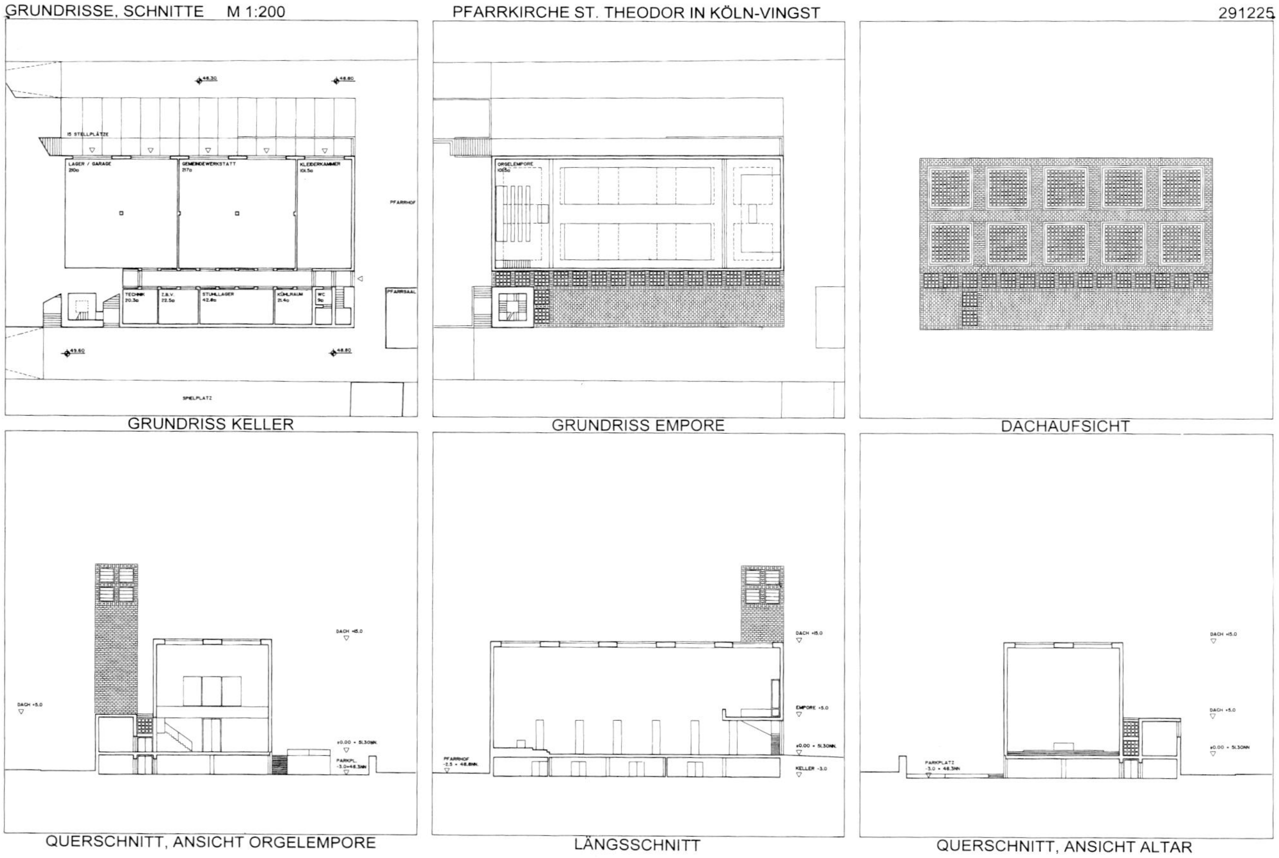

Competition Design for Dresdner Bank, Frankfurt am Main, 1997

Project team: Volker Diekmann, Marvin Keim

The site occupies an extremely sensitive location at the juncture of two important but completely different axes: Kaiserstrasse and the Gallusanlage. Kaiserstrasse is the central main street leading through the so-called Bahnhofsviertel to the train station. The Gallusanlage is a central, linear green area, not unlike Central Park in New York. Thus on the one hand, the plot marks the entrance to Kaiserstrasse; on the other, it articulates the edge of the park area.

There are three categories of high-rise architecture in Frankfurt: buildings over 200 meters in height, between 150 and 180 meters in height, and between 120 to 150. In view of the adjacent park and the neighboring historic buildings of high architectural quality, a building of the third category, about 120 to 130 meters in height, is most appropriate here.

A high-rise is a freestanding building whose character is determined not merely by an

Model view; site plan.

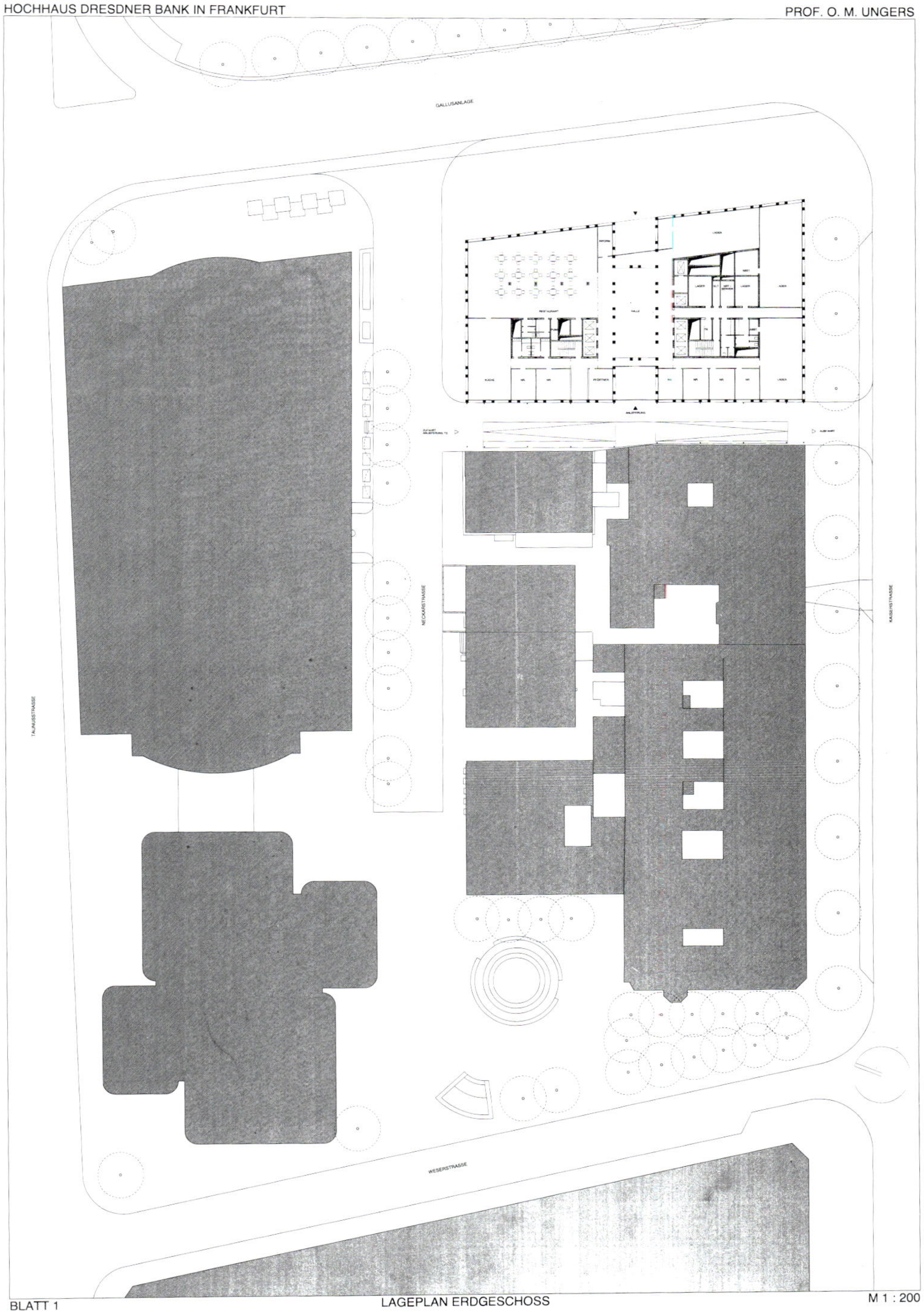

LUFTBILD - ZWILLINGSTURM

LUFTBILD - VARIANTE 1

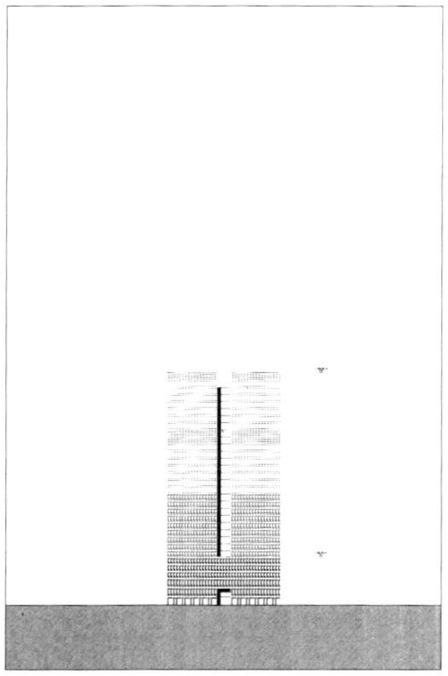

ZWILLINGSTURM

BGF oi = 59.200,98 qm / BGF ges = 67.313,09 qm

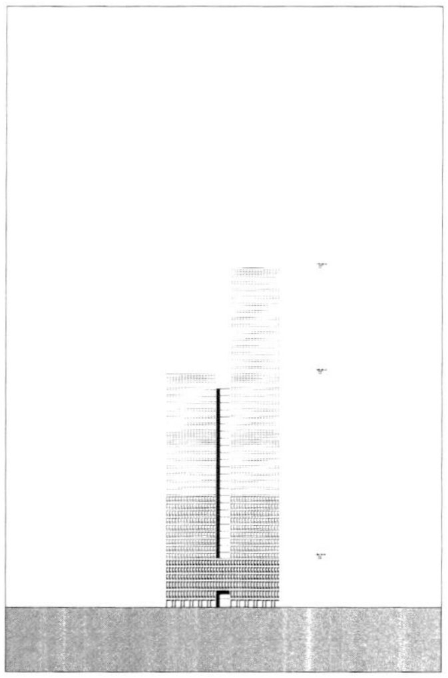

VARIANTE 1

BGF oi = 72.794,58 qm / BGF ges = 80.906,69 qm

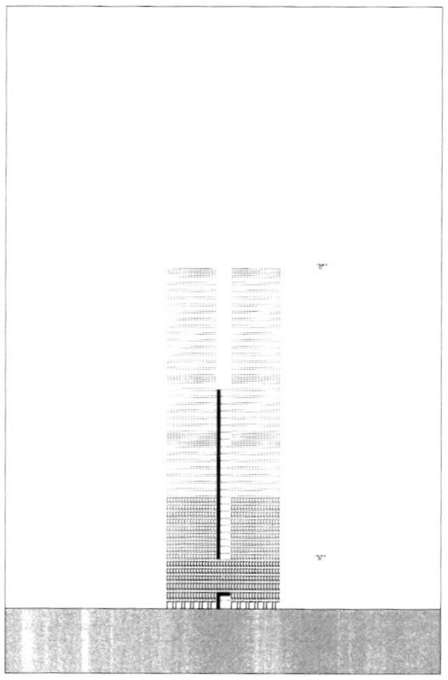

VARIANTE 2

BGF oi = 84.749,13 qm / BGF ges = 92.861,24 qm

EQUITABLE BUILDING, N.Y.

MÜNSTER, STRASSBURG

FRAUENKIRCHE, MÜNCHEN

Photomontages; elevations of variants; typological precedents.

Opposite: Elevations.

arbitrary number of stories, but by its own "identity," an image or a theme. The motif of a double tower on a single socle here serves as the point of departure for the architectural design. The socle structure corresponds to the dimensions of the street block on Kaiserstrasse, made visible in the facade. The two towers, separated by a vertical glass joint, extend to a height of 120 meters; the towers could also, however, have differing heights. The socle and towers are executed in the same material and share a common grid of 1.5 meters, on which the entire building is based. Differentiation is achieved through the articulation and plasticity of the building parts. According to the principle of "diversity in unity," three different zones are established. The recessed, conventional windows of the socle structure open onto balconies within the facade in a design that responds to the buildings of the surrounding blocks. The facade of the central area from the sixth to the fourteenth story is slightly profiled with simple casement windows. In the uppermost zone, the window surfaces are flush with the exterior and visually form a single skin with the stone facing. This triple articulation creates a facade that seems to grow narrower toward the top, giving the building a subtle scale. The exterior is faced in dark-colored clinkers.

The main entrance to the building is oriented to the Gallusanlage. The two-story entrance hall on the ground floor, however, which extends throughout the entire socle structure, also provides a protected rear entrance through a gallery between the socle structure and the existing buildings nearby. The exit from the underground garage and the service entrances are also located here. The entrance hall provides access to the elevators to the two towers and to a restaurant with a view of the Kaiserstrasse. The ground level also accommodates an exterior ring of shops and service areas. In the first upper story are conference rooms and the employee cafeteria; the second upper story accommodates meeting rooms and service installations. The remaining office levels are based on the regular grid system of 1.5 meters, permitting the space to be subdivided easily.

Facade prototype; plans.

Facade details;
use schemes.

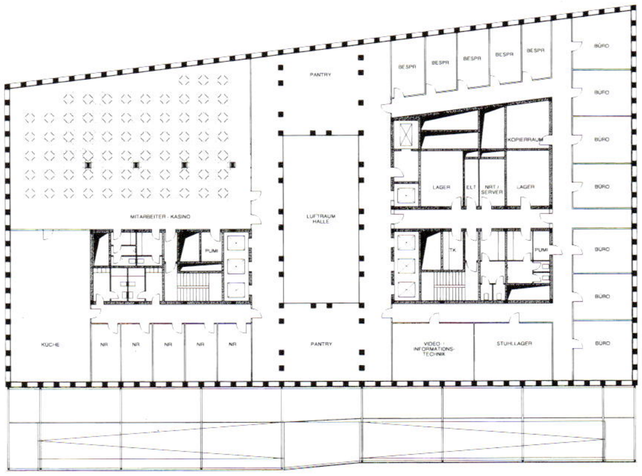

2. OBERGESCHOSS

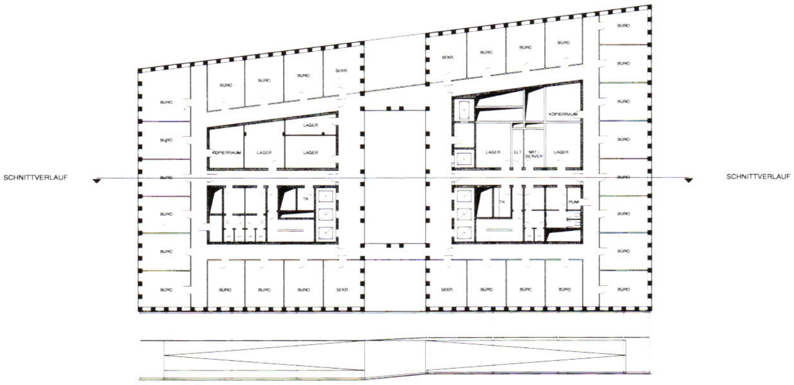

REGELGESCHOSS

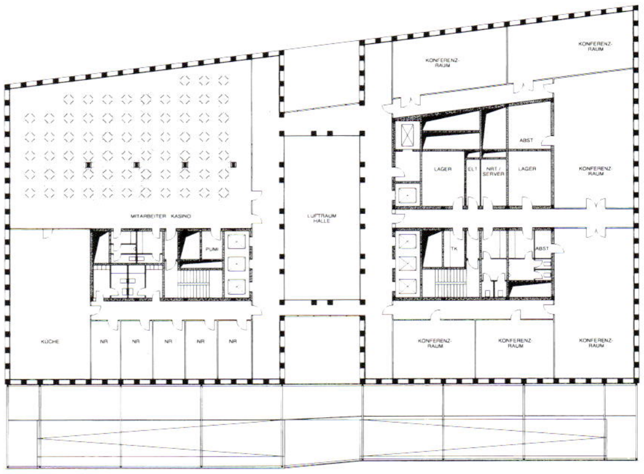

1. OBERGESCHOSS

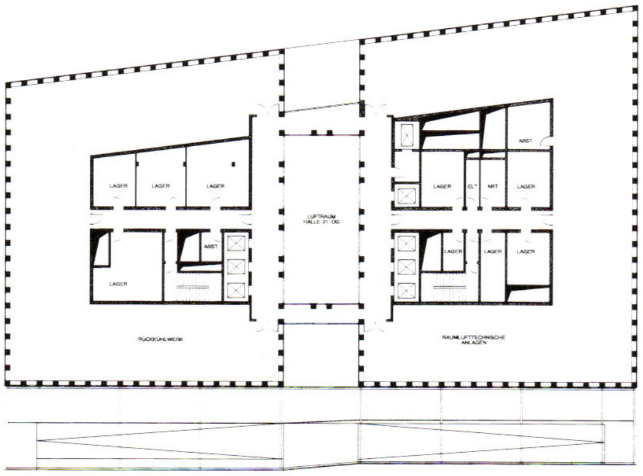

22. OBERGESCHOSS

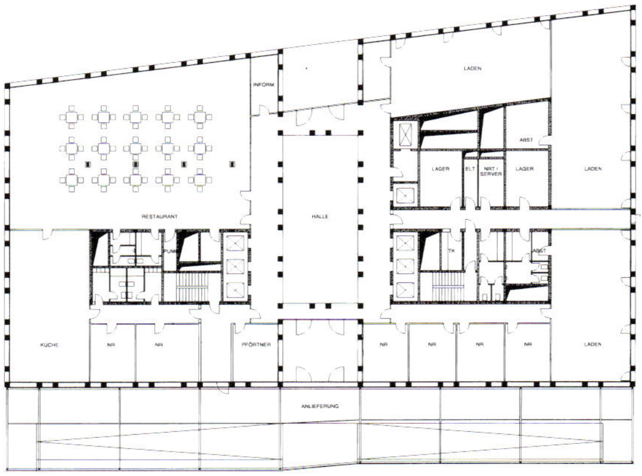

ERDGESCHOSS

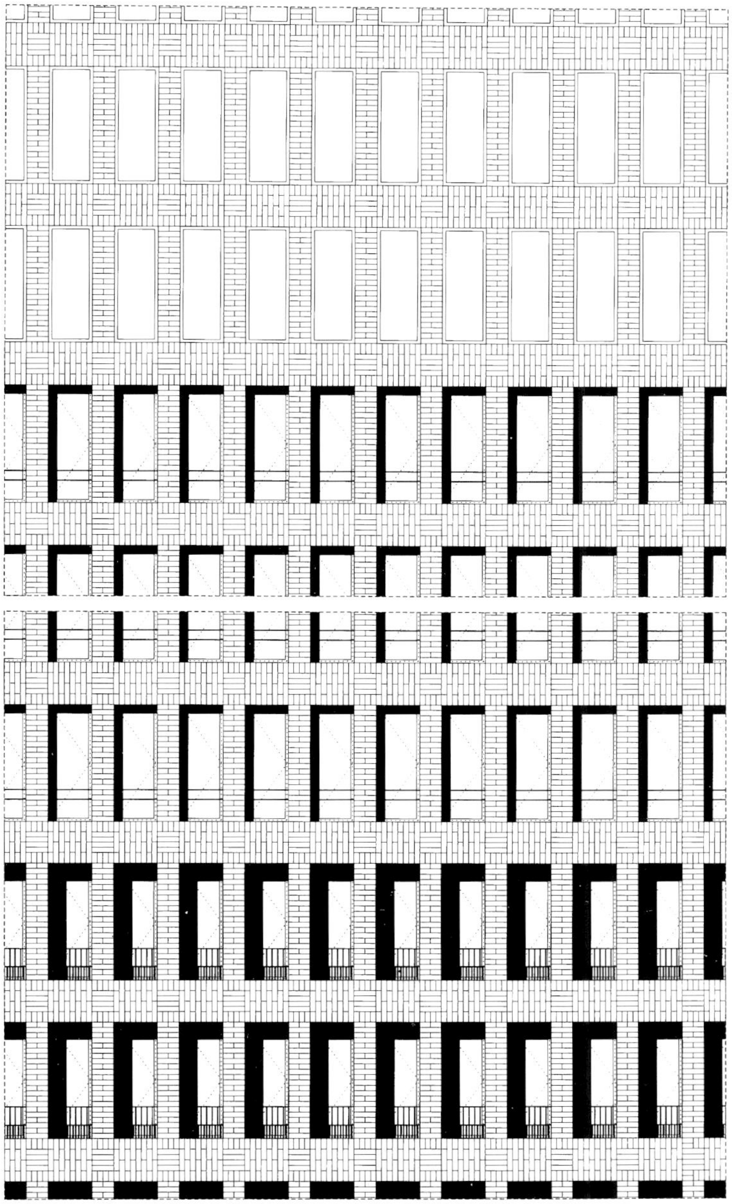

ANSICHT

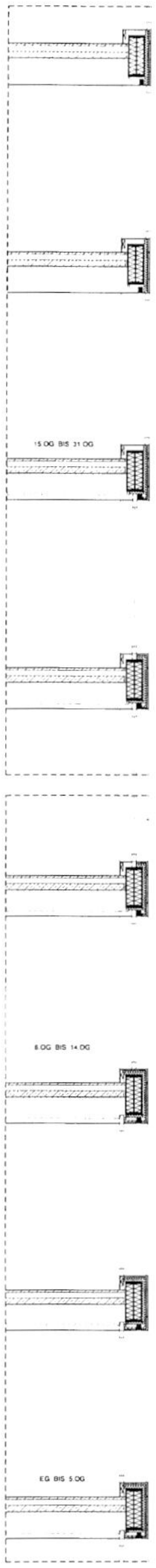

SCHNITT

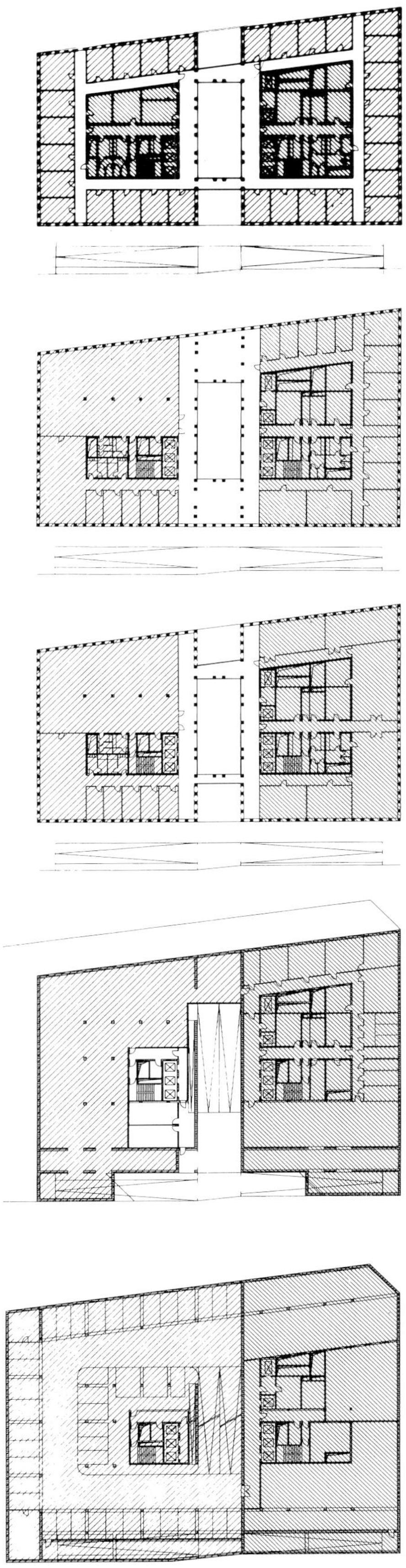

GRUNDRISS 15. BIS 31.OG

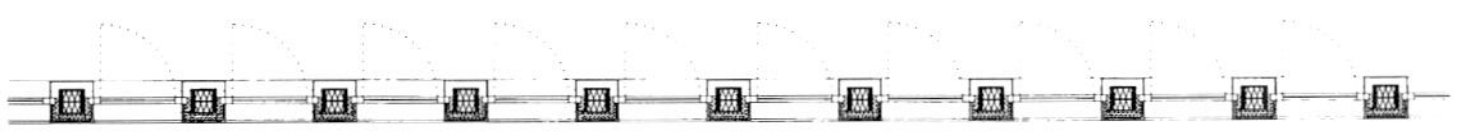

GRUNDRISS 6. BIS 14.OG

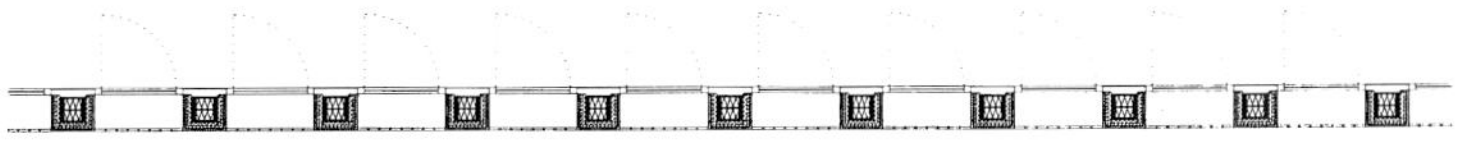

GRUNDRISS EG BIS 5.OG

Buildi

Badische Landesbibliothek, Karlsruhe, 1980–1991

Historic buildings across from the Stephanskirche; courtyard with gate structure on Erbprinzenstrasse.

Project team: Burkhard Meyer (construction supervision), Karl-Heinz Schmitz, Karl-Lothar Dietzsch

The scale and formal language of the design for the state library of Baden were defined by the existing urban situation, although the trees planted on the site, the dominant appearance of the Stephanskirche opposite, the predominantly classical character of the city of Karlsruhe, and the urban structure devised by Friedrich Weinbrenner also represented decisive influences.

The design consolidates the buildings on Erbprinzenstrasse, Ritterstrasse, Blumenstrasse, and Herrenstrasse into a single block structure. Most of the existing buildings and trees on the site were preserved and incorporated into the new ensemble. The buildings are divided into three formal zones, which complement one another and establish a morphological series. The small-scale residential architecture on Herrenstrasse is conceived as a closed volume with interior courtyards of varying form. The central zone is an open green space within which individual, self-contained architectural elements are placed; the latter include the gate structure on Erbprinzenstrasse, which marks the entrance to the garden courtyard and represents an architectural quotation of the "Ettlingen Gate," and the existing classical building marking the southern boundary. Finally, the library itself is a strictly geometric block surrounding an interior courtyard.

The arrangement of the individual buildings, which combine to form a complex overall morphology, resembles the dissection and reconstruction of Weinbrenner's Stephanskirche. The dome and facade articulation of the church are playfully adapted along with the passage, the four-columned hall, and the idea of the gatehouse. The library and church speak the same architectural language.

Passage between two buildings; library.

Wood construction of dome; interior view of dome; isometric of building complex.

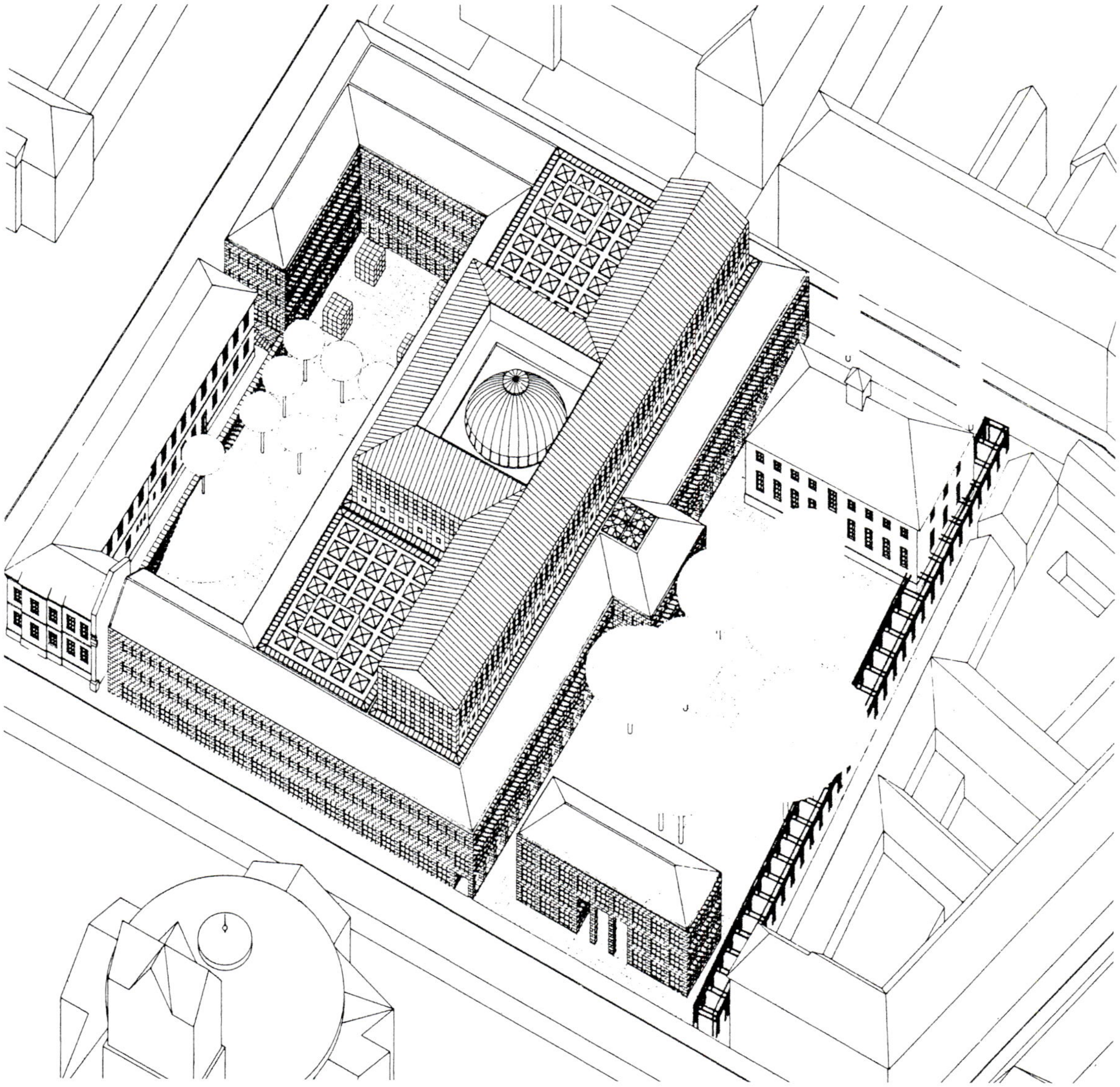

View into reading room of library with frieze by Günther Förge, and inscribed panels by Ian Hamilton Finlay.

Interiors.

Competition Design for Galerie der Gegenwart, Expansion of Kunsthalle, Kunstinsel Hamburg, 1986–1996

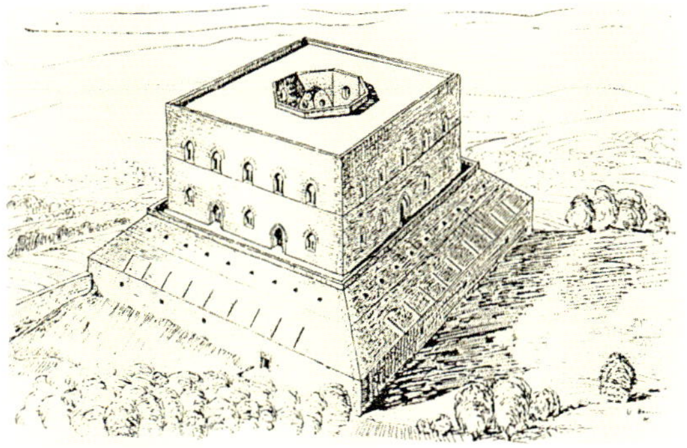

Project team: Joachim Sieber, Ingo Schweers, Andreas Geitner, Volker Diekmann, Frank Wieschemann, Peter Pfertner

The design for the expansion of the Kunsthalle is based on a revision of the competition design from 1986, which was modified in its spatial program. Construction was begun in 1992 and completed in August 1996.

The building stands on a plot measuring about seventy by one hundred meters, surrounded on three sides by streets and tracks and on the fourth by the east facade of the old nineteenth-century building. The new building consists of a socle structure whose outer walls are inclined at a forty-five-degree angle, with the main building positioned on it across from the old complex. In order to maintain the urbanistically dominant effect of the Kunsthalle, the new structure was placed as far away as possible from the facade of the old building, creating a spacious plaza between the old and new sections of the complex. The axial arrangement of the new building establishes it as a complement to the Kunsthalle complex; at the same time, it serves to mark the eastern boundary of the ensemble, setting off the entire museum area from the surrounding traffic zones like a kind of quay wall.

The socle, executed in red granite, contains the majority of the exhibition spaces, storerooms, depots, and administrative areas as well as an underground parking garage on a separate level. An axial passage connects the exhibition area to the old Kunsthalle. The exterior of the four-story main building is faced with white limestone. The ground level accommodates foyer, media spaces, bookshop, and café as well as a central hall uniting all the stories. In the three upper stories are exhibition areas with different systems of lighting for each level: sidelight through windows, artificial light, and overhead skylight. The design of the new building is reserved and austere. A counterpoint to the richly articulated facade of the Kunsthalle, it does not compete with but rather augments the existing architecture.

Sketch; Castello Lucera; aerial view; site plan.

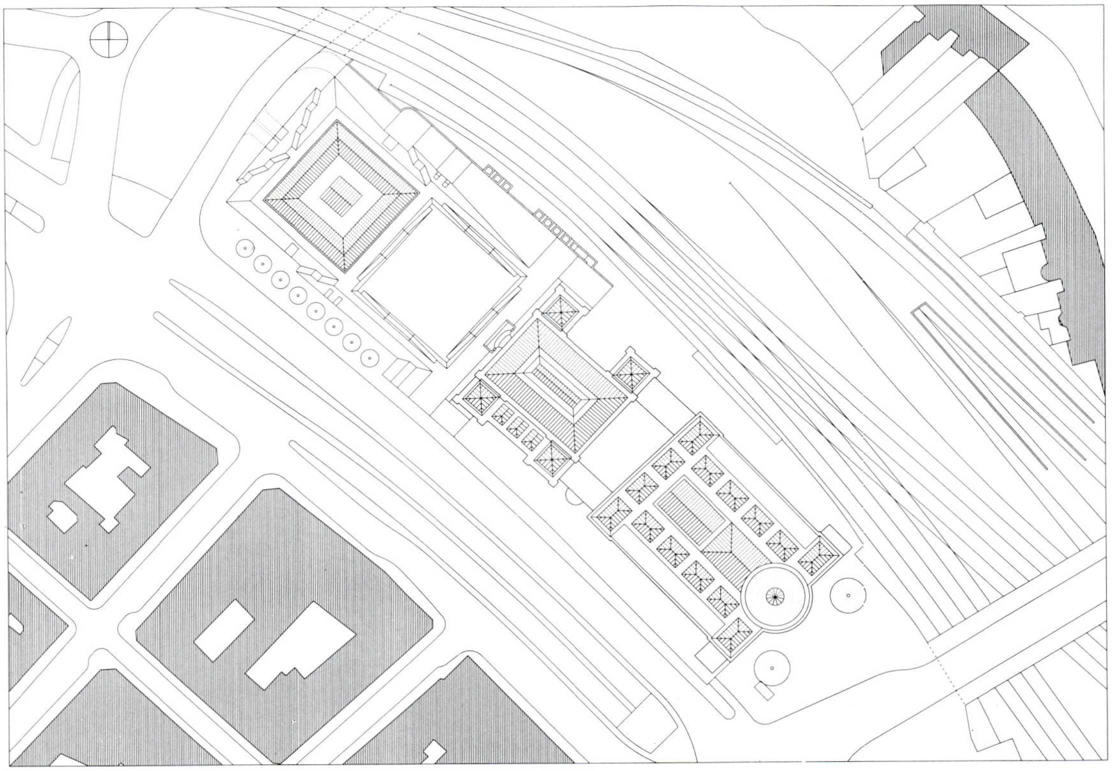

Sketches; first-upper-story plan; ground-level plan; basement-level plan.

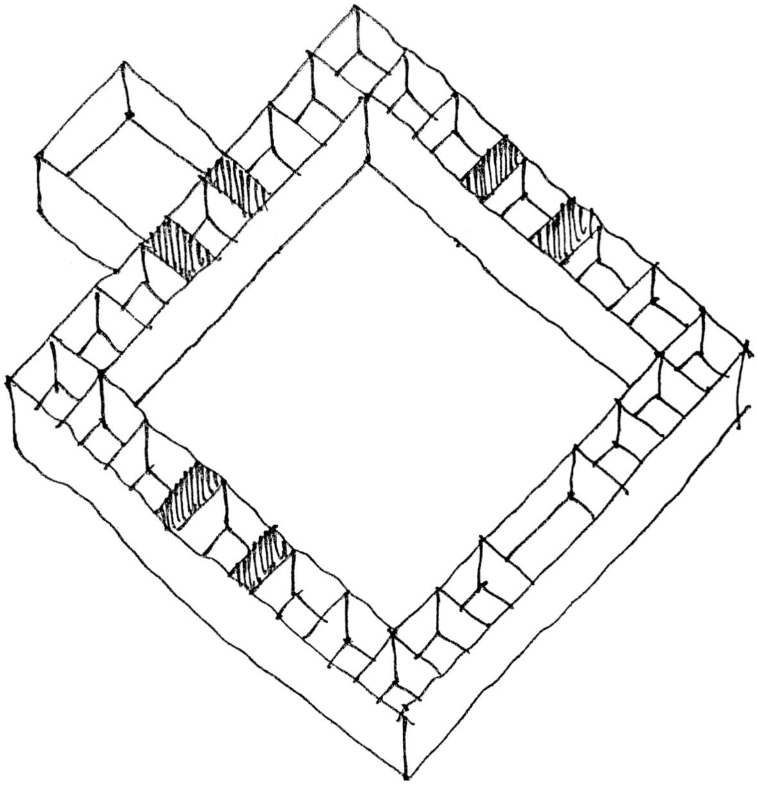

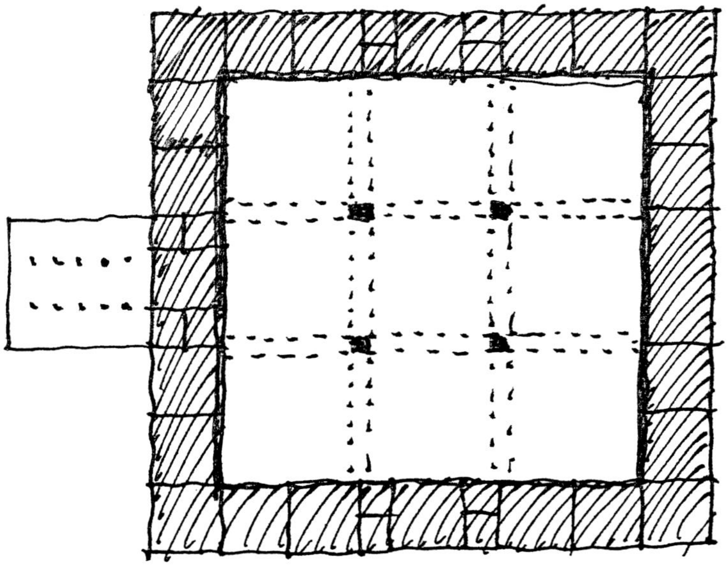

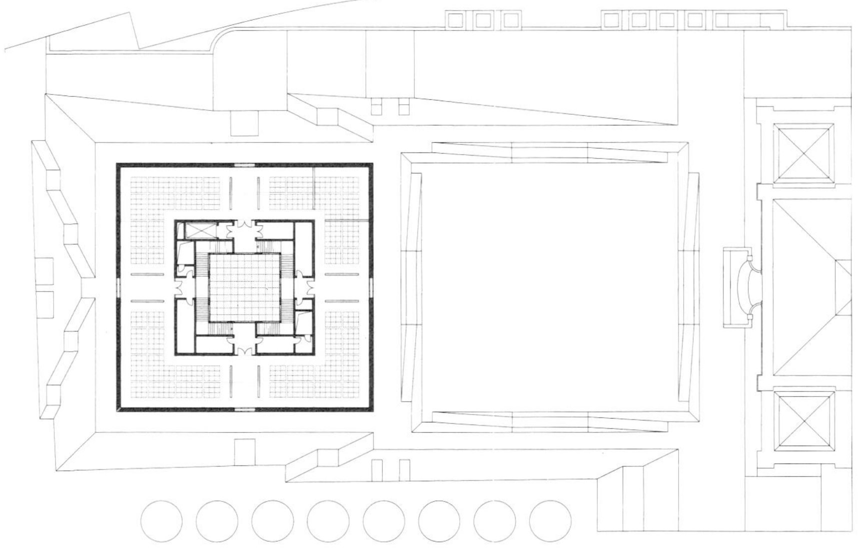

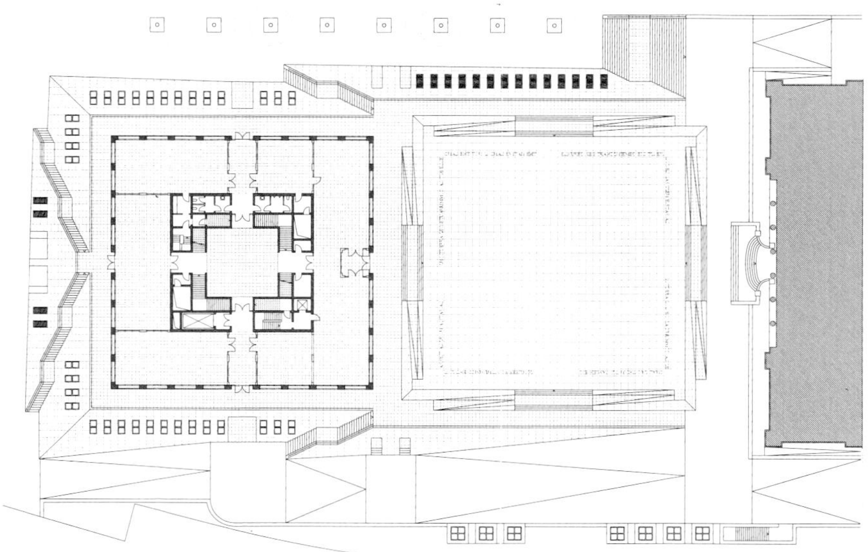

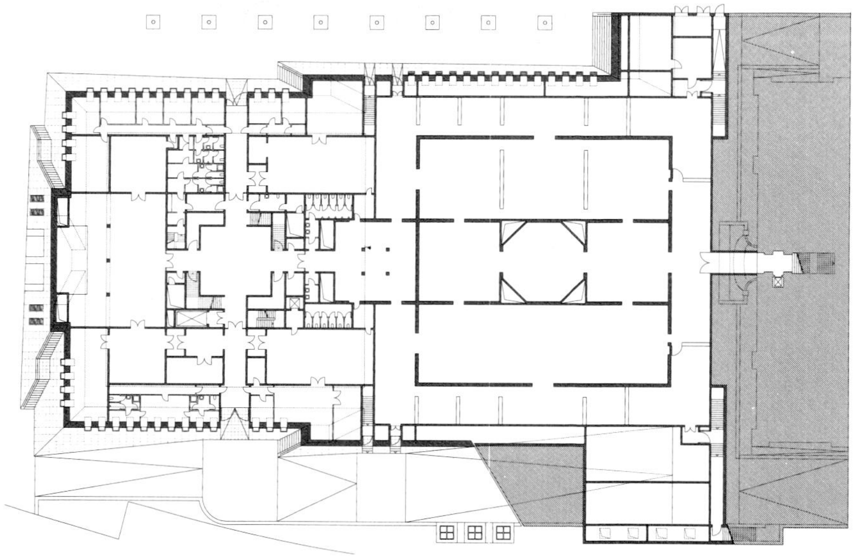

Perspective; exterior.

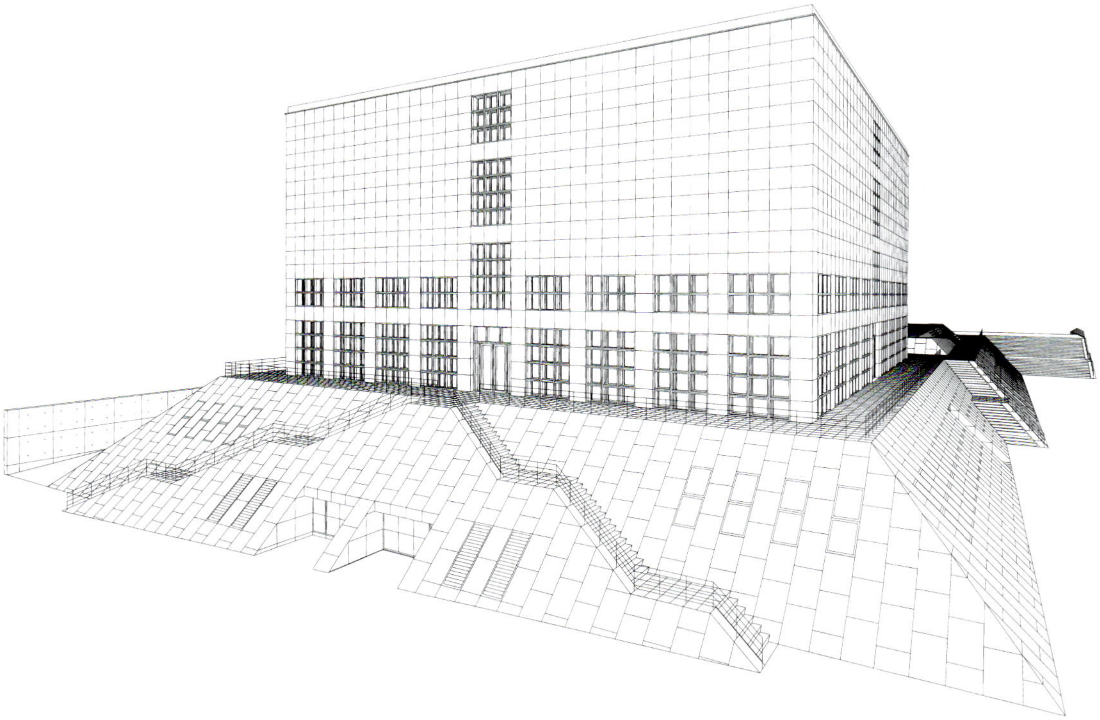

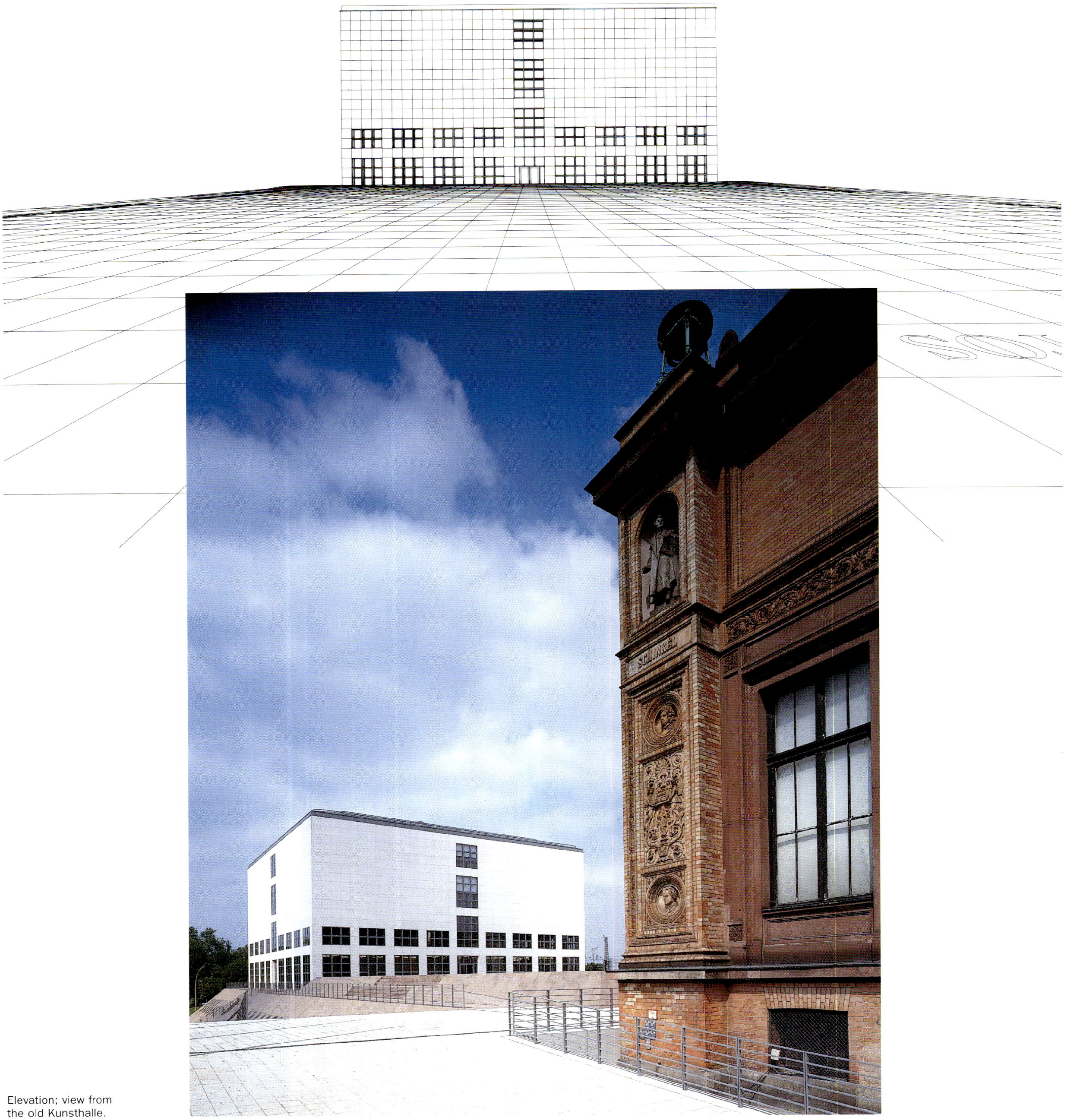

Elevation; view from
the old Kunsthalle.

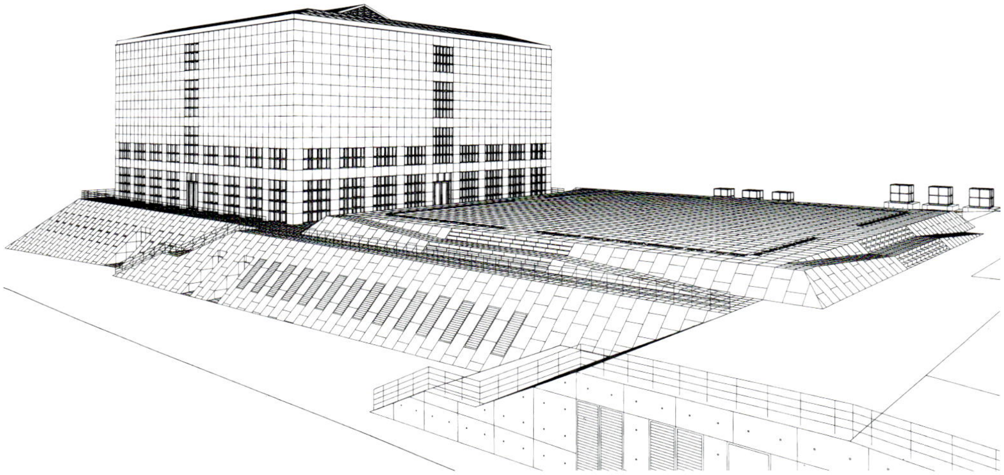

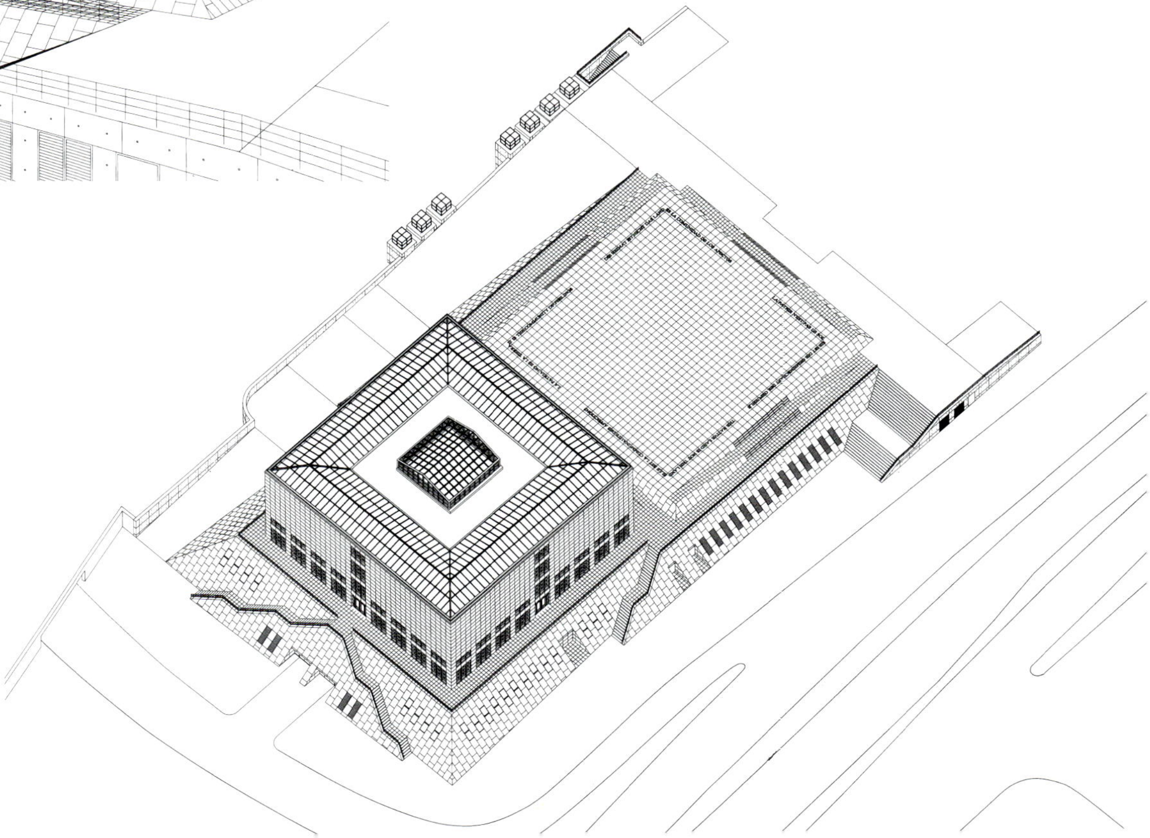

View from “Am Ferdinandstor”; perspectives showing plaza design with inscription in four languages by Ian Hamilton Finlay: “The native land is not the land; it is the community of feelings.”

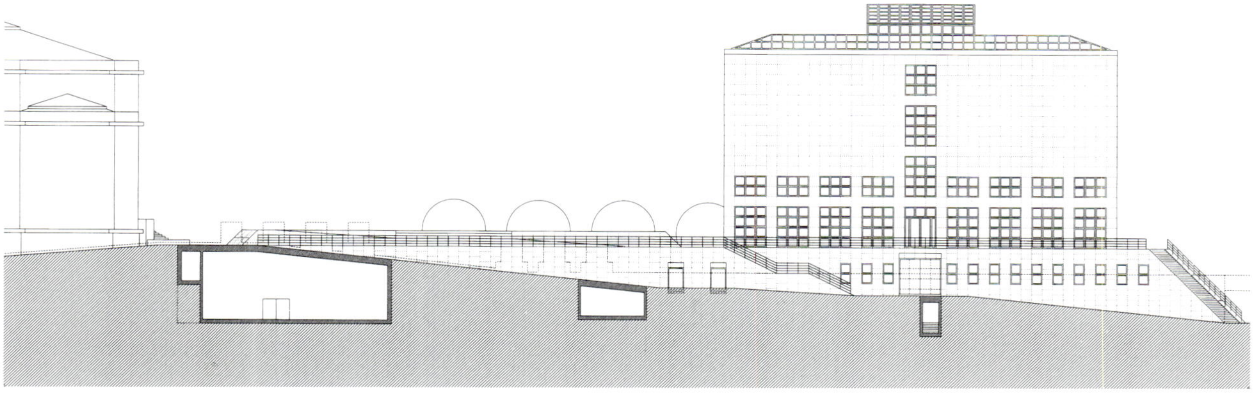

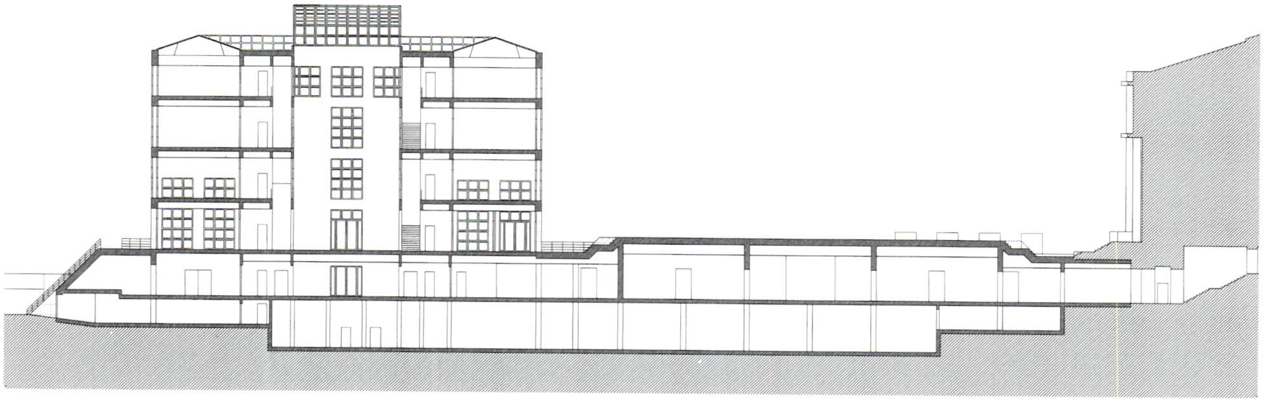

Elevations; views; sections.

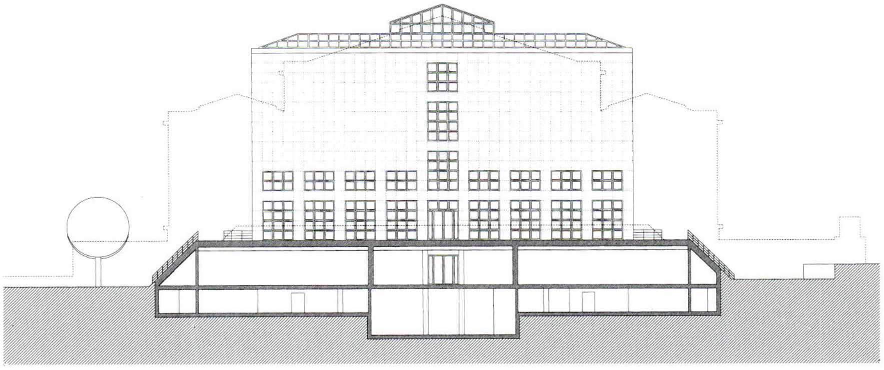

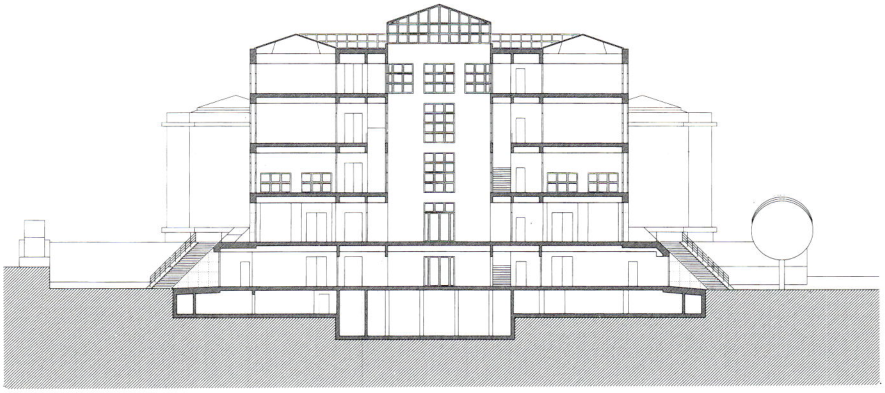

Views into central hall.

Exhibition spaces.

Residence of the German Ambassador, Washington, D.C., 1982, 1987–1995

Project team: Ingo Schrader, Peter Kretz, Ricardo Sargiotti

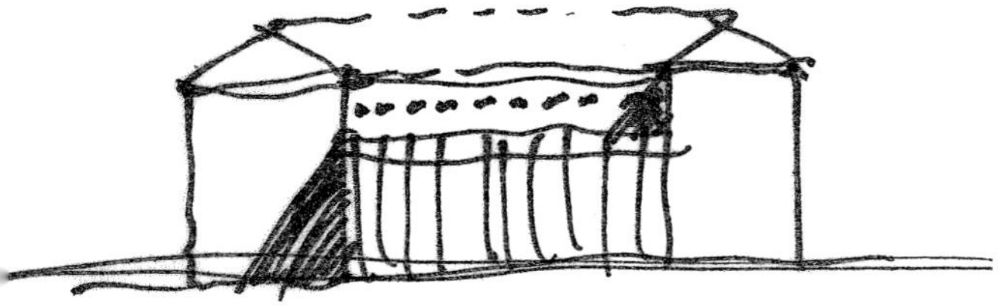

The residence of the German ambassador in Washington, D.C., is intended not merely as a functional building but as a mirror of German architectural culture. An ambassador's residence serves for political self-representation but also and above all as a cultural institution, manifesting the artistic, architectural, and technical achievement of a particular nation as well as its aspirations and self-understanding. The external appearance and interior design represent a "calling card" with which a land presents itself in the host country.

An imposing, extravagant architecture of the kind typical of such buildings in the nineteenth century seemed inappropriate for Germany, whose intellectual traditions are rooted in the Enlightenment. Nor did an exaggeratedly modern demeanor—all too optimistic, youthful, and future-oriented, perhaps with technological aspect in the foreground—necessarily appear suitable for a country with a two-thousand-year-old, dialectical history. Any kind of extreme conception—whether dominated by pure history or re-creating the supposed dynamism of futuristic visions—was rejected as inappropriate and not reflective of reality. Rather, the search for a suitable design led to a combination of tradition and the modern, in an effort to adequately represent both the presence of history and the progressive spirit of the land.

The building is intended to show that forms and typologies familiar from the history of architecture can indeed be brought together into a modern, rational combination, appropriate to the present time and purpose—not in the sense of quotations or copies of historical models but rather in an architectural language reduced to essentials. In this way, not only are old and new elements combined into a complex whole, but the interconnection of different building parts and architectural elements such as walls, arcades, stairs, facades, and spaces creates the impression not of a single house but of a compact aggregation of houses.

The Romanesque church with its westwork and east end, its nave and side aisles, as well as its towers, walls, and chapels, was conceived as the image of an ideal city; the Roman villa, which served as the model for the medieval palace, was not only a simple house but an interlocking, overlapping complex of different forms and parts. Accordingly, the ambassador's residence is conceived as the concentration and microcosm of a wide

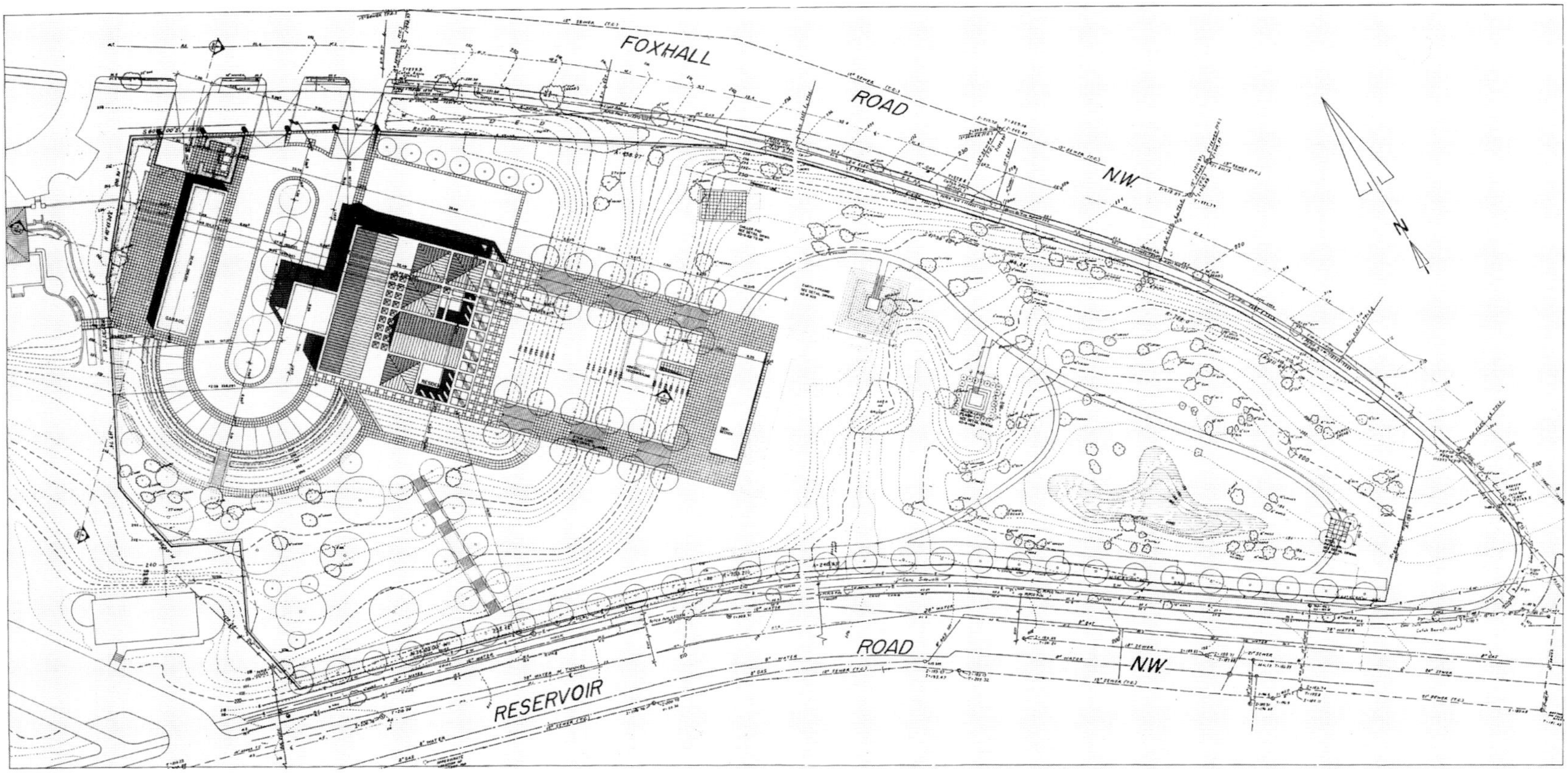

Sketches; site plan.

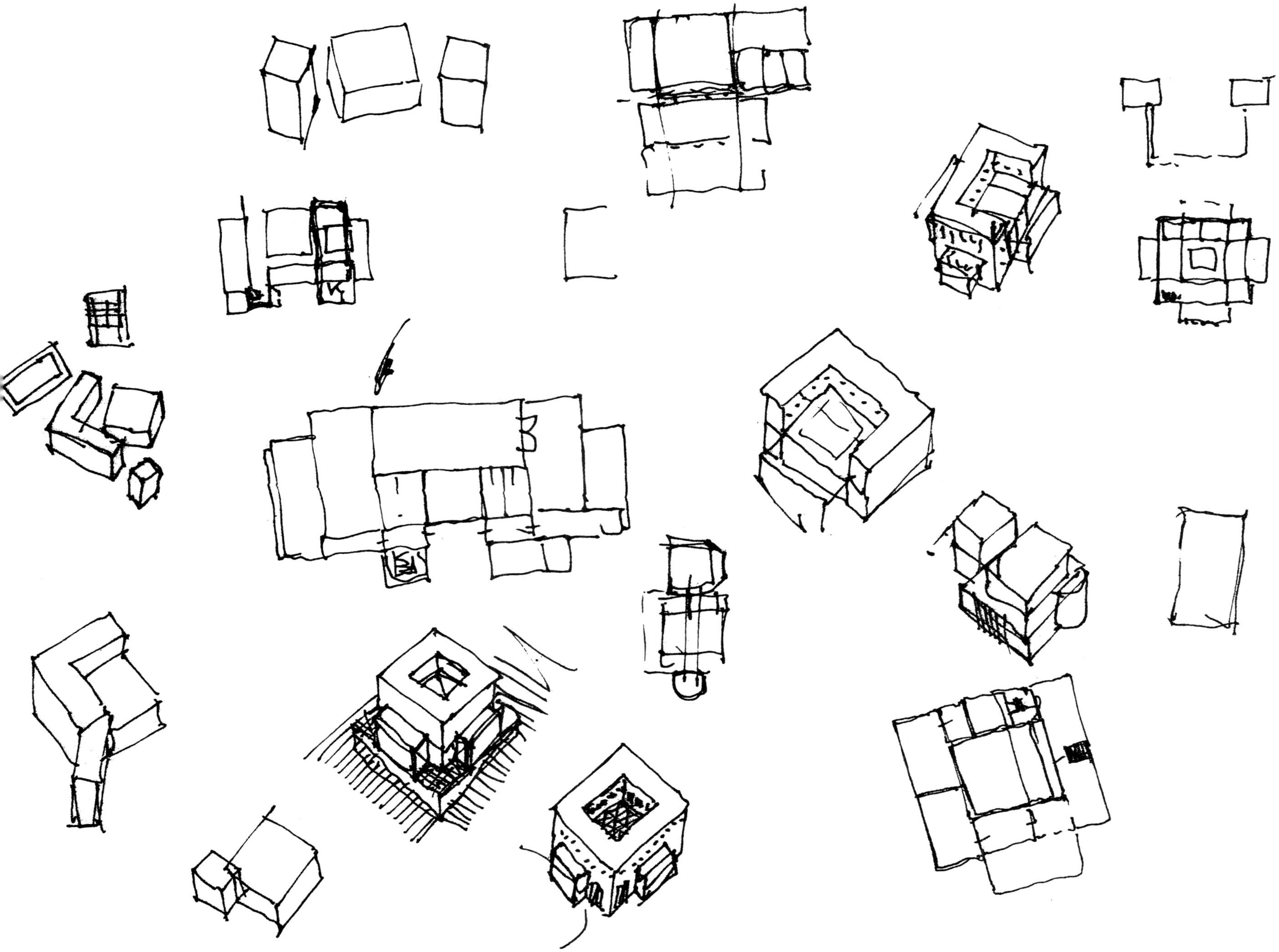

Sketch; views of
portico from lawn.

West elevation; portico details.

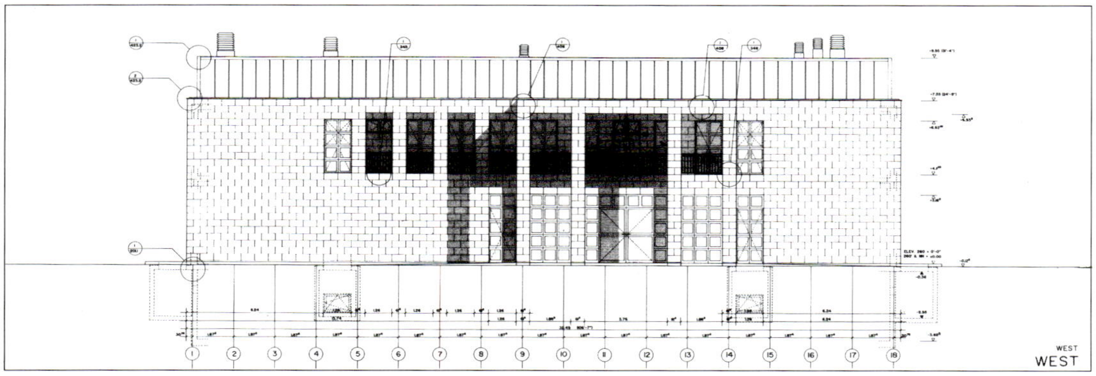

East, south, and north elevations and views.

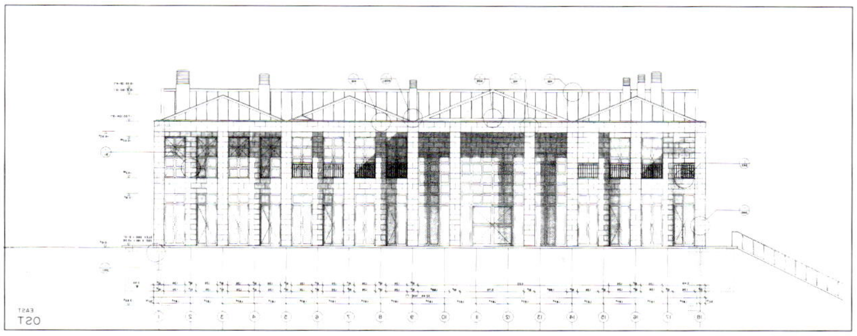

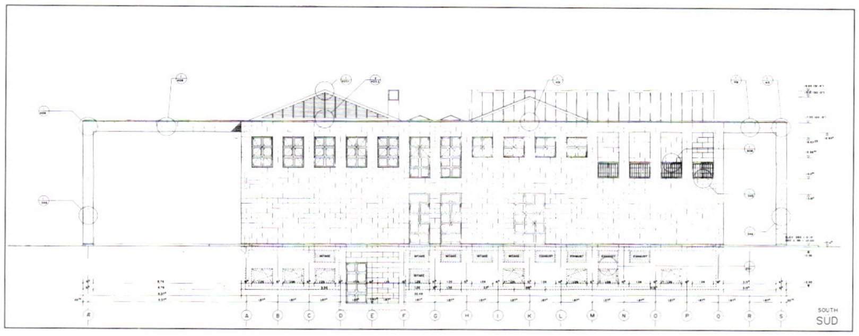

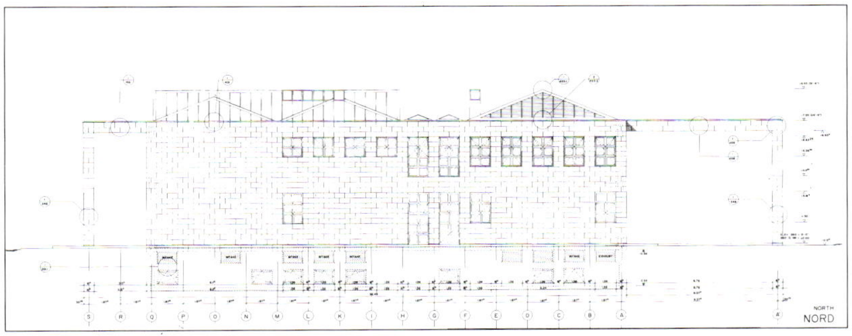

Overleaf:
Section; ground-level plan; view into reception hall with frieze by Markus Lüpertz.

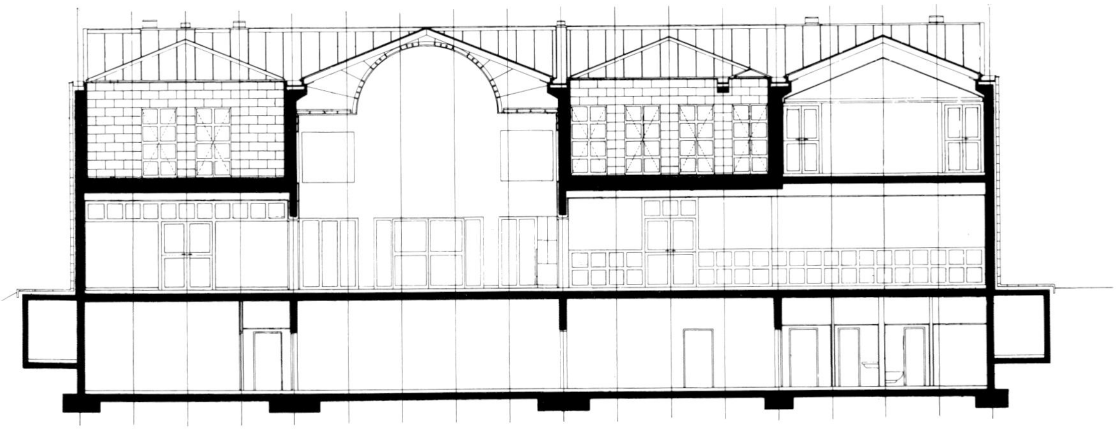

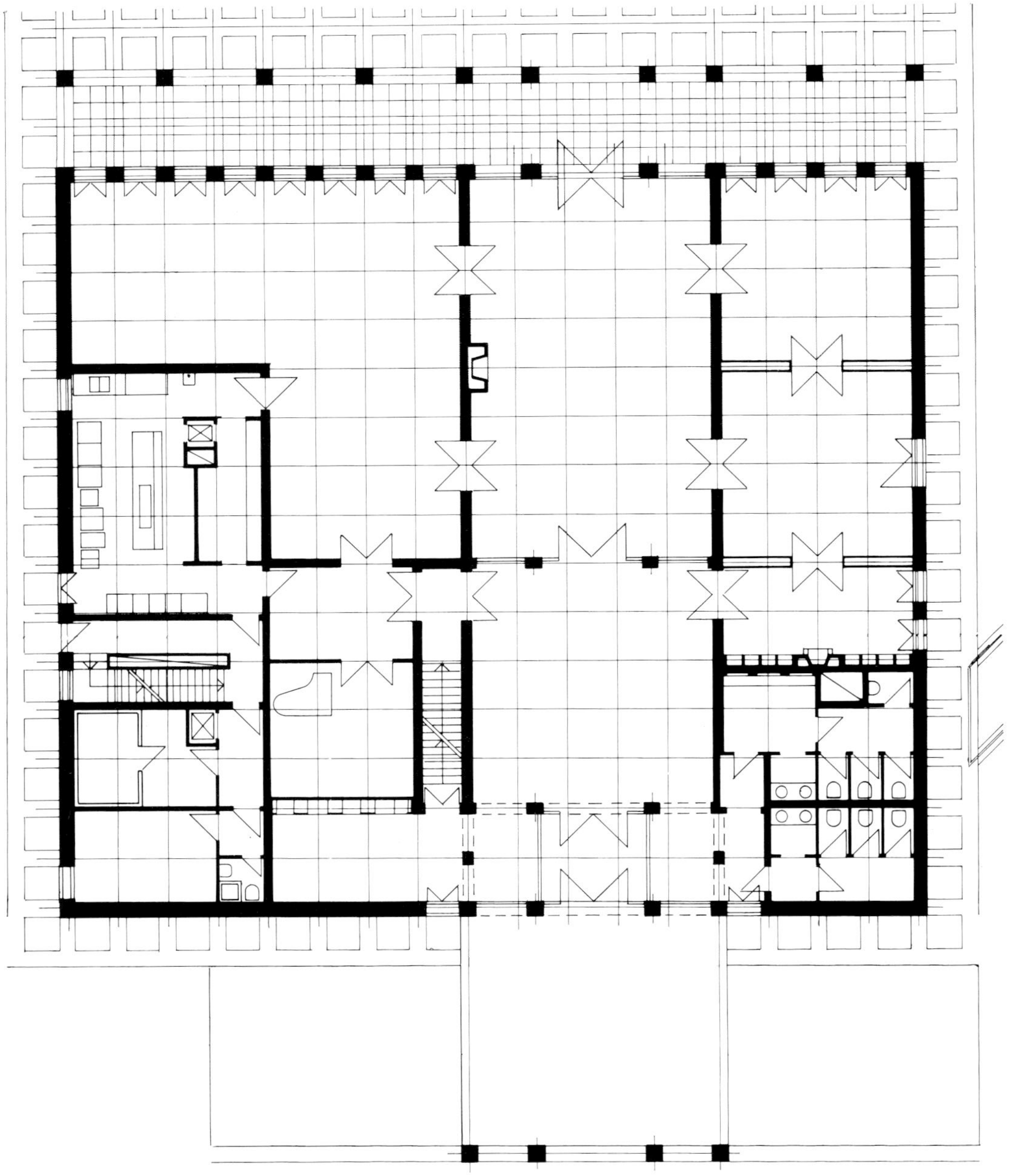

variety of functions—political representation and private dwelling, personal work and official ceremony—with all the adjacent and necessary facilities. In this way, a conceptual approach to an embassy building can be found in an age that tends toward randomness and a lack of identity, a means of transcending pure function to achieve a form of expression that is not arbitrary and interchangeable, suitable for any land and its history, but tailored solely to the particular country.

The plateau site of the old Harriman villa was chosen as the location for the residence. The driveway and approach to the complex have remained in their original location. The driveway approaches the building frontally, so that the visitor is directed into the entrance hall through a projecting structure. The main room of the house is the great reception hall, set off from the rest of the complex as an independent volume with a pitched roof. Its large glass front faces a terrace with a portico opening onto the lawn. Adjacent to the reception hall on one side are ladies' and gentlemen's chambers as well as a small library; on the other is a large dining hall that can be divided into three smaller spaces. The service facilities form a separate wing to the west. The upper story accommodates the private dwelling and sleeping rooms of the ambassador.

There are three separate entrances to the upper story: a direct connection from the reception hall for official guests and the ambassador, a private entrance for the ambassador's family on the east side, and an employees' entrance on the west from the service facilities. All of them lead into a large parlor that provides access to the individual rooms or groups of rooms. The living and dining rooms and sleeping areas are connected to a large terrace.

The building is integrated into the surrounding landscape in a variety of ways. To the southeast, toward the grounds of the park, a transition is achieved from architecture to nature, from artificial space to natural space. The closed volume of the building dissolves into the portico which is transparent even toward the top. The basalt socle develops into a continuous platform paved in basalt, from which two parallel stairways lead down into the lawn area. These stairways follow the slope and articulate the topography. At the bottom, a spacious terrace with an inset pool provides a rest area at the point of direct

transition to the open terrain. With its noble, reserved design and select materials—white limestone for the facades and dark oak wood for the windows and doors—the residence stands for the artisanal and architectural tradition of its land of origin; a symbol of cultural diversity, it manifests formal austerity and precision of craftsmanship.

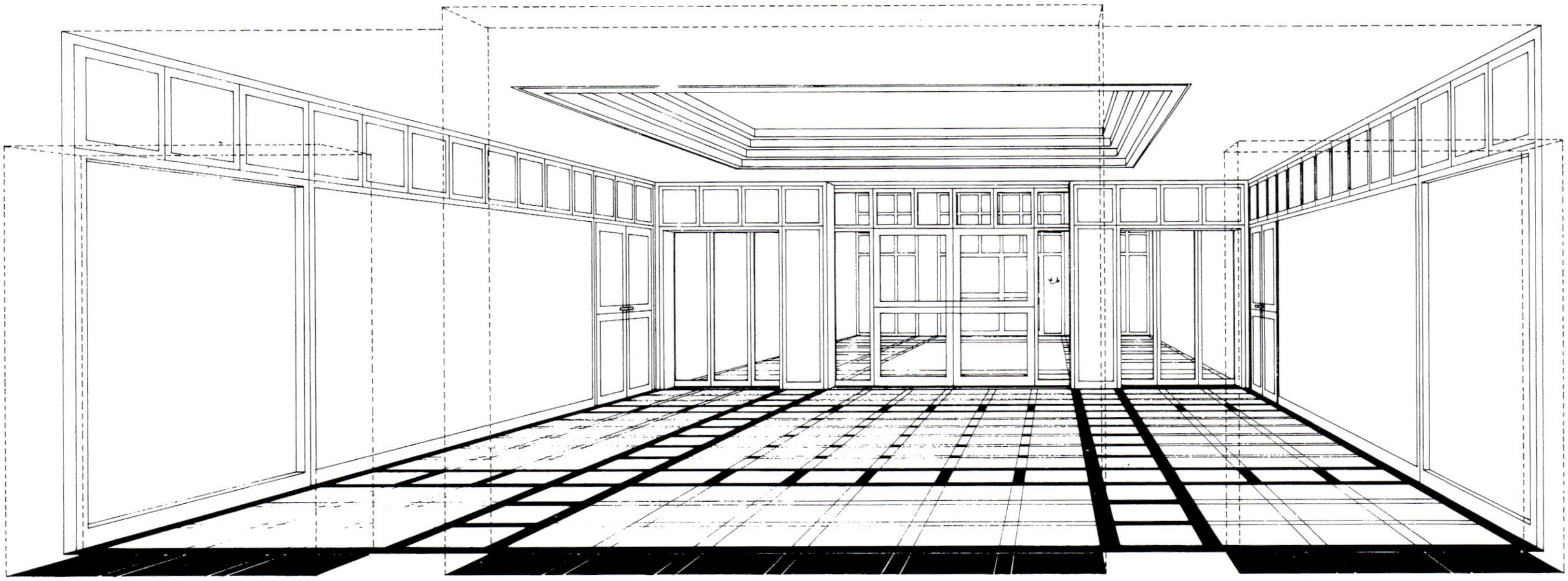

Gentlemen's chamber with frescoes by Christa Näher; ladies' chamber with carpet and ceiling design by Rosemarie Trockel.

Opposite:
Entrance hall with wall design by Gerhard Merz; perspective of entrance hall; library; dining room with paravent by Simone Ungers; corridor.

Redesign of Bayerische Hypotheken- und Wechselbank, Düsseldorf, 1988–1991

Project team: Karl-Lothar Dietzsch, Milan Pitlach, Ulrich Wiegmann, Bernhard Trübenbach, Barbara Taha, Volker Busse, Knud Ehm, Andreas Geitner, Claudia Henning, Martina Röhr, Detlef Porsch, Kaspar Steves

The redesign of the bank building in Düsseldorf involved a number of stipulations. The old Kirchfeld-Haus, a building by Helmut Hentrich and Hans Heuser located on the Königsallee, was to be expanded inward into an interior courtyard, provided with additional stories, restructured, and adapted to the new demands of the bank.

The objective was to adequately respond to the building's surroundings while at the same time creating spaces with a clear and striking individual identity.

The center-to-center distance and positioning of supports in the new building were established by the old structure. Ungers used these elements to develop the fundamental idea that gives the building its present character. The sequence of spaces and their specific structure were inherent in the existing layout. Ungers's careful search for basic architectural patterns brought to light a multiplicity of archetypes. The pronaos of the Greek temple and the portico of the Roman villa become a roofed-over porch area supported by pillars, accessible day and night. The rectangular main hall is surrounded by colonnades as in a Roman forum, though here they accommodate not shops but counters and desks. One of these colonnades leads into the interior courtyard square, crowned by a glass dome and surrounded by a two-story gallery like the colonnade of a Roman peristyle.

The basic module of the building is a square measuring 62.5 centimeters on each side, from which all the dimensions of the building are derived. It has often been said that the square is Ungers's obsession; it is an obsession that has not only found expression in many of his buildings but was also explicated in a small publication in which numerous

View; elevation; section.

Opposite:
View from above;
isometric studies; plan.

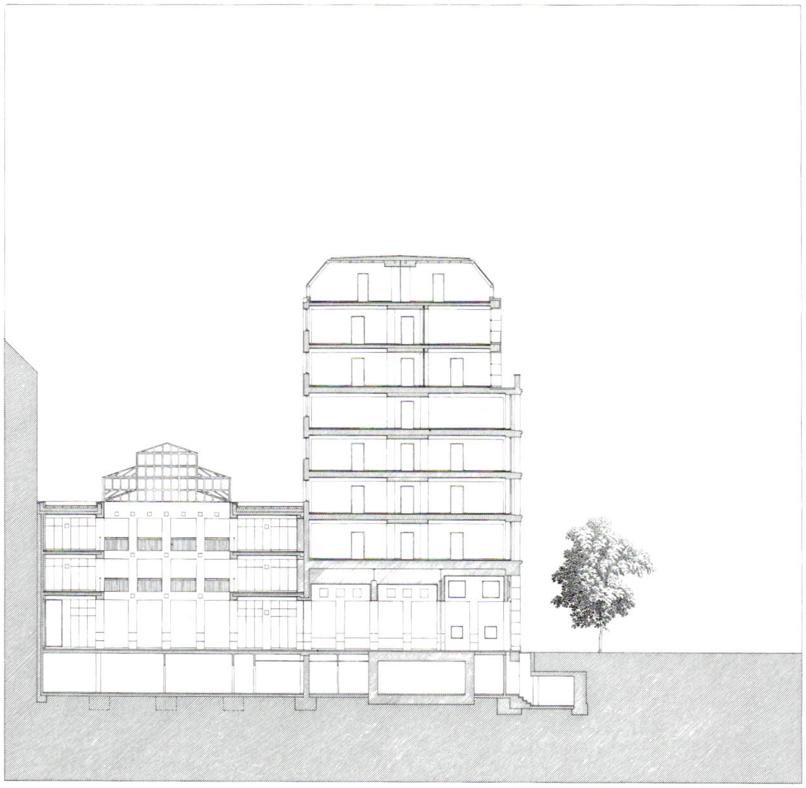

examples from prehistory to the twentieth century served to demonstrate the power of this basic geometric form since earliest times. As an eternal symbol of cosmic harmony and earthly existence—its four corners recalling the four seasons, the four elements, and the four cardinal points of the compass—the square speaks for itself. It needs no justification; it is a timeless form, one that has been predominant in all epochs of architecture.

Nonetheless, Ungers's choice of the square was not merely an arbitrary artistic decision. The form was not imposed upon the building but was already present in the existing layout. Here, Ungers responded to the variety of activities, transactions, and demands that converge in a bank with an architecture whose clarity and individuality unify this variety without limiting it. The main spaces of the bank—porch, hall, and interior courtyard—function as a marketplace, public plaza and meeting point. Off to the side, in the passages and colonnades that connect these centers, are spaces for private transactions. The diverse character of bank functions is reflected in the multiplicity of spatial and optical experiences that the building presents to its users.

In each space, art elaborates a different architectural element. In the porch, a continuous frieze appears in the area above the supports; the ceiling of the main hall has been accentuated; the floor surface beneath the glass cupola in the interior courtyard is an important dynamic element. Finally, in the colonnade farthest away from the entrance, the rear wall of the building is dissolved into shimmering surfaces. The linear sequence of spaces thus establishes an art axis with four essential stations that can be experienced individually but can also be related to each other from a variety of perspectives in ever new ways.—*Katarina Hegewisch*

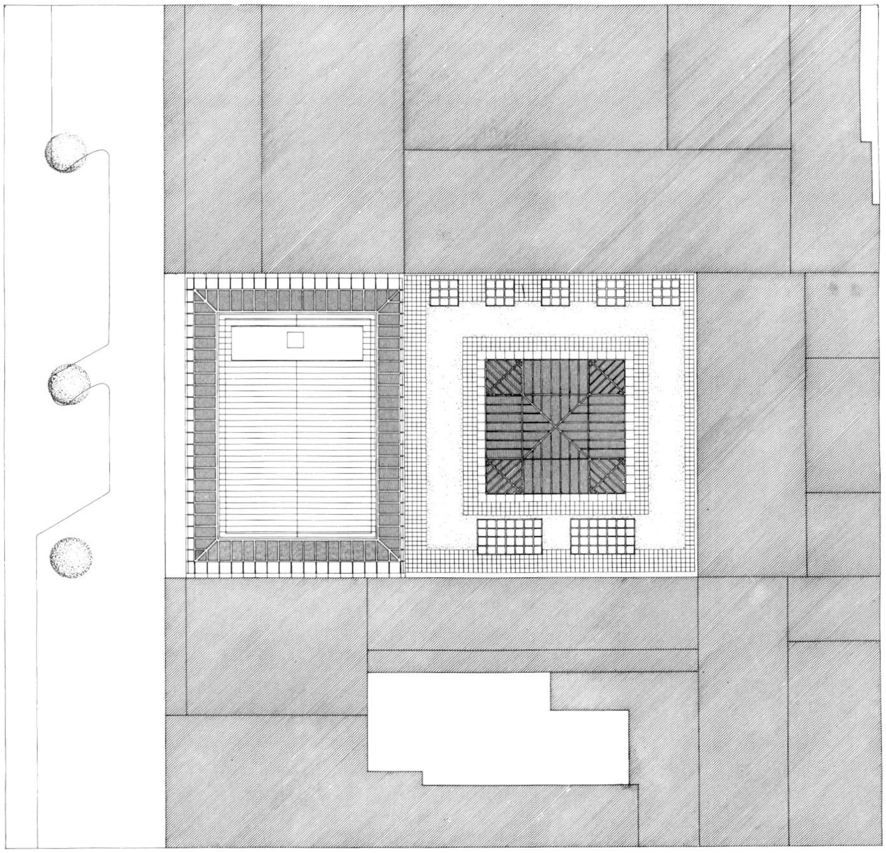

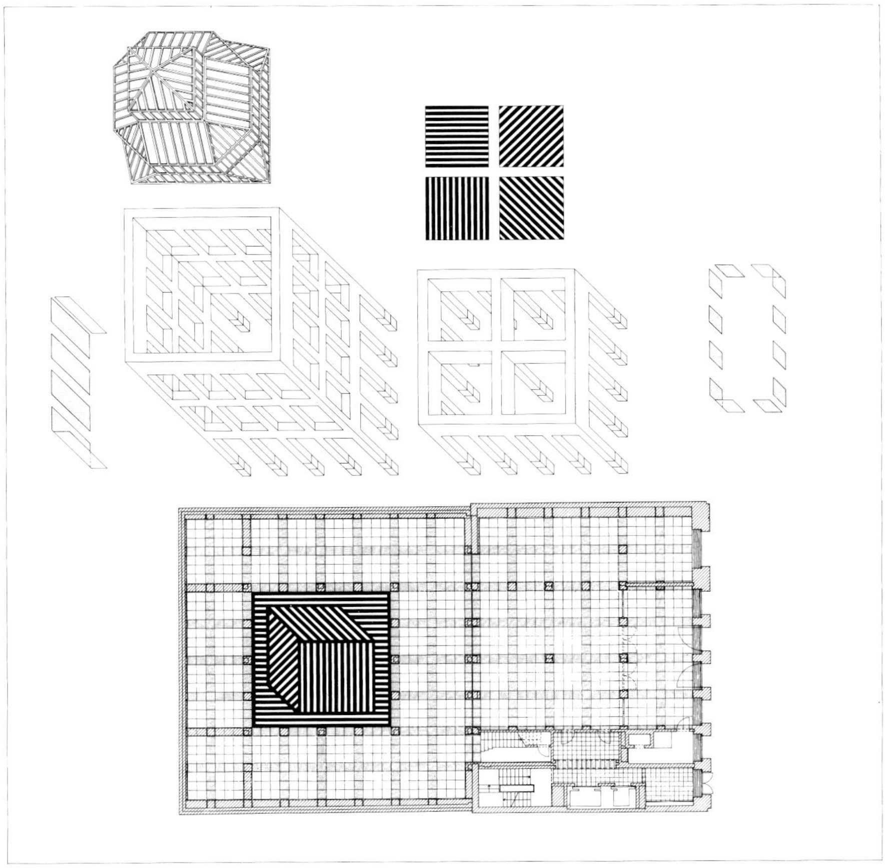

Axonometric showing floor design by Sol LeWitt; views of cupola from exterior and interior.

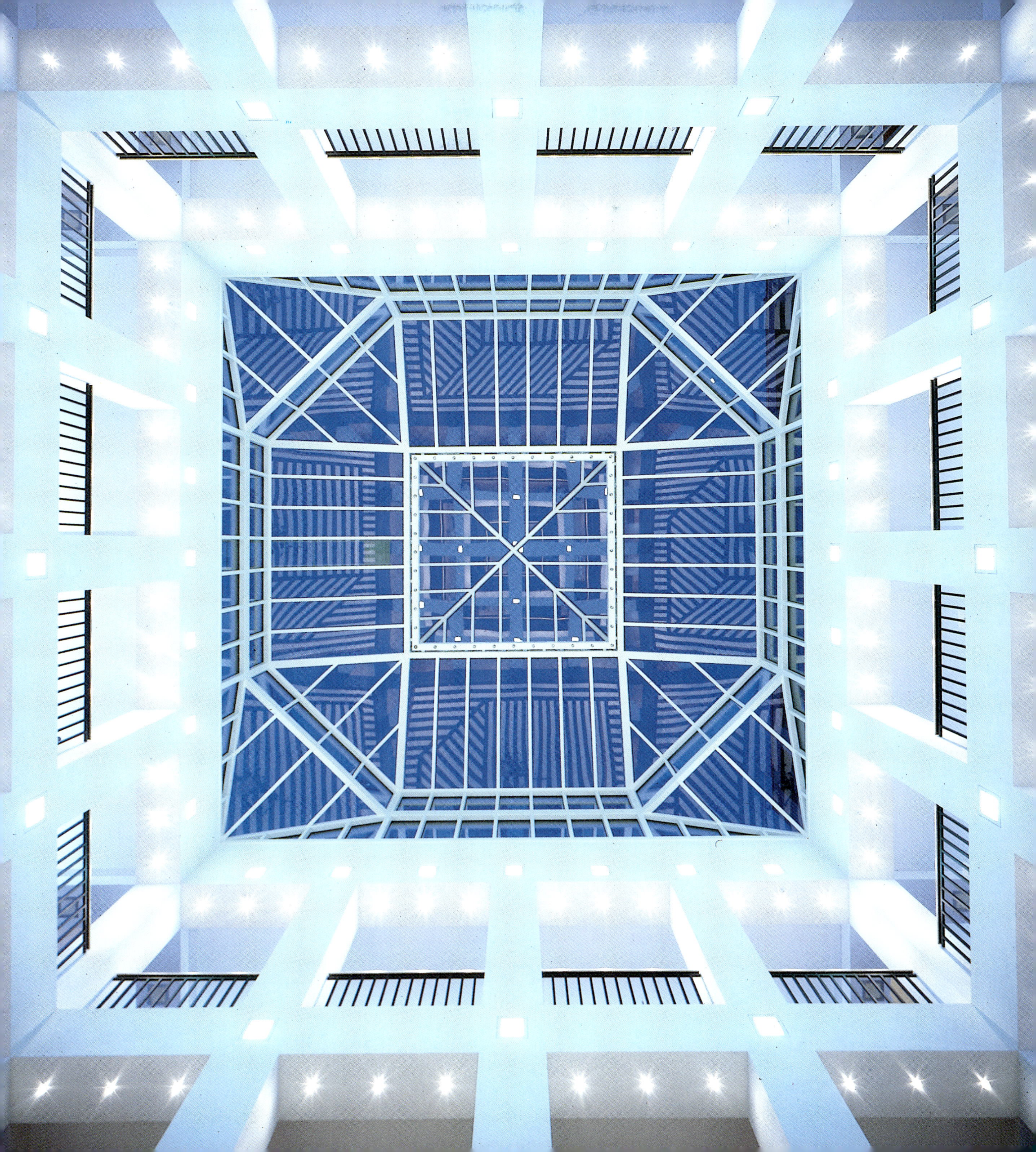

Views into main hall, tellers' area, and entrance hall.

GEW Thermal Plant, Cologne-Merheim, 1988–1990

Project team: Joachim Klose, Joachim Waack, Karl-Lothar Dietzsch, Andreas Geitner

The region around Cologne is marked by carbon and petrochemical factories that have settled in the lignite strip mining areas. The thermal plant in Cologne-Merheim is an experimental complex for recovering of heat and energy with a new coal-atomization technology. In this process, coal dust mixed with sand is whirled under high pressure and burned. The complex in Cologne-Merheim is the first in which the furnaces are arranged vertically.

The engineering-technical project and the accompanying architecture were already finished when Ungers was approached by the municipal administration. Thus the arrangement of the individual building parts had to be taken into consideration. With this first public commission in Cologne, Ungers thematically interprets the uniqueness of the building's function in a stepped form and places the fully self-contained object into the landscape, where it is visible from afar. The steel skeleton construction is faced with self-bearing prefabricated sections in a patented system. Square, intarsia-like surfaces faced in brick are articulated with divides painted petroleum green. With his typical rigor, Ungers recalls the tradition of early industrial architecture and positions a visible sign in the renaturalized expanse of the Rhenish lowlands. —*Walter A. Noebel*

Exterior.

Elevations; exteriors.

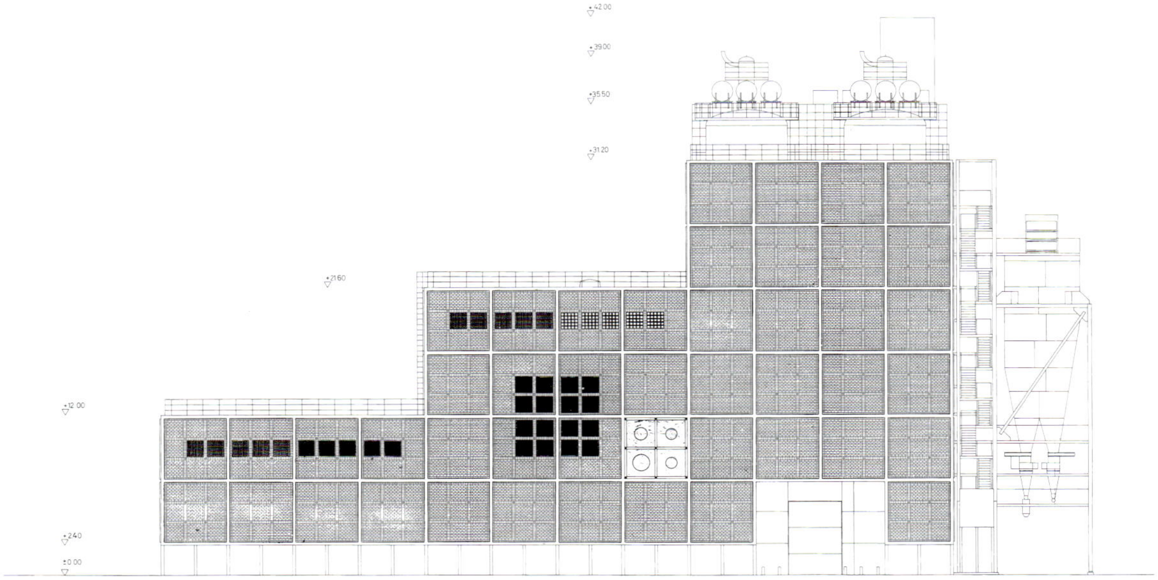

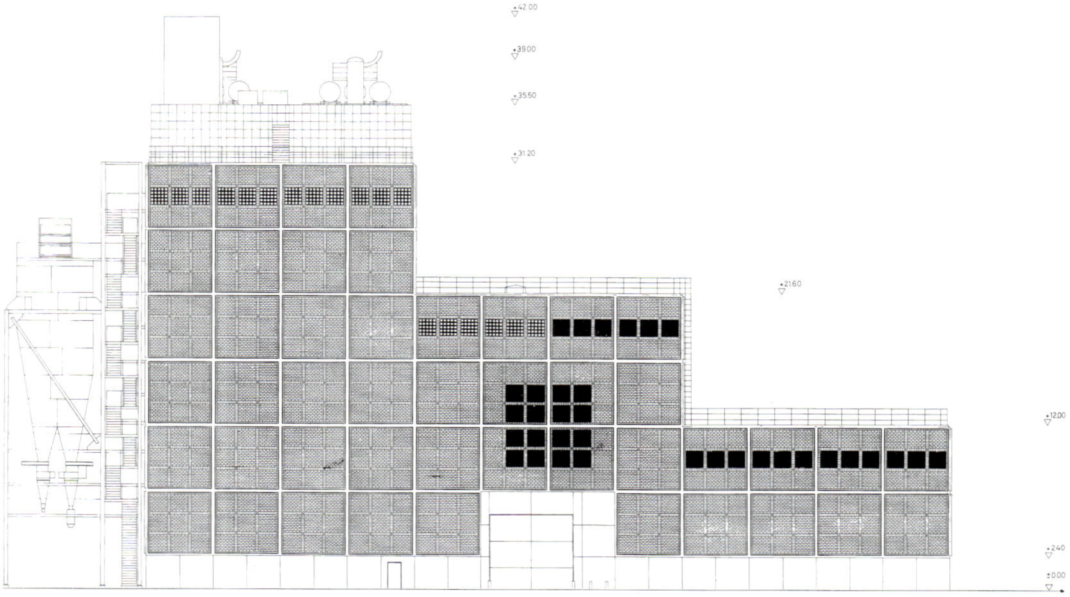

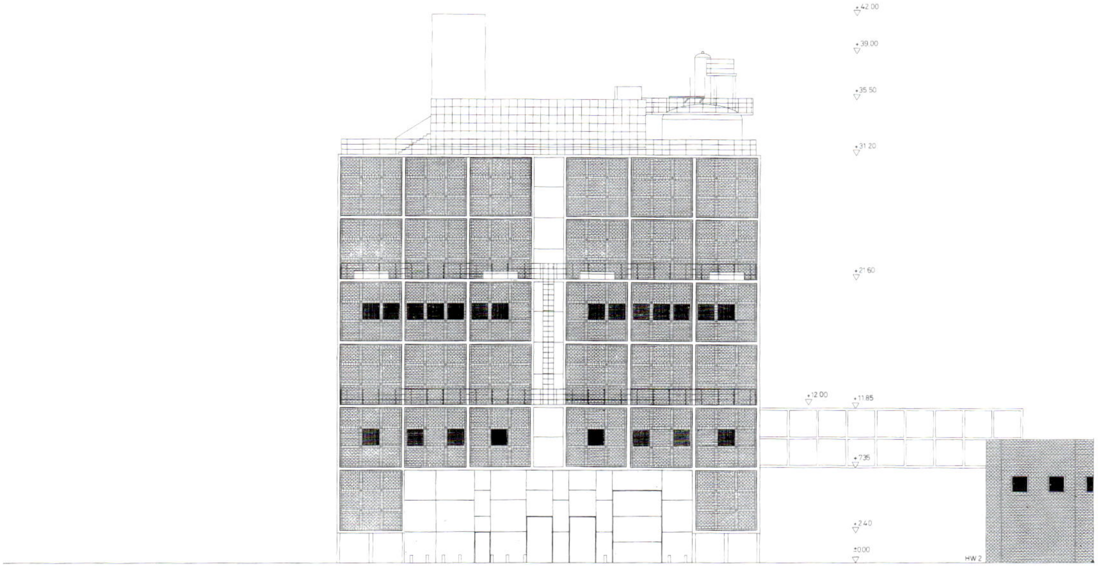
+42.00
+39.00
+35.50
+31.20
+21.60
+12.00
+11.85
+7.35
+2.40
±0.00
HW 2

Elevation; exterior.

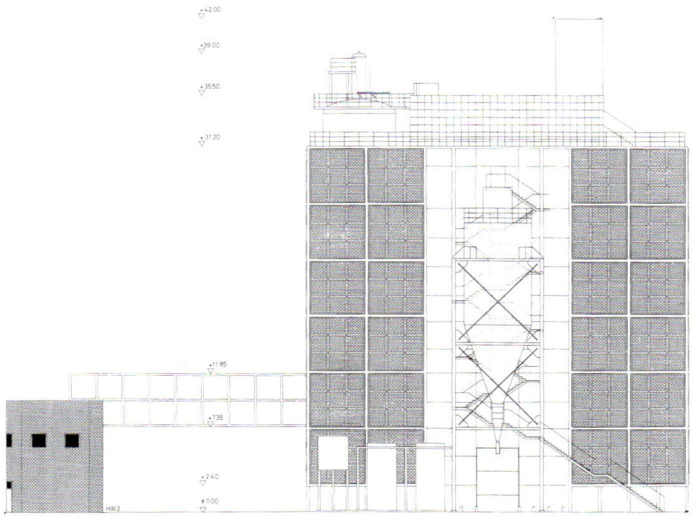

Competition Design for Thermenmuseum with Roman Baths, Trier, 1988-1996

Project team: Kai-Uwe Lompa, Johannes Götz

In 1988, excavations for an underground parking garage at the Viehmarktplatz in Trier uncovered Celtic and Roman ruins. Further archaeological excavations brought to light the well-preserved foundations, floors, and walls of the largest Roman baths north of the Alps.

In order to preserve this unique and historically significant find, the city announced a competition for the protection and public display of the ruins, a competition won by Ungers in 1989.

The urban character of the Viehmarktplatz is defined by the finely articulated facades on the southeast and southwest edges of the plaza. To the northwest, the St.-Antonius-Kirche forms a prominent element projecting into the plaza, while the northern boundary is established by the new bank building of the Sparkasse. For the most part, the Thermenmuseum is located below the surface of the plaza, covered by the inclined plane of the pavement. In the northeastern part, a square measuring thirty by thirty meters is cut out and elevated twelve meters, opening up a view into the lower-lying strata of urban history. This "lid" rests on a regular grid of supports, while the space between the "lid" and the plaza is protected on the exterior by a transparent glass facade. The glass cube alludes to the grid articulating the plaza parallel to the Viehmarktstrasse. Cutting through this newly defined grid are the Roman axes of the *cardo* and *decmanus*, a conscious evocation of the conflict between the grid of the plaza level and the coordinates of the ruins as well as between the ruins and the remains of a medieval monastery above it.

This theme defines the entire design of the building. In the above-ground section, the glass cube is oriented to the newly defined grid of the plaza; the passages cut through it, however, which enable the visitor to enter

Aerial view; sketch.

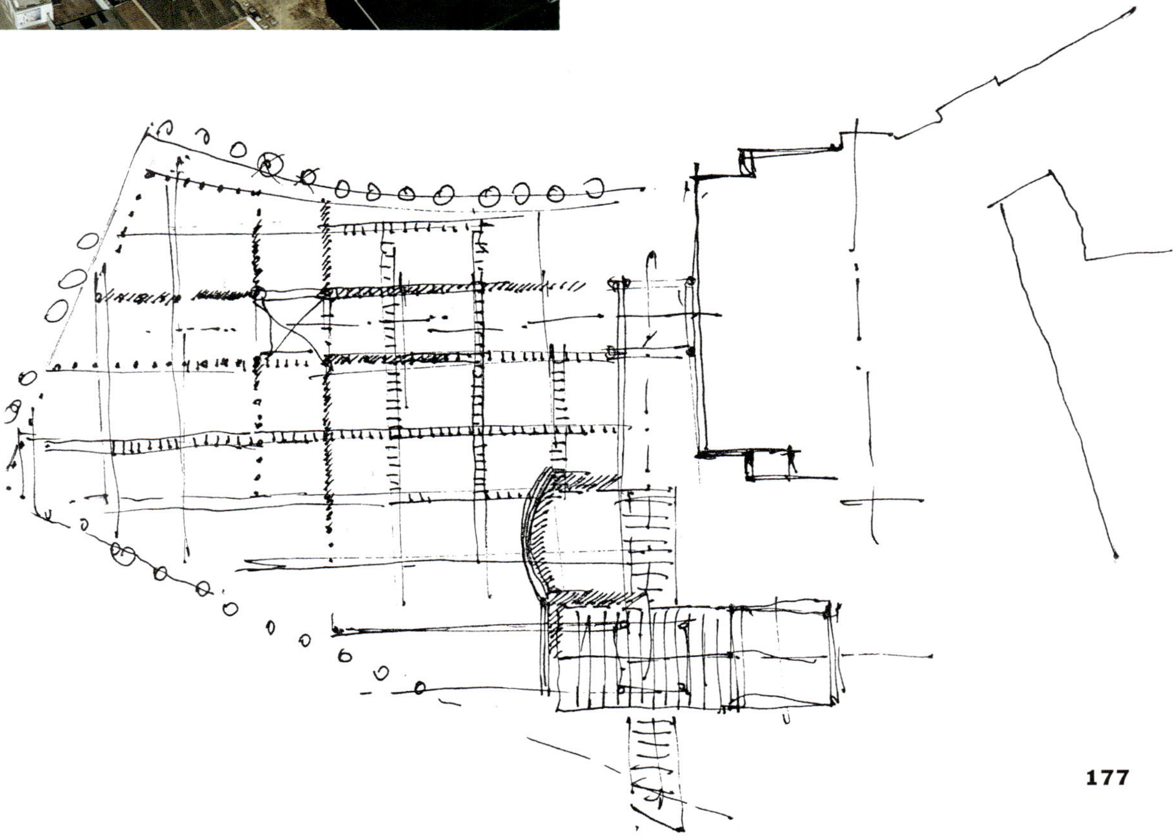

Site plan; exterior; ground level plan; basement-level plan.

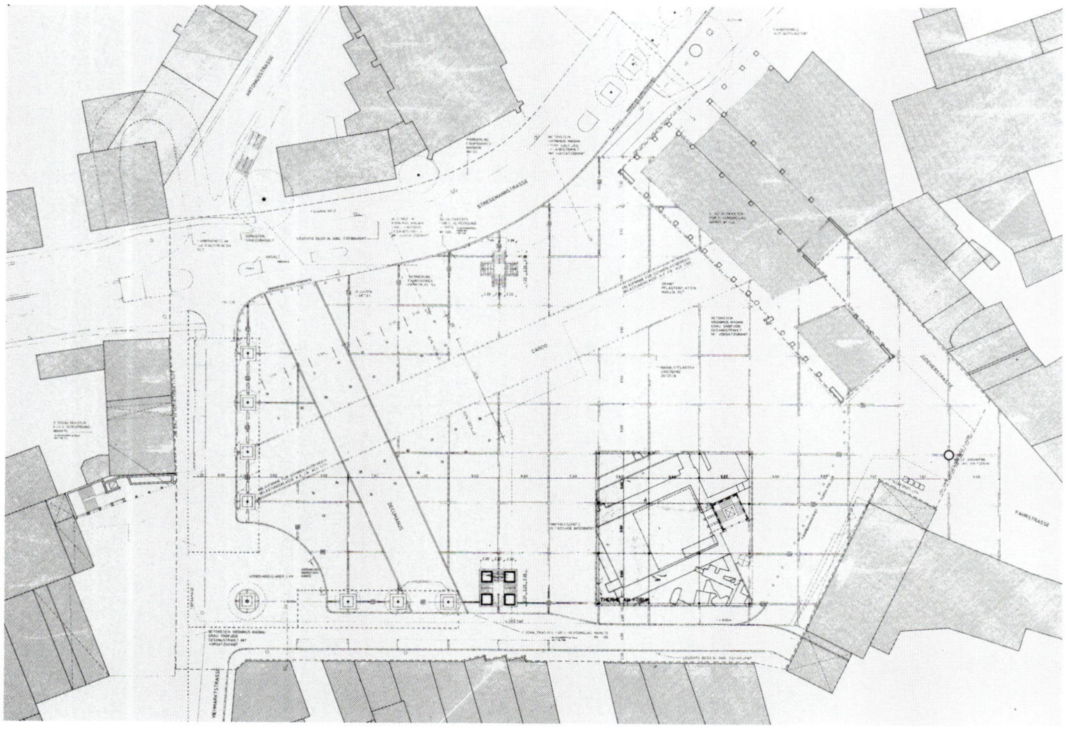

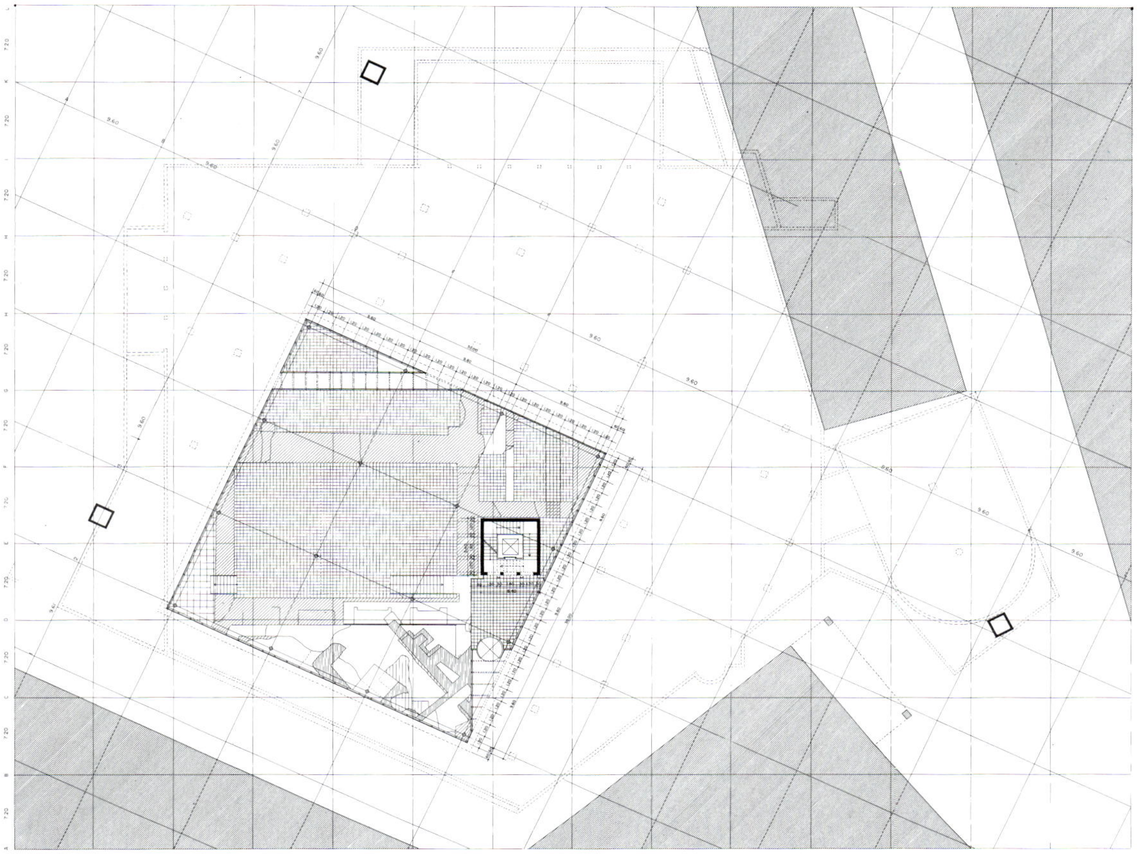

bank

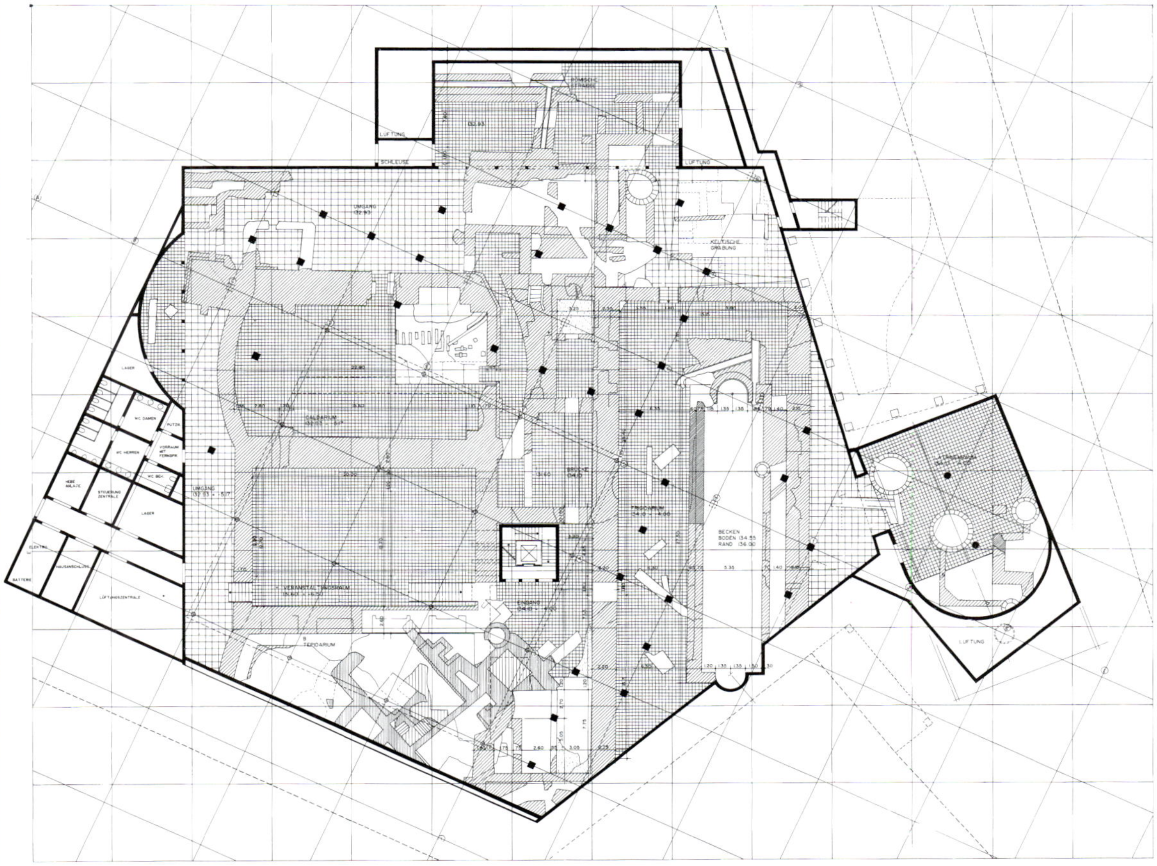

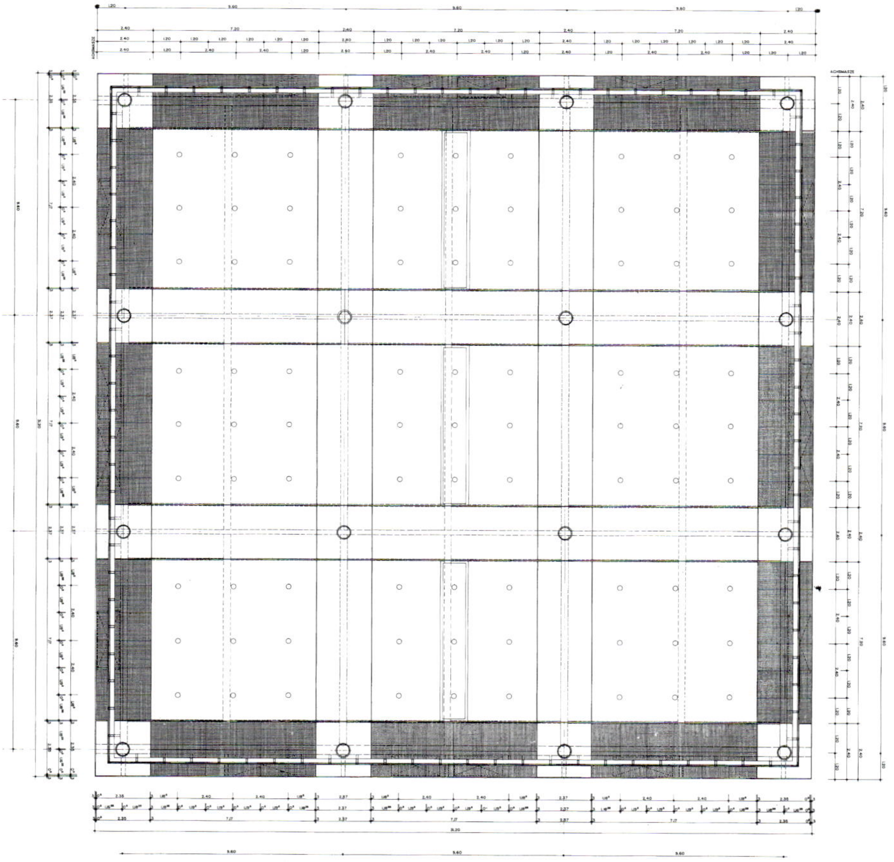

Exterior; reflected ceiling plan; sections.

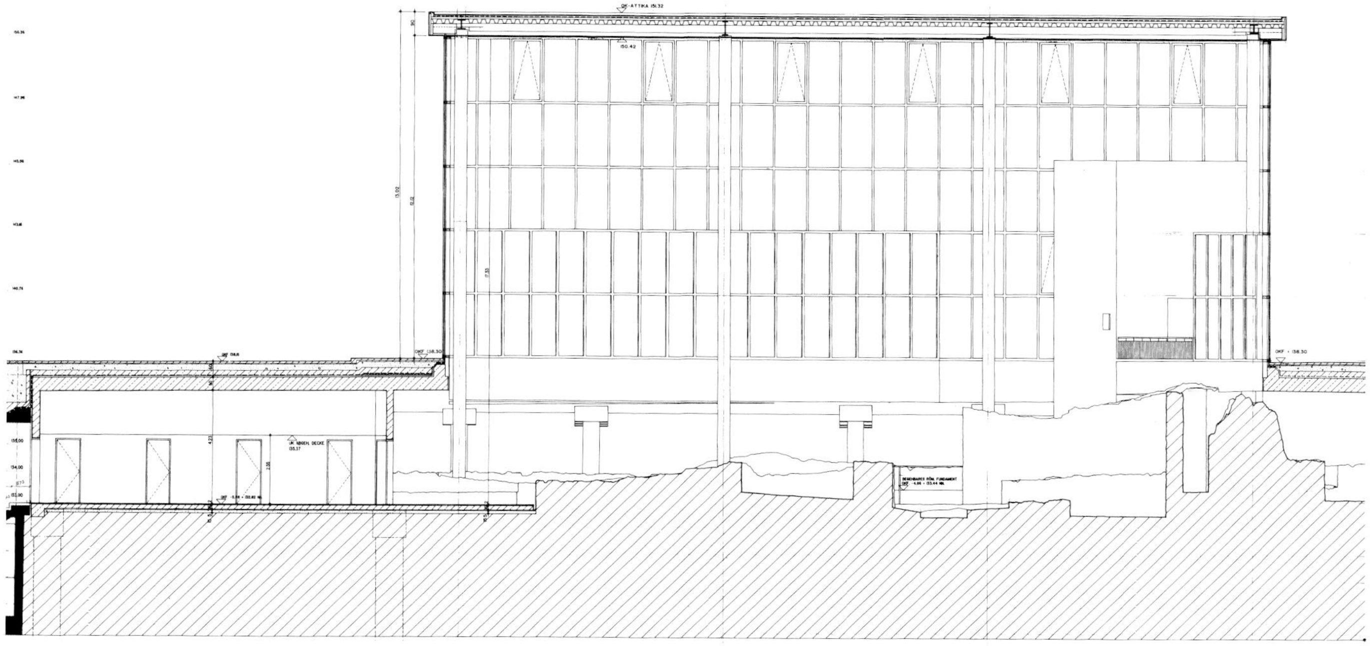

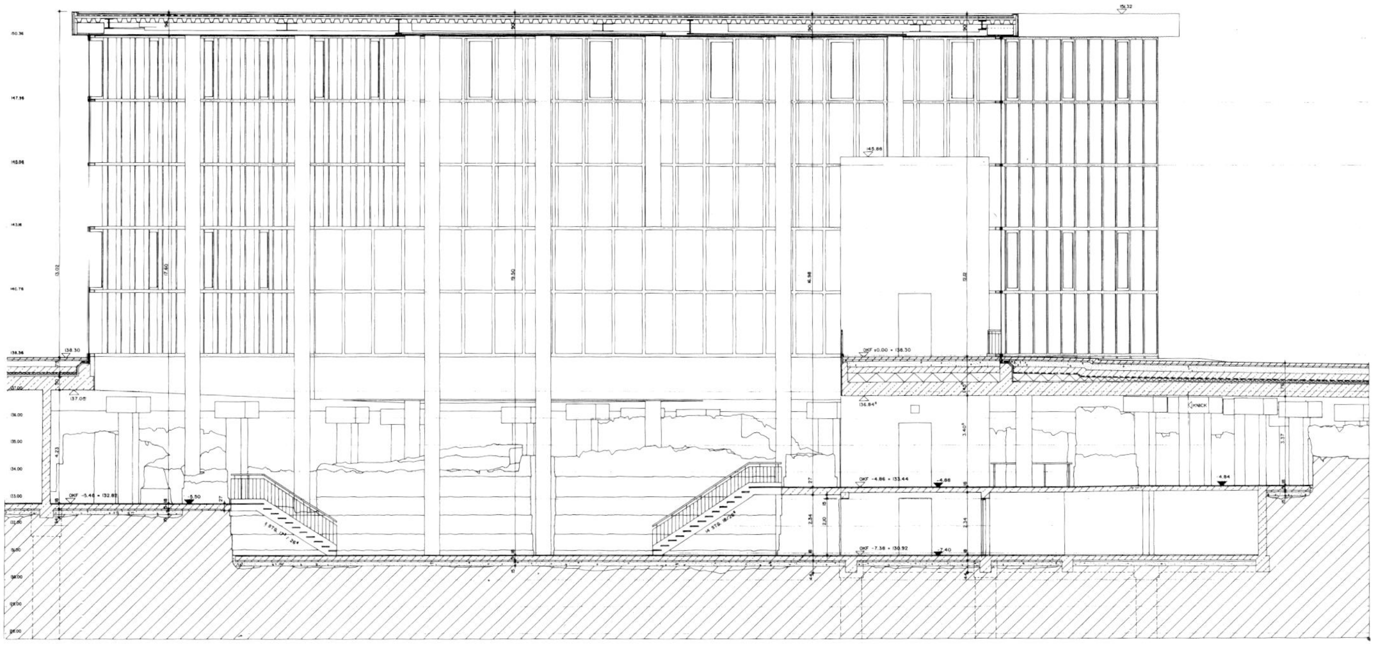

and traverse the cube, are oriented to the Roman grid, as is the stairwell providing access to the lower levels. There, all of the museum structures such as floor grid, paths, lighting, and ventilation are oriented to the new, above-ground grid, which repeatedly collides with the Roman walls and foundations. The resulting tension and opposition are intensified by the materials of the building, the warm reddish-yellows of the ruins contrasting with the cold gray of the precise, sharp-edged exposed concrete and steel of the new structure. The area beneath the plaza level is articulated by a large pentagonal space containing the warm-water bath, furnaces, calidarium, and frigidarium of the Roman baths along with the individual tubs and anterooms and the remains of the former medieval monastery. Two of the three smaller adjoining spaces present the remains of the Roman sewer system and the medieval cisterns and garbage trenches, while the third accommodates the necessary technical and sanitary facilities of the museum.

View into interior of
museum; passage.

Bremen Institute for Industrial Technology and Applied Ergonomics (BIBA), Technologiepark, Bremen, 1988–1991

Entrance facade; axonometrics; site plan.

Project team: Joachim Waack, Joachim Klose, Albert Brauns, Milan Pitlach, Michael Croce, Karl-Lothar Dietzsch, T. Meurer, A. Grond, Ulrich Wiegmann, A. Marchel, Barbara Taha, Claudia Henning

The urbanistic structure of the building for the Bremen Institute for Industrial Technology and Applied Ergonomics (BIBA) was predetermined by the block-edge construction of the university campus. In order to conform to this arrangement, priority had to be given to the definition of block edges on Hochschulring and Klagenfurter Strasse. In addition, the building for the Institute for Space Technology, under construction at the time, represented a prominent landmark on the university campus. The location of the BIBA building adjacent to this urbanistically dominant structure required a corresponding counterweight, adopting and continuing the established system of units and dimensions.

An architectural geometry based on the square was adopted as a modular system for the entire structure. The new building and extension areas, and hence the entire development of the block, are derived from the established geometry, resulting in a strict system of order suitable for both open areas and possible future additions.

The entrance to BIBA is located on Hochschulring, toward which the main facade is also oriented. On the exterior and particularly along Hochschulring, the building presents itself as a large, arcaded structure. The low height and broad expanse of the building made it difficult to find a significant expressive form; the location on Hochschulring, however, rendered the idea of an arcade—here associated with a tree-lined avenue as well—not only logical, but appropriate to both the place and the significance of the building.

BIBA contains three spatial complexes: spaces for the individual departments and the directorship, spaces for shared use, and the hall and workshop areas with the actual core of the complex, the great hall.

The arcaded wall marks the location of offices and work spaces. In the first stage of construction, it assumes the form of a U-shaped interior area opening toward the north. In a future stage, the continuous office tract can be expanded into a square enclosing a large interior space; in this form, it is accessible from both north and south, with a driveway through the center from Klagenfurter Strasse. The interior space enclosed by the arcaded wall contains halls, workshop areas, and mixed-use spaces. The center of the interior area is the semicircular multipurpose hall, which can be completed into a full circle in the future phase. The circular arrangement of the hall can be developed in a number of stages. Initially, it is possible to expand only the multipurpose hall itself by the same amount of space. Subsequently, two side wings for the expansion of the departments can be erected, and finally the entire block can be completed with additional departments and shared spaces.

The plan is organized in such a way that the spatial complex for the departments and directorship, consisting of offices of a relatively uniform type, forms a linear, U-shaped structure, accessible from a central entryway via an entrance hall and a single-loaded corridor. The spaces are naturally lit and ventilated and supplied with movable partition walls, so that their configuration can be changed at any time within the fixed exterior walls.

The spaces for mixed use are immediately adjacent to the great hall. The upper story accommodates the training rooms, while the ground level houses the construction office and computer laboratories. Since these spaces will likely be subject to continual alteration, they are articulated with a nonstructural wall system. The spaces are lighted from above or, on the ground level, from the side through the great hall. The technical and utility installations are accommodated on the ground level in the area of the delivery passages and are partially accessible from the exterior.

The actual center of the complex is the hall area with a crane runway system. The hall is spanned by radial girder construction; in the first phase, it rests on a central support, while in the future phase no supports will be necessary. The crane is a radial hanging crane; in its final form, it will be supplemented by a second, independently operating arm.

On the street and hall side, the outer wall is constructed of exposed masonry in a hard-burned, dark-colored brick. The windows are of steel and are painted white. The glass wall to the north is a lightweight construction that can be replaced in the future expansion.
In contrast to the more or less conventional architecture of the outer enclosure, the interior calls attention to the dialectic between masonry and high-tech construction.

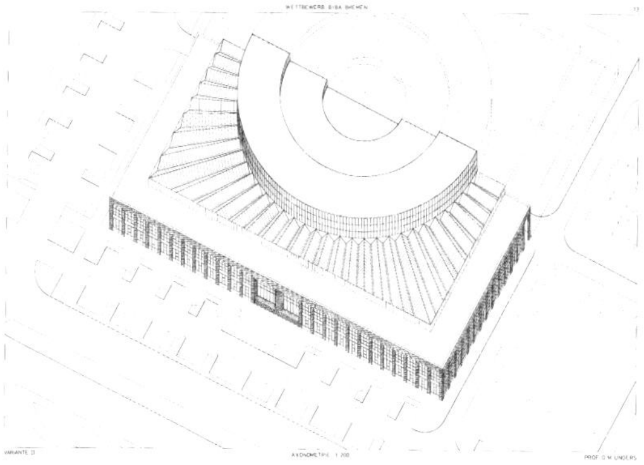

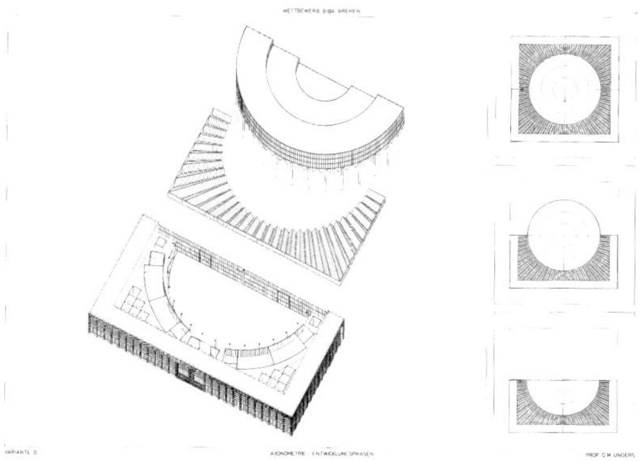

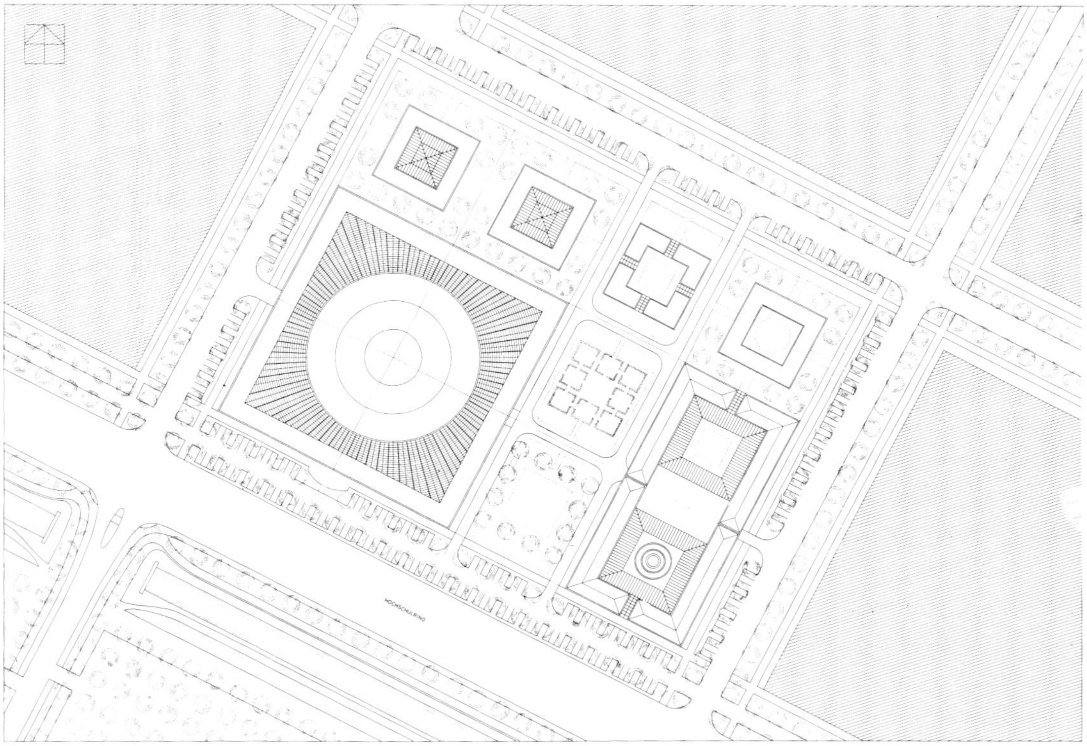

Plans of first upper story and ground level; construction of load-bearing structure.

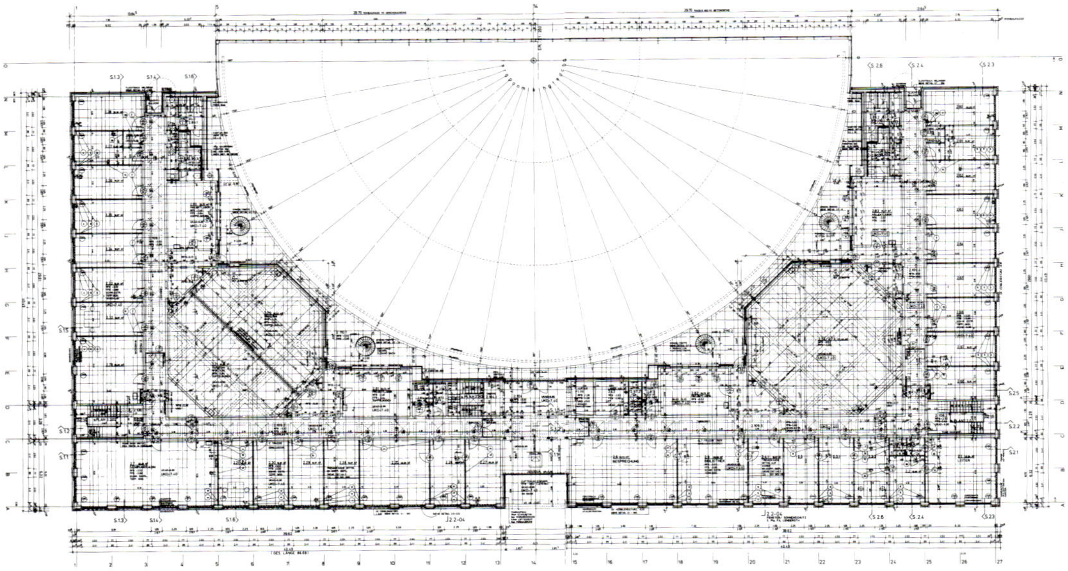

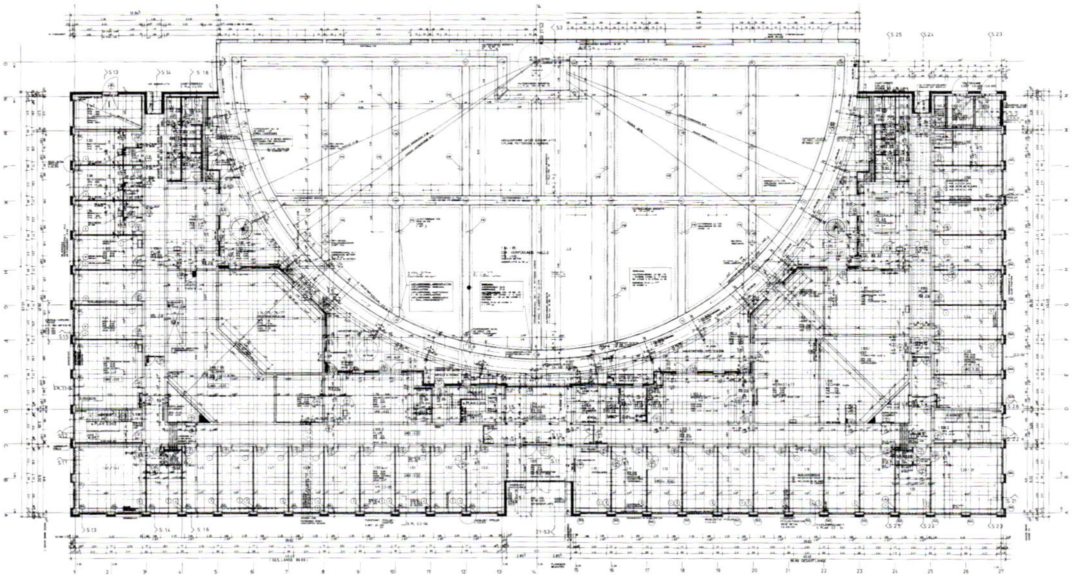

Exteriors; elevations;
section.

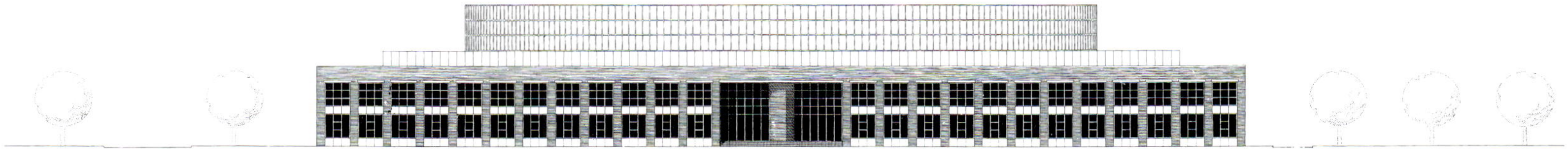

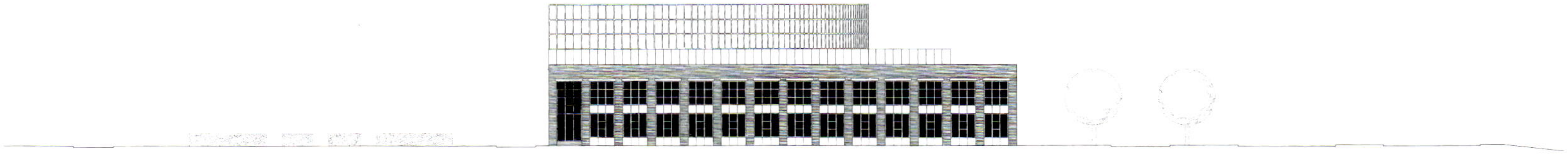

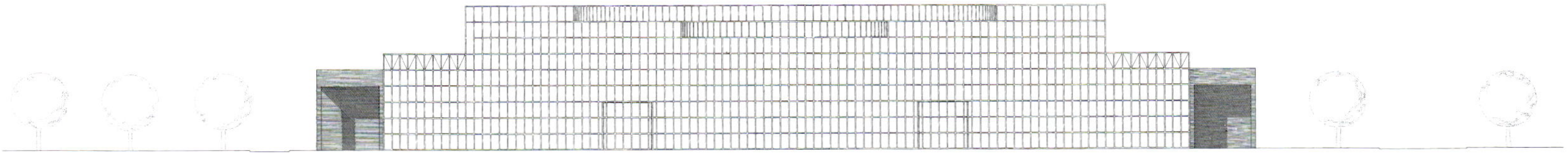

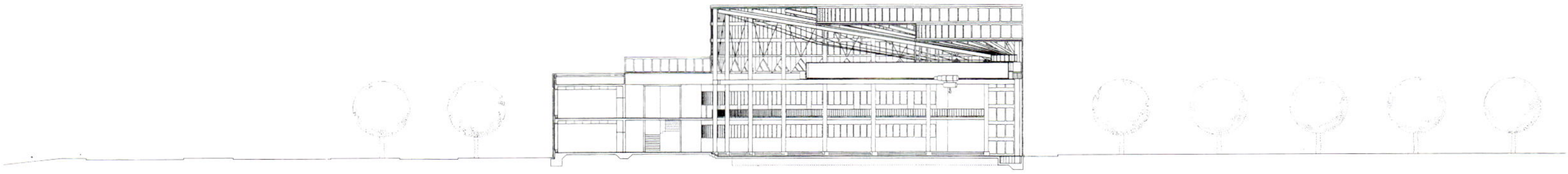

Sketch; glass front.

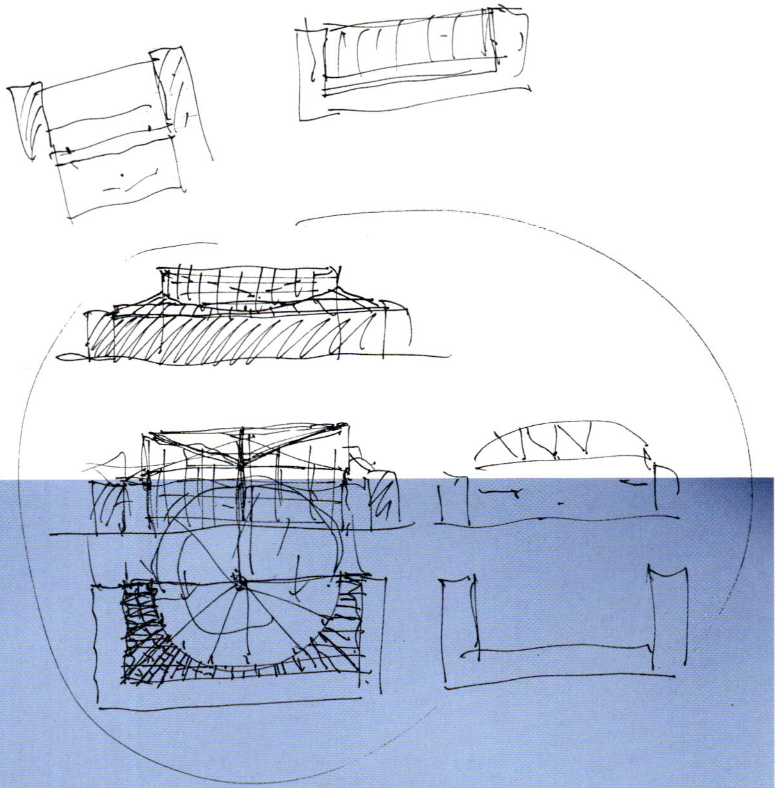

Views into office areas and main hall.

Bitz House, Galerie Kewenig, Cologne-Frechen, 1989–1992

Project team: Ulrich Wiegmann, Bernhard Trübenbach (execution and construction supervision)

The new residence is placed across from an existing manor house and a new gallery. The strict adherence to the right angle in the planning of the two new buildings means that only two of the exterior facades—the long side of the gallery and the long rear facade of the residence—lie directly atop the existing moat walls. All the other facades are set back from the edge of the moat, forming perspectivally narrowing spaces with stairs leading directly down to the water. The use of the same brick for all the buildings serves to unify the complex visually.

The homogeneity of the material contrasts with the differing design of the new buildings. The gallery building has unbroken walls and is illuminated by a glazed zone in the roof area. The walls of the residence, on the other hand, are dissolved into a kind of arcade with masonry pillars, with wall areas or glazed double doors visible between the supports. Only the two-story side wing and the area of the main entrance diverge from this regularity.

The plan of the residence consists of a sequence of equal square spaces with a ceiling-high door opening in the center of each wall. The entrance to the building leads into a central octagonal entrance hall. From here, the house is constructed symmetrically to either side. To the right and left of the hall lie the dining room and living room; adjacent to the living room are a library, bedrooms, and bath. On the other side are the kitchen and the children's rooms. The two-story section above the kitchen accommodates additional children's and guest rooms with small baths.

Preliminary sketch; ground-level plan.

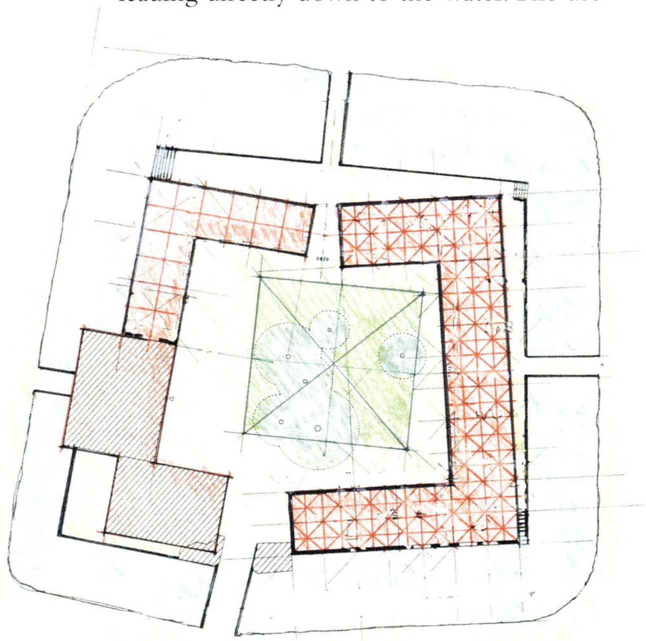

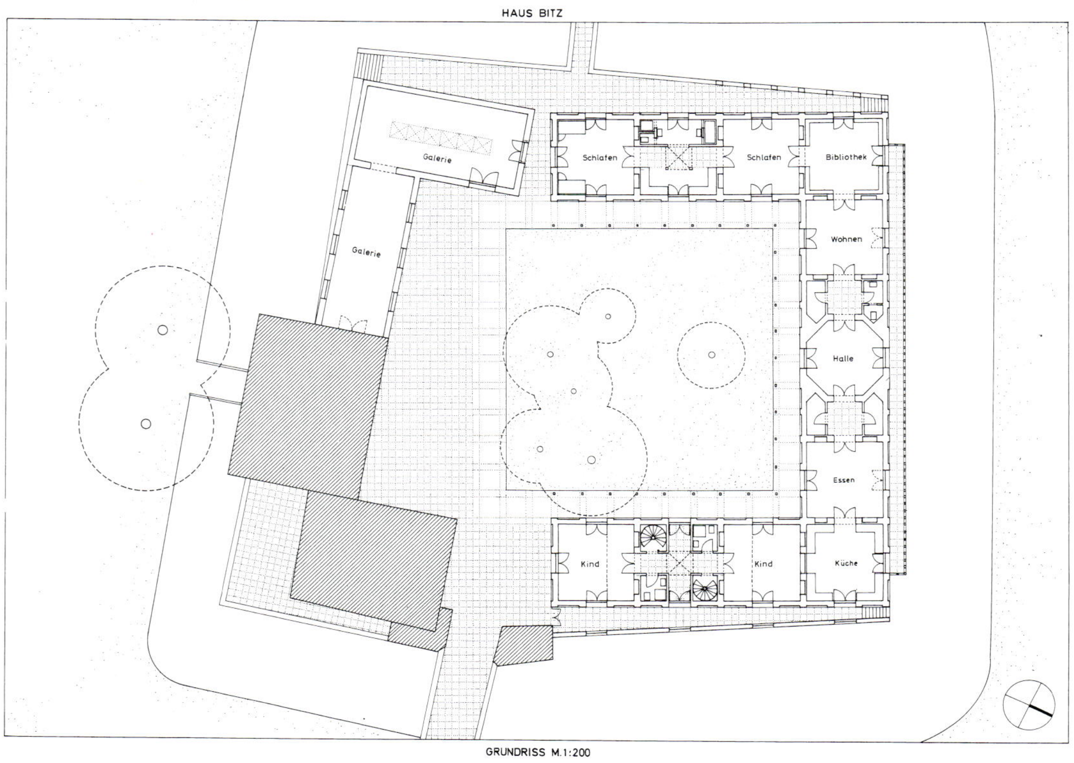

Elevation; views of waterfront facades of house and gallery with busts by Ian Hamilton Finlay.

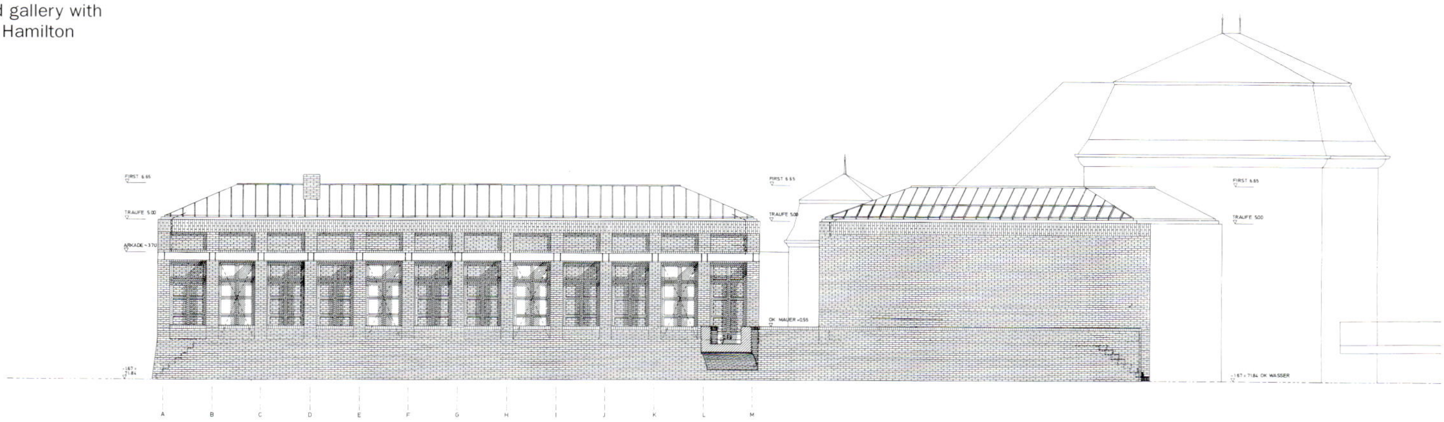

Elevations; exterior.

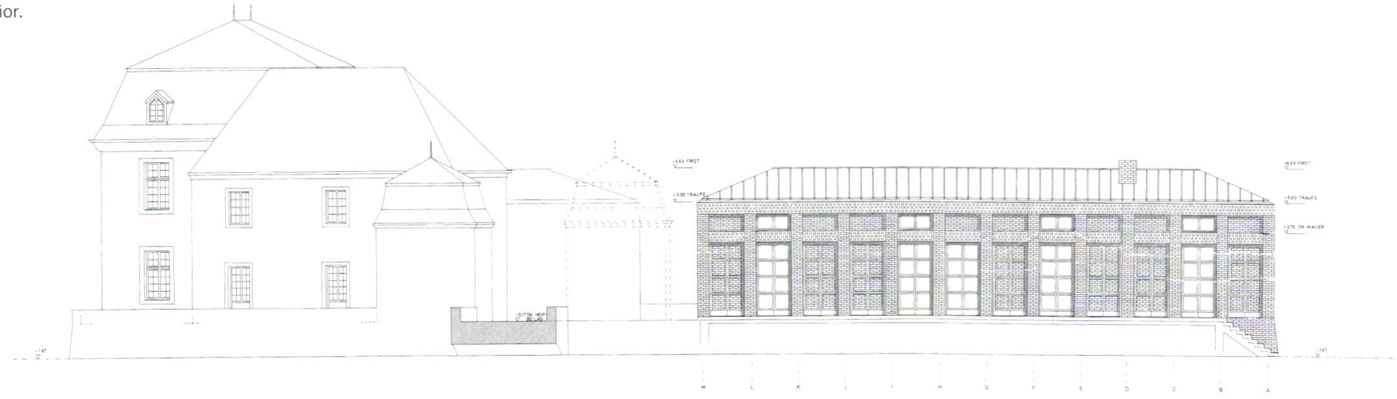

Elevations; view into courtyard.

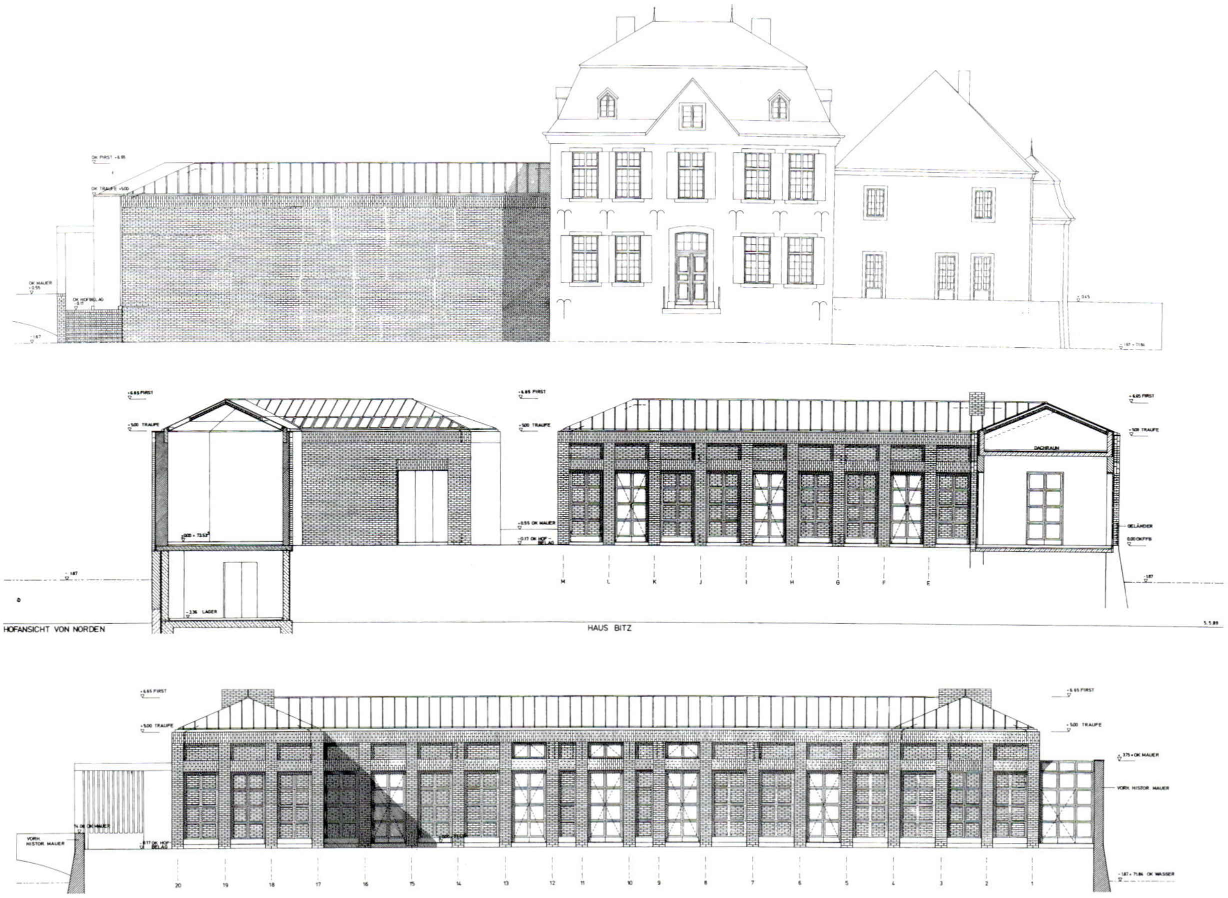

Section; views of living areas and gallery wing.

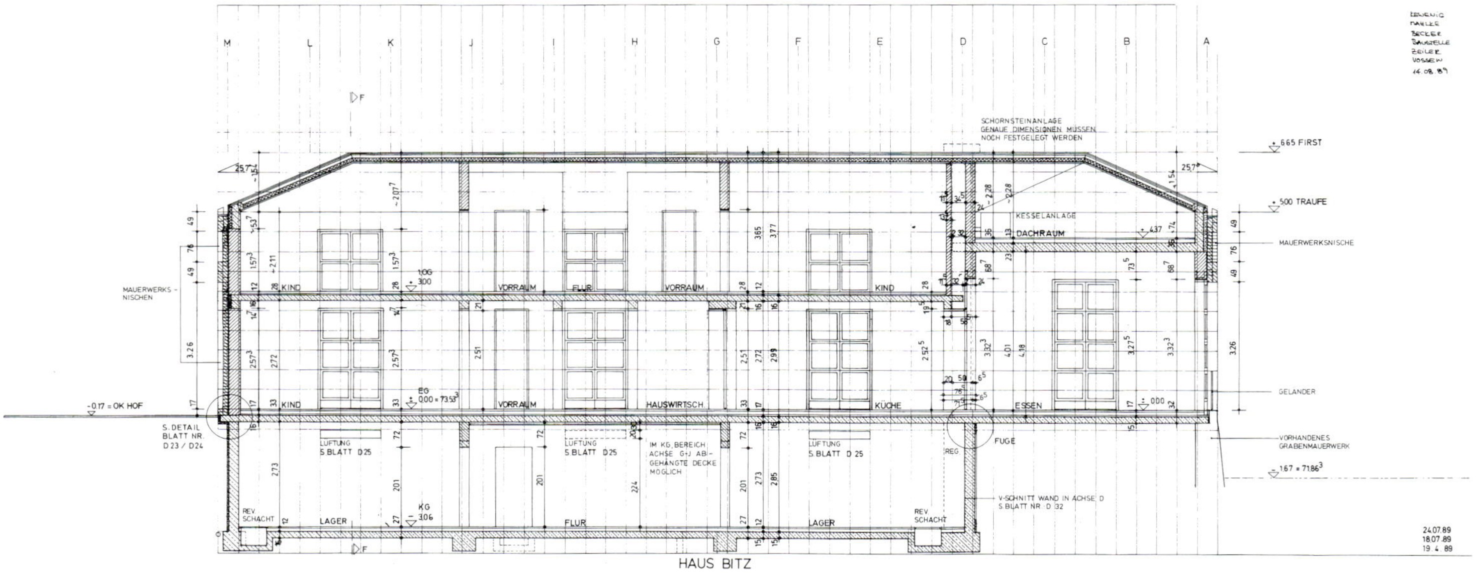

Competition Design for New Building for Domestic Court, Expansion of Tempelhof/Kreuzberg District Court, Berlin, 1989–1995

Project team: Karl-Heinz Winkens, Axel Balzereit, Claudia Euler, Michael Skadborg

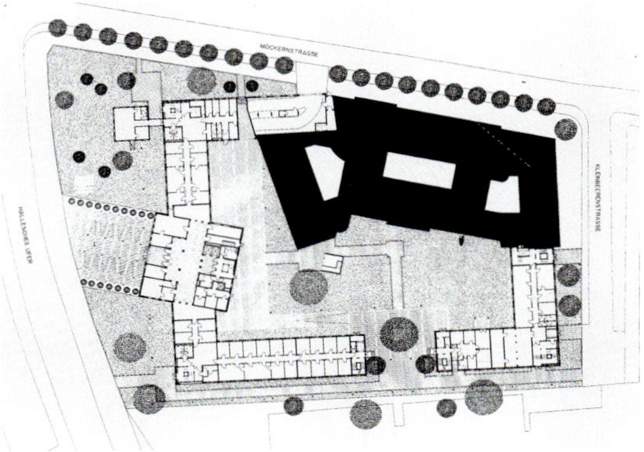

Site plan; aerial view.

The domestic court building is an administrative structure with halls and other facilities for court proceedings as well as a cafeteria, spaces for subordinate functions, and storage areas. The expansion of the district court is an extension of the existing functional spaces, with storage areas, an auction hall for pawned goods, and a residence for the head of maintenance. Both buildings have a shared underground garage.

The buildings were erected on a block delimited by Möckernstrasse to the west, Kleinbeerenstrasse to the north, the Postbank Berlin to the east, and the Landwehrkanal (Hallesches Ufer) to the south. The site lies at the southern edge of the Friedrichstadt district directly on the Landwehrkanal and U-Bahn Line 1, which here runs above ground. Adjoining to the west are the former tracks of the Anhalter Bahnhof railway station, which is to be transformed into a park. To the north, the site abuts the larger east-west strip of park area planned for the Kreuzberg section of Friedrichstadt.

The court building called for an inconspicuous exterior so as not to be imposing. The new design for the domestic court and the expansion of the district court uses narrow, five-story structures to form a rectangular block with the existing district court building as an independent volume in the northwest corner. This configuration results in a large, semipublic interior courtyard and a public open area on Hallesches Ufer and the Landwehrkanal. The uniform orientation of the buildings gives the new domestic court the appearance of a freestanding building toward the Landwehrkanal, while the expansion of the district court closes the block along Kleinbeerenstrasse. The new buildings adjoin the fire walls of the old structure and continue the historic rooflines: only the tower, rotated out of the grid, exceeds this height with the addition of two stories, one for technical facilities.

The placement of the buildings makes it possible to preserve almost entirely the existing trees and to incorporate the individual tree groups into the spatial design. In the locust tree grove on the southwest corner, a "children's house" is positioned as a freestanding volume. Paved area is reduced to a minimum. Steps, ramps, and elevators for the handicapped reconcile differences in level between old and new buildings.

Views and elevation of main facade with steel sculpture by Sol LeWitt.

Section; exterior.

Opposite:
Interiors.

Expansion of Gatehouse, Central Terminal of Trade Fair Complex, Frankfurt am Main, 1989–1997

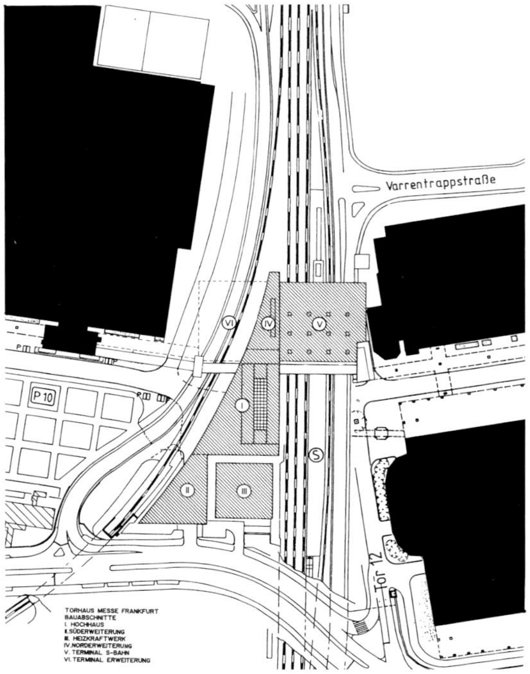

Project team: Ingo Schrader, Ricardo Sargiotti, Hikaro Hane, Maike Bräckerbohm, Raimund Fein, Guido Lohmann, Joachim Sieber, J. Engel

Despite its central location, the Frankfurt trade fair complex has heretofore been only insufficiently integrated into the public transit system.

Since a section of S-Bahn with a direct connection to the main railway station, airport, and comprehensive local transit network led directly past the gatehouse of the trade fair, the idea was conceived of creating an S-Bahn station at the trade fair grounds along with a new, more central entrance to the complex.

The six-story socle structure of the gatehouse is expanded to the north to accommodate the offices of the trade fair association as well as leased office space. Inserted horizontally through this socle structure, a platform penetrates the building about eight meters above the tracks. It serves as a distribution level and as the central entrance to the adjacent trade fair complex at the level of the "Via Mobile," the existing system of covered pedestrian walkways with moving sidewalks connecting all the halls of the fair grounds. In this way, direct access is provided from the S-Bahn station or the planned bus parking lot to the trade fair complex.

The one-story hall, illuminated with dome lights, accommodates the ticket offices, cloakrooms, a café, and sanitary facilities. A public distribution hall on the north side of the terminal, accessible at all times, makes it possible to cross the tracks outside the trade fair complex as well. The expansion of the gatehouse to the north augments the socle structure placed within the triangle formed by the tracks, its west side following the curve of the rail lines with a reflecting mirror facade. This second expansion of the socle intensifies the effect of the slightly curved facade.

The gatehouse proves itself both powerful and adaptable with the image of the gate as an architectural archetype. The clear, striking form of the building integrates functions such as thermal plant, service areas, offices and conference rooms, post office, restaurant, and now also the entrance terminal and S-Bahn station. Thus after more than ten years, the gatehouse finally fulfils, almost as an afterthought, the function visually evoked by its form.

Site plan; third-upper-story plan.

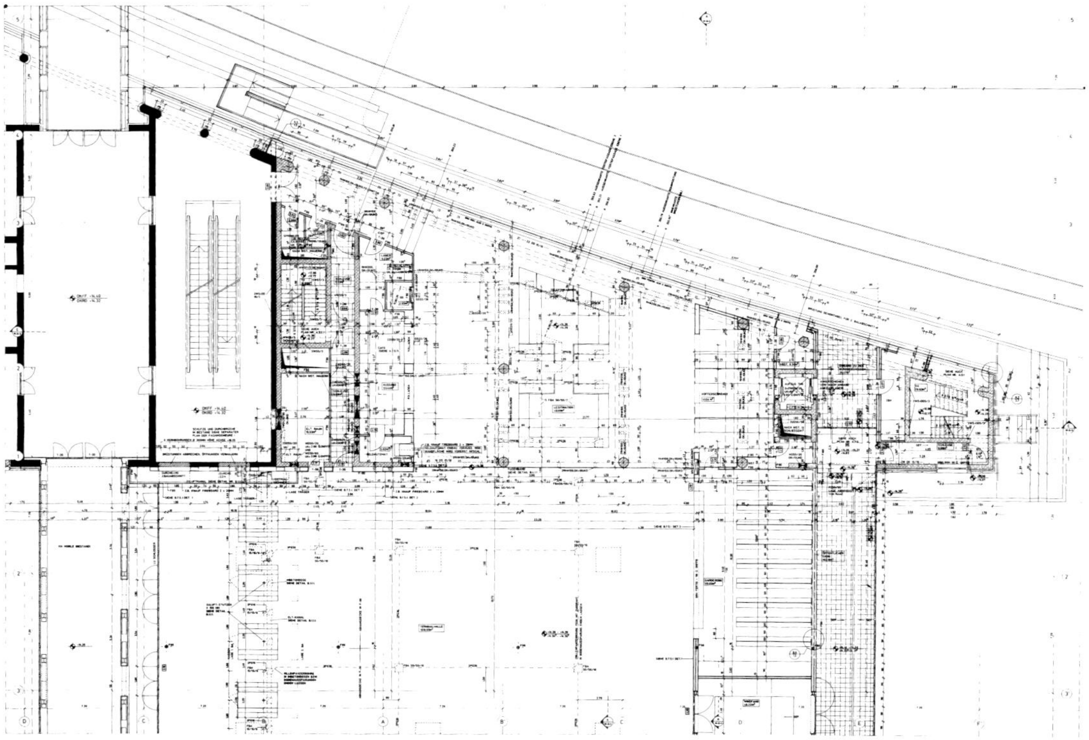

Detail of "Via Mobile";
exterior.

Exterior; section of platform and gatehouse expansion.

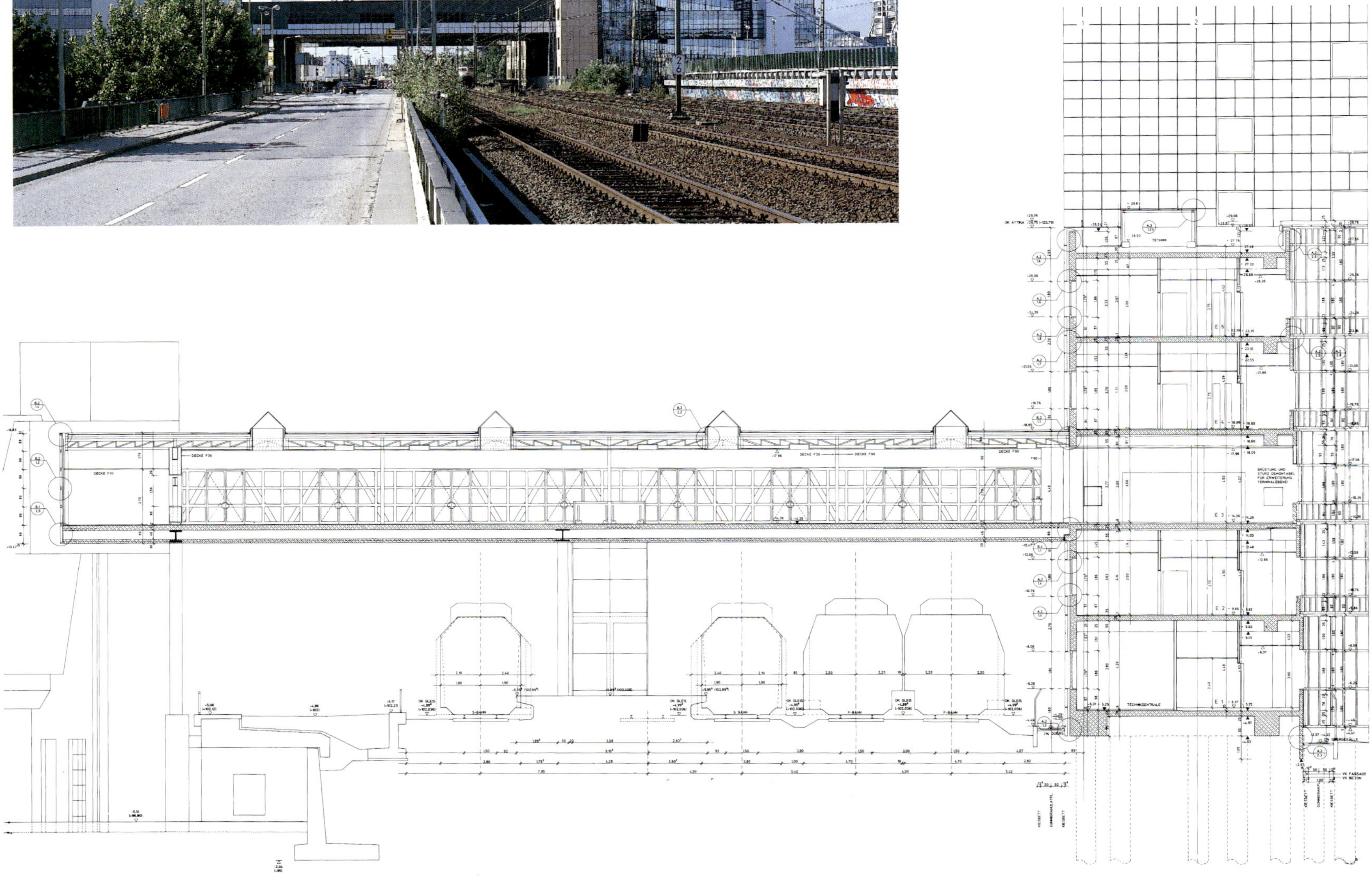

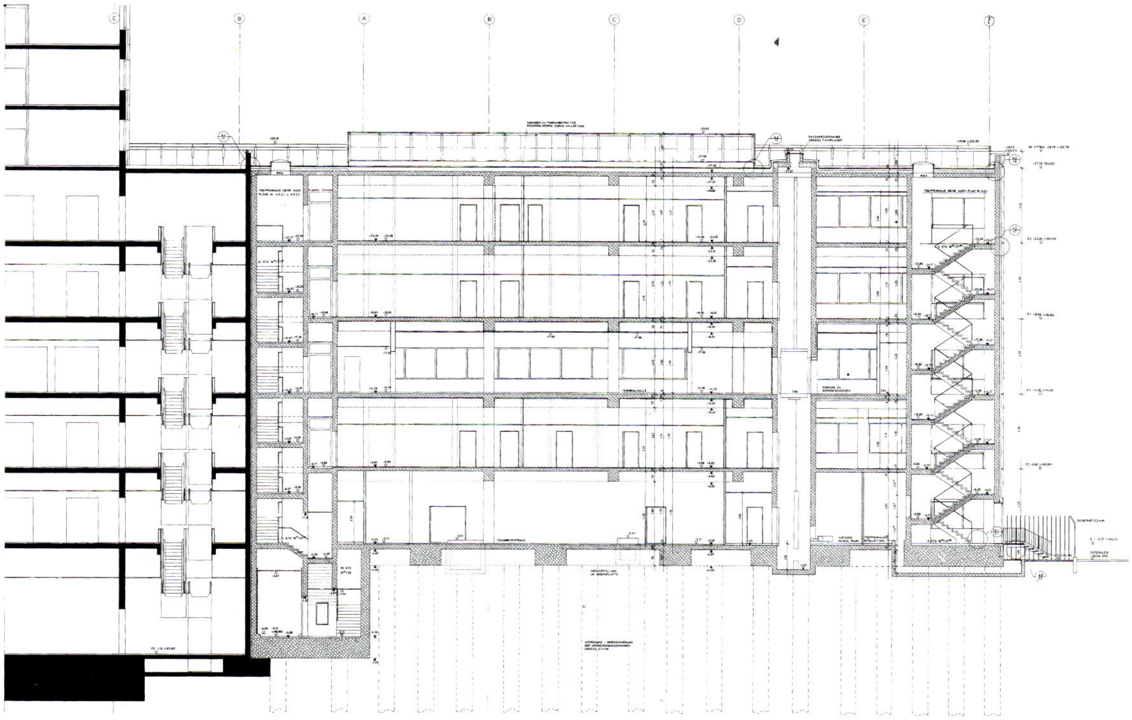

Section; view of stairwell.

Jeromin House, Königswinter, 1989–1992

Project team: Kaspar Steves, Ulrich Weigmann (execution: Wiegmann + Trübenbach, Cologne)

Elevation; section; plans of ground level and first upper story.

Opposite:
View from garden.

Overleaf: Views and details of interior.

The house, designed for a married couple who collect abstract art, stands on a slope above the city. The neighboring buildings consist primarily of villas from the turn of the century and recent years. In this setting, the villa is striking for its clearly formulated, abstract intellectuality. The unpretentious architecture is well-suited to the avocation and lifestyle of the owners, with a simplicity that leaves little room for superfluous representation, clearly articulated sequences of spaces, and a certain artificiality that provides an appropriate frame for the collection of pictures.

The central space is two stories high. Adjacent to it is a music or reading room. The lower level accommodates work spaces, the upper story the private chambers.
The rational spirit and consistent use of a thirty-by-thirty-centimeter module are so compelling that no other system is visible anywhere else. The modular system of order—Ungers's real passion, long with a "thematic architecture" obligated to pure idea—is here made perceptible for the first time on interior and exterior alike. All the elements are marvelously adapted to this idea. The house has no decorative elements inside or outside; the cube is articulated only by the window and door openings cut sharply into the white plaster. This almost reserved, yet friendly noblesse and the abstract, intellectual atmosphere—evoked and intensified by the perfection of the execution—is continued on the interior in the spare furnishings and pictures, so that one could almost characterize the owners as the ideal residents of an Ungers house.—*Martin Kieren*

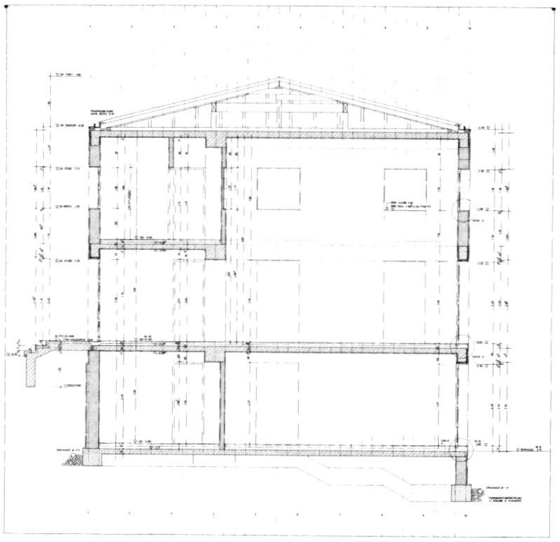

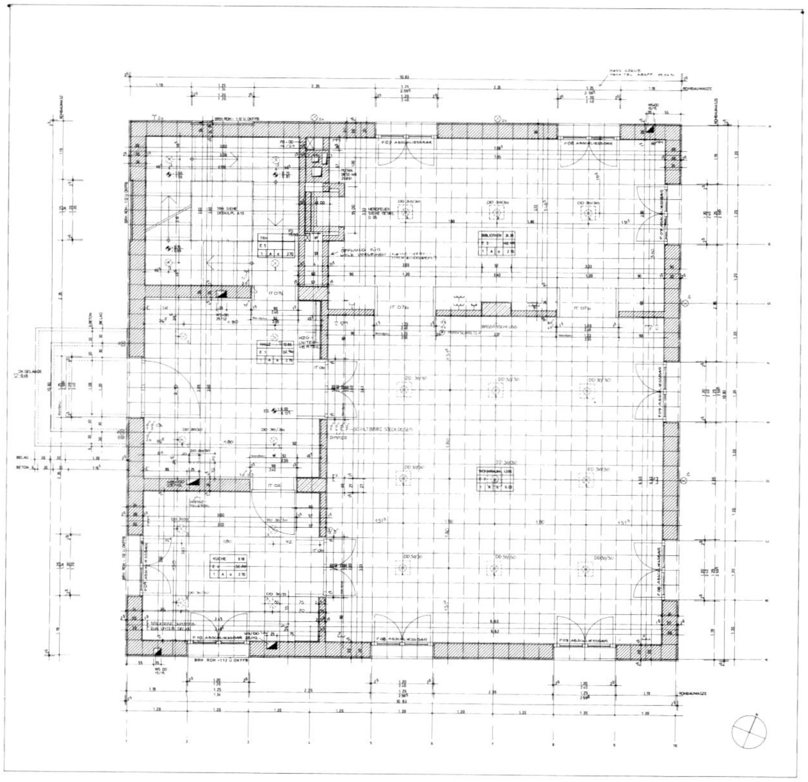

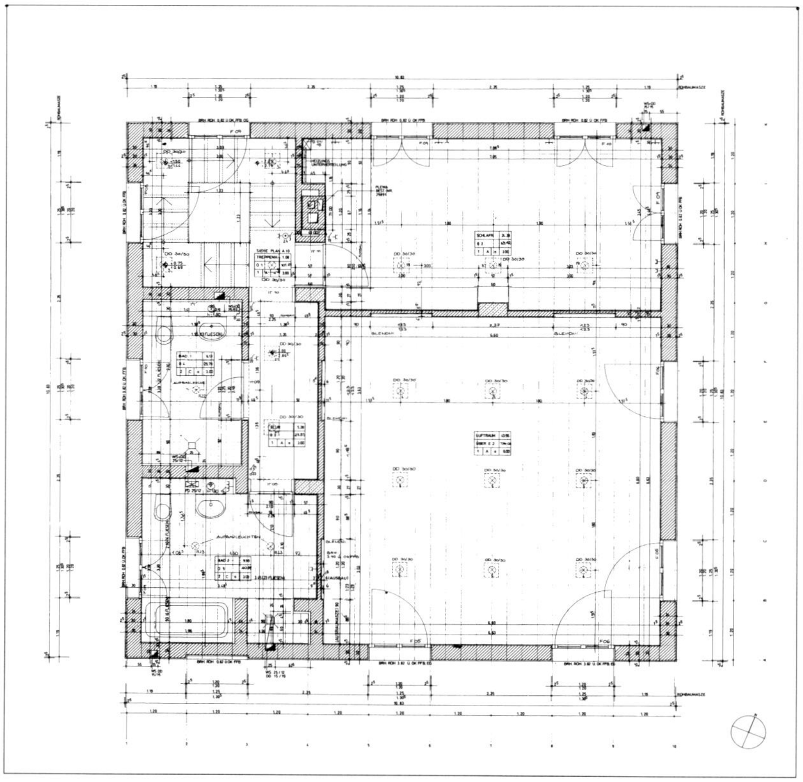

PTS Workshop, Frankfurt am Main, 1990–1994

Project team: Ingo Schrader, Walter Kohne, Hikaro Hane

Site plan; plans.

The Passagier-Transfer-System (PTS), a fully automatic railway traveling about seventeen meters above the ground, connects the two terminals of the Frankfurt airport. The PTS workshop accommodates the regular servicing, cleaning, and repair of the vehicles. Constructed on an otherwise unusable plot of leftover space on the airport grounds, the building was erected over a street and the existing entrance to an underground garage. It is a clear volume on a square plan, hollowed out almost sculpturally in the area of the street passages. A future expansion of the building is projected.

In addition to the main workshop hall on Level 4, the building also accommodates workshops for small-scale repairs and electronics, the main control office for the entire PTS system with its accompanying central computer, and office and training spaces including separate areas for offices, technical facilities, and storage. Stairs and elevator are located in a freestanding tower connected to the building by bridges; its upper part accommodates a push-back-control area for the surveillance and control of the shuttling movements of the airplanes in front of Terminal 2. These very different functions are expressed on the facades in a seemingly free arrangement of gates, ventilation screens, windows, and large areas of glass; all these elements, however, are subjected to a strict, unified grid, which underlies the entire building as an industrial invisible ordering principle. In accord with the purpose of the building, a few simple, robust materials were used: exposed concrete, dark gray painted steel, white plaster, and glass. For the facade, a radar-absorbing insulation system was developed in cooperation with the technical university in Aachen.

Within the heterogeneous, urbanistically and architecturally dissonant context of the airport, the workshop building asserts itself through its striking placement, solid yet interesting volumes, and straightforward appearance.

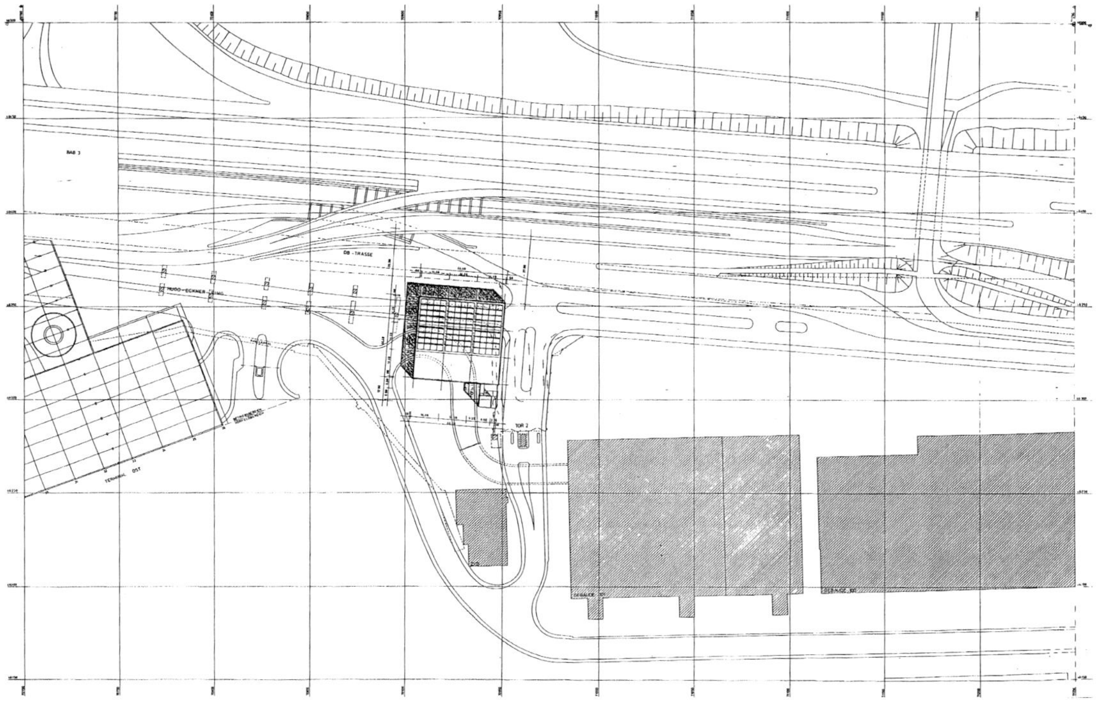

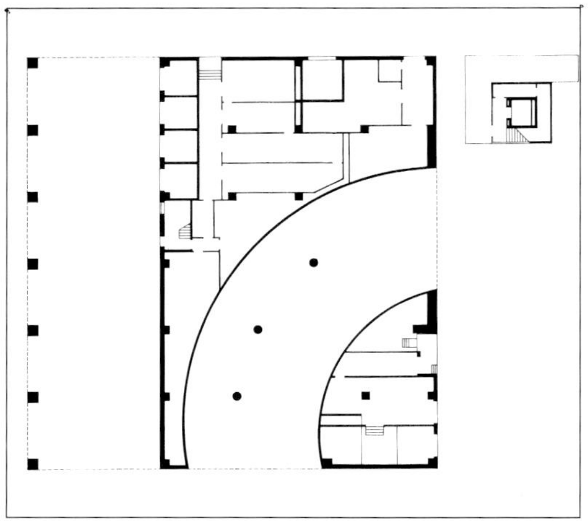

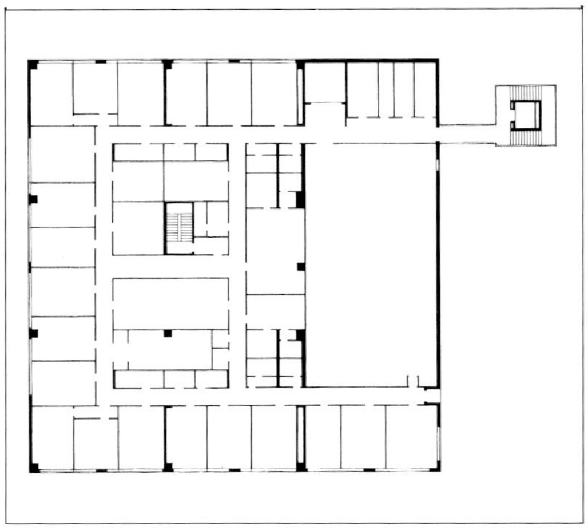

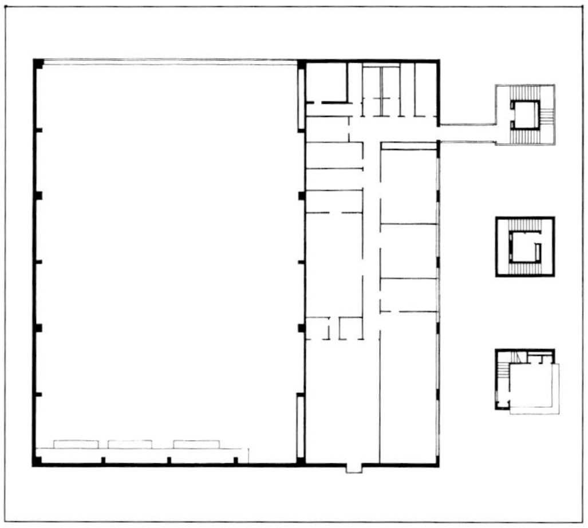

Workshop hall; stair tower.

Exteriors; elevations.

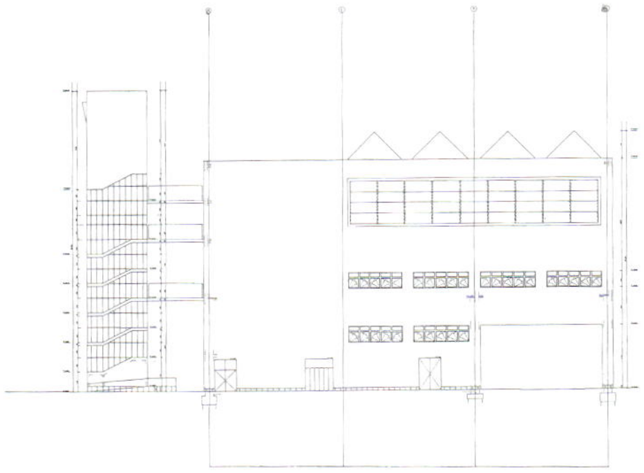

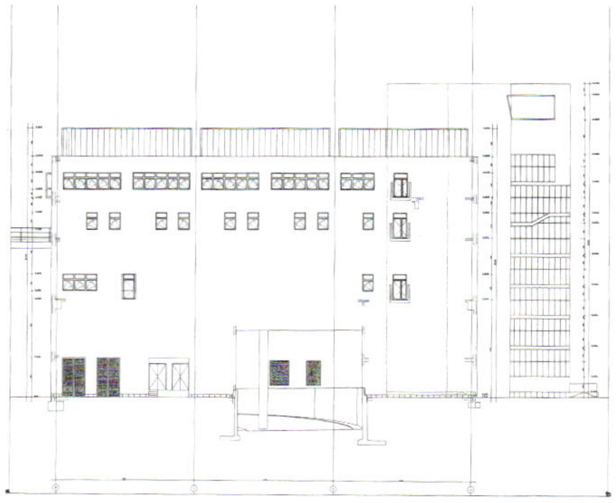

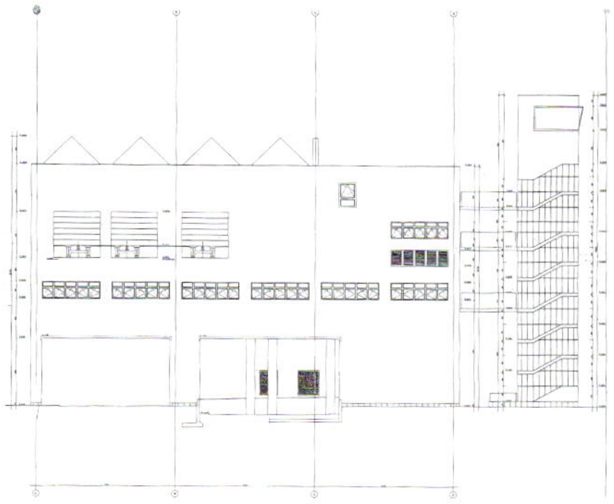

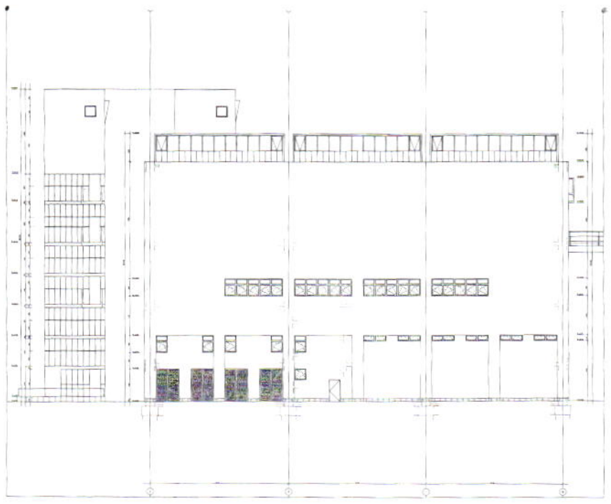

Residential, Office, and Commercial Building, Eschersheimer Landstrasse, Frankfurt am Main, 1989–1990

Project team: Peter Diehl, Helmut Kleine-Kraneburg

The two office and commercial buildings are located along Eschersheimer Landstrasse, with number 44 occupying a corner plot on Fichardstrasse. Number 42, a four-story office building, replaces a structure that was part of a larger complex worthy of preservation.

The new cubic building adopts the roof ridge height of the freestanding building next door. The lower socle of number 44 is likewise oriented to this height, while a second socle area corresponds to the roof ridge height of the row houses on Fichardstrasse. The two socle areas, which mark the six-story office and commercial part of the building, are surmounted by an additional two-story square of apartments. In this way—as well as through the recessed glass passage between the two buildings—the freestanding character of the tower is emphasized.

The two buildings share an entrance on Eschersheimer Landstrasse and are connected by a basement-level cellar and garage. The four-story building and lower socle of the tower have a curtain facade of large natural stone panels with staggered joints. Large window openings articulate the ground level and upper stories. The upper socle of the tower is made of brick, while the residential stories above have a curtain facade of large, square quarry tiles with cross joints.

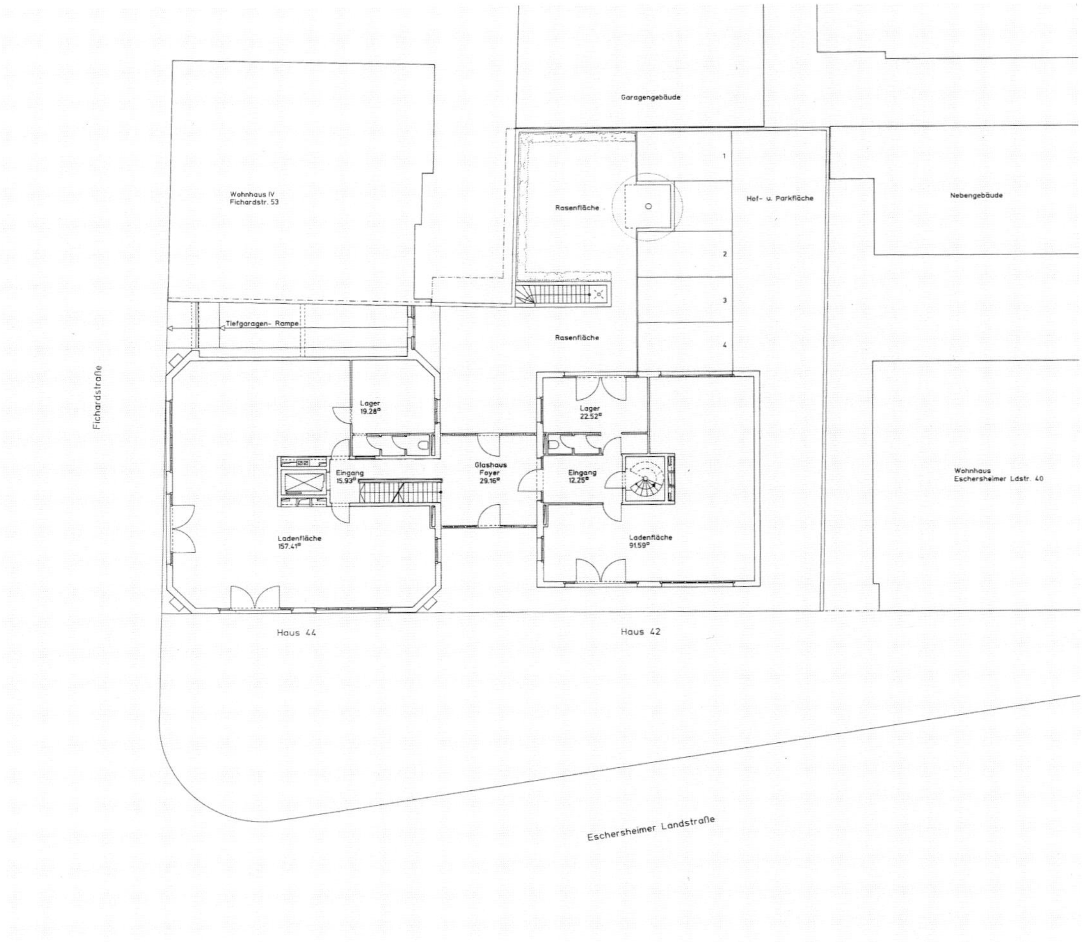

Plan; elevation.

Opposite:
Section; exterior.

Overleaf:
Detail of glass passage.

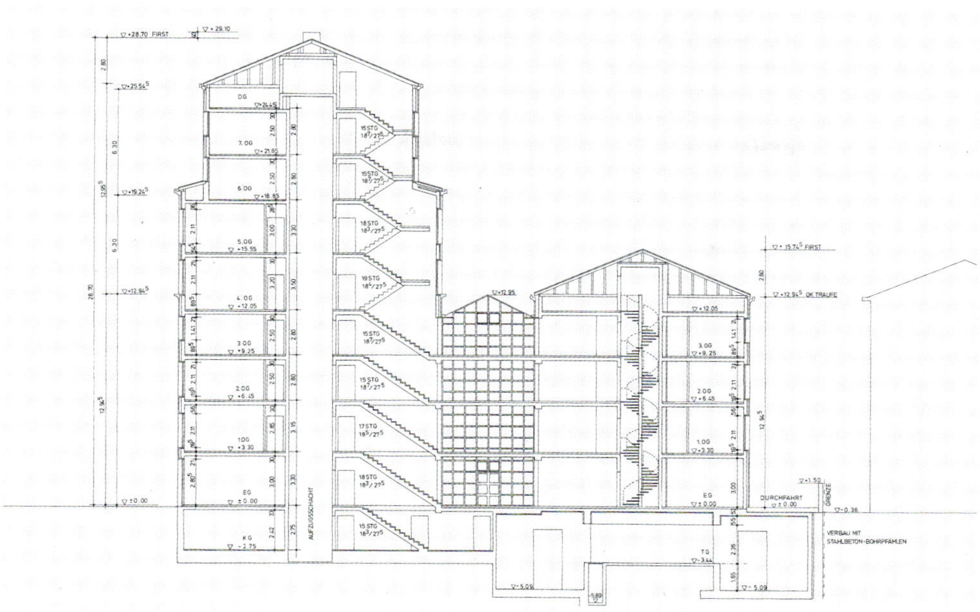

Competition Design for Expansion of South Trade Fair Complex, Hall A, Berlin, 1990–1999

With: Walter A. Noebel

Project team: Karl-Heinz Winkens, Jörg Lenschow, Peter Schmiedgen, Peter Wermund, Charly A. Pauly, Chase McCarthy, Jan Rogler, William Thomas Manarelli, Michael Ewerhardt, Iain May, Paul Panter, Luis Ocanto, Franco Bertossi, Thomas Möhlendick, Jost Westphal, Sylvia Becker, Niels Brockenhuis-Schack, David Koralek, Michael Pepper, Christine Brockenhuis-Schack, Hans Günther, Astrid Würdig, Mehmet Yalcin, Ross Carter Wingrove, John Bacus, Benjamin Thiele, Wilfried van der Bel, Martha Lewis, Jarno Nillesen

Photomontage; site plan.

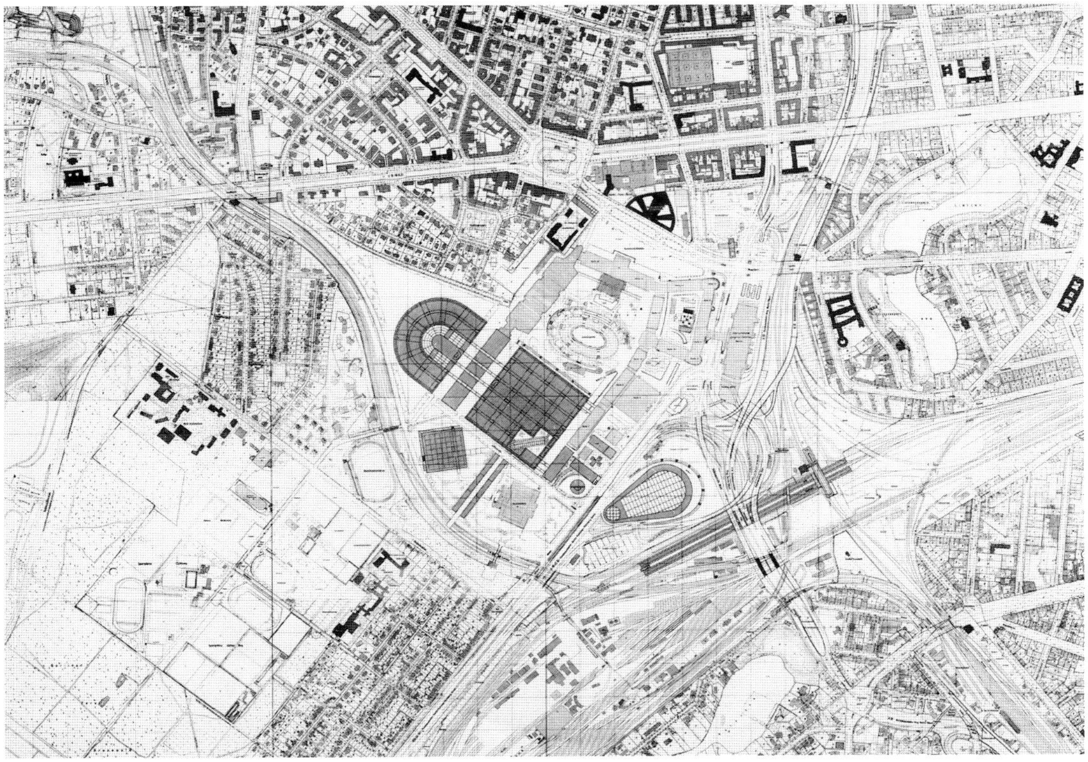

The Berlin trade fair complex is the result of an ad hoc building history that has produced an aggregation of halls of differing architectural character. Only the Sommergarten—the large enclosed space with the surrounding trade fair buildings—as well as the building on Hammerskjöldplatz (now Halls 18 to 20) and the pavilions around the radio tower (now Halls 11 to 17) on the Messedamm still manifest something of the clarity of the designs by Wagner, Poelzig, and Ermisch. In their architectural mediocrity, many of the newer halls cannot even compete with the makeshift structures of the 1950s and 1960s, now largely demolished. Above all, they are ill-suited to provide definition and a clear spatial frame for the large enclosed space of the Sommergarten. Apart from the central oval, moreover, the Sommergarten is still full of temporary pavilions and thus lacks a clear concept for circulation and open space. Particularly unsatisfactory is the spatial definition of the enclosed area in the southwest, which seems to be left over from the main site.

Instead of creating unconsidered expansions on an ad hoc basis, the project called for a long-term concept that would be viable, architecturally interesting, and unified, one that could be realized in stages and capable of lending architectural identity to the Berlin trade fair complex at each stage of construction. While still making use of the existing architecture and open spaces, the goal was to find an approach that on the one hand would reflect and continue the historical development of the trade fair grounds, and on the other, constitute an independent form of expression within the large areas of the expansion. Respect for the urban context required a clear sense of order, not the mere filling up of leftover areas with large-scale exhibition containers. What was needed was an architectural idea that was capable, even in the short term, of supplying the Berlin trade fair complex with a backbone for future development and above all with a new and memorable reference point.

The core of the configuration is a new Hall A, whose mid-term finished dimensions are 252 by 285 meters with a height of about 18 meters (21 meters along the edge). Located in the southern part of the fair grounds between Halls 25 and 7 and their possible expansions, it forms a new facade toward the

Elevations and sections of Hall A.

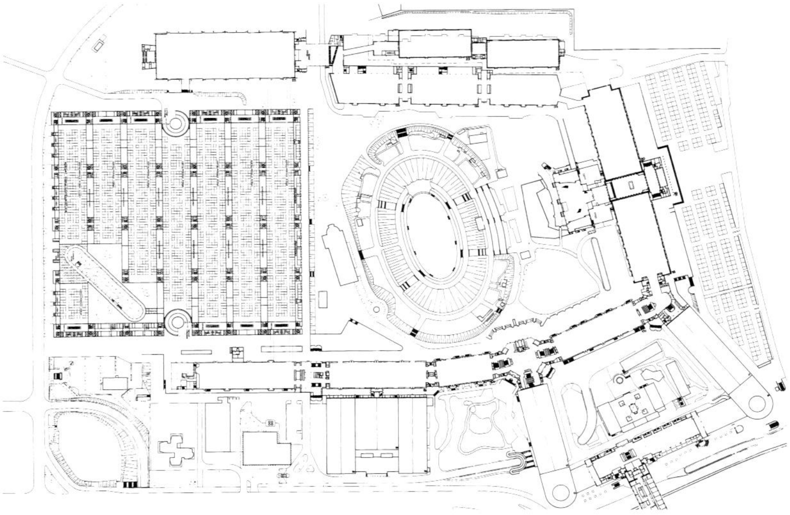

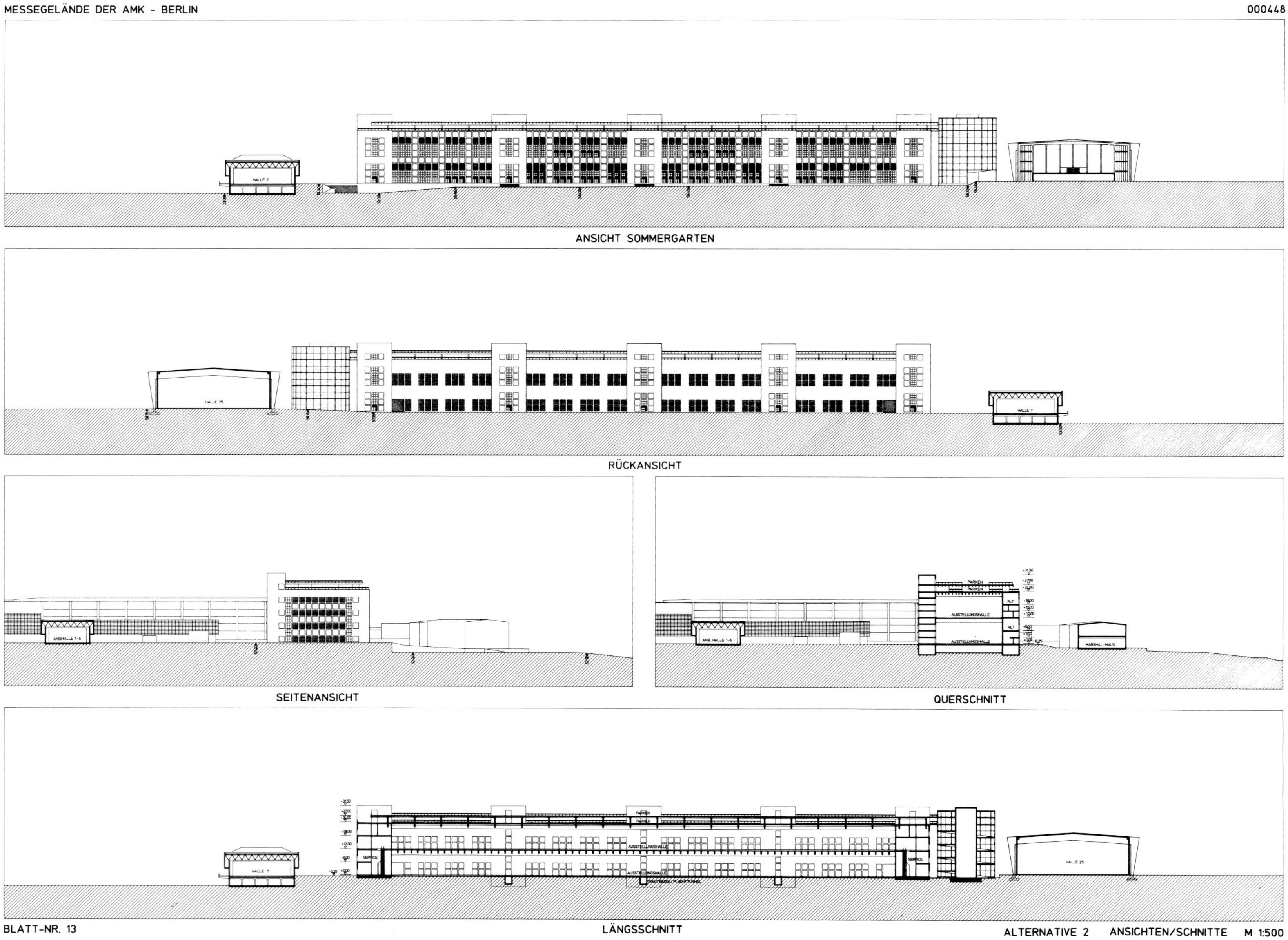

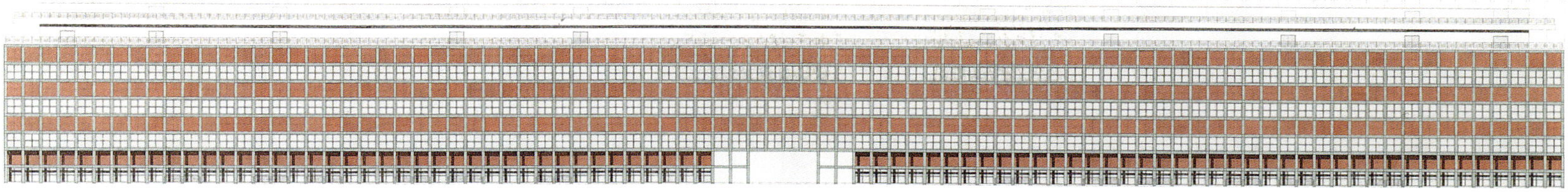

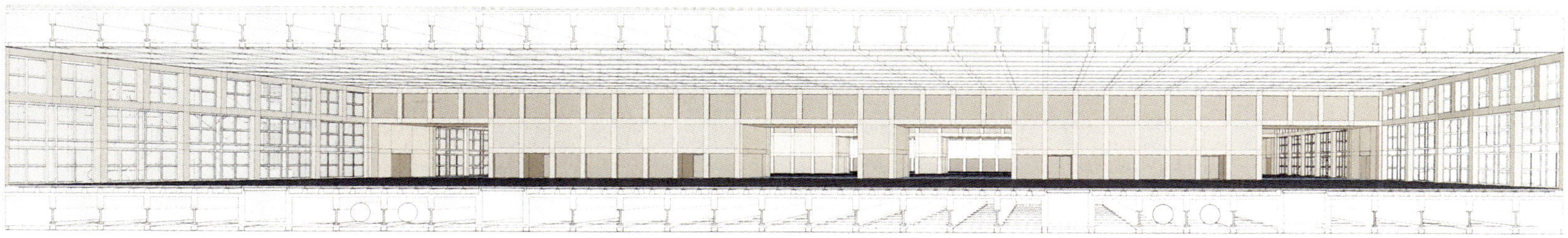

Elevation; interior perspectives; perspective of glass structure.

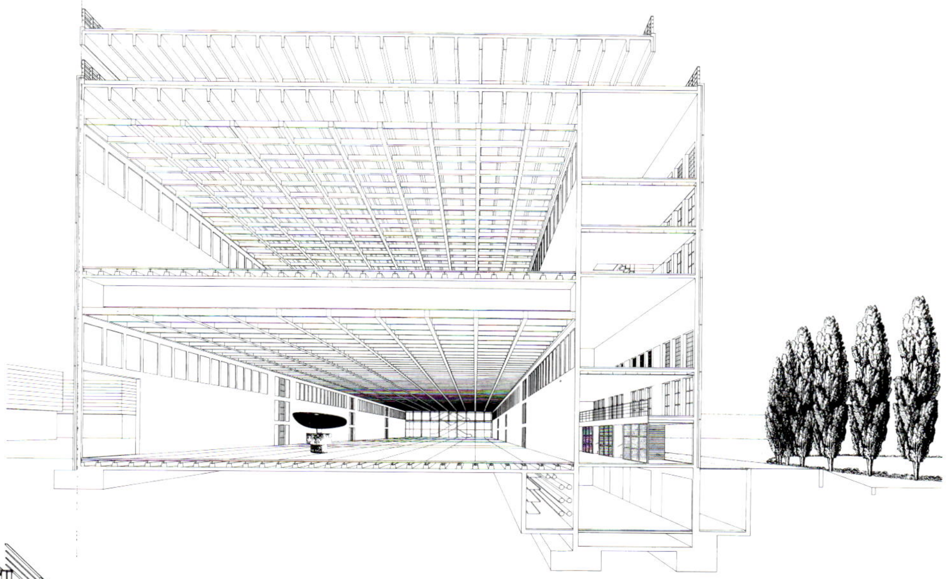

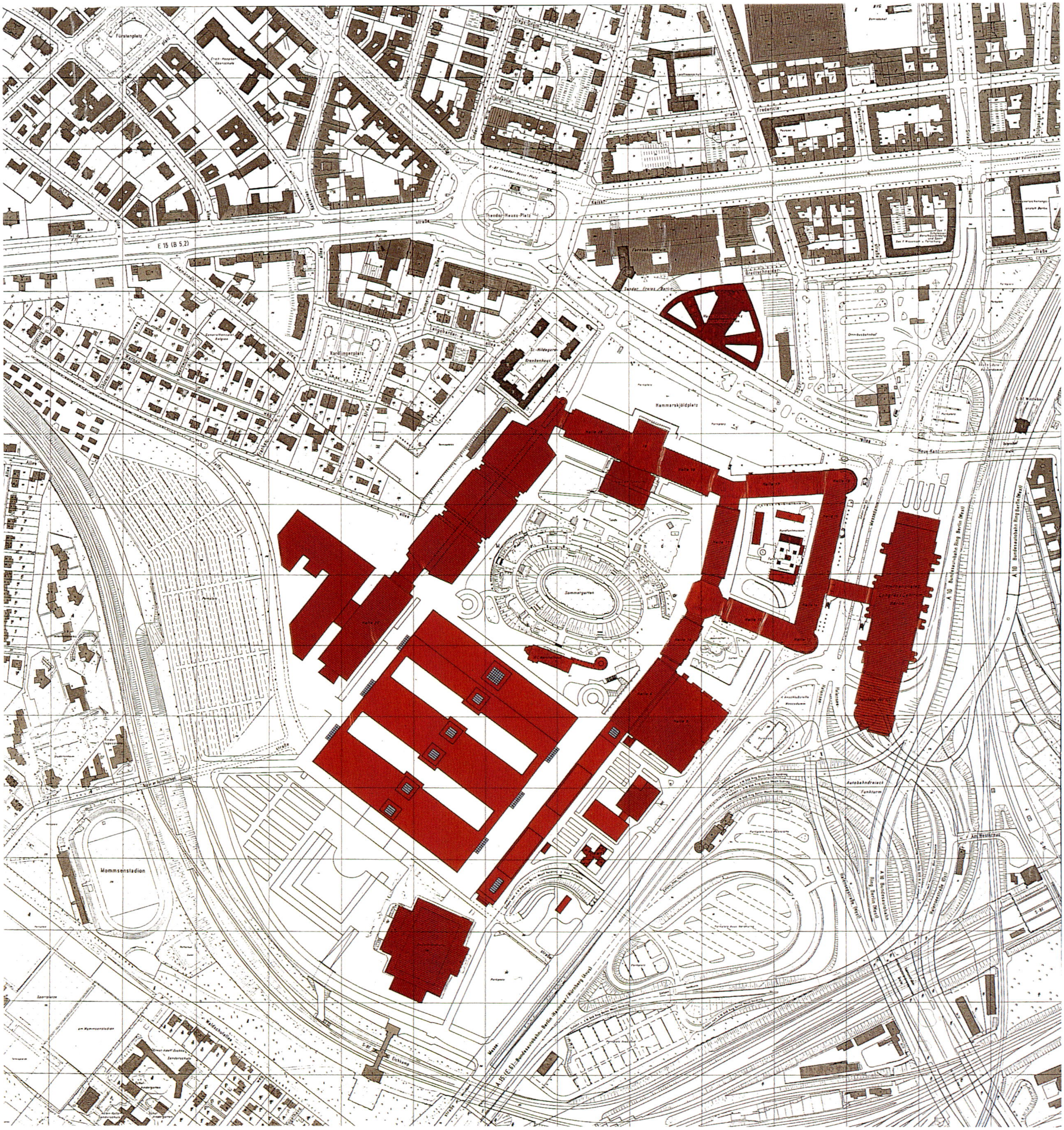
Fürstenplatz
Theodor-Heuss-Platz
E 15 (B 5.2)
Hammarskjöldplatz
Sommergarten
Mommsenstadion

Site plan of
existing buildings
and expansion.

Model view; plans.

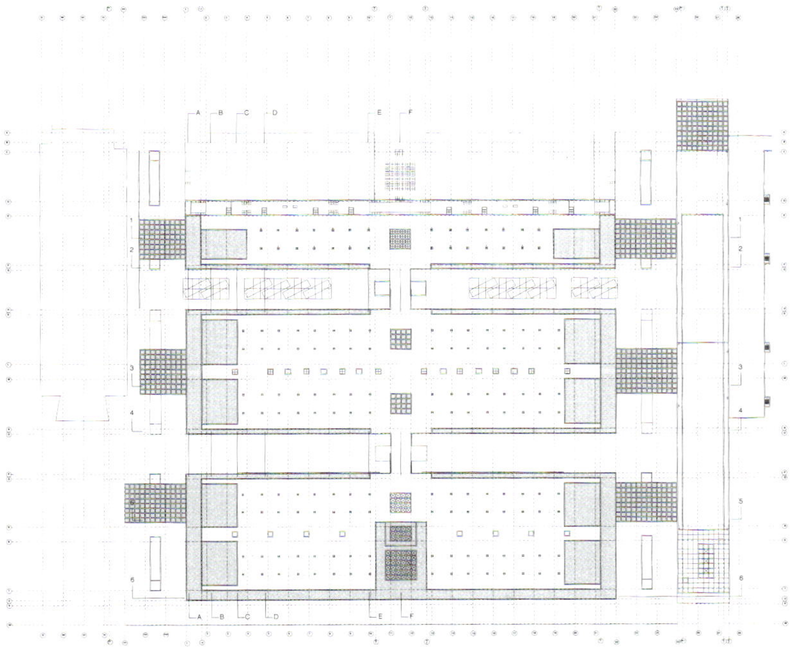

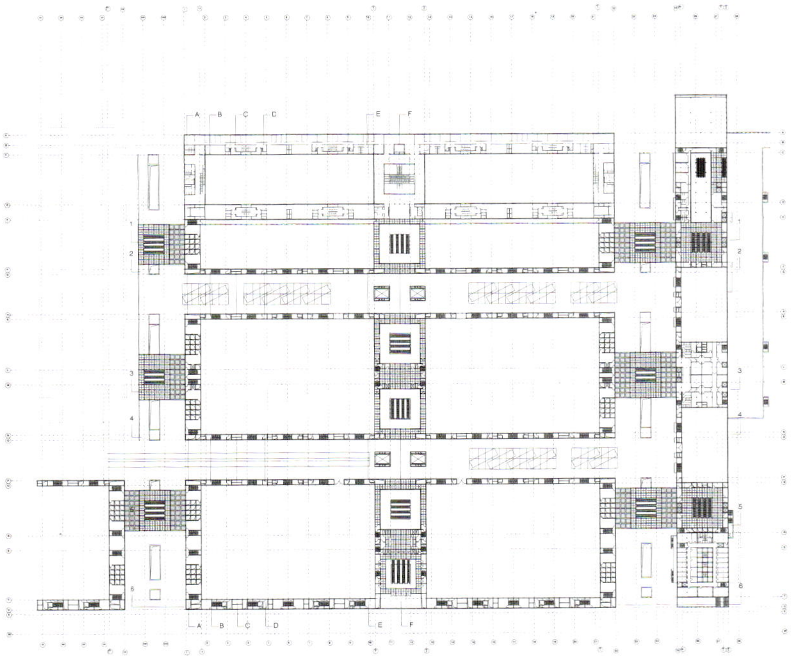

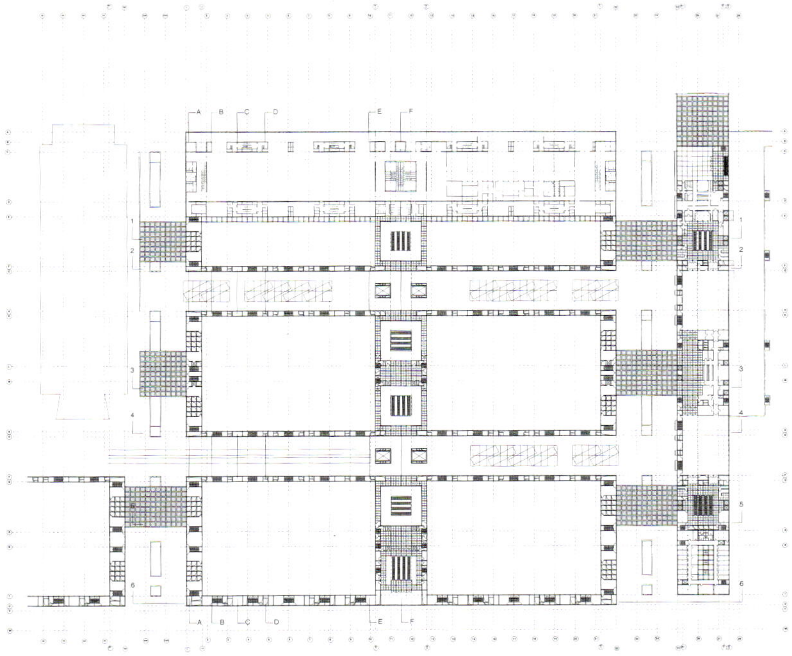

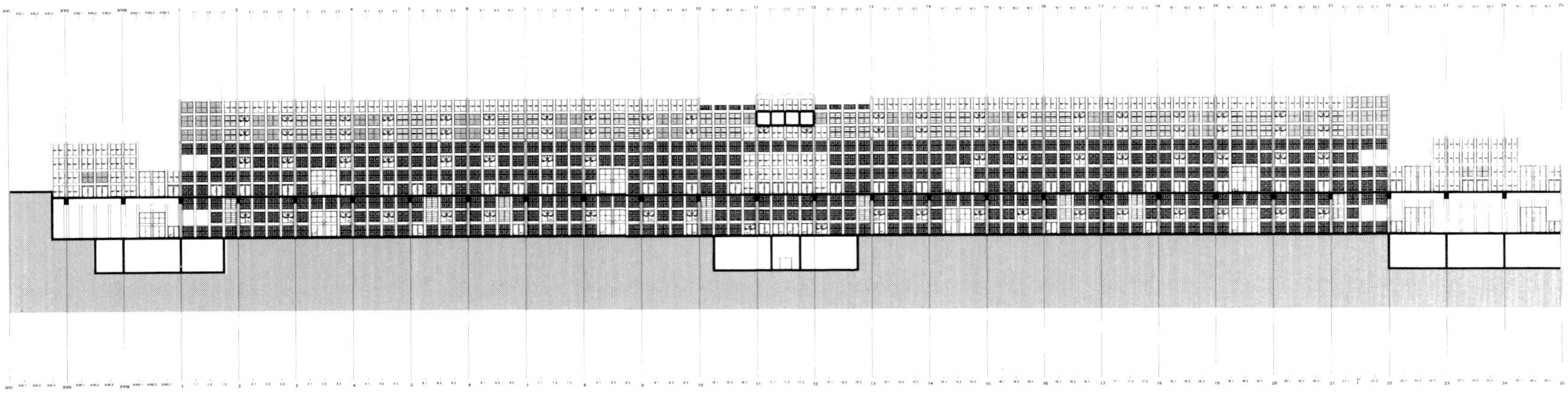

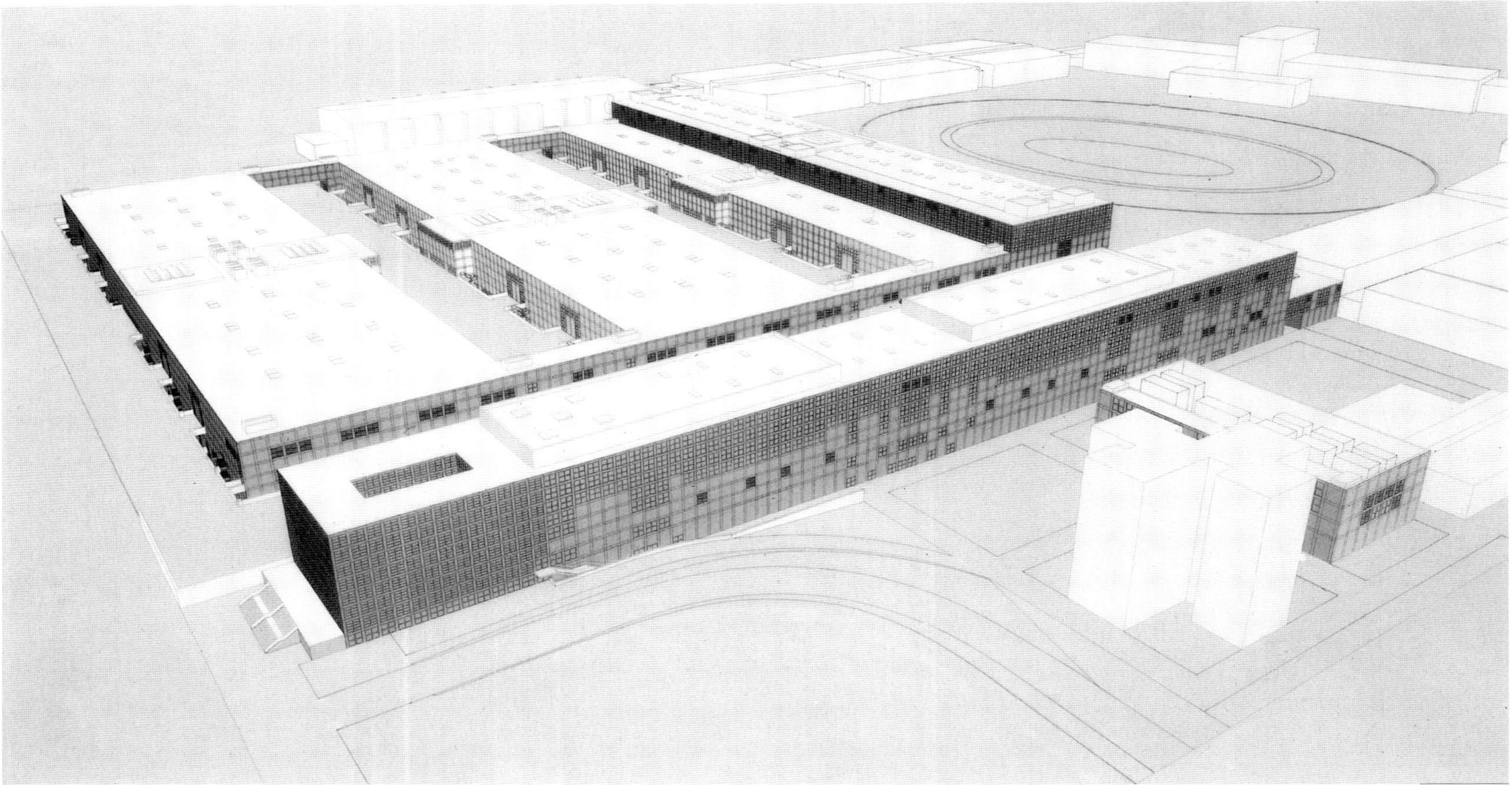

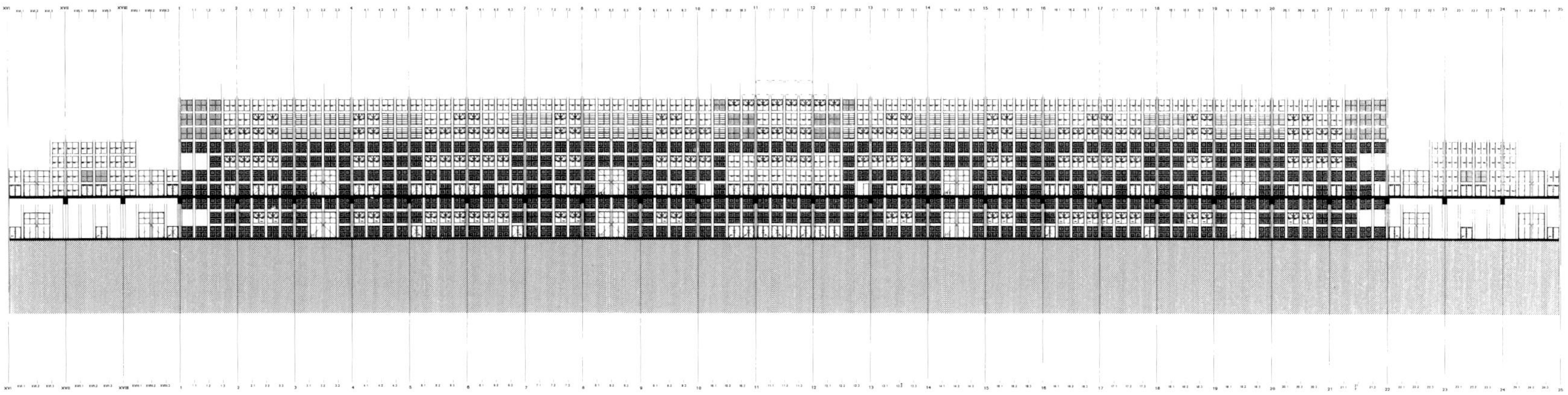

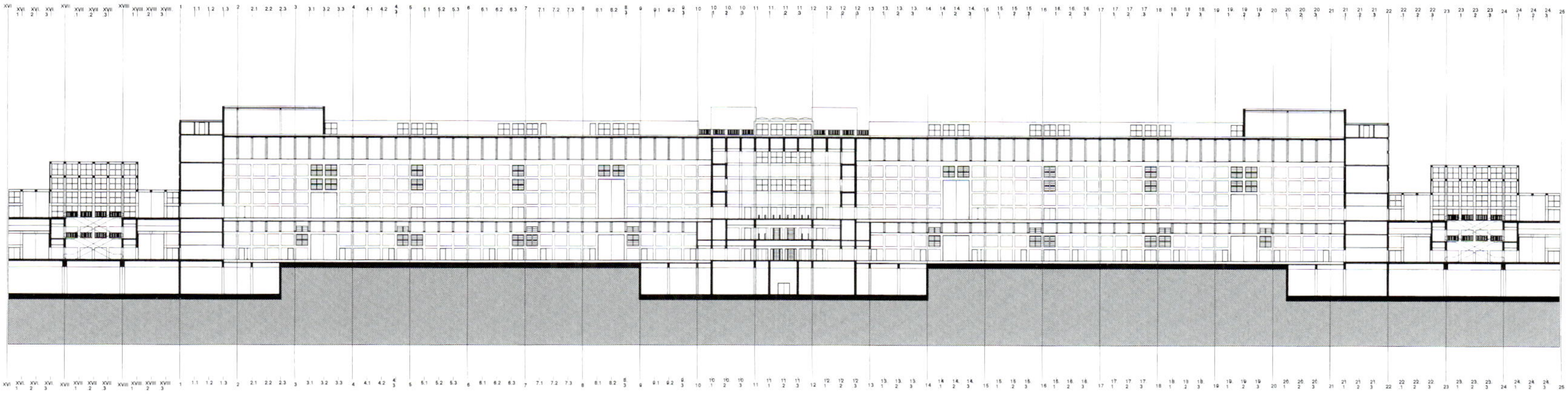

Elevations; perspective;
sections; model views.

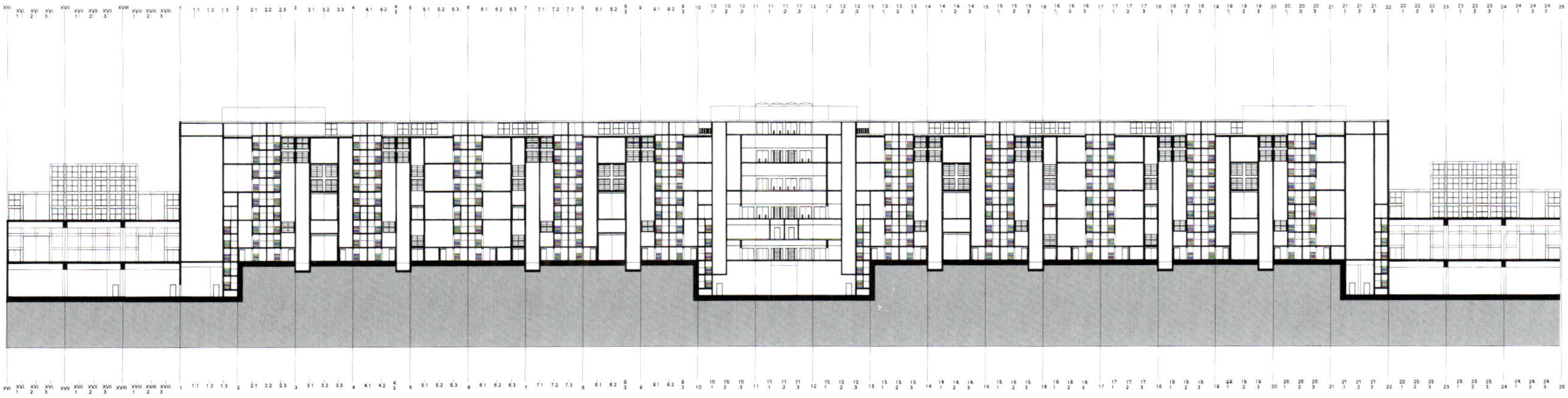

Trade fair halls.

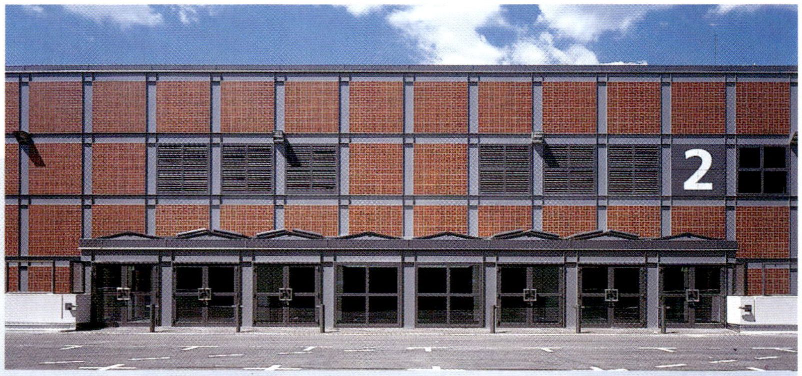

Sommergarten and the enclosed area to the north, as well as toward the open area and the Deutschlandhalle to the south. The entire structure is articulated into three wings, each of which is provided with delivery and service entrances on both sides.

The first wing is divided into six halls with three thousand square meters exhibition space each as well as two special-purpose areas of three thousand square meters each. The second and third wings each contain four large exhibition halls with 6,750 square meters over two levels each.

The entire new structure is two stories, thus continuing the principle of the existing Halls 8 to 10. The lower stories lie at the level of the interior courtyard of the radio tower, the upper ones at the level of the summer garden and of Halls 20 to 25 and 7, adjacent on either side. Hall A represents a complex answer to a complex problem: the space-saving accommodation of colossal exhibition areas and the management of a wide range of functions such as delivery, storage, visitors' and exhibitors' services, flexibility and connectability of exhibition spaces, circulation, and parking.

The three wings of Hall A find their logical continuation in the three wings of Hall B, adjoining to the west.

Facade details.

Interiors of trade fair halls.

Views of atrium.

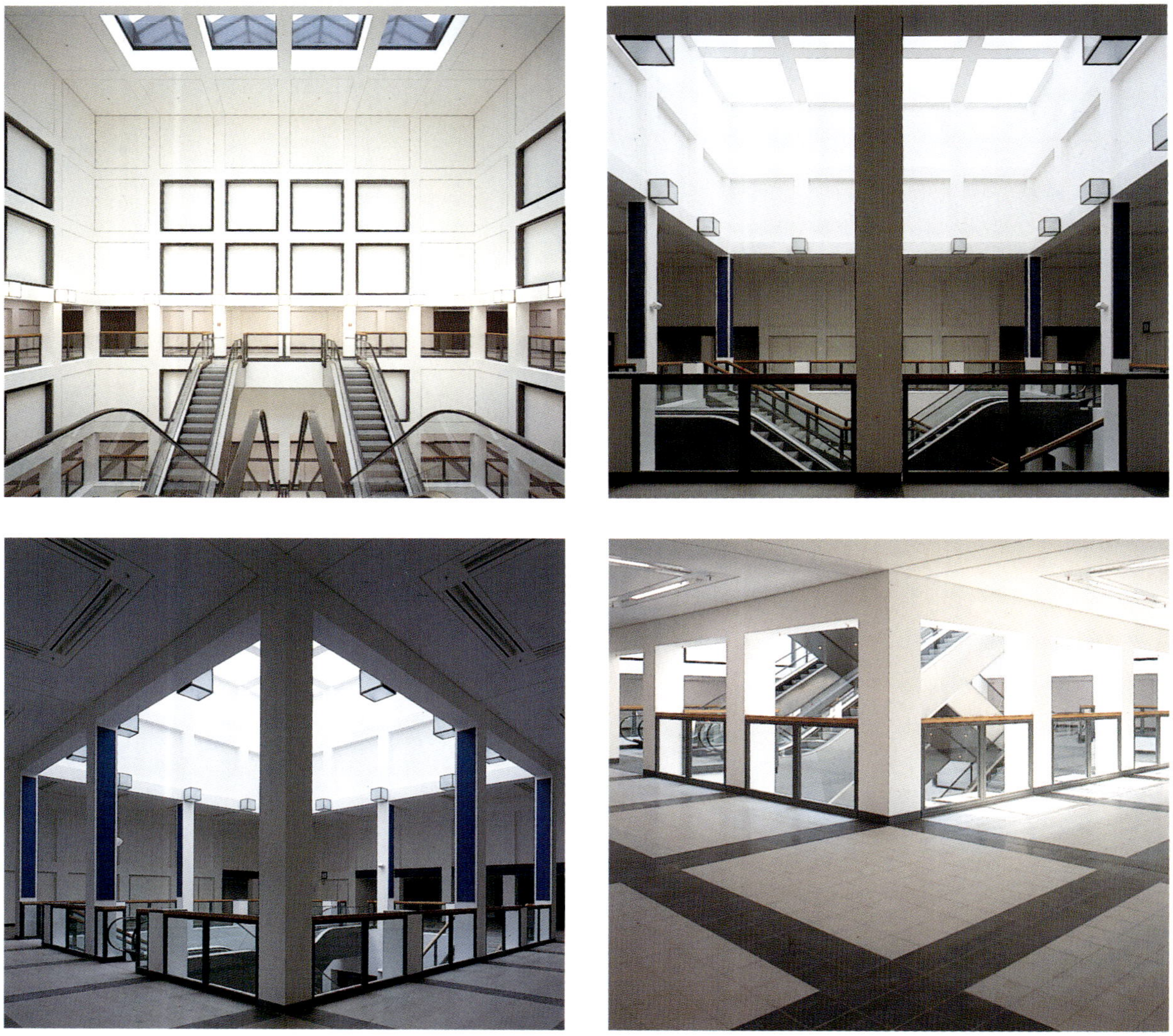

Federal Prosecutor's Office, Karlsruhe, 1985–1998

Isometric; site plan.

Project team: Kai-Uwe Lompa, Frank Wieschemann, R. Reingelhan, Helmut Kleine-Kraneburg, Martin Gruber
Construction supervision: Burckhard Meyer

The now realized design for the Federal Prosecutor's Office, in which the Federal Supreme Court still occupies its traditional site, is the third since the beginning of the competition in 1985. In 1989, the site was changed to the grounds of the Industriewerke Karlsruhe/Augsburg (IWKA) and the project was redesigned. In 1990, the building permit application for the now realized project was submitted. The building is now under construction on Block 4 of the IWKA grounds on Brauerstrasse on a plot measuring one hundred by one hundred meters.

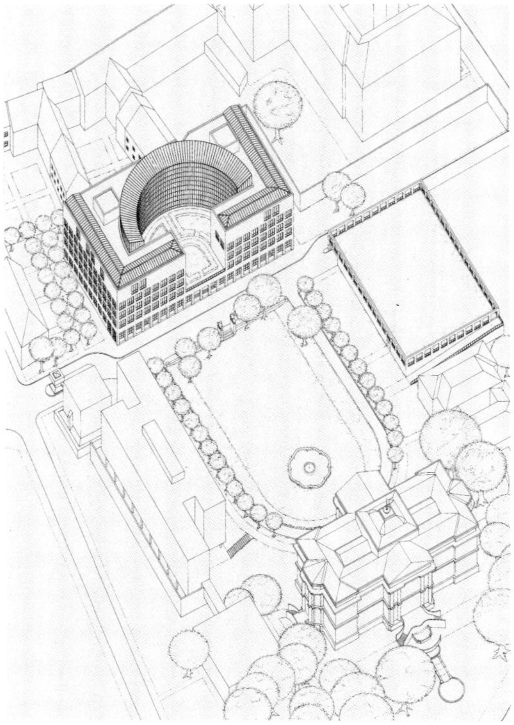

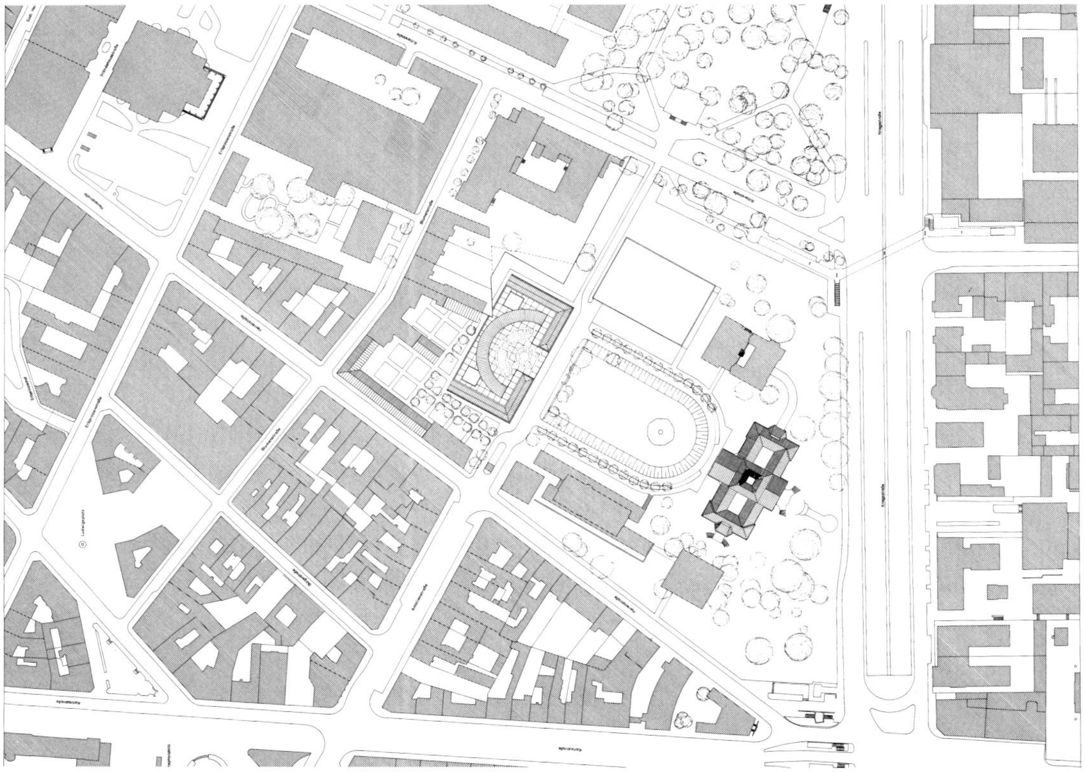

In order to demarcate the building line and satisfy security requirements, an outer enclosure five meters in height was conceived, a structure whose natural stone facade is articulated on both aides with an arcadelike configuration of fields, pilaster strips, and supports. Outside, it is covered on three sides with climbing plants, while its fourth, "public face" is on Brauerstrasse. The top of the enclosure is planted with a 1.8-meter-high hedge.

This arcade building encloses a square courtyard and parking area within which, in emulation of the "palace" building type, the main structure is symmetrically positioned. The building consists of a rectangle into which a round arch segment is inscribed. The spaces between the rectangle and arch form two interior courtyards extending the entire height of the five-story building, illuminated through a continuous band of skylights. The building thus has three basic elements: the rectangular building, the semicircular segment cut into it, and the two interior courtyards arising from the combination of rectangle and semicircle.

On the exterior, the rectangular building is faced with the same Jurassic stone as the arcade enclosure, though with a brighter surface. The semicircular building is covered in a fine, white plaster. Across from the main building, a symmetrical group of trees surrounded by a hedge mirrors the plan of the building. The driveways are paved with stone-filled asphalt.

The arcade enclosure accommodates parking areas, entrances to the underground garage, security systems, and side rooms. The ground floor of the main building houses the cafeteria and other generally accessible spaces, while the upper stories accommodate the main divisions of the Federal Prosecutor's Office, the central directorship, the conference hall, and a residence for the head of maintenance.

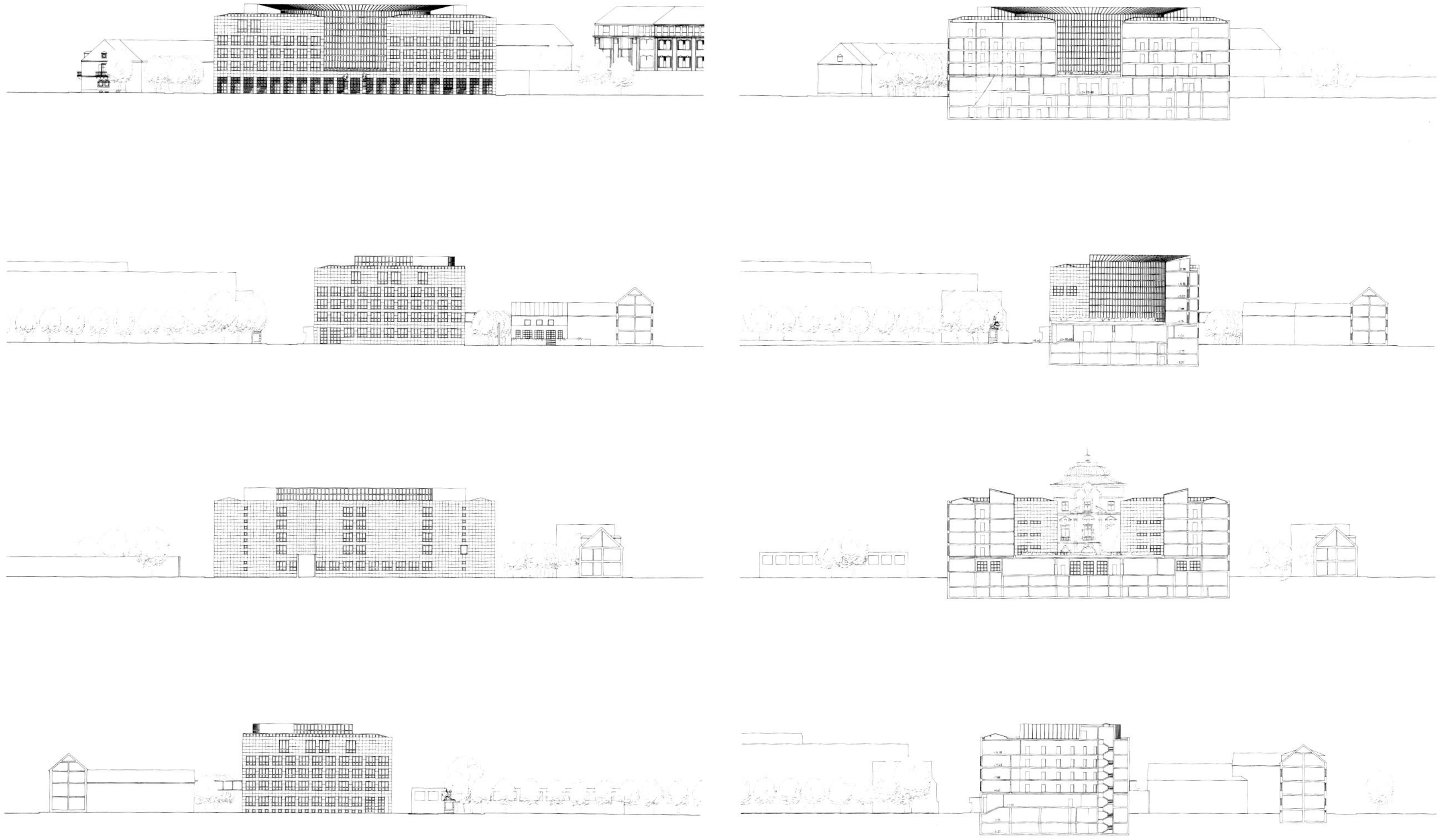

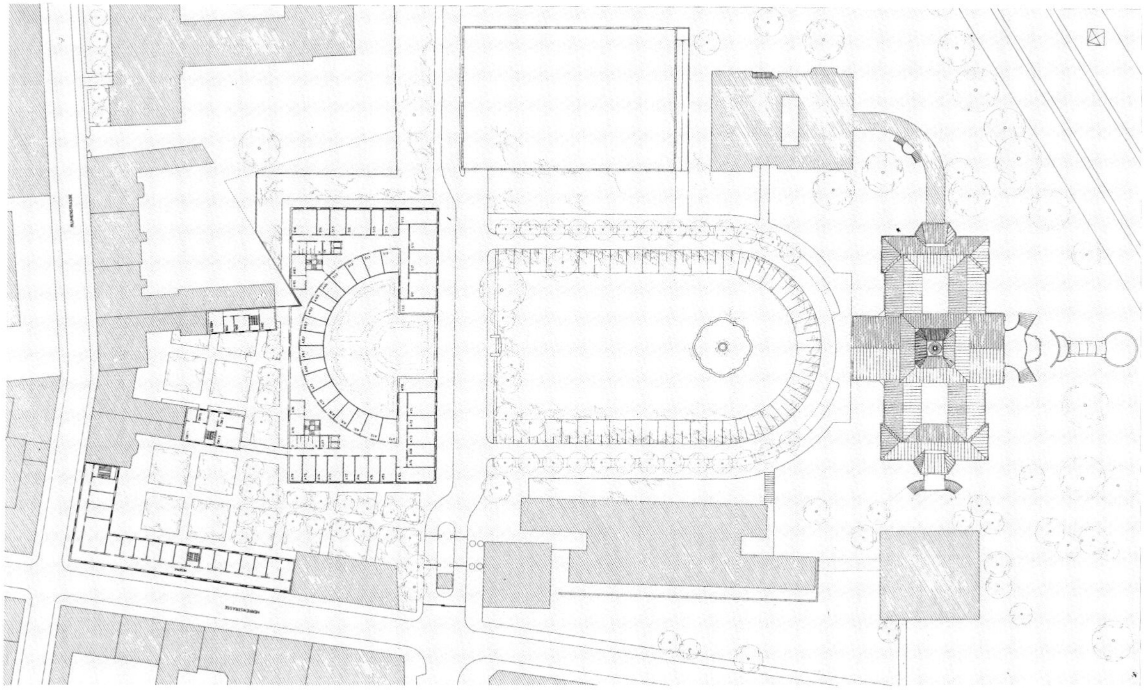

Elevations; sections; ground-level plan.

Model views; sketch.

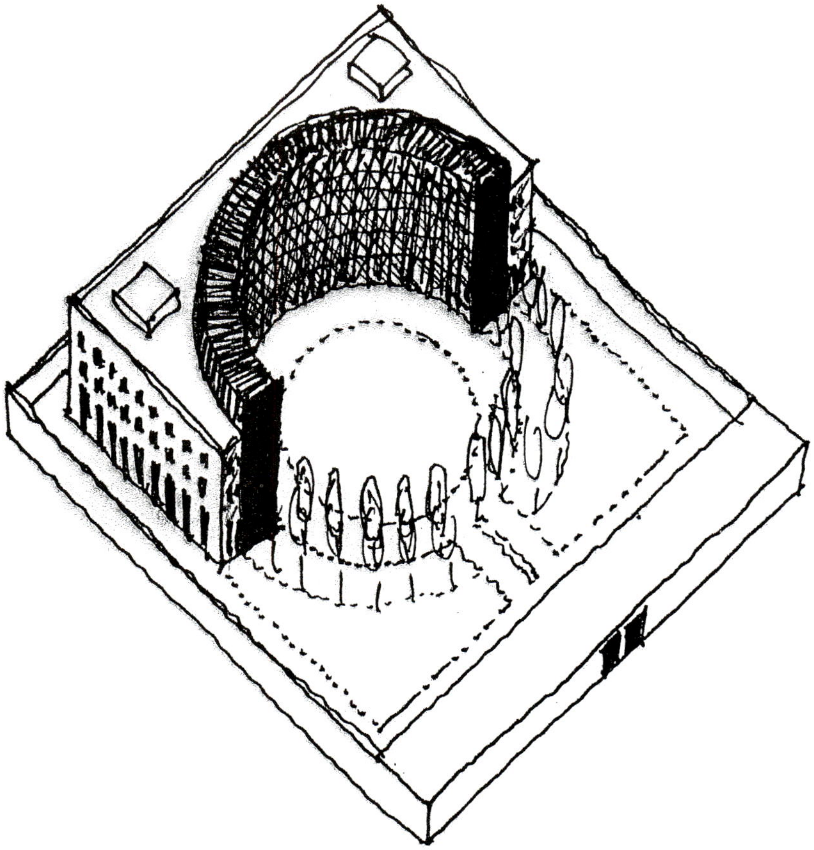

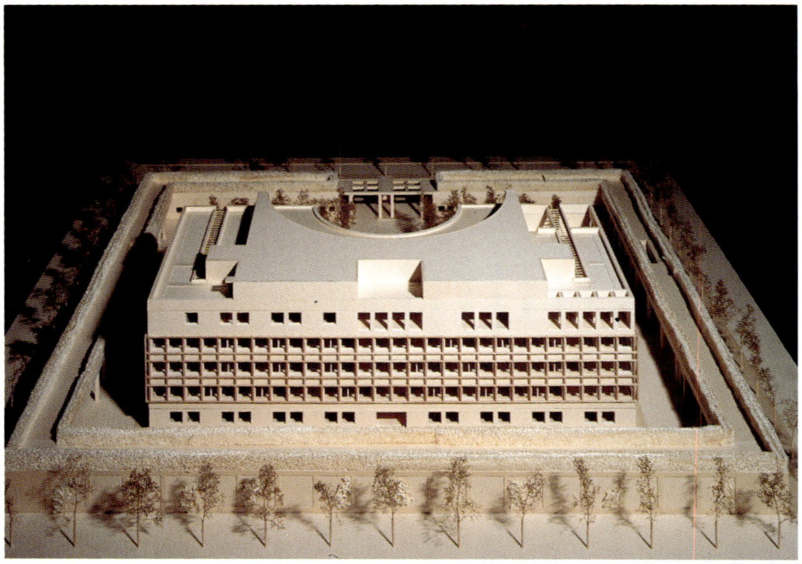

Plans; sketch.

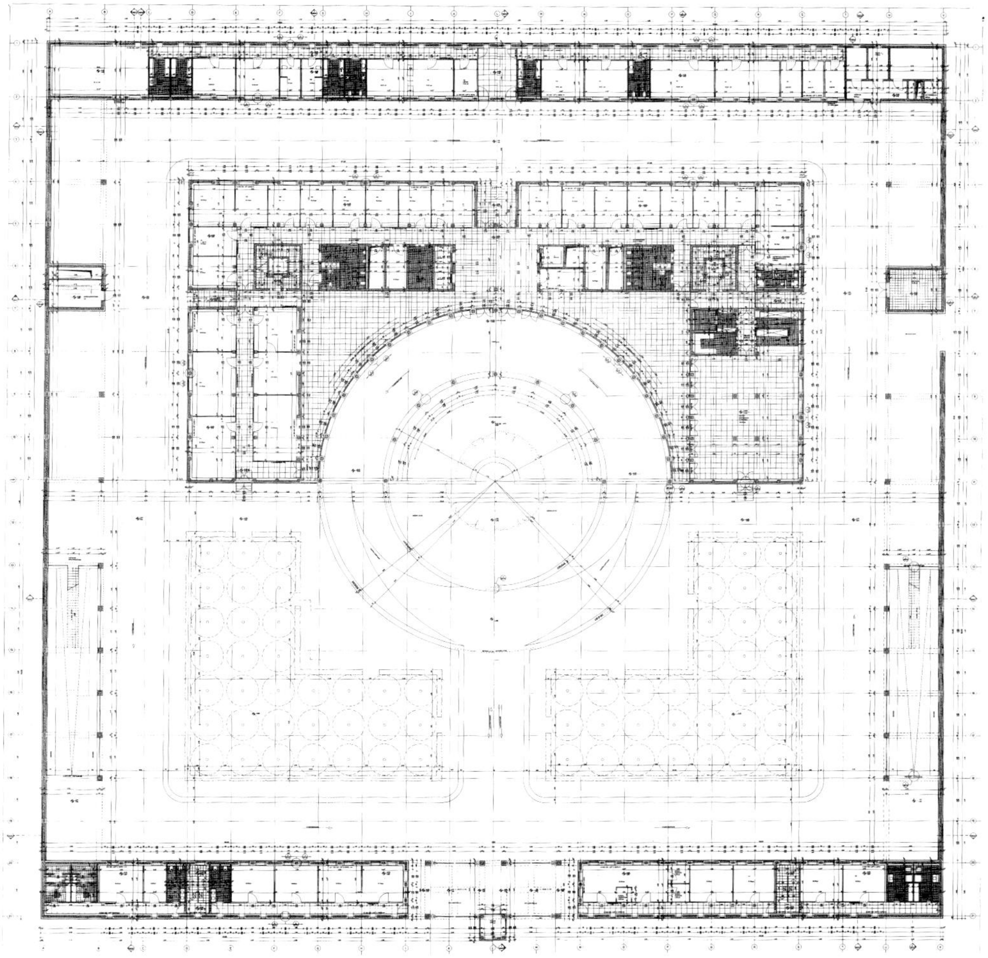

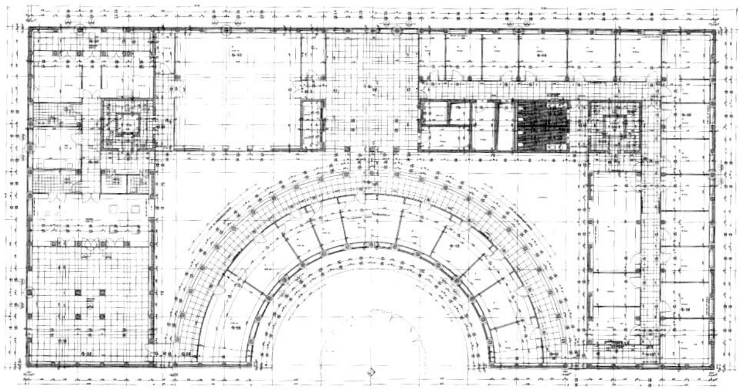

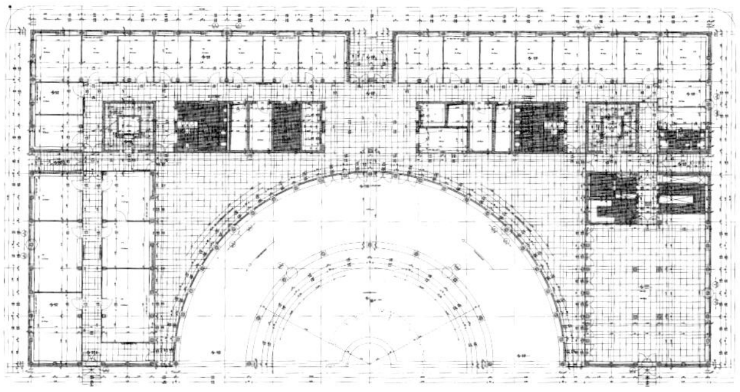

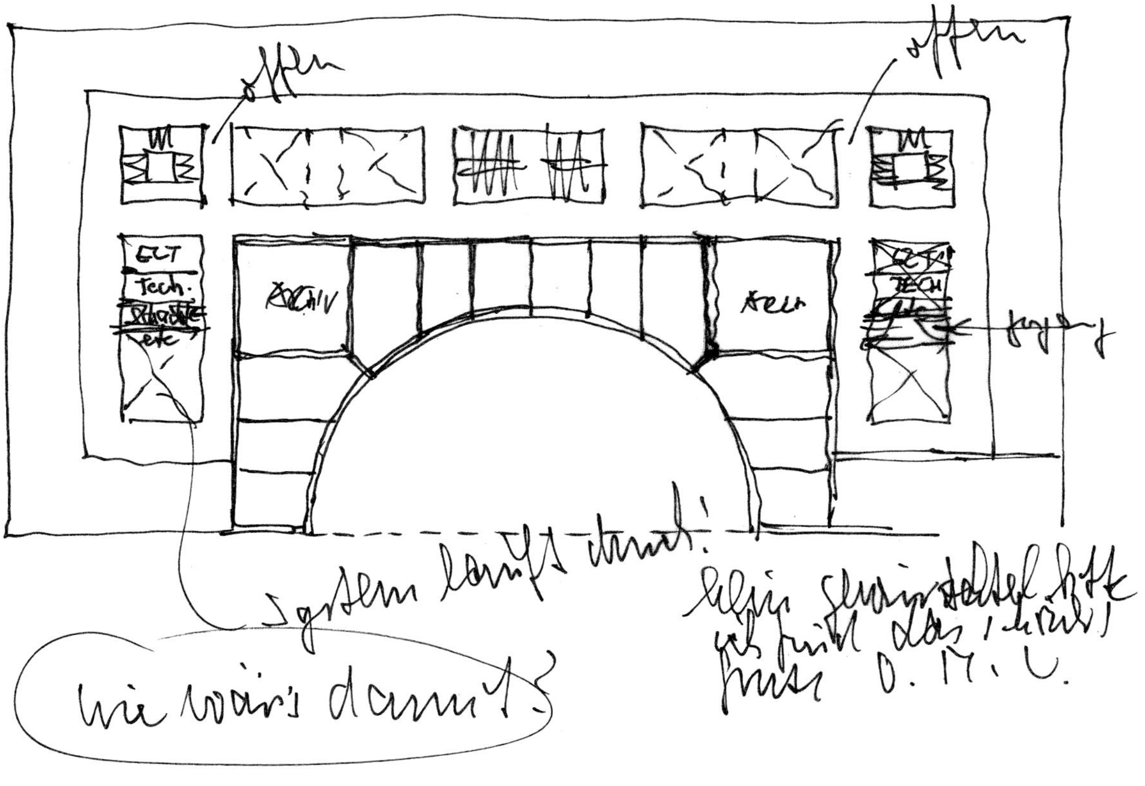

Sketches; section; exterior during construction.

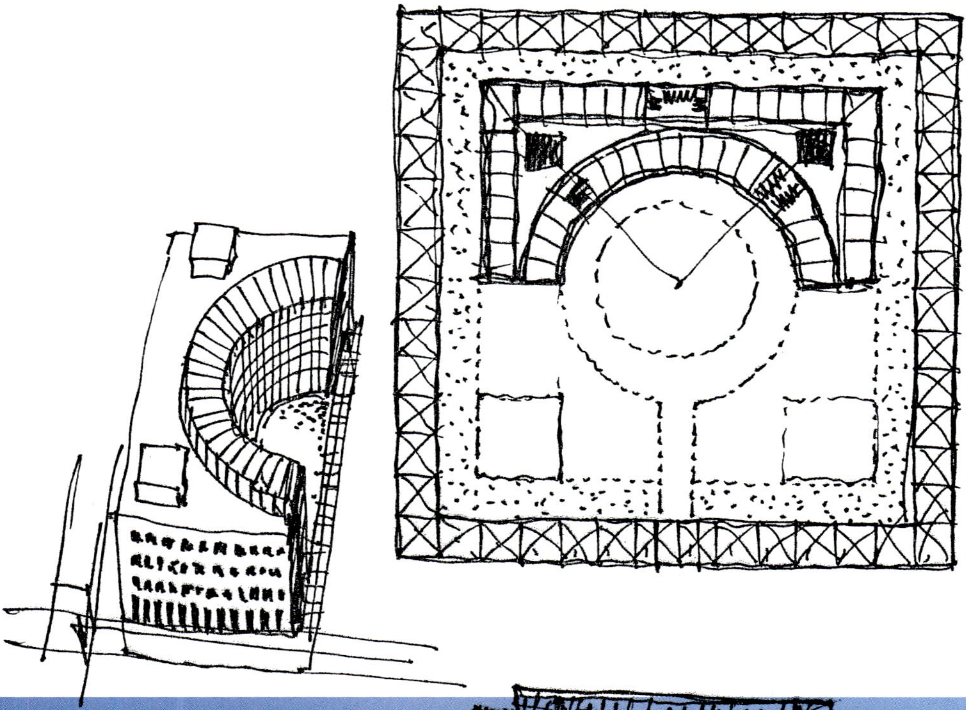

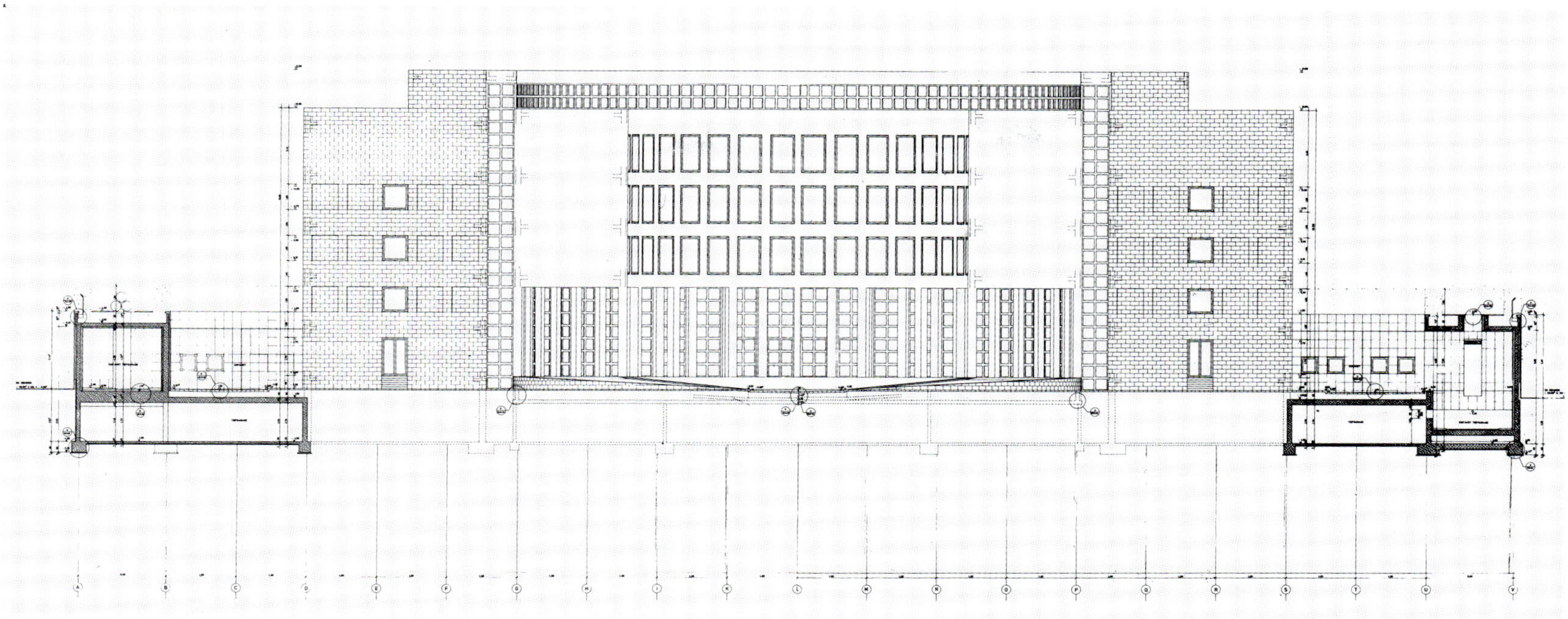

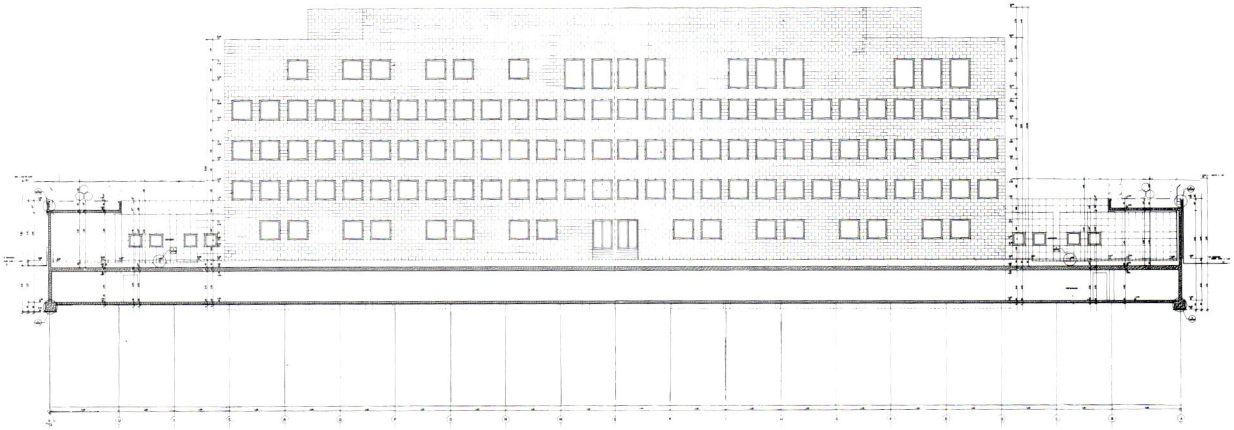

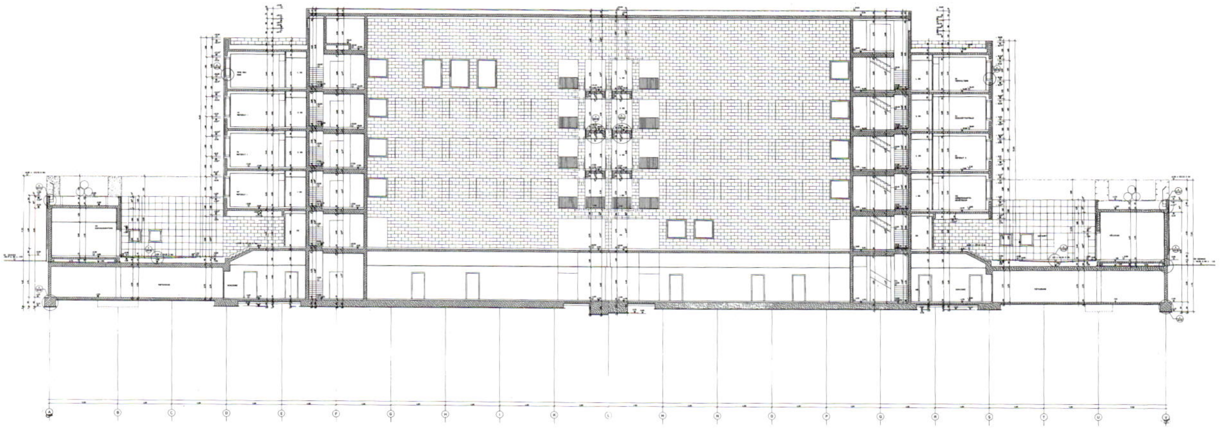

Elevation; exteriors; section; details of enclosure.

Roof terrace; view into entrance hall.

Expansion of Hall 10 and Galleria of Trade Fair Complex, Frankfurt am Main, 1990–1993

Project team: Peter Diehl, Ingo Schrader, Michael Winkelmann, Martin Gruber, Maike Bräckerbohm, Bernward Kraus, A. Resch

An existing trade fair hall from the 1960s was expanded to include an additional exhibition level and a ring-shaped technical level in the uppermost story. At the same time, all the technical facilities were modernized and the existing facade of asbestos-cement panels was replaced with a new, attractive, and environmentally friendly substitute. All the exhibition levels were technically and architecturally modified to accommodate two to three levels of temporary booths and eight levels with permanent booths.

The hall measures about 180 meters in length and 80 meters in width. The new facade has a classical tripartite division: a massive socle zone with isolated openings, a middle zone that dissolves into a pattern of large-scale, brightly colored glass surfaces, and an upper zone with a frieze of small plastered fields at the level of the technical story.

The new proportions and articulation of the building lend it a costly, precise appearance despite its extremely low-cost facade of mounted mineral panels and painted glass. During the construction of the new hall, the decision was made to erect a glazed hall as a foyer, a counterpart to the existing "Galleria." This extension stands on the exact axis of the existing Galleria, so the two structures can eventually be connected, as was proposed in the 1980 competition design for the trade fair grounds.

Plan; elevations.

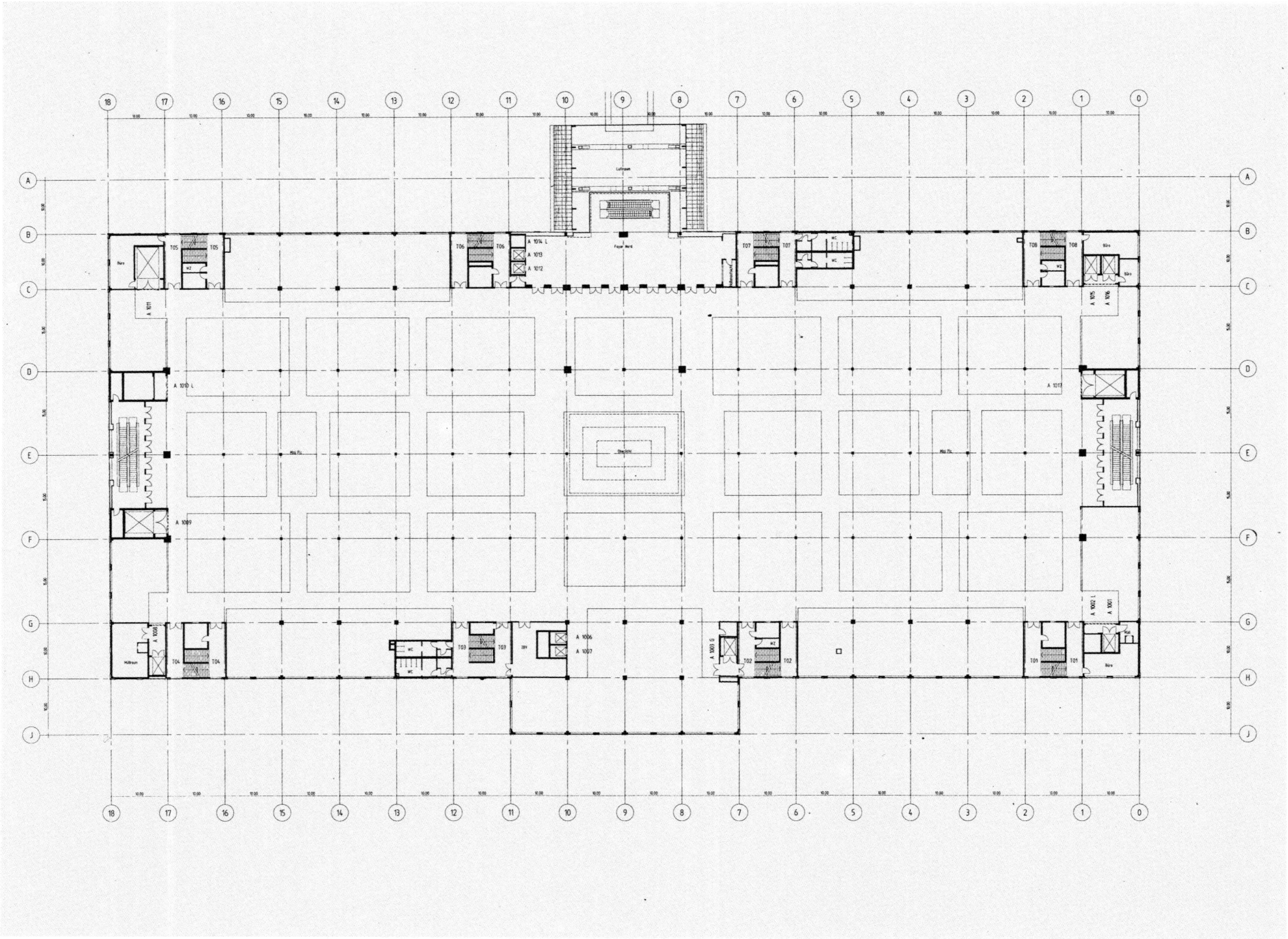

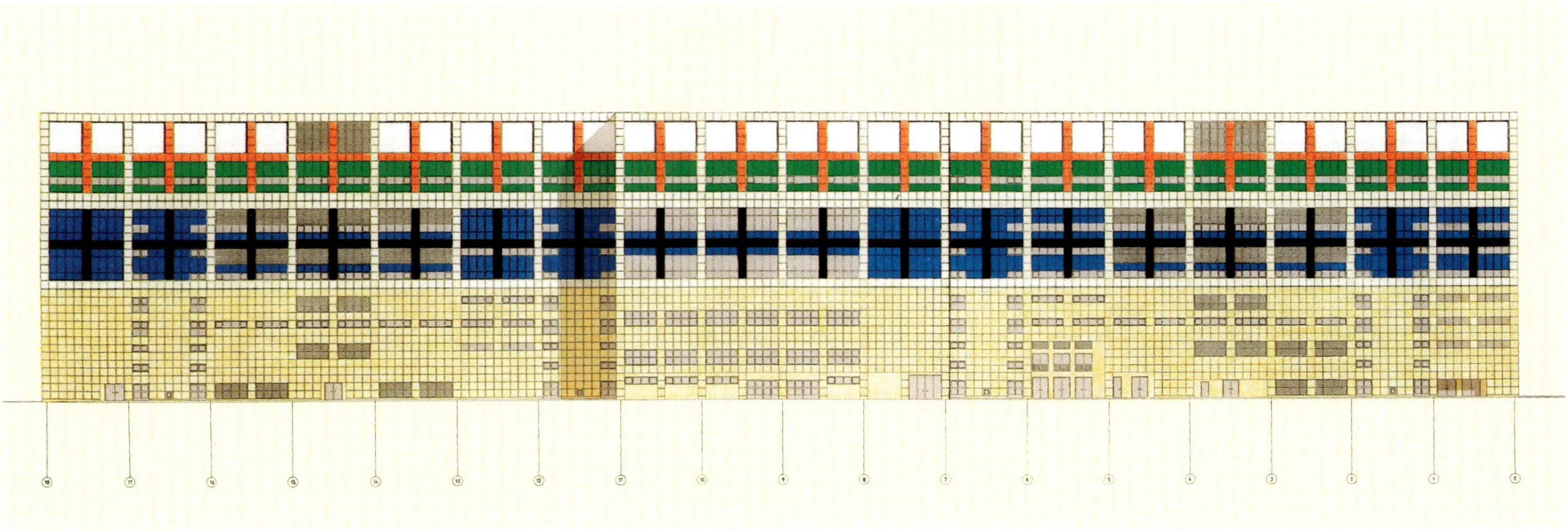

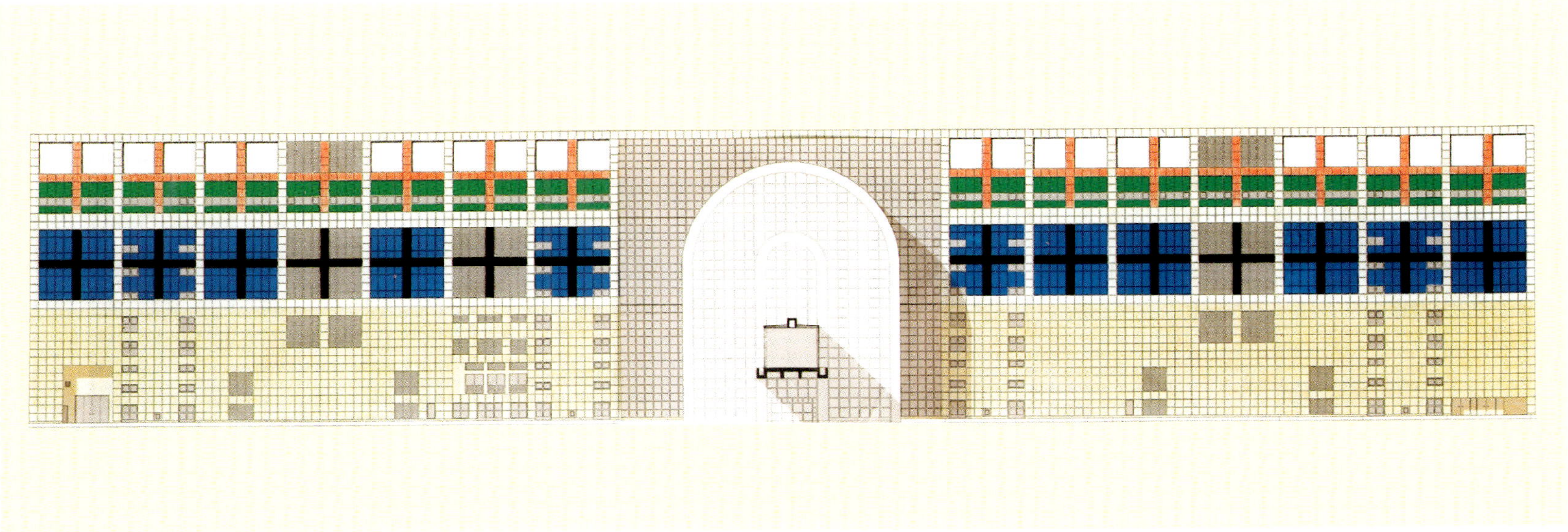

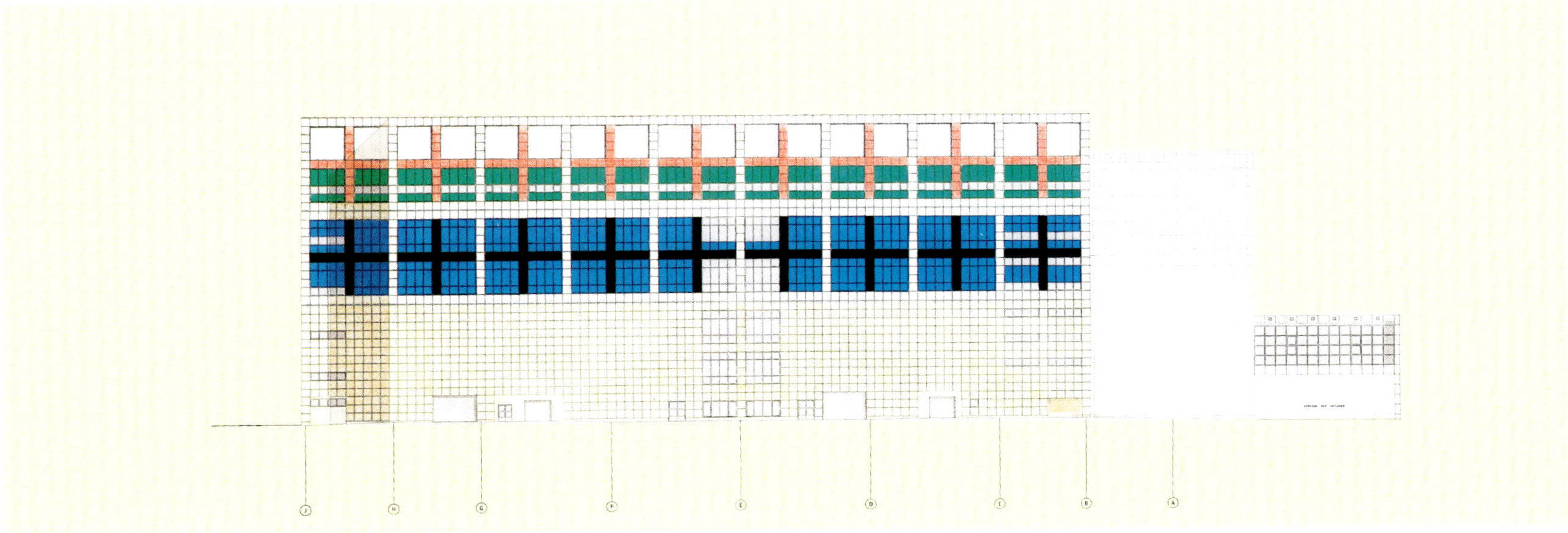

Views of Hall 10 with glazed foyer.

Competition Design for Friedrichstadt-Passagen, Block 205, Berlin, 1991–1995

With: Karl-Heinz Winkens, Sebastian Klatt

Project team: Robert Beyer, Hugo Daiber, Angela Leonhardt, Tobias Scheel, Birgit Schindler, Tanya Trevisan, Martin Weisser

Planning concept: In addition to the two original towns of Berlin and Cölln, the metropolis of Berlin grew out of the refugee cities of Friedrichswerder and Dorotheenstadt as well as Friedrichstadt, founded in the seventeenth century by Frederick William, the Great Elector. Despite many changes, the original urban structures are still clearly legible in the Berlin city center. The main streets from this early urban expansion are Unter den Linden, the former main axis leading to the Schloss, the Friedrichstrasse axis running perpendicular to it, and Leipziger Strasse, built at the king's expense.

Around 1730, Frederick William I initiated an expansion that called for the extension of these three main Friedrichstadt axes and the creation of three geometric plazas to serve as prominent entrance plazas to the city as well as military parade grounds: Pariser Platz, a square plaza on the axis of Unter den Linden, the octagon of Leipziger Platz on the axis of Leipziger Strasse, and the roundel of Belle-Alliance-Platz at the end of Friedrichstrasse. These plazas are not only characteristic of Friedrichstadt, but also represent a world-famous trademark of the Berlin metropolitan area. Friedrichstadt was a creation of the baroque era and shows a rational ground plan with regular block-edge construction. The central plaza of this urban district is Gendarmenmarkt with the two church towers by Gontard and the Schauspielhaus by Schinkel, originally planned as a market square with a church, town hall, and veterans' hospital.

The most important urbanistic criterion for the new design of Friedrichstadt was the preservation and reconstruction of the block-edge configuration and thus of the historic streets. Any modification of the historic block structure would be an unwarranted alteration of the inherited

Site plan; perspective.

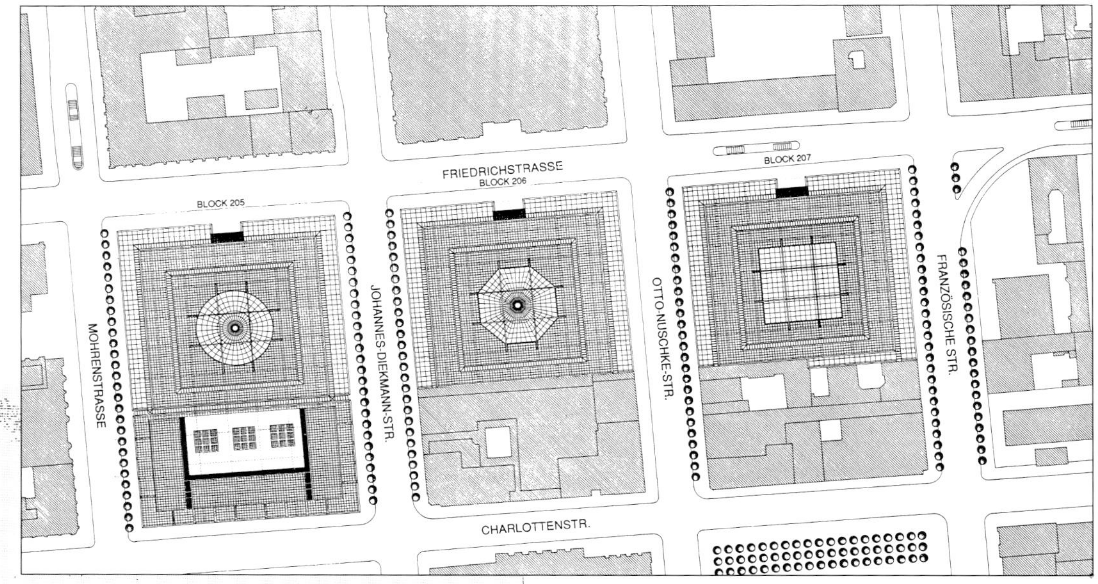

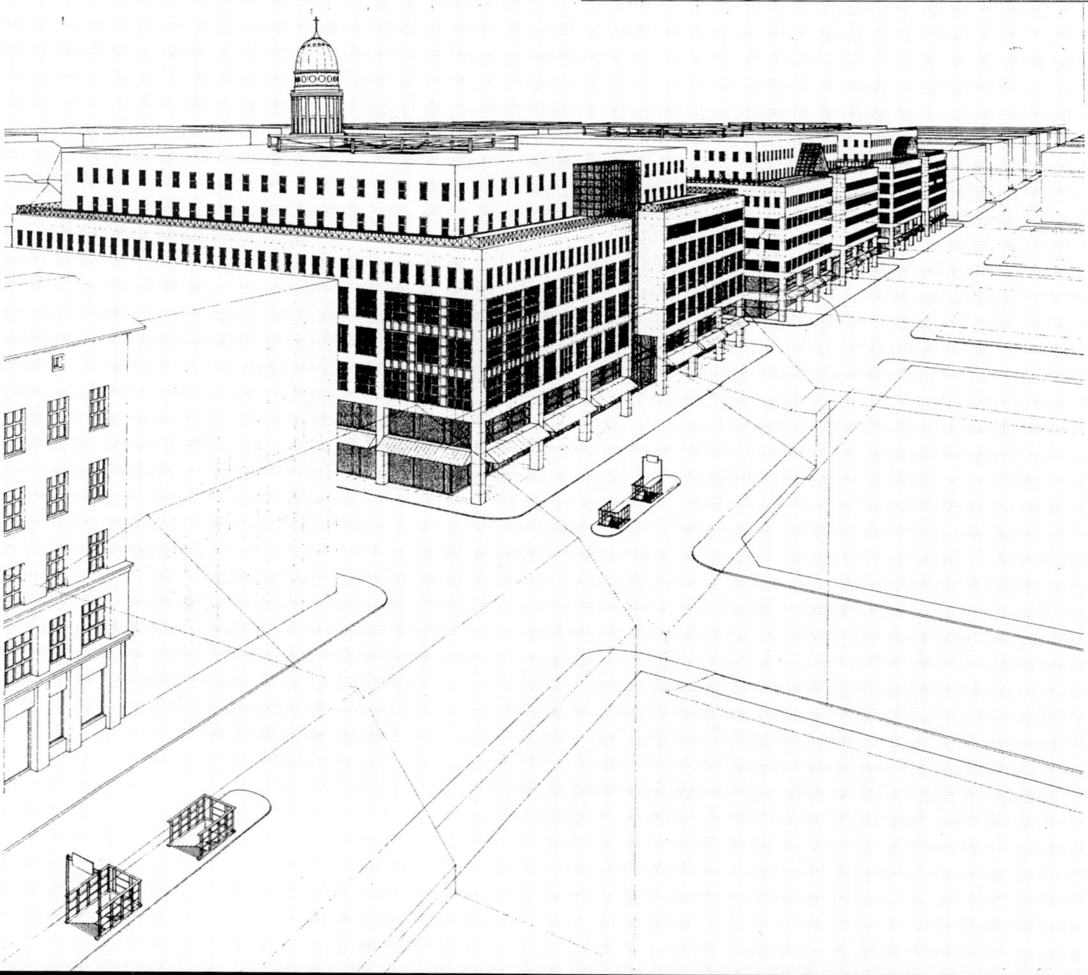

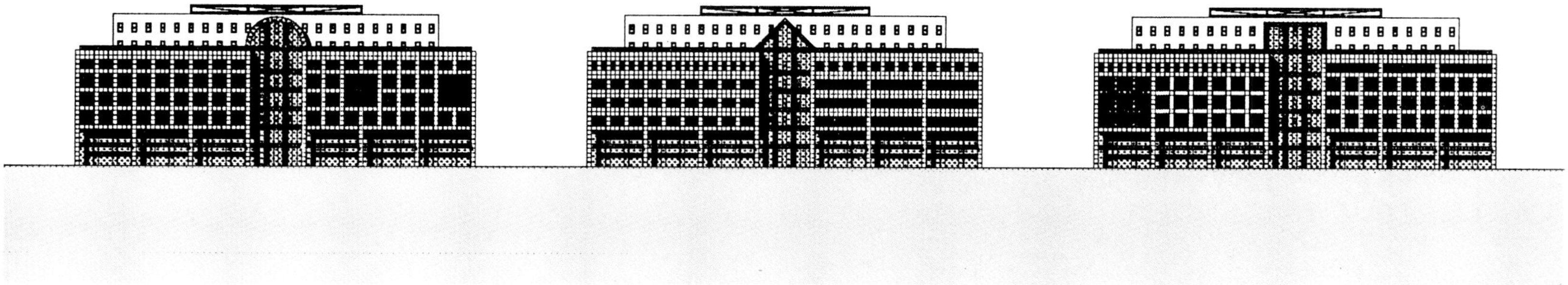

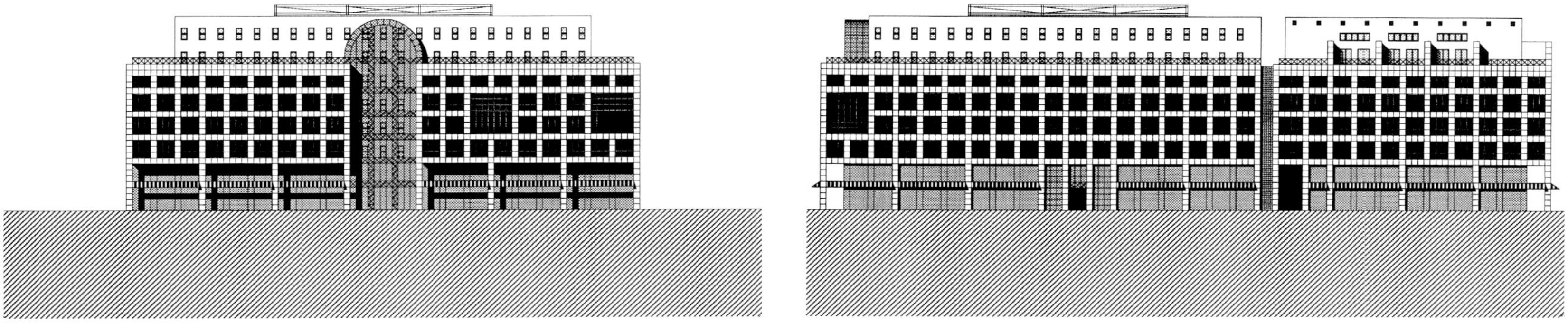

Elevations.

image of the city and would result in the destruction of a highly significant urban area. Neither the Marxist urbanistic experiments of Hilberseimer, the city-destroying landscape ideology of Scharoun, the movement patterns of the Smithsons, the bombardment of war, nor even socialist planning could completely alter the historic structure of Friedrichstadt. Its preservation was therefore the first and most important priority.

The demand for a Friedrichstadt-Passage clearly contradicted this imperative. The program called for a continuous shopping passage parallel to Friedrichstadt, a concept that was ill-advised for two reasons. On the one hand, the idea of a passage stood in direct conflict with the preservation of the block-edge structure and the street grid; on the other, Friedrichstrasse has historically been one of the main business streets of Berlin and should once again assume this role. All commercial and cultural activities along Friedrichstrasse should therefore be oriented to the street itself; a passage running parallel to it would relegate Friedrichstrasse to a secondary status, perhaps even degrading it to the level of a delivery street.

Instead of a Friedrichstadt-Passage, therefore, the concept of Friedrichstadt-Galerien was proposed. The galleries are accessed from Friedrichstrasse and form "pockets" opening off the street and leading to the interior of the block. Thus the significance of the street remains undiminished and is even intensified through the addition of interior gallery spaces. Blocks 205, 206, and 207 were designed accordingly. The block interior on Friedrichstrasse is formed by three glass galleries, whose differing geometric forms are signaled on the exterior by differing glass portals. The galleries represent enclosed piazzas and, with their three basic forms of square, octagon, and circle, recall the three historic plazas of Pariser Platz, Leipziger Platz, and Belle-Alliance-Platz. The content of the three galleries is differentiated as well. The Pariser Galerie in Block 207 focuses on commerce, the Leipziger Galerie in Block 206 on culture, and the Belle-Alliance-Galerie in Block 205

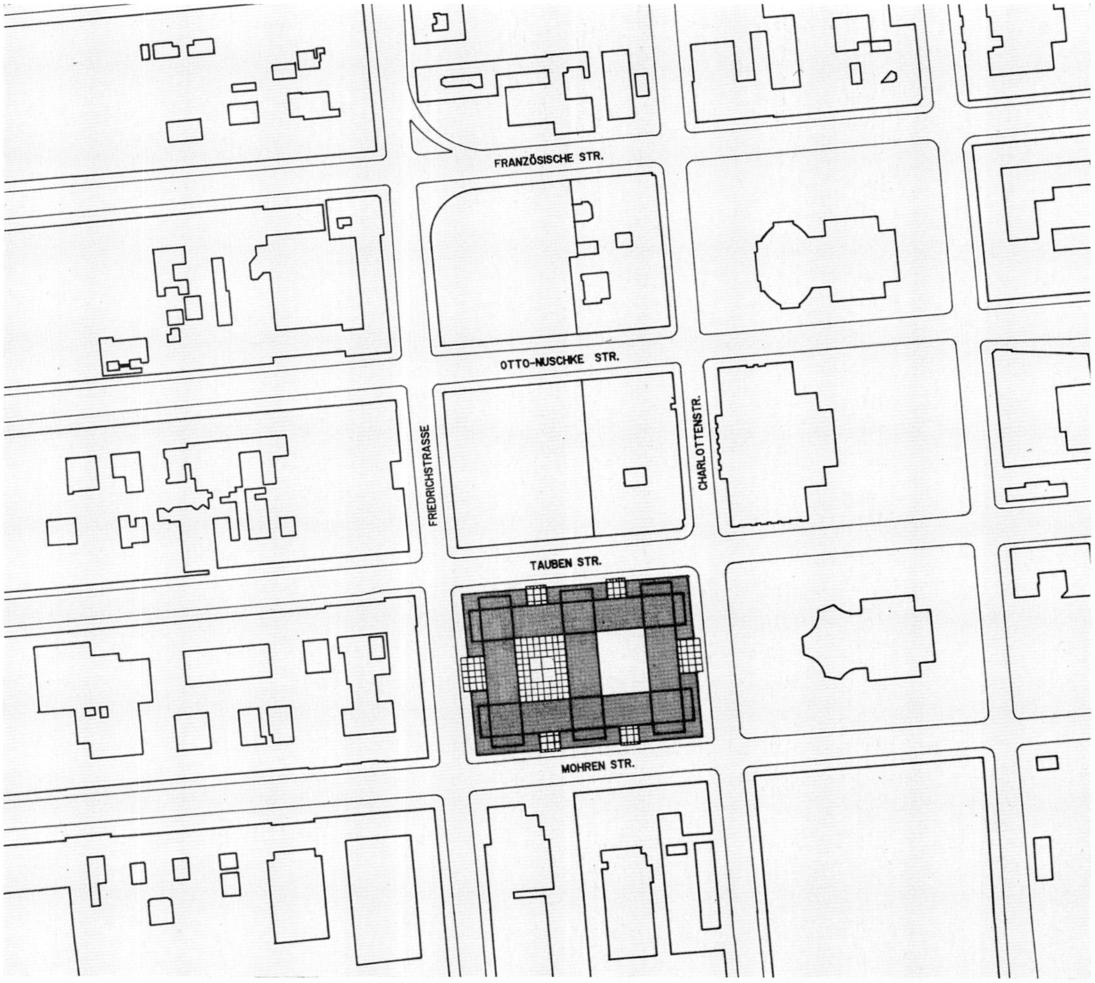

on gastronomy. At basement level, the three blocks and the galleries are connected by a continuous passage that also provides access to the Französische Strasse and Friedrichstrasse U-Bahn stations.

Realization, Block 205:
The plot Friedrichstrasse 66–70 lies between Mohrenstrasse and Taubenstrasse and is designated Block 205. It adjoins the rear side of Platz der Akademie along Charlottenstrasse. The rectangular site measures 109.60 by 76.61 meters and covers an area of about 8,400 square meters. Although the plot was already occupied by buildings, the structural shell completed in 1984 was torn down with a view to reconstructing the typical Friedrichstadt block structure, destroyed in World War II.

Block 205 uses two different elements to evoke the "Berlin block" motif. First, a tripartite, eight-story building set back from the block edge encloses two interior courtyards, or atriums. Then, around this core building are grouped six individual structures that delineate the block edge and continue the Friedrichstrasse roofline. Recessed areas between these buildings accommodate entrances to ground-level passages and permit a view through to the core building. The entrances are covered by canopies projecting 3.0 meters at the main entrances and 1.5 meters at the side entrances. Both atriums are roofed at the first upper story.
The roof of the atrium oriented toward Friedrichstrasse is glazed. The other atrium

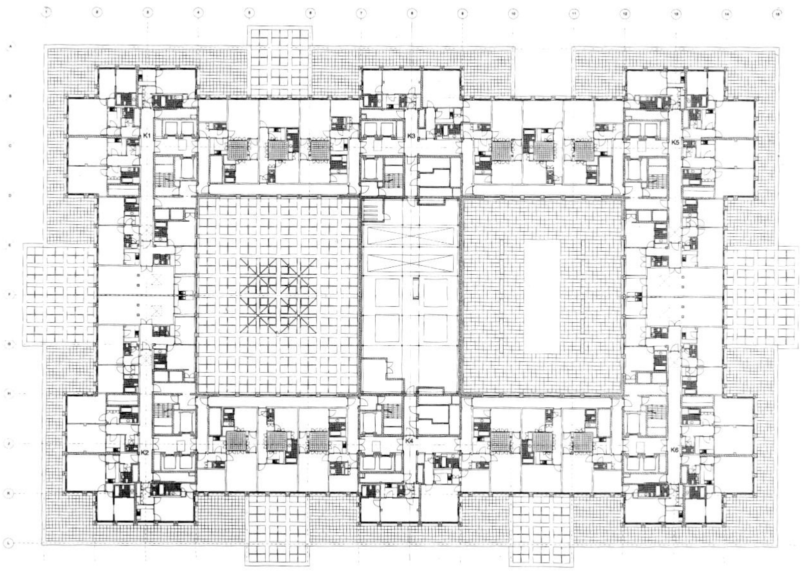

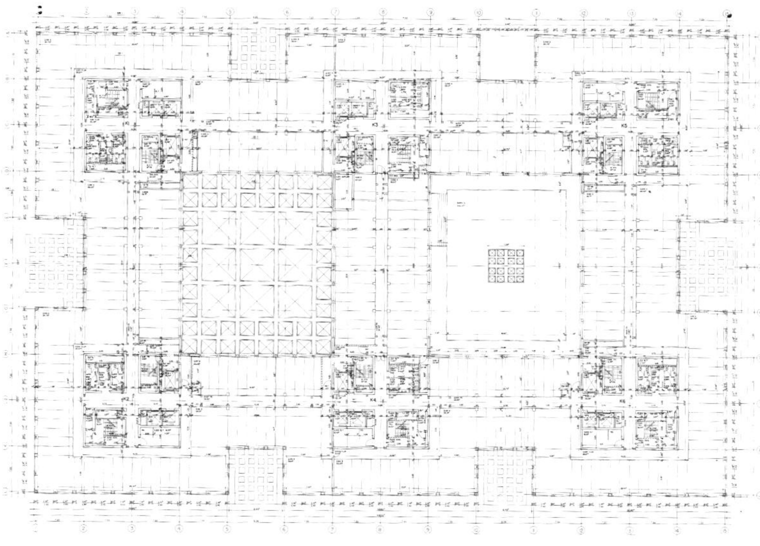

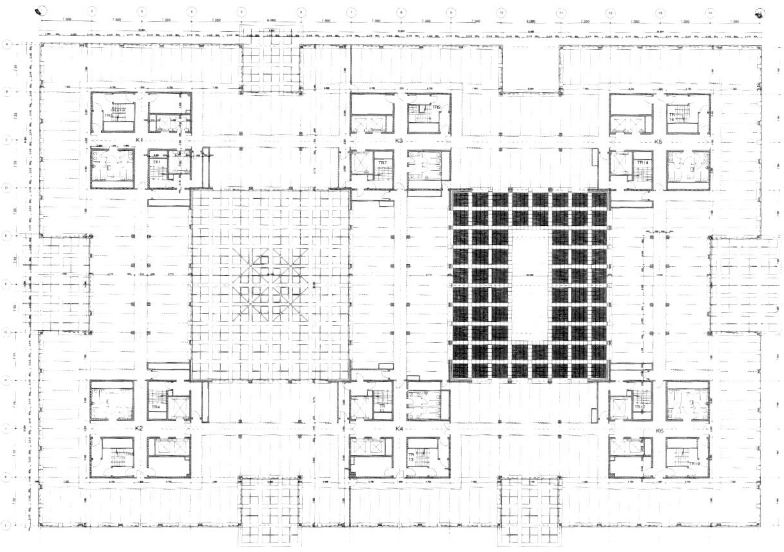

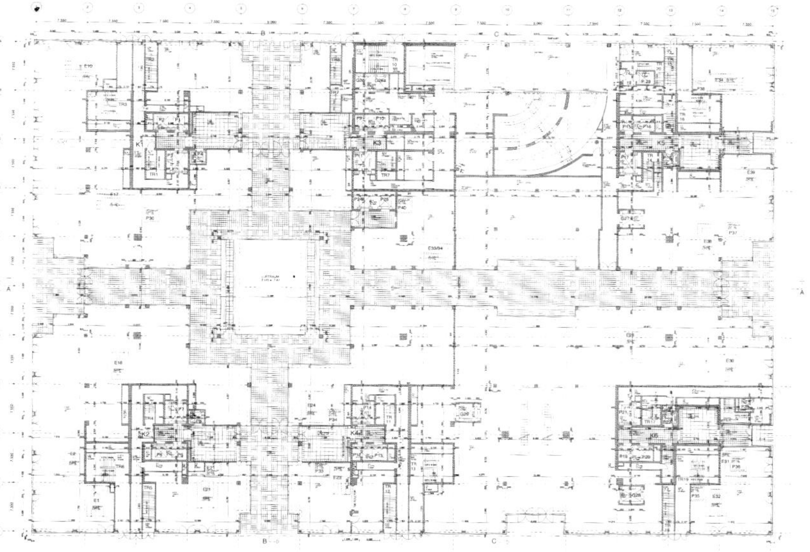

Block 205: aerial view; site plan; model view; plans.

roof is closed and serves as an exterior terrace for the gallery in the second upper story.

The facade is constructed around two opposing 1.5-meter grids. The inner framework of the building is reflected in the exterior design; nonetheless, the impression of a blocklike structure is preserved. Materials typical of Berlin differentiate between the six individual structures faced in dark limestone, and the core structure, of white limestone. The lower areas up to the first upper story are used for shops. Above are offices, and in the eighth, uppermost story are thirty-six apartments grouped around an open patio with access provided by a hallway around the atrium. Two ramps provide access to the two underground parking levels, which are also connected to the adjacent underground garages of Blocks 206 and 207. The shopping areas in the second basement level are entered either via the passage connecting all the blocks or via escalators from the ground level. A ring of storage and technical spaces surrounds the shop areas.

Elevation; crossection of model; exterior views; interior courtyard.

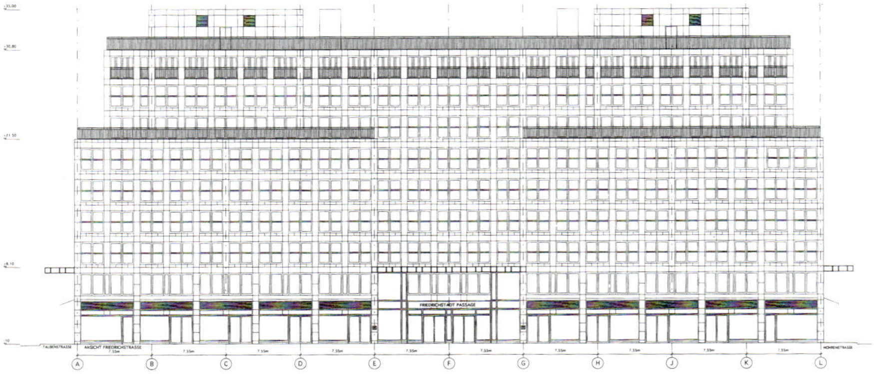

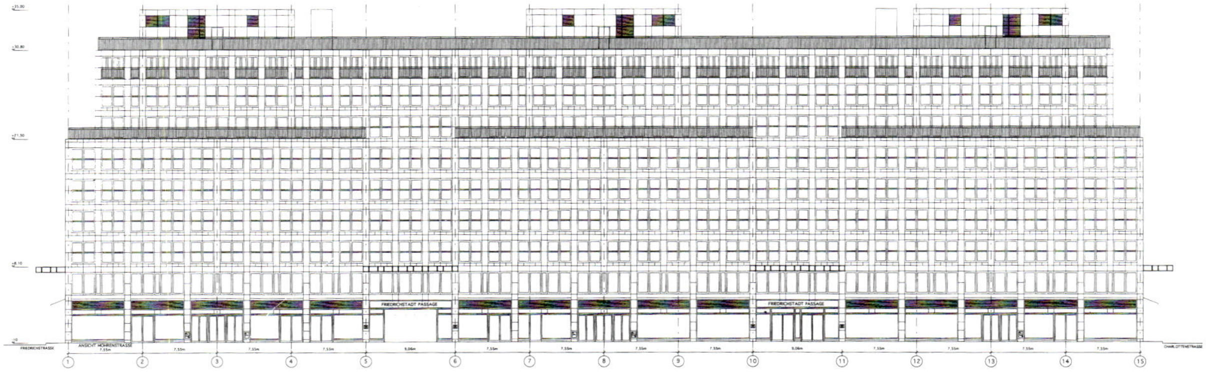

Views of central atrium.

Office and Commercial Building, Verband Kommunaler Unternehmen (VKU), Cologne, 1991–1994

Project team: Kai-Uwe Lompa, Ingo Schweers, Philippe Vernin, Joachim Sieber, Sharon Chung-Klatte, Lukas Baumewerd

Site plan; sketch; plans.

The project called for the expansion of the Verband Kommunaler Unternehmen (Association of Local Enterprises) building, erected in the 1970s. Ungers adopted the cubic form and eaves height of the existing building and created a mirror image of it. A glass hall positioned between the two halves serves as an axis and a link, and also marks the new entrance. The articulation of the exterior facade reflects the hierarchy of internal organization. The ground level accommodates service functions and thus has a symbolic character (in the entrance hall) as well as a public one (in the assembly room and cafeteria). Accordingly, the ground level is taller, as indicated by the proportions of the window muntins, while the normal office levels are somewhat shorter. The facade is marked only by this horizontal and vertical rhythm; it is a pure, brick facade with no socle, roof, eaves, or cornice. In this way, the opposition of old and new acquires a dynamic of its own in an almost classical articulation, entirely lacking in ornamentation: on the one hand the quietude of the "reposing cube," and on the other the building from the 1970s, now appearing almost as an afterthought. Only the symmetry and the glass hall indicate that the two belong together.—*Martin Kieren*

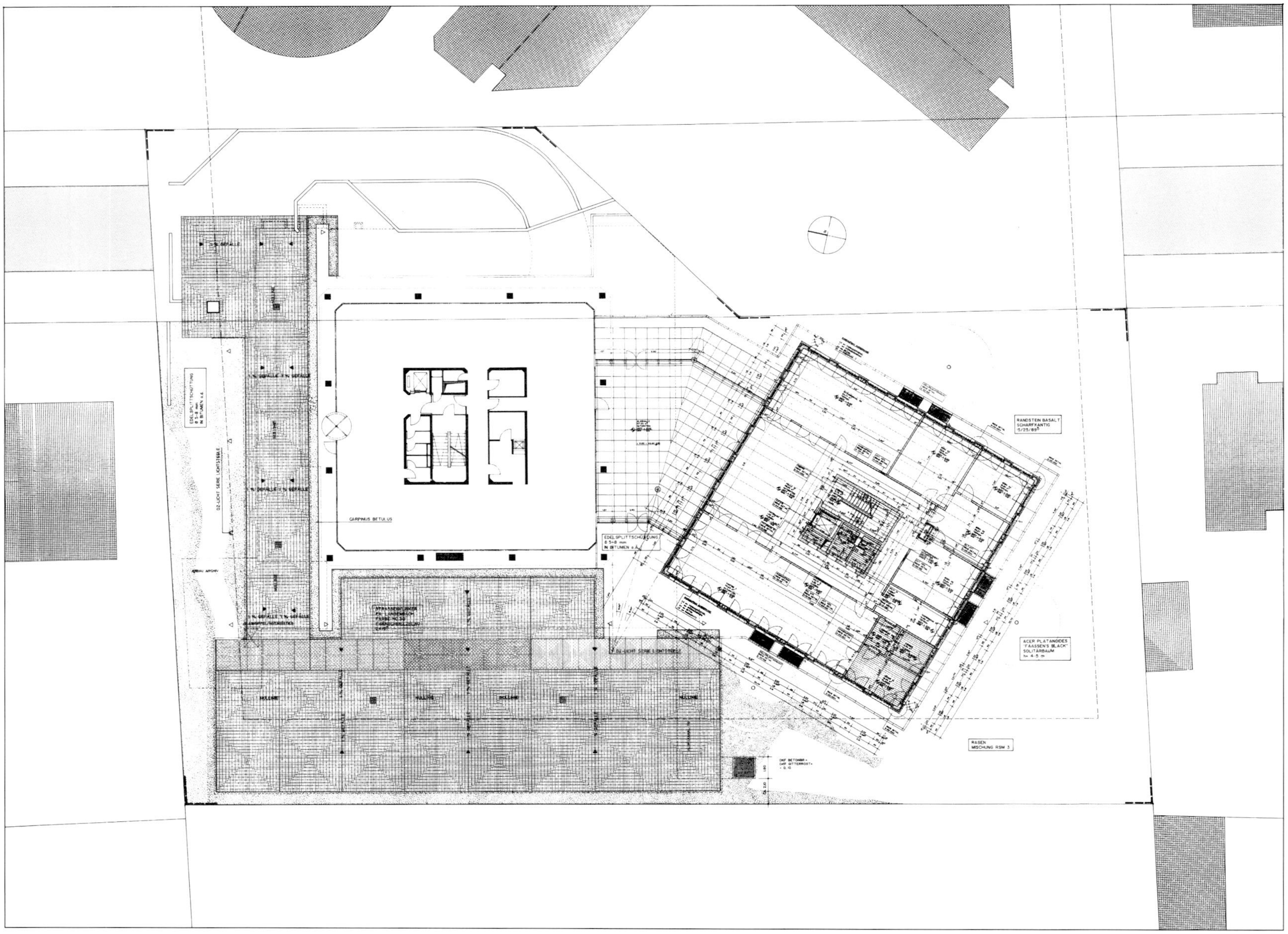

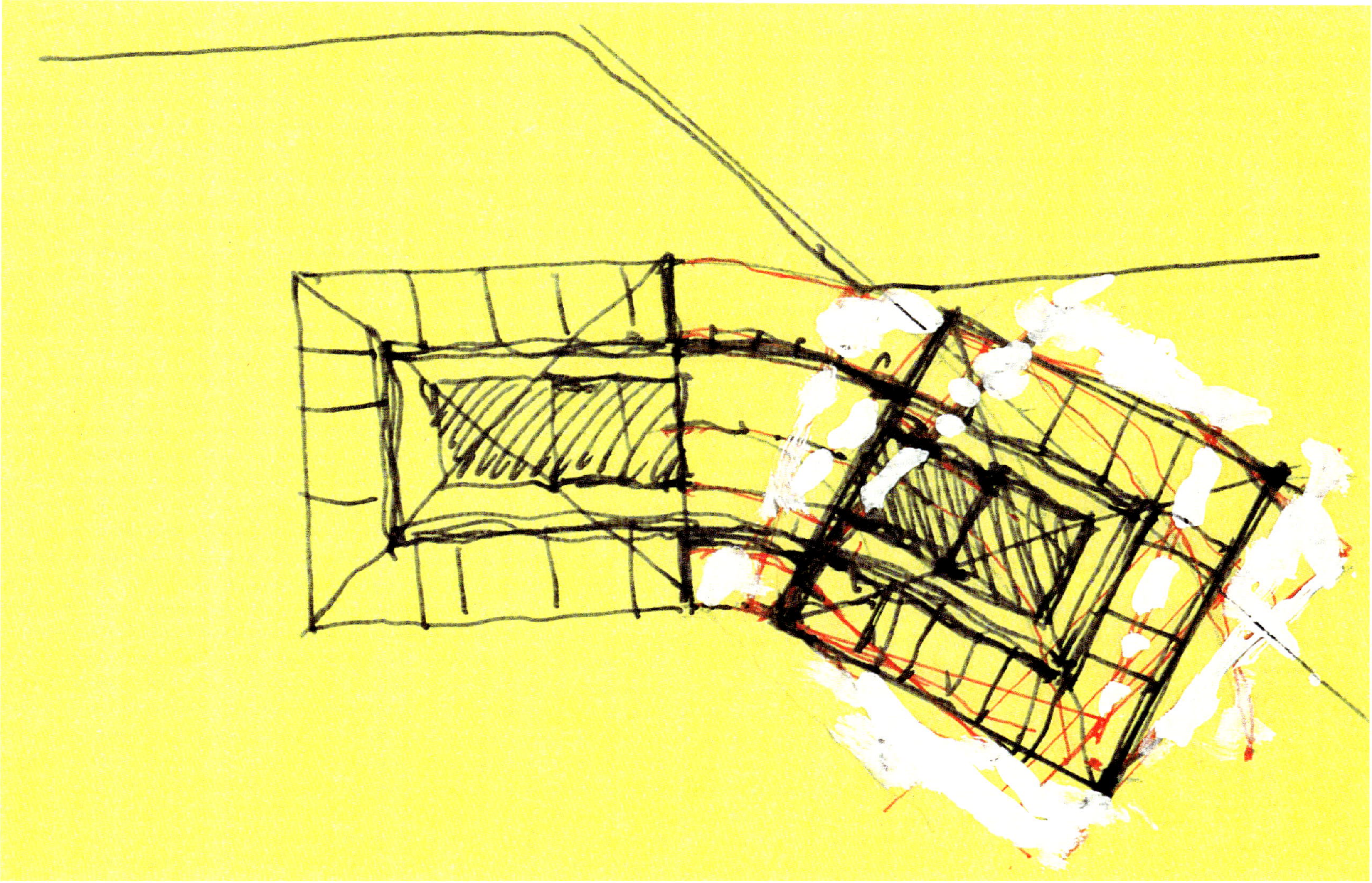

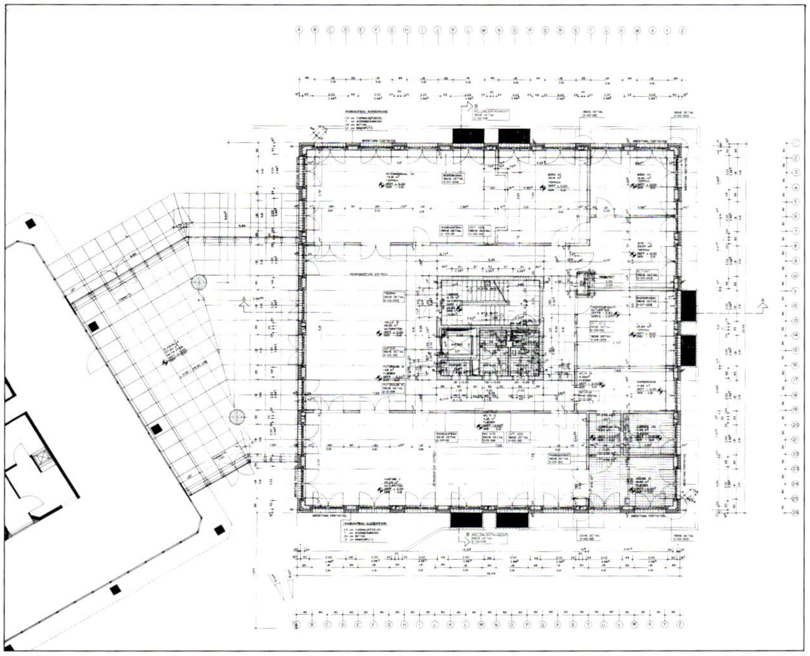

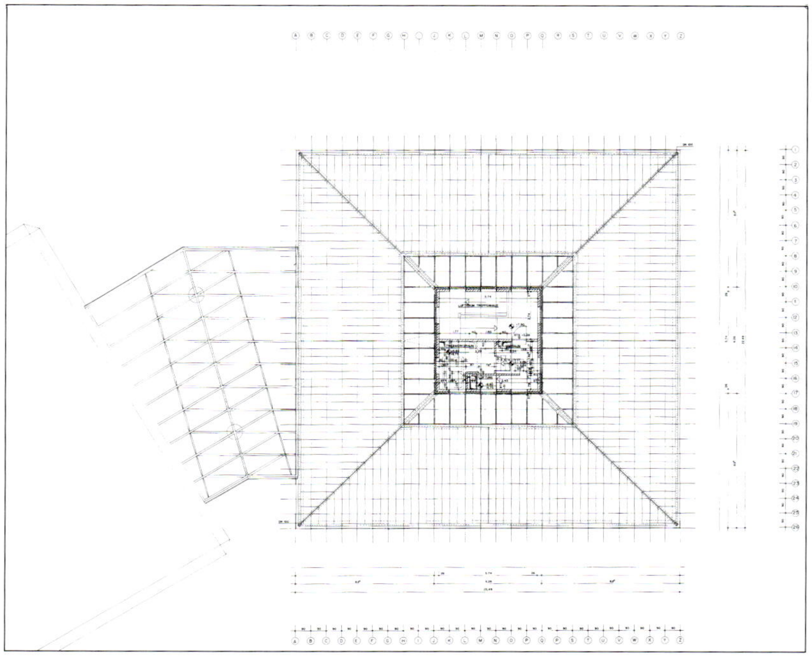

Section; exterior views; elevation.

Opposite:
Entrance hall.

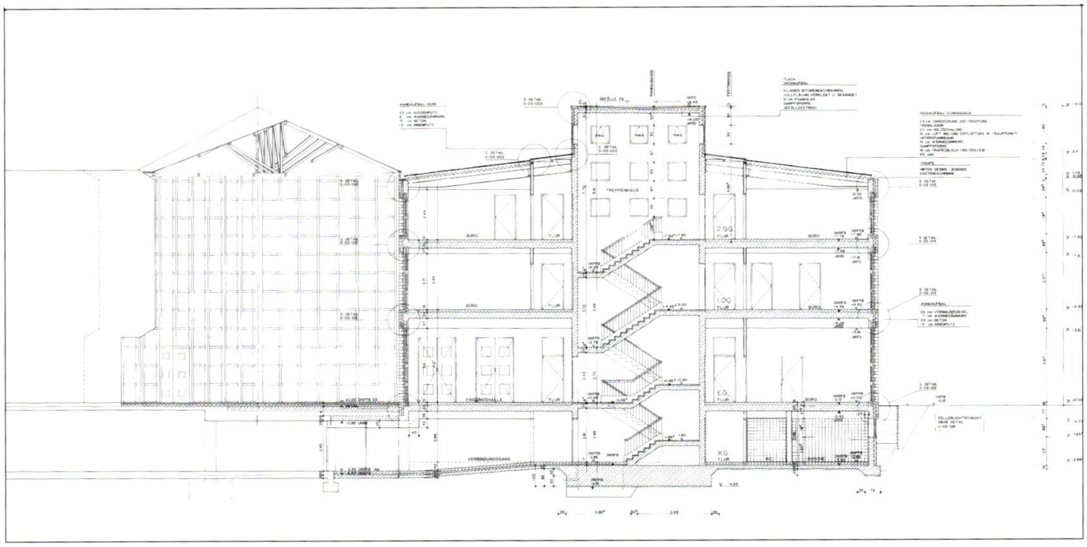

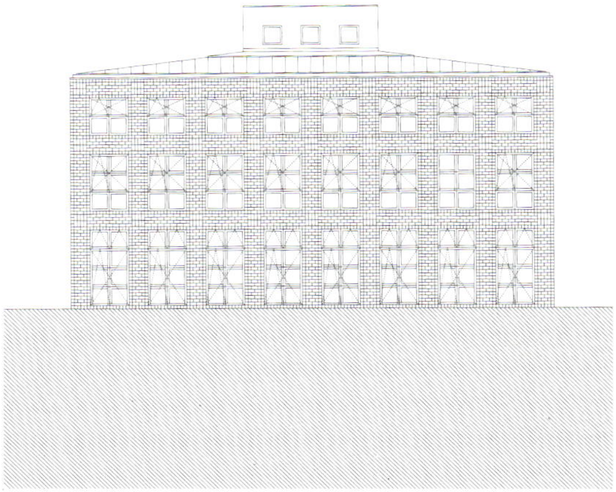

Entrance hall.

Johannishaus, Cologne, 1991–1994

Project team: Albert Brauns, Don Dimster, Knud Ehm, Claudia Henning, Jarno Nillesen, Axel Steudel, Philippe Vernin, Stefan Vieths

This administrative building for the city of Cologne is intended for the Office of Social Services, Youth Services, and Housing. The site lies north of the main railway station in the vicinity of the Rhine river. With respect to both the function and age of the surrounding buildings, the area is quite heterogeneous and is characterized by block-edge construction of three to four stories. In order to create space for the new building, the old "Johannishaus" from the 1950s—already in use as a social services office—had to be torn down as plans for renovation proved uneconomical.

The design calls for a building with a courtyard inserted into an existing block structure. The arena-shaped courtyard is defined by symmetrical building elements and spans the area between Johannisstrasse to the east and Am Alten Ufer to the west. The new building has a total of nine stories, including the underground garage. Due to the site's topography—it slopes downward toward the east from Johannisstrasse to Am Alten Ufer as well as from south to north—the new building has seven aboveground stories on Johannisstrasse and eight on Am Alten Ufer; here, the building recedes stepwise from the fourth to the sixth upper stories.

The exterior is articulated in reddish brick perforated by square window openings in a grid configuration; the interior "arena" facade, on the other hand, has a slightly reflective surface of steel and glass. Unlike the open area to the south of the building, which is conceived as a garden, the interior courtyard has the character of an urban plaza. The roof areas are planted as well.

The two-story entrance hall is positioned at one of the semicircular ends of the interior courtyard, offering a direct view into the courtyard. The upper stories are occupied almost exclusively by offices. An employee cafeteria is provided in the basement level, along with various business-related facilities. The lower basement level accommodates an underground garage and the archives.

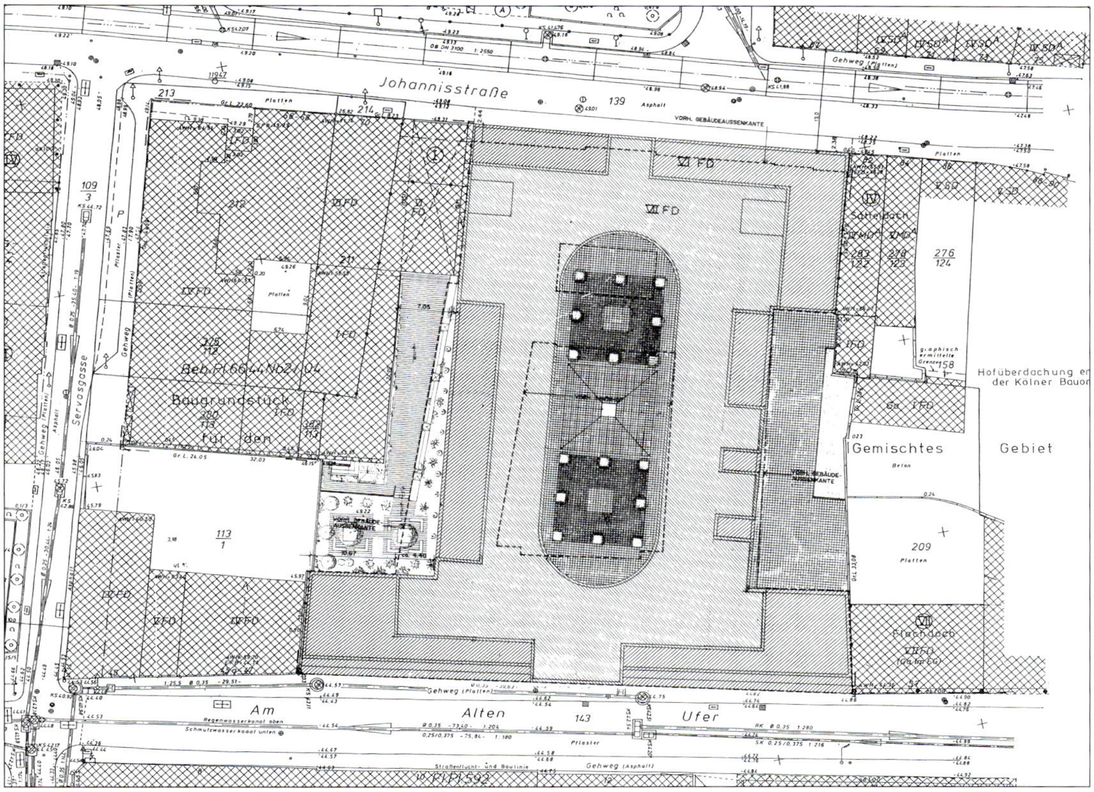

Perspective; site plan.

Elevation; exterior; section.

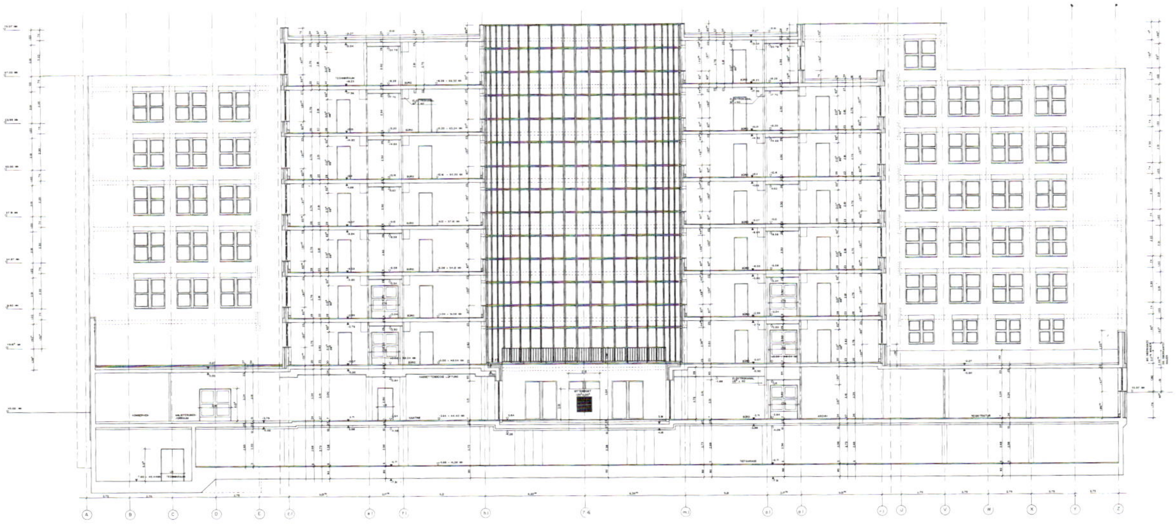

Views of interior courtyard with stele by Simon Ungers.

Interior courtyard; views of entrance hall with wall design by Gerhard Merz.

Competition Design for Office Building, Basler Versicherung, Cologne, 1993

With: Stefan Vieths

Project team: Christine Combe, Axel Steudel, Michael Garçon, Marvin Keim, Kai-Uwe Lompa

The site for the insurance company building is part of an urban block with an open structure consisting of individual buildings—some of them historic—and a dense growth of trees considered worthy of preservation.

The new building was conceived as a simple freestanding volume , complementing the heterogeneous structure of the block in a reserved and convincing way. The office building is typologically simple, reduced to its essential architectural elements. Despite this conscious simplicity, however, the building is given an independent character by the strict system of order, proportion, and fine articulation of the facade. The choice of materials (brick on interior and exterior facades) and additional detailing support this intention and give the building a striking sculptural quality.

The windows on all sides of the building are ceiling-high and can be opened completely, intensifying the sense of the pavilionlike structure and the parklike location of the site.

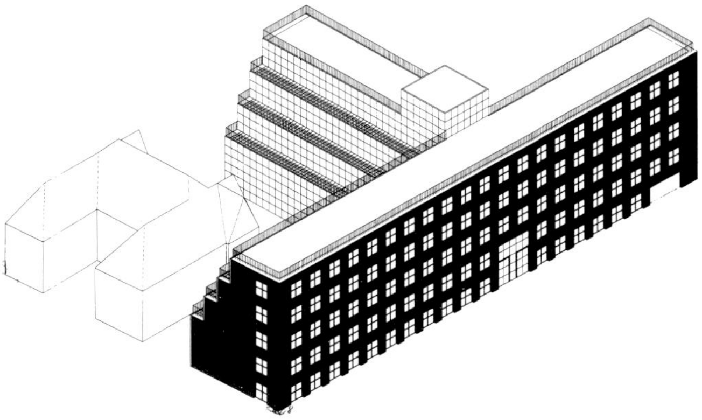

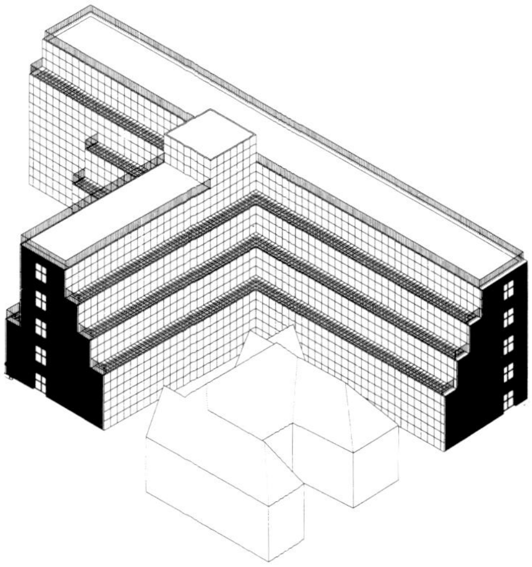

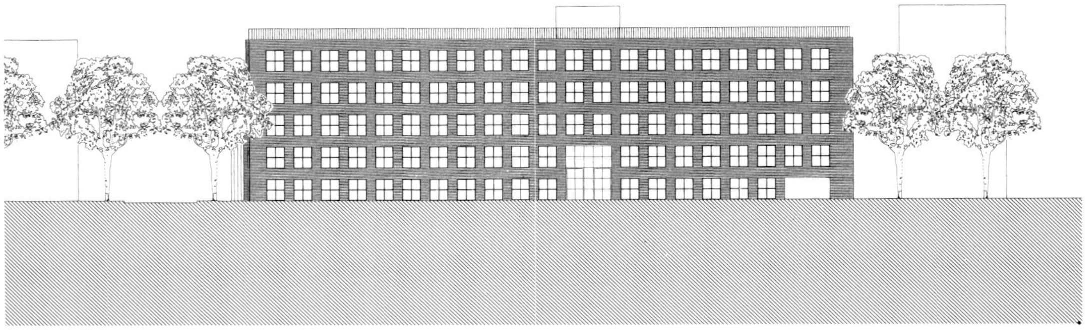

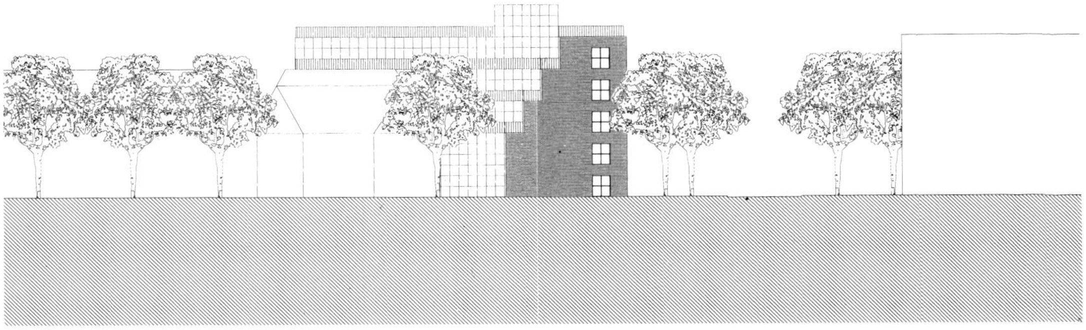

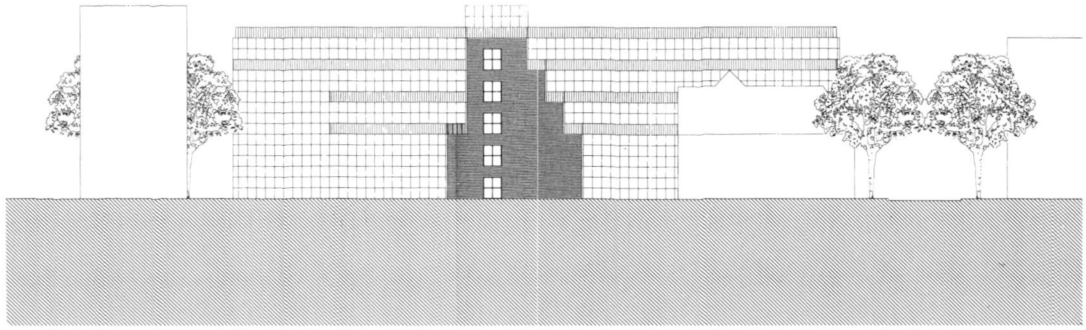

Axonometrics; elevations.

Opposite:
Perspective; exterior.

Elevation; ground-level plan; exteriors.

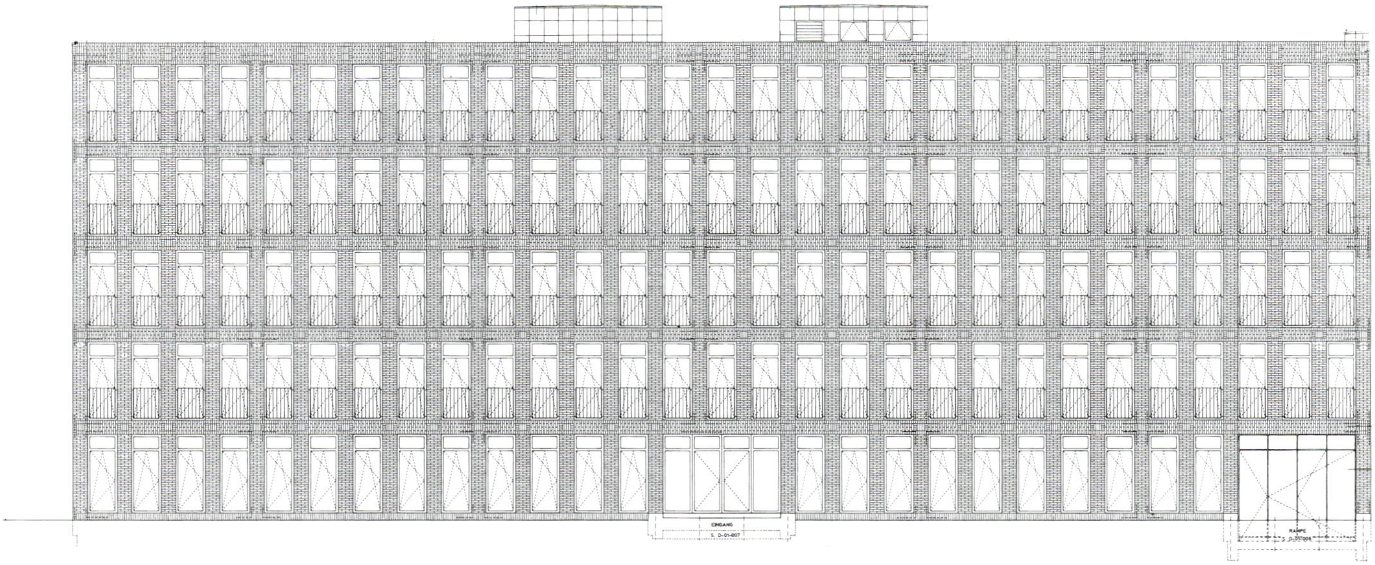

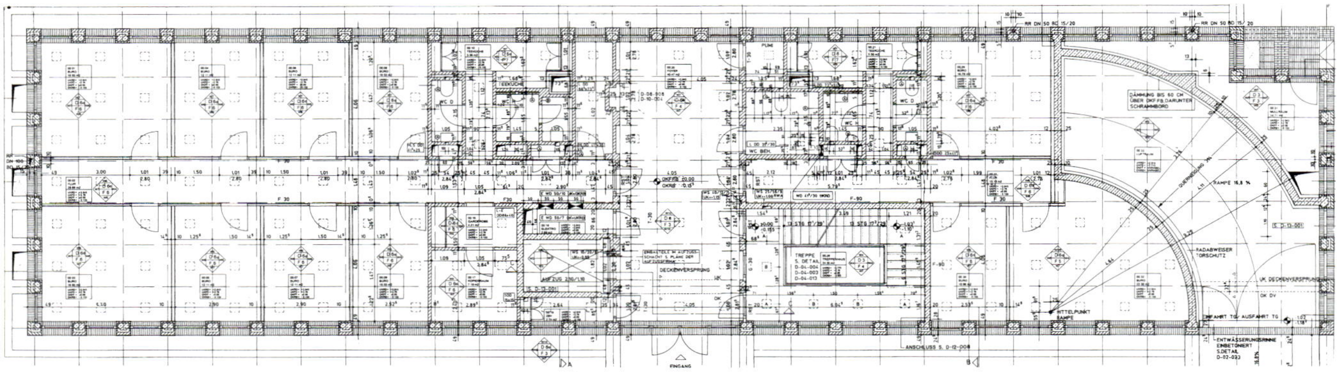

Overleaf:
Detail of entrance.

Redesign of Residential and Gallery Building, Schaafenstrasse, Cologne, 1993–1994

Execution and construction supervision: Rolf Bandus

The building was erected in the second half of the nineteenth century. It is most striking for the extreme, almost unprecedented narrowness of the site and the resulting tall, thin form of the building, which is wedged between two other structures.

No less remarkable is the picturesque ornamentation of the facade, which intensifies the effect of a stage set. The modest proportions of the site are transformed into an architecture of display, employing all elements that could possibly fit into the tall, narrow space: slightly rusticated pillars, pilasters, consoles, capitals, window ledge cornices, window caps, a triangular gable, cornices, dentils—an immodest historicism intended to draw attention to a house that would otherwise almost disappear among its neighbors.

Since the building stands under historic preservation, a careful approach was required from the beginning. First, the renovations of previous years had to be reversed. In its present form, the front facade is a reconstruction of the original: slightly rusticated pillars, display windows, and an entrance door, all with a narrow profile. The roof truss likewise represents a reconstruction—or rather an interpretation,

Street and courtyard elevations; section.

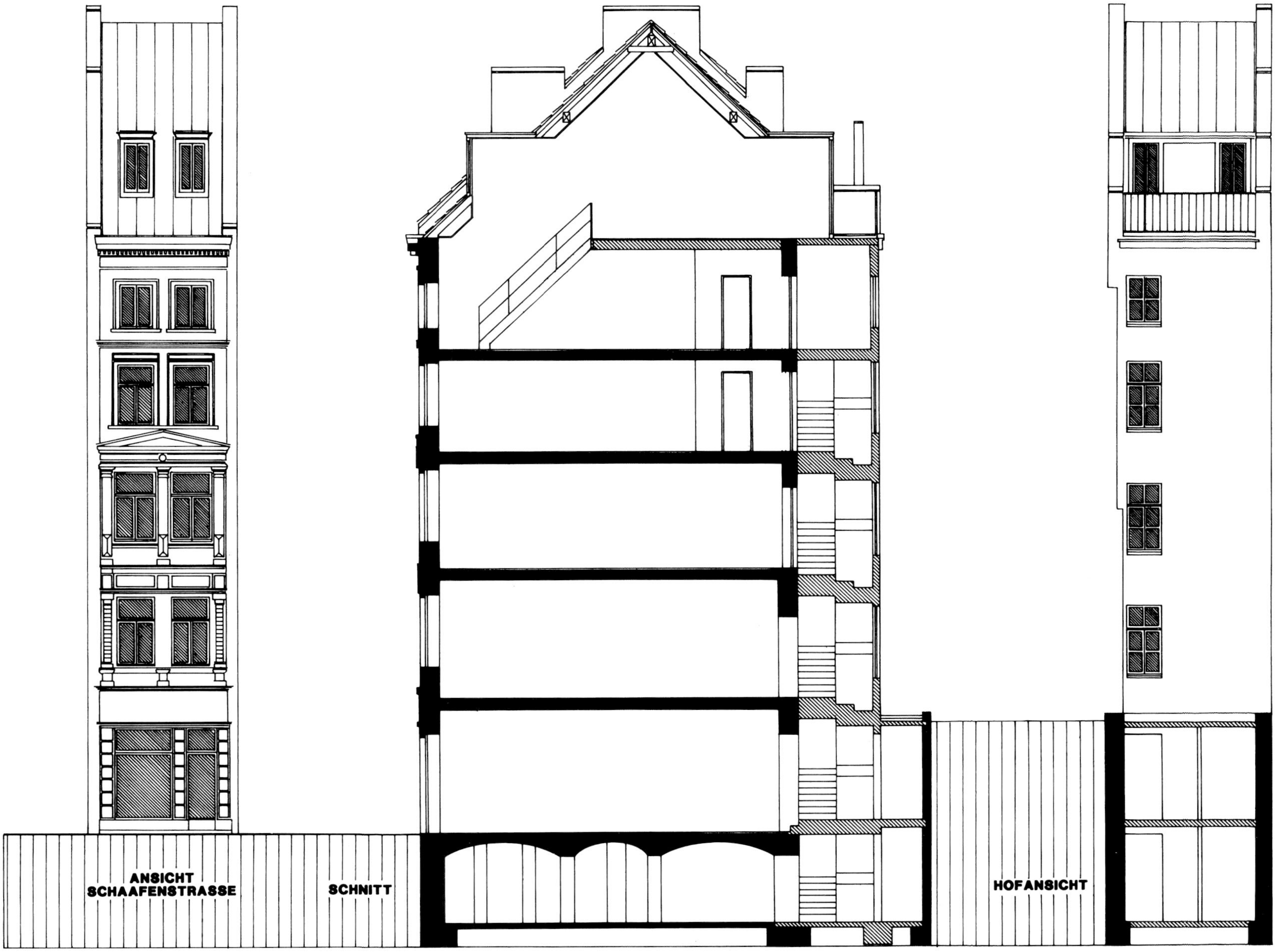

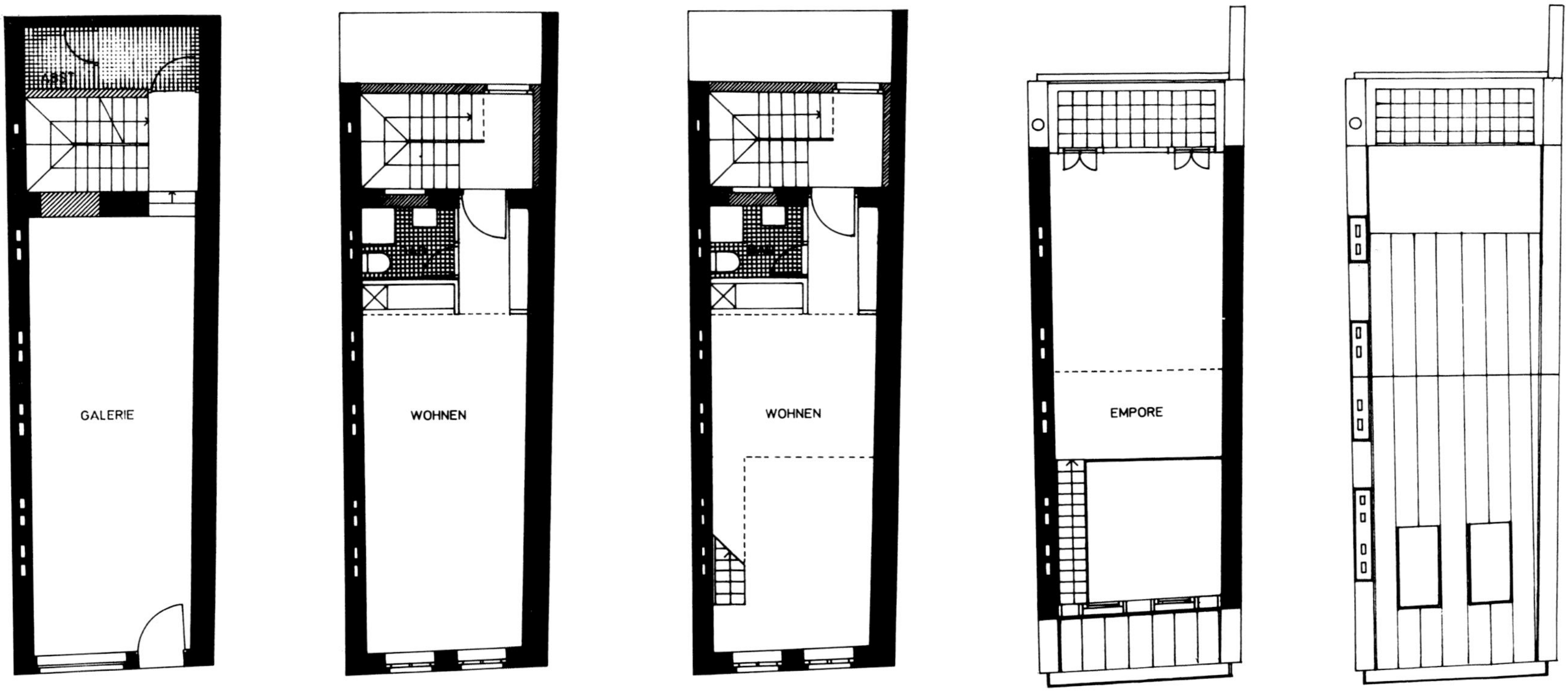

Plans.

Opposite and overleaf: Facade; interiors.

since no documentation for the original version could be found.

The basic layout is simple, and more or less corresponds to a plan Ungers once experimented with in a similar house, the gallery and residence of Max Hetzler in Cologne (1986): simple, layered spatial units whose clear, reserved character provides a suitable context for the works of art exhibited in them. Originally, circulation through the building was accommodated by a staircase positioned in the center of the building, which was later torn down in favor of a stairwell added to the rear. The lower gallery space is entered from the street. On each floor, the rear staircase of masonry and concrete with steps covered in black terrazzo panels leads from a landing to a passage and into the next two gallery levels and the three residential stories above. The first of these is a one-room residence.

The new construction of a steep roof made it possible to incorporate a studio apartment and a maisonette with a balcony in the two upper stories. Here the roof of the stairwell serves as a small terrace.

The rooms received a new wooden floor with the old beams remaining below; the oak windows varnished with linseed oil are likewise reconstructions with narrow profiles, double rabbets, weather grooves, and thermopane glass. The walls are finely plastered and painted white. With its combination of old and new and its mix of commercial and residential use, this is a successful, contemporary building.

The lower three stories of the facade show an extreme juxtaposition of decorative architectural elements in a wild but likeable, exaggerated but touching historicism. A triangular gable forms a sort of tympanum terminating this part of the facade in an appliquéd "idea of the house," an autonomous order. Behind this "house" on the facade lie the three stacked "boxes" of the contemporary gallery.

SCHADEN
SCHNELL
HILFE
KFZ UNFALL
Schaafenstr.

Redesign of Water Tower, Utscheid, 1993

Exterior.

Opposite:
Sketch; plans; elevation; section.

Overleaf:
Interiors; night view.

Project team: Johannes Götz

The tower, built in 1957, formerly supplied the town of Utscheid with water. Originally, there were only two upper floors with the water tank in the topmost space, the machine area below, and the entrance hall at the bottom. A new addition above the ground story now accommodates a kitchen with a gallery running parallel to the stairs providing a view into the kitchen from above. On the next level, a living unit was inserted with a shower, bath, and built-in cabinets, and behind it the sleeping area. The upper story is a tall space whose four windows face the four points of the compass. Frugally furnished with seating, it is a meditative space with a breathtaking view of the Eifel landscape.

The program is thus extremely simple; yet the existing situation would have permitted nothing more without extensive and visible alterations. The spaces and furnishings conform and rigorously subordinate themselves to the tower and its structure. Nothing on the exterior indicates that the building has become a residence and retreat. The sandstone walls, seventy to eighty centimeters thick, were preserved and in places repaired and newly pointed. The structurally necessary interior pier buttresses were integrated into the spatial design; they are autonomous, self-evident elements, modest and unobtrusive. The overall impression is not that of a house inside an old shell, but of an old water tower with individual elements added, derived from the existing structure.

Upon entering the tower, one is struck by the sequence of spaces, by the change from narrow to wide as well as from low to high. As one emerges from the low, narrow stair tower, an ever wider, higher space opens up with a distant view into the countryside. The plan consists only of stacked spaces, from which a tremendous visual effect—already inherent in the tower—was elicited. The art

lay in the exploitation of the existing aesthetic, functional, and structural energies, in filtering, exposing, and finally activating and refining them. In this process, the materials and forms were left as pure as possible: sandstone, the elementary form of the circle, the ascent, the verticality of the spatial arrangements, and the new elements, which leave the impression only of being inserted and thus merely complementing the existing structure.

The windows—one in the stairwell and one in the kitchen area—hold more or less their original positions. These windows serve not so much the idea of dwelling, drawing attention to the breathtaking view, but rather their original function of illuminating the interior. In the uppermost room, however, the relationship is reversed: here the four windows face the cardinal points of the compass, thus inscribing a conceptual figure into the circular ground plan.

3.OG WOHNRAUM

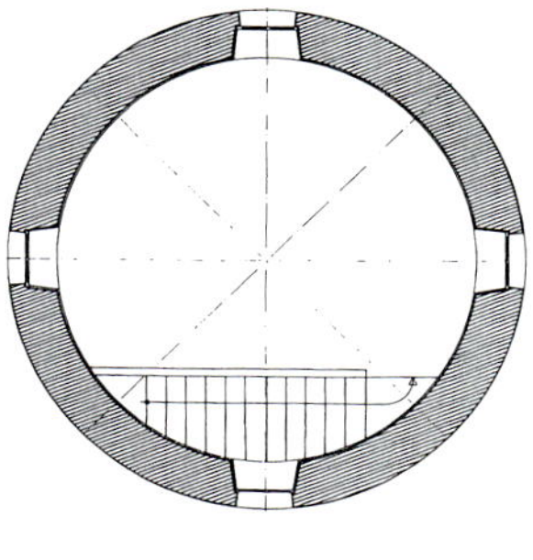

2.OG SCHLAFKAMMER

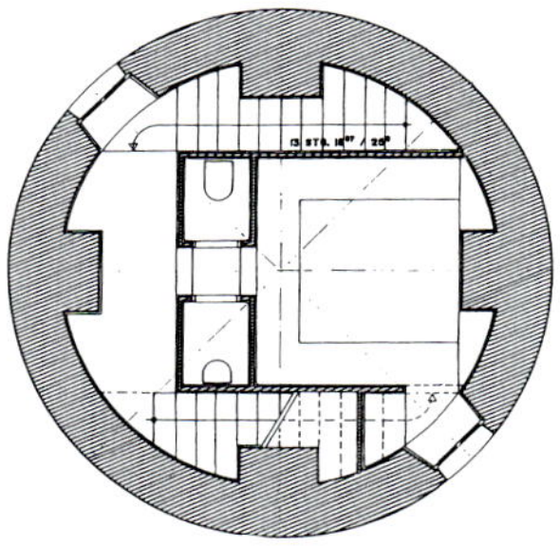

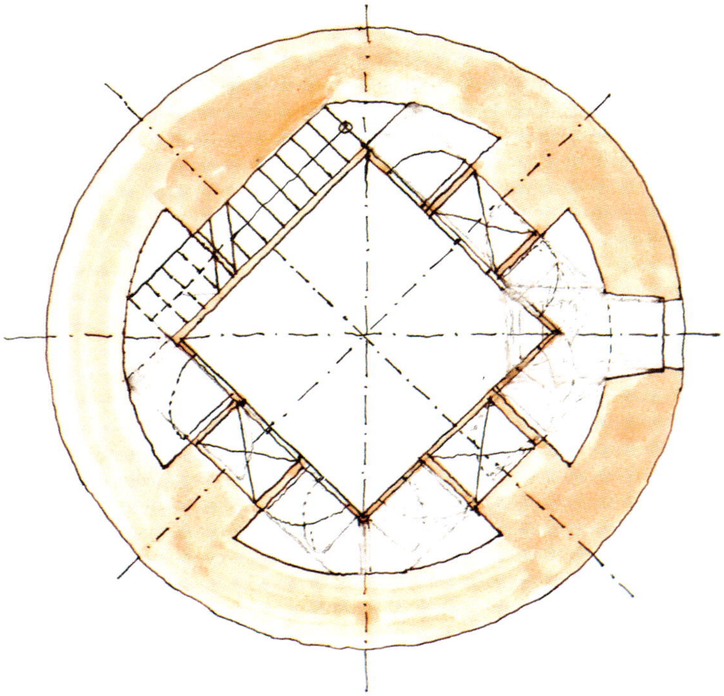

1.OG KÜCHE

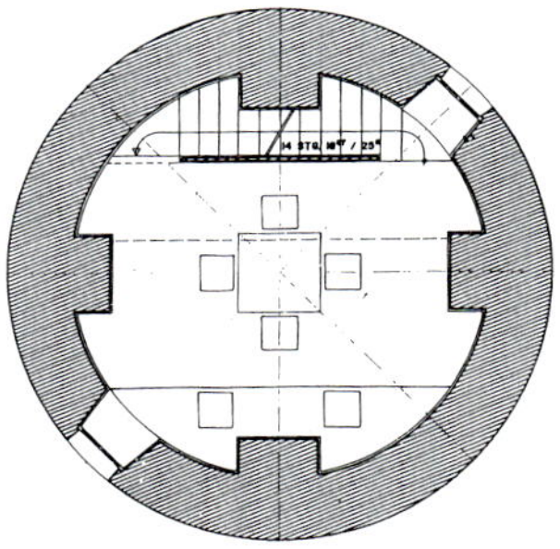

EG. EINGANG

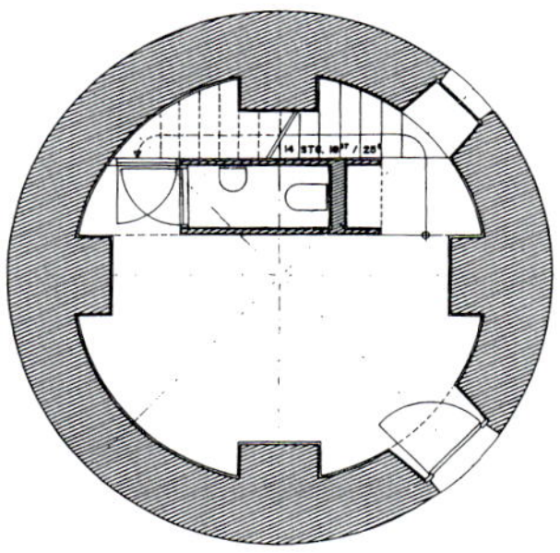

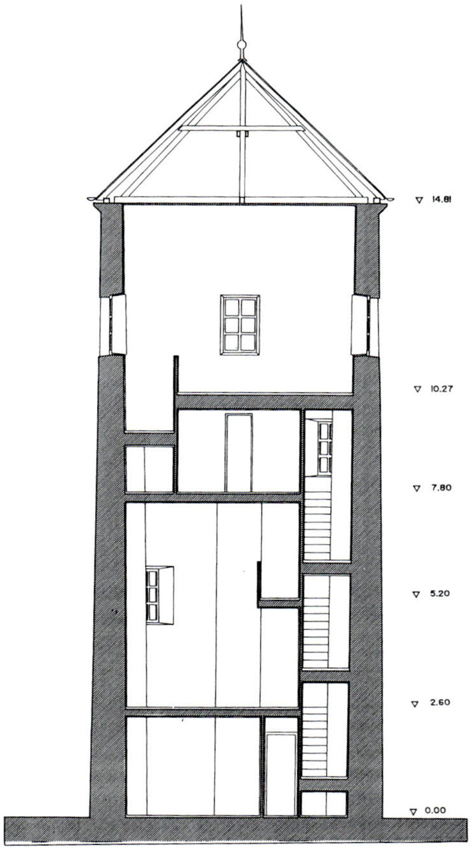

Ungers House III, Kämpchensweg, Cologne, 1994–1996

Sketch; garden facade; section; plans.

Project team: Johannes Götz, Bernd Grimm

The villa Ungers built for himself on Kämpchensweg in Cologne-Müngersdorf—only a few steps away from his first and now famous house on Belvederestrasse—recalls the villa that Ludwig Wittgenstein built for his sister Margaret on Kundmanngasse in Vienna. The association seems ineluctable with the discovery of a curious coincidence: Wittgenstein's house for Margaret was built in 1926, the same year Oswald Matthias Ungers was born. Ungers celebrated his seventieth birthday with the inauguration of his new house on Kämpchensweg. Here in the suburb of Müngersdorf, only a few meters separate the two houses which, like the fixed points of a far-flung parabola, represent the extreme poles of an oeuvre that Oswald Mathias Ungers has created in nearly half a century with almost dogged devotion.

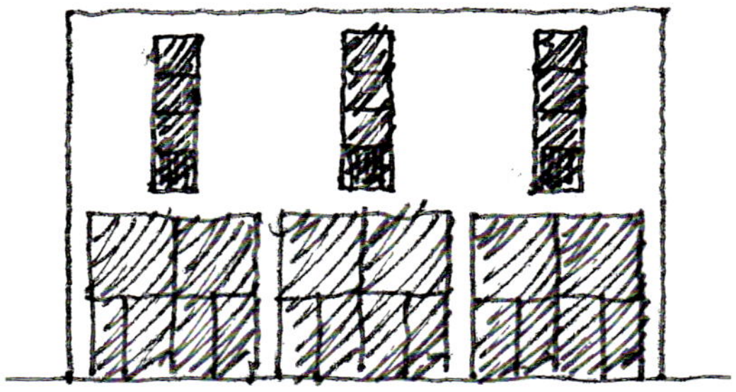

The house on Belvederestrasse, completed in 1959, was described by Reyner Banham as a "manifesto." It was subsequently remodeled on a number of occasions, including the addition of a sophisticated library structure in 1990. This house, articulated like a city or an ancient villa, most clearly represents the cultural climate of the 1950s. Yet as the history of CIAM (Congrès Internationaux d'Architecture Moderne) and the phenomenon of Brutalism show, architectural values subsequently reached a point of crisis. The villa on Kämpchensweg is the distillate of all Ungers's experience from then until now. While the house from the 1950s evinces an articulated structure of spatial units and building parts—an intentional display of structural logic and constructive openness—the newest villa is an untouchable, obsessive parallelepiped; it is as pure as the spaces of Adolf Loos, but without additives—a clinically pure figure. Yet the architecture

of the Ungers villa is entirely different from that of Adolf Loos. "Continuity" is not proven through forms, figures, and functional organization: nothing could be further removed from a Loos ground plan than the ice-cold geometry of the Ungers villa.

Nor does Ungers in any way rest on the potential of architectural tradition. The villa in Kämpchensweg is the outcome of a long process of development. It is the result of an intense struggle—much more intense than its rigid perfection would suggest. It is a purely intellectual dialogue, in which the forms play a purely incidental role. As Ungers himself describes it, it is the ultimate and final confrontation with Schinkel, in an extreme form; it is the desperate search for the *coincidentia oppositorum* of Nicolas of Cusa, the "spiritual unity of things, even in their formal difference."—*Francesco Dal Co*

Structural characteristics: Base module: forty-five centimeters. Cellar and inside walls in concrete, outside walls in brick, partition walls plastered with glossy marble finish; floors in white limestone, in red terracotta in the lateral rooms on the ground floor and in walnut in the lateral rooms on the second floor; windows and doors in white-lacquered oak; heating with panels, internal air-conditioning housed in the air spaces of the windows; swimming pool in the basement ventilated by four shafts located in the corners of the house that exploit temperature differences; the shafts also permit ventilation of the rooms in the house.

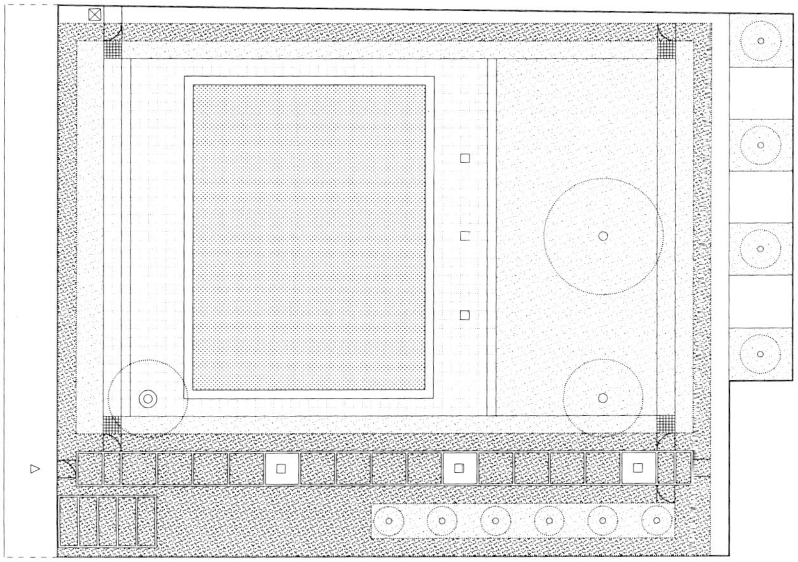

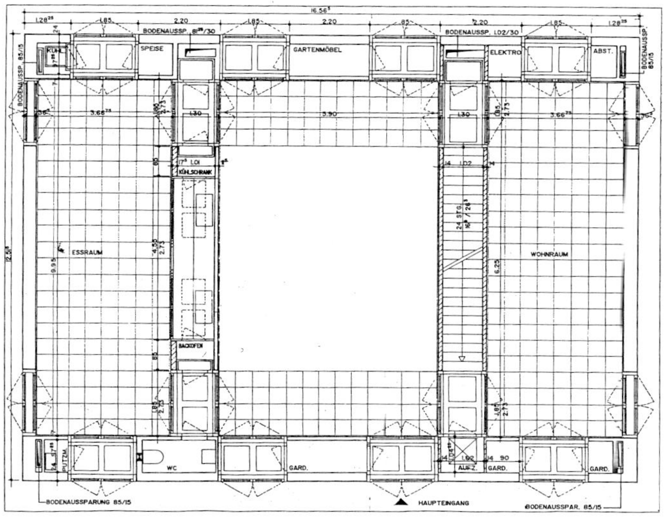

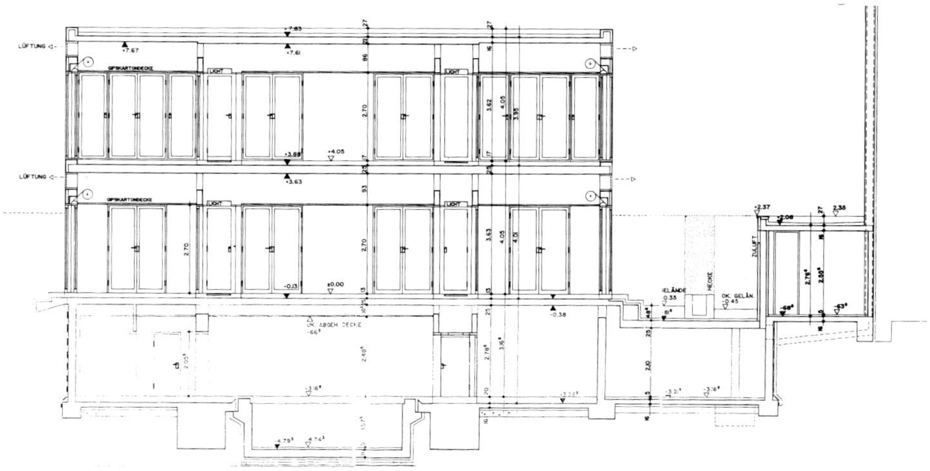

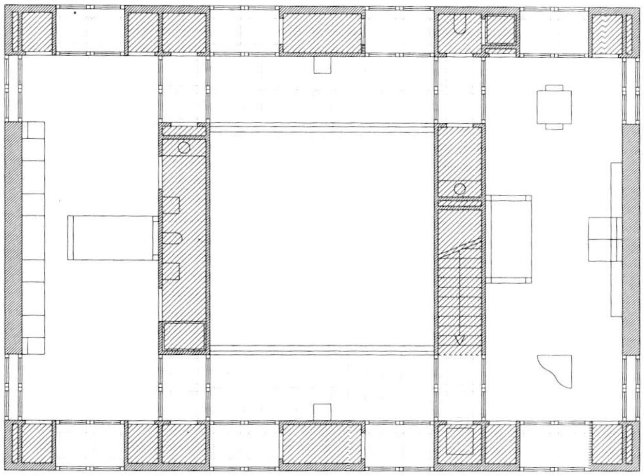

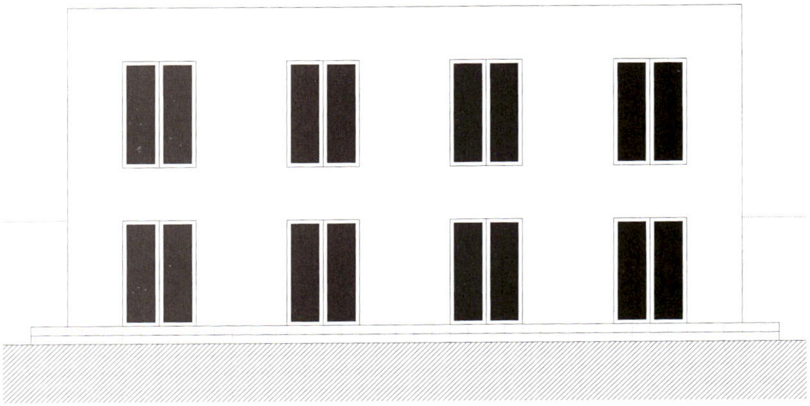

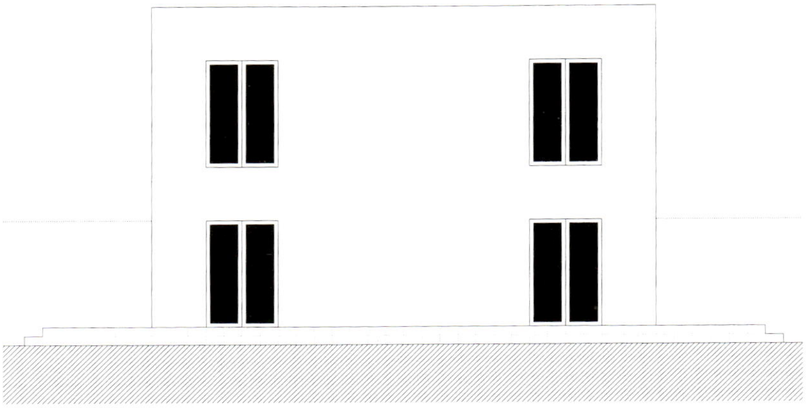

Elevations; exteriors; sections.

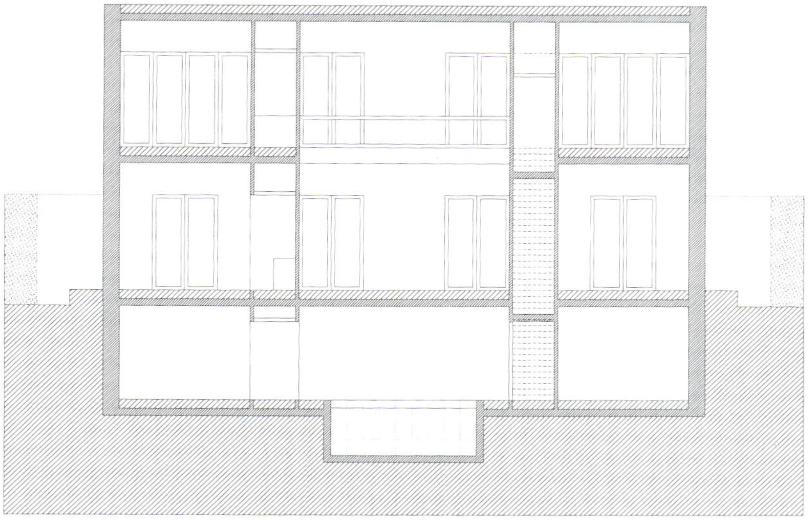

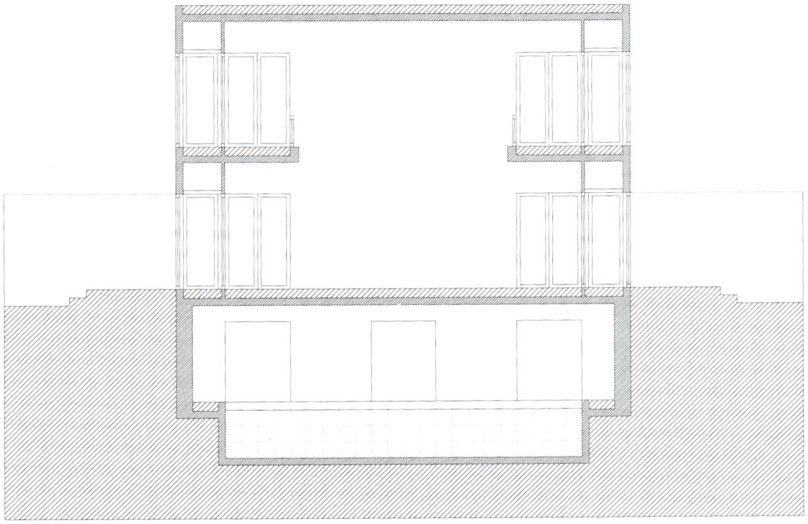

Sketches; interiors.

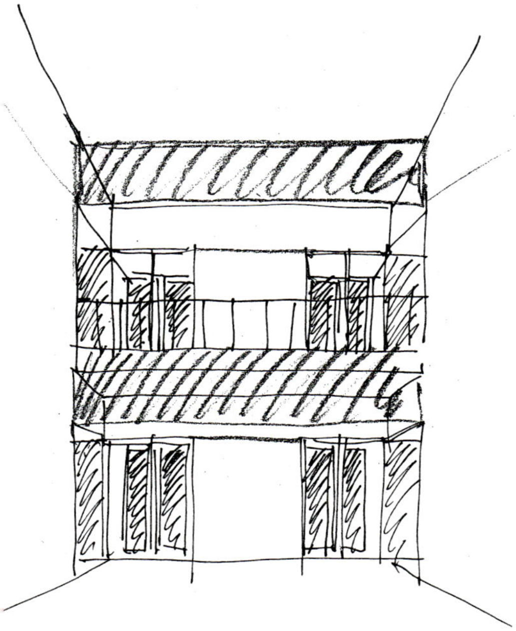

Views of swimming pool.

Furniture for Ungers House III (1994–1996).

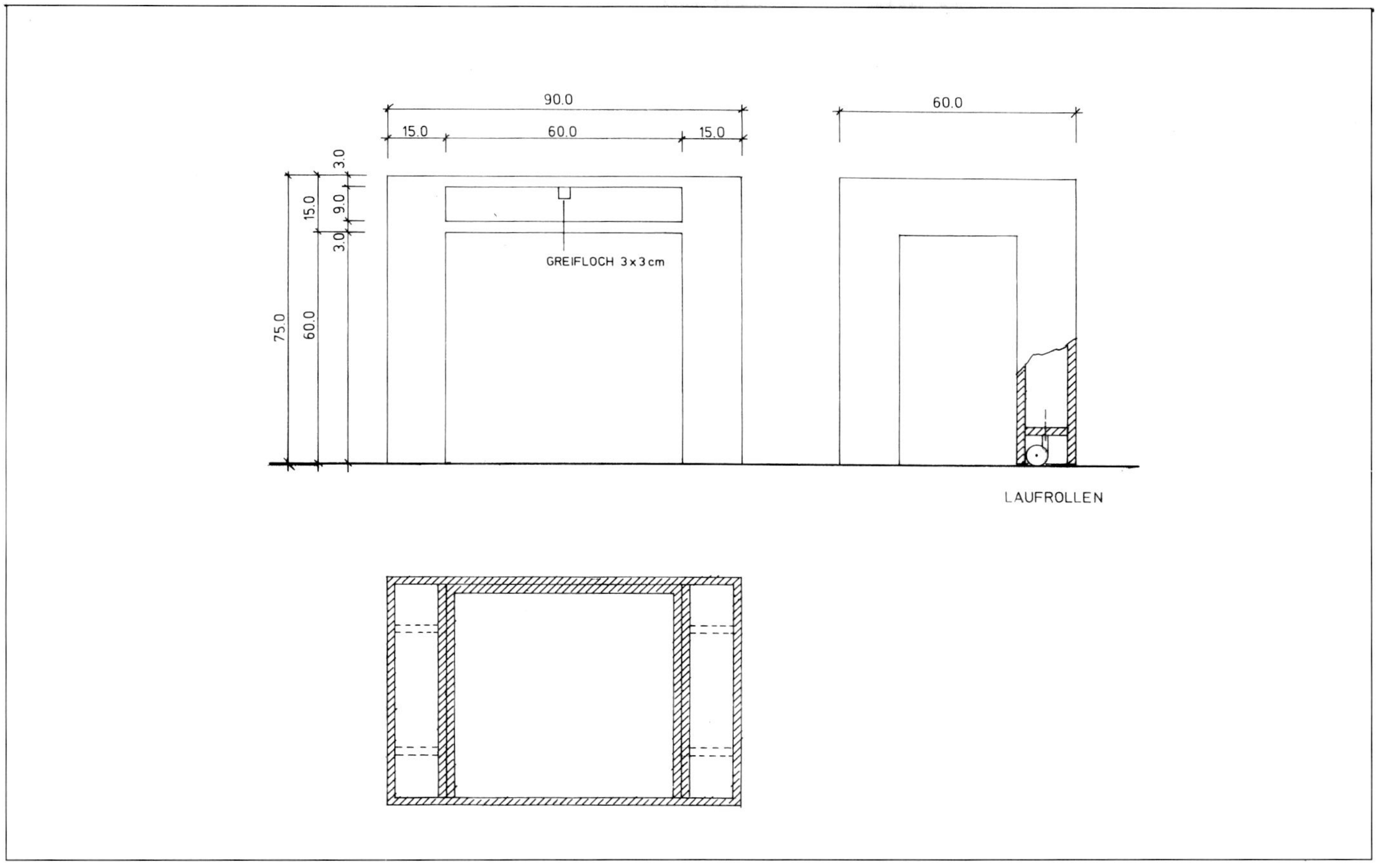
90.0
15.0
60.0
15.0
60.0
3.0
15.0
9.0
3.0
75.0
60.0
GREIFLOCH 3 x 3 cm
LAUFROLLEN

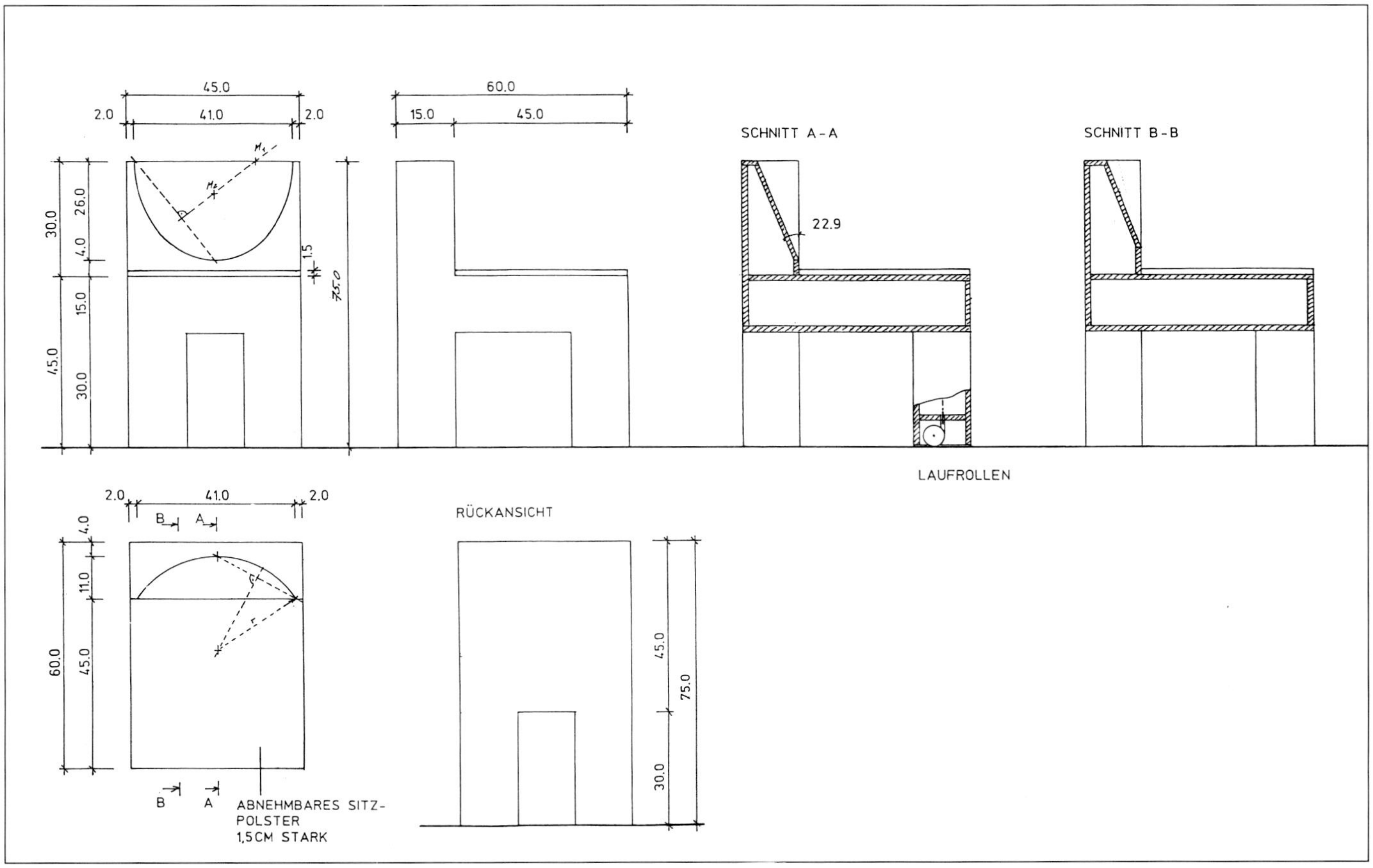
45.0
2.0
41.0
2.0
60.0
15.0
45.0
SCHNITT A-A
SCHNITT B-B
22.9
30.0
26.0
4.0
1.5
15.0
45.0
30.0
LAUFROLLEN
2.0
41.0
2.0
B
A
RÜCKANSICHT
4.0
11.0
60.0
45.0
45.0
75.0
30.0
B
A
ABNEHMBARES SITZ-
POLSTER
1,5CM STARK

Furniture for Ungers House III (1994–1996).

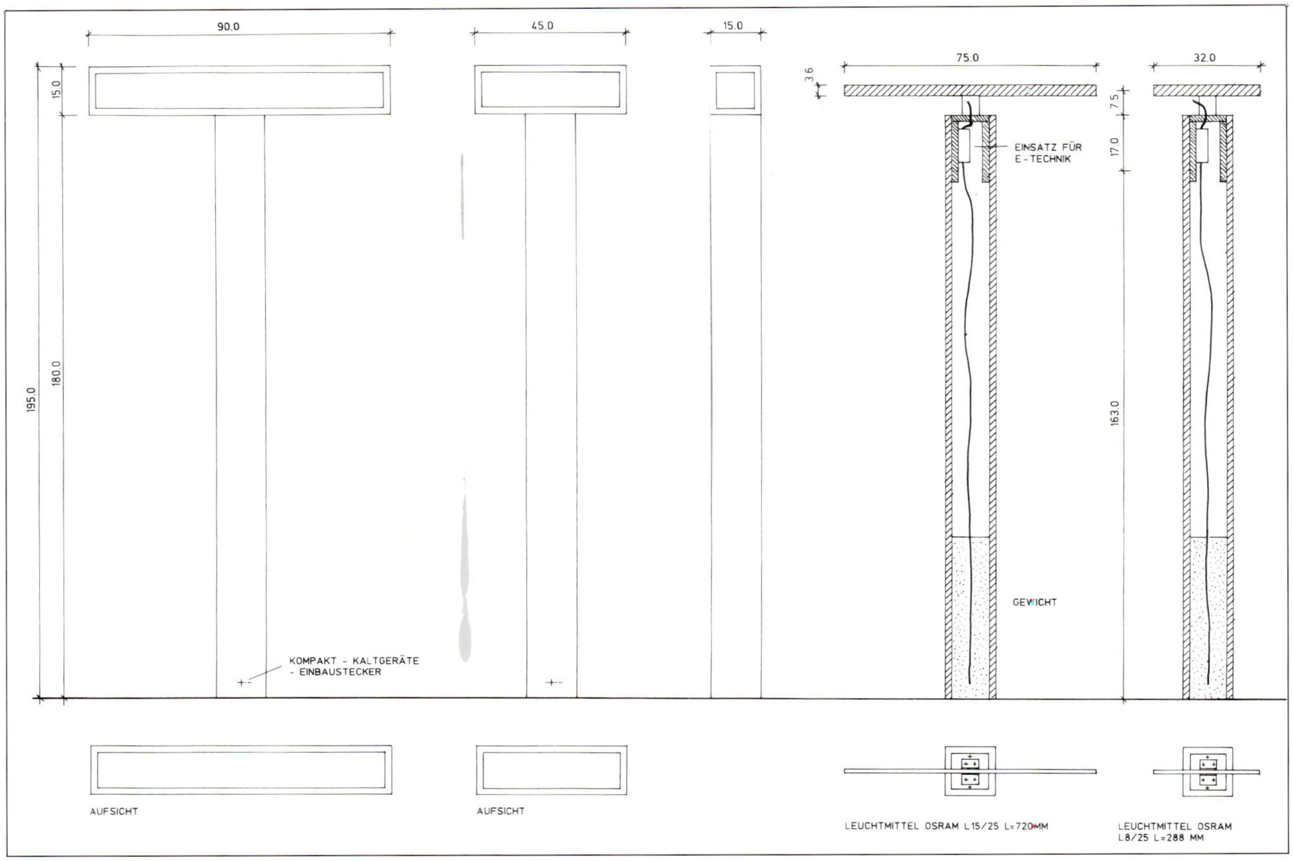

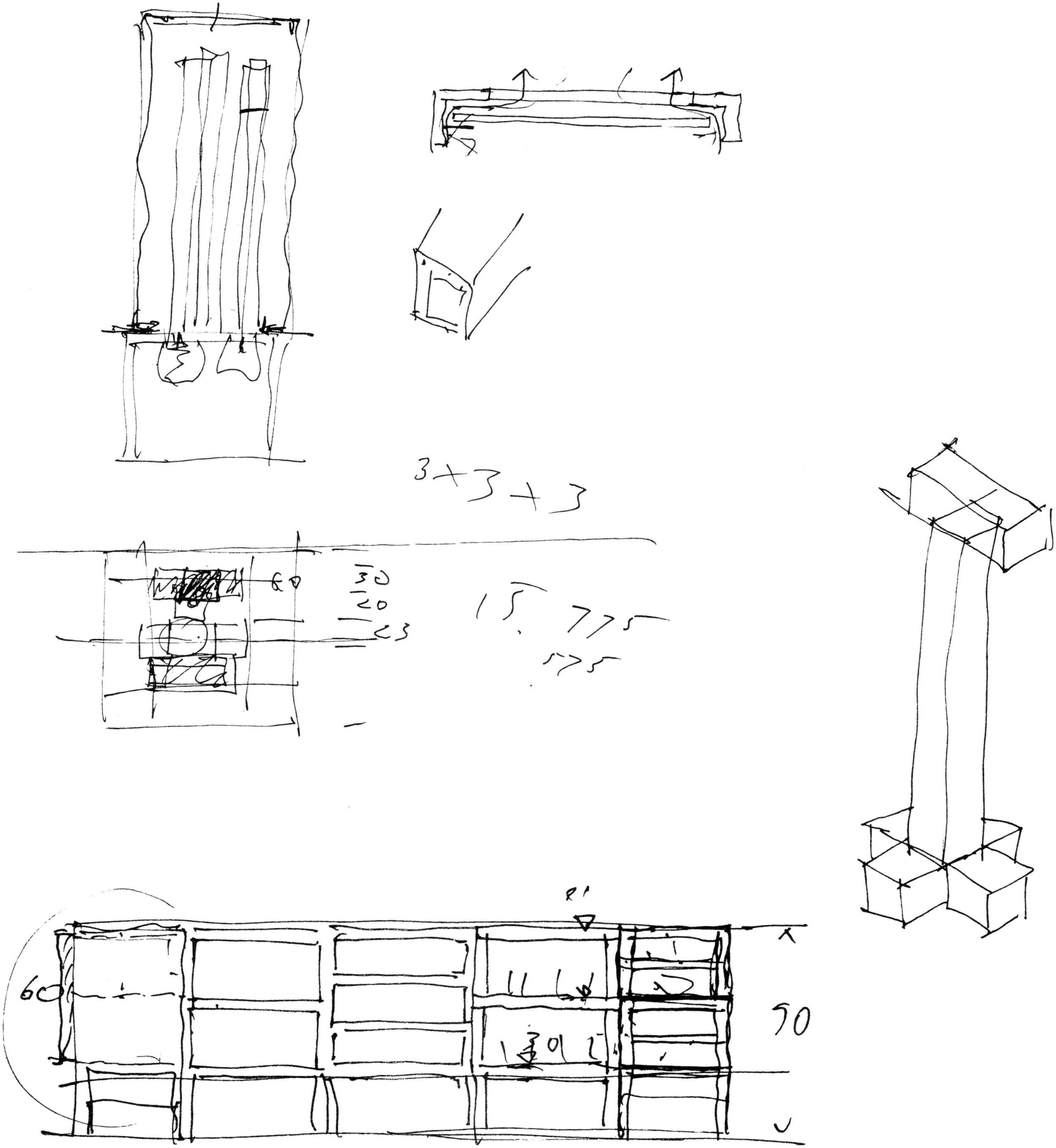
3+3+3
60
30
20
23
15
775
775
60
50

Concerto
Alt. II

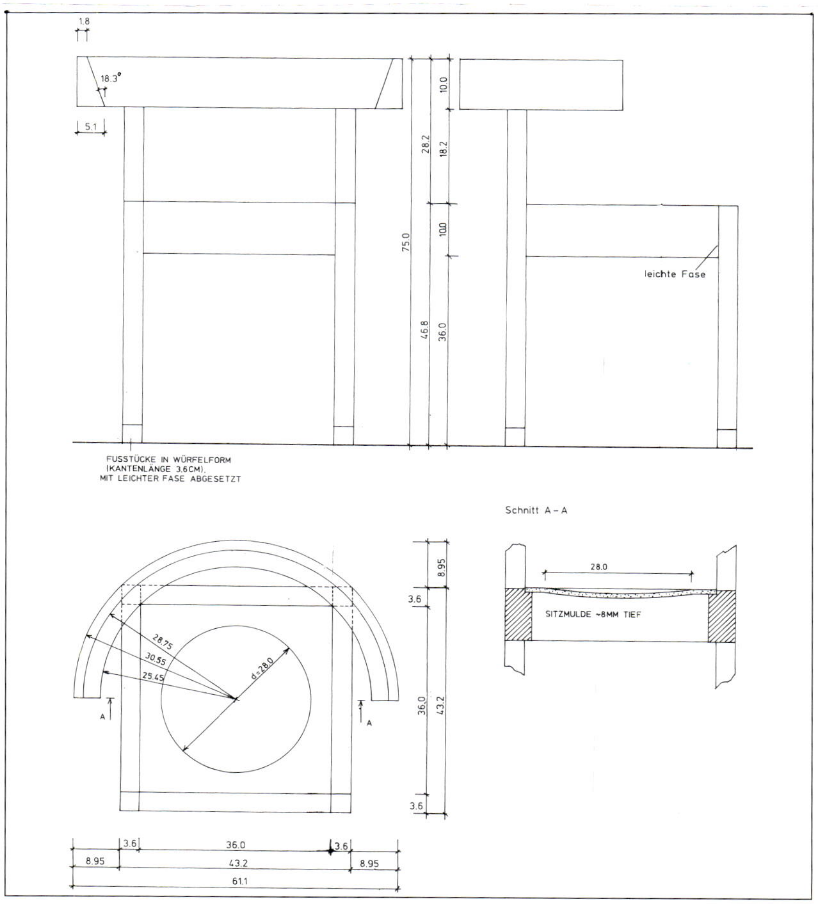
leichte Fase
FUSSTÜCKE IN WÜRFELFORM
(KANTENLÄNGE 3,6CM),
MIT LEICHTER FASE ABGESETZT
Schnitt A–A
SITZMULDE ~8MM TIEF

Furniture for cafeteria, domestic court building, Berlin (1989–1995); construction drawing and view of “Leonardo” chair; “Leonardo” chair with table.

Benches for domestic court building (1989–1995), Berlin.

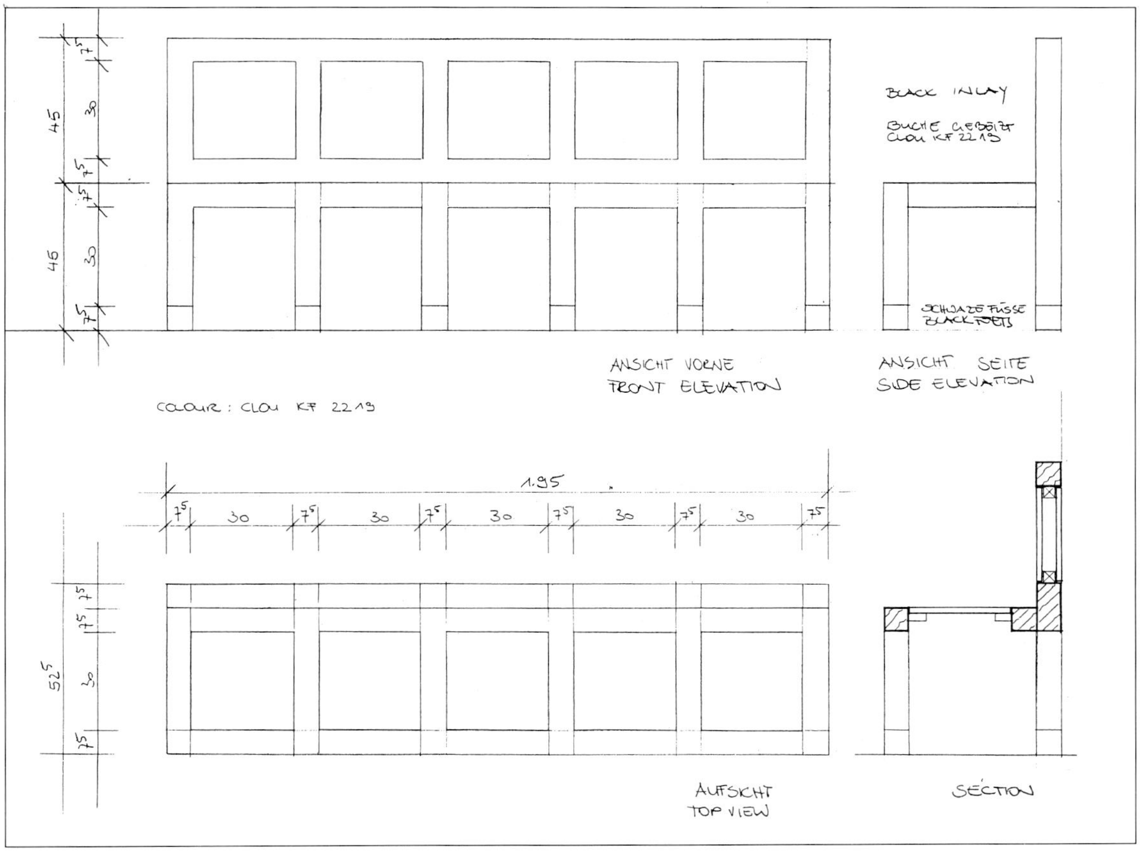
BLACK INLAY
BUCHE GEBEIZT
CLOU KF 2219
SCHWARZE FÜSSE
BLACK FEETS
ANSICHT VORNE
FRONT ELEVATION
ANSICHT SEITE
SIDE ELEVATION
COLOUR : CLOU KF 2219
1.95
AUFSICHT
TOP VIEW
SECTION

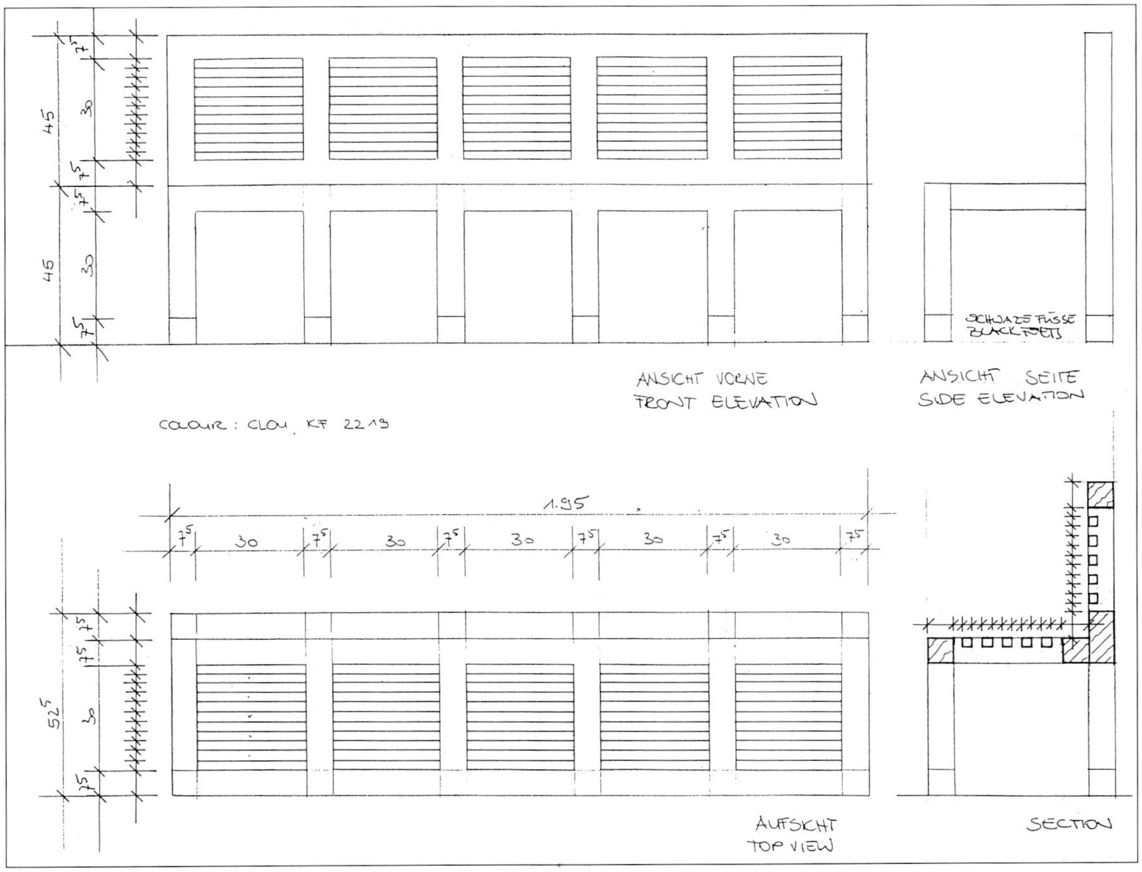
SCHWARZE FÜSSE
BLACK FEETS
ANSICHT VORNE
FRONT ELEVATION
ANSICHT SEITE
SIDE ELEVATION
COLOUR : CLOU KF 2219
1.95
AUFSICHT
TOP VIEW
SECTION

List of Works

1
Single-family House
Oderweg, Cologne-Dünnwald
1951
with O. Bosbach

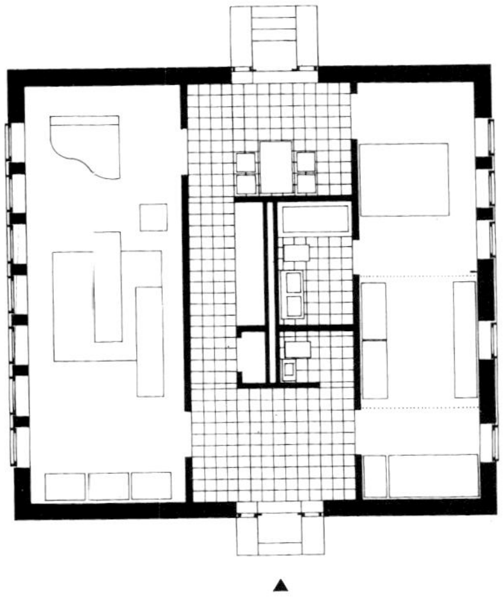

2
Multiple-family House
Hültzstrasse, Cologne-Lindenthal
1951
with O. Bosbach

3
Jobi Garment Factory and Residence
Aachener Strasse, Cologne-Braunsfeld
1951
with O. Bosbach

4
Dreesen Dance School
Hohenstaufenring, Cologne
1953

5
Bar "Moulin Rouge"
Maastrichter Strasse, Cologne
1953

6
Oberhausen Institute for the Attainment of University Qualification
Wehrstrasse, Oberhausen
1953–1958, 1967–1969
with S. Wewerka, L. Leo, K. L. Dietzsch

7
Multiple-family House
Brambachstrasse, Cologne-Dellbrück
1955–1957
with R. Gerber, C. Türke, H. Schultheiss

8
Apartment Building
Edenkobener Strasse, Cologne-Mauenheim
1955–1957
with R. Gerber, C. Türke, H. Schultheiss

9
Student Dormitory "Nibelungenhaus"
Goldenfelstrasse, Cologne-Lindenthal
1956
with C. Türke

10
Apartment Building
Garthestrasse, Cologne-Riehl
1956–1958
with R. Gerber, C. Türke, H. Schultheiss

11
Duplex
Werthmannstrasse, Cologne-Lindenthal
1957–1958
with C. Türke

12
Apartment Building
Mauenheimer Strasse, Cologne-Nippes
1957–1959
with C. Türke

13
Apartment Building
Aachener Strasse, Cologne-Braunsfeld
1958
with C. Türke, H. Schultheiss

14
Residential Complex
Jakob Kneip-Strasse, Cologne-Poll
1958–1959

15
Multiple-family House
Belvederestrasse, Cologne-Müngersdorf
1958–1959
with C. Türke, R. Gerber

16
Apartment and Commercial Building "Haus Reimbold"
Hansaring, Cologne City Center
1959
with C. Türke

18
Residential Complex
Eckewart Strasse, Cologne-Mauenheim
1959–1961
with K. L. Dietzsch

20
Competition Design for Kunsthalle
Düsseldorf
1960

22
Müller Publishing House and Printing Office
Stolberger Strasse, Cologne-Braunsfeld
1960–1964
with K. L. Dietzsch

17
Apartment Building
Mozartstrasse, Wuppertal-Elberfeld
1959
with K. L. Dietzsch

19
Competition Design for Römisch-Germanisches Museum
Cologne
1960

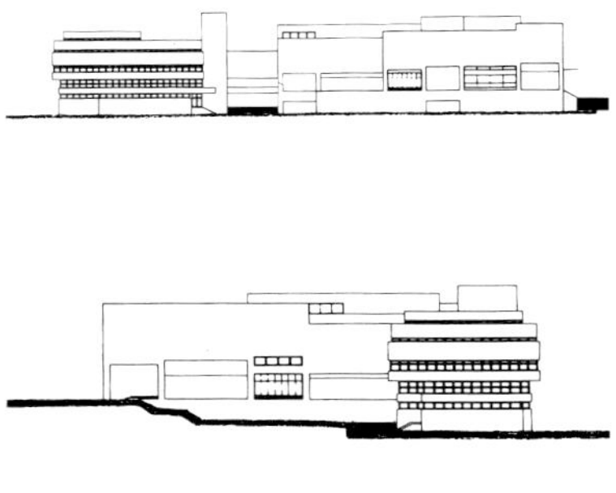

21
Single-family House
Schulstrasse, Overath
1960–1961
with J. P. Schori, K. L. Dietzsch

23
Competition Design for Secondary School Erzbischöfliches Gymnasium
Bonn-Beuel
1961
with K. L. Dietzsch

24
Competition Design for Student Dormitory "Schmalenbachhaus"
Cologne-Klettenberg
1961
with K. L. Dietzsch

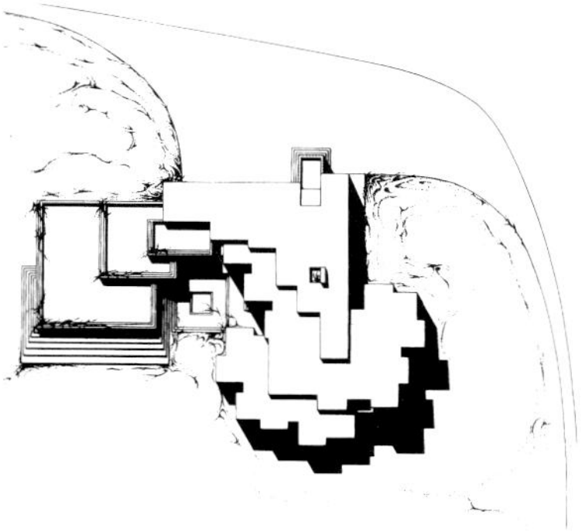

26
Single-family House
Wippenhohner Strasse,
Hennef-Sieg
1961–1962
with K. L. Dietzsch

28
Competition Design for Grünzug Süd
Cologne-Zollstock
1962–1965
with K. L. Dietzsch, F. Oswald,
R. Krier

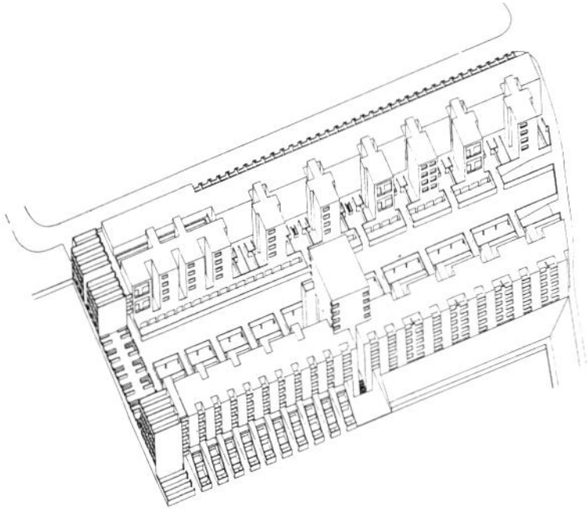

29
Märkisches Viertel Residential Complex
Berlin-Wittenau
1962–1967
with K. L. Dietzsch, F. Oswald,
J. P. Schori, J. Sawade, M. Wegener,
H. Schmetzer, K. Schallhorn,
K. Boje, U. Bangert, U. Flemming,
H. Schmalscheidt

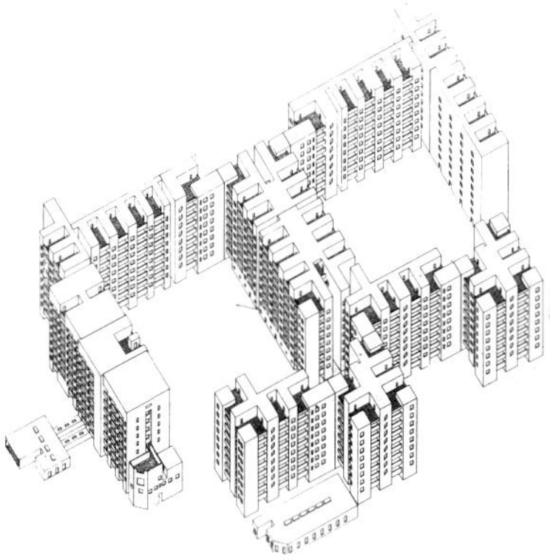

25
Wokan House
Bad Honnef
1961

27
Competition Design for Neue Stadt Residential Complex
Asternweg, Cologne-
Chorweiler/Seeberg
1961–1964
with K. L. Dietzsch

30
Competition Design for Student Dormitory, Technical University of Twente
Enschede, Netherlands
1964
with J. Sawade, J. Geist

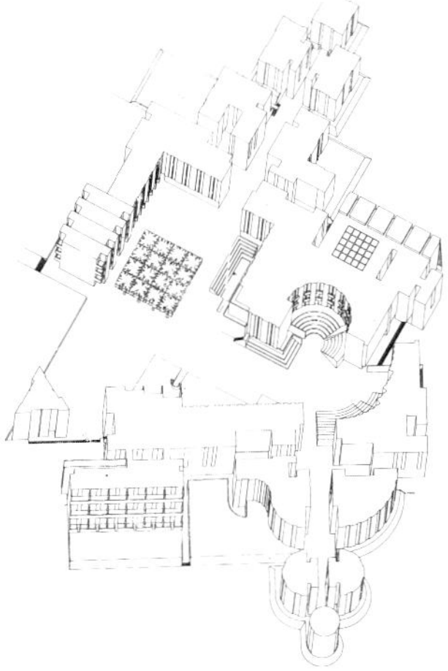

31
Competition Design for School Center
Mayen
1965
with U. Flemming

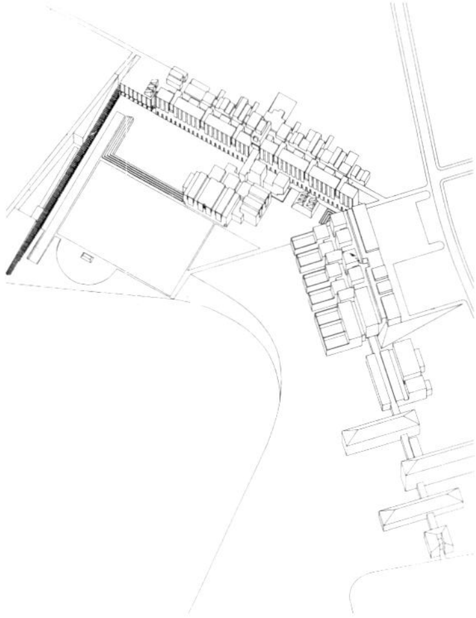

33
Competition Design for Museum Preussischer Kulturbesitz
Berlin
1965
with J. Sawade, U. Flemming

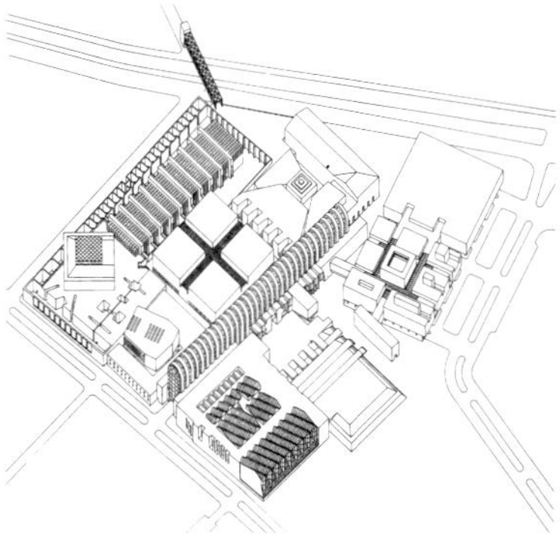

35
Urban Planning Design for Rupenhorn Residential Complex
Berlin
1965–1970
with U. Bangert, K. L. Dietzsch, J. Sawade

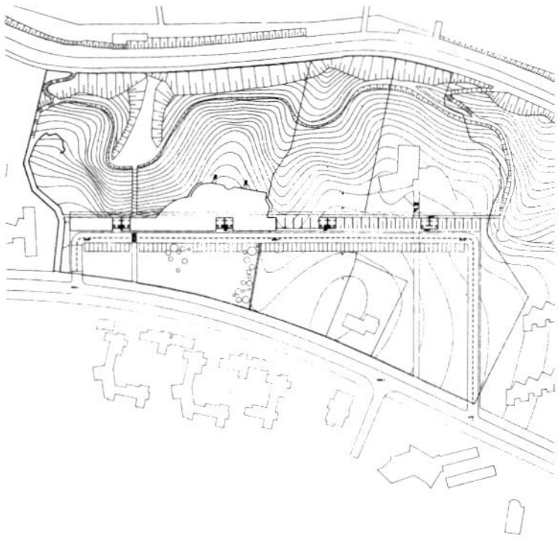

37
(Urban Planning) Competition Design for Blauer See Residential Complex
Rüsselsheim
1972

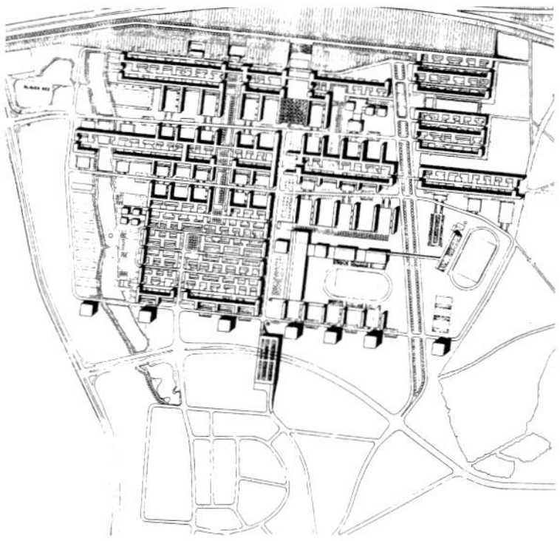

32
Competition Design for German Embassy to the Vatican
Rome
1965
with J. Sawade

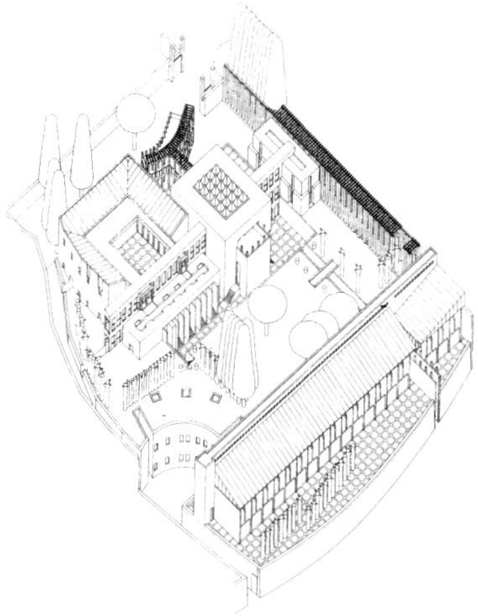

34
Urban Planning Design for Ruhwald Residential Complex (Two Versions)
Berlin
1965–1967
with H. J. Ehlers, D. Frowein, C. Meier, S. Patschkowski, V. Sayn, M. Wegener

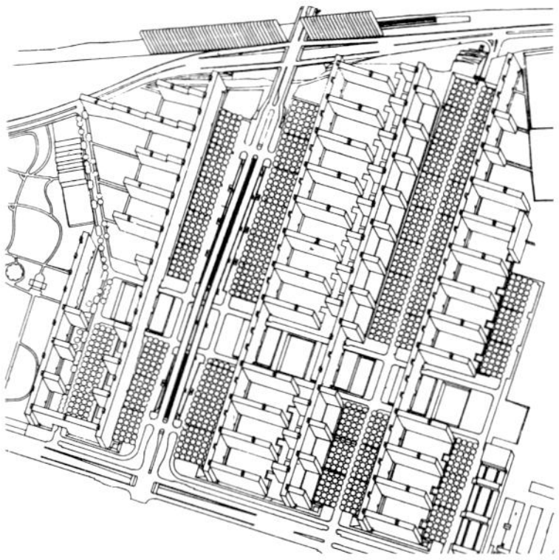

36
Competition Design for Expansion of Tegel Airport (Terminal Building)
Berlin
1966
with M. Wegener, H. Schmetzer

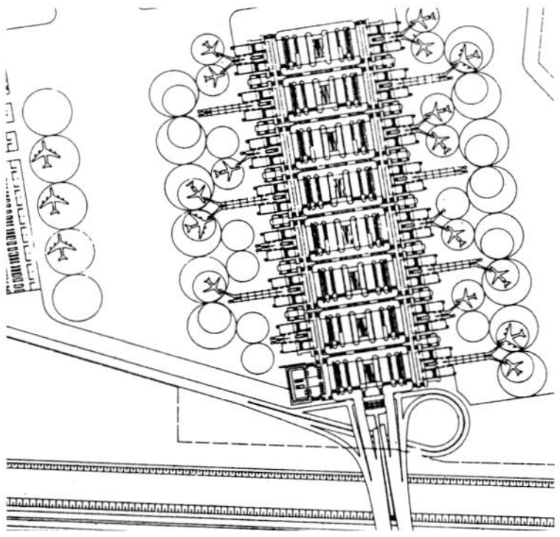

38
Design for Betzlin House
Kastanienallee, Berlin
1973

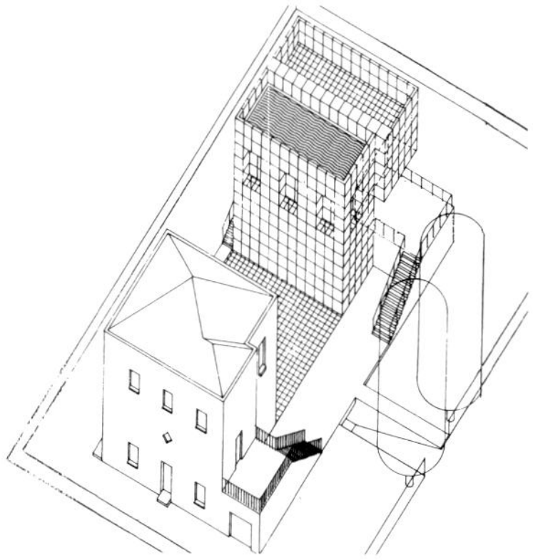

39
(Urban Planning) Competition Design for Kuhgassen District
Düren-Nord
1973
with K.-L. Dietzsch, M. Hornberger, A. Krieger, G. Brown-Manrique

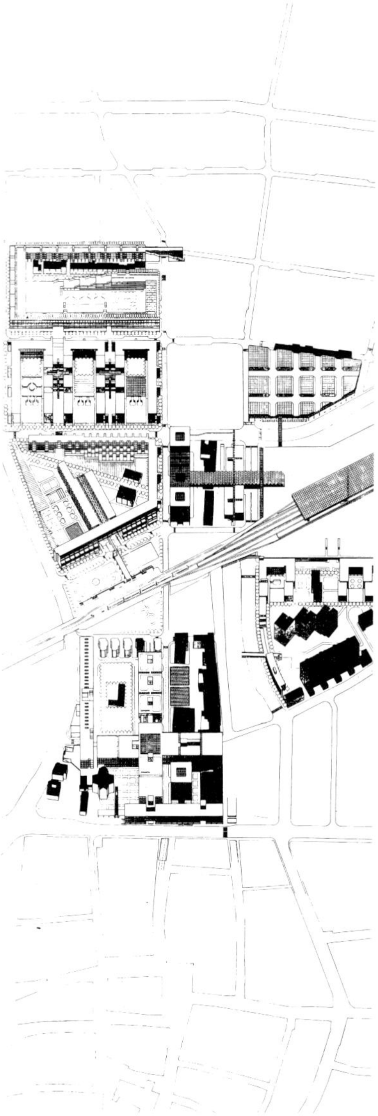

40
(Urban Planning) Competition Design for Landwehrkanal-Tiergarten District
Berlin
1973
with R. Koolhaas, P. Allison, D. Allison

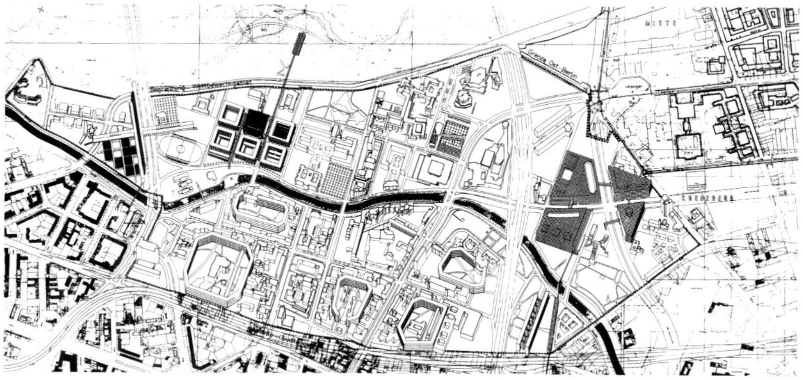

41
(Urban Planning) Competition Design for Billwerder Allerhöhe
Hamburg
1974

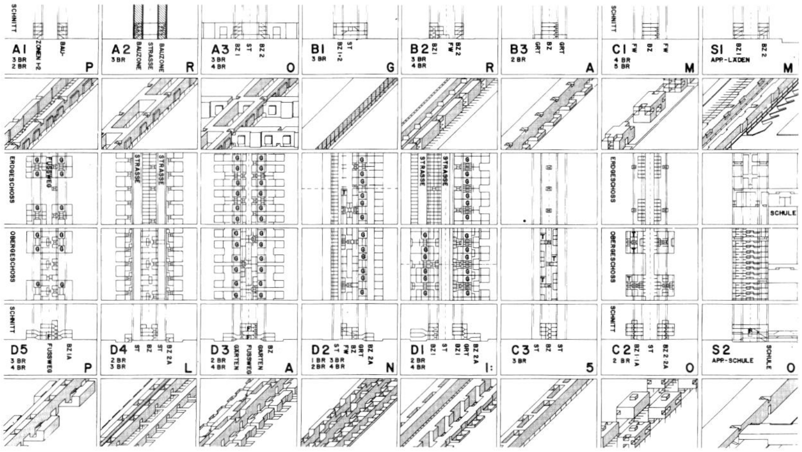

42
(Urban Planning) Competition Design for IV. Ring
Berlin-Lichterfelde
1974
with R. Koolhaas, K.-L. Dietzsch

43
(Urban Planning) Competition Design for Roosevelt Island
New York
1975
with J. Clark, K.-L. Dietzsch, A. Ovaska

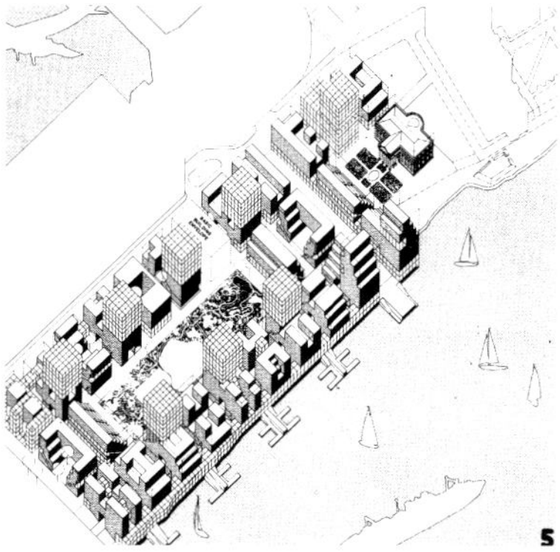

44
Competition Design for Wallraf-Richartz-Museum
Cologne
1975
with J. Clark, K.-L. Dietzsch

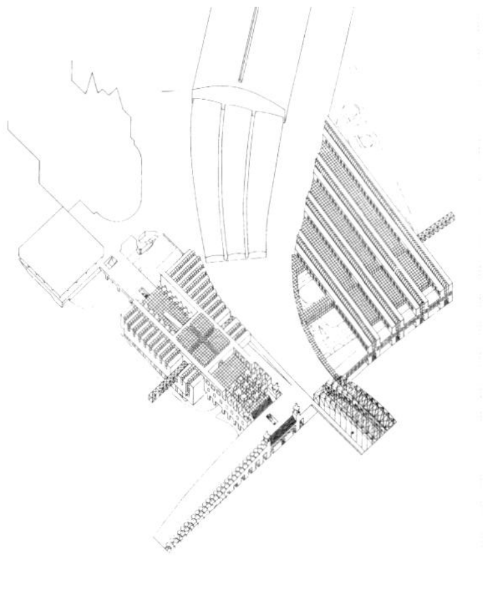

45
Planning for Mertenshof
Cologne-Widdersdorf
1975–1980
with K.-L. Dietzsch

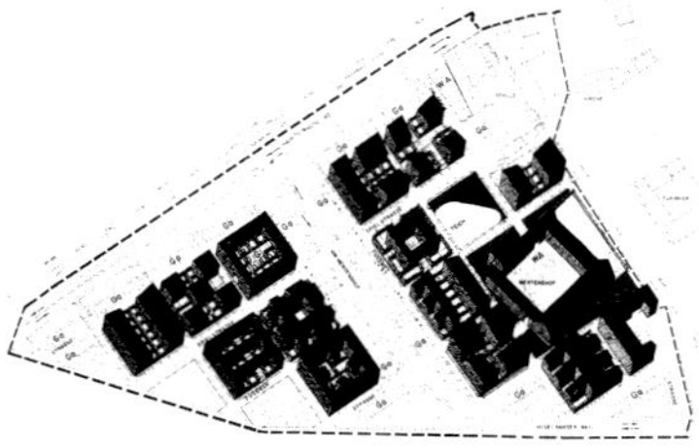

46
Planning for Residential Complex
Ritterstrasse, Marburg
1976
with K.-L. Dietzsch, H. Kollhoff, T. Will

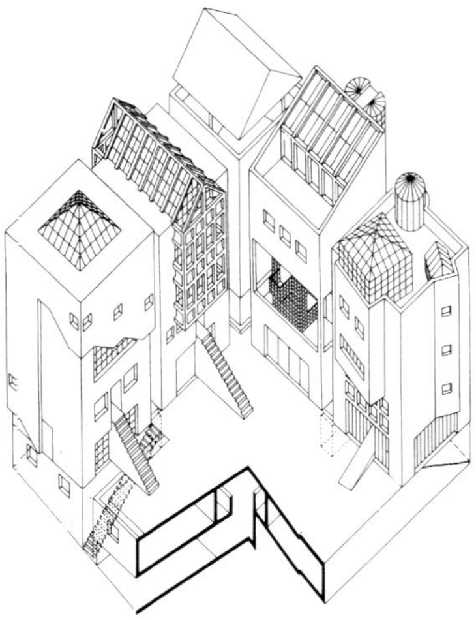

47
Planning for Schlosspark
Braunschweig
1976
with K.-L. Dietzsch, H. Kollhoff, T. Will

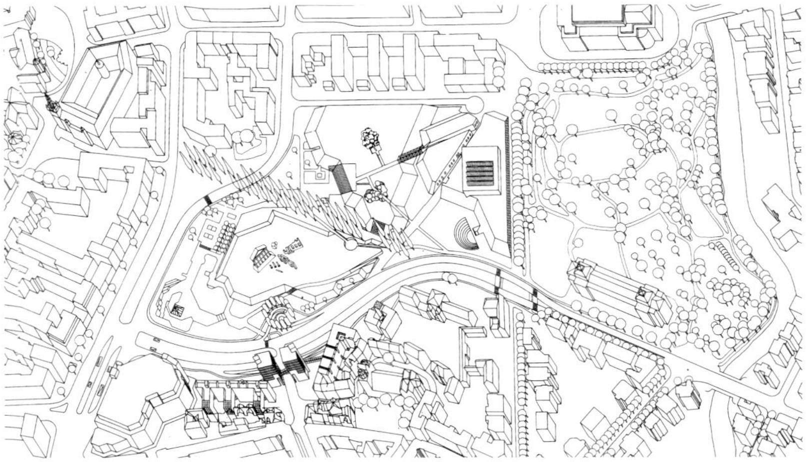

48
Competition Design for East University Grounds
Bremen
1976
with K.-L. Dietzsch, A. Ovaska

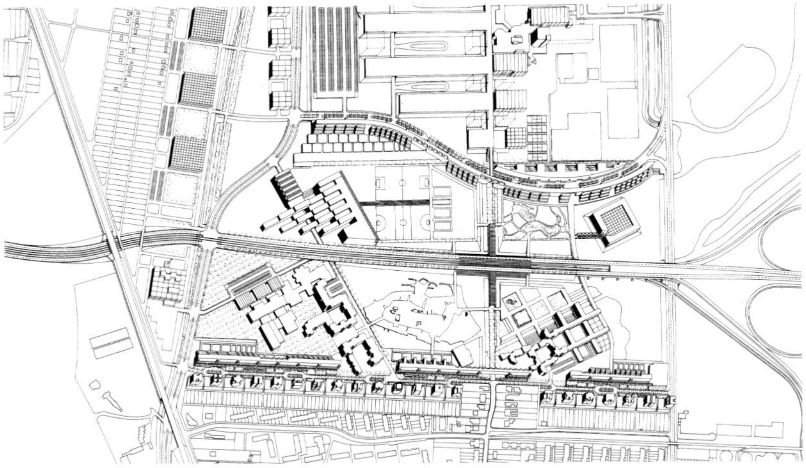

49
Exhibition Conception "City Metaphors"
Cooper Hewitt Museum of Design, New York; Smithsonian Institution, Washington, D.C.
1976–1977

50
Redesign and Construction of New Auxiliary Buildings for Museum Schloss Morsbroich
Leverkusen
1976–1980
with St. Böhm, K.-L. Dietzsch, K. Nagel, T. Will

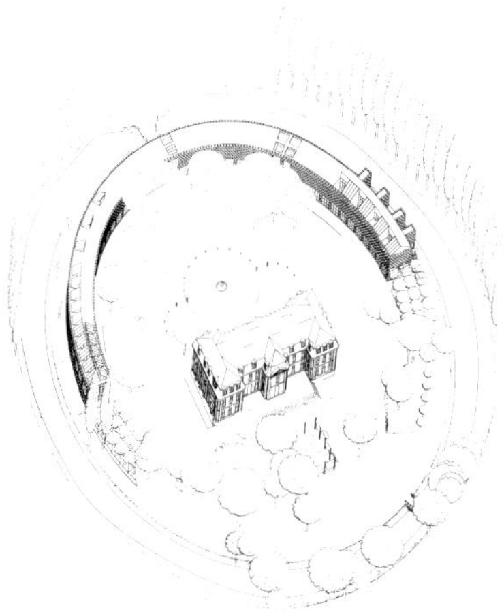

52
(Urban) Planning for South End of Friedrichstadt District
Berlin
1977
with H. Kollhoff, A. Ovaska, T. Will

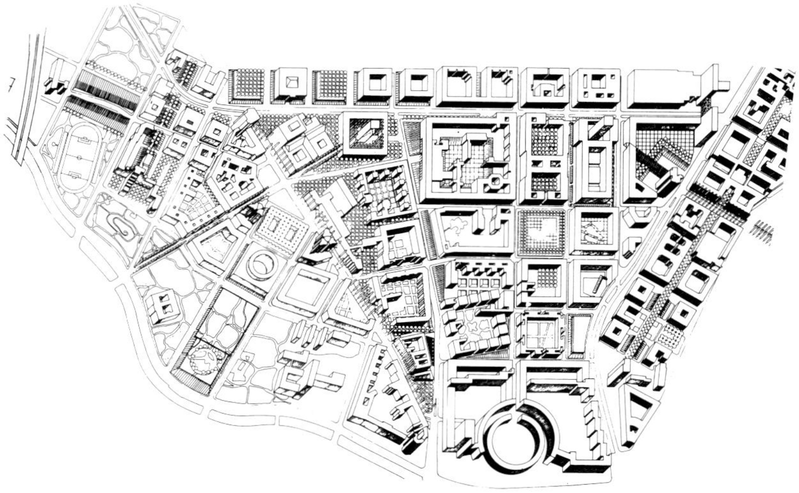

55
Tiergarten Sewage Pump Station
Berlin
1978
with M. Müller

51
Apartment and Commercial Building
Hoher Steinweg, Berlin-Spandau
1977
with H. Kollhoff, T. Will

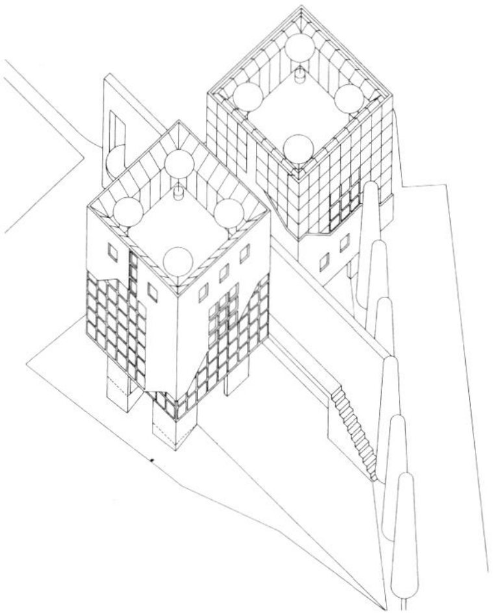

53
Competition Design for Hotel Berlin
Lützowplatz, Berlin
1977
with K.-L. Dietzsch, M. Kalsass, A. Ovaska

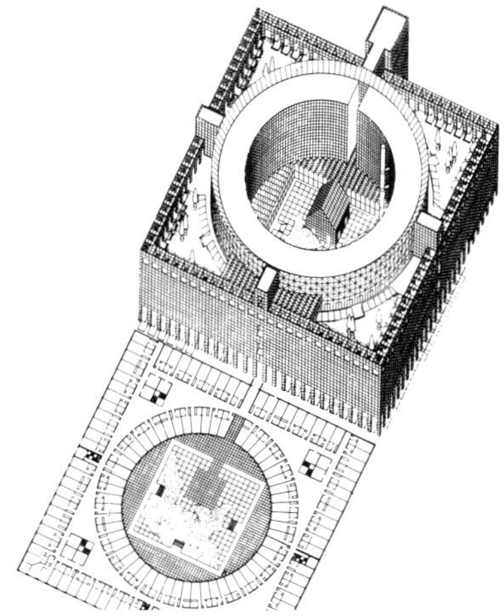

54
Competition Design for Hotel Budapester Strasse
Berlin
1978
with A. Ovaska

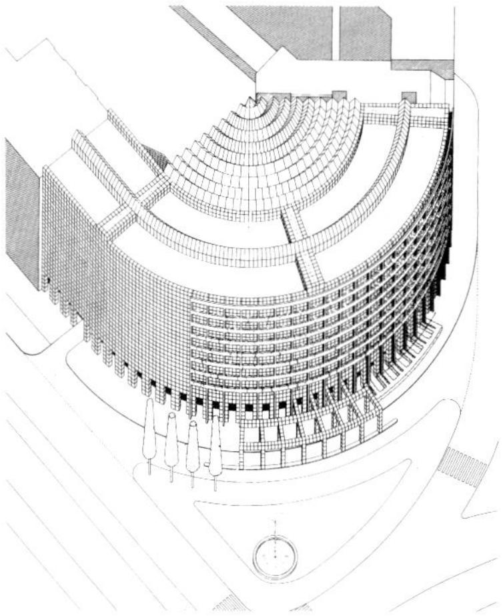

56
Competition Design for Severin District
Cologne
1979
with K.-L. Dietzsch, T. Will

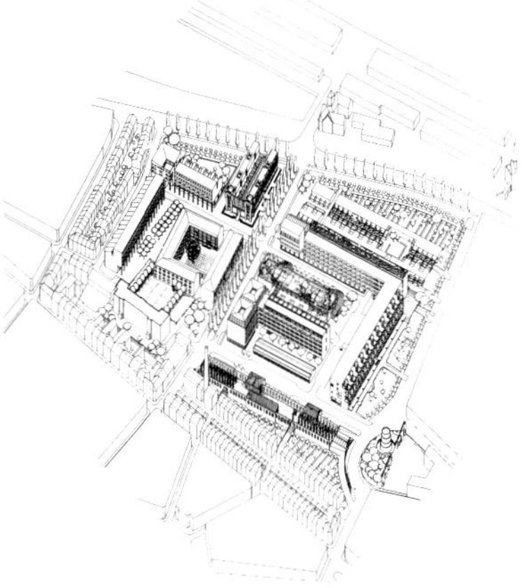

57
Competition Design for Superior Court
Berlin
1978–1979
with S. Ungers, L. Kiss

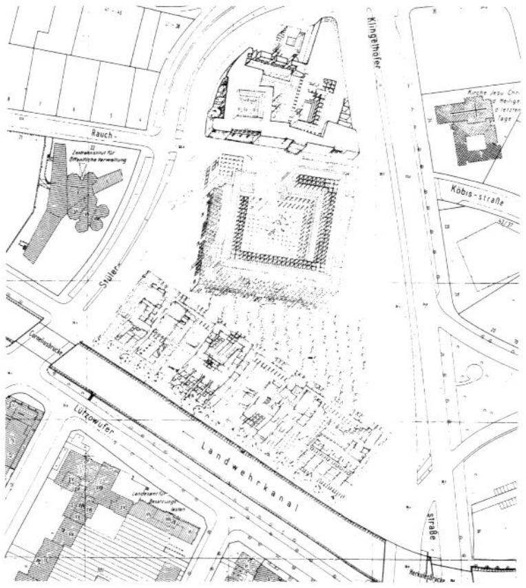

58
Apartment Building
Schillerstrasse, Berlin-Charlottenburg
1978–1979
with K.-L. Dietzsch, J. Essig, I. Keil, J. Leitner, B. Taha, B. Wippler

59
Design for Woolworth Store (Facade)
Berlin-Wedding
1978–1979
with K.-L. Dietzsch, T. Will, G. Wooding

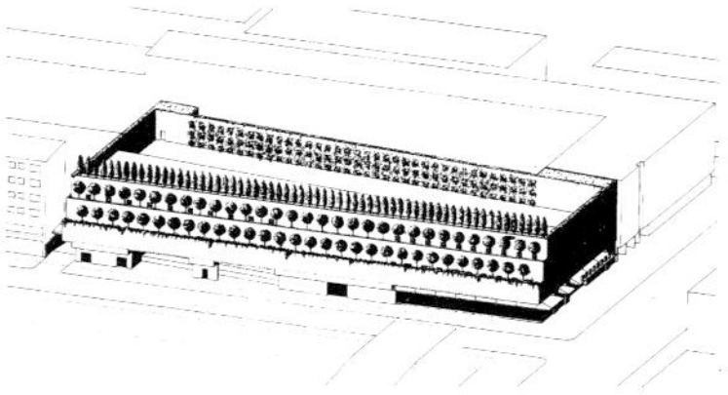

60
Competition Design for Sparkasse (Technical Center)
Berlin
1979
with K.-L. Dietzsch, L. Kiss, S. Ungers

61
(Urban Planning) Competition Design for Ackerhof
Braunschweig
1979
with S. Ungers, L. Kiss, G. Wooding

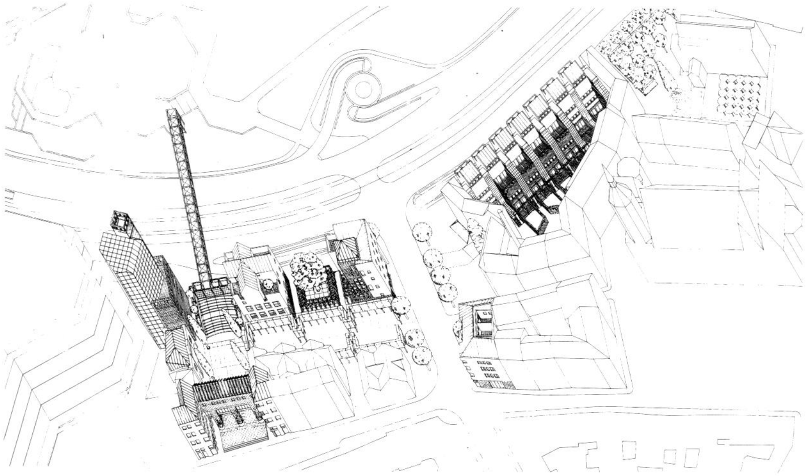

62
Competition Design for Melkerei Solar Buildings
Landstuhl
1979
with K.-L. Dietzsch, B. Faskel, J. Leitner, B. Meyer, M. Müller

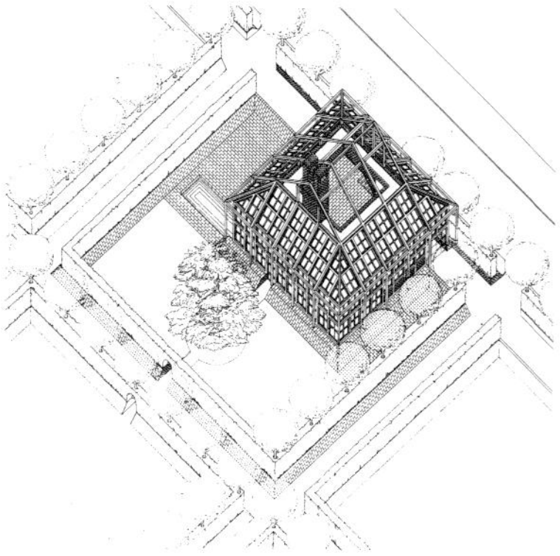

63
Competition Design for Technical College
Bremerhaven
1979–1980
with K.-L. Dietzsch, B. Taha, G. Wooding

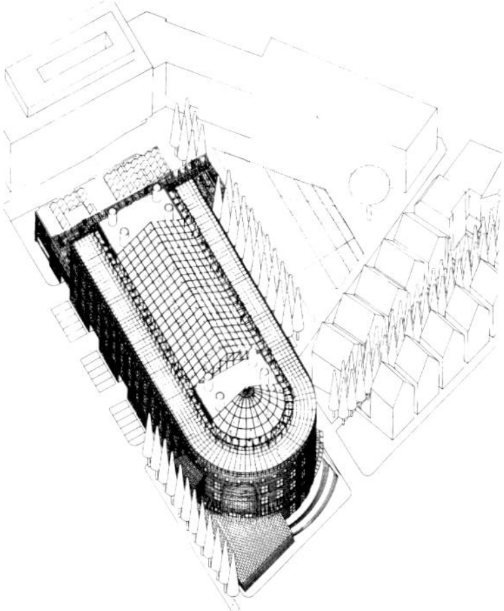

65
Deutsches Architekturmuseum
Schaumainkai, Frankfurt am Main
1979–1984
with K.-L. Dietzsch, K. Nagel, B. Taha

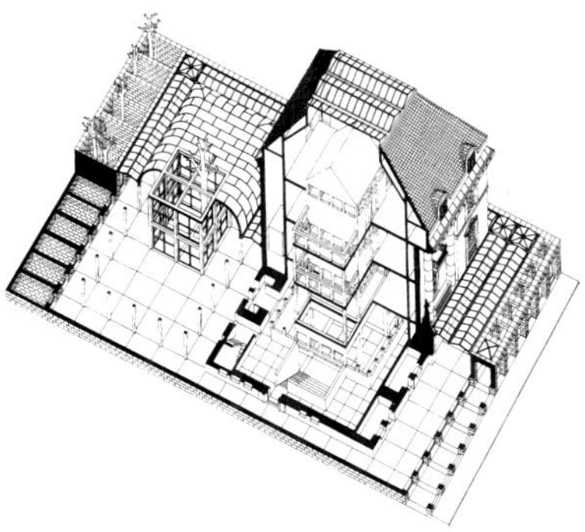

66
Competition Design for Market Square
Hildesheim
1980
with I. Keil, J. Leitner, B. Taha, G. Wooding

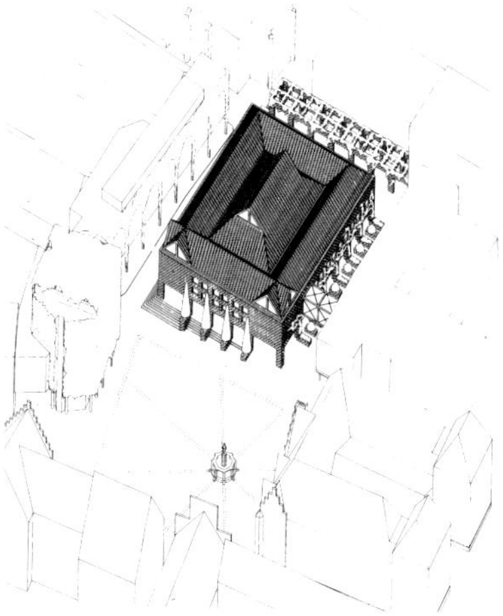

68
Trade Fair Hall 9 and Galleria for Trade Fair Complex
Frankfurt am Main
1980–1983
with W. Liebender, K. L. Dietzsch, B. Meyer, J. Franzke, M. Dudler, W. A. Noebel, A. v. Hoessle, T. Kubisch, J. Erb, F. Bucher, B. Operschalski, B. Petri, K. Junghans, E. Hadler, A. Keller, H. Lange, G. v. Lunteren, J. Leitner

64
Lützowplatz Residential Complex
Lützowplatz, Berlin
1979–1983
with K.-L. Dietzsch, G. Hagemann, B. Meyer, B. Taha, B. Wippler

67
Apartment Building
Miquellstrasse, Berlin
1980–1982
with K.-L. Dietzsch, G. Hagemann, B. Meyer, B. Wippler, G. Wooding

69
Alfred Wegener Institute for Polar Research and Oceanography
Am Alten Hafen, Bremerhaven
1980–1984
with J. v. Brand, K.-L. Dietzsch, B. Lehmann, C. Petzinka

70
Badische Landesbibliothek (State Library of Baden)
Karlsruhe
1980–1991
with B. Meyer (construction supervision), K.-H. Schmitz, K.-L. Dietzsch,

73
Temporary Museum Westkunst
Cologne Trade Fair Hall, Cologne-Deutz
1981
with B. Meyer

75
Redesign of Konstantinplatz
Trier
1981–1983
with K.-L. Dietzsch, B. Meyer, B. Taha

71
Competition Design for Karstadt Department Store
Berlin-Tempelhof
1981
with K.-L. Dietzsch, St. Braden

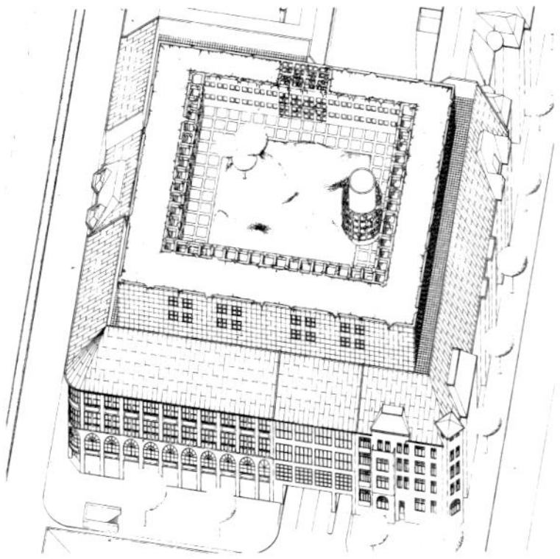

72
Competition Design for Barmer Ersatzkasse Building
Wuppertal-Elberfeld
1981
with K.-L. Dietzsch, B. Taha

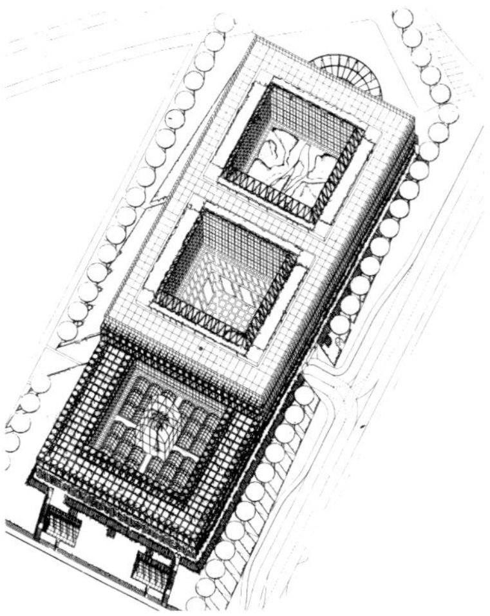

74
(Urban) Planning for Friedrichvorstadt District
Berlin
1981
with H. Timmermann, V. Eich, B. Faskel

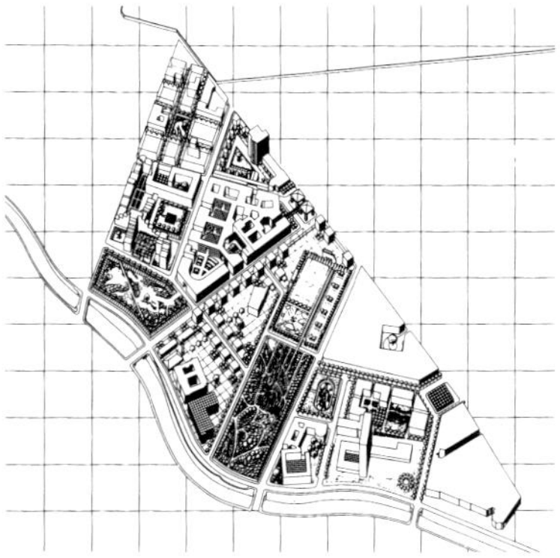

76
City Center Gibellina
Gibellina (Sicily)
1982
with S. M. Ungers, L. Kiss, D. Frederick, S. Bradic

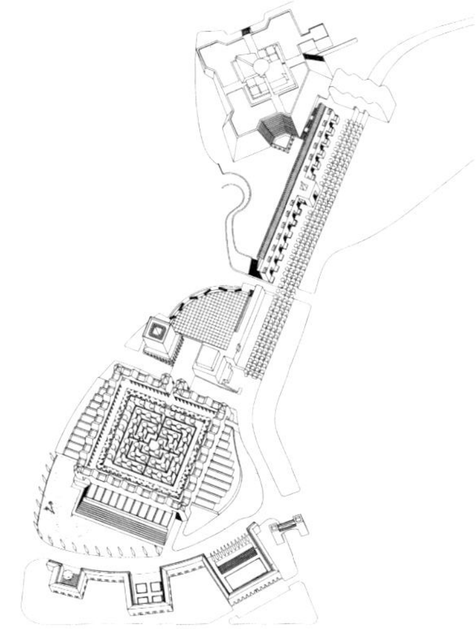

77
Competition Design for Deutsche Bibliothek
Frankfurt am Main
1982
with W. Liebender, B. Taha, K.-L. Dietzsch

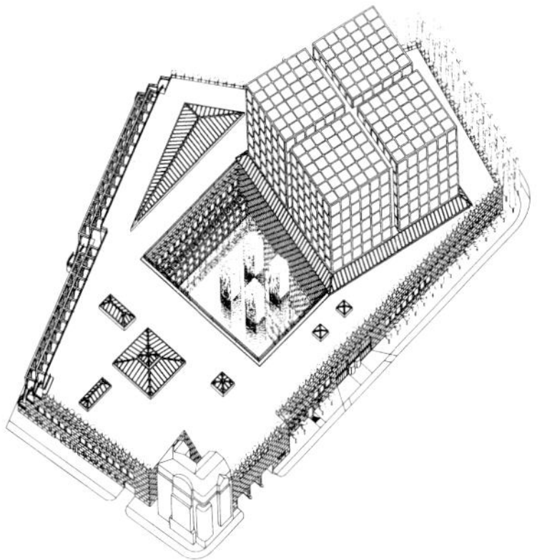

79
Competition Design for Bundespostmuseum
Frankfurt am Main
1982
with K.-L. Dietzsch, B. Meyer, B. Taha

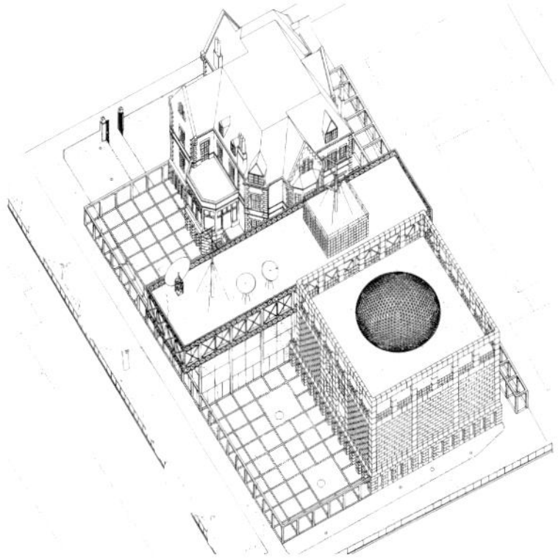

81
Urbanistic Redesign of Paulsplatz
Frankfurt am Main
1983
with B. Meyer, A. Keller, K.-L. Dietzsch

78
Competition Design for Residence of the German Ambassador (1st Phase)
Washington, D.C.
1982
with W. Liebender, B. Taha, K.-L. Dietzsch

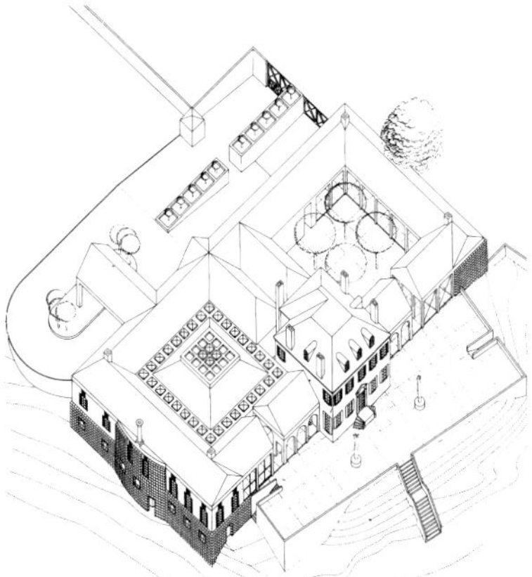

80
Competition Design for Kop van Zuid (Two Versions)
Rotterdam (Netherlands)
1982
with U. Bartelt, D. Frederick, A. Keller, L. Kiss, W. Liebender, S. Sterf, S. Ungers

82
Competition Design for Gruner + Jahr Publishing House
Hamburg
1983
with K. Wimmer, K.-L. Dietzsch, K. H. Wieland, W. Albrecht, B. Taha, B. Zens, S. Kolatan, K. Nagel, C. Petzinka, B. Meyer, J. v. Brandt, S. Ungers

83
Competition Design for Kulturforum
Berlin
1983
with M. Dudler, R. Vallebuona, H. Rübsamen, H. Jentschura, K. H. Wieland

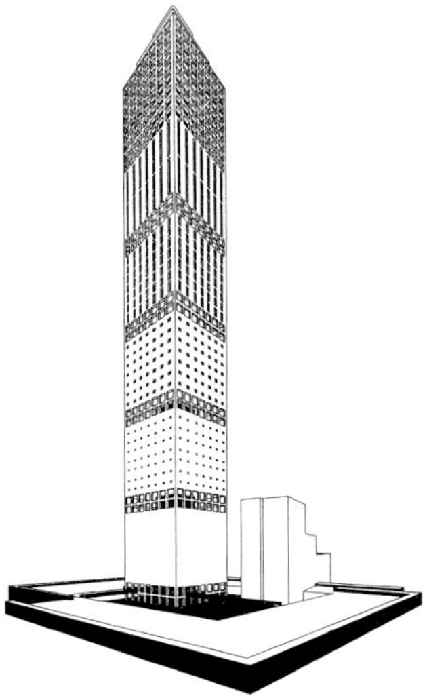

84
Competition Design for Museum für Moderne Kunst
Frankfurt am Main
1983
with K.-H. Schmitz, B. Meyer, B. Taha

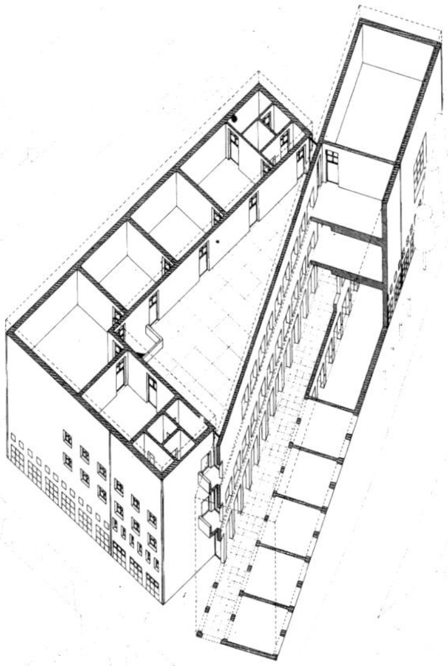

85
Gatehouse over Elevated Railway Tracks
1983–1984
with M. Dudler, W. A. Noebel, A. Bausinger, J. Franzke, K. H. Wieland, R. Bandus, A. Vorwerk, A. v. Hoessle, J. Jentschura, T. Kubisch

86
Planning for Forellenweg Residential Complex
Salzburg (Austria)
1984
with K.-L. Dietzsch, K. Wimmer, E. v. Branca

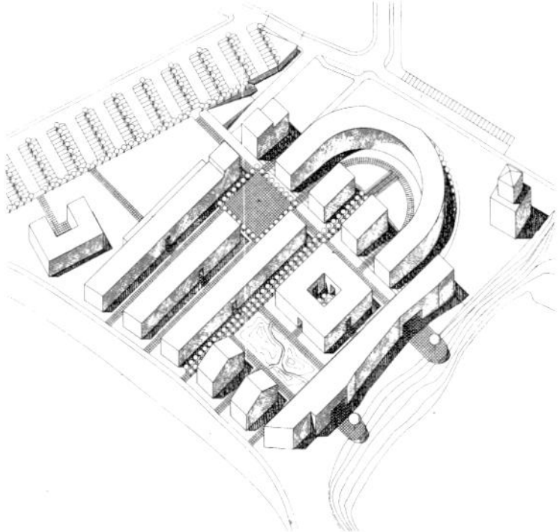

87
Competition Design for Albgrün Bridge
Ed. Züblin AG, Karlsruhe
1984
with M. Dudler, R. Vallebuona

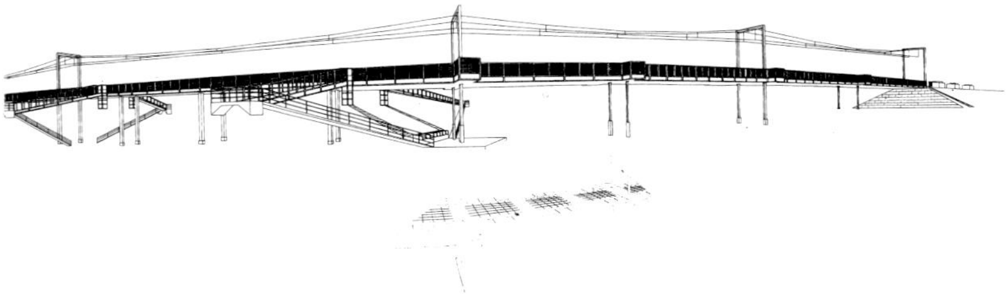

88
Competition Design for Silobad Gymnasium
Frankfurt am Main
1984
with M. Dudler, R. Vallebuona, K. Wimmer, B. Taha, K.-L. Dietzsch, A. Hierhölzer

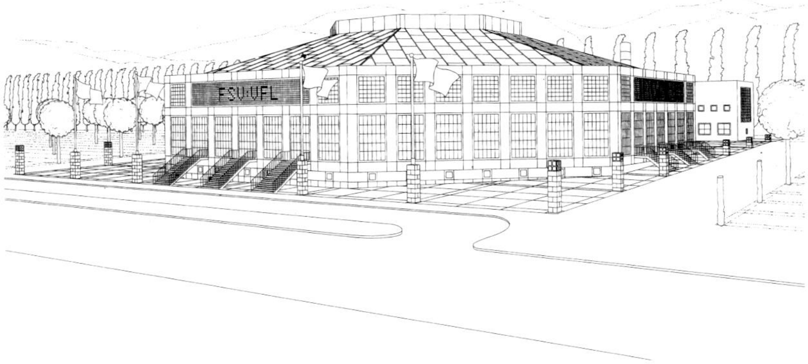

89
Cabinet Tower
Triennale di Milano
(Furniture Design)
1985

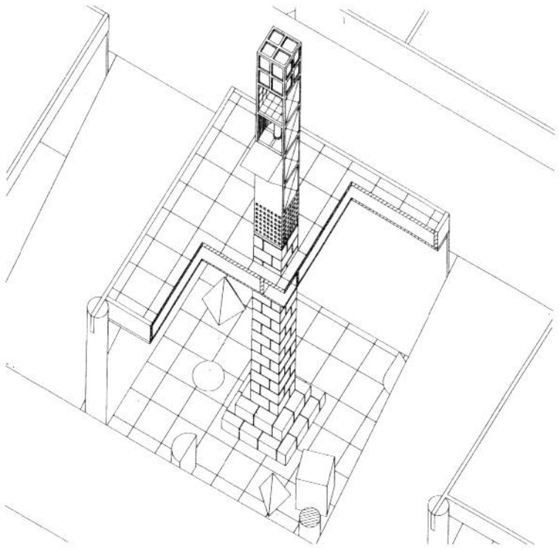

91
Thermal Plant
Frankfurt am Main
1985
with M. Dudler, J. Franzke, R. C. v. Bennewitz, M. Bräckerbohm

92
Feasibility Study for Battelle Grounds
Frankfurt am Main
1985
with M. Dudler, R. C. v. Bennewitz, J. Happ, M. Bräckerbohm

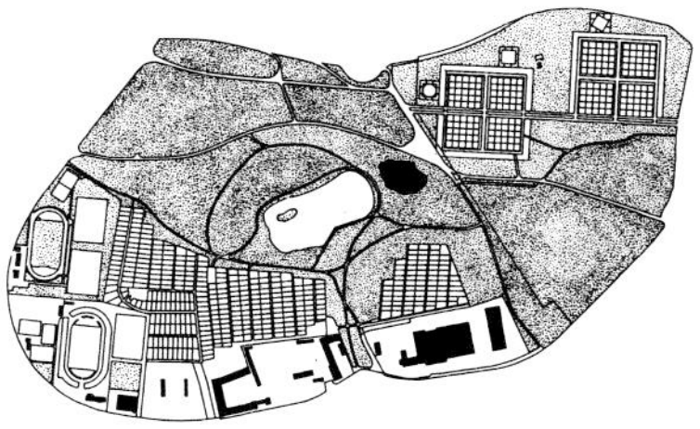

94
Competition Design for Festival Hall
Frankfurt am Main
1985
with J. Franzke, B. Kraus, P. Kupferschmidt, M. Bräckerbohm, R. C. v. Bennewitz, J. Engel, S. Canton, H. Rübsamen, A. Tillmann, P. Heidenreich, F. Stimmer, J. Schonerer, U. Bartelt

90
Competition Designs for Expansion of Federal Supreme Court and Federal Prosecutor's Office (1st Phase)
Karlsruhe
1985
with M. Pitlach, J. Klose, B. Taha

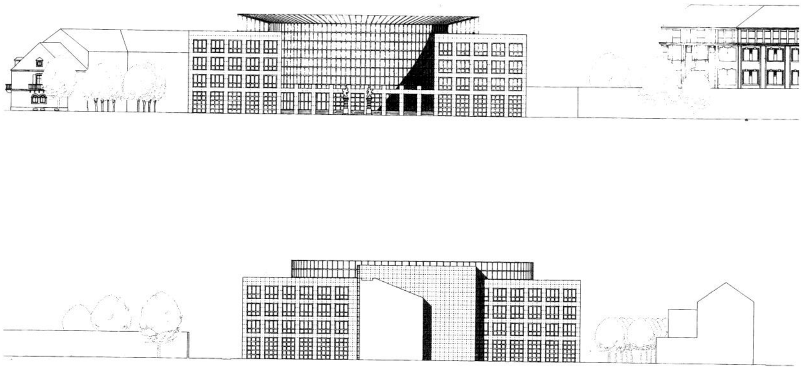

93
Competition Design for Eschenheimer Tor, Börsenplatz
Frankfurt am Main
1985
with M. Dudler, R. C. v. Bennewitz, M. Bräckerbohm, P. Kupferschmidt

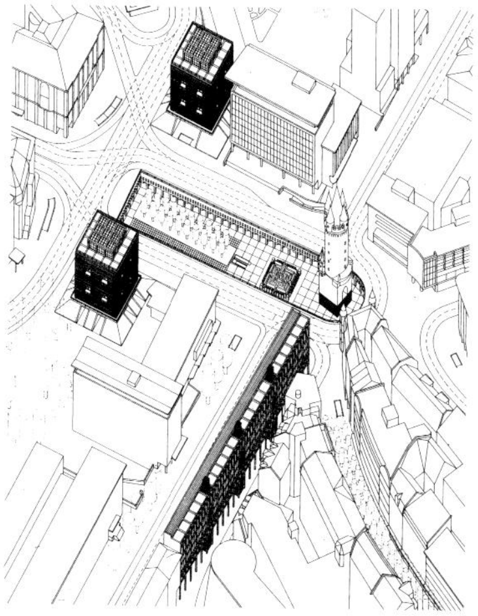

95
Competition Design for Landeshaus
Wiesbaden
1985
with E. v. Branca, P. Schmidt, K. Wimmer, B. Taha

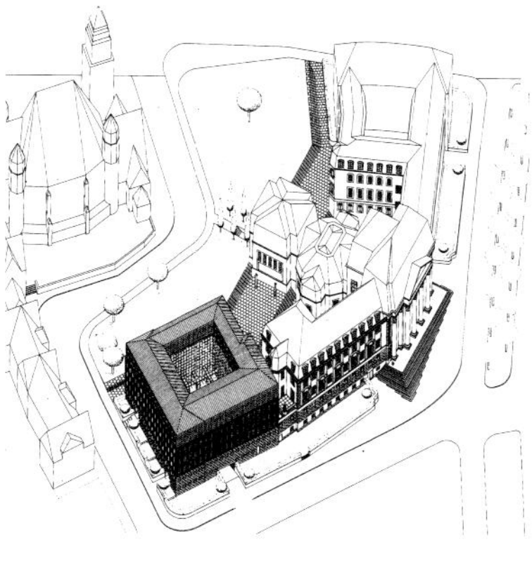

96
Competition Design for Railroad Depot
Frankfurt am Main
1985
with M. Dudler, R. C. v. Bennewitz, M. Bräckerbohm, B. Kraus

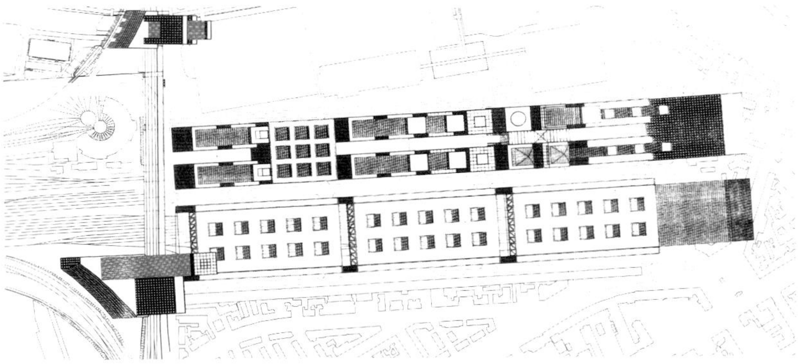

97
Design for City-West (Feasibility Study)
Frankfurt am Main
1985
with M. Dudler, R. C. v. Bennewitz, M. Bräckerbohm, J. Könz, S. Canton, P. Kupferschmidt

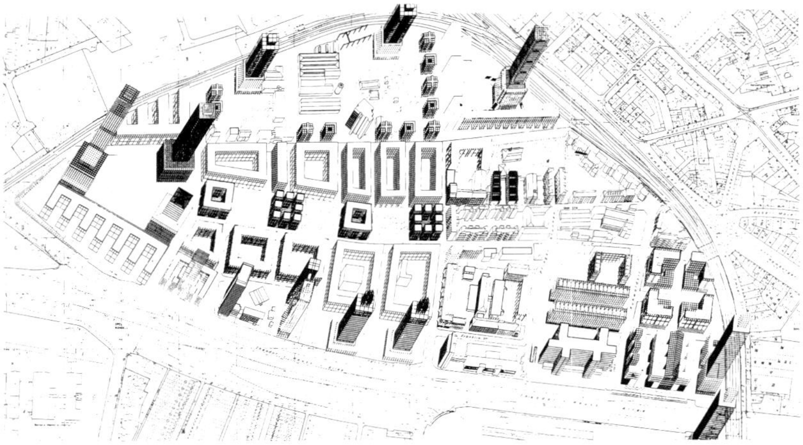

98
Competition Design for City Park
Salemi (Sicily)
1985
with M. Pitlach

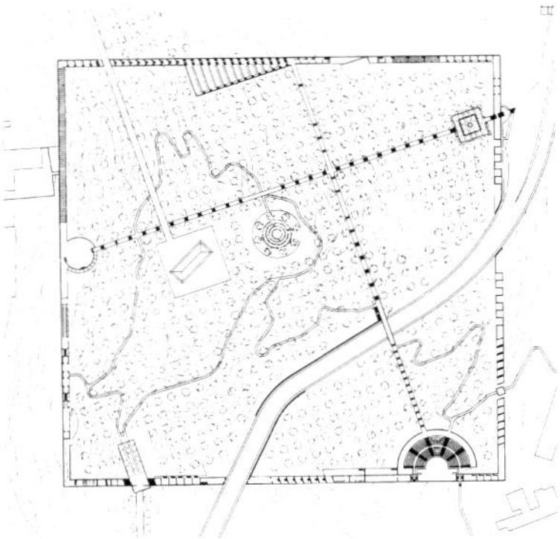

99
New Building for University Club
Bonn
1985–1988
with K.-L. Dietzsch, U. Wiegmann, K. Steves, A. Brauns

100
Competition Design for Shop Gallery
Rossmarkt, Frankfurt am Main
1986
with M. Dudler, R. Vallebuona, R. C. v. Bennewitz, J. Konz

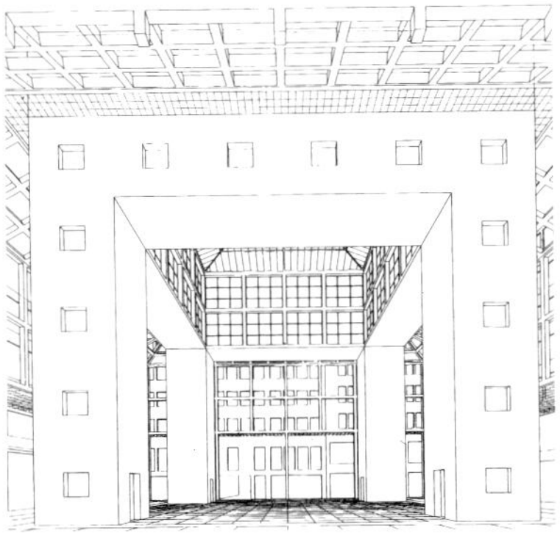

101
Competition Design for Galerie der Gegenwart Expansion of Kunsthalle
Kunstinsel, Hamburg, 1986–1996
with J. Klose, A. Geitner, K. Ehm, M. Röhr, B. Taha, R. Bandus, J. Nitsch, H. v. Dallwitz, C. Nieländer (design); J. Sieber, I. Schweers, A. Geitner, V. Diekmann, F. Wie Schenimann, P. Pfertner (execution)

102
Competition Design for Historisches Museum der Pfalz (Redesign and Expansion)
Speyer
1986
with R. Bandus, B. Taha, A. Tillmann

105
Design for Studio "Frog Design" (New Office Building)
Altensteig
1986
with J. Klose

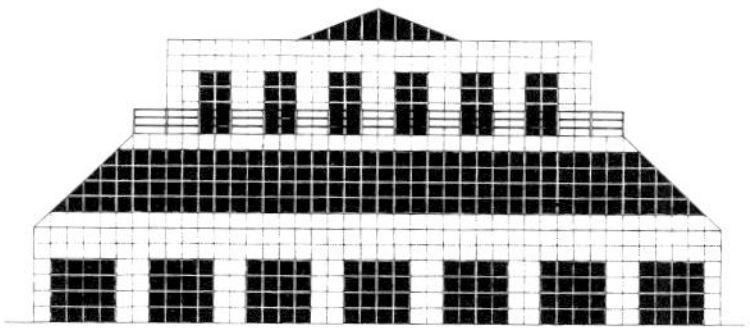

106
Glashütte House
Bitburg
1986–1988
with R. Bandus

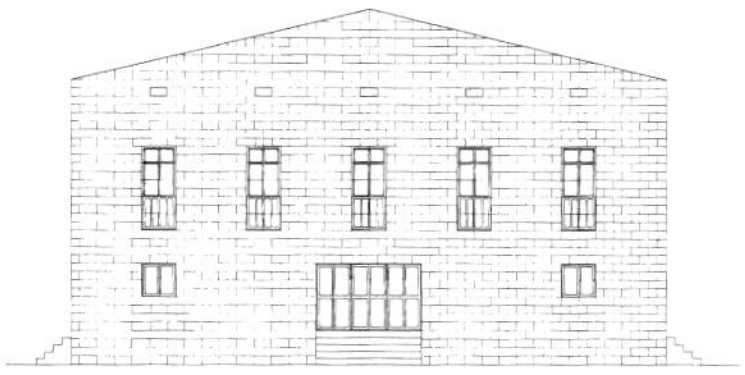

103
Competition Design for Building on Railway Station Plaza
Bonn
1986
with J. Klose, U. Wiegmann, B. Taha, C. Waser, T. Britz

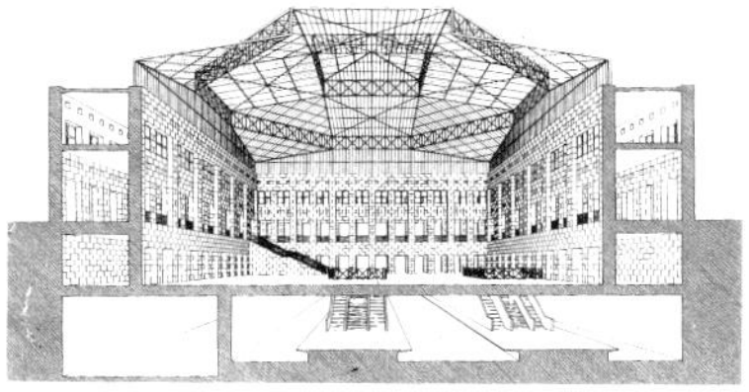

104
Competition Design for Württembergisches Staatstheater, Stage-set Building
Stuttgart
1986
with J. Klose, U. Wiegmann

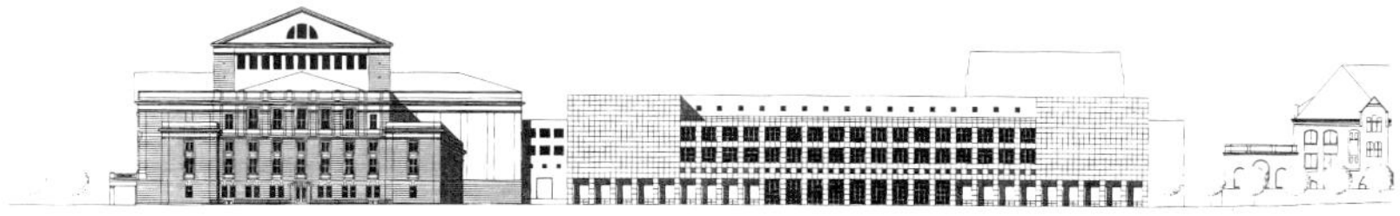

107
Competition Design for German Embassy
Helsinki (Finland)
1986
with M. Pitlach, B. Taha

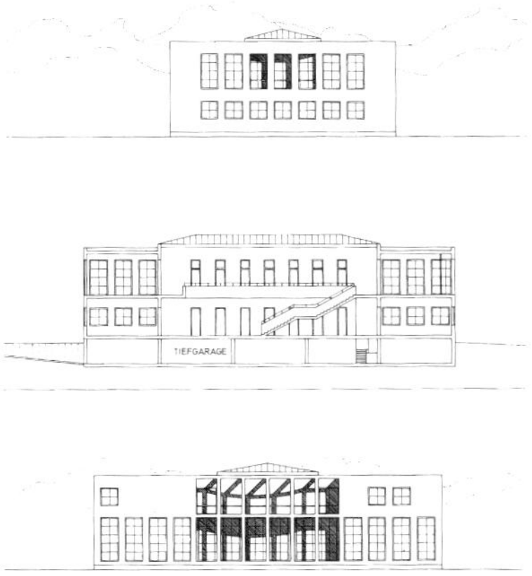

108
Competition Design for Expansion of Hessische Landesbibliothek (State Library of Hessen)
Fulda
1986

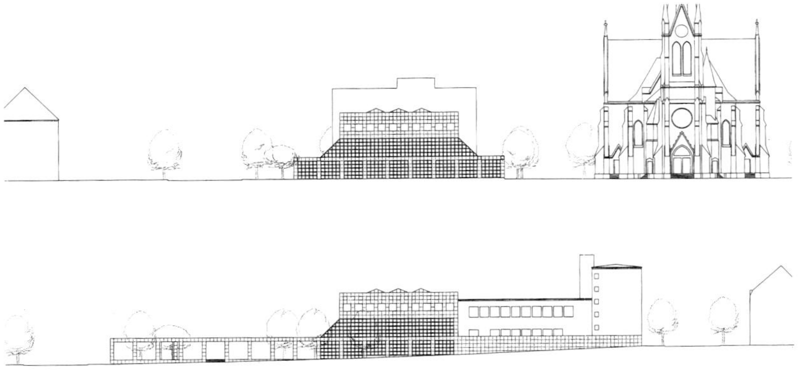

111
Competition Design for City Center
Cologne-Jülich
1986
with U. Wiegmann, K. Nieländer

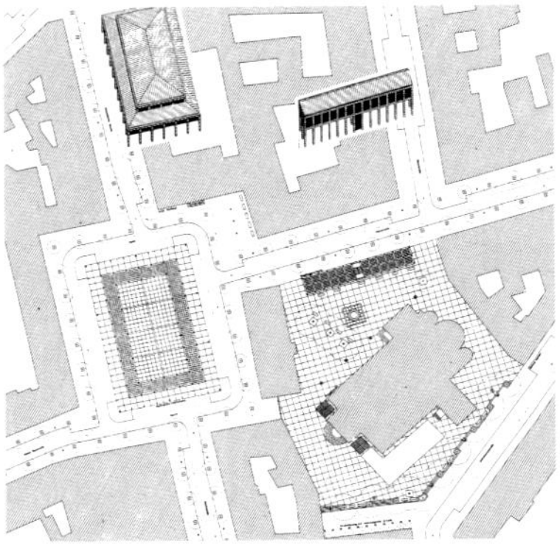

112
Design for Hotel Maritim Sassenhof
Cologne
1986
with M. Pitlach, J. Klose, T. Britz

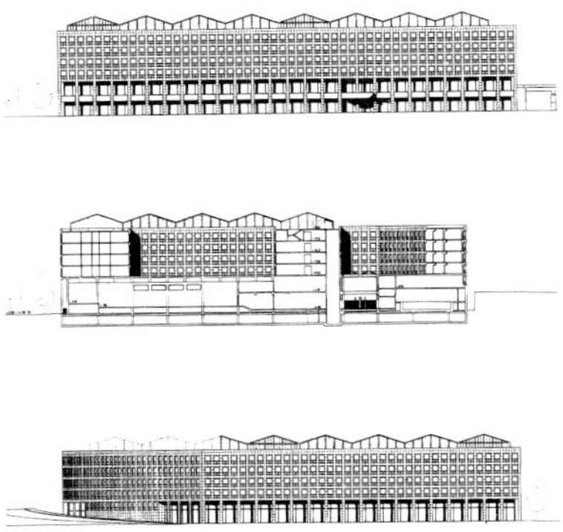

109
Feasibility Study for Transfer Center, Universität Dortmund
1986
with M. Pitlach, B. Taha, J. Nitsch, C. Nitsch, J. Klose

110
Competition Design for Cultural and Conference Center
Freiburg im Breisgau
1986
with M. Pitlach, U. Wiegmann, B. Taha

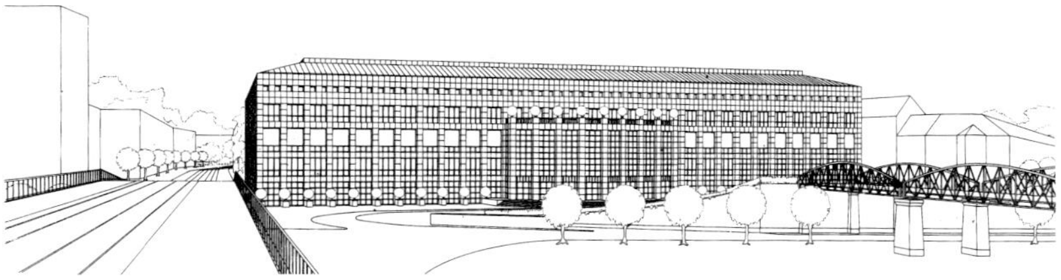

113
Competition Design for Stadtsparkasse
Mönchengladbach
1986
with M. Pitlach, U. Wiegmann

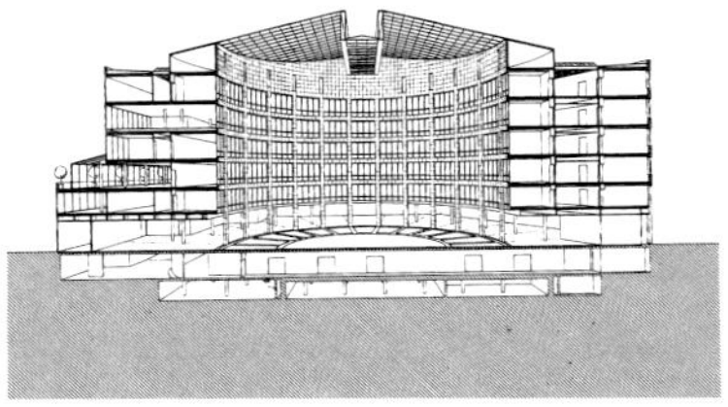

114
Feasibility Study for New Stadtsparkasse Building
Cologne
1986
with M. Pitlach, U. Wiegmann, J. Klose

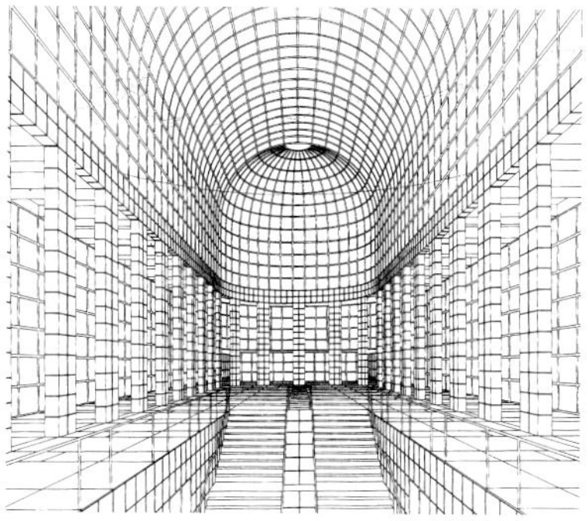

116
Competition Design for Media Center
Karlsruhe
1986
with W. A. Noebel, J. Schuster, B. Kraus, J. Schoyerer, M. Bräckerbohm

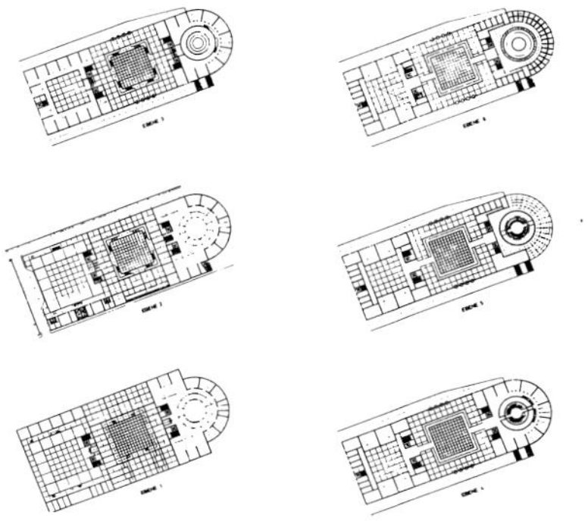

118
Competition Design for Lufthansa German Center
Peking (China)
1986
with M. Pitlach, U. Wiegmann, B. Trübenbach, J. Klose, B. Taha, K.-L. Dietzsch

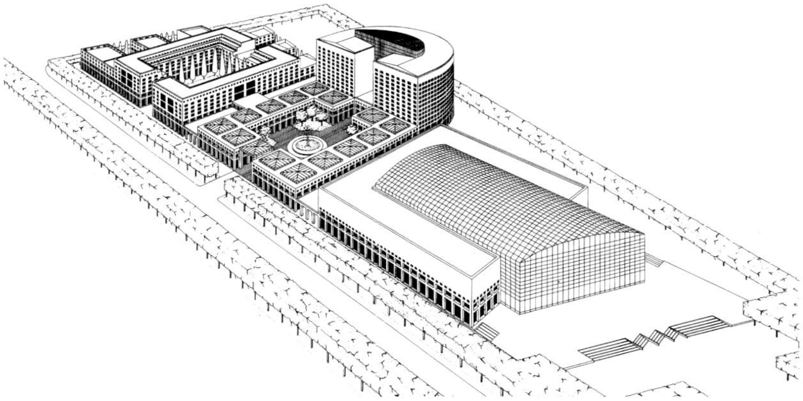

115
Competition Design for Kunstpalast
Düsseldorf
1986
with M. Pitlach, J. Klose, U. Wiegmann

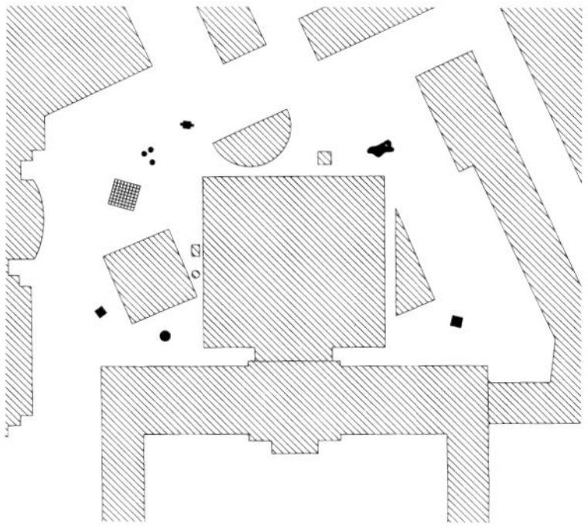

117
Competition Design for Administrative Building, Adolph Würth GmbH
Künzelsau-Gaisbach
1986
with M. Pitlach, J. Klose, B. Taha

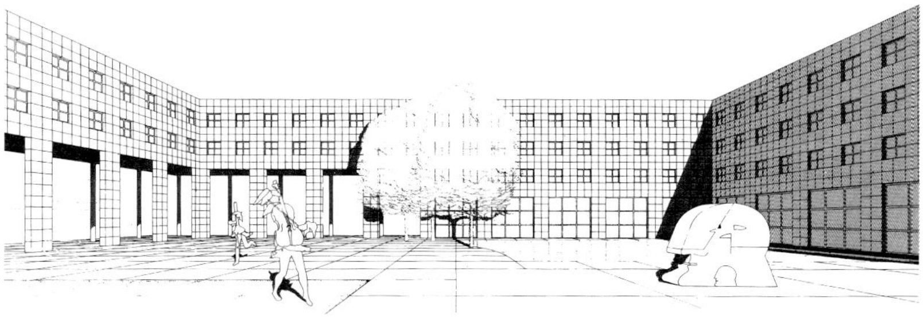

119
Competition Design for Pirelli-Bicocca
Milan (Italy)
1986
with M. Pitlach

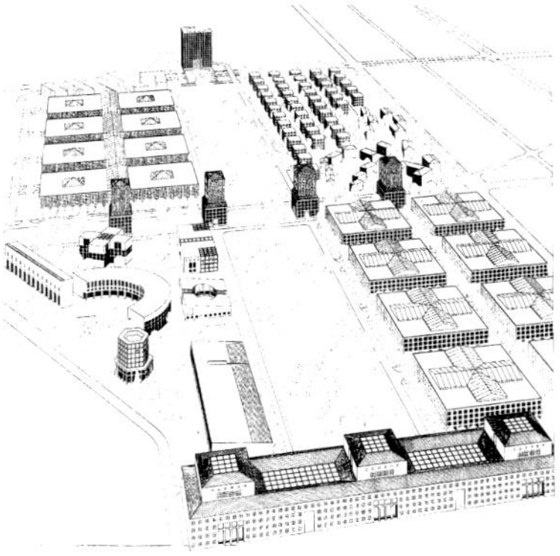

120
Max Hetzler Gallery and Apartment Building
Cologne
1986–1988
with K. L. Dietzsch, B. Taha, J. Klose

122
Design for Federal Supreme Court (Revision of Competition 1985 Design)
Karlsruhe
1987
with M. Pitlach, J. Klose, B. Taha

123
Design for Gallery Building
Marktplatz, Kornwestheim
1982
with J. Klose, J. de l'Or, B. Trübenbach, U. Wiegmann

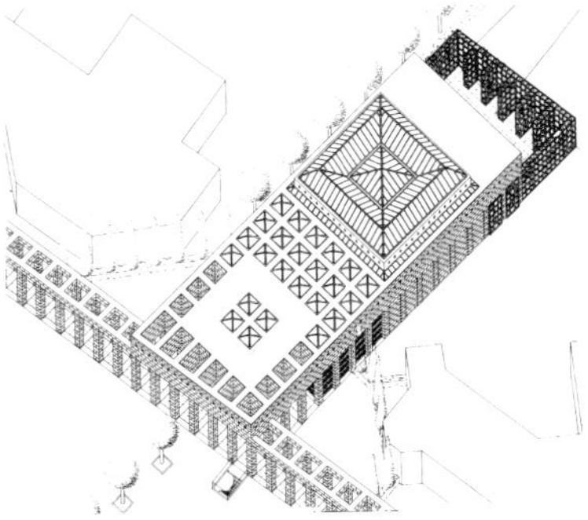

125
Design for Gallery Building
Marktplatz, Kornwestheim
1982
with J. Klose, J. de l'Or, B. Trübenbach, U. Wiegmann

121
Competition Design for New State Employment Office
Oldenburg
1987
with U. Wiegmann, K. Nierländer, J. Zadora

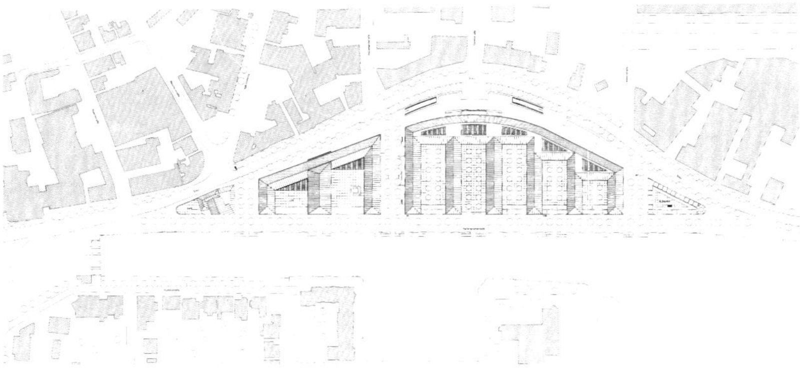

124
Design for Horten Administrative Building
Hannover
1987
with M. Pitlach, J. Klose

126
South Foyer, Via Mobile East for Trade Fair Complex
Frankfurt am Main
1987
with M. Dudler, J. Engel, J. Schuster, M. Bräckerbohm, B. Kraus

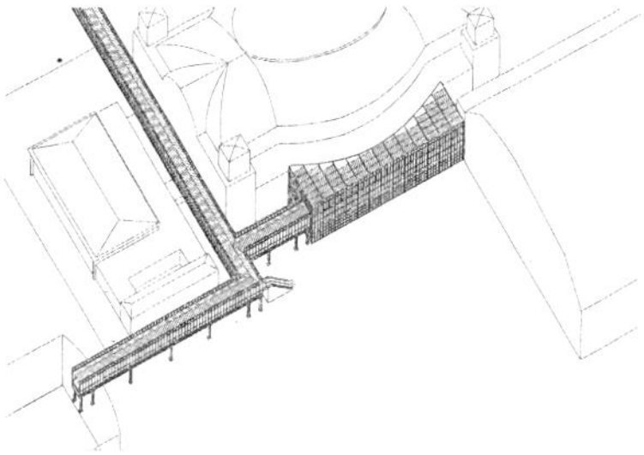

127
Trusthouse Forte – Ritters Parkhotel
Bad Homburg
1987
with J. Engel, J. Schuster, M. Bräckerbohm, C. Waser

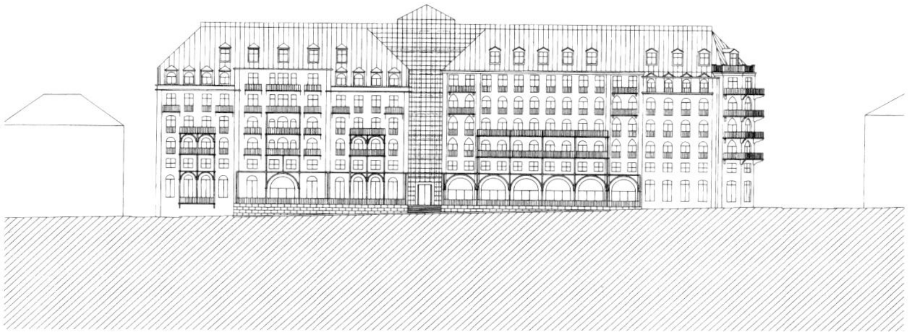

130
Design for Development of Eschborner Landstrasse (Feasibility Study)
Frankfurt am Main
1987
with J. Engel, M. Bräckerbohm

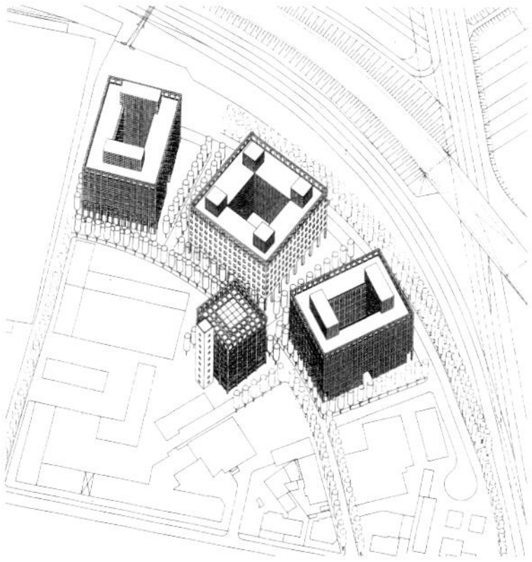

132
Design for Trade Fair Palace
Vienna (Austria)
1987
with M. Pitlach, J. Klose, J. de l'Or, U. Wiegmann, B. Trübenbach

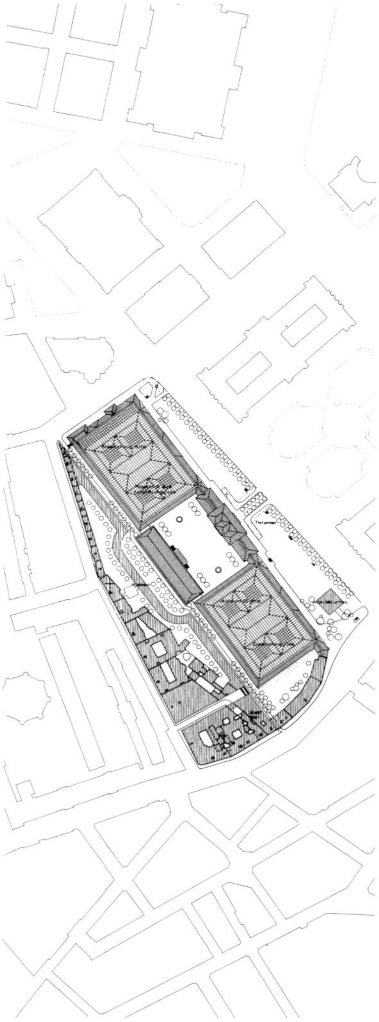

128
Design for Fair Grounds
Madrid (Spain)
1987
with J. Engel, R. C. v. Bennewitz, M. Bräckerbohm

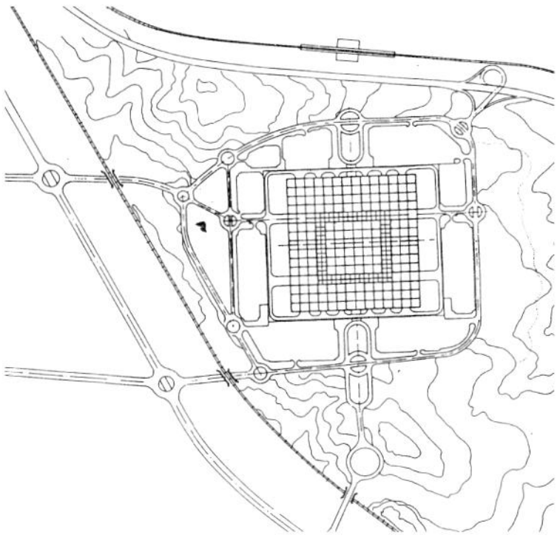

129
Competition Design for Facade of Hoechst Sales High-rise (Building C 660)
Frankfurt am Main
1987
with J. Engel, B. Kraus, M. Bräckerbohm, J. Schuster, U. Bartelt

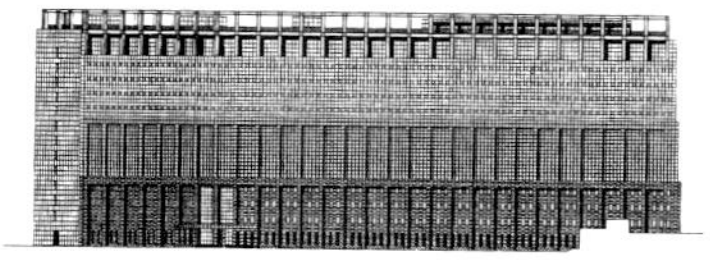

131
Design for Omega Bridge for Trade Fair Complex
Frankfurt am Main
1987
with J. Engel, M. Bräckerbohm, A. Hierholzer

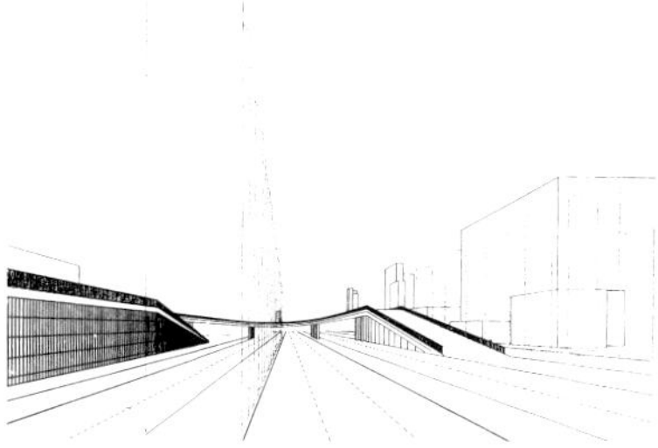

133
Competition Design for Deutsche Bank
Kurfürstendamm, Berlin
1987
with J. Engel, J. Schuster, M. Bräckerbohm, H. Hane

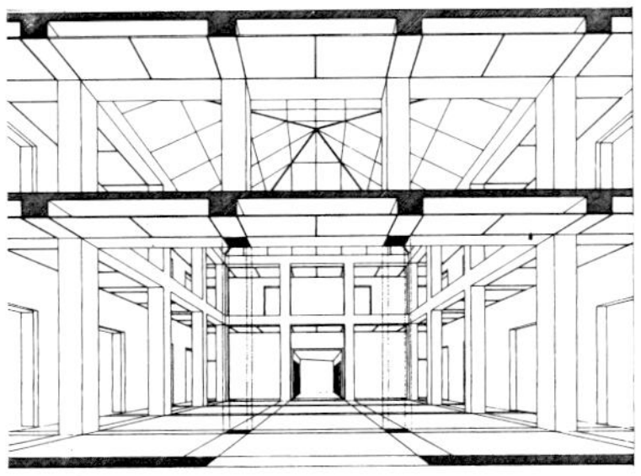

135
Feasibility Study for "Campanile"
Frankfurt am Main
1987
with U. Wiegmann, M. Pitlach, T. Britz, K.-L. Dietzsch, J. Klose, R. Bandus

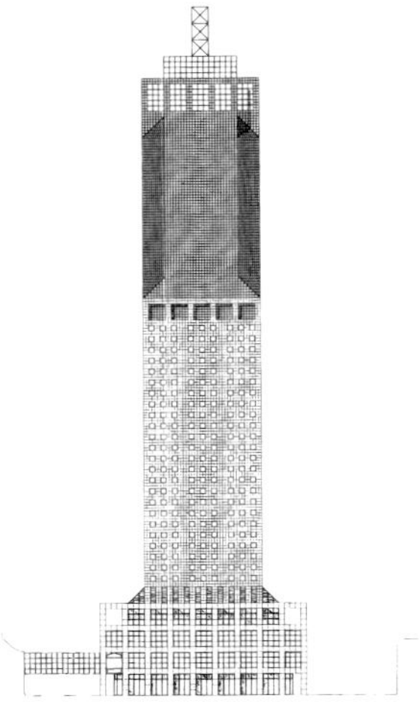

137
Feasibility Study for Kleiner Schlossplatz
Stuttgart
1987
with J. Klose, M. Pitlach, T. Britz

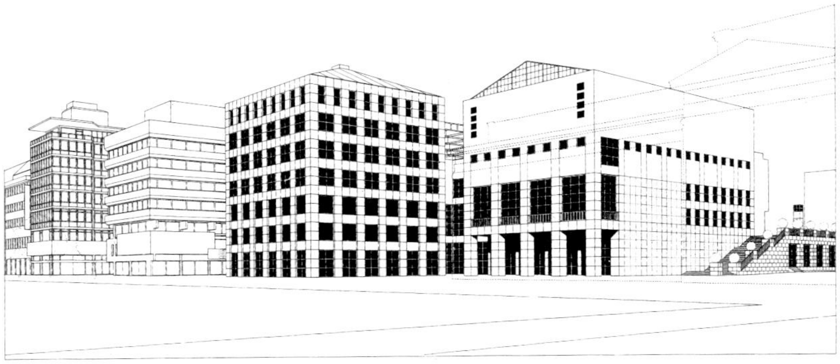

134
Urban Planning Competition for Media Park
Cologne
1987
with J. Klose, M. Pitlach

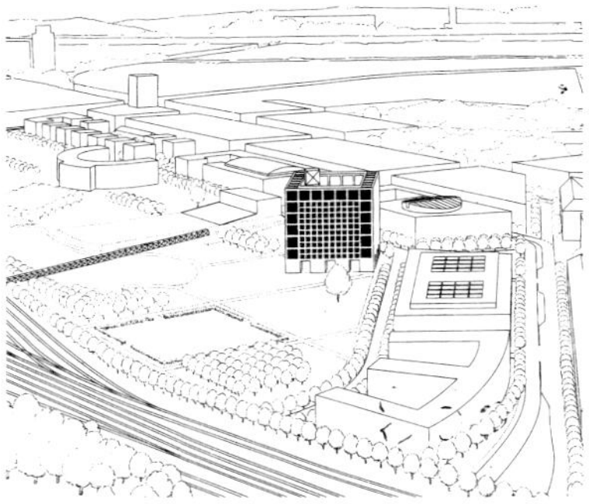

136
Competition Design for Residence of the German Ambassador (2nd Phase)
Washington D. C.
1987–1995
with J. Klose, A. Grond, M. Röhr, U. Wiegmann, B. Trübenbach, M. Pitlach, B. Taha, A. Hierholzer (planning); I. Schrader, P. Kretz, R. Sargiotti (execution)

138
Trade Fair Booth for Villeroy & Boch for Hall 9, Trade Fair Complex
Frankfurt am Main
1987–1989
with J. Engel, B. Kraus, M. Bräckerbohm, C. Waser

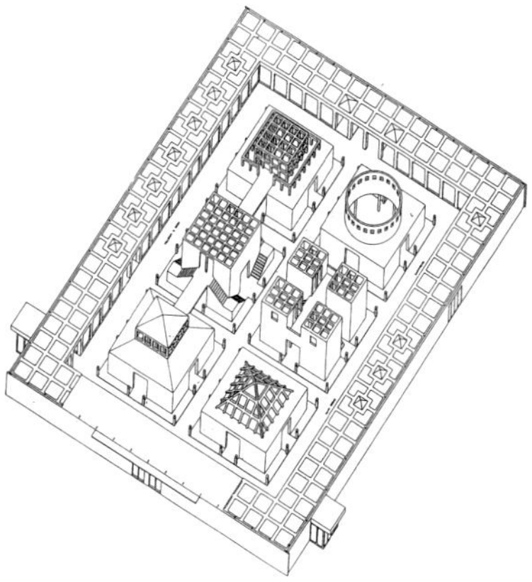

139
Competition Entry for Redesign of Maximilianstrasse – Cathedral Square
Speyer
1988
with K. L. Dietzsch, B. Taha, B. Meyer, T. Dietzsch, S. Moser

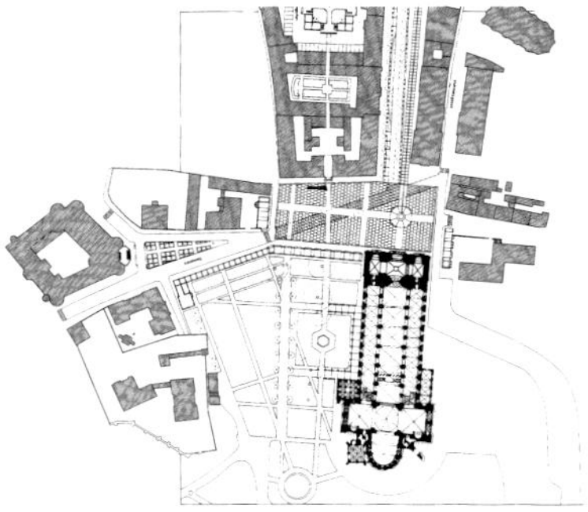

140
Competition Design for Deutsches Historisches Museum
Berlin
1988
with J. Klose, B. Trübenbach, M. Pitlach, U. Wiegmann, H. Hane

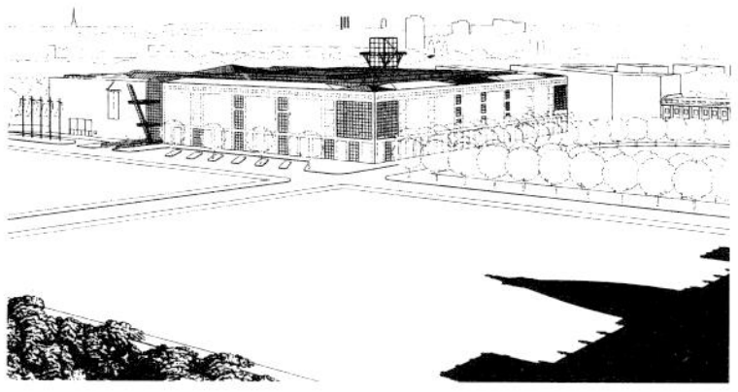

142
Redesign of Bayerische Hypotheken- und Wechselbank
Düsseldorf
1988
with K. L. Dietzsch, M. Pitlach, U. Wiegmann, B. Trübenbach, B. Taha, V. Busse, K. Ehm, A. Geitner, C. Henning, M. Röhr, D. Porsch, K. Steves

144
Designs for Fire Department
Frankfurt-Bornheim
1988
with J. Engel, M. Bräckerbohm, L. Busert

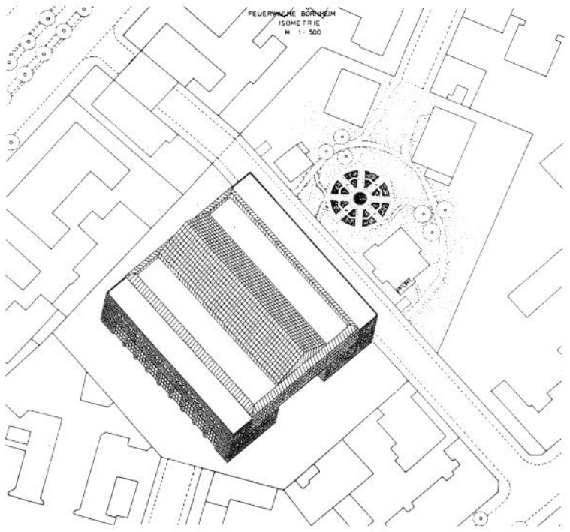

146
Competition Design for Kunsthalle (2nd Phase)
Düsseldorf
1988
with M. Pitlach, J. Klose, B. Trübenbach, U. Wiegmann

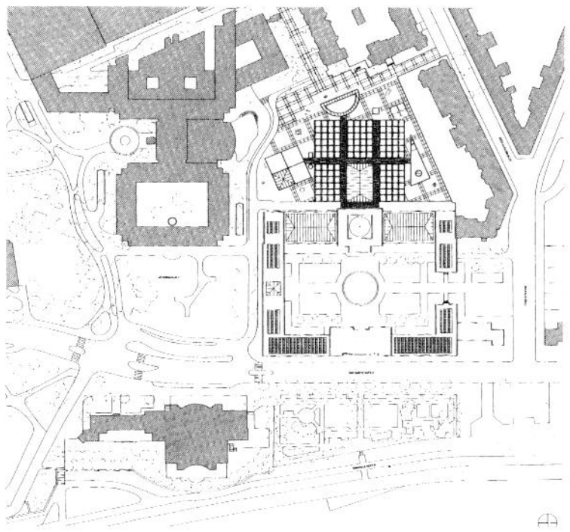

141
Design for the Milan Triennale: Fortezza de Basso, Florence
Milan (Italy)
1988
with M. Pitlach, W. A. Noebel, P. Schmidt

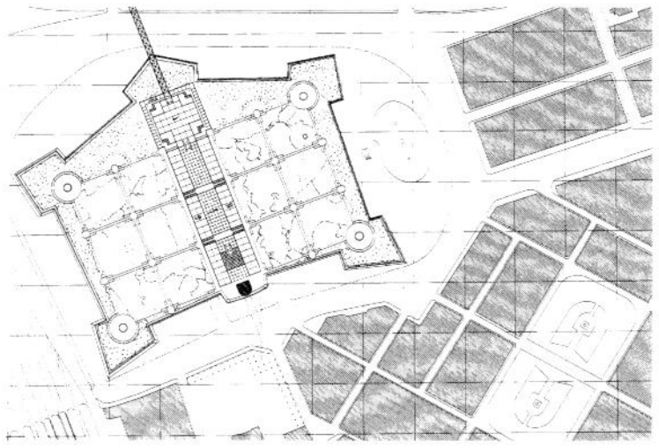

143
Competition Design for Deutsche Bank
Lörrach
1988
with J. Engel, H. Hane, P. Kretz, I. Eiben, B. Kraus, M. Bräckerbohm

145
GEW Thermal Plant
Cologne-Merheim
1988–1990
with J. Klose, J. Waack, K.-L. Dietzsch, A. Geitner,

147
Competition Design for Main University Grounds
Frankfurt am Main
1988
with M. Pitlach, J. Klose, B. Trübenbach, U. Wiegmann, K. L. Dietzsch

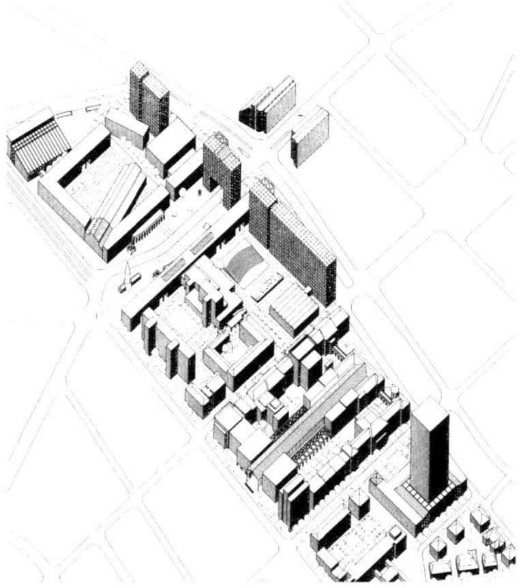

149
Design for Ikonenmuseum, Deutschordenshaus
Frankfurt am Main
1988
with J. Engel, H. Hane, J. Schuster, B. Kraus, M. Bräckerbohm

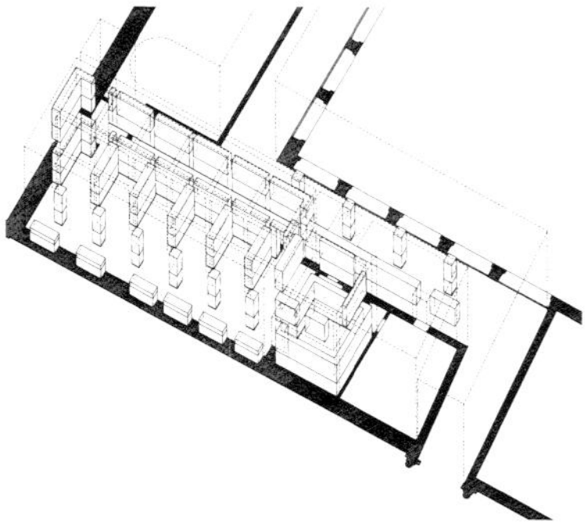

150
Competition Design for the Thermenmuseum with Roman Baths
Trier
1988–1996
with M. Croce, K. Steves, M. Röhr (design); K.-U. Lompa, J. Götz (execution)

152
Design for High-rise Building on Solmstrasse
Frankfurt am Main
1988, revised 1989
with W. A. Noebel, P. Diehl B. Taha, U. Wiegmann, K.-L. Dietzsch, A. Grond

148
Feasibility Study for International Airport Kansai
Osaka (Japan)
1988
with J. K. Engel, E. Balke, V. Busse, M. Chiaramonte, P. Diehl, A. Geitner

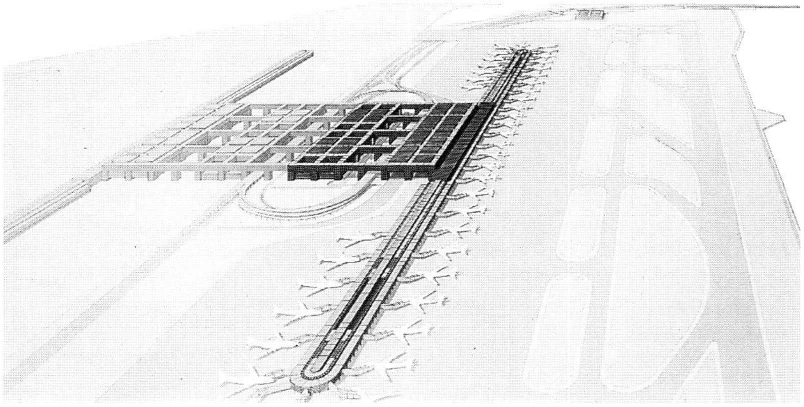

151
Competition Design for Depot Building and Forum Grounds of Johann Wolfgang Goethe-Universität (2nd Phase)
Frankfurt am Main
1988
with M. Croce, A. Grond, M. Pitlach, B. Taha

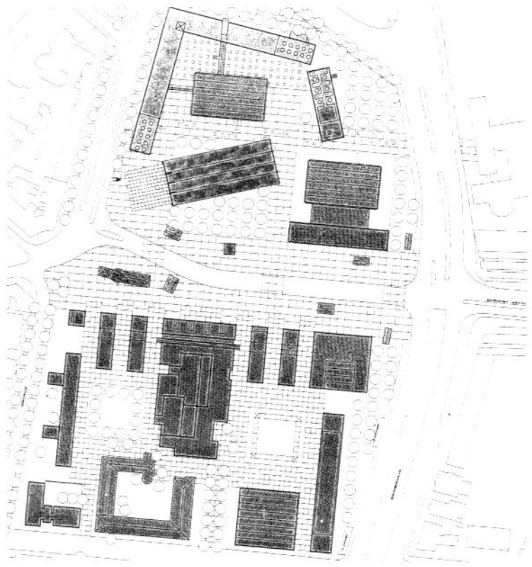

153
Feasibility Study for East Airport Terminal
Frankfurt am Main
1988
with J. K. Engel, E. Balke, V. Busse, M. Chiaramonte, P. Diehl, A. Geitner

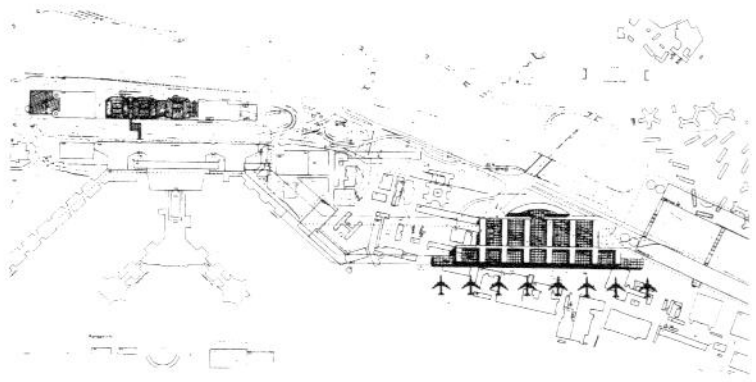

154
Bremen Institute for Industrial Technology and Applied Ergonomics (BIBA)
Technologiepark, Bremen
1988–1991
with J. Waack, J. Klose, A. Brauns, M. Pitlach, M. Croce, K. L. Dietzsch, Th. Meurer, A. Grond, U. Wiegmann, J. Waack, A. Marchel, B. Taha, C. Henning, A. Brauns

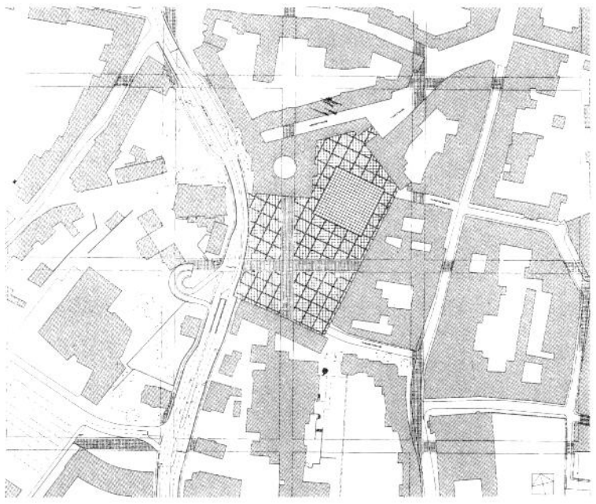

156
Competition Design for Piazza Matteotti (1st and 2nd Phases)
Siena (Italy)
1989
with W. A. Noebel, M. Bertolini, G. Bettini, M. Bräckerbohm, P. Diehl, H. Hane, H. Kleine-Kraneburg, P. Kretz, R. Sargiotti

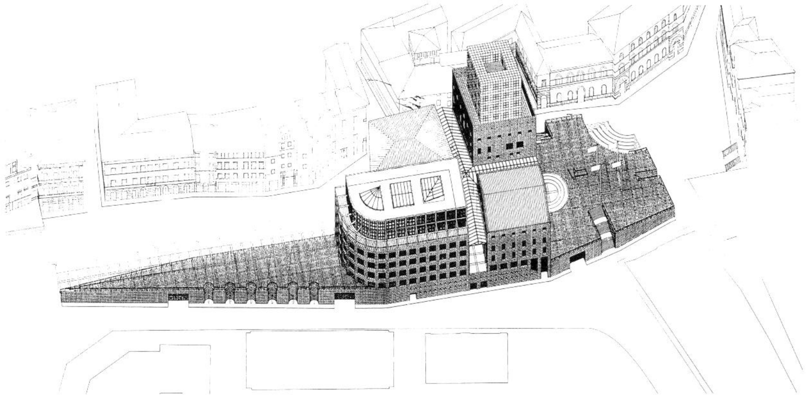

159
Design for East Depot
Frankfurt am Main
1989
with J. Engel, H. Hane, P. Kretz, W. A. Noebel, B. Kraus, I. Eiben, A. Becker-Bergemann

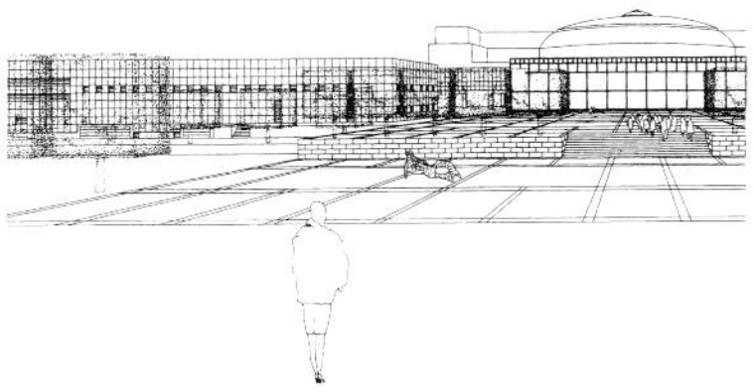

155
Bitz House, Galerie Kewenig
Cologne-Frechen
1989–1992
with U. Wiegmann, B. Trübenbach (execution and construction supervision)

157
Kubus-House (Library)
Quadrather Strasse, Cologne-Müngersdorf
1989–1990
with M. Croce, B. Grimm

158
Competition Design for Domestic Court, Expansion of Tempelhof/Kreuzberg District Court
Berlin-Kreuzberg
1989–1995
with M. Croce, K.-H. Winkens, C. Henning, A. Marchel, R. Thebrath (design); K.-H. Winkens, A. Balzereit, C. Euler, M. Skadborg (execution)

160
Design for Media Center
Kaistrasse, Düsseldorf
1989
with V. Busse, K. Ehm, A. Geitner

161
Expansion of Gatehouse, Central Terminal of Trade Fair Complex
Frankfurt am Main
1989–1997
with I. Schrader, R. Sargiotti, H. Hane, M. Bräckerbohm, R. Fein, G. Lohmann, J. Sieber, Engel

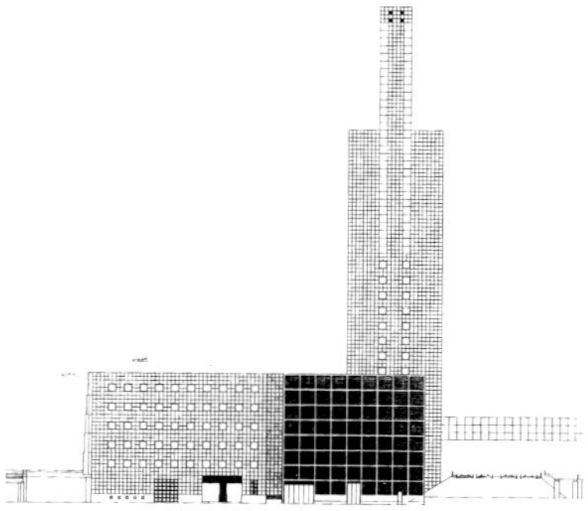

162
Competition Design for Römermuseum
Haltern
1989
with J. Klose, M. Pitlach

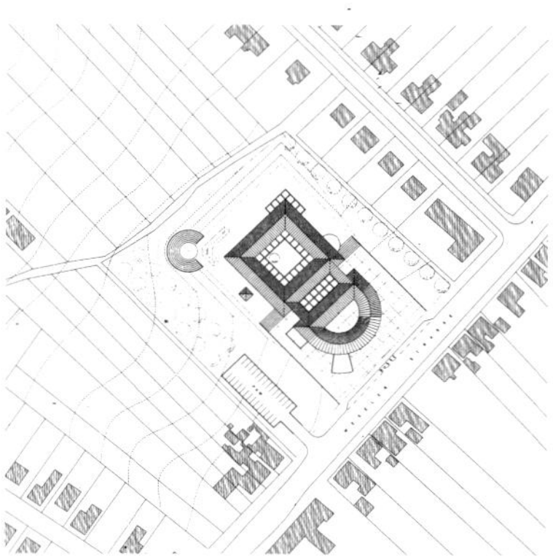

163
Competition Design for Deutsche Bundesbank
Frankfurt am Main
1989
with M. Croce, K. Steves, A. Geitner, V. Busse, J. Waack, A. Grond, P. Diehl

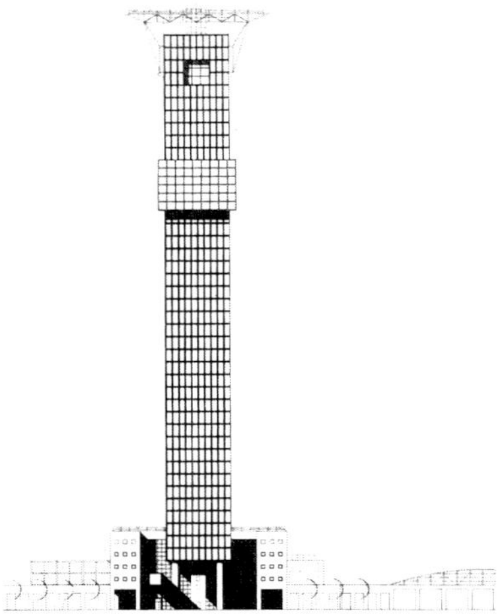

164
Competition Design for Court of Human Rights
Strasbourg (France)
1989
with M. Croce, A. Grond, M. Röhr, B. Taha, W. A. Noebel, K. Steves, P. Diehl, M. Bräckerbohm, H. Hane, P. Kretz

165
Competition Design for International Maritime Court
Hamburg
1989
with M. Croce, A. Grond, M. Röhr, C. Henning, B. Taha

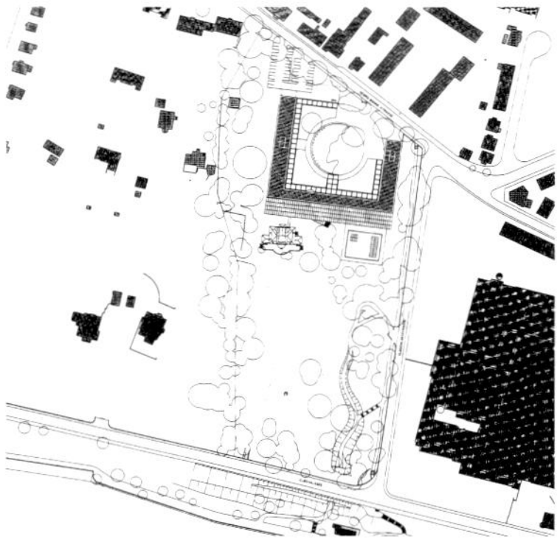

166
Competition Design for Mercedes Building
Frankfurt am Main
1989
with M. Croce, P. Diehl, M. Röhr, K. Steves, K. Ehm

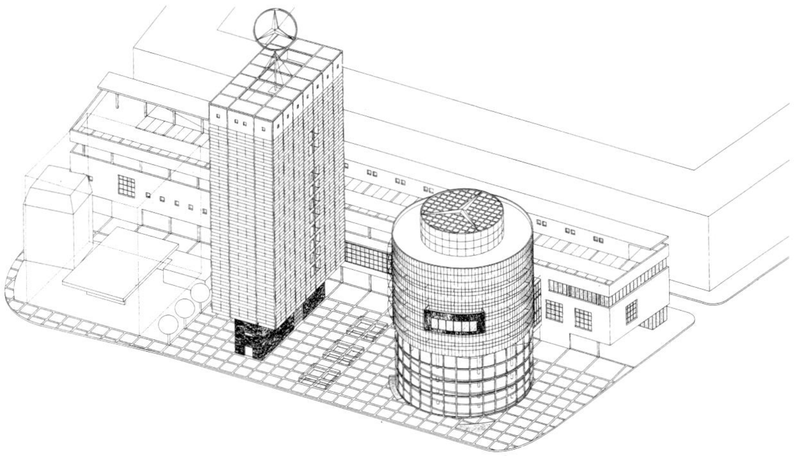

167
Design for Urban Planning Workshop for Former West Krupp Grounds
Bochum
1989
with A. Geitner, V. Busse, P. Diehl, K. Steves

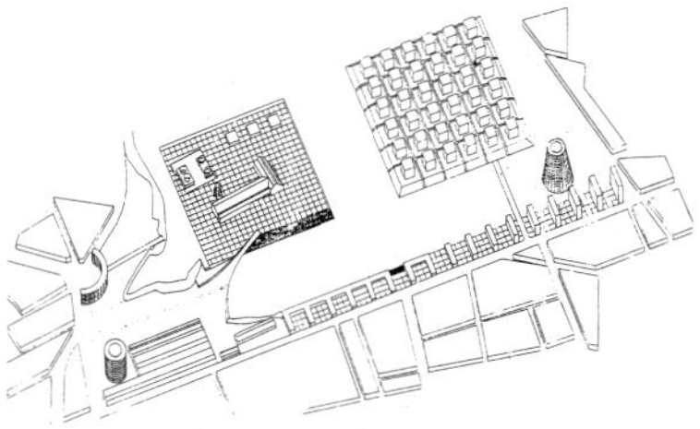

168
Design for Randwijk Noord
Maastricht (Netherlands)
1989
with J. von Brandt

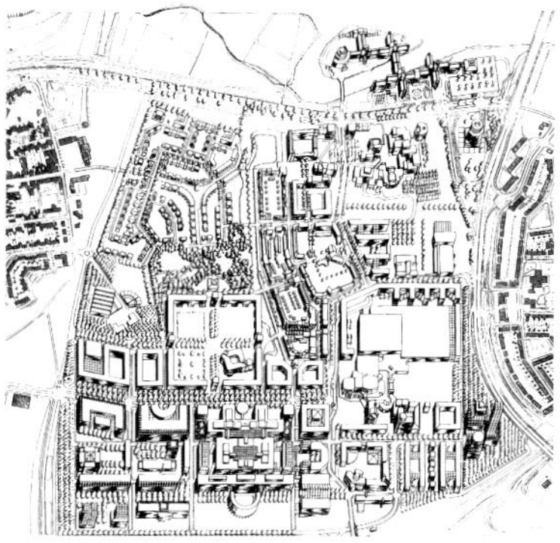

170
Competition Design for Hypolux
Kirchberg
1989
with V. Busse, A. Geitner, K.-H. Winkens

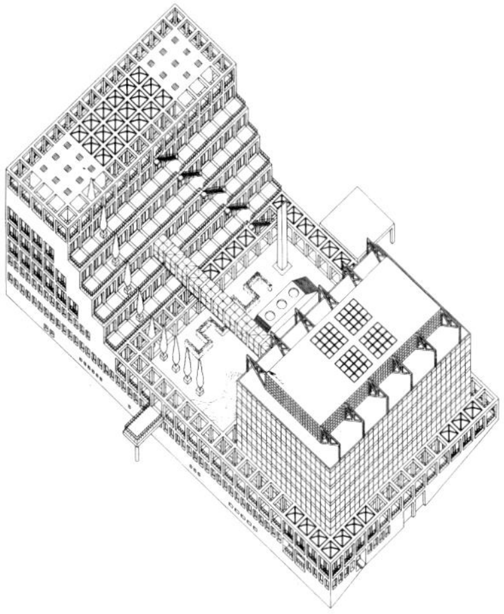

172
Competition Design for Hamburger Bahnhof (Museum für Gegenwartskunst)
Berlin
1989
with D. Alten, M. Croce

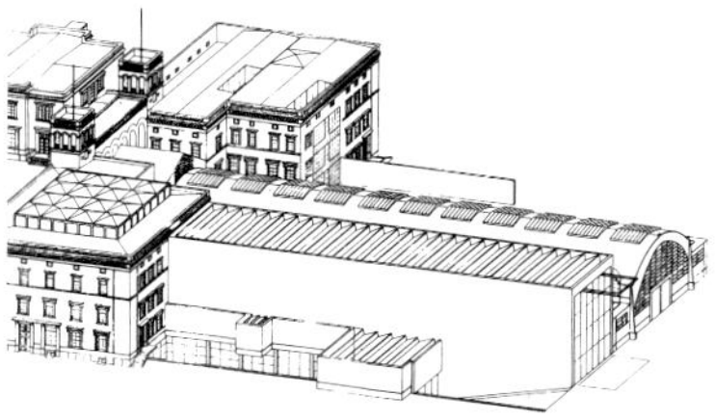

174
Competition Design for State Employment Office
Bremerhaven
1989
with M. Croce, M. Röhr, C. Henning, B. Taha

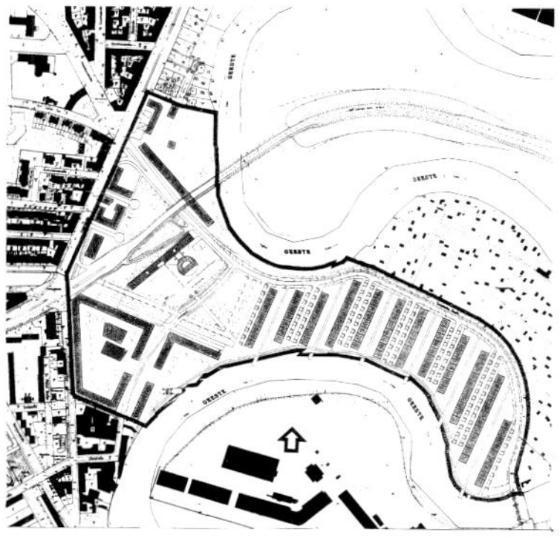

169
Design for Bauforum
Hamburg
1989
with V. Busse, A. Geitner, K.-H. Winkens

171
Competition Design for Horum Airport
Oslo (Norway)
1989
with Architektengruppe K 4, W. A. Noebel, P. Diehl, H. Hane, G. Priebe

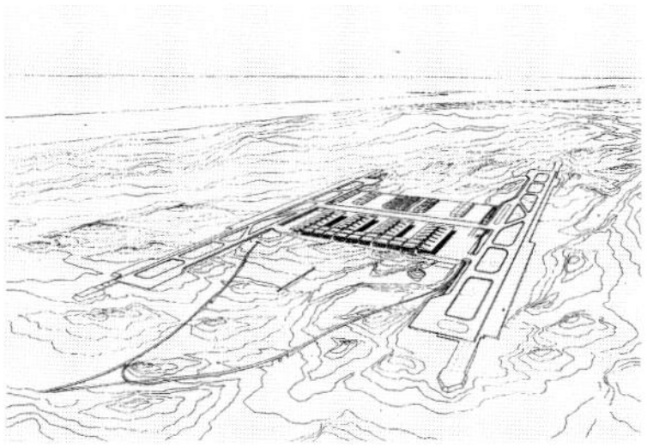

173
Design for Eumetsat
Darmstadt
1989
with W. A. Noebel, M. Bräckerbohm, P. Diehl, H. Kleine-Kraneburg, P. Kretz, R. Sargiotti

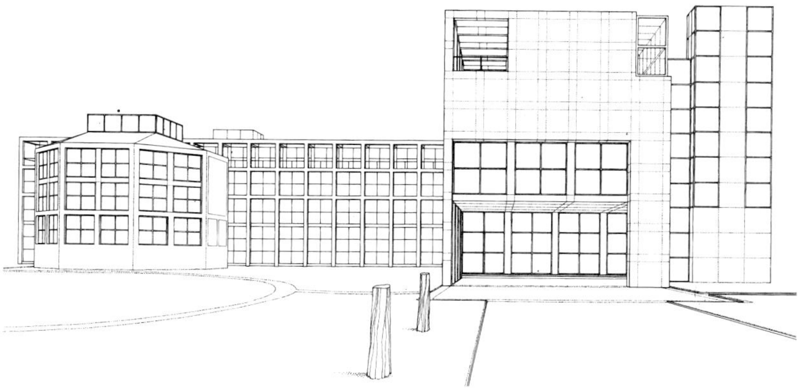

175
Feasibility Study for AMK Trade Fair Grounds
Berlin
1989
with W. A. Noebel, M. Bräckerbohm, P. Diehl, H. Hane, H. Kleine-Kraneburg, P. Kretz, B. Kraus, R. Sargiotti

178
PTS Workshop
Frankfurt am Main
1990–1994
with P. Diehl, I. Schrader, W. Kohne, H. Hane, S. Heinzl

180
Feasibility Study for Merowinger Platz
Düsseldorf
1990
with A. Geitner, M. Röhr, K. Steves

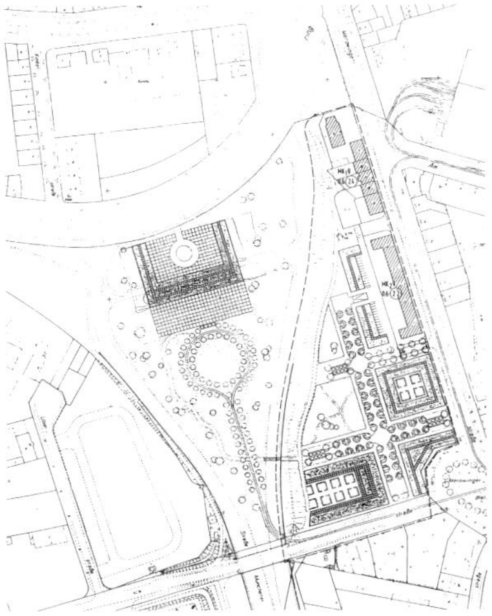

176
Jeromin House
Königswinter
1989–1992
with K. Steves, U. Wiegmann (execution: Weigmann + Trübenbach, Cologne)

177
Exhibition Hall for Galerie Hetzler
Cologne
1990
with K. Steves

179
Residential, Office, and Commercial Building
Eschersheimer Landstrasse, Frankfurt am Main
1989–1990
with P. Diehl, H. Kleine-Kraneburg

181
Competition Design for Haus der Geschichte Baden-Württemberg
Stuttgart
1990
with M. Croce, M. Röhr, K. Steves, D. Porsch

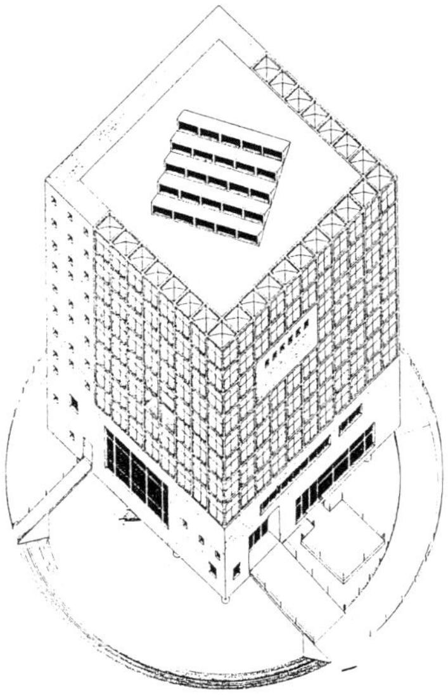

182
Design for ERC-Zentrale
Waterschei-Hasselt
1990
with W. A. Noebel,
M. Bräckerbohm, P. Diehl,
H. Kleine-Kraneburg, R. Sargiotti,
A. Stock

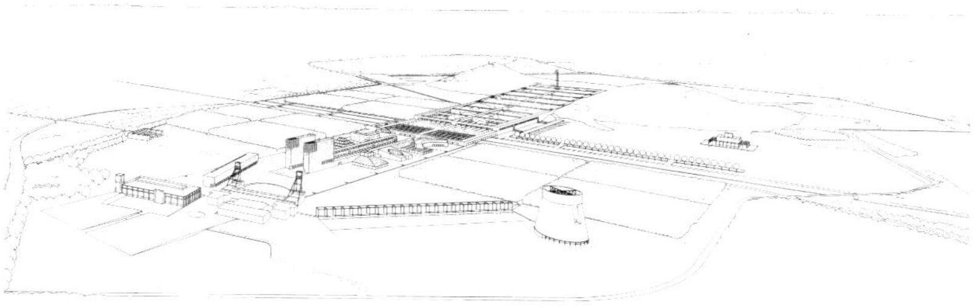

184
Feasibility Study for Hohenacker Commercial District
Pforzheim
1990
with W. A. Noebel,
M. Bräckerbohm, P. Diehl,
H. Hane, H. Kleine-Kraneburg,
P. Kretz

186
Feasibility Study for Schokoladenmuseum
Cologne
1990
with M. Röhr, M. Croce,
A. Geitner, Eun Young Yi

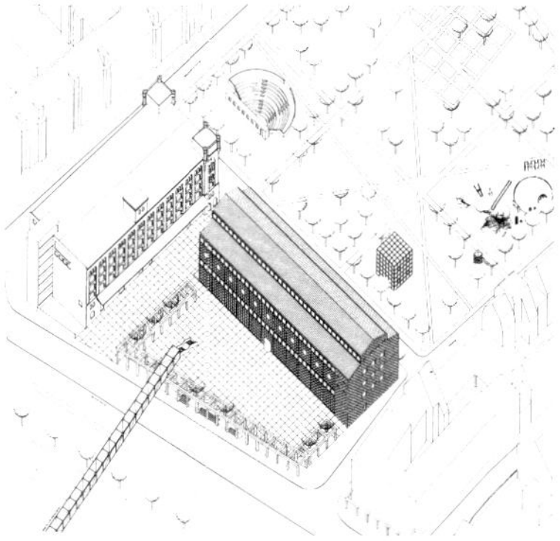

183
Competition Design for Expansion South Trade Fair Complex, Hall A
Berlin
1990–1999
with W. A. Noebel,
P. Diehl, M. Bräckerbohm, H. Hane,
H. Kleine-Kraneburg, P. Kretz,
R. Sargiotti, U. Schröder, A. Stock,
M. Biedermann; K.-H. Winkens,
J. Lenschow,
P. Schmiedgen, P. Wermund,
C. A. Pauly; C. McCarthy, J. Rogler,
W. T. Manarelli, M. Ewerhardt,
I. May, P. Panter, L. Ocanto, F.
Bertossi, T. Möhlendick, J. Westphal,
S. Becker, N. Brockenhuis-Schack,
D. Koralek, M. Pepper, C. Brockenhuis-Schack, H. Günther, A.
Würdig, M. Yalcin, R. C. Wingrove,
J. Bacus, B. Thiele, W. van der Bel,
M. Lewis, J. Nillesen

185
Design for Trade Fair Palace
Vienna (Austria)
1990
with W. A. Noebel, P. Diehl,
H. Hane, H. Kleine-Kraneburg,
P. Kretz, R. Sargiotti, U. Schröder,
A. Stock, C. Gensch

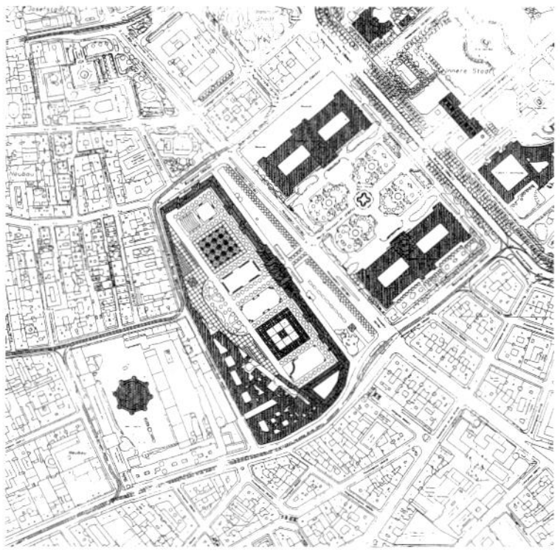

187
Competition Design for Palazzo del Cinema
Lido di Venezia (Italy)
1990
with W. A. Noebel, P. Diehl,
H. Hane, H. Kleine-Kraneburg,
P. Kretz, K. Lehmann, R. Sargiotti,
M. Biedermann, C. Gensch

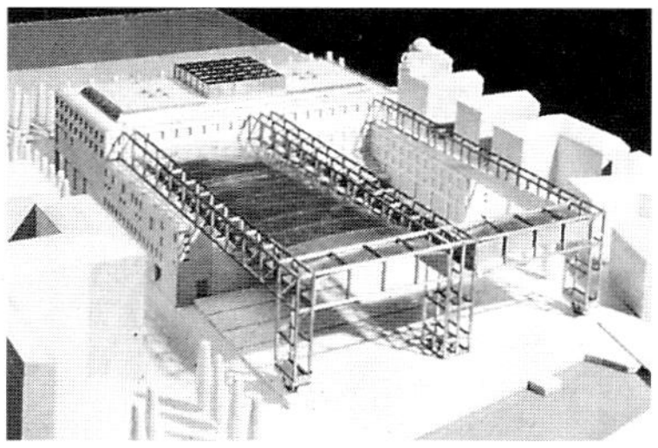

188
Competition Design for Innovation Center
Karlsruhe
1990
with L. Baumewerd

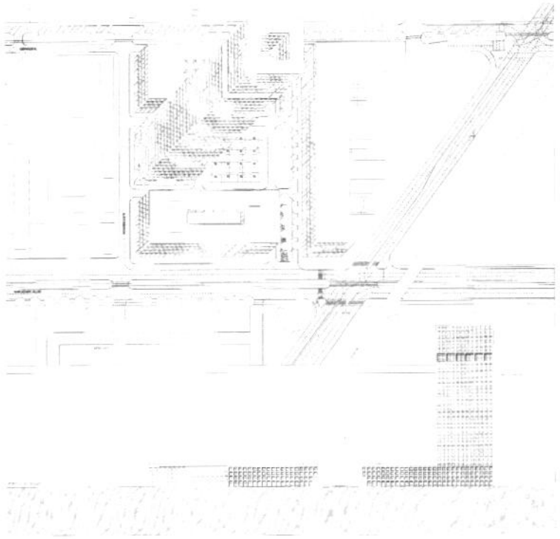

190
Expansion of Hall 10 and of Trade Fair Complex
Frankfurt am Main
1990–1993
with P. Diehl, I. Schrader, M. Winkelmann, M. Gruber, M. Bräckerbohm, B. Kraus, A. Resch

191
Berlin Tomorrow—The New Berlin
1990
with V. Busse, M. Croce, A. Geitner, W. Noebel, M. Röhr, K.-H. Winkens

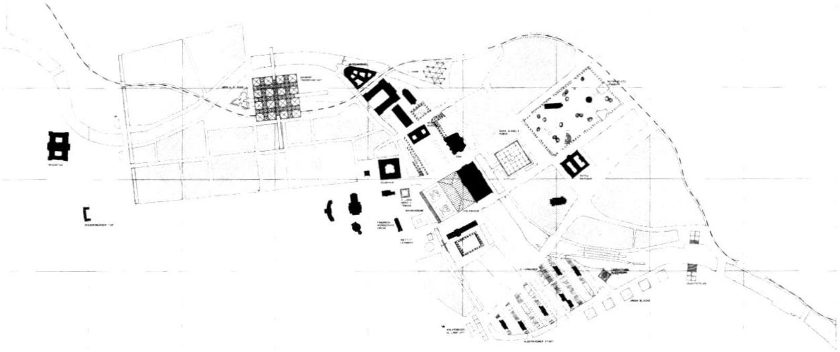

189
Federal Prosecutor's Office
Karlsruhe
1990–1998
with K.-U. Lompa, F. Wieschemann, G. Ringelhan, H. Kleine-Kraneburg, M. Gruber
B. Meyer (construction supervision)

192
Competition Design for Herz-Center
Heidelberg
1990
with P. Diehl, H. Hane, H. Kleine-Kraneburg, P. Kretz, R. Sargiotti, I. Schrader, M. Biedermann, J. Heemskerk
192

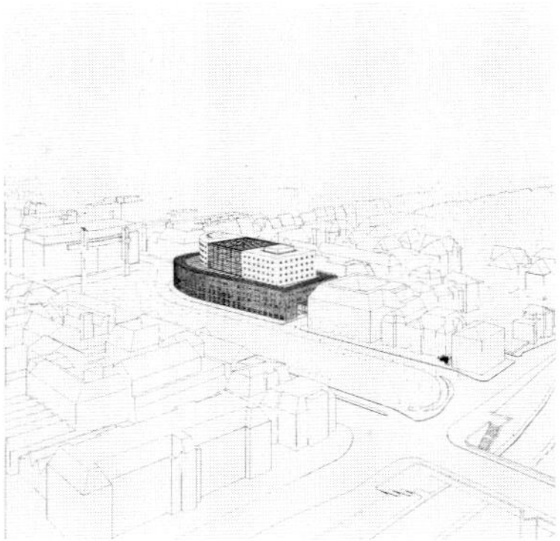

193
Competition Design for Trade Fair Grounds
Leipzig
1990
with W. A. Noebel, L. Ocanto

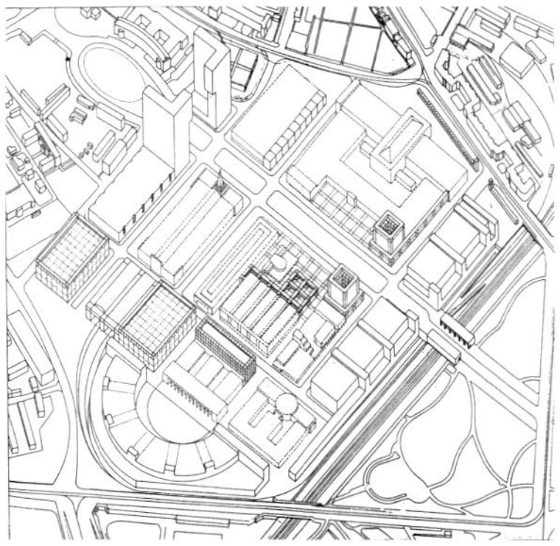

194
Competition Design for Office Building above Terminal 1
Frankfurt am Main
1990
with P. Diehl, I. Schrader, R. Sargiotti, H. Hane

196
Competition Design for Friedrichstadt-Passagen, Block 205
Berlin, 1991–1995
with B. Baumewerd, L. Baumewerd, A Brauns, V. Busse, A. Geitner, T. Röhr, R. Sargiotti, M. Wagner, K.-H. Winkens; K.-H. Winkens, S. Klatt, R. Beyer, H. Daiber, A. Leonhardt, T. Scheel, B. Schindler, T. Trevisan, M. Weiser (execution)

198
Competition Design for Olympia-Arena
Berlin
1991
with A. Balzereit, B. Baumewerd, L. Baumewerd, S. Chung-Klatte, J. Götz, S. Klatt, J. Lenschow, U. Müller, J. Sieber, D. Snellgrove, T. Treversian

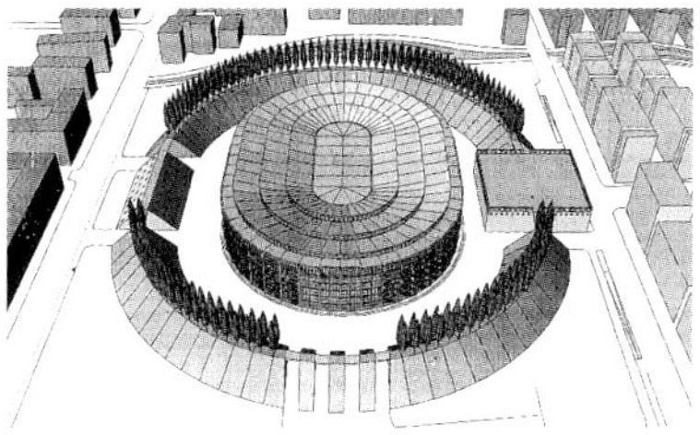

200
Competititon Design for City Portal Buildings
Frankfurt am Main
1991
with S. Vieths, B. Baumewerd, L. Baumewerd, K.-U. Lompa, M. Müller, A. Steudel

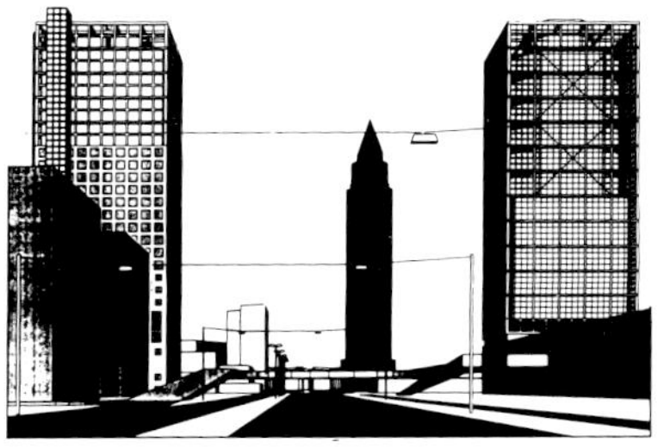

195
Design for Fiszman Office Building
Breitlacherstrasse, Frankfurt am Main
1990
with J. Engel, M. Bräckerbohm, P. Diehl, P. Kretz, I. Schrader

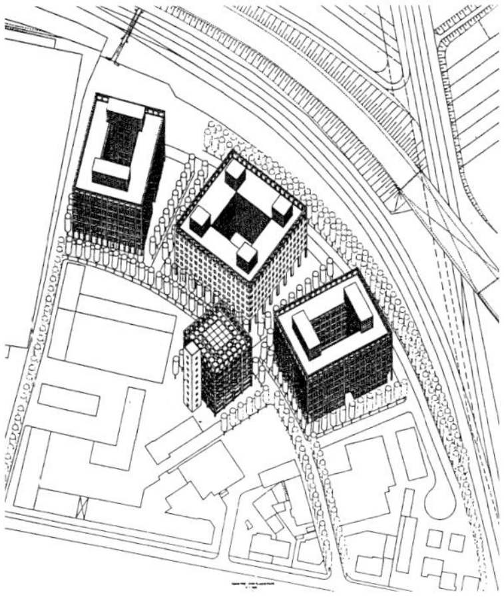

197
Competition Design for Potsdamer/Leipziger Platz
Berlin
1991, 1992
with S. Vieths, V. Busse, A. Geitner, J. Nillesen, L. Baumewerd, M. Müller, K. Schulz, T. Duda

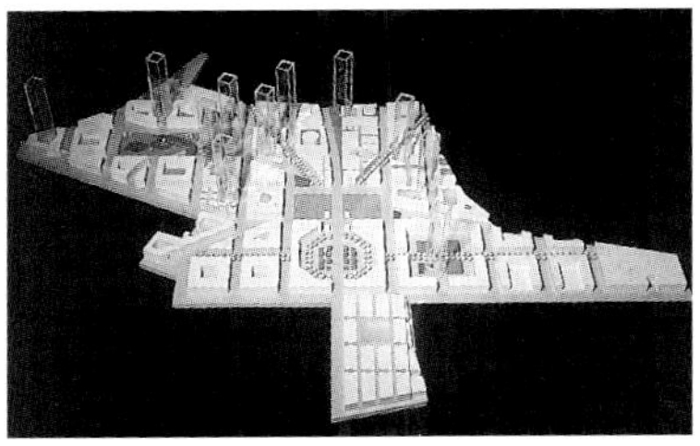

199
Competition Design for High-rise at Landtag
Düsseldorf
1991
with V. Busse, S. Vieths, L. Baumewerd, B. Baumewerd

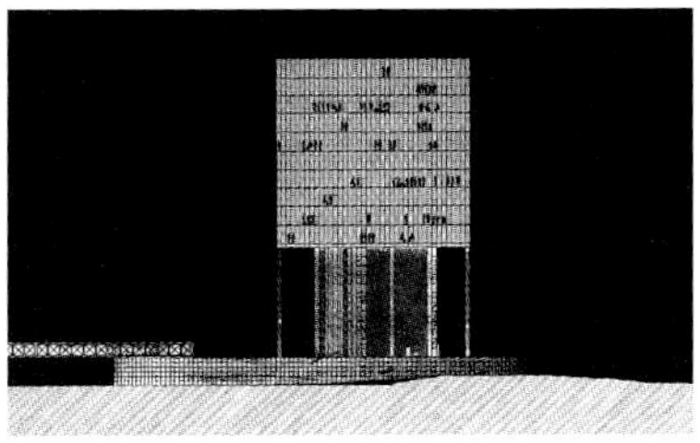

201
High-rise Project for Twin Towers
Hamburg
1991
with S. Vieths, B. Baumewerd

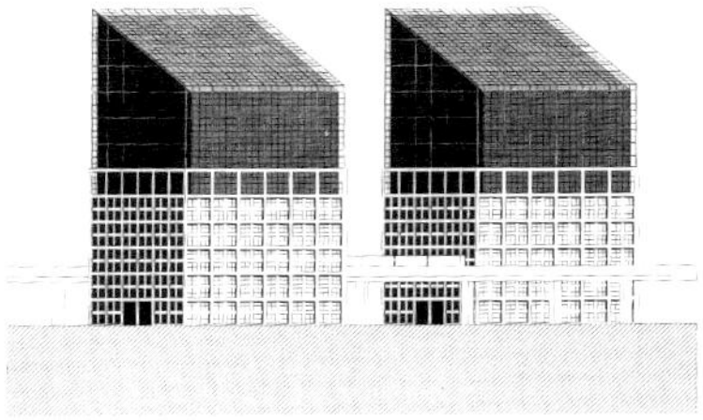

202
Feasibility Study for Sophiecenter
Eisenach
1991
with S. Vieths, B. Baumewerd, S. Chung-Klatte

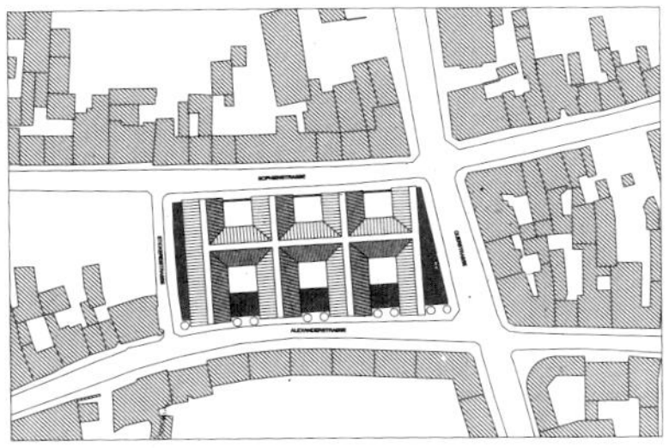

203
Competition Design for Radio Broadcaster Westdeutscher Rundfunk (WDR)
Cologne
1991
with K.-U. Lompa

204
St. Peter
Cologne
1991
with L. Baumewerd

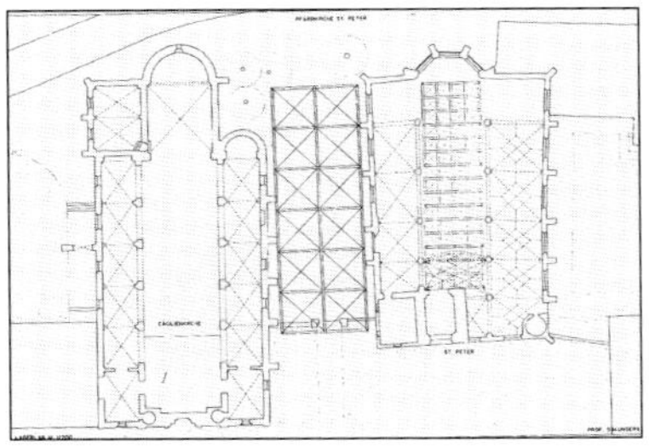

205
Office and Commercial Buildings Verband Kommunaler Unternehmen (Association of Local Enterprises; VKU)
Cologne
1991–1994
with K.-U. Lompa, I. Schweers, P. Vernin, J. Sieber, S. Chung-Klatte, L. Baumewerd

206
Johannishaus
Cologne
1991–1994
with A. Bauns, D. Dimster, E. Ehm, C. Henning, J. Nillesen, A. Steudel, P. Vernin, S. Vieths

207
Office and School Building
Magnusstrasse, Cologne
1991
with J. Götz, M. Laudert, R. Fein, K. Ehm, L. Baumewerd, P. Vernin, B. Baumewerd, D. Dimster, A. Steudel

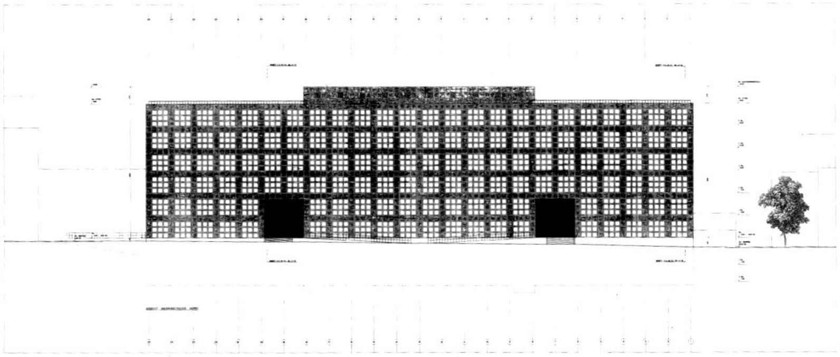

208
Design for a High-rise Building (Urban Development Master Plan)
Neuss-Hammfeld
1991
with L. Baumewerd, A. Geitner, V. Busse, E. Young Yi

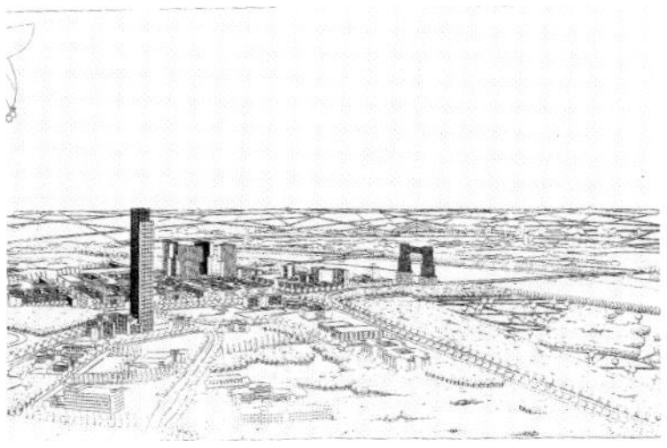

209
Competition Design for City Hall
Dessau
1991
with S. Vieths, B. Baumewerd,
K.-H. Winkens, S. Chung

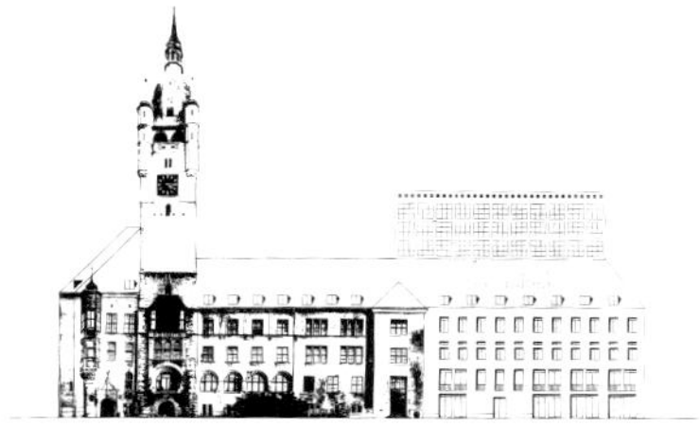

210
Competition Design for Daimler-Benz, Potsdamer Platz
Berlin
1992
with S. Vieths,
B. Baumewerd, L. Baumewerd,
A. Brauns, V. Diekmann, K. Ehm,
J. Götz, K.-U. Lompa, G. Malat,
J. Martini, J. Nillesen, I. Schweers,
J. Sieber, P. Vernin, F. Wieschemann

211
Competition Design for Max-Planck-Institut
Bremen
1992
with V. Busse

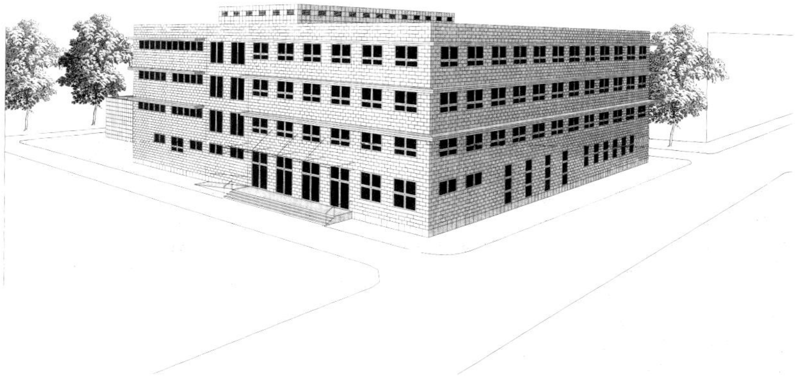

212
Feasibility Study for Hotel Building on the Banks of the Saar
Merzig
1992
with S. Vieths, B. Baumewerd,
S. Chung-Klatte

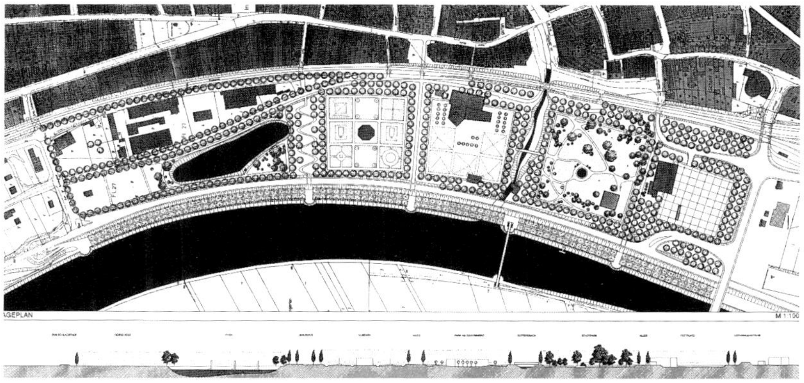

213
Feasibility Study for Urban Development Master Plan
Heerlen (Netherlands)
1992
with J. Nillesen, J. v. Brandt

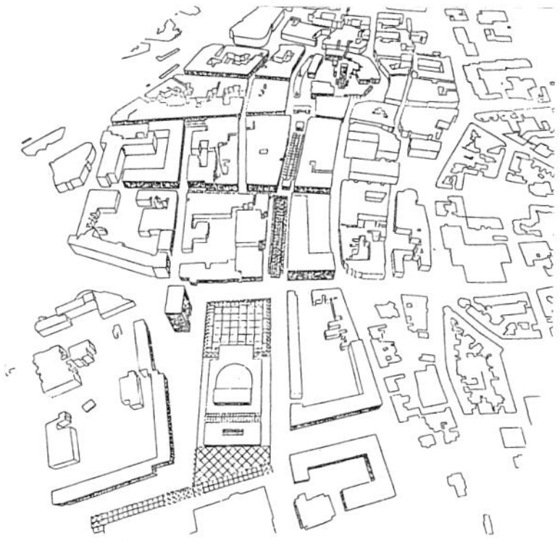

214
Competition Design for Expo 2000
Hannover
1992
with S. Vieths, H. Martini,
F. Wieschemann, L. Baumewerd,
V. Diekmann, H. Gietmann,
J. Götz

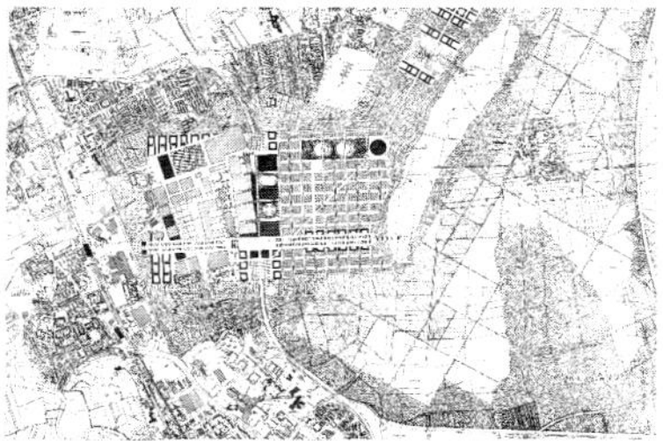

215
Competition Design for Office and Commercial Complex
Oskar-Jäger-Strasse, Cologne
1992
with S. Vieths, L. Baumewerd, J. Götz, J. Martini, K. Schultz

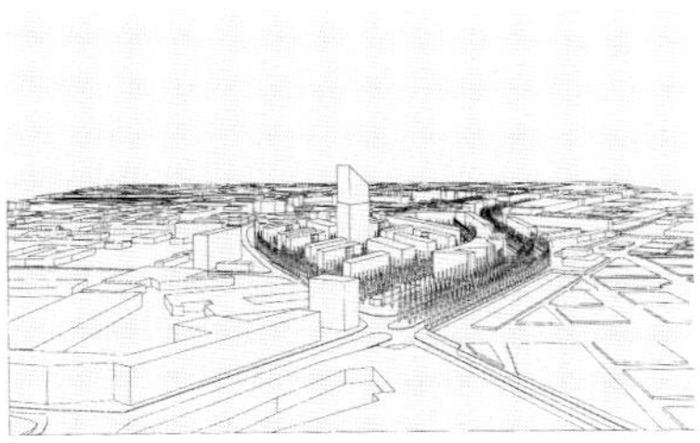

216
Feasibility Study for Bosch Buildings
Frankfurt am Main
1992
with S. Vieths, I. Schrader

217
Competition Design for Nord-Süd-Fahrt
Cologne
1992
with S. Vieths, F. Wieschemann, L. Baumewerd, J. Götz, J. Sieber

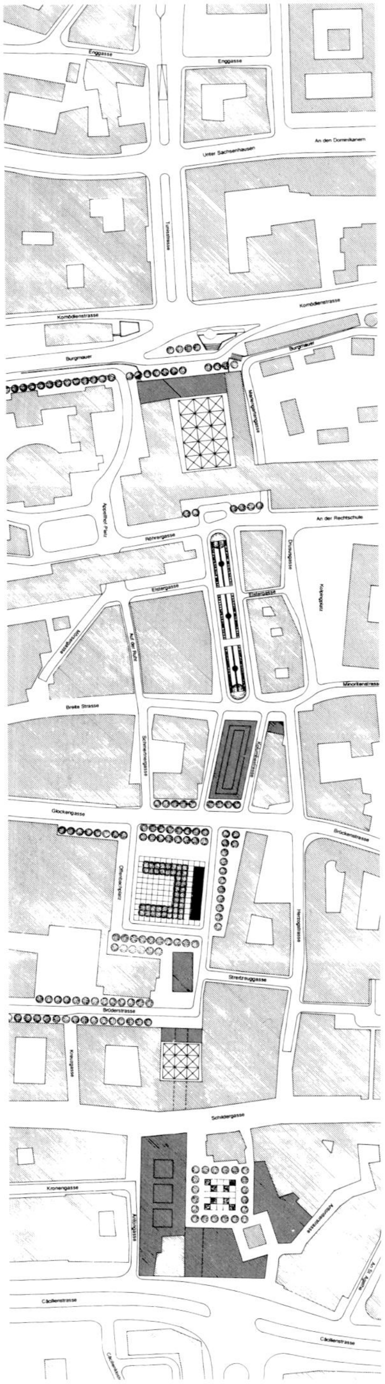

218
Competition Design for Urban Planning of KHD Euroforum, Musical Theater
Cologne
1992
with S. Vieths, F. Wieschemann, D. Dimster, L. Baumewerd, J. Götz, J. Sieber, P. Vernin, A. Brauns, K.-U. Lompa

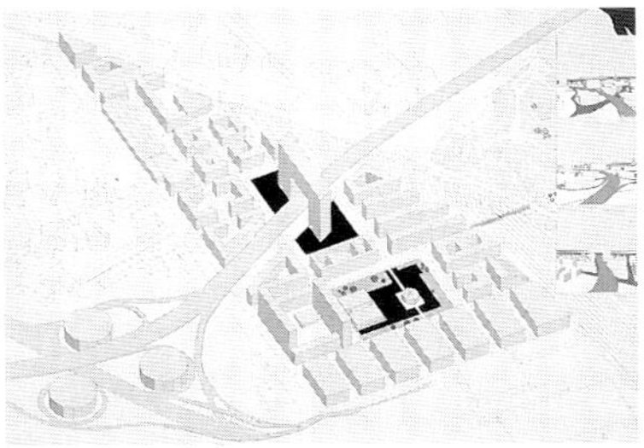

219
Workshop "Alte Messe Leipzig"
Leipzig
1992
with K.-H. Winkens, S. Klatt, R. Eastwood

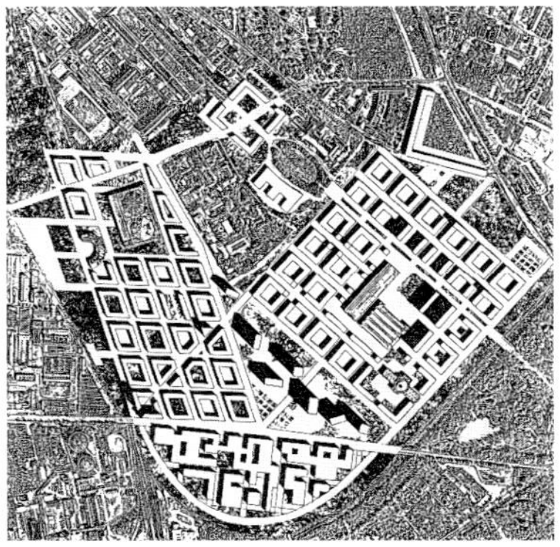

220
Competition Design for Residential Complex
Solmstrasse, Frankfurt am Main
1992
with R. Sargiotti, P. Kretz, H. Kleine-Kraneburg, H. Hane, M. Bräckerbohm, W. Kohne, M. Winkelmann, M. Gruber, C. Gröpl, I. Mauruschat, P. W. Garcia

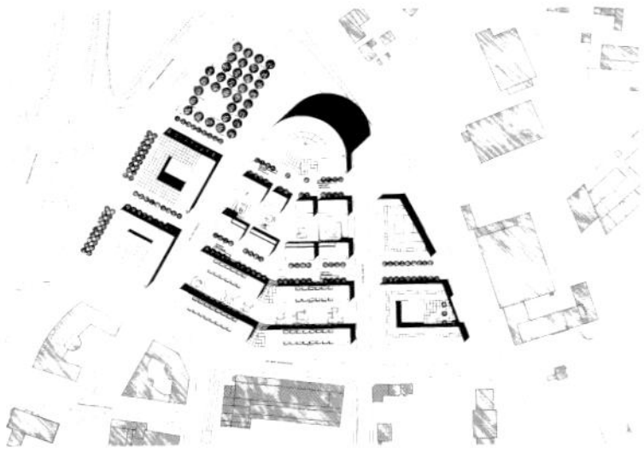

221
Competition Design for Expansion of City Hall
Saarbrücken
1992
with I. Schrader, H. Kleine-Kraneburg, P. Kretz, R. Sargiotti, S. Blümm, P. W. Garcia, C. Gröpl

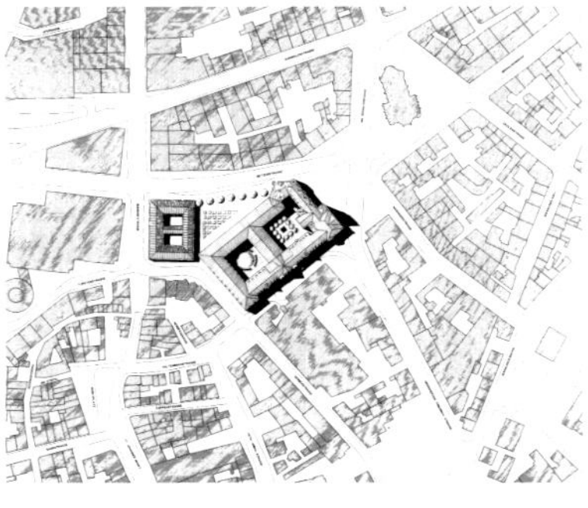

222
Pavilions
Heerlen (Netherlands)
1993
with B. von Glasenapp

224
Competition Entry for Redesign of Schrangen
Lübeck
1993
with S. Vieths, D. Dimster

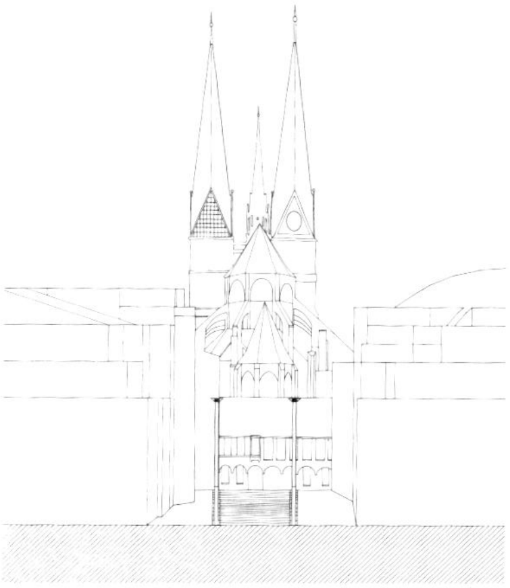

226
Competition Design for Cathedral Square
Magdeburg
1993
with S. Vieths,
D. Dimster, L. Baumewerd, J. Götz,
F. Wieschemann, R. Fein,
M. Haase, V. Diekmann

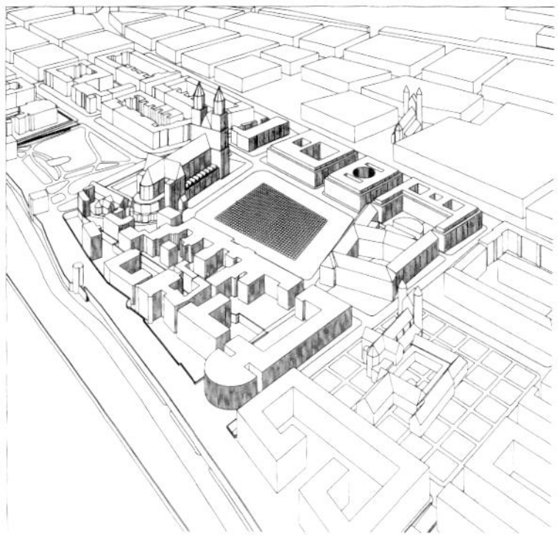

227
Residential Complex for Daimler-Benz Project
Potsdamer Strasse, Berlin
1993
with S. Vieths, D. Dimster

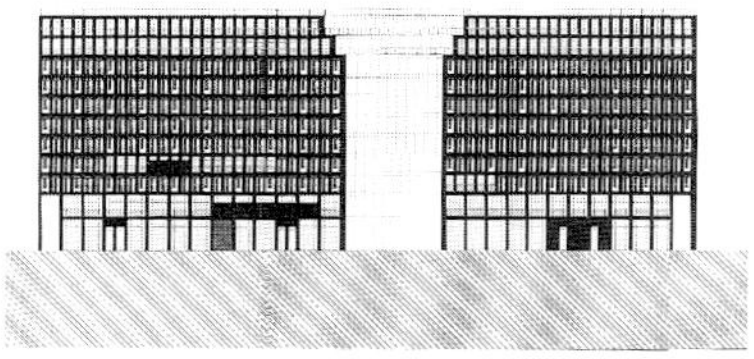

223
Competition Design for Office Building for Basler Versicherung
Cologne
1993
with S. Vieths, C. Combe,
A. Steudel, M. Garcon, M. Keim,
K.-U. Lompa

225
Competition Design for Golf and Country Club
Berlin-Wannsee
1993
with K.-H. Winkens, H. Daiber,
N. Zarratini, R. Beyer,
A. Leonhardt, C. McCarthy,
T. Scheel

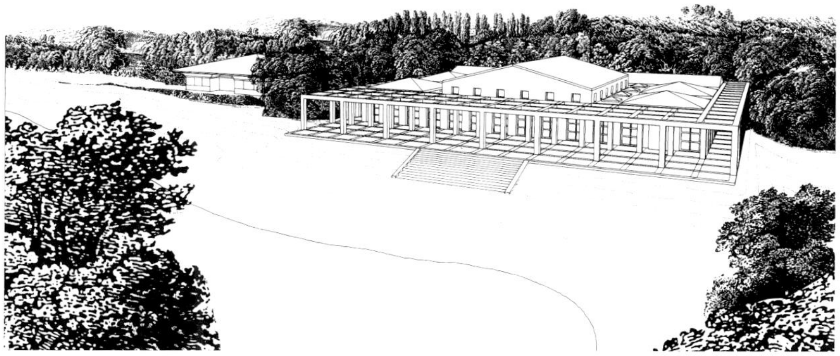

228
Redesign of Gallery Building
Schaafenstrasse 43, Cologne
1993-1994
with R. Bandus (execution and construction supervision)

229
Redesign of Water Tower
Utscheid
1993
with J. Götz

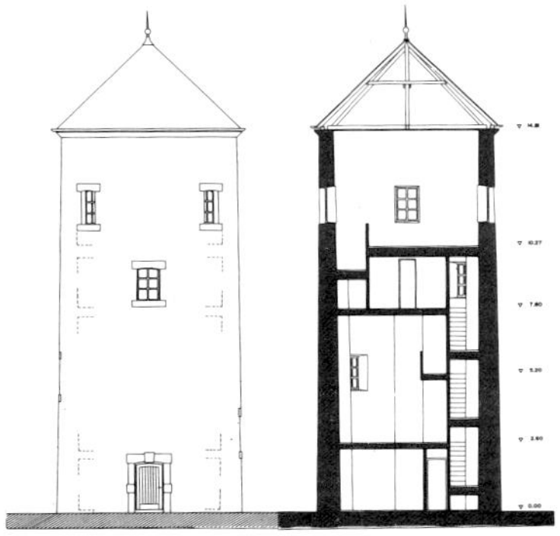

230
Competition Design for Expansion of Königliche Porzellan-Manufaktur (KPM)
Berlin
1993
with S. Vieths, D. Dimster, A. Steudel, J. Götz, F. Wieschemann

231
Competition Design for Spreeinsel (First Phase)
Berlin
1993, 1994
with S. Vieths, P. Pfertner, J. Götz, A. Steudel, F. Wieschemann

232
Feasibility Study for Alfred-Wegener-Institut
Potsdam
1993–1998
with T. Scheel, B. Schindler, K.-H. Winkens

233
Feasibility Study for Alfred-Wegener-Institut
Bremerhaven
1993
with S. Vieths, D. Dimster

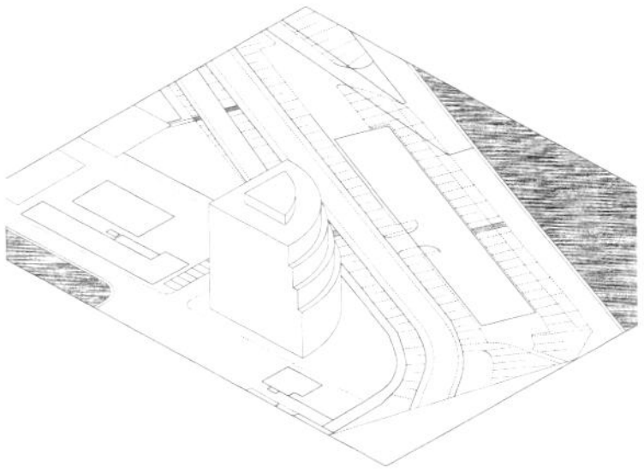

234
Feasibility Study for Hotel Izmailova
Moscow (Russia)
1994
with K.-H. Winkens, S. Walk

235
Competition Design for Architectural Exhibition Kleinmachnow
Berlin
1994
with K.-H. Winkens, S. Walk

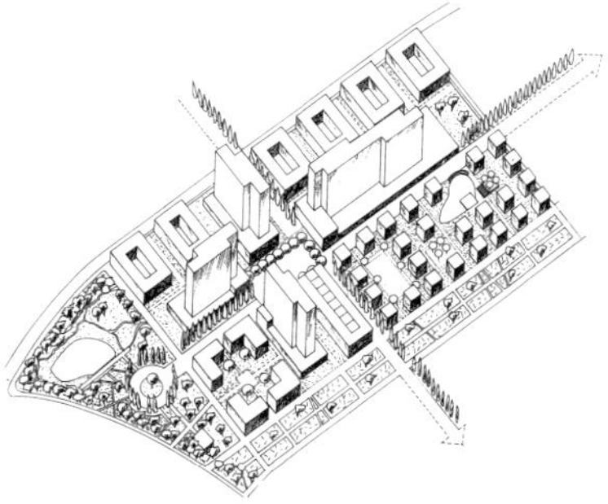

236
Competition Design for Museumsinsel
Berlin
1994
with S. Vieths, P. Pfertner, A. Steudel, D. Dimster, K.-U. Lompa, J. Götz, F. Wieschemann, M. Laudert, R. Fein, E. Stumm, V. Diekmann, J. Sieber

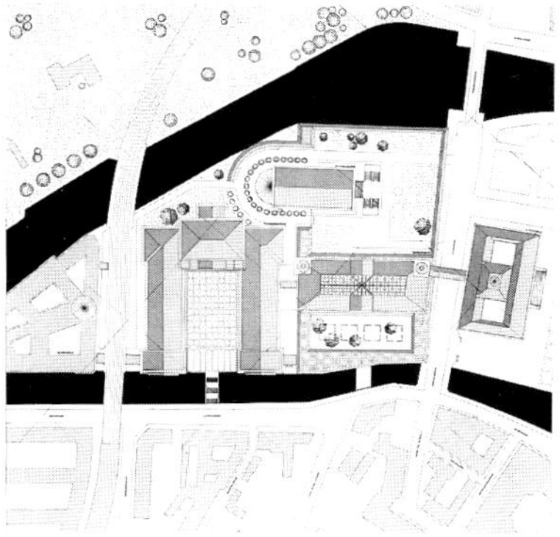

238
Competition Design for Spreeinsel (2nd Phase)
Berlin
1994
with S. Vieths, P. Pfertner, M. Keim, D. Dimster, K.-U. Lompa, A. Steudel, E. Stomm, F. Wieschemann, J. Götz, M. Laudert

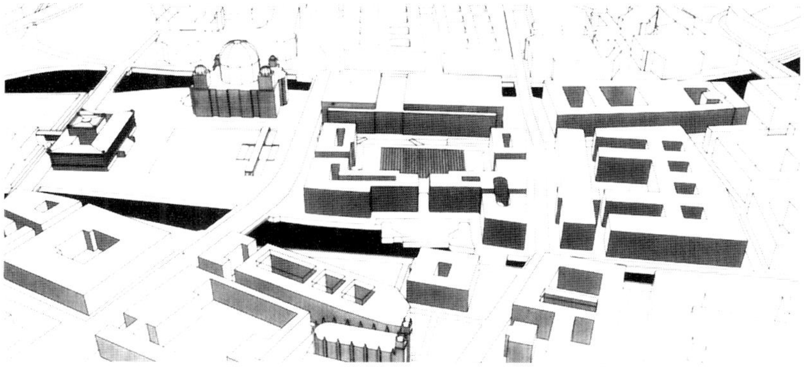

240
Competition Design for Dresdner Bank (Third Prize)
Dresden
1994
with S. Vieths, M. Keim, P. Pfertner, D. Dimster, J. Götz, A. Steudel, P. Vernin, K.-U. Lompa

237
Exhibition of Plaster Models, Kunsthalle
Hamburg
1994
with A. Albers, B. Grimm, J. Sieber

239
Hanstein House
Cologne
1994
with S. Vieths

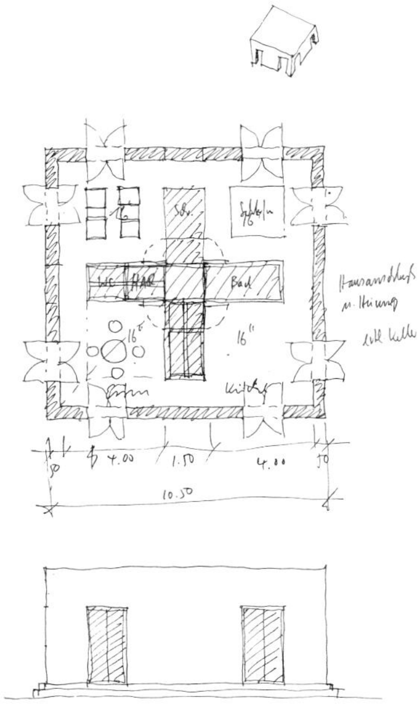

241
Competition Design for Deutsche Bauindustrie
Berlin
1994
with S. Vieths, M. Keim, P. Pfertner, D. Dimster

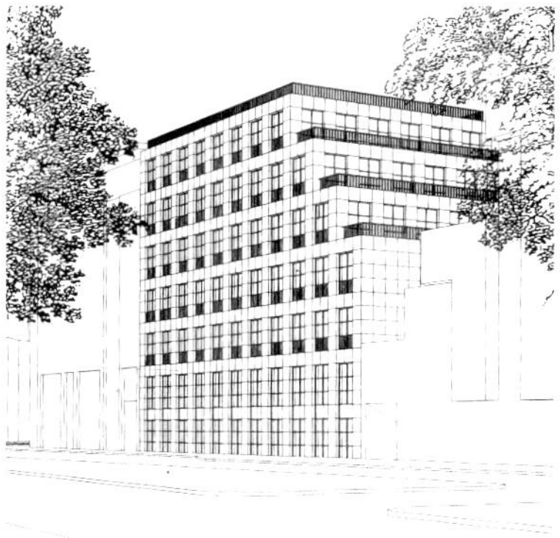

242
Design for Fiszman Complex
Breitlacherstrasse, Frankfurt am Main
1994
with J. Engel, M. Bräckerbohm, B. Kraus, I. Schrader, M. Gruber, H. Kleine-Kraneburg, P. Kretz

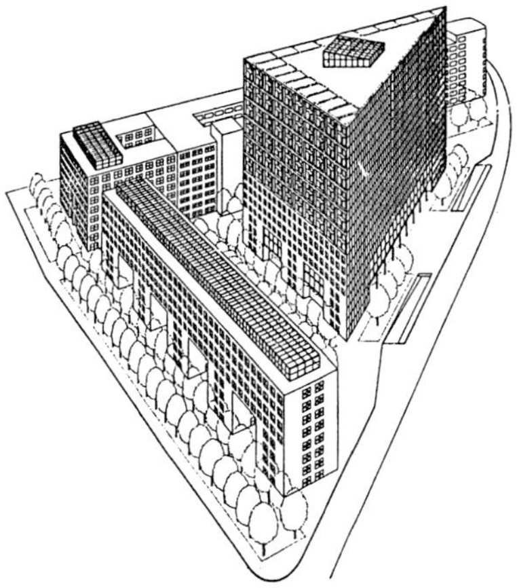

244
Competition Design for Lehrter Bahnhof District (1st Phase)
Berlin
1994
with S. Vieths, K.-H. Winkens, M. Keim, D. Koralek, A. Steudel, P. Pfertner, P. Vernin, M. Laudert, F. Wieschemann, C. McCarthy, B. Mannarelli, V. Diekmann, K.-U. Lompa

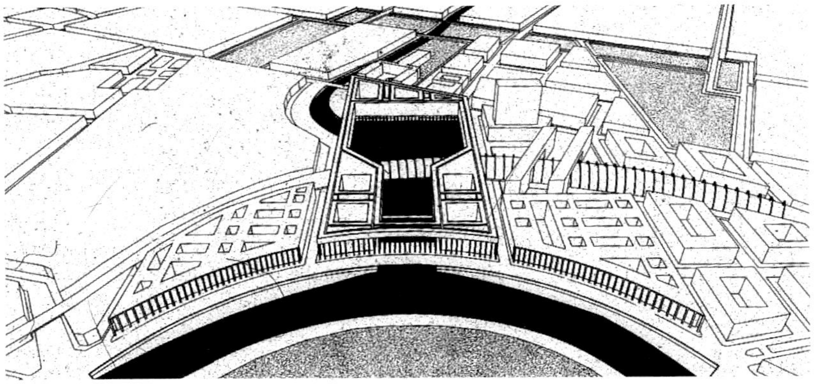

247
Competition Design for Dresdner Bank
Pariser Platz, Berlin-Mitte
1994
with K.-H. Winkens, T. Scheel, C. McCarthy, C. Sauter

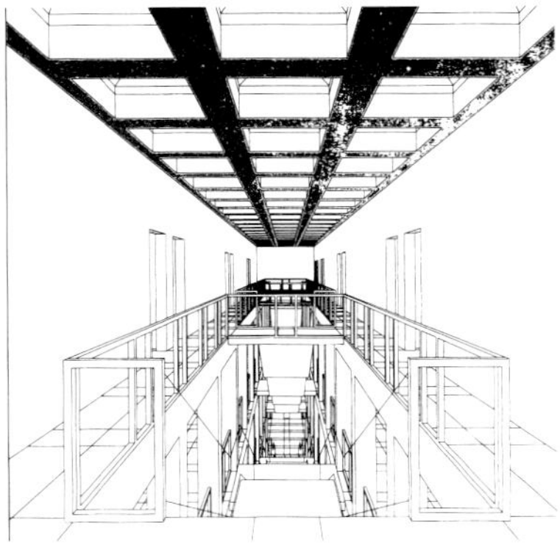

243
Feasibility Study for Neuss-Hammfeld II and III
Neuss-Hammfeld
1994
with S. Vieths, M. Keim, P. Pfertner, D. Koralek, P. Vernin, K.-U. Lompa, F. Wieschemann, M. Laudert

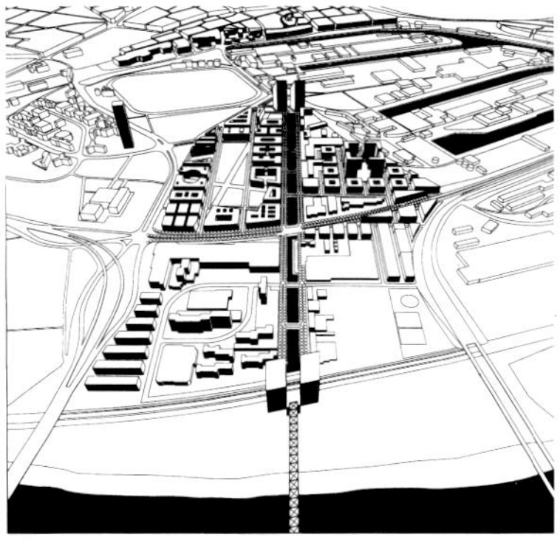

245
Competition Design for Federal Chancellery
Berlin
1994
with S. Vieths, P. Pfertner, M. Keim, A. Steudel, D. Koralek, K.-U. Lompa, P. Vernin, F. Wieschemann, M. Laudert, J. Sieber, V. Diekmann

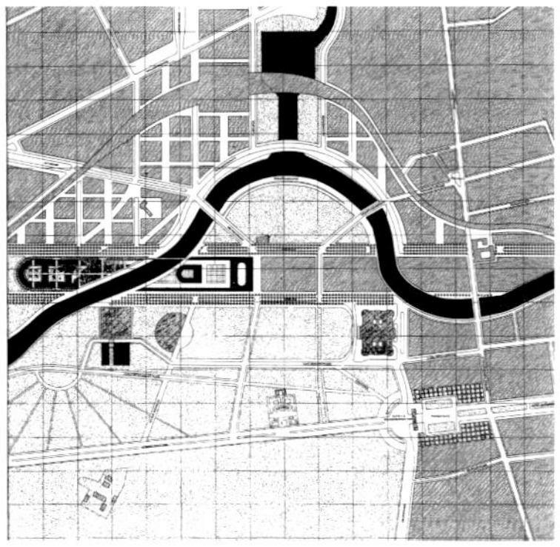

246
Competition Design for Lehrter Bahnhof District (2nd Phase)
Berlin 1994
S. Vieths with K.-H. Winkens, N. Cadez, A. Steudel, D. Koralek, M. Keim, C. McCarthy, P. Catoir, V. Diekmann, J. Götz, M. Laudert, K.-U. Lompa, B. Mannarelli, P. Pfertner, J. Sieber, P. Vernin, F. Wieschemann

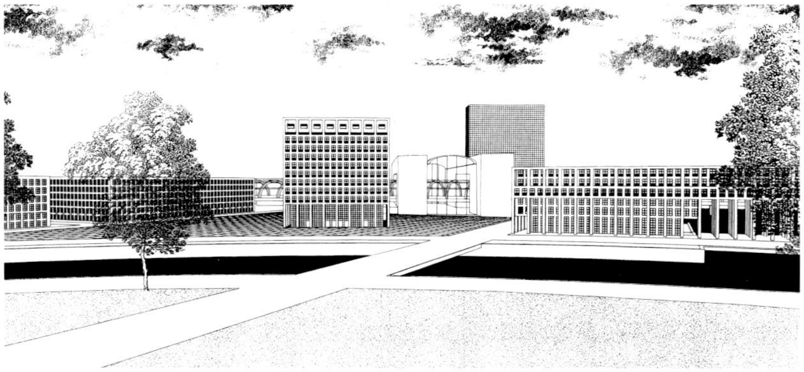

248
Ungers House III
Kämpchensweg, Cologne
1994–1996
with J. Götz, B. Grimm

249
Design for Residential Tower
Heerlen (Netherlands)
1995
with B. v. Glasenapp

250
Design for Kubus,
Lehrter Bahnhof District
Berlin
1995
with K.-H. Winkens,
H. Daiber, T. Scheel, R. Beyer

251
Master Plan for Euroforum
Cologne
1995
with S. Vieths, P. Pfertner

252
Design for Hotel, Euroforum
Cologne
1995
with S. Vieths,
A. Steudel, K.-U. Lompa,
M. Laudert, R. Fein

253
Design for Musical Theater,
Euroforum
Cologne
1995
with S. Vieths, M. Keim,
A. Steudel, K.-U. Lompa,
D. Koralek, F. Wieschemann,

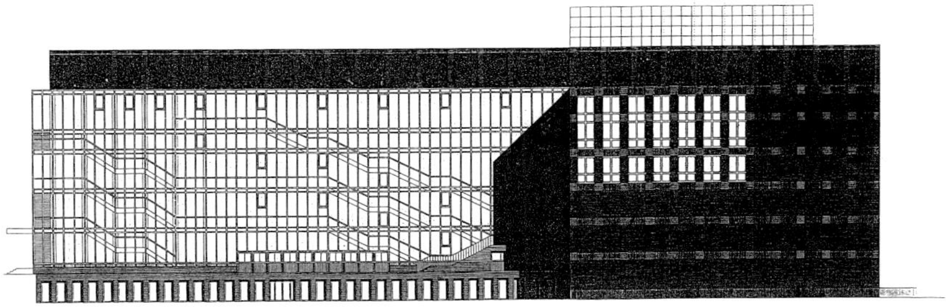

254
Design for Office Building,
Euroforum
Cologne
1995
with S. Vieths,
V. Diekmann, M. Laudert,
P. Vernin

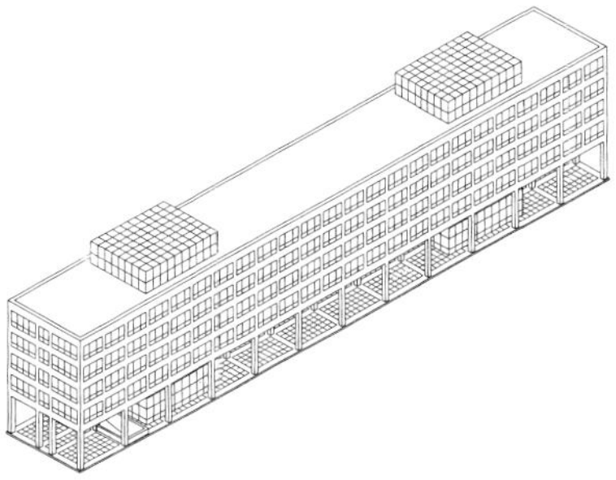

255
Design for Neuss Tower
Neuss-Hammfeld
1995
with L. Baumewerd,
B. v. Glasenapp

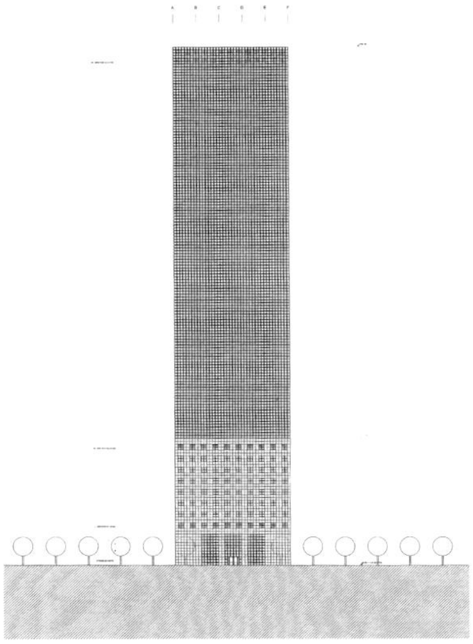

256
Competition Design for Railway Plaza
Bremen
1995
with S. Vieths, N. Cadez, R. Fein,
J. Sieber

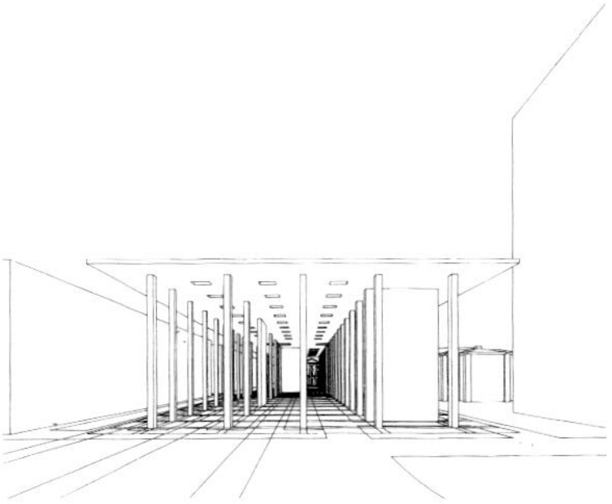

257
Feasibility Study for Rostock-Reutershagen
1995
with S. Vieths, A. Steudel,
M. Keim, C. Combe, P. Pfertner,
V. Diekmann, F. Wieschemann,
A. Albers

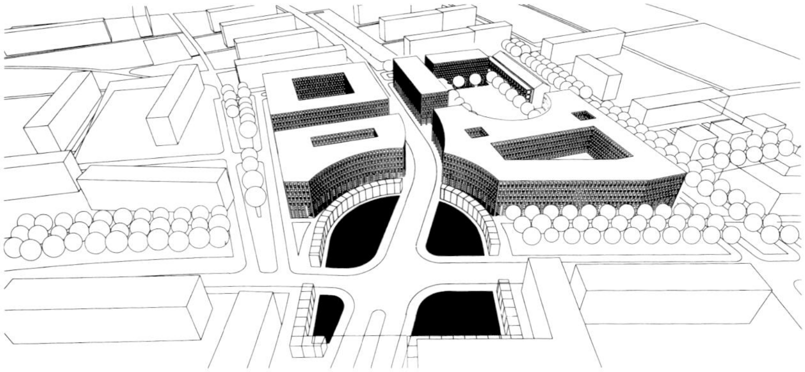

258
Urban Villas
Bramsche
1995
with J. Götz, S. Vieths

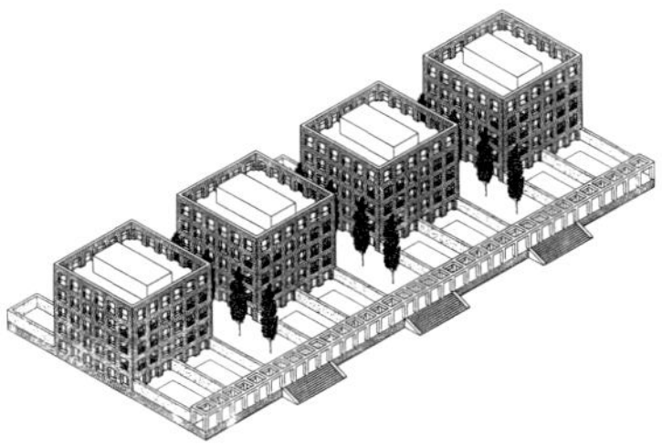

259
Competition Design for Kunstpalast
Düsseldorf
1995–2000
with S. Vieths, K.-U. Lompa,
B. v. Glasenapp, F. Wieschemann,
M. Keim, J. Götz, G. Lohmann,
M. Weiher, G. Amling

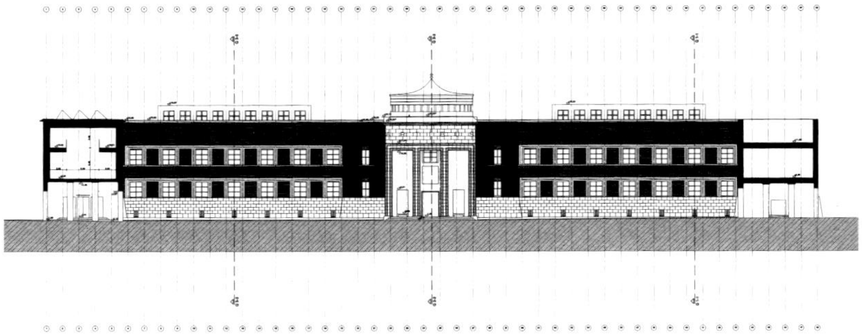

260
Competition Design for Kavallierstrasse
Düsseldorf
1995
with S. Vieths, D. Dimster,
M. Keim

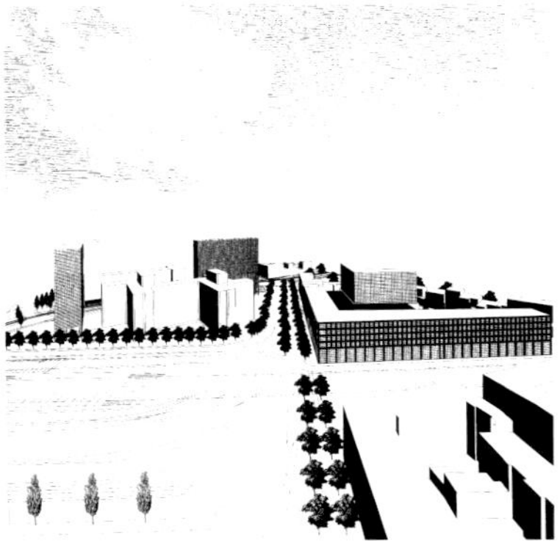

261
Feasibility Study for Gatehouses at Leipziger Platz (Entrance to Potsdamer Platz U-Bahn Station)
Leipziger Platz, Berlin
1995
with S. Vieths, M. Keim

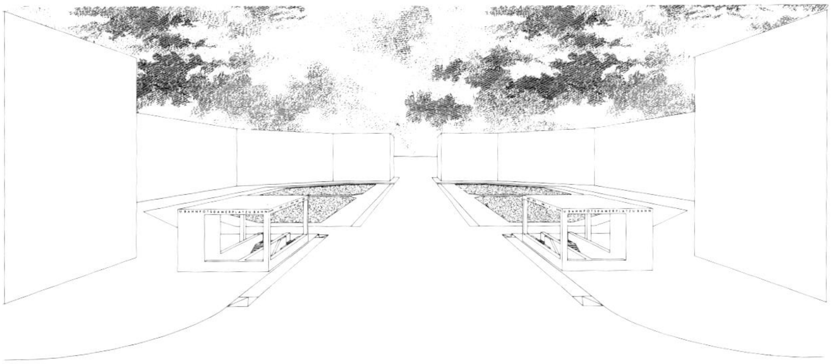

264
Fasieco Finger Office and Workshop Building
Cologne
1995
with S. Vieths, B. v. Glasenapp, J. Götz, A. Steudel

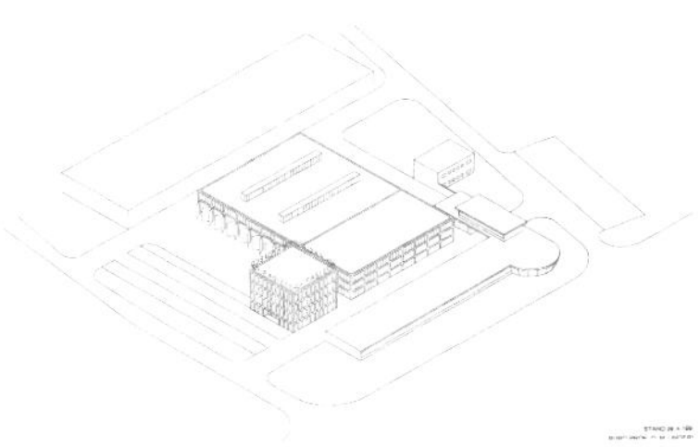

265
Feasibility Study for Fürstenbergpassage
Bonn
1995–1999
with C. Combe, W. van der Bel

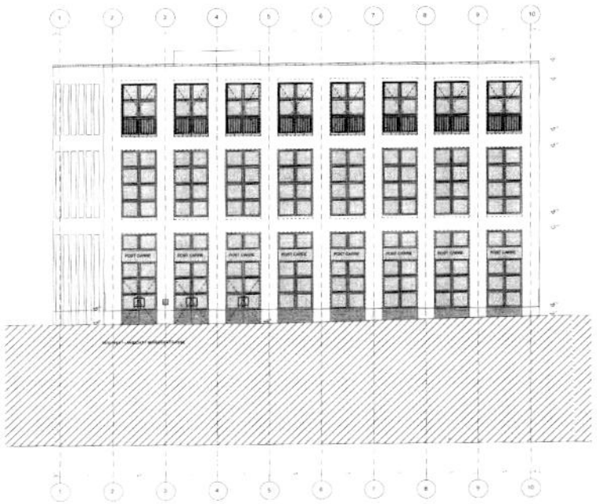

262
Feasibility Study for Postcenter at Münsterplatz
Bonn
1995
with S. Vieths, M. Keim, M. Garçon

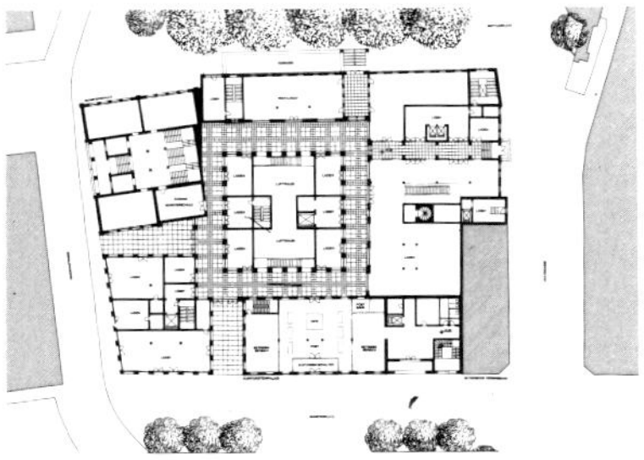

263
Residential Complex on Fraunhoferstrasse
Berlin
1995
with K.-H. Winkens, B. Schindler

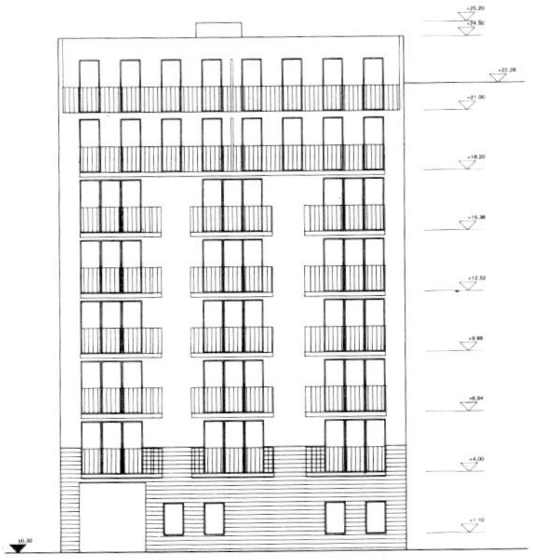

266
Exhibition Architecture for Speck Collection
Cologne
1996
with S. Vieths

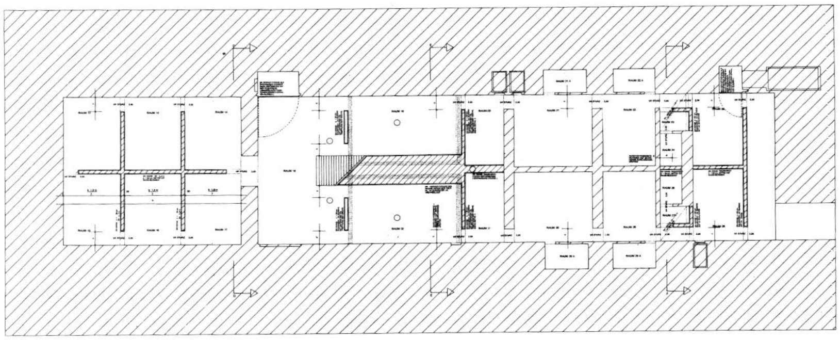

267
Competition Design for Federal Foreign Office
Berlin
1996
with S. Vieths, M. Keim

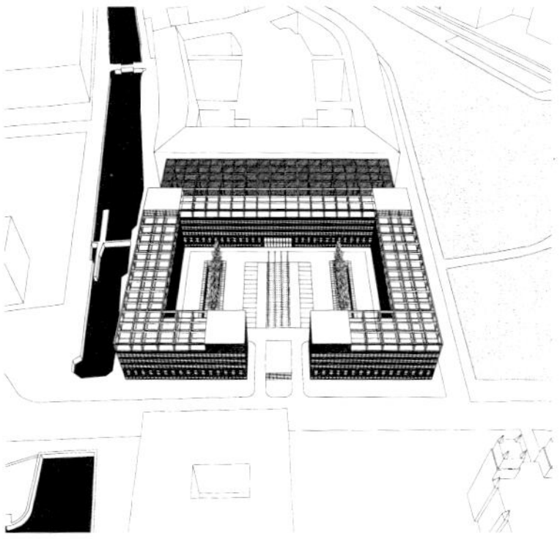

269
Airport Center
Bremen
1996
with B. v. Glasenapp

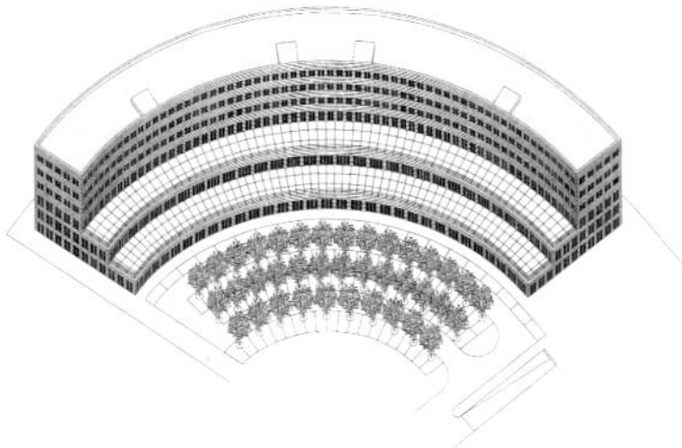

270
Competition Design for Rautenstrauch-Joest-Museum
Cologne
1996
with S. Vieths, M. Keim

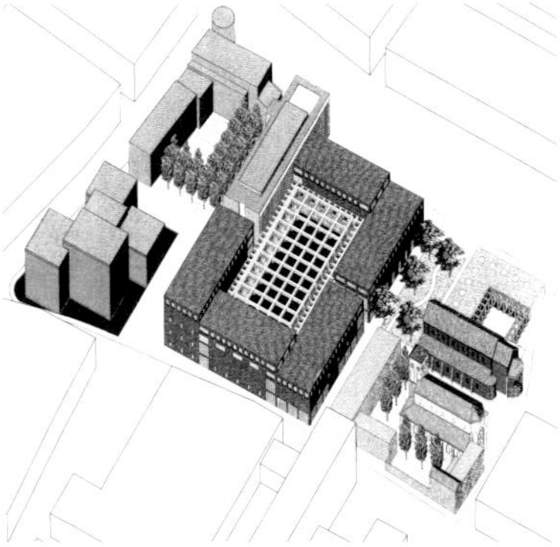

271
Urban Planning Competition Design for Löwen-Brauerei
Trier
1996
with J. Götz, P. Pfertner

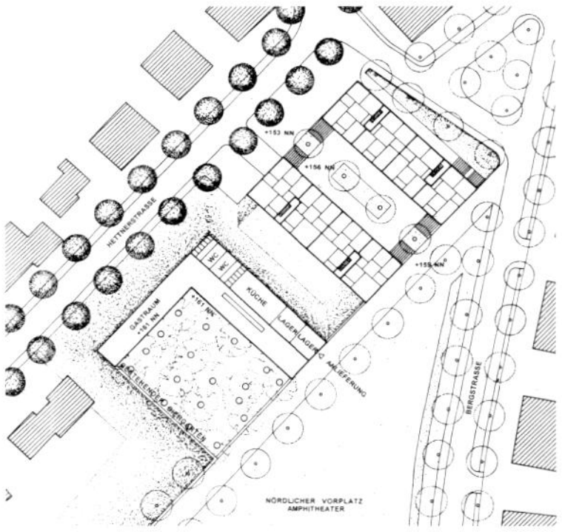

268
Competition Design for Wallraf-Richartz-Museum
Cologne
1996–1999
with S. Vieths, M. Garçon, M. Keim, D. Koralek, P. Pfertner, J. Rogler, A. Steudel, W. van der Bel, M. Yalcin

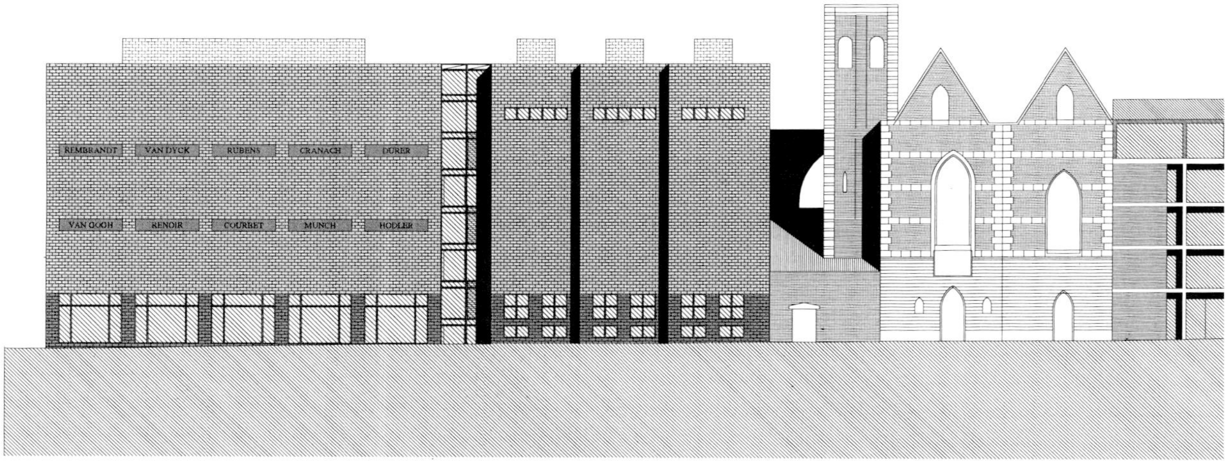

272
Competition Design for Parish Church of St. Theodor
Cologne-Vingst
1997
with J. Götz, V. Diekmann

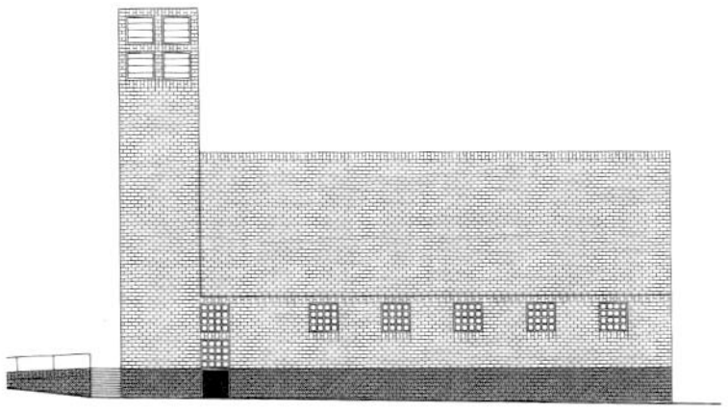

273
Competition Design for Diözesanmuseum/ St. Kolumba
Cologne
1997
with J. Götz

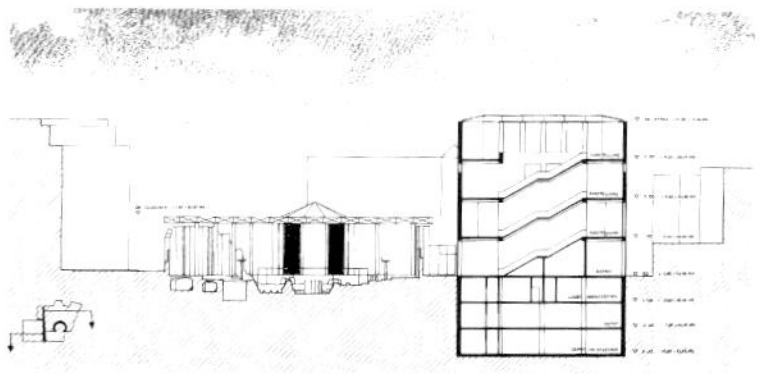

275
Humboldt Colonnades, Spreeufer Bridge
Berlin
1997
with K.-H. Winkens, T. Scheel

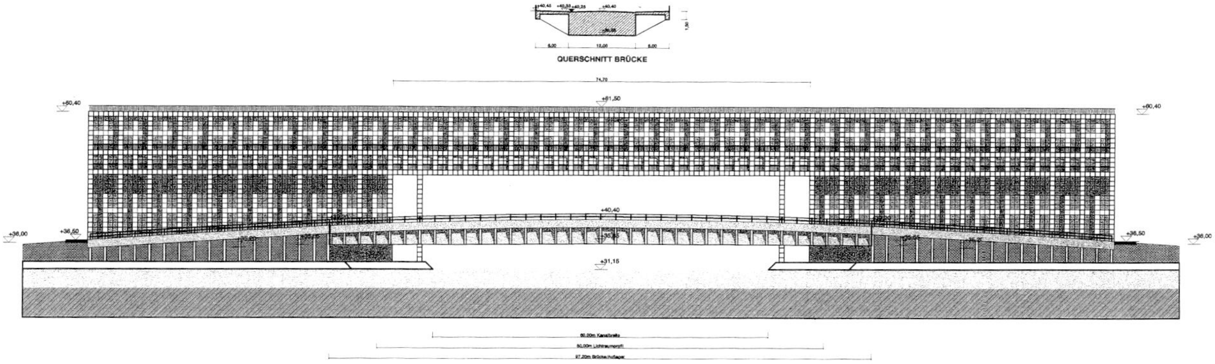

274
Competition Design for Dresdner Bank High-rise
Frankfurt am Main
1997
with V. Diekmann, M. Keim

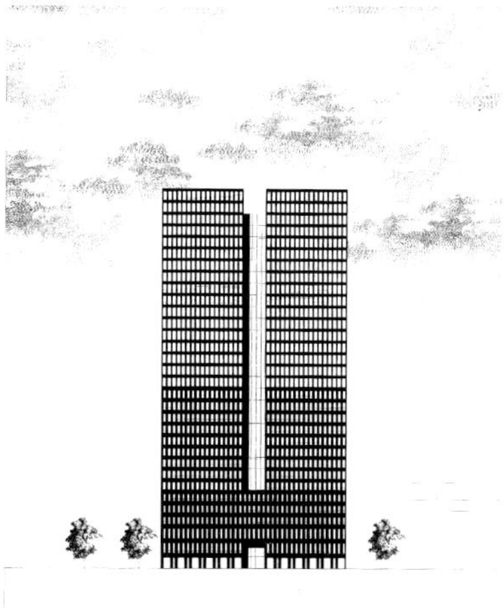

276
Competition Design for State Office of Rhineland-Palatinate
Berlin
1997
with K.-H. Winkens, T. Scheel, B. Mannarelli

277
Competition Design for Trade Fair Hall
Rimini (Italy)
1997
with K.-H. Winkens, F. Bertossi, J. Lenschow, B. Mannarelli, I. May

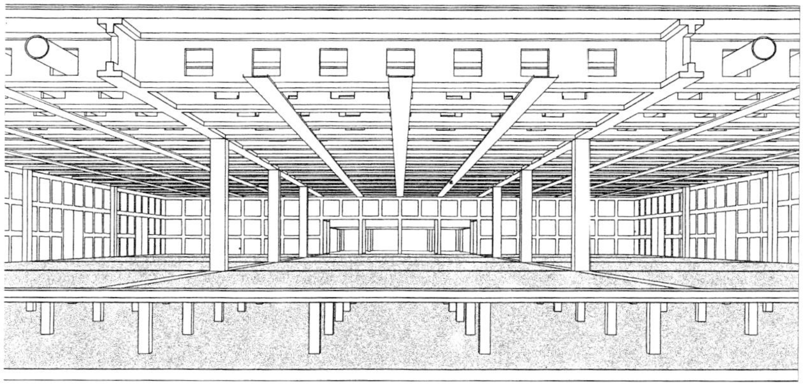

278
Hall Building
Essen
1997
with V. Diekmann, M. Yalcin,
G. Lohmann

280
Competition Design for Trade Fair Complex
Freiburg im Breisgau
1997
with K.-H. Winkens, J. Lenschow,
B. Schindler, B. Mannarelli

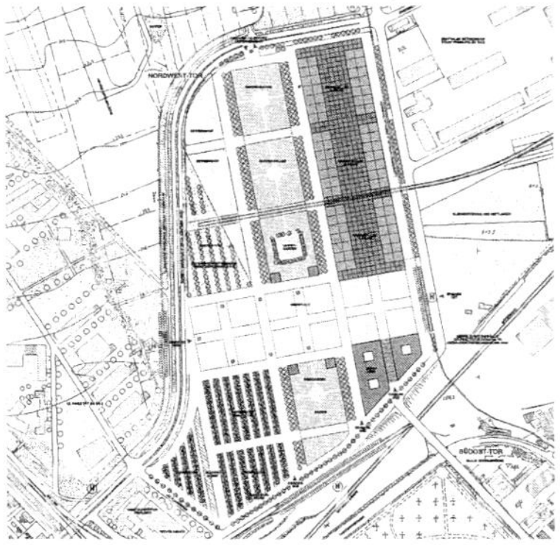

281
Competition Design for Trade Fair Complex
Düsseldorf
1997
with K.-H. Winkens, T. Scheel,
B. Schindler, B. Mannarelli

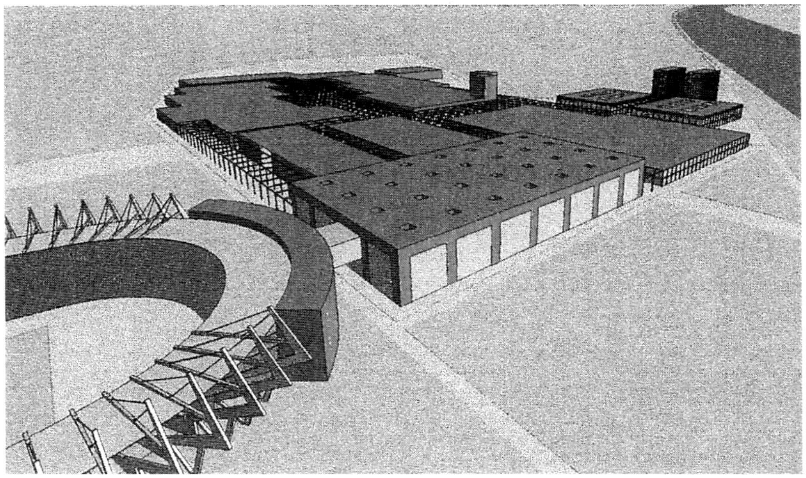

279
Competition Design for Trade Fair Complex
Vicenza (Italy)
1997
with K.-H. Winkens, F. Bertossi,
J. Lenschow, B. Mannarelli

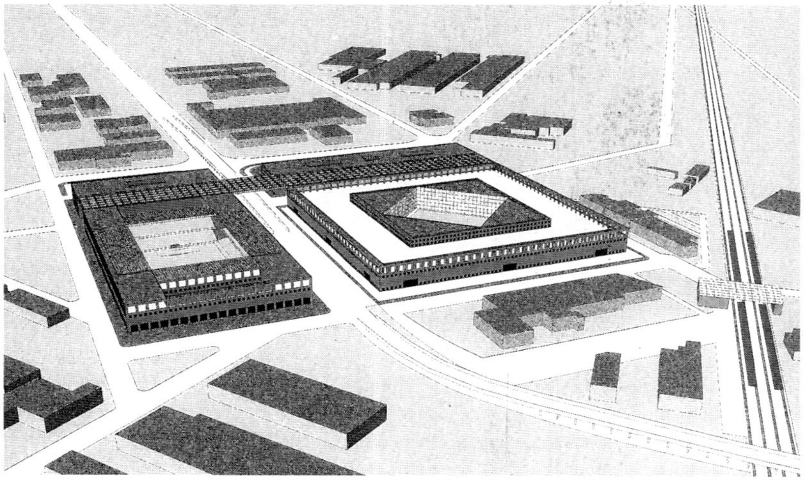

282
Municipal Building
Utscheid
1997
with J. Götz, M. Garcon

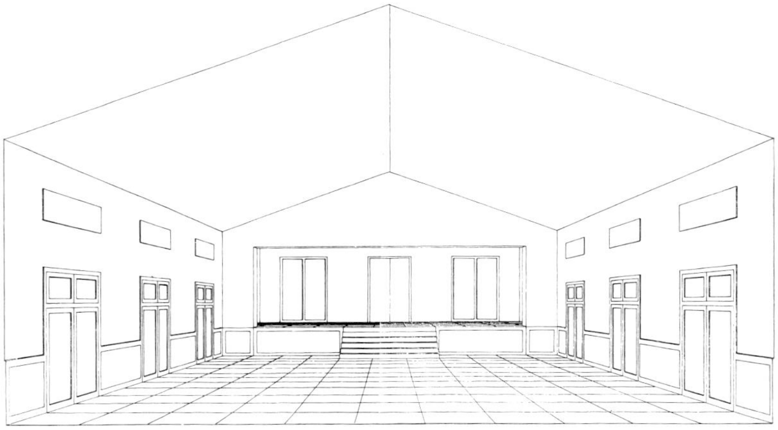

Appendices

Biography

July 12, 1926
Born in Kaisersesch/Eifel

1947
School-exit examination

1947–50
Studies in architecture at the Technische Hochschule in Karlsruhe; final examination with Prof. Eiermann

1950
Opens architectural offices in Cologne and Berlin

1963
Appointed full professor at Technische Universität Berlin

1965, 1967
Visiting Critic at Cornell University, Ithaca

1965–67
Dean of the faculty of architecture at the Technische Universität Berlin

1969–75
Professor of architecture at Cornell University, Ithaca

1970
Licensed architect in New York State

1971
Member of the American Institute of Architects (AIA)

1973, 1978
Professor of architecture at Harvard University

1974, 1975
Professor of architecture at the University of California, Los Angeles

1975–86
Emeritus professor of architecture (Chair) at Cornell University, Ithaca

1979, 1980
Professor of architecture at the Hochschule für Angewandte Kunst in Vienna

1982
Accademia di San Luca, Rome

1986–90
Professor of architecture at the Kunstakademie Düsseldorf (emeritus)

1987
Akademie der Wissenschaften, Berlin
Grand Prize of the BDA (German Architects' Association)

1988
Honorary member of the Bund Deutscher Architekten BDA (German Architects' Association), Berlin

1989
Prix Rhenan, Strasbourg

1992
Member of the Moscow branch of the International Academy of Architects

1994
BDA Prize, Bremen

1997
Grand Cross of the Order of Merit of the Federal Republic of Germany

Bibliography

Gerardo Brown-Manrique

1989

M. Dannemann. *Fotographische Portraits.* Düsseldorf: Stadtmuseum der Landeshauptstadt Düsseldorf.

Design Heute. Tokyo, 51ff.

H. Dominik, J. Maes, J. M. Nebe. *Der Viehmarkt im Brennpunkt von Planung und Interessen.* Trier: Selbstverlag des Trier Forum e.V.

V. Fischer, ed. *Bodenreform: Teppichboden von Künstlern und Architekten/Moquettes par des artists et des architectes/Carpets by artists and architects.* Berlin: Ernst & Sohn, 38.

V. Fischer, ed., V. Albus, J. Gros, M. Thun. *Design Now: Industry or Art?* New York: Prestel, 116–24, 242–57.

Ironimus. *Architekten sind auch nur Künstler.* Berlin: Ernst & Sohn.

H. Klotz. *Architektur des 20. Jahrhunderts.* Frankfurt am Main: Deutsches Architekturmuseum/ Stuttgart: Klett-Cotta.

H. Klotz, ed. *Jahrbuch für Architektur 1989.* Braunschweig/Wiesbaden: Friedrich Vieweg & Sohn, 127–30, 131–37, 138–42.

H. Klotz. *20th Century Architecture: Drawings, Models, Furniture from the Exhibition of the Deutschen Architekturmuseums, Frankfurt am Main.* New York: Rizzoli.

Magistrat der Stadt Marburg, ed. *Neues Bauen in der alten Stadt: Geplantes und Gebautes: Ausstellung zu Projekten für die Marburger Altstadt: Skizzen, Entwürfe, Modelle und Objekte.* Marburg: Dr. Wolfgang Hitzeroth Verlag, 27–29.

"Den Ort suchen, den Ort setzen: Günther Behnisch und Oswald Mathias Ungers im Gespräch." In W. Pehnt, *Die Erfindung der Geschichte: Aufsätze und Gespräche zur Architektur unseres Jahrhunderts,* Munich: Prestel-Verlag, 171ff.

H.-P. Schwarz. *Deutsches Architekturmuseum Frankfurt am Main.* Frankfurt am Main: Deutsches Architekturmuseum.

Stadt Speyer, ed., V. Fouquet. *Straße und Platz: Dokumentation, Neugestaltung Maximilianstraße und Domplatz, Speyer: Dokumentation Planung, Band 1.* Mannheim: Edition Quadrat.

C. Van de ven, ed. *Museumsarchitectuur.* Rotterdam: Uitgeverij 010, 164.

P. Wels. "Das Projekt für die Erweiterung der Museumsbauten auf der Museumsinsel von Oswald Mathias Ungers." In E. Kossak, M. Markovic, *Hamburg: Stadt im Fluß,* Hamburg: Ellert & Richter Verlag, 156–57.

M. Worner, D. Mollenschott, eds. *Architekturführer Berlin.* Berlin: Dietrich Reimer Verlag, 16 (24), 55 (83), 218 (344), 264–65 (423–24).

"Zwischen individueller Pragmatik und professioneller Utopie: Das Architektenhaus in der Gegenwart." In H.-P. Schwarz, *Künstlerhäuser: Eine Architekturgeschichte des Privaten,* Braunschweig/Wiesbaden: Friedrich Vieweg & Sohn, 164–92.

Einladung, Museum Leverkusen, Ausstellungseröffnung, Freitag, dem 27. Januar 1989 (Invitation, Museum Leverkusen, exhibition opening, Friday, January 27, 1989), Leverkusen, Städtisches Museum Leverkusen.

"Badische Landesbibliothek Karlsruhe." *Detail,* January–February, 31–38.

M. Champenois, P. Andreu. "Aeroport du Kansai: Competition for Island Airport, Osaka Bay, Japan." *Architecture d'Aujourd'hui,* February, 42–53.

"Platz und Verkehr." *Baumeister,* February, 30–43.

"Trier: Oswald Mathias Ungers baut das Thermenmuseum: Gläserne Vitrine für Mauern aus römischer Zeit." *Art: Das Kunstmagazin,* February, 18.

Frankfurt: Museen, Architektur, Künstler, Galeristen: Die neuen Museen am Main, special issue of *Pan, Zeitschrift für Kunst und Kultur,* March, 72.

T. Norweg. "Das Ausbaukonzept des Flughafens Frankfurt." *Bauwelt,* March 24, 492–96.

"Kansai International Airport." *Architectural Design,* March–April, 42–61.

O. M. Ungers. "Viehmarktplatz Trier Museum, Trier, West Germany, Design: 1988." *GA Document,* April, 65–67.

B. Kauhsen. "Konstantinplatz: O. M. Ungers a Treviri." *Arredo Urbano* 9, no. 32 (April–May): 94–105.

V. Magnago Lampugnani. "Il concorso per l'aeroporto internazionale di Kansai, Osaka." *Domus,* May, 35–51.

"Oswald Mathias Ungers." *Architektura ČSR,* May, 42ff.

J. Isasi. "La torre de la feria: O. M. Ungers en Frankfurt." *Arquitectura Viva,* June, 18–21.

M. Le Gans. "Das Bonner Loch: der Bonner Bahnhofsvorplatz." *Deutsche Bauzeitung* 123, no. 8 (June): 18–21.

H. Matsui. "International Competition of Invitation for New Architectural Solution of Urbanisation at the Piazza Matteotti–La Lizza Area in Siena: Un progetto per Siena." *Architecture + Urbanism,* June, 3–14.

N. Miller. "Architecture on Film." *Progressive Architecture,* June, 127–28.

"Museumsneubau nun auch für Hamburg." *Baumeister,* June, 10.

O. M. Ungers. "Archeologia a Treviri: I progetti di O. M. Ungers: Museo delle Terme, Trier, Germany." *Casabella,* June, 39.

O. M. Ungers. "L'Europe de ville en ville: Grands projets, grandes formes/Major Projects, Large Constructions." *Architecture Intérieure Crée,* June–July, 116–23.

"Oswald Mathias Ungers, lauréat du prix Rhénan d'architecture, Hans Hollein, lauréat du Prix Soprema." *Techniques et Architecture,* June–July, 21.

Verband Rheinischer Museen, ed. "Enge und Zwänge am Viehmarkt in Trier: Die Suche nach dem Raum." *Rheinische Heimatpflege,* July–September, 182.

"Zweck-Tempel." *Baumeister,* August, 50–55.

"MediaPark Köln." *Architektur + Wettbewerbe,* September, 66–72.

"Messepalast, Areal der ehemaligen Hofstallungen in Wien, Österreich, 1. Stufe." *Architektur + Wettbewerbe,* September), 28–35.

K.-D. Weiss. "Zwischen Ordnung und Konflikt: Oswald Mathias Ungers im Gespräch mit Klaus-Dieter Weiss." *Werk, Bauen + Wohnen,* September, 4–11.

"Spitzenheizwerk Messe Frankfurt." *Bauwelt,* 80, no. 36 (September 22): 1711–12.

"Hotel Berlin." *Prolegomena, Arbeitsblätter des Instituts für Wohnbau an der Technischen Universität Wien,* October, 36.

"'Die Deutschen kommen,' Design Made in Germany." *Ambiente,* November, 172.

R. Brüning. "Das Märkische Viertel in Berlin wird 25." *Bauwelt* 80, no. 43 (November 10): 2057–59.

R. Scharfenorth. "Boden-Kür." *Architektur & Wohnen,* November–December, 148–52.

"IBA, die jüngsten Wohnbauten: 33 Projekte in Berlin." *Baumeister,* December, 24–55.

H. Ahuis. "Krupp-Gelände-West in Bochum: Der Städtebauliche Workshop 1989." *Bauwelt* 80, no. 48 (December 22): 2282–89.

"Einchecken unterm Glasdach. Ost-Terminal umgeplant. Flughafen–Neues Modell nach dem Streit um die Architektur/ Baubeginn im Sommer." *Frankfurter Rundschau* 108, 13.

M. Mönninger. "Ehrentempel als Stadttor. Bonn plant ein neues Bahnhofsportal." *Frankfurter Allgemeine Zeitung* 55, 31.

H. Müller-Schliepe. "Stadtplanung in Frankfurt am Main." *Garten und Landschaft* 99, no. 4, 53–58.

"Museo de Arquitectura, Frankfurt." *Escala* 21, no. 144, 15–16.

K. Wagner. "Anstifter. Das neue Ausstellungszentrum am Hamburger Delchtormarkt." *Frankfurter Allgemeine Zeitung* 201, 23.

M. Zardini. "Ontologia dello spazio urbano? Tre progetti per Siena." *Lotus International* 61, 42–61.

1990

"1968–1975 Vielfalt in neuen Ansätzen/Diversity in Initial Attempts." In *Ideen Orte Entwürfe: Architektur und Städtebau in der Bundesrepublik Deutschland/Ideas Places Projects: Architecture and Urban Planning in the Federal Republic of Germany.* Exh. cat., Berlin: Ernst & Sohn, T51.

"1975–1990 Internationale Bauausstellung Berlin als Modellversuch/International Architectural Exhibition Berlin as a Model Project." In *Ideen Orte Entwürfe: Architektur und Städtebau in der Bundesrepublik Deutschland/ Ideas Places Projects: Architecture and Urban Planning in the Federal Republic of Germany.* Exh. cat., Berlin: Ernst & Sohn, T61.

"1975–1990 Museumsbau–Bewahren als gesellschaftliche Aufgabe/Museum Architecture–Safekeeping as a Social Duty." In *Ideen Orte Entwürfe: Architektur und Städtebau in der Bundesrepublik Deutschland/Ideas Places Projects: Architecture and Urban Planning in the Federal Republic of Germany.* Exh. cat., Berlin, Ernst & Sohn, T67.

"1975–1990 V. Rationalismus: Abstraktion des Quadrats/V. Rationalism: Abstraction of the Square." In *Ideen Orte Entwürfe: Architektur und Städtebau in der Bundesrepublik Deutschland/Ideas Places Projects: Architecture and Urban Planning in the Federal Republic of Germany.* Exh. cat., Berlin: Ernst & Sohn, T73.

"Abwasserpumpwerk Tiergarten." In *Architekturpreis Berlin 1989.* Berlin: Aedes, Galerie und Architekturforum, 86–87.

"Alfred-Wegener-Institut für Polarforschung, Bremerhaven." In J. Joedicke, Ruhrgas AG, Essen, eds., *Architektur in Deutschland '89–Deutscher Architekturpreis '89.* Stuttgart: Karl Krämer, 32–39.

"Deutsches Architekturmuseum Frankfurt am Main." In H. Klotz, ed., E. Hils, *Von der Urhütte zum Wolkenkratzer.* Frankfurt: Deutsches Architekturmuseum.

"Deutsches Architekturmuseum Frankfurt am Main 1984–Architekt Oswald Mathias Ungers Köln und Frankfurt am Main." In J. Schilgen, *Neue Häuser für die Kunst: Museumsbauten in Deutschland.* Dortmund: Harenburg Edition, 68.

A. J. Estrada Uribe. "La vivienda en la continuidad del movimiento moderno: 1957–1987." Ph.D. diss., Universidad de Navarra.

G. Fioravanti. *La composizione contemporanea: una strumentazione disciplinare e didattica per la progettazione architettonica.* Rome: Gangemi Editore, 15, 17–18, 21, 28–29, 31 (nos. 5–6), 35, 44–45, 47, 49–51, 53 (no. 11).

G. Forg. *O. M. Ungers: Kubus.* Cologne: Galerie Max Hetzler.

"Gatehouse, Frankfurt am Main 1983–1986." In *Mies van der Rohe Award for European Architecture.* London: Butterworth Architecture, 114–17.

D. Henzel. *Architekten Oswald Mathias Ungers.* Stuttgart: IRB Verlag.

"Hinweis auf Literatur: Die Thematisierung der Architektur: DVA Stuttgart 1983." In F. Kind-Barkauskas, ed., *Architektur im Wandel: Beispiele und Meinungen.* Düsseldorf: Beton, 10–11.

Ideen Orte Entwürfe: Architektur und Städtebau in der Bundesrepublik Deutschland/Ideas Places Projects: Architecture and Urban Planning in the Federal Republic of Germany: 1949–1990. Berlin: Ernst & Sohn, T51, T61, T67, S04, A07.

Institut für Wohnbau, Technische Universität Wien, ed. *Bewohnbare Architektur: Festschrift für Reinhard Gieselmann.* Vienna: Picus.

P. Jesberg. "Eine neue Dimension des Ästhetischen von der Konstruktion zur Dekonstruktion." In F. Kind-Barkauskas, ed., *Architektur im Wandel: Beispiele und Meinungen.* Düsseldorf: Beton, 79–88.

J. Joedicke. *Architekturgeschichte des 20. Jahrhunderts: Von 1950 bis zur Gegenwart.* Stuttgart/Zurich: Karl Krämer, 210–11, 238, 242, 245–47.

C. Kranz. *O. M. Ungers–951–1984 Bauten und Projekte.* Cologne: Fachhochschule Köln.

G. Lueg. *'90 Möbeldesign aus Europa.* Cologne: Museum für Angewandte Kunst Köln.

V. Magnago Lampugnani, ed. *Museumsarchitektur in Frankfurt 1980–1990.* Munich: Prestel, 96–103, 104–5, 138–49, 150–51, 197.

Medienzentrum Düsseldorf. Düsseldorf: Philipp Holzmann AG.

"O. M. Ungers–Teppichentwürfe." In Vorwerk & Co., *Pressearbeiten für Vorwerk Dialog.* Hameln: Editorial publications of Vorwerk Dialog.

Oswald Mathias Ungers–Möbel-Collection "cubo und sfera." Milan: Sawaya & Moroni.

J. Pahl. "Architektur im Raum–Raum in der Architektur." In F. Kind-Barkauskas, ed., *Architektur im Wandel: Beispiele und Meinungen.* Düsseldorf: Beton, 47–56.

P. Peters. "Es gibt keine Wahrheiten in Extremen." In F. Kind-Barkauskas, ed., *Architektur im Wandel: Beispiele und Meinungen.* Düsseldorf: Beton, 57–63.

Postmoderne: 1975–1990; Signale Deutscher Baukunst. Dortmund: Signal Versicherungen.

Stefan Polónyi: Festschrift zu seinem

sechzigsten Geburtstag. Cologne, 355.

Prix Rhénan d'Architecture 89. Strasbourg: Prix Rhénan d'Architecture, 8–9, 32–33.

"Realisierungswettbewerb für die Büroüberbauung der Besucherterrassen A und C des Terminals Mitte am Flughafen Frankfurt Main." In *Flughafen Frankfurt Main AG.* Frankfurt: O. M. Ungers + Partner.

Straße und Platz Neugestaltung Maximilianstraße und Domplatz, Speyer: Dokumentation Ausführung Band 2. Speyer: Stadtverwaltung Speyer.

"Teppichdesign von Künstlern und Architekten." In *Das Bilderbuch für Vorwerk Dialog.* Hameln: Vorwerk & Co. Teppichwerke KG, 43, 60.

"Das Thermenmuseum in Trier–Oswald Mathias Ungers." In A. Preiß, K. Stamm, F. G. Zehnder, eds., *Das Museum: Die Entwicklung in den 80er Jahren. Festschrift für Hugo Borger zum 65. Geburtstag–eit Zeuge Kunst.* Munich: Klinkhardt & Biermann, 434–39.

O. M. Ungers, W. A. Noebel. *Messe Leipzig–Entwicklungsvorschlag.* Berlin: O. M. Ungers + Partner.

K.-H. Volkmann. "Vorstellung der ausgezeichneten Arbeiten." In J. Joedicke, Ruhrgas AG, Essen, eds., *Architektur in Deutschland '89–Deutscher Architekturpreis '89.* Stuttgart: Karl Krämer, 8–10.

"Werner Strodthoff: 20 Jahre Bauen in Nordrhein-Westfalen." In *20 Jahre Architektenkammer Nordrhein-Westfalen.* Düsseldorf: Architektenkammer Nordrhein-Westfalen, 19ff.

Wert und Design: Wilkens Tafelsilber-Objekte. Bremen: Wilkens.

M. Wörner, D. Mollenschott, eds. *Architekturführer Berlin.* Berlin: Dietrich Reimer, 16 (24), 55 (83), 218 (344), 264–65 (423–24).

Zur Einweihung des Universitäts-Clubhauses Bonn am 20. Oktober 1990. Bonn: Universitätsclub Bonn e.V.

"Unger's Collection." *Casa Vogue,* January, 57ff.

"BAK: Deutscher Architekturpreis 1989 verliehen." *Deutsches Architektenblatt* 22, no. 2 (February 1): 224–26.

"Hochhaus in Frankfurt am Gleisdreieck, Sohnsstraße [*sic*]." *Baumeister,* February, 16.

"Hochhäuser: Deutsche Bundesbank in Frankfurt." *Baumeister,* February, 22.

"Progetti di aeroporti di Oswald Mathias Ungers." *Casabella,* February, 10–22, 59–60.

"Richard Meier baut Hypobank in Luxemburg." *Baumeister,* February, 11.

O. M. Ungers. "Forms as Symbols." *Casabella,* February, 10, 22.

"Sonderbriefmarke zum 750-jährigen Jubiläum der Messe Frankfurt." *Galleria/Zeitschrift der Messe Frankfurt* 190 (February–May): 7, 14, 43, 52.

P. M. Bode. "Erfolg für jedermann sichtbar." *Art: Das Kunstmagazin,* March, 108–16, 162.

"Completato un edificio di Ungers a Berlino (Architetture in breve: Argomenti)." *Casabella,* March, 26.

"O. M. Ungers Möbel-Collection Vorwerk-Teppich: design O. M. Ungers." *Casa Vogue,* March.

"Primo Piano: 'Il Capitolato tecnico come supporto alla progettazione.'" *Casabella,* March.

"Verpackung für die Phantasie: Würfelgedanken/Wrapping for Imagination: Cubic Thoughts." *Daidalos,* March 15, 110–15.

D. Steiner. "Der Salzbuger Forellenweg: Ein kommunalpolitischer Kriminalroman." *Bauwelt* 81, no. 12 (March 30): 601–3.

"Wettbewerb Erweiterung Messegelände Berlin." *Bauwelt* 81, no. 12 (March 30): 532–33.

D. Dunster. "Profile: Oswald Mathias Ungers: The Romance of the Grid." *Architecture Today,* April, 38–43.

"Sawaya & Moroni Contemporary Furniture." *Casa Vogue,* April.

"Frankfurt–Die Braut des Geldes–kühl und verschwiegen." *Bunte,* April 26, 59.

L. Kelly. "Spiel mit dem Quadrat." *Atrium: Haus & Wohnen International,* April–May–June, 20–27.

"Ein Portrait von Oswald Mathias Ungers und sein Wohnhaus in Köln." *Atrium: Haus & Wohnen International,* April–May–June, 3.

"Beschränkter Realisierungswettbewerb: Haus der Geschichte Baden-Würtemberg, Stuttgart." *Wettbewerbe Aktuell,* May, 315–22.

V. Fischer. "'Honni soit qui mal y pense' (Pamphlet gegen den Minderwertigkeitskomplex der deutschen Architekten)." *Der Architekt–Zeitschrift des BDA,* May, 235.

"Über 30.000 Aussteller, mehr als 2,4 Millionen Besucher und eine Gesamthallenfläche von ca. 260.000 m²–das ist die Messe Frankfurt heute." *Frankfurter Allgemeine Zeitung,* May 11.

V. Magnago Lampugnani. "La terminal de la isla: concurso del aeropuerto de Kansai." *Arquitectura Viva,* May–June, 14–18.

"Der 'Forellenweg' in Salzburg: Viel Lärm um wenig." *Baumeister,* June, 56–62.

"Museum für Völkerkunde in Frankfurt." *Baumeister,* June, 40–45.

"Concurso de ideas en la zona industrial de Hohenäcker, Pforzheim, Republica Federal Alemana, marzo 1990." *Arquitectura* 72, no. 285 (July–August): 28–31.

"Stadt und Verkehr." *Baumeister,* August, 13–53.

P. Jesberg. "Das Frankfurter Museumsufer." *DBZ–Deutsche Bauzeitschrift,* October, 1356–57.

K. Wohlhage. "Das Objekt und die Stadt: Erinnerungen an eine Berliner Tradition." *Arch+,* October, 51–58.

K. Schmid. "Köln Galerie–Parade Galerie Sophia Ungers." *Kunst Intern,* November–December, 14.

K. Schmid. "Kooperation als Strategie: Max Hetzler, der Galerist der neuen Generation." *Kunst Intern,* November–December, 9–11.

"Konstantinplatz in Trier." *Architektur + Wettbewerbe,* December, 25.

"Neugestaltung Domplatz in Speyer." *Architektur + Wettbewerbe,* December, 20–21.

"Piazza Matteotti und Piazza Gramsci in Siena, Italien." *Architektur + Wettbewerbe,* December, 44–48.

"Technologiepark Universität Bremen." *Baumeister,* December, 32–41.

W. M. Chramosta. "Wettbewerb Museumsquartier." *Architektur & Bauform* 23, no. 138, 9–13.

"Plaza Matteotti: La Lizza, Siena, Italia." *Escala* 22, no. 151, 25–30, 71.

1991

Berlin 1991, Sonderheft: Sammlung verschiedener Hefte zum Thema "Berlin." Berlin: Bauwelt, 972–77, 2107, 2210–29, 2231.

R. Burgard, R. Sommer, eds. *Ikonen-Museum der Stadt Frankfurt am Main. Stiftung Dr. Schmidt-Voigt, Abteilung des Museums fur Kunsthandwerk.* Frankfurt am Main: Magistrat der Stadt Frankfurt am Main.

Concorso internazionale per il nuovo Palazzo del Cinema al Lido di Venezia. Milan: Edizioni La Biennale di Venezia/Electa.

"Ein Kleinod an der Kö." In H. Achenbach, ed., *Achenbach Art Report 2.* Düsseldorf: Achenbach Art Consulting, 4.

H. Hall, W. Baecker. *Köln: Seine Bauten 1928–1988.* Cologne: J. P. Bachem Verlag, 383–87.

K. Hegewisch. *Oswald Mathias Ungers, Gerhard Richter, Sol LeWitt.* Düsseldorf: HypoBank.

U. Hohns. *Das Ungebaute Hamburg: Visionen einer anderen Stadt in architektonischen Entwürfen der letzten hundertfünfzig Jahre.* Hamburg: Junius Verlag, 15, 146, 147, 154.

"Hypobank, Düsseldorf." In *Annual ufficio 1991–1992: La qualità totale.* Milan: Electa, 35.

Internationale Bauausstellung Berlin 1987: Projektübersicht. Berlin: Internationale Bauausstellung Berlin 1987, 48–49, 100–101, 122–23.

H. Klotz, E. Hils. *Von der Urhütte zum Wolkenkratzer: Geschichte der gebauten Umwelt. 24 Modelle zur Geschichte der Architektur.* Munich: Prestel.

J. Krichbaum, V. Magnago Lampugnani. *Baumeister im Profil: Architektenforum Dresden 1990.* Stuttgart: Verlag Gerd Hatje, 161, 172–73, 176–79, 180–83, 190.

V. Magnago Lampugnani, M. Mönninger. *Berlin Morgen: Ideen für das Herz einer Großstadt.* Stuttgart: Verlag Gerd Hatje.

"O. M. Ungers: Urban Islands in a Metropolitan Sea." In A. Papadakis, V. Magnago Lampugnani, eds., *Berlin Tomorrow.* London: Academy Editions/New York: St. Martin's Press, 92–96.

"Palacio Morsbroich, Leverkusen (RFA)–Museo en el edificio principal; Arquitecto: O. M. Ungers, Colonia/RFA." In *Reabilitación des edificios.* Barcelona: Ediciones CEAC, 21–22.

A. Papadakis, J. Steele. *A Decade of Architectural Design.* London: Academy Editions, 134–35.

A. Phillips. *The Best in Lobby Design, Hotels & Offices.* London: Batsford/New York: Rotovision, 166.

J. Robertson, S. Tigerman, eds. *Der Postmoderne Salon: Architekten über Architekten.* Basel/Berlin/Boston: Birkhäuser Verlag, 50–59.

Senatsverwaltung für Bau- und Wohnungswesen, ed. *Berlin: Werkstatt für Architektur: Katalog zum 4. Internationalen Architektur-Salon vom 28.09.–06.10. in Mailand.* Berlin: Senatsverwaltung für Bau- und Wohnungswesen, 77–81, 102–12.

O. M. Ungers. *Architekturmodelle und -zeichnungen.* Neuß: Kulturforum Alte Post.

O. M. Ungers. "Stadtinseln im Meer der Metropole." In M. Mönninger, *Das Neue Berlin: Baugeschichte und Stadtplanung der deutschen Hauptstadt.* Frankfurt am Main/Leipzig: Insel Verlag, 214.

O. M. Ungers, J. von Brandt. *Eenheid in verscheidenheid: Randwyck Noord naar 2000.* Maastricht: Gemeente Maastricht.

O. M. Ungers, F. Neumeyer. *Oswald Mathias Ungers: Architektur 1951–1990.* Stuttgart: Deutsche Verlag.

O. M. Ungers, F. Neumeyer. *Oswald Mathias Ungers: Architetture 1951–1990.* Milan: Electa.

M. Wörner, D. Mollenschott, K.-H. Hüter, eds. *Architekturführer Berlin.* Berlin: Dietrich Reimer Verlag, 16 (24), 55 (83), 218 (344), 264–65 (423–24).

B. J. Zikesch. *Die Badische Landesbibliothek in Karlsruhe von Oswald Mathias Ungers–eine Hommage an Friedrich Weinbrenner.* Heidelberg: Ruprecht-Karls-Universität Heidelberg.

M. Mönninger. "Zwölf Architekten entwerfen 'Berlin Morgen,' das Herz einer großen Stadt"; "Von Vakuum zur Weltstadt." Special insert, *Frankfurter Allgemeine Zeitung,* January 5, 5.

"Realisierungswettbewerb Büroüberbauung der Besucherterrassen A und C und des Terminal Mitte am Flughafen Frankfurt am Main." *Wettbewerbe Aktuell,* January, 10–16.

P. M. Bode. "Das neue Berlin: Gegen die dritte Zerstörung der geschundenen Stadt." *Art: Das Kunstmagazin,* February, 52–55.

L. Dawson. "Berlin Games." *Building Design,* February 22, 16–17.

N. Di Battista, "Berlino domani: Idee per il cuore di una metropoli." *Domus,* March, xxii, 54–63.

"Klassiker von Heute." *Atrium: Haus & Wohnen International,* March, 42.

R. Lautenschläger, "Keine Architektur für Todesstreifen." *Profil: Das Architektur-Magazin,* March, 32–35.

"Sulla nuova monumentalità urbana." *Industria delle costruzioni* 25, no. 233 (March): 56–57.

O. M. Ungers, "O. M. Ungers: Museumsisland Hamburg, Germany, design: 1986 (Competition); construction: 1991–92." *GA Document* 29 (April): 92–95.

W. Strodhoff, "Eine Privatbibliothek in Köln-Müngersdorf." *Bauwelt* 82, no. 16 (April 26): 830–33.

U. Hansen, "Gesamtkunstwerk: Die HypoBank bekennt Farbe." *Capital,* May, 132–34, 136.

D. Mandolesi, "Istituto di ricerche a Bremerhaven." *Industria delle costruzioni* 25, no. 235 (May): 42–49.

W. Strodthoff, "Oswald Mathias Ungers: La biblioteca dell'architetto a Colonia." *Domus,* May, 38–43.

P. Rumpf, "Die Friedrichstadtpassagen in Berlin Mitte." *Bauwelt* 82, no. 1819 (May 17): 972–77.

"Auf oder zwischen den Stühlen: Dreizehn Architekten suchen eine Position/Sitting on or between chairs: Thirteen architects in search of a position." *Daidalos* 40 (June 15): 52–79.

"Die neue Bau-Art Campanile-Projekt." *Merian,*

Frankfurt am Main, July, 104.

A. Loeckx, "ERC Waterschei opnieuw ter discussie." *Archis,* July, 8–9.

V. Gregotti, "Libertà al quadrato." *Panorama* 29 (July 14): 34.

" 'Who will design the new EC HQ?' Zeichnung: Louis Hellmann aus: élan." *Bauwelt* 82, no. 27 (July 19).

"Bremerhaven: il mare, i commerci." *Abitare,* July–August, 92–99.

S. Cassarà, "O. M. Ungers: L'assoluto dell'Architettura." *Parametro,* July–August, 2–3.

O. Aicher, "Berlin wird Hauptstadt." *Arch+,* August, 20–25.

"Messehalle 10." *Messezeitung Herbst* (August 24), 5.

N. Di Battista, "Biennale di Venezia: 10 architetti per il nuovo Palazzo del Cinema al Lido." *Domus* 730 (September), 54–56.

D. Mandolesi, "Berlino: idee per una metropoli." *Industria delle costruzioni* 25, 239 (September), 72–75.

G. Owen, "Projects: a film palace on the Lido." *Progressive Architecture* 72, 9 (September), 142–45.

"Ungers: Rigueur et Diversité." *D'Architectures: D'A* 18 (September), 44–45.

F. Apollonio, "L'architettura dei concorsi." *Parametro* 186 (September–October), 2–3.

"Köln: Eine Halle für die Kunst." *Zyma: Art Today* 4 (September–October), 37–38.

"Interview with O. M. Ungers." *Archidea* (Autumn), 2–7.

"Architekten als Designer: Sie entwerfen die bedeutendsten Bauten der Gegenwart ebenso wie die einfachen Dinge des Alltags." *Vogue* 10 (October), 162.

K. Schalhorn, "Mode und Entwerfen." *RO: Rosenheimer Hochschulhefte* (October), 10–19.

" 'Was halten Sie von Schinkel?' PAN fragte zeitgenössische Architekten." *Pan* (October 25), 58.

E. von Radziewsky, G. Wohman, F. J. Raddatz, "Mit Büchern leben: 'Der Bücherwürfel,' " *Architektur & Wohnen* 5 (October–November), 4, 102–20, 122, 124.

"Keine Gewalt!: Internationaler Wettbewerb 'Potsdamer und Leipziger Platz' in Berlin." *Bauwelt* 82, 41 (November 1), 2210–31.

"Internationaler engerer Wettbewerb Postdamer und Leipziger Platz, Berlin." *Wettbewerbe Aktuell* 21, 11 (November), 727–46.

"Photographs, Hypobank Düsseldorf and Messe Frankfurt." *Trockenbau Akustik* 9 (November), 6, 40.

"Potsdamer Platz Berlin." *Wettbewerbe Aktuell* 21, 11 (November), 727–35.

F. Strauven, "Een zuiver type in een suburbane verhulling: Ungers' bibliotheek in Keulen." *Archis* 12 (December), 39–43.

N. Messler, "Erkenntnisfalle und Illusion: Oswald Mathias Ungers' Bibliothek in Köln-Müngersdorf." *Kunst & Antiquitäten* 6, 28–30.

1992

80–90 Architektur (Salzburg: Informationszentrum der Landeshauptstadt Salzburg).

"AMK-Messehallen Berlin." in *Centrum: Jahrbuch Architektur und Stadt 1992* (Braunschweig/ Wiesbaden: Friedrich Vieweg & Sohn), 86–91.

"Ansprache des Architekten Prof. Oswald Mathias Ungers." in O. M. Ungers, *Badische Landesbibliothek: Reden zur Einweihung des Neubaus der Badischen Landesbibliothek in Karlsruhe am 17. Januar 1992* (Karlsruhe: Badische Landesbibliothek), 43–51.

Daimler-Benz-Wettbewerb Potsdamer Platz (Berlin: Daimler-Benz AG Projektgruppe Potsdamer Platz).

Das 2. Internationale Architektur-Forum in Potsdam: "Die Zukunft bauen" (Potsdam), 7.

"European Qualities." in *Intérieur 92* (Kortrijk: Fondation Intérieur), 57. "Hochhaus am Landtag, Düsseldorf, 1991." in *Centrum: Jahrbuch Architektur und Stadt 1992* (Braunschweig/Wiesbaden: Friedrich Vieweg & Sohn), 52–63.

Landeshauptstadt Hannover und Land Niedersachsen, Baudezernat, *Weltausstellung EXPO 2000 Hannover* (Hannover: Landeshauptstadt Hannover und Land Niedersachsen, Baudezernat).

Magistrat der Stadt Frankfurt am Main, *Dezernat Bau–Hochbauamt: Frankfurter Architektur Sommer '90* (Frankfurt am Main: Magistrat der Stadt Frankfurt am Main), 4–5, 28–31.

"Oswald Mathias Ungers: Progettista della Fiera di Francoforte e della nuova Fiera delle Germanie unificate di Berlino." in *Fiere in Italia* (Milan), 19–25 and plates 1–8.

"Privathäuser: Haus Ungers, Müngersdorf, Belvederestraße 60, 1958 (Oswald Mathias Ungers)." in *Der Oberstadtdirektor, Verkehrsamt: Architektur in Köln: Anfänge der Gegenwart* (Cologne: Verkehrsamt Stadt Köln).

"Sawaya & Moroni, Mailand; Designer: Oswald Mathias Ungers." in *Euro Design Guide Ambiente; Teil 5: M-Z Shopping* (Munich: Ambiente), 114.

H. Schubert, "Oswald Mathias Ungers, Deutsches Architekturmuseum Frankfurt/Main." in *Räume für die Kunst: Eine Ausstellung des Förderkreises der Leipziger Galerie für zeitgenössische Kunst e. V.* (Leipzig: Stadtgeschichtliches Museum Leipzig), 54–55.

H. Schubert, "Oswald Mathias Ungers, Deutsches Architekturmuseum Frankfurt am Main." in *Räume für Kunst. Museumsmodelle. Europäische Museumsarchitektur der Gegenwart* (Hannover: Kestner Gesellschaft), 72–73.

B. Secchi, C. Merlini, *Un progetto per Siena: Il concorso internazionale per piazza Matteotti–La Lizza* (Milan: Electa).

Staatliches Hochbauamt Karlsruhe, O. M. Ungers, *Die Badische Landesbibliothek Karlsruhe: Architekt Oswald Mathias Ungers* (Stuttgart: Verlag Gerd Hatje).

"Stadtportalhäuser, Frankfurt am Main, 1991." in *Centrum: Jahrbuch Architektur und Stadt 1992* (Braunschweig/Wiesbaden: Friedrich Vieweg & Sohn), 78–85.

A. Tzonis, L. Lefaivre, *Architecture in Europe Since 1968: Memory and Invention* (New York: Rizzoli International), 134–35.

A. Tzonis, L. Lefaivre, *Architektur in Europa seit 1968* (Frankfurt am Main: Campus Verlag), 134–35.

O. M. Ungers, "Der Genius loci als Thema der Gestaltung." in L. Buch, *Bibliothek: Festschrift der Badischen Landesbibliothek zum Neubau* (Karlsruhe: Badische Landesbibliothek), 63–70.

O. M. Ungers, "Das Janusgesicht der Architektur." in *Räume für die Kunst: Eine Ausstellung des Förderkreises der Leipziger Galerie für zeitgenössische Kunst e. V.* (Leipzig: Stadtgeschichtliches Museum Leipzig), 60–61.

O. M. Ungers, "Das Janusgesicht der Architektur." in *Räume für Kunst. Museumsmodelle. Europäische Museumsarchitektur der Gegenwart* (Graz: Neue Galerie am Landesmuseum Joanneum), 72–73.

O. M. Ungers, B. Gravagnuolo, *Oswald Mathias Ungers: Quattro Opere/Four Works* (Milan: Clean Edizioni).

"Westkunst in Köln; Konstantinplatz, Trier; Festhalle FFM Messe; Hypobank Düsseldorf." in I. Flagge, ed., *Jahrbuch für Licht und Architektur 1992* (Berlin: Ernst & Sohn), 60–61, 98–99, 112–13, 142–43.

C. Hein, "Berlijn: prijsvraag Potsdamer en Leipziger Platz." *Archis* 1 (January), 6–7.

"Hochhäuser als Stadtportale." in *Galleria* 1 (January), 36.

"Interview mit Kultursenatorin Christina Weiss: 'Hamburgs Kunstmeile kommt,'" *Art: Das Kunstmagazin* 1 (January), 68.

M. Mönninger, "Berlino: progetti per il Potsdamer/Leipziger Platz." *Domus* 734 (January), 36–49.

"Hauptsache Kultur: Frankfurter Riesen-Parade." *Forbes: Das Wirtschaftsmagazin fur Europa* 2 (February), 92.

K. Hegewisch, "Umbau einer Bank Düsseldorf." *Baumeister* 89, 2 (February), 21–25, 95.

R. R. Lauterschläger, "Museumsarchitektur, Entkernte Villen." *VfA Profil* 2 (February), 20–24.

V. Magnago Lampugnani, "Dall'imago al progetto: l'architettura come scoperta archeologica: Oswald Mathias Ungers." *Domus* 735 (February), 17–28.

"Oswald Mathias Ungers Architetture 1951–1990: Electa 1991." *Bollettino della Biblioteca del Dipartimento di Architettura e Analisi della Città* 1 (February), 117.

G.-A. Joas, "Olympiahalle Berlin." *Bauwelt* 83, 9 (February 28), 410–11.

"Disziplin Schulbau." *Leonardo: Magazin für Architektur* 1 (February–March), 20–25.

I. Bohning, "Klassizismus und Ungers." *Baumeister* 89, 3 (March), 6–7.

D. Meyhöfer, "O. M. Ungers: Architektur für Bücher. Ein Würfel für die Welt des Wissens." *Ambiente* 3 (March), 64–71.

"Perle an der Kö." *Beton* 3 (March), 128–30.

"Ungers-Stiftung in Köln." *Pan: Zeitschrift für Kunst und Kultur* 3 (March), 109.

"Literaturblatt der Bauwelt Nr. 14: Oswald Mathias Ungers Architektur 1951–1990" (review), *Bauwelt* 83, 11 (March 13), 13.

"Banque conceptuelle: Bayrische Bank (Düsseldorf)." *Architecture Intérieure Crée* 247 (March–April), 146–49.

W. Oechslin, "Städtebau: In Berlin erfunden, in Berlin desavouiert?" *Archithese* 22, 2 (March–April), 34–38.

M. Tschanz, "Nochmals Potsdamer Platz." *Archithese* 22, 2 (March–April), 44–56.

"Stadtportalhäuser." *Deutsche Bauzeitschrift* 40, 4 (April), 448.

M. Schreiber, "Der Turm im Kopf der Haupstädter." *Der Spiegel* 46, 15 (April 6), 266.

"Der Klassizismus und seine Folgen: die Badische Landesbibliothek Karlsruhe." *Bauwelt* 83, 14 (April 10), 798–803.

"Proposte per il Potsdamer–Leipziger Platz a Berlino." *Industria delle costruzioni* 26, 247 (May), 76–79.

G. Zohlen, "Mies resurrexit: Podiumsdiskussion in Berlin." *Baumeister* 89, 5 (May), 4.

"Zum Quadrat: Badische Landesbibliothek Karlsruhe." *AIT Architektur Innenarchitektur Technischer Ausbau* 100, 5 (May), 142–45.

"Eine Bank als 'Gesamtkunstwerk,'" in *Stein* 6 (June), 18–20.

"Friedrichstadtpassagen, Berlin." in *Architektur + Wettbewerbe* 150 (June), 17–21.

F. Jaeger, "Rekomposition mit höheren Weihen." *Deutsche Bauzeitschrift* 6 (June), 850–51.

F. Jaeger, "Wärmekraftwerk in Köln-Merheim: Maß und Zahl in der Industriebaukunst." *Baumeister* 89, 6 (June), 17–21.

P. Jesberg, "Zwischen Ratio und Phantasie: Über Oswald Mathias Ungers." *Deutsche Bauzeitschrift* 40, 6 (June), 853–60.

T. Metz, "The New Downtown (Frankfurt am Main)." *Architectural Record* 180, 6 (June), 80–89.

"Potsdamer Platz, Leipziger Platz, Berlin." *Architektur + Wettbewerbe* 150 (June), 52–61.

O. M. Ungers, "Die Kunst der Ordnung." *Deutsche Bauzeitschrift* 6 (June), 844–45.

O. M. Ungers, F. Jaeger, "Badische Landesbibliothek in Karlsruhe." *Deutsche Bauzeitschrift* 40, 6 (June), 841–52.

"Il fascino della semplicità." *Costruire* (July–August), 122–25.

Villa palladienne: vision bucolique." *Architecture Intérieure Crée* 249 (August–September), 58–61.

W. Hafner , "Steinregion: Rotweiß und rot, Der Sandstein vom Main." *Stein Time* 1, 1 (September), 60–64.

Jürgensen K., "Das Haus des Architekten: Wohnhaus Ungers in Köln (1957–59)." *Deutsche Bauzeitung* 126, 9 (September), 100–102, 104.

"Die Fünf Grossen: Oswald Mathias Ungers (66)." *Scala* 5 (September–October), 37.

"Architektur unterwegs." *Deutsches Architektenblatt* 24, 10 (October 1), 1493–96.

"Daimler-Benz Wettbewerb." *Bauwelt* 83, 38 (October 9), 2202–17.

D. Hoffmann-Axthelm, "Mit dem Fernrohr auf dem Leipziger Platz: Kommentar zu den Wettbewerben Daimler-Benz und Sony am Potsdamer Platz." *Bauwelt* 83, 38 (October 9), 2196–2201.

D. Hoffmann-Axthelm, "Plaza und Piazza (Berlin)." *Bauwelt* 83, 38 (October 9), 2196–2226.

"Beschränkter Realisierungswettbewerb Potsdamer Platz Berlin: Daimler Benz AG." *Wettbewerbe Aktuell* 22, 10 (October), 50–51.

J. Esche, "Landhaus im Quadrat."

Architektur & Wohnen 5 (October–November), 132–38, 140.

"Wettbewerb Potsdamer Platz in Berlin." *Detail* 32, 5 (October–November), 452.

"Daimler-Benz baut am Potsdamer Platz." *Deutsches Architektenblatt* 24, 11 (November), 1773–74.

"Tra Karlsruhe e Babele: O. M. Ungers, biblioteca a Karlsruhe." *Abitare* 312 (November), 138–45.

P. Rumpf, "Progetti per l'area della Potsdamerplatz." *Domus* 744 (December), 44–55.

Senatsverwaltung für Bau- und Wohnungswesen, "Wettbewerbe kein Allheilmittel." *Foyer Berlin: Magazin der Senatsverwaltung für Bau- und Wohnungswesen* (December), 31.

"From the square to the cube: Oswald Mathias Unger's [sic] home library." *Lotus International* 72, 50–55.

"Messehochhaus." *L'Architecture Tertiaire en Europe et aux Etats Unis* 24, 84–85.

"Oswald Mathias Ungers, Germany." *Design Journal* 45, 55.

1993

Architektur & Wirtschaft Journal Köln (Wiesbaden: VWAT), 16–17.

J. Cejka, *Tendenzen zeitgenössicher Architektur* (Stuttgart/Berlin/Cologne: W. Kohlhammer), 55–56.

Deutsches Architekturmuseum: DAM Architektur Jahrbuch 1993 (Munich: Prestel), 144–52, 180–83.

G. G. Feldmeyer, M. Sack (introduction), C. C. M. Mathewson (essay), *Die Neue Deutsche Architektur* (Stuttgart/Berlin/Cologne: W. Kohlhammer), 9, 17–31, 32–51, 216–23.

G. G. Feldmeyer, M. Sack (introduction), C. C. M. Mathewson (essay), *The New German Architecture; From city planning to urban design: rebuilding Germany 1945–1992* (New York: Rizzoli International), 9, 17–31, 32–51, 216–23.

"Il quartiere modello di Forellenweg." in A. Rocca, *Salisburgo la verde* (Milan: Electa), 99–119.

Jahrbuch für Licht und Architektur (Cologne: Ernst & Sohn), 60–61, 98–99, 112–13, 189–92.

H. Kollhoff, *Über Tektonik in der Baukunst* (Braunschweig/Wiesbaden: Friedrich Vieweg & Sohn), 37.

J. Krichbaum, V. Magnago Lampugnani, U. M. Schumann, A. Meseure, *Architektur im Profil: 35 Projekte für Berlin* (Stuttgart: Verlag Gerd Hatje), 182–89, 246–49.

V. Pasca, "La radicalità della geometria/Radical Geometry: Intervista con/Interview with Oswald Mathias Ungers." in *Annual Ufficio 1993–94* (Milan: Electa), 18–23.

S. Polónyi, "Die Tragkonstruktion als architektonischen Dominant." in H. Kollhoff, ed., *Über Tektonik in der Baukunst* (Braunschweig/Wiesbaden: Friedrich Vieweg & Sohn), 26–37.

Progetti e Territori '93 (mostra realizzata nell'ambito di "Abitare il Tempo") (Verona: Edizioni Grafiche Zanini), 29.

"Rationalismus." in *Tendenzen zeitgenössischer Architektur* (Stuttgart: W. Kohlhammer), 55–56.

Räume für Kunst. Museumsmodelle: Europäische Museumsarchitektur der Gegenwart (Groningen: Groninger Museum), 72–73.

J. Schilgen, *Das neue Frankfurt: Vom Funktionalismus zur Postmoderne* (Dortmund: Harenberg Edition), 17–23, 78–79.

L. Semerani, *Dizionario critico illustrato delle voci più utili all'architetto moderno* (Faenza: Gruppo Editoriale Faenza Editrice), 111–13.

C. Steckweh, P. Neitzke, eds., *Centrum: Jahrbuch Architektur und Stadt 1993* (Braunschweig/Wiesbaden: Friedrich Vieweg & Sohn), 192–95, 236–37.

D. Steiner, "Un programma di salvataggio: La Salisburgo di Johannes Voggenhuber." in A. Rocca, *Salisburgo la verde* (Milan: Electa), 8–15.

O. M. Ungers, "The City as a Work of Art." in J. Ockman, E. Eigen, eds., *Architecture Culture, 1943–1968: A Documentary Anthology* (New York: Rizzoli International), 361–64.

O. M. Ungers, "'Ikonen der Architektur' für Berlin Morgen 1990." in *Mies-van-der-Rohe-Symposium; Fritz Neumeyer: Ludwig Mies van der Rohe; Hochhaus am Bahnhof Friedrichstraße; Dokumentation des Mies-van-der-Rohe-Symposiums in der Neuen Nationalgalerie, Berlin* (Berlin: Ernst Wasmuth Verlag), 27, 31–75.

P. Wels, *Architekturzeichnungen* (Hamburg: Junius Verlag), 81.

J. Goetz, "Perfektion in Weiß." *Wohn! Design!* 5 (December–January), 12–20.

"Wettbewerb zur Weltausstellung EXPO 2000 in Hannover entschieden." *Deutsches Architektenblatt* 25, 1 (January 1), 39–41.

D. Cruickshank, "Friedrichstraße." *Architectural Review* 192, 1151 (January), 29–35.

"Die Schachtel: Heizwärmekraftwerk Köln-Merheim." *Industriebau* 39, 1 (January).

"Stadt- und Landschaftsplanerischer Ideenwettbewerb Weltausstellung Expo 2000, Hannover." *Wettbewerbe Aktuell* 1 (January), 21–32.

L. E. Nesbitt, "The German museum building boom: a look back." *Newsline* 5, 3 (January–February), 8.

O. Bouman, R. van Toorn, "'Ik probeer de fenomenologie van de architectuur te redden.' Interview met Oswald Mathias Ungers." *Archis* 2 (February), 58–65.

M. Heuser, "Hochhausmodelle aus Alabastergips von O. M. Ungers." *Objekt* 49 (February), 17–19.

"Nicht jeden Montag muß Architektur neu erfunden werden." *Living: Das Kulturmagazin* 6, 2 (February), 8–13.

"Heizwärmekraftwerk in Köln-Merheim." *Deutsche Bauzeitschrift* 41, 3 (March), 429–31.

G. Römer, "2–Ein Bibliotheksbau zwischen Funktion und Historie–der Neubau für die Badische Landesbibliothek." *Bibliothek: Forschung und Praxis* 17, 3 (March), 341–45.

H. Stimmann, "Berlin: Wiederaufbau ohne Zerstörung." *Der Architekt* 3 (March), 158–61, 190.

"Wie aus einem Guss–Zuwachs für ein Wasserschloss: Haus Bitz bei Köln nach Plänen von O. M. Ungers." *Häuser* 3 (March), 22–29.

"Nicht Kuppel und nicht Glasdach: Persönlichkeiten aus

Politik, Wissenschaft und Kultur zum Umbau des Reichstags." *Der Tagesspiegel* (March 12), 13.

R. Cowan, "Architecture centres: The German Architecture Museum, Frankfurt." *Architectural Review* 192, 1154 (April), 72–73.

W. A. Noebel, "Centrale termoelettrica a Colonia di Oswald Mathias Ungers." *Casabella* 57, 600 (April), 65–67.

Photograph, Messehalle 10, *Licht und Technik* (April).

"Comments on æsthetics." *Wohn! Design!* 5 (May), 12–22.

"Der Kontrakt des Zeichners: Wettbewerbszeichnungen lesen." *Baumeister* 90, 5 (May), 46–50.

Photograph of the Messehochhaus, *Fokus: Glas* 19 (May).

K. J. Phillip, "Architektenporträts." *Bauwelt* 84, 19 (May 14), 1015–19.

"Nicht Ganz Dicht: Der Kölner Architekt Oswald Mathias Ungers, 66, über vergängliche Neubauten." *Der Spiegel* 47, 21 (May 24).

M. Düttmann, "Die neue Friedrichstraße." *Bauwelt* 84, 21 (May 28), 1108–27.

"Beschränkter städtebaulicher Ideenwettbewerb Domplatz Magdeburg." *Wettbewerbe Aktuell* 23, 6 (June), 45–47 (52).

"Berliner Allgemein: Was ein Gerüst alles bewirkt... O. M. Ungers, Bebauung am Bahnhofsvorplatz Bonn." *Berliner Morgenpost* (June 5), 13.

R. Frank, "Domplatz in Magdeburg." *Bauwelt* 84, 27 (July 16), 1450–51, 1456.

C. Caldenby, "Tyskland genom 5 (En spegling av nutid)." *Arkitektur: The Swedish Review of Architecture* 93, 5 (July–August), 10–31, 71–72.

F. Jaeger, "Från Modernism till Pluralism." *Arkitektur* 93, 5 (July–August), 4–9.

"Oswald Mathias Ungers." *Arkitektur* 93, 5 (July–August), (1) 18–21.

R. K. Lewis, "German Ambassador's Residence: A Hilltop Villa." *AIA/DC* (August–September), 1, 4.

"Bücher: Wer liest Was? Prominente Zeitgenossen verraten neugierigen Vogue-Leserinnen ihre aufregendste Lektüre." *Vogue* 9 (September), 182.

"Il mobile a Francoforte." *Domus* 752 (September).

A. Piva, "Un difficile equilibrio/A Difficult Balance: The architecture of the Contemporary Museum as a means of communication between the world of art and everyday life." *Ottagono* 28, 108 (September), 105–8.

"Deutsches Architekturmuseum." *Daidalos* 49 (September 15), 7.

"Architektur; Köln: Kubus aus Glas und Klinkern." *Ambiente* 10 (October), 18.

"War das schön... Architektenfußball in Berlin." *Baumeister* 90, 5 (November), 9.

"Magdeburgs Staadtbaugeschichte." *Basler Magazin* 266, 44 (November 13), 15.

S. Polónyi, "Interpretare le strutture portanti dell'architettura/ Interpreting the Supporting Structure of Architecture." *Lotus International* 79 (December), 78–87.

O. M. Ungers, "Il Biba di Brema/The biba of Bremen." *Lotus International* 79 (December), 70–77.

"Die Sammlung von O. M. Ungers, Bedeutende Sammlung zur Architektur." *Köln: Zeitschrift der Stadt Köln* 38 , 39–44.

"Euroforum Köln." *Architektur & Wirtschaft: Journal Köln*, 16–17.

"Hochhaus am Westbahnhof/Highrise at Westbahnhof." *Archigrad–Architekturmagazin: Planen und Bauen am 50. Breitengrad* 3, 34–43.

"Interview with O. M. Ungers." *Corpus* 1, 20–25.

"Oswald Mathias Ungers: Badische Landesbibliothek Karlsruhe." *Materia* 12, 24–29.

H.-P. Schwarz, "Ein grüner Archipel für Frankfurt? Zur Planung der City West/A Green Archipelago for Frankfurt? On Planning City West." *Archigrad–Architekturmagazin: Planen und Bauen am 50. Breitengrad* 3, 24–27.

H.-P. Schwarz, "Eine Planung mit Folgen: Die Messepläne von Speer und Oswald Mathias Ungers/ Planning with results: Trade Fair Plans by Speer and Ungers." *Archigrad–Architekturmagazin: Planen und Bauen am 50. Breitengrad* 3, 4–17.

"Torhaus." *Archigrad–Architekturmagazin: Planen und Bauen am 50. Breitengrad* 2, 51.

1994

Arbeitsgruppe Berlin-Wettbewerbe, F. Zwoch, *Hauptstadt Berlin/Capital Berlin: Stadtmitte Spreeinsel/Central District Spreeinsel: Internationaler Städtebaulicher Ideenwettbewerb 1994/International Competition for Urban Design Ideas 1994* (Berlin: Birkhauser).

"Badische Landesbibliothek/State Library of Baden, Karlsruhe." in I. Flagge, ed., *Jahrbuch für Licht und Architektur 1993/Annual of Light and Architecture 1993* (Berlin: Ernst & Sohn/London: Academy Editions/New York: St. Martin's Press), 189–91, 195.

Bund Deutscher Architekten BDA der Hansestadt Hamburg, ed., *Architektur für Hamburg: Geplantes, Gebautes, Ungebautes: 1984–1994–2004* (Hamburg: Bund Deutscher Architekten BDA der Hansestadt Hamburg), 132–33.

Bundesbaudirektion Berlin, ed., *Museumsinsel Berlin: Wettbewerb zum Neuen Museum/Competition for the Neues Museum* (Stuttgart: Avedition, 90–91.

B. Jacob, "Die Friedrichstadt: Pläne und Projekte für Berlins Mitte." in Architektenkammer Berlin, ed., *Architektur in Berlin: Jahrbuch 1993/1994* (Hamburg: Junius Verlag), 70–81.

M. Kieren, *Oswald Mathias Ungers* (London/Zurich: Artemis StudioPaperback).

B. Kolb, *Wintergärten und Glasanbauten im Detail* (Munich: WekaBaufachverlage), 9, 12.

S. Nagbøl, *Berøvende Arkitektur: En oplevelsanalyse af Arkitekturnuseet i Frankfurt am Main* (Copenhagen: Arkitektens Forlag).

"Oswald Mathias Ungers: 'Le Style, c'est l'Homme,'" in O. Bouman, R. van Toorn, eds., *The Invisible in Architecture* (London: Academy Editions/ New York: St. Martin's Press), 52–65, 502.

"Oswald Mathias Ungers, Stefan Vieths (2. Preis): Oswald Mathias Ungers, 2. Preis." in V. Magnago Lampugnani, R. Schneider, eds., *Ein Stück Großstadt als Experiment: Planungen am Potsdamer Platz in Berlin*

(Stuttgart: Verlag Gerd Hatje), 74–77, 92–95.

"Preis: Bremer Institut für Betriebstechnik und angewandte Arbeitswissenshaft (biba)." in *Bund Deutscher Architekten im Lande Bremen: BDA-Preis 1994* (Bremen: Bund Deutscher Architekten im Lande Bremen), 16–17.

Stadt Köln, ed., *Das Neue Köln 1945–1995* (Cologne: Stadt Köln), 278, 602.

J. Steele, ed., *Museum Builders* (London: Academy Editions), 244–45.

O. M. Ungers, "Ordo, pondo et mensura." in H. Millon, V. Magnago Lampugnani, eds. *The Renaissance from Brunelleschi to Michelangelo: the representation of architecture* (New York: Rizzoli International/London: Thames & Hudson), 307.

O. M. Ungers, "'Ordo, pondo et mensura': criteri architettonici del Rinascimento." in H. Millon, V. Magnago Lampugnani, eds., *Rinascimento, da Brunelleschi a Michelangelo: La rappresentazione dell'Architettura* (Milan: Bompiani), 306–17.

O. M. Ungers, "Und immer noch kein Plan für Berlin." in P. Neitzke, C. Steckeweh, eds., *Centrum: Jahrbuch Architektur und Stadt 1994* (Braunschweig/Wiesbaden: Friedrich Vieweg & Sohn), 45–54.

O. M. Ungers, "Verband kommunales Unternehmen, Köln, 1993; Johannishaus, Köln, 1994." in P. Neitzke, C. Steckeweh, eds., *Centrum: Jahrbuch Architektur und Stadt 1994* (Braunschweig/Wiesbaden: Friedrich Vieweg & Sohn), 160–65.

K. Winkler, ed., *Archigrad Nr. 3: Planen und Bauen am 50. Breitengrad* (Frankfurt am Main: Verlag AFW), 4–15.

M. Wörner, D. Mollenschott, K.-H. Hüter, eds., *Architekturführer Berlin/Architectural Guide to Berlin, English Supplement* (Berlin: Dietrich Reimer Verlag), 16 (24), 55 (83), 218 (344), 264–65 (423–24).

O. M. Ungers, "Berlino: quale piano?/Berlin: what plan?." *Domus* 756 (January), 81.

K. Ronneberger, P. Noller, "Instant City–Instant Culture: Frankfurt als gemütliches New York." *Bauwelt* 85, 12 (January 7), 30–35.

C. Rademacher, "Kunst: Highlights der Architekturfotographie." *VfA Profil* 7, 2 (February), 8–9.

"Im Nächsten Heft." *Art: Das Kunstmagazin* 3 (March), 138.

"Berlin 1994 (Stadtbauwelt 121)." *Bauwelt* 85, 12 (March 25), 578–660.

"Bauplatz Berlin: Hauptstadt muß Berlin erst noch werden." *Art: Das Kunstmagazin* 4 (April), 26–41.

J. Müller, "Die größte Baugrube Berlins." *Baumeister* (April), 12–17.

"Neubau Familiengericht und Erweiterung Amtsgericht Tempelhof/Kreuzberg." *Foyer Berlin: Magazin der Senatsverwaltung für Bau- und Wohnungswesen* 4, 1 (April), 31.

C. Rudeck, "Architektur: Poesie nach Plan." *Ambiente* 4 (April), 20, 22.

O. M. Ungers + Partner, "Archäologie und Baustelle." *Baumeister* 91, 4 (April), 24–25, 96, 101.

P. Rumpf, "Das Schiff auf Kurs halten (DAM)." *Bauwelt* 85, 1617 (April 29), 930–33.

C. Kapplinger, "Jenseits des Backsteins." *Bauwelt* 85, 22 (June 3), 1184.

H. Bodenschatz, "Wettbewerbsgebiet 'Spreeinsel': Vergangenheit, Gegenwart, Zukunft." *Bauwelt* 85, 25 (July 1), 1414–35.

"Bauausstellung 1995 in Kleinmachnow." *Bauwelt* 85, 26 (July 8), 1458–59.

D. Reinsch, "Diebstahl im Staatsrat: Der Palast der Republik ist weg." *Foyer Berlin: Magazin der Senatsverwaltung für Bau- und Wohnungswesen* 4 (September), 16–18.

A. G. Sullivan, "New Embassies Open in Washington, D.C.." *Architecture (AIA)* 83, 9 (September), 28–29.

"Berlin 1999: Messeerweiterung von O. M. Ungers." *AIT Architektur Innenarchitektur Technischer Ausbau* 102, 10 (October), 38.

T. Gill, "Hoodfdstad Berlijn: Spreeinsel-Prijsvraag/Capital City Berlin: The Spreeinsel Competition." *Archis* 10 (October), 2–4.

L. D. Jensen, "Konkurrencer-fortiden i troldspejlet." *Arkitekten* 96, 14 (October), 463–68.

M. Miyawaki, ed., "Rebirth of a City of the Arts: Gibellina Nuova, Italy." *Space Design* 361 (October), 41–84.

M. Kieren, "Berühmte Lehrer–berühmte Schüler: Egon Eiermann und Oswald Mathias Ungers." *Bauwelt* 85, 38 (October 7), 2093, 2118–43.

H. Niederwohrmeier, "Residenz der Deutschen Botschaft Washington." *Bauwelt* 85, 4041 (October 28), 2240–49.

D. Reinsch, "Architektur: Berlin im Jahre 2010." *Architektur & Wohnen* 5 (October–November), 99–114.

H.-W. Hämer, B. Riese, "Beinahe Überrollt ... Verkehrsplannung contra Geschichtspark." *Stadtforum Berlin* 17 (November), 15.

M. Kieren, "Residenza dell'ambasciatore tedesco a Washington DC." *Casabella* 58, 617 (November), 60–66, 71.

J. von Uthmann, "Wie der Tempel eines fremden Gottes: Neue Residenz des deutschen Botschafters in Washington." *Baumeister* 91, 11 (November), 4–5.

"Berlino: i nuovi sviluppi urbanistici e architettonici." *Domus* 766 (December), 68–72.

A. Denk, O. M. Ungers, "Die Ratio muß die Phantasie kontrollieren." *Der Architekt* 12 (December), 697–700.

K. Frampton, "'In nome del padre'/'In the Name of the Father.'" *Domus* 766 (December), 19–22.

B. Knauf, R. Renger, "Architektur: Poesie nach Plan." *Ambiente* 12 (December), 64–70, 72.

"La nuova residenza dell'Ambasciatore della Germania a Washington DC/The German Ambassador's new residence in Washington DC." *Domus* 766 (December), 5, 7–18.

M. Sack, "Architektur: Der Anspruch auf Kunst rangiert vor Bequemlichkeit." *Art: Das Kunstmagazin* 12 (December), 24.

S. G. Nayhauß, "Dr. Immo Stabreit: So residiert unser Mann in Washington." *Gala: Leute der Woche* (December 8), 38–42.

M. Sack, "Berlin für alle."

Die Zeit 50 (December 9), 57–58.

"Daimler Benz: Concurso del sector." *A&V: Monografías de Arquitectura y Vivienda* 50, 36–37.

"Friedrichstraße." *Lotus International* 80, 110–17.

D. Hoffmann-Axthelm, "Un caso extremo de crisis urbana." *A&V: Monografías de Arquitectura y Vivienda* 50, 4–9, 113–15.

B. Korte, "Eine Landschaft der beschnittenen Bezirke/Un paysage fait de lieux tailles/A landscape of pruned areas." *Anthos: Garten- und Landschaftsgestaltung* 33, 3, 38–40.

V. Magnago Lampugnani, "Una nueva simplicidad: Reflexiones ante el cambio de milenio." *A&V: Monografías de Arquitectura y Vivienda* 50, 100–103, 119–20.

"Potsdamer Platz." *Lotus International* 80, 100–101, 106.

"Potsdamer Platz: El concurso general." *A&V: Monografías de Arquitectura y Vivienda* 50, 34–35.

"PTS-Werkstatt am Flughafen Frankfurt/Main." *Umeni/The art* 42, 3, 2541.

"Una mastaba comercial: Friedrichstadt Passagen." *A&V: Monografías de Arquitectura y Vivienda* 50, 74–77.

O. M. Ungers, "Ancora una volta, nessun piano per Berlino/Once Again, no Plan for Berlin." *Lotus International* 80, 6–23.

1995

A. Caragonne, *The Texas Rangers: Notes from an Architectural Underground* (Cambridge, Mass.: The MIT Press), 353–56.

F. Jaeger, "Familiengericht, Berlin, 1989–1995." in *Centrum: Jahrbuch Architektur und Stadt 1995* (Braunschweig/Wiesbaden: Friedrich Vieweg & Sohn), 156–59.

F. Pesch, *Neues Bauen in historischer Umgebung* (Cologne: Rudolf Müller), 48, 152–53.

H. Stimmann, ed., *Berlin Mitte: Die Entstehung einer urbanen Architektur/Downtown Berlin: Building the Metropolitan Mix* (Basel/Boston: Birkhäuser).

S. Ehrlinger, "Letztes Wort beim Kanzler." *Deutsche Bauzeitung* 129, 1 (January), 14, 16.

"Stadtquartier Lehrter Bahnhof, Berlin." *Bauwelt* 86, 12 (January 13), 2–3.

"Wettbewerb Bundeskanzleramt: Ein Kommentar." *Bauwelt* 86, 12 (January 13), 62–65.

"Baumeister Exkursion 2: Hochhäuser in Frankfurt am Main." *Baumeister* 92, 2 (February).

"Bundeskanzleramt Berlin." *Wettbewerbe Aktuell* 25, 2 (February), 27–43.

"Friedrichstraße." *Architecture d'Aujourd'hui* 297 (February), 84–85, 88–89.

E. Santifaller, "Kommentar: Sparen mit Sponsoren?" *Deutsche Bauzeitung* 129, 2 (February), 3.

B. Schulz, "Die Haupstadtkolumne." *Baumeister* 92, 2 (February), 8.

H. Wefing, "Kommentar: Sparen mit Sponsoren?" *Deutsche Bauzeitung* 129, 2 (February), 14–15.

P. Goldberger, "Reimaging Berlin." *The New York Times Magazine* (February 5), 45–53.

J. Giovannini, "Unverstandene Botschaft." *Architektur & Wohnen* 1 (February–March), 100–104.

T. Schröder, "Im Dreieck: Lehrter Bahnhofsquartier, Alsenblöcke und Bundeskanzleramt-Wettbewerbe bringen neue Stadtkronen zu Papier." *Stadtforum Berlin* 18 (March), 10–11.

O. M. Ungers, "Residence of the German Ambassador in Washington, D.C.; Washington, D.C., 1994." *A+U: Architecture + Urbanism* 294 (March), 4–35.

"Frankfurt Messe." *ArtFair* 2, 3 (March–May).

S. Collyer, "An exercise in futility? The Berlin Spreeinsel competition." *Competitions* 1 (Spring), 56–61.

"Novità da Dieter Sieger/News from Dieter Sieger." *Abitare* 340 (May), 66.

M. Kieren, "Eine Wiese, ein Haus: ein Versuch mit der Form zu überleben: Oswald Mathias Ungers' Haus in der Eifel." *Deutsche Bauzeitung* 129, 6 (June), 84–91.

S. Protasoni , "Oswald Mathias Ungers [by] Martin Kieren [book review]." *Domus* 772 (June), 95–96.

U. Kleefisch-Jobst, "Die Planungen in der City West von Frankfurt." *Deutsche Bauzeitschrift* 43, 10 (October), 187–90, 193–94.

I. Breccia Fratadocchi, "Dal Reno al Tevere: nuove chiese della diocesi di Colonia." *Parametro* 211 (November–December), 58–64.

"Berlin." *Domus Dossier* 3.

1996

S. Behling, S. Behling, *Sol Power. Die Evolution der solaren Architektur* (Munich: Prestel Verlag).

Bund Deutscher Architekten with Meinhard von Gerkan, ed., *Renaissance der Bahnhöfe. Die Stadt im 21. Jahrhundert* (Braunschweig/Wiesbaden: Friedrich Vieweg & Sohn), 122–25.

G. de Bruyn, *Zeitgenössische Architektur in Deutschland 1970–1995* (Bonn: Inter Nationes), 126–29.

M. De Michelis, *Tendenze dell'architettura europea. Gli anni novanta. Atlante* (Venice: Marsilio), 82–87.

Deutsches Architekturmuseum, Frankfurt am Main, ed., *Architektur-Jahrbuch 1996*, (Munich: Prestel Verlag), 140–43, 170, 173.

U. Drost, ed., *Schwerin. Zwischen Geschichte und Gegenwart. Ergebnisse des IAAS Institute for Advanced Architectural Studies/Internationalen Städtebauworkshops 1996* (Hamburg: IAAS Press), 92–97.

M. Düttmann, F. Zwoch, eds., *Bauwelt Berlin Annual 1996: Chronology of Building Events 1996–2001* (Boston/Berlin: Birkhäuser).

Garpa, Garten & Park Einrichtungen: Objekte 1997 (Escheburg bei Hamburg: Garpa), 8, 9.

K. Harpprecht, in *Centrum: Jahrbuch Architektur und Stadt 1996* (Braunschweig/Wiesbaden: Friedrich Vieweg & Sohn), 246–51.

J. J. Holland, J. Strassel, *Zur semantischen Analyse neuerer öffentlicher Plätze in europäischen Städten* (Hannover: Universität Hannover), 51–66, 155.

B. Katz, *Souvenirs*, ed. P. Feierabend (Cologne: Könemann), 102.

B. F. Löwenberg, *Kölner Persönlichkeiten. Menschen mit Engagement, Ideen und Schaffenskraft* (Cologne: Edition Cologne), 186–87.

W. Nerdinger, C. Tafel, *Germania. Guida all'architettura del Novecento* (Milan: Electa), 21, 24, 156, 172, 250, 276, 303 (German ed. Basel: Birkhäuser Verlag).

"Oswald Mathias Ungers. Qualität und Qualitäten. Das "Haus ohne Eigenschaften", Köln-Müngersdorf 1994–1995." in *Masse–Körper–Gewicht* (Sulgen: A. Niggli), 44–47.

O. M. Ungers, *Museumsinsel Hamburg. Erweiterung der Kunsthalle* (Freiburg im Breisgau: *Wettbewerbe Aktuell* Verlagsgesellschaft), 85–88.

R. Wulf, *Über Dächern von Berlin* (Hamburg: Junius), 90–93.

A. Zabalbeascooa, *El taller del arquitecto* (Barcelona: G. Gili), 164–67, 190.

S. Stucchi, "Residenza dell'ambasciatore tedesco a Washington, D.C./German ambassador's residence Washington, D.C." *Industria delle costruzioni* 30, 291 (January), 44–50.

D. van den Heuvel, "Ungers versus Libeskind: twee interpretaties van de geschiedenis." *Architect* 27, 1 (January), 12–13.

"Opinioni e progetti/Opinions and projects." *Casabella* 60, 630–31 (January–February), 106–17.

H. Reyelts, "Tradiciones alemanas: Ungers y Behnisch, orden formal y expresividad espacial." *Arquitectura viva* 47 (March–April), 21–25.

C. Luchsinger, "Zurück zur Form." *Werk, Bauen + Wohnen* 4 (April), 28–45.

D. Mandolesi, "Tribunale della famiglia a Berlino/Family court in Berlin." *Industria delle costruzioni* 30, 295 (May), 32–37.

"Friedrichstadtpassagen Berlin—Quartier 205/Friedrichstadt passages Berlin–Quartier 205." *Architektur + Wettbewerbe* 166 (June), 22–24.

A. Ruby, "Wir in Köln: Ein Nachruf auf den Wettbewerb zum Neubau des Wallraf-Richartz-Museums." *Deutsche Bauzeitung* 130, 7 (July), 33.

W. Zahner, "Wettbewerb für das neue Wallraf-Richartz-Museum in Köln." *Baumeister* 93, 7 (July), 77.

"Umzug: das Wallraf-Richartz-Museum in Köln." *AIT Architektur Innenarchitektur Technischer Ausbau* 104, 7 (July–August), 18.

D. Meyhofer, "Das Quadrat in Zeiten fliessender Räume." *Deutsche Bauzeitung* 130, 9 (September), 14–15.

P. Rumpf, "Was gibt es Geheimnisvolleres als die Klarheit: Kunsthalle Hamburg." *Bauwelt* 87, 35 (September 13), 1970–77.

M.V. Engelberg, "Zum Wettbewerb für den Neubau Wallraf-Richartz-Museum, Köln 1996." *Kunstchronik* 49, 9–10 (September–October), 440–46.

U. M. Schumann, "Qualität und Qualitäten." *Archithese* 26, 5 (September–October), 44–47.
L. Dawson, "Ungers in Hamburg." *Architectural Review* 200, 1196 (October), 9.

"Kunstkiste: Erweiterungsbau Kunsthalle Hamburg." *AIT Architektur Innenarchitektur Technischer Ausbau* 104, 10 (October), 24.

Stein-Time (October) 48–52, 64.

W. Wang, M. Eichel, "Kunst-Tempel oder Festung?." *Architektur & Wohnen* 5 (October–November), 122–[124], 126.

"Oswald Mathias Ungers: House Ungers, Cologne, Germany 1994–1995." *A+U: Architecture + Urbanism* 11, 314 (November), 96–103.
R. Ryan, "Rational experiment: Ungers House, Cologne, Germany, O. M. Ungers, architect." *Architecture* 85, 12 (December), 70–73.

"Architettura nelle capitali." *Materia* 22, 24–29.
Bauwelt 33, 1840.

F. Dal Co, "O. M. Ungers, Schinkel als Erzieher. Casa Ungers a Köln-Müngersdorf, Kämpchensweg." *Casabella* 635, 4–9.

Golf Report Köln 5, 22–23.
"House Ungers." *A+U* 11, 96–103.

"Mit Noblesse und Jagdistinkt: Der Kölner Urologe Reiner Speck." *Art* 9, 32–34, 128.

"Naturwerkstein-Architektur", 2, 23–27.

"Oswald Mathias Ungers. Klares Votum für moderne Kunst." *Kulturchronik* 6, 40–43.

"Oswald Mathias Ungers. Müngersdorf. Aforismi sul costruire case." *Lotus International* 90, 6–33.

M. Sack, "Hamburger Kunsthalle: Kühl bis an den First." *VfA Profil* 12, 12–14.

Wettbewerbe Aktuell 12, 85–88.

1997

C. Broto, *Rehabilated Buildings. Architectural Design* (Barcelona: Links International), 158ff.

Centrum: Jahrbuch Architektur und Stadt 1997–1998 (Braunschweig/Wiesbaden: Friedrich Vieweg & Sohn), 138–40, 141, 143.

Deutscher Naturstein Preis 1997–Dokumentation (Würzburg: Deutscher Naturwerkstein-Verband e.V.), 4–7.

Erzbischöfliches Diözesanmuseum Köln, ed. *Kolumba. Ein Architekturwettbewerb in Köln 1997.* Cologne: Walther König Verlag, 194.

G. Feuerstein. *Androgynos. Das Mann-Weibliche in Kunst and Architektur.* Stuttgart/London: Edition Axel Menges, 192, 193, 203, 204.

Förderverein Deutsches Architektur Zentrum Berlin, ed. *Neue Architektur, Berlin 1990–2000.* Berlin: Jovis Verlagsbüro, 57, 66, 115, 172.

Frontiers: Artists & Architects. London: Academy, I, VI–XI, 47–51.

H. Fußroich. *Architekturführer Köln. Profane Architektur nach 1990.* Cologne: J. P. Bachem Verlag.

C. Gunßer. *Einfamilienhäuser.* Stuttgart: Deutsche Verlags-Anstalt, 148–53.

C. Haberlik, G. Zohlen. *Die Baumeister des neuen Berlin. Porträts–Gebäude–Konzepte.* Berlin: Nicholaische Verlagsbuchhandlung, 178–85.

Hamburger Kunsthalle–Galerie der Gegenwart (press release on the occasion of the inauguration of the new Kunsthalle in February) (Hamburg: Galerie der Gegenwart).

G. Kähler, *"Die ewige Form?" Kunsthalle in Hamburg von Oswald Mathias Ungers*, 22–29.

M. Kieren et al., *Houses for Sale* (Cologne: Galerie Sophia Ungers).

V. Magnago Lampugnani, R. Schneider, *An Urban Experiment in Central Berlin. Planning Potsdamer Platz* (Frankfurt am Main: Deutsches Architekturmuseum/Stuttgart: Institut für Auslandsbeziehungen), 92–95.

W. Meyer-Bohe, *Grundrisse öffentlicher Gebäude. Synoptische Gebäudetypologie* (Berlin: Ernst & Sohn), 122–23.

S. Redecke, R. Stern, eds., *Foreign Affairs. Neue Botschaftsbauten und das Auswärtige Amt in Berlin* (Berlin: *Bauwelt*, Birkhäuser), 90.

A. Rocca, M. Zardini, eds., *Fiere e città* (Milan: Triennale di Milano), 8–23, 101.

K. Schalhorn, H. Schmalscheidt, *Raum–Haus–Stadt* (Stuttgart: Kohlhammer), 26.

U. M. Schneede, R. Leppien, eds., *Die Hamburger Kunsthalle. Bauten und Bilder* (Leipzig: E. A. Seeman).

O. M. Ungers, "Der Bahnhof ist nicht die Stadt." in *Deutsche Bahn–WorkShop 2* (Berlin: Deutsche Bahn AG), 14.

O. M. Ungers, "Die dialektische Stadt." in J. Posener, M. Mislin, eds., *Laßt mir doch, Kinder, hier komme ich wahrscheinlich ne wider her!* (Berlin: jovis Verlagsbüro), 193–202.

O. M. Ungers, "Prolog." in J. Sawade, *Bauten und Projekte 1970–1995*, ed. Wolfgang Schäche (Berlin: Gebr. Mann Verlag), 7–9.

O. M. Ungers, C. Herstatt, *Hamburger Kunsthalle–Galerie der Gegenwart* (Stuttgart: Verlag Gerd Hatje).

O. M. Ungers, M. Kieren, *Oswald Mathias Ungers* (Bologna: Zanichelli).

O. M. Ungers, S. Vieths, *Oswald Mathias Ungers. La città dialettica* (Milan: Skira).

D. W. von Goddenthow, ed., *Solange ich hoffe, lebe ich* (Munich: Kösel Verlag), 39–40.

Willkommen in der Galerie der Gegenwart (Hamburg: Hamburger Kunsthalle).

P. Winter, "Friedrichstadt Passagen–Quartier 205. Die rationale Ästhetik von Baustelle und Bau." in M. Düttmann, F. Zwoch, eds., *Bauwelt Berlin Annual 1996* (Basel: Birkhäuser Verlag), 38–47.

M. Nadler, "Kunst im Quadrat. Die Galerie der Gegenwart im Erweiterungsbau der Kunsthalle." *Zug* (February), 36–38.

A. Lösel, "Hamburger Allerlei." *Stern* 9 (February 20), 136.
H. T. Flemming, "Galerie der Gegenwart. Der Ungers-Neubau der Hamburger Kunsthalle."

Weltkunst 7 (April), 707.

"L'immagine del potere." *Domus* 793 (May), 52–60.

A. Denk, "Pfarrkirche St. Theodor in Köln-Vingst." *Bauwelt* 19 (May), 980–82.

Der Spiegel 51 (December 15), 212.

Art: Das Kunstmagazin 2, 16–31.
Bunte 44, p. 72.

C. Claussen, "Oswald Mathias Ungers. Kunst im Quadrat." *Stern* 3, p. 71.

"Die Magie der edlen Kiste." *Der Spiegel* 8, 194–98.

"Dünner Geduldsfaden." *Der Spiegel* 10, p. 14.

K. Heckes, "Ein schlichter Rahmen für die Kunst. Ungers Neubau der Hamburger Kunsthalle." *Der Kunsthandel* 5, 14–15.

"Hier wohnt der Architekt." *Stern* 46, 158ff.

G. Kähler, "Der Bau: Kunst-Tempel. Die neue Hamburger Kunsthalle." *Der Architekt* 4, p. 199.
Kunstforum International 37, 441–49.

Kunstmagazin 33, 4, p. 39.

K. Lore, "Kraft durch Reduktion." *Raum und Wohnen* 11, 60–71.

D. Meyhöfer, "Gegensatz. Galerie der Gegenwart in Hamburg."

Deutsche Bauzeitschrift 3, 43–48.
Museumskunde 62, 1, 1, 4, 5.

"Oswald Mathias Ungers. Gebäude ohne funktionelle Zwänge. Thermen am Forum in Trier." *Die Bauverwaltung–Bauamt & Gemeindebau* 10, 480–81.

"Oswald Mathias Ungers. Kunsthalle Hamburg." *Stein, Keramik & Sanitär*, 6–7, 9–12.

P. Sager, "Was die neue Hamburger Kunstkiste alles in sich hat." *Die Zeit* 9, 24–34.

R. Stadler, "Deutscher Natursteinpreis 1997. Fassaden mit massiven Elementen."

Naturstein Architektur 1, 30–31.
H. Stimmann, "'Das steinerne Berlin,' ein Mißverständnis." *Der Architekt* 3, 164–69.

VfA Profil 3.

Wettbewerbe Aktuell 8.

Abridgement of G. Brown-Manrique, O. M. Ungers. A Comprehensive Bibliography 1953–1995, *published by Interalia Design Books.*

Illustration Credits

We wish to thank the O. M. Ungers Studio for kindly providing all of the illustrations, and especially the photographer Stefan Müller of Berlin, who took most of the photographs, and Dieter Leistner of Mainz. Thanks also go to:
Willi Bosl, Trier
Uwe Dettmar, Frankfurt am Main
Franz Josef Hering, Werl
Dieter Klein
Grimm Kraege, Cologne
Christoph Lison, Frankfurt am Main
Tom Lingnau, Frank Schumacher, Cologne
Magnus Müller - Werkfotos
Hans-Joachim Wuthenow, Berlin.